NIELS J. BLUNCH

SECOND EDITION
INTRODUCTION TO
STRUCTURAL
EQUATION
MODELING
USING IBM SPSS
STATISTICS AND AMOS

Los Angeles | London | New Delhi
Singapore | Washington DC

SAGE

Los Angeles | London | New Delhi
Singapore | Washington DC

SAGE Publications Ltd
1 Oliver's Yard
55 City Road
London EC1Y 1SP

SAGE Publications Inc.
2455 Teller Road
Thousand Oaks, California 91320

SAGE Publications India Pvt Ltd
B 1/I 1 Mohan Cooperative Industrial Area
Mathura Road
New Delhi 110 044

SAGE Publications Asia-Pacific Pte Ltd
3 Church Street
#10-04 Samsung Hub
Singapore 049483

Editor: Katie Metzler
Editorial assistant: Anna Horvai
Production editor: Vanessa Harwood
Copyeditor: Neville Hankins
Proofreader: Derek Markham
Marketing manager: Ben Sherwood
Cover design: Wendy Scott
Typeset by C&M Digitals (P) Ltd, Chennai, India
Printed by MPG Books Group, Bodmin, Cornwall

Library of Congress Control Number: 2011945856

British Library Cataloguing in Publication data

A catalogue record for this book is available from
the British Library

MIX
Paper from
responsible sources
FSC
www.fsc.org   FSC® C018575

ISBN 978-1-4462-4899-7
ISBN 978-1-4462-4900-0 (pbk)

ION
N TO
RAL
ON
NG
PSS
MOS

SAGE has been part of the global academic community since 1965, supporting high quality research and learning that transforms society and our understanding of individuals, groups, and cultures. SAGE is the independent, innovative, natural home for authors, editors and societies who share our commitment and passion for the social sciences.

Find out more at: **www.sagepublications.com**

Connect, Debate, Engage on Methodspace

 Connect with other researchers and discuss your research interests

Keep up with announcements in the field, for example calls for papers and jobs

 Discover and review resources

Engage with featured content such as key articles, podcasts and videos

Find out about relevant conferences and events

Methodspace
Connecting the Research Community

www.methodspace.com

brought to you by

Contents

About the author

Niels J. Blunch has a MSc in Business Administration from Copenhagen School of Business.

After a few years working in industry Niels went to Aarhus School of Business, Department of Marketing and Statistics in 1965, where he taught and carried out research in marketing research and in research methodology in general. In parallel with his academic work he has worked as a consultant. He retired in 2007.

Structural Equation Modeling Using IBM SPSS and AMOS is his seventh book, but his first in English.

Preface to the first edition (abridged)

This book contains what I consider to be the essentials for a non-mathematical introductory course in structural equation modeling (SEM) for the social and behavioral sciences.

It builds on material that I have used during the years in a compulsory course in behavioral science methods for first year graduate students at Aarhus School of Business (Denmark).

The book should be well suited for introductory courses in SEM for last year undergraduate or first year graduate students who have had an introductory course in statistics up to and including multiple regression. The book contains an appendix on statistical prerequisites that could be used as a refresher. The appendix could be read as an introduction to the text or consulted when necessary during reading.

The examples in the book are real life examples taken from a wide range of disciplines – including psychology, political science, marketing and health – and the same goes for the exercises down-loadable from the book's homepage: they build on real data.

A book on SEM could either illustrate the programming aspects by showing examples on how models are programmed in the various computer programs available (e.g. LISREL, EQS, AMOS, Mplus, Mx Graph) – or one could concentrate on one and only one computer program and use it all through the book.

I have chosen the last-mentioned method using SPSS and AMOS as the workhorses: SPSS is a statistics program used at most universities and it should be well-known to many students in the social and behavioral sciences. AMOS is now sold as an add-on to SPSS and it is very easy to use as it was originally developed with a view to its use in the classroom.

I would like to thank my two reviewers, professor Dale R. Fuqua of Oklahoma State University (US) and research associate Elizabeth Ackerly of Lancaster University (UK) for helpful comments and suggestions. The same thanks go to professor Joachim Scholderer from Aarhus School of Business (Denmark), who have done careful reading of the first three chapters at an early stage of the project, and professor Carsten Stig Poulsen from Aalborg University (Denmark) who despite a busy life found time to work his way through the complete manuscript in its (nearly) final form.

I would also like to thank the many persons, who have allowed me to use their data for examples and exercises – without them it would have been impossible to write the book. They are too many to mention here, but credits are given where the data are introduced.

Last – but not least – my thanks go to my wife Anne-Marie for her loving support during the long writing process.

Niels J. Blunch

Preface to the second edition

This second edition differs from the first in several respects:

1. In the first edition all programming was in Visual Basic (VB), and a demonstration of the graphic interface was relegated to an appendix.
   Realizing that many newcomers to AMOS would probably prefer the graphic interface, AMOS Graphics is now fully integrated in the main text and used throughout the book together with VB.
2. As the amount of panel data is growing steadily, a new chapter on the analysis of such data using latent curve models has been added.
3. A section on multiple imputation has been added to the chapter on analysis of data with missing values.
4. There have been a number of changes in most of the chapters, the most dramatic being in the first chapter, where students will appreciate a 'softer' and more pedagogical introduction to the complicated subject of structural equation modeling (SEM).

The book is now organized in three parts.

Part 1 comprises three chapters and introduces you to SEM and the preparation of your data.

Part 2 contains four chapters and introduces AMOS with three model 'prototypes': path models, confirmatory factor models and full SEM with latent variables.

Part 3 comprises three chapters and deals with more advanced subjects: analysis of several samples in order to judge whether the model is invariant across the groups from which the samples were taken, problems with missing and non-normal data, and analysis of panel data.

Niels J. Blunch

Part 1
Preparing Yourself and Your Data

1

Introduction

After a presentation and an overview of the contents of the whole book, this chapter goes on with an intuitive introduction to *structural equation modeling* (SEM) by presenting a few examples of such models.

The models are *very* simple, but chosen to illustrate the broad spectrum of research problems that can be analyzed by the collection of tools in the bag called SEM. This will not only acquaint you with prototypes of problems and models taken up in more depth in later chapters, but also stress the way SEM solves the problem of measuring the vague concepts you often meet in the social and behavioral sciences (intelligence, preference, social status, attitude, literacy and the like) for which no generally accepted measuring instruments exist.

A short outline of the history of SEM follows subsequently.

Then you will learn how to cope with another problem. Unlike the natural sciences, the ideal way of doing causal research, namely experimentation, is more often than not impossible to implement in the social and behavioral sciences. This being the case, we face a series of difficulties of a practical as well as a philosophical nature.

As you will observe in the first part of this chapter, depiction of the models plays a large role in SEM, and AMOS (Analysis of MOment Structures) has a complete drawing environment 'AMOS Graphics' to which you will be introduced next.

You will also encounter a short introduction to the matrices found in the output from AMOS, the computer program used in this book.

Rather than presenting a deep discussion of the mathematical and statistical calculations, which are the basis for SEM estimation, a brief, intuitive explanation of the principles is presented instead.

1 Purpose and Plan of the Book

As you can see from the title, this book is an *introduction* to structural equation modeling – or SEM for short. SEM is a very large subject indeed. It is not just one statistical method, such as regression analysis or analysis of variance techniques that you should know from your introductory course in statistics. In fact these two statistical techniques can be shown to be special cases of SEM, and the same goes for more advanced statistical models that you might have met, such as MANOVA, discriminant analysis and canonical correlation.

So, you can see that general SEM is a rather big toolbox that can serve you in lots of different data analysis situations. This means that it is impossible to cover in a rather slim volume like this one the more advanced and complicated topics in this rapid developing area.

Furthermore, this is a *non-mathematical* introduction, which means that you will encounter very few formulae, but instead of mathematical deductions, you will find verbal explanations often of a more intuitive character.

The reader I have in mind is a student within the social and behavioral sciences who has completed an introductory course in statistics up to and including multiple regression analysis, and also has some experience of the IBM statistics program SPSS.

Plan of the book

The book consists of three parts.

Part 1 includes three chapters. The first chapter starts by presenting a few simple examples, each being a prototype of the kind of more complicated problems you will meet in later chapters. As you will learn from these examples, a central problem in SEM is the extent to which you can draw causal conclusions based on non-experimental data. A discussion of the problems involved takes up a good deal of space.

The variables you want to enter into your structural equation model must be measured. Chapter 2 considers problems connected with judging the quality of your measurements, by introducing the concepts of reliability and validity, and Chapter 3 presents principal components analysis and exploratory factor analysis as simple tools for examining the dimensionality in your data.

You should now be well equipped to embark on Part 2 of the book, where in Chapter 4 you are introduced to the steps in SEM and to the various problems that can arise as you go through the steps. In the process you will also be introduced to AMOS programming by means of a very simple multiple regression example similar to those that you have probably met several times before.

The next three chapters (5, 6 and 7) present the three 'main models' of SEM, the prototypes of which you met in Chapter 1 but now in more realistic (and complicated) forms. The examples are taken from a variety of disciplines: psychology, political science, health and marketing.

Part 3 of the book moves on to more advanced topics. In Chapter 8 the analysis is extended to deal with the *values* of the variables and not just the *relations* between them (as is most often the case in SEM). Chapter 8 also deals with models based on data from more than one population in order to compare populations and examine the extent to which the same model can be used to describe them all.

Chapter 9 will show you how to deal with problems caused by incomplete and non-normal data, while Chapter 10 introduces you to the so-called latent curve model used to model trends based on panel data.

2 Theory and Model

This is a book about drawing conclusions based on non-experimental data about relationships between non-measurable concepts – and about using the computer program AMOS to facilitate the analysis.

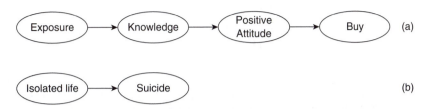

Figure 1 (a) The hierarchy-of-effects model; (b) Durkheim's suicide model

Scientific work is characterized by the fact that a scientist works with *models*, i.e. simplified descriptions of the phenomenon in 'the real world' that is the object of the research. An example of such a model is the hierarchy-of-effects model depicting the various stages through which a recipient of an advertising message is supposed to move from awareness to (hopefully) the final purchase (e.g. Lavidge & Steiner, 1961). See Figure 1a.

Another example comes from the theory of the pioneering French sociologist and philosopher, Emile Durkheim, that living an isolated life increases the probability of suicide (Durkheim, 1897). This theory can be depicted as in Figure 1b.

We can see that a scientific theory may be depicted as a graphic model in which the hypothesized connections among the concepts of the theory are shown as arrows.

What then is SEM?

SEM is a collection of tools for analyzing connections between various concepts in cases where these connections are relevant either for expanding our general knowledge or for solving some problem.

Examples of such problems are as follows:

1. Health officials might be interested in mapping a *possible* connection between smoking during pregnancy and infant health.
2. School authorities might be interested in examining the effects of various factors having a *possible* impact on students' academic achievement.
3. A psychologist might be interested in developing a questionnaire that could 'measure' the respondent's 'style of information processing', i.e. whether the respondent prefers a verbal and/or visual modality of processing information about his or her environment. In that connection the psychologist is interested in mapping the *possible* connection between a person's 'style of information processing' and the same person's answers to the various proposed questions.
4. A health researcher might be interested in mapping a *possible* connection between a person's psychical well-being and the same person's physical reactions.
5. An advertising manager or a health official might (for different reasons) be interested in mapping a *possible* connection between cigarette advertising and cigarette sales.

The key term is the word *possible*. We are not sure that a connection exists, but we want to find out whether it exists and, if so, to measure the strengths of the connection in numerical form.

So, SEM is a set of tools for verifying theories. In principle we start out with an a priori theory about the system we want to map, and then use SEM to test our model against empirical data – SEM is a *confirmatory* rather than an *exploratory* technique.

Our hope is that we can *confirm* our model and as a result be able to measure the *strength* of the various 'connections', and in that way be able to answer questions such as 'By how much can we expect each extra pack of cigarettes smoked during pregnancy to reduce birth weight?'

However, this does not exclude the possibility that our analysis might lead to modifications of the original model as we gain more insight while working with our model – so the distinction between confirmatory and exploratory is not a sharp one.

As the name 'structural equation *modeling*' suggests, the first step is to form a graphic depiction – *a model* – showing how the various concepts fit together.

Let us look at the first example above.

Example 1
Cigarette smoking during pregnancy and infant health
(Mullahy, 1997)

If we measure cigarette smoking in 'total number of cigarettes smoked during pregnancy' and infant health by 'birth weight' we can suggest the model shown in Figure 2a. The concepts are shown in rectangles and the 'connection' between them is depicted as an arrow indicating the direction of a possible causal effect: we suspect the mother's cigarette smoking to affect the child's birth weight and not the other way round.

In this example it is easy to decide on the direction of a (possible) effect, but at times this can be more problematic, e.g. Example 5 in the list above, where an advertising manager hopes that advertising will promote sales – but we cannot rule out the possibility that a positive covariation between advertising and sales figures could be due to the way the advertising budget is compiled, e.g. using a fixed percentage of sales income for advertising. That is why I have avoided words like 'cause' and 'effect' in the list of examples above and used the more vague expression 'connection'. As you will learn in Section 4, it takes more than covariation to confirm a possible causal effect, and SEM is (in principle) only the analysis of covariations.

β is a measure of the strength of the connection and δ (*disturbance*) depicts the combined effect of all other factors influencing the child's birth weight.

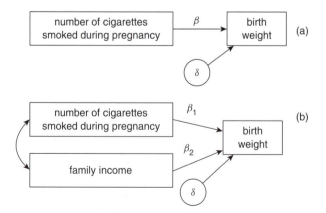

Figure 2   Example 1: a traditional regression model

There are many such other causes, most of which (in order to keep the model simple) could be summed up in economic power as measured by total family income, so let us modify our model by including 'family income' as shown in panel (b). In this way we reduce the 'noise' summed up in δ. The two-headed arrow depicts a possible covariation between 'total number of cigarettes smoked during pregnancy' and 'family income', a covariation not 'explained' by the model. You may know this phenomenon under the name of *multicollinearity* from when you learned multiple regression in your introductory statistics course. If you need a refresher, consult Appendix A.

So much for the word 'model' in 'structural equation modeling'. What about the words 'structural equation'?

If we let the Greek letters β_1 and β_2 stand for the strength of the two effects while β_0 is a constant, we can just as well express our model in the *structural equation*

$$Y = \beta_0 + \beta_1 X_1 + \beta_2 X_2 + \delta \tag{1}$$

where Y is 'birth weight', X_1 is 'number of cigarettes smoked during pregnancy' and X_2 is 'family income'.

This is a traditional multiple regression model that most of us should know from our introductory course in statistics. So, you can see that multiple regression is a special case of SEM. As mentioned above, SEM is about mapping 'relations', so the regressions coefficients β_1 and β_2 are the parameters of interest here (I have, however, added the intercept β_0 just to make the equation look familiar to you).

An obvious way to judge the correctness of the model in Figure 2b is to take a sample of mothers from the relevant population and question them about the three variables 'birth weight', 'number of cigarettes smoked during pregnancy' and 'family income'.

You can therefore test the model's agreement with empirical data by multiple regression and in that way verify the model.

In this case you do not need AMOS to estimate the parameters (β_0, β_1, β_2 and the variance of δ) in the model, but if you do you will get exactly the same result as if you used traditional regression analysis.

(Note that covariances between independent variables are not considered parameters of the model in regression analysis – but they are in SEM, a point worth remembering!)

Usually, however, our models are a bit more complicated – and then regression analysis will not do the job. This can be illustrated using the second example above.

Example 2
Students' academic achievements

The model shown in Figure 3 was used by Joireman and Abbott (2004) – using AMOS – to examine the impact of various factors they suggested affected students' academic achievements.

This model is more representative of the complexity usually met in SEM – and here traditional regression analysis will (in general) not do the job.

In Example 1, 'number of cigarettes smoked' and 'family income' are traditionally called *independent variables* while 'birth weight' is the *dependent variable*; it depends on 'number of cigarettes smoked' and 'family income' – or at least that is what we think may be the case.

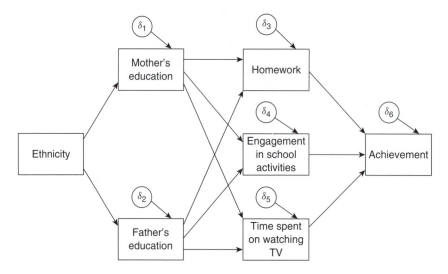

Figure 3 Example 2: model used to explain the impact of factors affecting students' academic achievements

A glance at the model in Figure 3 reveals that here things are a bit more complicated. Looking only at the connection between 'mother's education' and 'homework' you could say that 'mother's education' is the independent variable and 'homework' the dependent variable. However, 'mother's education' is dependent on 'ethnicity', so it is *also* a dependent variable.

This shows that we have to draw a very important distinction between *exogenous variables*, whose values are determined by variables not included in the model, and *endogenous variables*, the values of which are determined by other variables in the model.

In the model in Figure 3 (apart from δ-variables) the only exogenous variable is 'ethnicity' – all other variables are endogenous.

Example 3
Constructing a measuring instrument

A psychologist is constructing a questionnaire that can 'measure' a person's 'style of processing', i.e. the person's preference to engage in a verbal and/or visual modality of processing information about his or her environment.

The psychologist decides on using a summated scale.

A summated scale is compiled by adding up scores obtained from answering a series of questions. One of the most popular scales is the *Likert scale*. Here the respondents are asked to indicate their agreement with a series of statements by checking a scale from, say, 1 (strongly disagree) to 5 (strongly agree) and the scores are then added to make up the scale. The scale values are in the opposite direction for statements that are favorably worded versus unfavorably worded in regard to the concept being measured.

Examples of such questions – or *items* as they are called in this connection – to measure 'style of processing' are as follows:

1. I enjoy work that requires the use of words.
2. There are some special times in my life that I like to relive by mentally 'picturing' just how everything looked.
3. When I'm trying to learn something new, I'd rather watch a demonstration than read how to do it.

The psychologist has formulated around 50 such items (statements), and is now wondering which of them should be chosen for inclusion in the questionnaire – the criteria of course being that the ones with the strongest 'connection' to the concept 'style of processing' should be the preferred ones.

The problem can be modeled as in Figure 4.

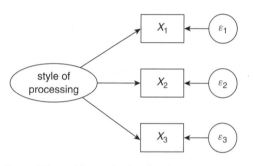

Figure 4   Example 3: model used in scale development

The X-variables in the figure are three items supposed to measure 'style of processing', and the three ε-variables indicate that factors other than the variable 'style of processing' affect how people answer a question. The error, ε, is the combined effect of all such 'disturbing' effects. In other words, ε is the measurement error of the item in question.

You may wonder why the variable 'style of processing' in the model in Figure 4 is shown as an ellipse (just like the concepts in Figure 1), while the concepts in Figure 2 are depicted as rectangles. This is done because there is a fundamental difference between 'number of cigarettes', 'family income' and 'birth weight' on the one hand, and 'style of processing' on the other.

The first-mentioned concepts are *measurable*, i.e. there exist well-defined ways of measuring them. They are measured in number of cigarettes, in dollars (or whatever currency is relevant) and in pounds or kilograms. Such measurable variables are called *manifest variables*, and they are traditionally depicted as squares or rectangles.

A characteristic of the concept 'style of processing' in the model in Figure 4 is that it is not directly measurable by a generally accepted measuring instrument, a characteristic it shares with many concepts from the social and behavioral sciences – satisfaction, preference, intelligence, lifestyle, social class and literacy, just to mention a few. Such non-measurable variables are called *latent variables*. Latent variables are traditionally depicted as circles or ellipses.

As such concepts cannot be measured directly, they are measured indirectly by *indicators* – in this case items in a Likert scale – and such indicators are *manifest variables*.

The arrows connecting a latent variable to its manifest variables should be interpreted as follows.

If a latent variable were measurable on a continuous scale – which of course is not the case as a latent variable is not (directly) measurable on *any* scale – variations in a person's (or whatever the analytical unit may be) position on this scale would be mirrored in variations in its manifest variables. This is the reason why the arrows point *from* the latent variable *towards* its manifest indicators and not the other way round.

The purpose is now to estimate the parameters in the model in Figure 4, these parameters being the three regression coefficients and the variances of the ε-variables, and then use the result to select the 'best' items (i.e. the ones with the strongest connection to 'style of processing') for use in the summated Likert scale.

In this case we cannot use traditional regression analysis, because one of the variables is latent, but AMOS can do the job.

In fact, the three items in this example are taken from the 22-item SOP (Style of Processing) scale by Childers, Houston, & Heckler (1985). We will return to this example in Chapter 6.

Selection of items for summated and non-summated scales is discussed in the next chapter.

Example 4
The effects of depression on the immune system

A health researcher is interested in evaluating the (possible) connection between depression and the state of the immune system, and tentatively suggests the model shown in Figure 5 (this figure is part of a more complicated model, to which we will return in Chapter 7).

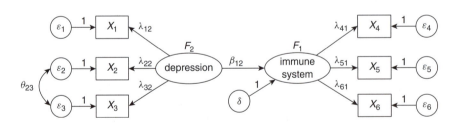

Figure 5   Example 4: a model with latent variables

As can be seen, the model contains the hypothesized effect of 'depression' on 'immune system' as well as the connections between the two latent (non-measurable) variables and their manifest (measurable) indicators.

The model thus consists of two parts:

1. The *structural model* describing the (causal?) connections between the latent variables. Mapping of this connection is the main purpose of the analysis.
2. The *measurement model* describing the connections between the latent variables and their manifest indicators.

We can translate the graphic model into a set of equations:

$$F_1 = \beta_{12}F_2 + \delta$$

$$X_1 = \lambda_{12}F_2 + \varepsilon_1 \qquad X_4 = \lambda_{41}F_1 + \varepsilon_4$$

$$X_2 = \lambda_{22}F_2 + \varepsilon_2 \qquad X_5 = \lambda_{51}F_1 + \varepsilon_5 \qquad (2)$$

$$X_3 = \lambda_{32}F_2 + \varepsilon_3 \qquad X_6 = \lambda_{61}F_1 + \varepsilon_6$$

where F_1 is the state of the immune system and F_2 depression. The first equation describes the structural model and the last six the measurement model.

We note that a hypothesized causal structure can be depicted in two ways:

1. As a graph with variables shown as circles (or ellipses) and squares (or rectangles), (possible) 'causal' links shown as arrows, and covariation not explained by the model shown as two-headed arrows.
2. As a system of equations.

Both ways of depicting models have their advantages. The graph has great communicative power, and the equations make it possible to use traditional algebraic manipulations. Usually during a study you sketch one or more models, and then translate the drawings into equations, which are used as input to calculations. Newer computer programs (such as AMOS) also make it possible to draw a graph of the model, which the program then translates into program statements ('equations') and carries out the calculations necessary to estimate the parameters.

Throughout the book I will use the notation in Figure 5. Latent variables are depicted by circles or ellipses and manifest variables by squares or rectangles. A one-headed arrow depicts a hypothesized relationship between two variables, the arrow pointing from the independent to the dependent variable, while a two-headed arrow indicates covariance unexplained by other variables in the model. β denotes a coefficient in the structural model and λ a coefficient in the measurement model.

Coefficients usually have a subscript with two digits, the first indicating the head of the arrow and the second the foot. However, if no risk of misunderstanding exists, only one subscript is used.

Covariances between exogenous (predetermined) variables are denoted by ϕ and covariances between error terms are denoted by θ. Subscripts indicate the variables involved. If the two digits of the subscript are the same, it indicates a variance. Variances are not shown in the figure.

In this case we have several latent variables:

1. The two variables that are the center of our research: 'depression' and 'state of the immune system'.
2. The δ (*disturbance*) is the combined effect of all factors having an effect on the dependent variable, but not explicitly included in the model.
3. The six ε-variables indicate that factors other than the latent variable ('depression' or 'state of the immune system') affect the result of a measurement – ε (*error*) is the combined effect of all such 'disturbing' effects.

Depression could be measured by Likert items such as:

X_1. I am sad all the time and I cannot snap out of it.
X_2. I am so restless and agitated that I have to keep moving or doing something.
X_3. I have as much energy as ever.

Most often you will have more than three items in a scale, but three will do as an illustration (in fact the three items mentioned above are taken from one of the most widespread scales for measuring the strength of depression: 'Beck's Depression Inventory' (Beck, Ward, Mendelson, & Erbaugh, 1961)). Observe that the variables X_1 to X_3 are expected to correlate, because they are all functions of the same variable 'depression' – they are measuring the same concept. However a glance at the wording of X_2 and X_3 shows that they are indeed very similar, and they could be expected to correlate *more* than by their mutual cause 'depression'. If that should be the case X_2 and X_3 measure not only the same latent variable 'depression', but also the same aspect of that concept, therefore the double-headed arrow in Figure 5.

A characteristic of the summated scale is that in taking an unweighted sum of the various scores you implicitly assume that all the questions (or items) making up the scale measure the concept to the same precision. An advantage of SEM is that instead of summing the various items, you can use the items separately, and in that way weight them in accordance with their quality in measuring the concept in question.

Now, we cannot measure the state of the immune system by using a questionnaire. Instead we carry out a few tests to measure variables that could be used as indicators, such as number of leukocytes, number of lymphocytes and PHA-stimulated T-cell proliferation.

To sum up, a theory is a number of hypothesized connections among conceptually defined variables. These variables are often latent, i.e. they are not directly measurable and must be operationalized in a series of manifest variables.

These manifest variables and their interrelations are all we have at our disposal to uncover the connections among the latent variables.

The benefits of using latent variables

The variables with which the social science researcher works are usually more diffuse than concepts such as weight, length and the like, for which well-defined and generally accepted measuring methods exist. Rather, the social scientist works with concepts such as attitudes, literacy, alienation, social status, etc. Concepts are not directly measurable and therefore must be measured indirectly via indicators, whether they are questions in a questionnaire or some sort of test.

If we compare SEM with a traditional regression model, such as

$$Y_i = \beta_0 + \beta_1 X_i + \delta_i \tag{3}$$

it is obvious that the latter is based on an assumption which is rarely mentioned but is nevertheless usually unrealistic: that is, all variables are measured without error. (The assumption of no measurement error always applies to the independent variable, whereas you can assume that δ_i includes measurement error in the dependent variable as well as the effect of excluded variables.)

An assumption of error-free measurements is of course always wrong in principle, but it will serve as a reasonable simplification when measuring, e.g. weight, volume, temperature and other variables for which generally agreed measurement units and measuring instruments exist.

On the other hand, such an assumption is clearly unrealistic when the variables are lifestyle, intelligence, attitudes and the like. Any measurement will be an imperfect indicator of such a concept. Using more than one indicator per latent variable makes it possible to assess the connection between an indicator and the concept it is assumed to measure and in this way evaluate the quality of the measuring instrument.

Introducing measurement models has the effect of freeing the estimated parameters in the structural model from the influence of measurement errors. Or – put another way – the errors in the structural model ('errors in equations' δ) are separated from the errors in the measurement model ('errors in variables' ε).

What then is SEM?

As should be clear from the examples, SEM is not a single statistical model, but rather a collection of models originated in different disciplines at different times and brought together, because they can be shown to be special cases of a general model.

In Example 1 you met the traditional regression model that you should already know from your introductory statistics course, and in Example 2 several such models were put together to form a system of regression functions. Such systems are known in psychology and related fields as *path models* and in economics as *simultaneous equation models* or *econometric models*.

The model in Example 3 is generally known as the *confirmatory factor model*, and in Example 4 the path model and the confirmatory factor model are brought together to form *the general structural equation model*, of which the models in the first three examples are special cases. In fact, the general model can be shown to include many of the linear models that are bases for statistical techniques you may already know: analysis of variance, canonical correlation and discriminant analysis, to mention a few. So the structural equation model is very general indeed, and well suited for analyzing a broad spectrum of problems in many disciplines.

3   A Short History of SEM

SEM can trace its history back more than 100 years.

At the beginning of the twentieth century C. Spearman laid the foundation for factor analysis and thereby for the measurement model in SEM (Spearman, 1904). He tried to trace the different dimensions of intelligence back to a general intelligence factor. In the 1930s L. L. Thurstone invented multi-factor analysis and factor rotation (more or less in opposition to Spearman), and thereby founded modern factor analysis where intelligence, for instance, was thought of as being composed of several different intelligence dimensions (Thurstone, 1947; Thurstone & Thurstone, 1941).

About 20 years after Spearman, S. Wright developed so-called *path analysis* (Wright, 1918, 1921). Based on box-and arrow-diagrams like those in Figure 3, he formulated a series of rules that connected correlations among the variables to parameters in a model of the assumed data-generating process. Most of his work was on models with only manifest variables, but a few also included models with latent variables.

Wright was a biometrician and it is amazing that his work was more or less unknown to scientists outside this area, until it was taken up by social researchers in the 1960s (Blalock, 1961, 1971; Duncan, 1975).

In economics a parallel development took place in what came to be known as *econometrics*. However, this development was unaffected by Wright's ideas, and was characterized by an absence of latent variables – at least in the sense of the word used in this book. However, in the 1950s econometricians became aware of Wright's work, and some of them found to their surprise that he had pioneered estimation of supply and demand functions and in several respects was far ahead of econometricians of that time (Goldberger, 1972).

In the early 1970s path analysis and factor analysis were combined to form the general SEM of today. Foremost in its development was K. G. Jöreskog, who created the well-known LISREL (LInear Structural RELations) program for analyzing such models (Jöreskog, 1973).

However, LISREL is not alone in this. Among other similar computer programs mention can be made of EQS (EQuationS) (Bentler, 1985) and RAM (Reticular Action Model) (McArdle & McDonald, 1984) included in the SYSTAT package of statistics programs under the name RAMONA (Reticular Action Model Or Near Approximation), and of course AMOS (Arbuckle, 1989).

Jöreskog was a statistician but published much of his research in psychological journals. No wonder then that psychology was the area where this 'new' way of thinking first gained widespread use.

The first discipline to 'import' SEM – and the area where it has found most use outside of psychology – is marketing. One of the first articles on SEM in the *Journal of Marketing Research* was by Bagozzi (1977), and three years later this author published a book on the use of SEM in marketing (Bagozzi, 1980).

Since then there is hardly any area within the social and life sciences where SEM is not gaining more and more appreciation.

The reasons for this are very simple: we often have to struggle with measurement problems, and the possibilities to perform experiments are often limited.

Last but not least, SEM forces you to think in terms of hypotheses, models and verification, i.e. it *speaks* the language of science and forces you to think as a scientist.

There is an exception to the development sketched above, namely *economics*, where the use of latent variables (in the SEM sense) is not apparent, despite modern economists are spending more and more time analyzing 'soft' variables like health, values, etc.

4   The Problem of Non-experimental Data

Basing causal conclusions on non-experimental data usually necessitates statistical models comprising several equations as opposed to traditional regression analysis and analysis of variance, which serve us so well in the simpler situations we meet when we analyze experimental data. Besides, the statistical assumptions underlying the models used are more difficult to fulfill in non-experimental research, and last but not least, the concept of causality must be used with greater care in non-experimental research.

As is well known, we are not able to observe causation – considered as a 'force' from cause to effect. What we *can* observe is:

1. *Covariation* – the fact that two factors A and B covary is an indication of the possible existence of a causal relationship – in one direction or the other.
2. *The time sequence* – the fact that the occurrence of A is generally followed by the occurrence of B is an indication of A being a cause of B (and not the other way round).

However (and this is a crucial requirement):

3. These observations must be made under conditions that rule out all other explanations of the observations than that of the hypothesized causation.

These three points could be used as building blocks in an operational definition of the concept of causation, even if this concept 'in the real world' is somewhat dim and perhaps meaningless except as a common experience facilitating communication between people (Hume, 1739).

It is clear from the above that we can never *prove* a causal relationship; we can only render it probable. It is not possible to rule out all other explanations, but we can try to rule out the ones deemed most 'probable' to the extent that makes the claimed explanation 'A is the cause of B' the most probable.

The extent to which this can be done depends on the nature of the data from which the conclusions are drawn.

The data

The necessary data can be obtained in one of two different ways:

1. Data can be 'historical' in the sense that they mirror 'the real world', e.g. the actual consequences that a firm's pricing policy has had on sales.
2. Data can be experimental: you can make your own 'world' in which you can manipulate the variables whose effects you want to investigate.

Historical data are often called *observational* data in order to indicate that while in an experiment you deliberately manipulate the independent variables, you do not interfere with the variables in non-experimental research more than necessary in order to observe (i.e. measure) them.

The necessity of a closed system

To rule out all possible explanations except one is of course impossible, and since we can examine only a subset of (possible) explanations it is obvious that causal relationships can only be mapped in isolated systems. Clearly, experimental data are to be preferred to non-experimental data, because in an experiment we create our own world in accordance with an experimental plan designed to reduce outside influences.

It is much more difficult to cut out disturbing effects in a non-experimental study. In an experiment we create our own little world but when we base our study on the real world, we must accept the world as it is. We deal with historical data and cannot change the past.

While it seems obvious that causality can only be established – or according to Hume (1739) only be meaningful – in a scientific model which constitutes a closed system, it is a little more complicated to define 'closed'.

Example 5
The determinants of cigarette sales

In Figure 6 – inspired by Bass (1969) – some of the factors determining cigarette sales are depicted. There are an enormous number of possible factors influencing cigarette sales – many more than shown in the figure. It would not be very difficult to expand the model to cover several pages of this book. In causal research it is necessary to keep down the number of variables – in this example (as Bass did) to the variables on the gray background.

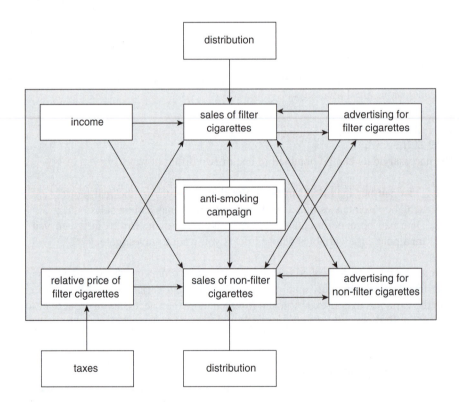

Figure 6   Example 5: The demand for cigarettes (δ-terms not shown)

As any limit on the number of variables must necessarily cut causal relations, we cannot demand that the system has no relation to the surrounding world. What we require is that all effects on a variable, in the model from outside the model can be summarized in one variable which is of purely random (i.e. non-systematic) nature, and with a variance small enough not to 'drown' effects from variables in the model in 'noise'. If we use the Greek letter δ (disturbance) to designate the combined effects of excluded independent variables (noise), we can write

$$Y = f(X_1, X_2, X_3, \ldots, X_j, \ldots, X_p) + \delta \qquad (4a)$$

where Y is the dependent variable in the model, and X_j ($j = 1, 2, \ldots, p$) are exogenous variables included in the model and supposed to influence Y. If the model is really 'closed', X_j and δ must be stochastically independent. This is the same as demanding that for each and every value of X_j the expected value of δ is the same and consequently the same as the unconditional expected value of δ. This can be written as

$$E(\delta \mid X_j) = E(\delta) = 0 \quad \text{for all values of } j \qquad (4b)$$

(for a definition of *expected value*, see Appendix A).

If condition (4b) is not met, a *ceteris paribus* interpretation of the parameters indicating the influence of the various independent variables is not possible, because the effects of variables included in the model are then mixed up with the effects of variables *not* included in the model.

Simon (1953, 1954) has given Hume's operational definition of causality a modern formulation.

Example 6
The disturbance must be independent of exogenous variables

As is well known (Appendix A), least squares estimation in traditional regression analysis forces δ to be independent of the exogenous variables $X_1, \ldots, X_j, \ldots, X_p$ *in the model* – and so do the estimation methods used in AMOS. But the point is that this condition must hold in the population and not just in our model. So be careful in specifying your model.

Consider the following model:

score obtained at exam $= f(\textit{number of classes attended}) + \delta$

Think about what variables are contained in δ: intelligence, motivation, age and earlier education, to name but a few. Do you think that it is likely that 'number of classes attended' does not depend on any of these factors?

Three different causal models
Figure 7 shows three causal models from marketing, depicting three fundamentally different causal structures.

Dominick (1952) reported an in-store experiment concerning the effect on sales of four different packages for McIntosh apples. The experiment ran for four days in four retail stores. The causal model is shown in Figure 7a. In order to reduce the noise δ, the most influencing factors affecting sales (apart from the package) were included in the experiment, namely the effects on sales caused by differences among the shops in which the experiment was conducted, the effects caused by variations in sales over time, and the varying number of customers in the shops during the testing period.

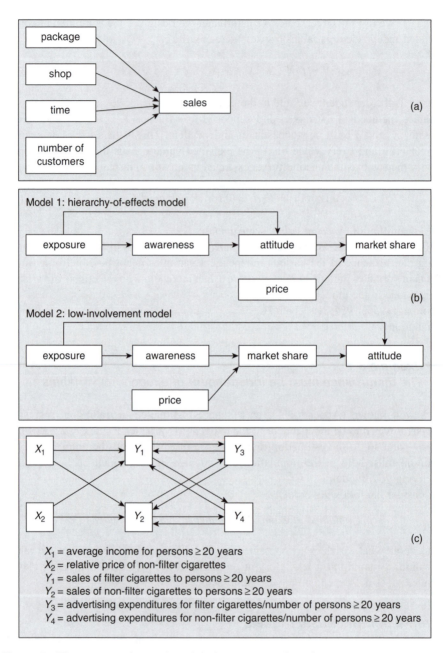

Figure 7   Three types of causal models (δ-terms not shown)

Aaker and Day (1971) tried to decide which of the two models in Figure 7b best describe buying behavior in regard to coffee. The question is whether buying coffee is considered a *high-involvement activity* (in which an attitude towards a brand is founded on assimilated information prior to the actual buying decision), or the buying of coffee is a *low-involvement activity* (where the attitude towards the brand is based on the actual use of the product). The non-experimental data came partly from a store panel (market shares and prices) and partly from telephone interviews (awareness and attitude). The models in the figure are somewhat simplified compared with Aaker's original models, which additionally included a time dimension showing how the various independent variables extend their effects over subsequent periods of time.

Bass (1969) analyzed the effects of advertising on cigarette sales using the model in Figure 7c based on time series data.

The three examples illustrate three types of causal models of increasing complexity.

The model in Figure 7a has only one box with ingoing arrows. Such models are typical of studies based on experimental data, and the analysis is uncomplicated, since:

1. There is no doubt about the orientation of the arrows – they depart from the variables being manipulated and from variables incorporated in the model in order to reduce the amount of noise.
2. The model can be expressed in only one equation.
3. The parameters in this equation can (subject to the usual assumptions) be estimated with regression analysis or analysis of variance (or in this case analysis of covariance) – simple statistical techniques which can be found in any introductory statistics text.

In Figure 7b and c there are several boxes with both ingoing and outgoing arrows, so the model translates into more than one equation, because every box with an ingoing arrow is a dependent variable, and for every dependent variable there is an equation. For example, the hierarchy-of-effects model can be expressed by the following equations:

$$awareness = f_1(exposure) + \delta_1$$
$$attitude = f_2(exposure, awareness) + \delta_2$$
$$market\ share = f_3(attitude, price) + \delta_3$$

Such a system of equations, where some of the variables appear as both dependent and independent variables, is typical of causal models based on non-experimental data. This complicates the analysis, because it is not obvious a priori that the various equations are independent with regard to estimation, so can we then estimate the equations one by one using traditional regression analysis?

While the graphs in Figure 7b are *acyclic* (i.e. it is not possible to pass through the same box twice by following the arrows), the graph in 7c is *cyclic*: you can walk your way through the graph by following the arrows and pass through the same box several times. In a way you could say that such a variable has an effect on itself – a problem that I return to in Chapter 5. In the example the cyclic nature comes from reciprocal effects between advertising and sales: not only does advertising influence sales – which is the purpose – but sales could also influence advertising through budgeting routines.

We therefore have *two* (possible) causal relationships between advertising and sales, and the problem is to separate them analytically – to *identify* the two relationships.

This identification problem does not arise in acyclic models, at least not under certain reasonable assumptions. The causal chain is a 'one-way street', just as in an experiment. This means that not only is the statistical analysis simpler, but also the same thing applies to the substantive interpretation and the use of the results.

Causality in non-experimental research

Care must be taken in interpreting the coefficients in a regression equation, when using non-experimental data.

To take a simple example from marketing research, suppose a market researcher wants to find the influence of price on sales of a certain product. The researcher decides to run an experiment in a retail store by varying the price and noting the amount sold. The data are then analyzed by regression analysis, and the result is

$$sales = a_0 + a_1(price) \qquad (5a)$$

where a_0 and a_1 are the estimated coefficients.

Suppose the same researcher also wants to estimate the influence of income on sales of the same product. Now, the researcher cannot experiment with people's income, so he or she takes a representative sample from the relevant population and asks the respondents – among other things – how much of the product they have bought in the last week, and also asks them about their annual income. The researcher then runs a regression analysis, the result of which is

$$sales = b_0 + b_1(income) \qquad (5b)$$

How do we interpret the regression coefficients a_1 and b_1 in the two cases?

The immediate answer you would get by asking anyone with a knowledge of regression analysis is that a_1 shows by how many units sales would change if the price were changed by one unit and b_1 by how many units sales would change if income were changed one unit.

However, this interpretation is only valid in the first case, where prices were actually changed.

In the second case, income is not actually changed, and b_1 depicts by how many units we can expect a household's purchase to change if it is *replaced* by another household with an income one unit different from the first.

Therefore the word 'causality' must be used with great care in non-experimental research, if we cannot rule out the possibility that, by replacing a household (or whatever the analytical unit may be) with another, the two units could differ on other variables than the one that is of immediate interest.

This is exactly the reason why an earlier name for SEM – 'causal modeling' – went out of use.

It is only fair to mention that the use of SEM is in no way restricted to non-experimental research, although this is by far its most common use. Readers interested in exploring the possible advantages of using SEM in experimental research are referred to Bagozzi (1977) and Bagozzi and Yi (1994).

However, in this book you will find SEM used only on non-experimental data. The point to remember is that SEM is based on relations among the manifest variables measured as covariances, and (as you have probably heard several times before) 'correlation is *not* causation'. Therefore – as pointed out at the beginning of this section – it takes more than statistically significant relations to 'prove' causation.

If time series data are available you can also use the time sequence to support your theory, but – and this is the crucial condition – you cannot for pure statistical reasons rule out the possibility that other mechanisms could have given rise to your observations.

A claimed causal connection should be based on substantiated theoretical arguments.

5 Drawing Structural Equation Models in AMOS Graphics

Picturing a model – such as the one in Figure 5 – gives you an impression of the model structure that is harder to obtain by reading through a series of equations.

AMOS has a drawing environment, 'AMOS Graphics', that is particularly suited for drawing structural equation models. Furthermore, it is possible to program AMOS by just drawing the model, so that you do not need to learn a long list of program statements in order to do SEM.

When you click the AMOS Graphics icon, the window shown in Figure 8 appears.

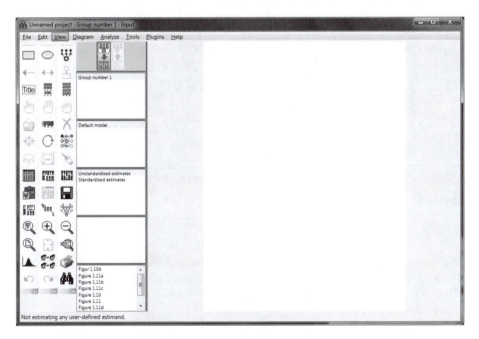

Figure 8 The opening page of the AMOS Graphics interface

To the right you will see your working place and, to the left, there is your toolbox. I will not go deeply into the functions of the various tools, because, when you point at a tool, a short text will pop up telling you the function of the tool. If you move your pointer around in the toolbox, you will observe that some of the tools are not really drawing tools at all but programming tools, the use of which I will postpone until you have been introduced to programming in Chapter 4.

So, let us concentrate on drawing, and let us draw the model from Figure 5.

As the model is wider than it is tall, it is a good idea to change the orientation of the drawing area, and choose 'landscape' instead of the default 'portrait'. Choose 'View/ Interface Properties', and when the window shown in Figure 9 appears, choose 'Landscape - A4'.

Start by choosing the 'indicator tool' 👹, and place the mouse pointer where you want your first latent variable – in this case the variable 'depression'. Then click

Figure 9   Choosing paper orientation

four times. The first click produces an ellipse (the size of which you determine by dragging the mouse) to symbol the latent variable, and each of the following three clicks adds an indicator. After four clicks, your window should look as shown in Figure 10a.

Now choose the 'rotate tool' ↻ and click in the ellipse. This click will rotate the diagram clockwise by 90°. Then choose the 'reflect tool' ▧ and click the ellipse once more, and your screen should look as in panel (b). Of course, you could instead have clicked the rotate tool three times.

Now choose the 'select all tool' 🖑 and click the ellipse. Then each time you click and drag the selected objects using the 'duplicate tool' 🖺, you produce a copy. In this case you only make one copy and drag it to the right. Should you by accident drop it in the wrong position, you can always pick it up again using the 'removal van' 🚚. Then, after having reflected the dependent variable, your screen should look like panel (c).

As your next steps you add a disturbance to the endogenous variable, connect the exogenous variables to the endogenous variable by a single-headed arrow, and connect the two error terms to each other by a two-headed arrow (cf. Figure 5).

To add the disturbance term choose the 'error tool' 🔺 and click in the (latent) endogenous variable. To add one- and two-headed arrows, choose the 'path tool' ← or the 'covariance tool' ↔, move the mouse pointer to the starting variable, press the button

Figure 10 Using the 'indicator tool' (a). Using the 'rotate' and the 'reflect tools' (b). Using the 'select all' and 'duplicate tool' (c). Using the 'error', 'path' and 'covariance tools' (d)

and hold it down while you move the mouse pointer to the target variable, where you release the button. Your diagram should now look like panel (d).

What remains in order to complete the drawing is to name the various variables. Double-click the left latent variable symbol, and a dialog box like the one in Figure 11 appears. As you can see, I have filled out the variable name box, after which the model looks as in Figure 12a.

With the dialog box still open, repeat this procedure for the other latent variable, for the manifest variables and for the disturbance and error symbols, naming them as in Figure 5 (but remember, no Greek letters), and your screen should look as in Figure 12b.

You will have noted that AMOS by default set the regression coefficients for errors at '1'. An explanation of the other two '1s' will have to wait until Section 4.2.

Now, experiment with the drawing tools on your own!

Figure 11   Naming the latent variables

6   The Data Matrix and Other Matrices

In the computer output from AMOS, in the AMOS manual and whenever you read an article where SEM is used, you will come across a wide variety of matrices. Therefore a few words on vectors and matrices are in order.

A *matrix* is a rectangular arrangement of numbers in rows and columns. In the data matrix in Table 1, X_{ij} is the value of variable j on observation i. In this book the observation is most often a person, and the variable is an answer to a question in a questionnaire.

The need to be able to describe manipulations, not of single numbers but of whole data matrices, has resulted in the development of *matrix algebra*. Matrix algebra can be considered a form of shorthand, where every single operator (e.g. + or −) describes a series of mathematical operations performed on the elements in the matrices involved. So, matrix algebra does not make it easier to do actual calculations, but it makes it easier to describe the calculations.

Table 1   Data matrix

Variable → Observation ↓	1	2	...	j	...	p
1	X_{11}	X_{12}	...	X_{1j}	...	X_{1p}
2	X_{21}	X_{22}	...	X_{2j}	...	X_{2p}
⋮	⋮	⋮		⋮		⋮
i	X_{i1}	X_{i2}	...	X_{ij}	...	X_{ip}
⋮	⋮	⋮		⋮		⋮
n	X_{n1}	X_{n2}	...	X_{nj}	...	X_{np}

Figure 12 Naming the variables

In matrix notation the data matrix is

$$\mathbf{X} = \begin{bmatrix} x_{11} & x_{12} & \cdots & x_{1j} & \cdots & x_{1p} \\ x_{21} & x_{22} & \cdots & x_{2j} & \cdots & x_{2p} \\ \vdots & \vdots & & \vdots & & \vdots \\ x_{i1} & x_{i2} & \cdots & x_{ij} & \cdots & x_{ip} \\ \vdots & \vdots & & \vdots & & \vdots \\ x_{n1} & x_{n2} & \cdots & x_{nj} & \cdots & x_{np} \end{bmatrix} \tag{6}$$

Matrices are denoted by uppercase boldface letters and ordinary numbers (called *scalars*) by lowercase italicized letters. The matrix $\mathbf{X}$ is a $n \times p$ matrix, i.e. it has n rows and p columns.

A single row in the matrix could be considered as a $1 \times p$ matrix or a *row vector*, the elements of which indicate the coordinates of a point in a p-dimensional coordinate system in which the axes are the variables and the point indicates an observation. In this way we can map the data matrix as n points in a p-dimensional space – the *variable space*. Vectors are denoted by lowercase boldface letters:

$$\mathbf{x}_i = \begin{bmatrix} x_{i1} & x_{i2} & \cdots & x_{ij} & \cdots & x_{np} \end{bmatrix} \tag{7}$$

Alternatively, we could consider the data matrix as composed of p *column vectors*, and map the data as p points each representing a variable in an n-dimensional coordinate system – the *observation space* – the axes of which refer to each of the n observations:

$$\mathbf{x}_j = \begin{bmatrix} x_{j1} \\ x_{j2} \\ \vdots \\ x_{ij} \\ \vdots \\ x_{nj} \end{bmatrix} \tag{8}$$

It is often an advantage to base arguments on such geometrical interpretations.

In addition to the data matrix you will meet a few other matrices. The *sum of cross-products (SCP)* for two variables X_j and X_k is defined as

$$SCP = \sum_{i=1}^{n}(X_{ij} - \overline{X}_j)(X_{ik} - \overline{X}_k) \tag{9}$$

If $j = k$ we obtain the *sum of squares (SS)*. The $p \times p$ matrix

$$\mathbf{C} = \begin{bmatrix} SS_{11} & SCP_{12} & \cdots & SCP_{1j} & \cdots & SCP_{1p} \\ SCP_{21} & SS_{22} & \cdots & SCP_{2j} & \cdots & SCP_{2p} \\ \vdots & \vdots & & \vdots & & \vdots \\ SCP_{i1} & SCP_{i2} & \cdots & SCP_{ij} & \cdots & SCP_{ip} \\ \vdots & \vdots & & \vdots & & \vdots \\ SCP_{p1} & SCP_{p2} & \cdots & SCP_{pj} & \cdots & SS_{pp} \end{bmatrix} \tag{10}$$

containing the SCP and – on the main diagonal (the northwest–southeast diagonal) – the SS of p variables is usually called the *sum of squares and cross-products (SSCP) matrix.*

If all elements in **C** are divided by the *degrees of freedom* $n-1$ (see Appendix A), we obtain the *covariance matrix* **S**, containing all covariances and, on the main diagonal, the variances of the p-variables:

$$\mathbf{S} = \begin{bmatrix} s_{11} & s_{12} & \cdots & s_{1j} & \cdots & s_{1p} \\ s_{21} & s_{22} & \cdots & s_{2j} & \cdots & s_{2p} \\ \vdots & \vdots & & \vdots & & \vdots \\ s_{i1} & s_{i2} & \cdots & s_{ij} & \cdots & s_{ip} \\ \vdots & \vdots & & \vdots & & \vdots \\ s_{n1} & s_{n2} & \cdots & s_{nj} & \cdots & s_{np} \end{bmatrix} \tag{11}$$

If all variables are standardized

$$X_{std} = \frac{X_{ij} - \overline{X}_j}{s_j} \tag{12}$$

where $\overline{X}_j$ is the mean and s_j the standard deviation of X_j, to have mean 0 and variance 1.00 before these calculations, **S** becomes the *correlation matrix* **R**:

$$R = \begin{bmatrix} 1 & r_{12} & \cdots & r_{1j} & \cdots & r_{1p} \\ r_{21} & 1 & \cdots & r_{2j} & \cdots & r_{2p} \\ \vdots & \vdots & & \vdots & & \vdots \\ r_{i1} & r_{i2} & \cdots & r_{ij} & \cdots & r_{ip} \\ \vdots & \vdots & & \vdots & & \vdots \\ r_{n1} & r_{n2} & \cdots & r_{nj} & \cdots & 1 \end{bmatrix} \tag{13}$$

By default AMOS calculates covariance matrices and correlation matrices by dividing by the number of observations, n, and not by *degrees of freedom*, $n-1$ (see Appendix A).

Often you will not need to input the raw data, only the covariance matrix. In this case AMOS will as a default assume that the variances and covariances in the input matrix are calculated using $n-1$ as the denominator. AMOS will then transform this matrix to one where n is used as the denominator and base the following calculations on that. You can of course override the default. Generally, however, it does not make a great difference which of the two is used as the denominator in sample sizes sufficiently large for this kind of analysis.

7 How Do We Estimate the Parameters of a Structural Equation Model?

At first it seems impossible to estimate, for example, the regression coefficient β_{12} in Figure 5. After all, β_{12} connects two latent (i.e. non-measurable) variables. To give you an intuitive introduction to the principle on which estimation of parameters in models with latent variables is based, consider the simple regression model

$$Y = \beta X + \delta \tag{14}$$

where both X and Y are measurable and assume – without loss of generality – that both variables are measured as deviations from their average. Under this assumption we have the following *expected values* E (see Appendix A):

$$E(Y) = E(X) = E(\delta) = 0 \tag{15}$$

Further,

$$Var(Y) = E(Y^2) \tag{16a}$$

$$Var(X) = E(X^2) \tag{16b}$$

$$Cov(YX) = E(YX) \tag{16c}$$

Now

$$Var(Y) = Var(\beta X + \delta) = \beta^2 \sigma_X^2 + \sigma_\delta^2 \qquad (17a)$$

because $E(X\delta) = 0$ following the usual assumption of regression analysis, and from (16c) we get

$$
\begin{aligned}
Cov(YX) = E(YX) &= E\big[(\beta X + \delta)X\big] \\
&= \beta E(X^2) + E(X\delta) \qquad (17b) \\
&= \beta \sigma_X^2
\end{aligned}
$$

We can then write the two covariance matrices

$$
\begin{bmatrix} \sigma_X^2 & \\ \sigma_{YX} & \sigma_Y^2 \end{bmatrix} = \begin{bmatrix} \sigma_X^2 & \\ \beta \sigma_X^2 & \beta^2 \sigma_X^2 + \sigma_\delta^2 \end{bmatrix} \qquad (18)
$$

The model (14) implies a functional connection between the theoretical covariance matrix and the parameters of the model – here β and σ_δ^2.

If the empirical values are substituted for the theoretical ones, (18) becomes

$$
\begin{bmatrix} s_X^2 & \\ s_{YX} & s_Y^2 \end{bmatrix} \cong \begin{bmatrix} s_X^2 & \\ b s_X^2 & b^2 s_X^2 + s_\delta^2 \end{bmatrix} \qquad (19)
$$

The 'approximately equals' sign $\cong$ has been substituted for = because we cannot in general expect the two matrices to be exactly equal, but the better the model describes the data, the more equal the matrices will be.

To generalize, if there is a one-to-one correspondence between the *sample covariance matrix* and the parameters of a model assumed to have generated the sample (i.e. if the model is *identified*) – which is not always the case – then the model can be estimated, its fit tested, and several measures of fit can be calculated based on the difference between the sample covariance matrix and the matrix implied by the model. This difference is called the *residual matrix*:

$$
\begin{bmatrix} s_X^2 & \\ s_{YX} & s_Y^2 \end{bmatrix} - \begin{bmatrix} s_X^2 & \\ b s_X^2 & b^2 s_X^2 + s_\delta^2 \end{bmatrix} = \begin{bmatrix} 0 & \\ s_{YX} - b s_X^2 & s_Y^2 - b^2 s_X^2 + s_\delta^2 \end{bmatrix} \qquad (20)
$$

Therefore SEM is often called *analysis of covariance structures*.

In the regression case above, we can see that minimizing the elements of the residual matrix leads to the traditional estimates of β and σ_δ^2:

$$
\beta \approx b = \frac{s_{YX}}{s_X^2} = \frac{SCP_{YX}}{SS_{XX}} \qquad (21)
$$

$$
\sigma_\delta^2 \approx s_y^2 - s_{yx}^2
$$

which makes all entries in the residual matrix equal to zero.

You can therefore look at least squares not as a method to minimize the sum of squares for the residuals, but to minimize the difference between the two matrices in (19).

This is the basis on which estimation in SEM is built. Every model formulation implies a certain form for the covariance matrix of the manifest variables, and the parameters are estimated as the values that minimize the difference between the sample covariance matrix and the implied covariance matrix, i.e. the residual matrix – or to put it more precisely, a function of the residual matrix is minimized.

In this chapter you met the following concepts:

- theory and model
- exogenous and endogenous variable
- summated scale, Likert scale
- manifest and latent variable- structural model and
- measurement model
- cyclic and acyclic models

- data matrix, SSCP matrix, covariance matrix and correlation matrix
- population and sample covariance matrix
- implied covariance matrix
- residual matrix

- and you have been introduced to AMOS Graphics

Questions

1. Why should a researcher prefer to work with latent variables? (List all the reasons you can.)

2. Explain the concepts 'measurement model' and 'structural model'.

3. To what extent is it possible to support a hypothesis of causal connections using SEM?

4. Explain the difference between cyclic and acyclic models.

5. Explain the various matrices: **X**, **C**, **S** and **R**.

6. Look at Figure 3. Do you have any comments on the model? Do you have any suggestions for modifications of the model?

References

Aaker, D. A., & Day, D. A. (1971). A recursive model of communication processes. In D. A. Aaker (Ed.), *Multivariate analysis in marketing*. Belmont, CA: Wadsworth.

Arbuckle, J. L. (1989). AMOS: Analysis of moment structures. *American Statistician, 43*, 66–67.

Bagozzi, R. P. (1977). Structural equation models in experimental research. *Journal of Marketing Research, 14*, 202–226.

Bagozzi, R. P. (1980). *Causal models in marketing*. New York: Wiley.

Bagozzi, R. P., & Yi, Y. (1994). Advanced topics in structural equation models. In R. P. Bagozzi (Ed.), *Advanced methods of marketing research* (pp. 1–51). Oxford: Blackwell.

Bass, F. M. (1969). A simultaneous study of advertising and sales – analysis of cigarette data. *Journal of Marketing Research, 6*(3), 291–300.

Beck, A. T., Ward, C. H., Mendelson, M., & Erbaugh, J. (1961). An inventory for measuring depression. *Archives of General Psychiatry, 4*, 561–571.

Bentler, P. M. (1985). *Theory and implementation of EQS: A structural equation program*. Los Angeles: BMDP Statistical Software.

Blalock, H. M. (1961). *Causal inferences in non-experimental research*. Chapel Hill, NC: University of North Carolina Press.

Blalock, H. M. (1971). *Causal models in the social sciences*. Chicago: Aldine-Atherton.

Childers, T. L., Houston, M. J., & Heckler, S. (1985). Measurement of individual differences in visual versus verbal information processing. *Journal of Consumer Research, 12*, 124–134.

Dominick, B. A. (1952). *An illustration of the use of the Latin square in measuring the effectiveness of retail merchandising practices*. Ithaca, NY: Department of Agricultural Economics, Cornell University Agricultural Experiment Station, New York State College of Agriculture, Cornell University.

Duncan, O. D. (1975). *Introduction to structural equation models*. New York: Academic Press.

Durkheim, E. (1897). *Suicide*. Available is e.g. (2002). London: Routledge.

Goldberger, A. S. (1972). Structural equation methods in the social sciences. *Econometrica, 40*, 979–1001.

Hume, D. (1739). *A Treatise of human nature*. Available is e.g. (2000) ed. D. Norton. Oxford: Oxford University Press.

Joireman, J., & Abbott, M. (2004). *Structural Equation Models Assessing Relationships Among Student Activities, Ethnicity, Poverty, Parents' Education, and Academic Achievement* (Technical Report #6). Seattle, OR: Washington School Research Center.

Jöreskog, K. G. (1973). A general method for estimating a linear structural equation system. In A. S. Goldberger & O. D. Duncan (Eds), *Structural equation models in the social sciences* (pp. 85–112). New York: Seminar Press.

Lavidge, R. C., & Steiner, G. A. (1961). A model for predictive measurement of advertising effectiveness. *Journal of Marketing, 25*(Oct.), 59–62.

McArdle, J. J., & McDonald, R. P. (1984). Some algebraic properties of the Reticular Action Model for moment structures. *British Journal of Mathematical and Statistical Psychology, 37*, 234–251.

Mullahy, J. (1997). Instrumental-variable estimation of count data models: Applications to models of cigarette smoking behavior. *Review of Economics and Statistics, 79*, 586–593.

Simon, H. A. (1953). Causal ordering and identifiability. In W. C. Hood & T. C. Koopmans (Eds), *Studies in Econometric Method*. New York: Wiley.

Simon, H. A. (1954). Spurious correlation: A causal interpretation. *Journal of the American Statistical Association, 49*(Sept.), 467–479.

Spearman, C. (1904). General intelligence, objectively determined and measured. *American Journal of Psychology, 15*, 201–293.

Thurstone, L. L. (1947). *Multiple factor analysis*. Chicago: University of Chicago Press.

Thurstone, L. L., & Thurstone, T. (1941). *Factorial studies of intelligence*. Chicago: University of Chicago Press.

Wright, S. (1918). On the nature of size factors. *Genetics, 3*, 367–374.

Wright, S. (1921). Correlation and causation. *Journal of Agricultural Research, 20*, 557–585.

2

Measuring Your Variables:
Reliability and Validity

The concepts in your model will usually be rather diffuse (attitude, skill, preference, democracy), i.e. concepts for which no generally agreed measuring instruments exist. In such situations, therefore, you have to make your own measuring instruments – be they questions in a questionnaire or some sort of test.

The first requirement for such an instrument is that if you repeat the measurement under identical conditions, then you will end up with nearly the same result: your instrument must be *reliable*.

Another requirement – which seems just as obvious – is that the instrument should measure exactly what it is intended to measure and nothing else: the instrument must be *valid*.

Reliability and validity are the two main standards by which we evaluate a measuring instrument.

You will learn the classical versions of the two concepts, and you will learn how the use of SEM can illustrate the weaknesses of the classical ways of measuring reliability and validity and perhaps lead to more useful ways of judging these two central concepts.

In Example 1.3 in the previous chapter mention was made of the SOP scale as an example of a summated scale. You will also learn how to construct such scales and how special computer programs can be used to that end.

From now on, you will need access to the companion website in order to carry out some of the activities used to demonstrate concepts and techniques and to take advantage of the exercises.

1   Reliability

We evaluate a measuring instrument by its reliability. The reliability of an instrument is its ability to give nearly identical results in repeated measurements under identical conditions. In other words, reliability is about reproducibility.

Let us consider the simple measurement model in Figure 1 as our point of departure.

Figure 1   A simple measurement model

We can write

$$X = \lambda F + \varepsilon \tag{1a}$$

with the usual conditions

$$E(\varepsilon) = 0 \quad \text{and} \quad Cov(\varepsilon, F) = 0 \tag{1b}$$

The expectation of (1a) is

$$E(X) = E(\lambda F) = \lambda E(F) \tag{2a}$$

and the variance is

$$Var(X) = Var(\lambda F) + Var(\varepsilon) = \lambda^2 Var(F) + \sigma_\varepsilon^2 \tag{2b}$$

While we are able only to observe variation in X, it is of course the latent variable F and its variance – often referred to as the *true variance* – that is the center of our interest. I will now define the *reliability coefficient* ρ_{XX} as the proportion of measured variance that can be traced back to F:

$$\rho_{XX} = \frac{\lambda^2 Var(F)}{\lambda^2 Var(F) + Var(\varepsilon)} = \frac{\lambda^2 Var(F)}{Var(X)} = 1 - \frac{Var(\varepsilon)}{Var(X)} \tag{3a}$$

It is obvious that (1) is an analogue of the simple regression model, and that ρ_{XX} is the squared correlation coefficient in this model. Unlike the traditional regression model, however, the independent variable F is unobservable.

When – as in this case – a latent variable has only one indicator, λ is only a scale factor the value of which is arbitrary. Usually λ is then taken to have the value 1.00, in which case (3a) can be written as

$$\rho_{XX} = \frac{Var(F)}{Var(X)} = 1 - \frac{Var(\varepsilon)}{Var(X)} = \rho_{XF} \tag{3b}$$

Variances, covariances and reliability

Analysis of quantitative empirical data is basically analysis of variation and covariation. By how much do the attributes vary among observations, and to what extent do they covary?

Suppose you are interested in measuring the structural correlation $\rho_{F_1 F_2}$ between the two latent variables F_1 and F_2 in Figure 2. However, since you are able only to observe the empirical correlation r_{XY} between the manifest variables X and Y, you will underestimate the structural covariation.

Figure 2   Correlation and reliability

As you can see from the figure

$$\rho_{XY} = \sqrt{\rho_{XX}} \; \rho_{F_1 F_2} \sqrt{\rho_{YY}} = \rho_{F_1 F_2} \sqrt{\rho_{XX} \rho_{YY}} \tag{4}$$

From which you get

$$\rho_{F_1 F_2} = \frac{\rho_{XY}}{\sqrt{\rho_{XX} \; \rho_{YY}}} \tag{5}$$

As the denominator is generally less than one you will underestimate the structural correlation, the size of underestimation depending on the reliability of the two measurements. It is therefore quite possible to overlook an existing correlation because of unreliable measurements.

In order to develop satisfactory measuring instruments we must find a way to estimate their reliability. This, however, means that we must have at least two measurements as shown in Figure 3.

From (3a) the reliability coefficients of the two measurements X_1 and X_2 are $\rho_{X_1 X_1} = \rho_{X_1 F}$ and $\rho_{X_2 X_2} = \rho_{X_2 F}$, respectively. However, because F is non-observable you cannot use (3a) for computation.

From Figure 3 it is evident that X_1 and X_2 – both being influenced by F – must correlate, and the more they correlate with F, the stronger their mutual correlation. It should therefore be possible to judge the reliabilities of the two measurements based on the empirical correlation between X_1 and X_2.

Figure 3   A measurement model with two indicators

We can now write

$$\begin{aligned} X_1 &= \lambda_1 F + \varepsilon_1 \\ X_2 &= \lambda_2 F + \varepsilon_2 \end{aligned} \tag{6a}$$

with the usual regression assumptions

$$\begin{aligned} E(\varepsilon_1) &= E(\varepsilon_2) = 0 \\ Cov(\lambda_1, \varepsilon_1) &= Cov(\lambda_2, \varepsilon_2) = 0 \end{aligned} \tag{6b}$$

to which we add one further assumption:

$$Cov(\varepsilon_1, \varepsilon_2) = 0 \tag{6c}$$

This leaves us with four possibilities:

$$
\left.\begin{array}{l} \lambda_1 = \lambda_2 \\ \sigma_{\varepsilon_1}^2 = \sigma_{\varepsilon_2}^2 \end{array}\right\} \text{ the measurements are strictly parallel}
$$

$$
\left.\begin{array}{l} \lambda_1 \neq \lambda_2 \\ \sigma_{\varepsilon_1}^2 = \sigma_{\varepsilon_2}^2 \end{array}\right\} \text{ the measurements are weakly parallel}
$$

$$
\left.\begin{array}{l} \lambda_1 = \lambda_2 \\ \sigma_{\varepsilon_1}^2 \neq \sigma_{\varepsilon_2}^2 \end{array}\right\} \text{ the measurements are tau-equivalent} \qquad (7)
$$

$$
\left.\begin{array}{l} \lambda_1 \neq \lambda_2 \\ \sigma_{\varepsilon_1}^2 \neq \sigma_{\varepsilon_2}^2 \end{array}\right\} \text{ the measurements are congeneric}
$$

If the measurements are strictly parallel or tau-equivalent, the values of λ are arbitrary and are usually set to 1.00 – a tradition I will follow.

In classical test theory the latent variables F are not formally taken into account, which means that the coefficients λ are not known.

Consequently, classical theory builds on strictly parallel (and to a lesser extent tau-equivalent) measurements, where values of λ can be set to 1.00. Therefore, unless otherwise stated, parallel in the following means *strictly* parallel.

Parallel tests

Setting $\lambda = 1$, it follows from (6) and (7) that if X_1 and X_2 are parallel measurements, then

$$
\begin{array}{l} E(X_1) = E(X_2) = E(F) \\ Var(X_1) = Var(X_2) = Var(F) + Var(\varepsilon) \qquad (8) \\ Cov(X_1, X_2) = Var(F) \end{array}
$$

It should be possible to use parallel measurements to evaluate the reliability. I will therefore calculate their correlation:

$$
\rho_{X_1 X_2} = \frac{\sigma_{X_1 X_2}}{\sigma_{X_1} \sigma_{X_2}} = \frac{\sigma_{X_1 X_2}}{\sigma_X^2} = \frac{\sigma_F^2}{\sigma_F^2 + \sigma_\varepsilon^2} = \frac{\sigma_F^2}{\sigma_F^2 + \sigma_\varepsilon^2} \qquad (9)
$$

or, read from right to left,

$$
\rho_{X_1 X_1} = \rho_{X_2 X_2} = \rho_{X_1 X_2} \qquad (10)
$$

In other words, parallel measurements have the same reliability, which is equal to their correlation.

If you are able to create parallel measurements, you can estimate their reliability. In the following subsections, I will show three different ways of doing so.

Test-retest

The obvious way to create parallel measurements is to repeat the measurement using the same instrument on the same respondents with a shorter or longer interval, and then estimate the reliability as the correlation coefficient between the two. The problem with this method is that it is difficult to say whether we are measuring reliability or changes in the latent variable. If the value of the latent variable has changed between the two points in time, the correlation could be small even if the measurements are reliable.

The correlation could also be large if a respondent could remember his or her answer to the first measurement, when the second is taken.

Alternative forms method

In order to rule out the possibility that the respondents at the second measurement remember their answer to the first – which will contradict assumption (6c) – it is necessary to construct another measuring instrument, which is parallel to the first, and use that in the second round.

If for instance you intend to measure the skills of children in arithmetic by administering a test comprising various arithmetic problems, you can let the children do another test with different problems at a later time. Of course the two tests have to be of the same difficulty in order to obtain parallelism. One way to achieve this in both tests is to split the pool of problems between the two tests by randomization.

If you are interested in measuring attitudes or other more diffuse concepts it is difficult enough to construct one measuring instrument, so to construct two parallel ones can be a formidable task.

Split-half method

Both the above-mentioned methods require that two measurements are taken at shorter or longer intervals.

This is a drawback, but instead you can randomize the indicators of the latent variable in question into two equal-sized parts and calculate the correlation between these two measures. This can be considered as an approximation to the alternative forms method.

Let the two indicators X_1 and X_2 in Figure 3 be the results obtained by splitting the pool of arithmetic problems (after they have been administered) in the above example into two. If the two measurements can be considered parallel, the correlation between them is an estimate of the reliability of the two separate tests. However, we are interested in the reliability of the combined test. What then is the connection between the reliability of the two part-tests and the total, combined, test?

This, of course, depends upon how the two half-tests are combined, but if the combination is a simple addition $X = X_1 + X_2$, the reliability can be expressed as

$$\rho_{XX} = \frac{2\rho_{X_1 X_2}}{1 + \rho_{X_1 X_2}} \tag{11}$$

This is the so-called *Spearman-Brown formula*.

Let the correlation coefficient between the number of correct answers to the two part-tests be 0.75. Since this is an estimate of the reliability of the part-tests, the reliability of the total test will, according to the Spearman-Brown formula, be

$$\rho_{XX} = \frac{2 \times 0.75}{1 + 0.75} = 0.86 \tag{12}$$

A drawback with the split-half method is that the estimated reliability depends on how the test battery is split. I shall return later with a possible solution to this problem.

2 Summated and Non-summated Scales

Adding together the number of correct answers to a test is an example of a *summated scale*. The answers are coded as '0' if the answer is wrong and as '1' if it is correct, and the total score is then taken to be the sum of the *item scores*.

We met another summated scale in Example 1.3, where a psychologist used SEM to develop a scale to measure 'style of processing'.

It is unrealistic to expect one question in a questionnaire to uncover all facets of complicated concepts such as 'style of processing'. A solution to the problem could be to use several questions – or *items* as they are called in this connection – per concept and to combine the scores obtained on each item into one measurement, usually by adding together the separate scores.

By adding several item scores we obtain a larger differentiation in the measurements. While a variable measured on a single five-point scale can have five different values (usually the values 1–5), a variable measured by summing over 10 five-point scales can take on 41 different values (usually the values 10–50), and thus give a more differentiated picture.

A further advantage is that while several objections could be raised against treating the separate items as interval scaled or even as normally distributed (a precondition for many statistical procedures including SEM), things look different when it comes to the sum of several items.

The central limit theorem (Appendix A) states that under fairly general conditions the sum of several stochastic variables will approach a normal distribution (and consequently be interval scaled) as the number of addends tends to infinity.

However, the following objections against the use of summated scales have been raised:

1. The simple summation of item scores presupposes that all items are equally good in measuring the underlying concept.
2. The respondents are scaled solely on their total score irrespective of how this score is obtained. Consequently, different respondents could have obtained the same score in very different ways. Are they then similar with regard to the attribute we intend to measure?

This last question can also be formulated as: 'Do the various items in the battery measure one and the same concept, or do they measure more concepts than one?' In the latter case it could, depending on the circumstances, be meaningless to add item scores that measure different concepts.

SEM offers a solution to both problems. By working with the individual items the coefficients linking the latent variable to its manifest indicators (the λ_{ik} in Figure 5) are the 'optimal' ones, and *if* you choose to sum the items, you can use SEM to calculate an optimally weighted sum of item scores instead of a simple sum. Also (as we shall see in Chapter 6), SEM makes it possible to check whether a series of items are unidimensional, i.e. they all measure one and the same concept. However, a simpler method to deal with these two problems is to use factor analysis, the subject of the next chapter.

Nevertheless it has become quite common in recent years to use summated scales as indicators. Most often this is done by grouping items from a long scale (such as the 22-item SOP scale mentioned in Example 1.3) into bundles – or *parcels* as they are called – of 4–8 items and using a simple or weighted sum of the item scores as manifest indicators. The advantages of such a procedure are as follows:

1. The central limit theorem mentioned above could ensure that such indicators are 'more normal' than the separate items – especially if you group right skew and left skew distributed item scores into the same *parcel*.
2. You can reduce the number of λ-parameters to be estimated, which could be an advantage, especially if the sample size is small.
3. It could be that *parceling* increases the stability of parameter estimates.

If your scale is very short – the extreme being binary variables of the yes/no type – parceling could also be an advantage.

Consider a test consisting of five yes/no questions. If you let 'No' count as '0' and 'Yes' as '1', summating the scores will give you a scale ranging from zero to five.

So, summated scales is not an obsolete technique as it was possibly regarded when SEM was considered to be the answer to all problems.

Lastly, it should be mentioned that even if you have decided to use a summated scale in your research (e.g. for easier comparison with other research), it could still be an advantage to use SEM as a means of constructing the scale as mentioned in Example 1.3 and which will be demonstrated in Chapter 6.

However, parceling is not to be done carelessly: grouping the items could cover up problems that you should try to solve instead of hiding them. One such problem is *multidimensionality*. It should be obvious that if the concept you intend to measure is not unidimensional, there is a large risk that some or all of the parcels will also be multidimensional, i.e. cover more than one aspect of the concept. Then it could be difficult to find out what your latent concept really is, and there is a great chance that you will end up with a misspecified model.

So, discovering multidimensionality is an important issue in SEM, an issue that will be taken up in the next chapter.

My advice is: do not use parceling if you are working in a field that is new to you and/or you are developing a measurement model for a construct whose nature you are uncertain about. Only use parceling in situations where you are sure about the structure of the construct you are working with.

The many problems in parceling are summarized in the excellent article by Bandalos and Finney (2001).

Conceptual and operational definitions

It should be clear that it is very important for you to spend a good deal of time on defining your concepts and making their nature clear.

Traditionally you distinguish between a *conceptual definition* and an *operational definition*.

A *conceptual definition* is what you will find in a math book or in an encyclopedia. New concepts are defined with reference to concepts defined earlier or (in the case of an encyclopedia) to concepts that are assumed to be better known.

An *operational definition* defines a concept through the method used to measure it: 'temperature' is what you measure using *this* thermometer, 'intelligence' is what you measure using *this* test.

As it is impossible to trace a concept back to a few primitive concepts, the contents of which are interpreted by everyone in the same way, you could say that every conceptual definition is a circular definition – but then you will fail to see that during the process you are not moving in a plane but in a space. Therefore, when you have gone around the circle, you will be 'higher up' than when you started. The mental processes you have gone through will have given you a clearer understanding of the original concept as well as the auxiliary concepts you have had to introduce in order to clear your thoughts.

If you skip conceptual defining and go right to operationalization, it should be obvious that there will be a great risk that you will end up with an inconsistent measuring instrument.

The conceptual definition tells you *what* to measure, and the operational definition tells you *how* to measure – but of course it is problematic to answer 'how' before 'what'.

Choosing items

Whether you choose to use the items separately or to summarize them in some way, you must be careful in the selection of items.

'Good' items require:

1. Large variances.
2. Expected values near the middle value.
3. All correlations between items to be about the same numerical magnitude, and if you choose to sum the items all the correlations should be positive.
4. All items to correlate with the sum of the rest.

The more these conditions are met, and the more the number of items, the larger the reliability.

As mentioned earlier, analysis of empirical data is basically analysis of variation and covariation. If a variable does not vary it is of no interest, because then it is part of the definition of the elements making up the population – and if a variable does not vary it cannot covary.

If the average of a variable is near one of the endpoints of a scale, we have denied respondents with more extreme attitudes the option to express their opinion. If a reformulation of the item brings the average nearer the midpoint of the scale, this will in most cases also increase the variance.

The correlations should be about the same (numerical) size. Two items having a numerically larger correlation between them than the rest indicate that they – apart from measuring the intended concept – also measure something else not measured by the other items, i.e. the scale is not unidimensional.

In a summated scale the inter-item correlations must necessarily all be positive. If an item shows negative correlations with the other items the most obvious reason is that you have forgotten to reverse the scale of an item, which is worded in the opposite direction to the others. Another possibility is that the majority of respondents have failed to see a negation in the item. This risk is of course larger if only a few items have negations, so that the respondents do not get used to them. Good advice is to avoid negations altogether. An item having both positive and negative correlations to other items should be discarded.

Point 4 above is, of course, a logical consequence of point 3. Nevertheless, I mention it as a separate point because it expresses in a single number the value of adding an item to a scale.

The reliability of summated scales

In connection with the split-half method at the end of Section 1, mention was made of the Spearman-Brown formula

$$\rho_2 = \frac{2\rho}{1+\rho} \tag{13}$$

You can consider (13) to express the reliability of a scale that has twice the length (therefore ρ_2) of a scale with reliability ρ. If a summated scale has a reliability coefficient of 0.75, a scale of double the length will have a reliability of 0.86, provided the items are parallel.

Equation (13) is a special case of the general formula

$$\rho_k = \frac{k\rho}{1+(k-1)\rho} \tag{14}$$

expressing the reliability of a summated scale with k times the length of a scale with reliability ρ. If a summated scale has a reliability of 0.40, then the reliability of a scale five times as long is

$$\rho_5 = \frac{5 \times 0.40}{1+(5-1)0.40} = 0.77 \tag{15}$$

assuming parallel measurements. We see that – other things being equal – the longer the test battery, the larger the reliability.

Cronbach's α

Let the reliability of a single item X_j be ρ. The reliability of a scale made by the simple summation of k items is then

$$\rho_k = \frac{k\rho}{1+(k-1)\rho_{ii}} \tag{16}$$

If we use the simple correlation coefficient r_{ij} between two arbitrary items as an estimate for ρ, we can estimate the reliability of the summated scale as

$$\hat{\rho}_k = \frac{kr_{ij}}{1+(k-1)r_{ij}} \tag{17}$$

In other words, in a test battery of k items we can calculate $k(k-1)/2$ different estimates of the reliability of the summated scale. But even if the tests are parallel these estimates will differ, so it is natural to insert the average correlation $\bar{r}$ in (17):

$$\hat{\alpha}_{std} = \frac{k\bar{r}}{1+(k-1)\bar{r}} \tag{18}$$

This is *Cronbach's* α (Cronbach, 1951). The subscript *std* (for standardized) indicates that Cronbach's α also exists in an unstandardized version based, not on correlations, but on covariances. It is possible to prove that $\hat{\alpha}_{std}$ equals the average of the $k(k-1)/2$ reliability coefficients that can be computed using (17).

If the measurements are not parallel the standardized version of α is of course not appropriate, and an unstandardized version based on the covariance matrix is to be preferred.

Then (18) becomes

$$\hat{\alpha} = \frac{k\bar{c}}{\bar{v}+(k-1)\bar{c}} \tag{19}$$

where $\bar{v}$ is the average of the elements in the main diagonal and $\bar{c}$ is the average of the off-diagonal elements in the covariance matrix for X_j. If (19) is used on a correlation matrix, we get (18).

Equation (19) is a measure of the reliability of a summated scale whether the measurements are parallel or tau-equivalent. Moreover, (19) can be proved to indicate a lower limit of the reliability if the measurements are only congeneric (Bollen, 1989).

Usually (19) is written as

$$\hat{\alpha} = \frac{k}{k-1}\frac{s_L^2 - \sum s_i^2}{s_L^2} \tag{20}$$

I leave it to you to demonstrate the equality of (19) and (20).

3   Computer-based Item Analysis

The process of choosing the 'best' items from a pool of items to be used in a research project is called *item analysis* or *reliability analysis*. Item analysis is usually done on a computer, and routines for this sort of analysis when using summated scales can be found in some of the most widespread statistics packages, e.g SPSS, STATA and SYSTAT.

Example 1
Constructing a summated scale

Strangely enough, the consumption of fresh fish is much smaller in Denmark than in the surrounding countries in spite of the fact that no Dane lives more than 60 miles (96 km) from the sea.

A research project was therefore launched in order to map the possible barriers for an increase in the consumption of fresh fish (Bredahl & Grunert, 1995; Grunert, Bisp, Bredahl, Sørensen, & Nielsen, 1995). Part of the project was a survey of the Danish population's attitudes towards fish and the use of fish in the household; one variable of interest was 'general experience/competence regarding preparation of fish'. Respondents were presented with the questionnaire in Table 1, and asked to check their agreement with the sentences on a scale from 1 (strongly agree) to 7 (strongly disagree). After reversal of item 36, the seven points were added, and the sum was proposed as a measure of a respondent's 'general experience/competence'.

Table 1   Example 1: extract from questionnaire

35.	I don't feel quite sure of how to clean fish:	❑
36.	It is quite natural for me to clean and fillet fish:	❑
37.	I think that fresh fish are unpleasant to touch:	❑
38.	I don't like the smell of fish:	❑
39.	I only rarely clean fresh fish:	❑
40.	If I want fresh fish, I usually get the fishmonger (or somebody else) to clean the fish, so that I don't have to handle it myself:	❑
41.	When I buy fish, I prefer ready-made dishes, so that I don't have to do anything myself:	❑
42.	I have never learned how to clean and fillet fish:	❑

Figure 4   Example 1: reliability analysis using SPSS

Figure 5   Example 1: reliability analysis using SPSS – the main window and dialog box

Now open the SPSS file 'Fish1' containing the data from the book's website. Choose 'Analyze/Scale/Reliability Analysis' as shown in Figure 4, and the dialog box shown in Figure 5a will appear.

Select the items in the left column and click the little arrow (or double-click the selected items), whereby they are moved to the right column. In the model pane choose 'Alpha' (the default) and click 'Statistics', which makes the dialog box in Figure 5b to appear. As you can see, SPSS offers a wide range of possibilities, which you can explore on your own. In order to keep things simple, you should check only the three boxes shown, which results in the output given in Table 2, which I shall briefly comment upon as follows:

1. First in the output is Cronbach's α in unstandardized and standardized form. The two are of about equal size as a consequence of the items having nearly the same standard deviations.
2. Then average, standard deviation and number of answers to every single item are stated. We see that item 41 has a relatively small standard deviation and therefore is a candidate for exclusion. The average is very extreme, so perhaps a reformulation of the item would be a good idea. Both items 37 and 38 also have extreme averages.
3. Next the correlation matrix is shown. All the correlations are positive after reversal of item 36 (hence 36r). However, item 41 correlates poorly with the other items, and a few of the correlations are a little too high compared with the rest, e.g. (forb35, forb42) and (forb39, forb40).
4. Towards the end of the output you will see the most interesting results of the analysis, where you can evaluate the consequences of deleting an item from the battery. Shown first for each item are the mean and variance for the summated scale if the item is deleted. 'Corrected Item-Total Correlation' is the simple correlation between the item and the sum of the rest, and 'Squared Multiple Correlation' is the coefficient of determination when the item is regressed on the others. Finally, the last column shows the size of (unstandardized) α, if the item is deleted.

Table 2 Example 1: reliability analysis using SPSS

Reliability Statistics (1)

Cronbach's Alpha	Cronbach's Alpha Based on Standardized Items	N of Items
.831	.823	8

Item Statistics (2)

	Mean	Std. Deviation	N
forb35	3.93	2.662	89
forb36r	3.00	2.454	89
forb37	5.56	2.164	89
forb38	5.22	2.152	89
forb39	2.31	2.156	89
forb40	2.57	2.235	89
forb41	6.15	1.736	89
forb42	4.21	2.643	89

Inter-Item Correlation Matrix (3)

	forb35	forb36r	forb37	forb38	forb39	forb40	forb41	forb42
forb35	1.000	.607	.326	.245	.538	.442	.179	.698
forb36r	.607	1.000	.439	.310	.689	.541	.240	.604
forb37	.326	.439	1.000	.524	.276	.280	.153	.249
forb38	.245	.310	.524	1.000	.264	.370	.171	.237
forb39	.538	.689	.276	.264	1.000	.691	.209	.484
forb40	.442	.541	.280	.370	.691	1.000	.119	.385
forb41	.179	.240	.153	.171	.209	.119	1.000	.043
forb42	.698	.604	.249	.237	.484	.385	.043	1.000

Item-Total Statistics (4)

	Scale Mean if Item Deleted	Scale Variance if Item Deleted	Corrected Item-Total Correlation	Squared Multiple Correlation	Cronbach's Alpha if Item Deleted
forb35	29.03	109.783	.671	.570	.795
forb36r	29.967	109.283	.760	.635	.782
forb37	27.40	127.016	.463	.375	.823
forb38	27.74	128.717	.429	.343	.827
forb39	30.65	117.389	.690	.632	.795
forb40	30.39	119.696	.605	.524	.805
forb41	26.82	142.263	.218	.111	.846
forb42	28.75	113.620	.598	.561	.806

If you remove item forb41, you can expect α to increase from 0.831 to 0.846. Also notice that the 'Corrected Item-Total Correlation' and 'Squared Multiple Correlation' are very small for this item. Often a minimum of 0.40 for the two is used as a rule of thumb.

If you remove item 41 and repeat the analysis, you get the output shown in Table 3.

Table 3 Example 1: reliability analysis using SPSS (second run)

	Scale Mean if Item Deleted	Scale Variance if Item Deleted	Corrected Item-Total Correlation	Squared Multiple Correlation	Cronbach's Alpha if Item Deleted
forb35	22.89	99.419	.674	.564	.814
forb36r	23.82	99.308	.755	.627	.801
forb37	21.26	116.148	.460	.375	.845
forb38	21.60	117.971	.421	.334	.850
forb39	24.51	106.935	.688	.630	.814
forb40	24.25	108.597	.615	.520	.824
forb42	22.61	101.991	.623	.545	.823

I will leave it to you to convince yourself that α can be further increased (to 0.866) by deleting both items 37 and 38.

It is also worth noting that these two items, together with item 41, are the only ones that mention reasons for (low) experience with preparation of fish; that is, they are unpleasant to touch and do not smell good – and in the case of item 41 that ready-made dishes are preferred. These are not the reasons in the majority of cases (cf. the high means), hence the rather small 'Corrected Item-Total Correlation' and 'Squared Multiple Correlation' of these items.

Now, you could draw up a long list of reasons why a person would avoid preparing fish, but *there is no reason a priori to expect that the various reasons should correlate with each other or with any other item in the battery.*

The three items should never have been entered into the scale in the first place.

Item analysis is usually done on a small sample – a so-called *pilot sample* – prior to the main study. This was probably also done in this case, but the three items nevertheless made their way to the main study.

A final warning: remember that the last column in Table 3 shows the expected change in α *if a single item is removed*. Sometimes α cannot be increased by removing just one item, but can still be increased if more than one item is removed simultaneously. Therefore also look at the 'Corrected Item-Total Correlation' and the 'Squared Multiple Correlation'.

As mentioned, 'Alpha' is the default in SPSS, but it is also possible (in the window in Figure 5a) to specify other measurement models:

1. *Split-half* calculates the split-half coefficient between the first and the second half of the items. In addition the Spearman-Brown coefficient (11) and the Guttman-Rulow coefficient, which only assumes tau-equivalence, are calculated.
2. *Guttman's lower bound on true reliability* calculates lower bounds for test-retest reliability under six different sets of assumptions, which are all weaker than the traditional assumption of parallel measurements. Besides, they are based on only one sample (Guttman, 1945).
3. *Parallel* estimates reliability under the assumption of weak parallel measurements and tests this hypothesis.
4. *Strictly parallel* estimates reliability under the assumption of strictly parallel measurements and tests this hypothesis.

It should be mentioned that the way SPSS calculates split-half is not the wisest one, as there could be a fatigue factor. It is preferable to calculate split-half between odd- and even-numbered items.

As should be evident, there is no such thing as 'the true reliability'. The various methods for calculating reliability measure different aspects of reliability: 'test-retest' is a measure of the *stability* of the measuring instrument, whereas 'alternative forms' measures the *equivalence* of two measuring instruments. In a way 'split-half' measures the equivalence of the two halves of the same measuring instrument and alpha the equivalence of the separate items. In that way 'split-half' and alpha are measures of the *internal consistency* of the measuring instrument.

4   Validity

It is of course not sufficient for a measuring instrument to be reliable, it must also be valid – it must measure what is intended. If your instrument is not reliable it measures only *uncertainty* or *noise* – and then it is of course meaningless to ask whether the instrument is valid. If on the contrary your measuring instrument is reliable, it measures something – but what? In other words, to be valid, a measurement must be reliable.

I have hitherto assumed that a measurement measures one and only one concept. However, this is not always the case. Often an indicator is connected to more than one latent variable, as is pictured in Figure 6.

This is not a problem if you can name the two factors, which usually can be done only if they both have several indicators. If, however, the measurement X_1 in addition to measuring the factor F is also influenced by the unknown factor F_*, for which it is the only indicator, then things become more complicated. A factor such as F_* is called measurement X_1's *specific factor*.

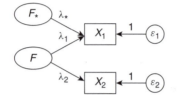

Figure 6   An indicator measures two different factors

The answer to the question 'How many times in the last five years have you been stopped by the police for drunken driving?' will not only be influenced by the true driving habits of the respondent (F), but also by his or her tendency to play down drunk-driving (F_*). We can write

$$X_1 = \lambda_1 F + \lambda_* F_* + \varepsilon_1 \qquad (21a)$$

with expected value

$$E(X_1) = \lambda_1 E(F) + \lambda_* E(F_*) \qquad (21b)$$

and variance

$$Var(X_1) = \lambda_1^2 Var(F) + \lambda_*^2 Var(F_*) + Var(\varepsilon_1) \qquad (21c)$$

$\lambda_1^2 Var(F)$ is called the *common variance* or *communality*. It is that part of the variable's variance that it shares with F and thus with the other variables, measuring the same factor (or factors). $\lambda_*^2 Var(F_*)$ is called the *specific variance*, as it relates to the specific factor, and $Var(\varepsilon_1)$ is the *error variance*.

In this notation

$$\rho_{X_1 X_1} = \frac{\lambda_1^2 Var(F) + \lambda_*^2 Var(F_*)}{Var(X_1)} \qquad (22)$$

constitutes the reliable share of the variance, but only a share of

$$h^2 = \frac{\lambda_1^2 Var(F)}{Var(X_1)} \qquad (23)$$

is valid.

As the validity of a measuring instrument expresses the agreement of the reading of the instrument with the true value, you could – at least in principle – judge the validity by comparing the imperfect measurement with that of a totally valid instrument. For example, the validity of the question 'How many times in the last five years have you been stopped by the police for drunken driving?' can be judged by comparing the answers with police reports.

However, this method presupposes that:

1. a totally valid measuring instrument exists; and
2. it is possible to get access to it.

Usually at least one of these conditions will not be met. In such situations the concept of validity becomes ambiguous, and you talk about:

1. content validity;
2. criterion validity; and
3. construct validity.

A measurement has large *content validity* if it covers all (or many) aspects of the concept being measured. A trivial example is a test to measure children's ability in arithmetic. Such a test has content validity if it covers all of the examination require- ments. On the other hand, if the test only covers a small part of the requirements, the content validity is low. Now, this example is special because the content of the concept 'examination requirements' is laid down in the curriculum. It is, however, very seldom that you are that lucky. In most cases content validity is evaluated in discussions with colleagues or other experts.

Criterion validity of a measuring instrument is evaluated by comparing the actual measurement with a criterion variable. We distinguish between *concurrent validity*, where the criterion is measured at the same time as the variable we wish to evaluate, and *predictive validity*, where the criterion is measured at a later time. A concurrent criterion is usually a measurement of the same concept with a different measuring instrument, while an example of a predictive criterion is the final exam result from a university as predicted by the entrance examination.

If a measurement is a valid measurement of construct F_1 it should correlate – posi- tively or negatively – with measurements of other constructs $(F_2, F_3, F_4, ...)$ with which concept F_1 is related in exactly the same way as the constructs $F_1, F_2, F_3, F_4, ...$ are expected to correlate, based on theory. A measuring instrument which stands such a test is said to have (a large) *construct validity*.

You could say that content validity is theoretically based and usually not measurable, while criterion validity is purely empirical, and construct validity is theoretically as well as empirically based.

Weaknesses of traditional validity measures

Criterion validity is fundamentally an empirical concept without much theoretical con- tent. Concurrent validity is measured by the correlation coefficient between two or more simultaneous measurements assumed to measure the same theoretical construct. Let X_1 be the measurement whose validity you want to judge, and X_2 the criterion.

Then it is apparent that the correlation between the two, apart from the reliability of X_1, also depends on the reliability of X_2, and that the correlation could be inflated if the two measurement methods are not sufficiently different.

Construct validity suffers from many of the same weaknesses as criterion validity. Let F_1 with indicator X_1 and F_2 with indicator X_2 be two theoretical constructs, which – based on sound, substantiated theory – are expected to correlate. However, the correlation between X_1 and X_2 depends not only on the correlation between X_1 and F_1, but also on the correlation between X_2 and F_2, and on the correlation between F_1 and F_2.

Convergent and discriminant validity: the multitrait-multimethod technique

Cambell and Fiske (1959) proposed the so-called *multitrait-multimethod technique* for assessing validity: each of several concepts (traits) is measured by several methods.

Let three traits (latent variables) each be measured by two methods (manifest variables), and let the correlation matrix be as shown in Table 4.

Table 4   Multitrait-multimethod matrix

	X_1	X_2	X_3	X_4	X_5	X_6
method 1, trait 1 X_1	1.00					
method 1, trait 2 X_2	ρ_{21}	1.00				
method 1, trait 3 X_3	ρ_{31}	ρ_{32}	1.00			
method 2, trait 1 X_4	ρ_{41}	ρ_{42}	ρ_{43}	1.00		
method 2, trait 2 X_5	ρ_{51}	ρ_{52}	ρ_{53}	ρ_{54}	1.00	
method 2, trait 3 X_6	ρ_{61}	ρ_{62}	ρ_{63}	ρ_{64}	ρ_{65}	1.00

In order for the methods to be valid, Campbell and Fiske state the following requirements:

1. *Convergent validity*: The correlations of measurements of the same traits using different methods should be statistically significant and 'sufficiently large'. In this case these so-called convergent correlations are ρ_{41}, ρ_{52} and ρ_{63}.
2. *Discriminant validity*: Convergent correlations should be larger than correlations among measurements of different traits using the same method. In this case ρ_{41}, ρ_{52} and ρ_{63} should be larger than ρ_{21}, ρ_{31} and ρ_{32}.
3. *Discriminant validity*: Convergent correlations should be larger than correlations of measurements having neither trait, nor method in common. i.e. ρ_{41}, ρ_{52} and ρ_{63} should be larger than $\rho_{51}, \rho_{61}, \rho_{42}, \rho_{52}, \rho_{43}$ and ρ_{53}.
4. The pattern of correlations among traits should be the same across methods.

The multitrait-multimethod technique is an attempt to support the researcher in evaluating construct validity, but some of the fundamental problems still persist. This is easiest to see if we sketch the method in an SEM diagram as shown in Figure 7.

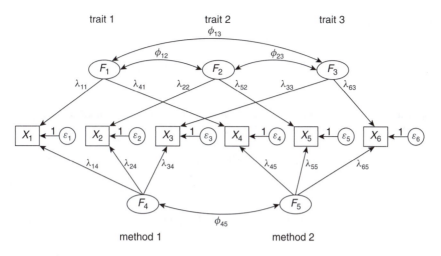

Figure 7 SEM model of multitrait-multimethod validation

Assuming all variables are standardized, we can write

$$\rho_{X_1 X_4} = \lambda_{11}\lambda_{41} + \lambda_{14}\lambda_{45}\phi_{45} \tag{24}$$

and see that the convergent correlation $\rho_{X_1 X_4}$ does depend not only on F_1's influence on X_1 and X_4, which is implicit in the multitrait-multimethod philosophy, but also on the correlation ϕ_{45} between the two methods and their effects on X_1 and X_4.

The fundamental problem with the classical methods of validity assessment discussed so far is that they are all based exclusively on relations among manifest variables without explicitly taking the latent variables into account.

In Chapter 6 you will learn how SEM, by introducing latent variables, opens up for evaluations of reliability and validity that are based directly on the theoretical definition of these concepts.

In this chapter you met the following concepts:

- reliability and reliability coefficient
- parallel, tau-equivalent and congeneric measurements summated and non-summated scale
- parcel and parceling
- common variance
- specific variance

- error variance
- conceptual and operational definitions
- item analysis
- pilot sample
- validity
- content, criterion and concept validity
- convergent and discriminant validity

Questions

1. Define reliability and validity.

2. Discuss the various ways in which you can judge the reliability of a measuring instrument.

3. Discuss the demands that an item should meet in order to be included in a summated and/or unsummated scale.

4. List the various steps you would take in constructing a summated scale.

5. Explain the concepts 'common variance', 'specific variance' and 'error variance'.

6. Explain the various forms of validity using examples from your own area of study or research.

References

Bandalos, D. L., & Finney, S. J. (2001). Item parceling issues in structural equation modeling. In G. A. Marcoulides & R. E. Schumacker (Eds.), *New developments and techniques in structural equation modeling*. Mahwah, NJ: Erlbaum.

Bollen, K. A. (1989). *Structural equations with latent variables*. New York: Wiley.

Bredahl, L., & Grunert, K. G. (1995). Determinants of the consumption of fish and shellfish in Denmark: An application of the theory of planned behavior. Paper presented at the International Seafood Conference: Seafood from producer to consumer, integrated approach to quality, Noordwijkerhout.

Campbell, D. T., & Fiske, D. W. (1959). Convergent and discriminant validation by the multitrait-multimethod matrix. *Psychological Bulletin, 56*, 81–105.

Cronbach, L. (1951). Coefficient alpha and the internal structure of tests. *Psychometrika, 16*, 297–334.

Grunert, K. G., Bisp, S., Bredahl, L., Sørensen, E., & Nielsen, N. A. (1995). *En undersøgelse af danskernes køb af fisk og skaldyr*. Aarhus: Aarhus School of Business. MAPP project paper.

Guttman, L. (1945). A basis for analyzing test-retest reliability. *Psychometrika, 10*(4), 255–282.

Further Reading

DeVellis, R. F. (2011). *Scale development* (3rd edn). Thousand Oaks, CA: Sage.

de Gruijter, N. M., & van der Kamp, L. J. Th. (2008). *Statistical test theory for the behavioral sciences*. Boca Raton, FL: Chapman & Hall.

The first book is a rather elementary introduction, while the second is more advanced.

3
Factor Analysis

As mentioned in the previous chapter, we ideally require that a scale (summated or not, weighted or not) measures one and only one concept – that the scale is unidimensional. Another problem you faced was that of finding the optimal item weights when using parcelling or other summated scales.

In this chapter you will therefore learn how to employ two classical and easy-to-use techniques for mapping the dimensionality of a data set and for calculating item weights.

The first technique is *principal components analysis* whereby a set of manifest variables (e.g. items) are transformed into new and fewer uncorrelated variables called *principal components*, each representing a dimension in the data.

The other is *exploratory factor* analysis where the roles, so to speak, are inverted. Instead of the 'new' variables being functions of the original manifest variables, the original variables are considered to be indicators (and thus functions) of underlying dimensions called *factors*.

This latter technique will, however, only be scantily treated as an introduction to *confirmatory factor analysis* in Chapter 7. The reason is that component analysis is less complicated and usually will give the same results as exploratory factor analysis. As the reason is purely pragmatic, you will no doubt find several examples on the use of component analysis, where factor analysis would have been more 'correct'.

Most often component analysis and exploratory factor analysis both go under the name of factor analysis, hence the name of this chapter.

1 Optimal Scales

In connection with Example 1.3, mention was made of summated scales as a means for measuring latent variables, and, in Chapter 2, you saw how item analysis based on a pilot sample could help you pick the 'best' items for use in the main study.

It was mentioned that a large variance is an essential attribute of a 'good' scale. As the aim is to study variations and covariations in variables across respondents or other objects, you could in fact consider the variance of a variable as an expression of the amount of information contained in that variable. The larger the variance, the larger the amount of information.

This, perhaps, might sound a bit strange to the reader who is used to looking at the variance as a measure of uncertainty or noise: the larger the variance, the larger the uncertainty, and thereby the less information. This, however, is only correct as long as we talk about the variance of a sampling distribution for an estimator (see Appendix A), but in scale construction we are interested in the variance in the population.

If all objects had the same value on a variable (in which case the variance is zero), measuring this variable would be of no interest, because the population would then partly be defined as the collection of objects having that value on the variable.

If we let X_j be the score on item j in a summated scale and L the total score, we can write

$$L = X_1 + X_2 + X_3 + \cdots + X_j + \cdots + X_p \tag{1}$$

and ask the question: 'Is it possible to obtain a larger variance (and thus a larger amount of information) by using a weighted sum?'

$$Y_1 = a_{11}X_1 + a_{12}X_2 + \cdots + a_{1j}X_j + \cdots + a_{1p}X_p \tag{2}$$

The answer is yes, and a simple example will illustrate the idea.

Example 1
Calculating the optimal weighting of a written and an oral exam

A class has obtained the marks shown in Figure 1 in an exam in French (measured on a 13-point scale as used in Denmark until 2007).

Most often the average of the two marks will appear on the certificate, i.e.

$$Y = 0.5X_1 + 0.5X_2 \tag{3}$$

A glance at the graph in Figure 1 will convince you that the points are more spread out along the X_1-axis than along the X_2-axis.

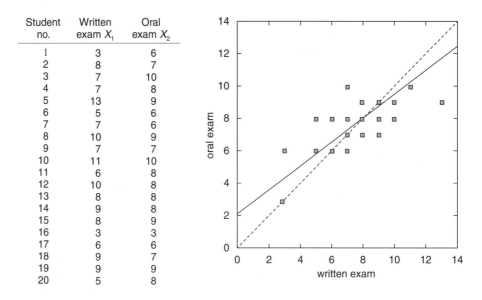

Student no.	Written exam X_1	Oral exam X_2
1	3	6
2	8	7
3	7	10
4	7	8
5	13	9
6	5	6
7	7	6
8	10	9
9	7	7
10	11	10
11	6	8
12	10	8
13	8	8
14	9	8
15	8	9
16	3	3
17	6	6
18	9	7
19	9	9
20	5	8

Figure 1   Example 1: data and graphics

X_1 has a variance of 6.37 and X_2 a variance of 2.79. The written exam does a better job in discriminating between the students, so should it then not also count more in the calculation of the combined mark for French?

In the figure a solid line is drawn through the cluster of points in such a way that the points are spread out more along this line than along any other line that could be drawn. If you project the points onto this line and provide a suitable scale, you might perhaps have a better expression of the students' abilities in French than if you use an unweighted average, which is tantamount to projecting the points onto the dashed 45° line.

The solid line has the equation

$$Y_1 = 0.64X_1 + 0.36X_2 \qquad (4)$$

and expresses the optimal weighting scheme for the two variables. Y_1 is called *the first principal component*.

Note that the Y_1-line is *not* the regression line. We can estimate two regression lines: the regression of X_1 on X_2 and the regression of X_2 on X_1. The first of these is placed so that the sum of squared *horizontal* distances from the points to the line is minimized, and the second so that the sum of the squared *vertical* distances is minimized. Both these lines pass through the point $(\bar{X}_1, \bar{X}_2)$. The Y_1-line also passes through this point minimizing the sum of squared *orthogonal* distances from the points to the line. See Figure 2.

So, a correlation (see Appendix A) between two or more variables could be considered a sign of a cause-effect relation – as in the structural part of a SEM model – in which case you can use regression analysis to map the relationship, or it could be interpreted as a sign that the variables measure the same underlying concept – as in the measurement part of the model – in which case the measurements could be combined to include as much information as possible from the original variables, using *principal components analysis*.

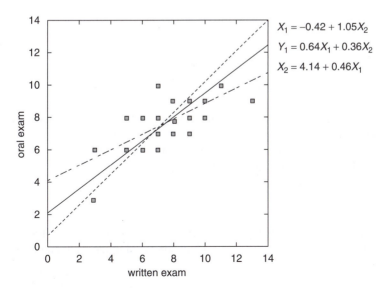

$X_1 = -0.42 + 1.05X_2$

$Y_1 = 0.64X_1 + 0.36X_2$

$X_2 = 4.14 + 0.46X_1$

Figure 2   Example 1: the two regression lines and the (first) principal component

When marks obtained in written and oral exams in French were combined into a single mark using the formula $Y = 0.64X_1 + 0.36X_2$, we treated the observations as if they were all placed on the Y_1-line, and thereby ignored the information contained in the distance from the various points to the Y_1-line.

This information can be utilized by introducing a Y_2-line perpendicular to the Y_1-line, thereby constructing a new coordinate system as shown in Figure 3. This Y_2-line is *the second principal component.*

It is obvious that Y_1 (by a suitable choice of scale) has a much larger variance than Y_2 (and any of the two original variables). Therefore Y_1 discriminates better among the students than any of the other three variables – it thus has the largest amount of information of the four variables and Y_2 the least. Also observe that Y_1 and Y_2, contrary to X_1 and X_2, are uncorrelated (a regression line would coincide with the Y_1-axis).

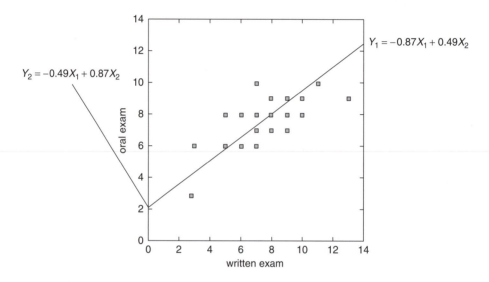

Figure 3   Example 1: the two principal components

The two components have the equations

$$Y_1 = 0.87X_1 + 0.49X_2 \quad \text{and} \quad Y_1 = -0.49X_1 + 0.87X_2 \tag{5}$$

The first equation describes the same line as (4), because only the relative size of the coefficients matters.

If we measure the amount of information in the data by the variances of the variables, then the total amount of information in the X-variables is

$$VAR(X_1) + VAR(X_2) \tag{6}$$

As the Y-coordinate system is just a rotation of the X-system, this transformation should not change the amount of information contained in the data, and consequently the coefficients in (5) are chosen so that

$$VAR(X_1) + VAR(X_2) = VAR(Y_1) + VAR(Y_2) \tag{7}$$

In the present case

$$6.37 + 2.78 = 8.00 + 1.15$$

As our goal was to find the optimal weighting of the marks in the written and oral exam, we can disregard Y_2 and still keep

$$8.00 / (8.00 + 1.1.5) = 87\% \tag{8}$$

of the total amount of information in the X-variables. That is a lot more than the 41% kept in the simple average, which has a variance of 3.74.

2   Principal Components Analysis

The primary goal of component analysis is to reduce a number of correlating variables (i.e. variables sharing a certain amount of information) to a smaller number of – usually uncorrelated – variables. The p original variables X_j are transformed to p new variables Y_i called *principal components*:

$$
\begin{aligned}
Y_1 &= a_{11} X_1 + a_{12} X_2 + \cdots + a_{1j} X_j + \cdots + a_{1p} X_p \\
Y_2 &= a_{21} X_1 + a_{22} X_2 + \cdots + a_{2j} X_j + \cdots + a_{2p} X_p \\
&\ \ \vdots \\
Y_i &= a_{i1} X_1 + a_{i2} X_2 + \cdots + a_{ij} X_j + \cdots + a_{ip} X_p \\
&\ \ \vdots \\
Y_p &= a_{p1} X_1 + a_{p2} X_2 + \cdots + a_{pj} X_j + \cdots + a_{pp} X_p
\end{aligned} \tag{9}
$$

The total amount of information in the original variables (the X-variables) is then the sum of their variances, and the scales of the new variables (the Y-variables) are chosen to make

$$\sum_{i=1}^{p} Var(Y_i) = \sum_{i=1}^{p} Var(X_j) \tag{10}$$

in order to preserve the amount of information measured in this way. We have therefore not reduced the amount of data *unless we disregard some of the Y-variables*.

   If we choose to keep only Y_1, then the coefficients a_{1j} are chosen so as to maximize the amount of information in Y_1 (i.e. to maximize $Var(Y_1)$ under the restriction (10)). If we also wish to keep the second principal component Y_2, then a_{2j} must be chosen so as to maximize $Var(Y_2)$ under the restriction that Y_2 is not correlated with Y_1 so that Y_2 only contains new information – and of course also under the restriction (10). This process is then continued with Y_3, Y_4, ...

   In other words, the coefficients are chosen so that the principal components, the Y-variables, are not correlated and are ordered by decreasing variance. The values of the Y-variables are called *component scores*, the coefficients a_{ij} are called *component score coefficients* and the covariances or correlations (depending on whether the analysis is based on a covariance or a correlation matrix) between the Y-variables and the X-variables are called *component loadings*.

The whole process groups the *X*-variables according to which component they correlate strongest with – *load most on*. By examining the variables loading on the same component it should be possible to interpret the component, i.e. to name it.

If the variables entering into a component analysis are very different in size (size of household, income, amount spent on a certain product or activity) it could be advantageous to standardize the variables to a variance of 1.00 before the analysis, because the variables with the largest variances would otherwise have the strongest influence on the outcome. This is tantamount to basing the analysis on the correlation matrix instead of the covariance matrix.

Although several good statistical reasons could be given in favor of basing component analysis on the covariance matrix (see e.g. Morrison, 2003), the use of correlations is almost universal – at least in the social and behavioral sciences.

Example 2
Interpreting dimensions in physical measurements

The correlations in Table 1 are based on measurement of eight physical variables on 305 individuals (Harman, 1976).

Table 1 Example 2: correlations of eight physical measurements

	1	2	3	4	5	6	7	8
1. Height	1.000							
2. Arm span	0.846	1.000						
3. Forearm length	0.805	0.881	1.000					
4. Lower leg length	0.859	0.826	0.801	1.000				
5. Weight	0.473	0.376	0.380	0.436	1.000			
6. Bitrochanteric diameter	0.398	0.326	0.319	0.329	0.762	1.000		
7. Chest girth	0.301	0.277	0.237	0.327	0.730	0.583	1.000	
8. Chest width	0.382	0.415	0.345	0.365	0.629	0.577	0.539	1.000

From a correlation matrix of eight variables you can extract eight principal components, but the real question is: 'How many of these shall you keep in order to retain most of the information in the data?' You can find some support for this decision in Figure 4.

Component	Variance	Variance in pct.
1	4.67	58
2	1.77	22
3	0.48	6
4	0.42	5
5	0.23	3
6	0.19	2
7	0.14	2
8	0.10	1
Total	8.00	100

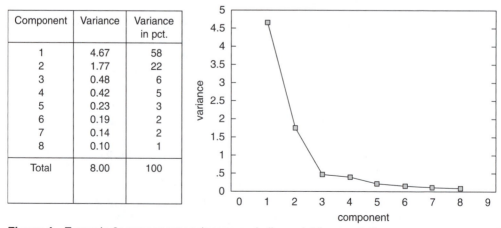

Figure 4 Example 2: component variances and elbow plot (scree plot)

The sum of the component variances is equal to the number of components. This comes as no surprise, as the original variables were standardized to have variance 1.00.

When deciding how many of the components to retain, the following rules of thumb are often used as starting points:

1. Extract components until a satisfactory share of the total information has been picked up. From the figure we see that by extracting one component we keep 58% of the information (variance), while extraction of two components brings this figure up to 80%:

$$\left(\frac{4.67+1.77}{8.00}\right)100\% = 58\% + 22\% = 80\%$$

2. From component 3 the variances are smaller than the average variance of the original variables (in this case 1.00). In other words, the last six components each contain less information than an average X-variable, and should therefore be discarded. According to this so-called *Kaiser criterion*, only the first two components should be retained.
3. If we look at the discarded components as uncertainty or noise, we should extract components until the next component is mainly made up of noise. But when is that? Usually you consider remaining components to be noise, when the component variances begin to level off and have about the same size. This point is easier to find if the variances are depicted in an *elbow plot* (or *scree plot* as it is called in SPSS) as shown in Figure 4. The curve has a distinctive bend – an elbow – after the second component. According to this criterion a two-component solution should be chosen.

In this case the last two rules (and possibly also the first) lead to the same conclusion: extraction of two components. We measure two different attributes and not one or eight.

However, these are only rules of thumb – in the end the decision of how many components to retain depends on whether the components are substantively meaningful.

The transformation from the original variables to the first two principal components is

$$Y_1 = 0.4X_1 + 0.39X_2 + 0.38X_3 + 0.39X_4 + 0.35X_5 + 0.31X_6 + 0.29X_7 + 0.31X_8$$
$$Y_2 = 0.28X_1 + 0.33X_2 + 0.34X_3 + 0.30X_4 - 0.39X_5 - 0.40X_6 - 0.44X_7 - 0.31X_8$$
(11)

Example 2 (continued)
Rotation of Components

In order to interpret the components – to name them – we group the X-variables according to which component they correlate strongest with – *load most on*. The variables loading on the same component should have something in common, which could be used to name the component and thereby give it a substantive meaning. However, more often than not, the picture will be rather confusing.

The transformation (11) from *X*-variables to *Y*-variables is a mechanical process, and there is no reason to believe that the new variables should have any substantive meaning.

You might expect the variables to load most on the first component, and a look at the component loadings in Figure 5a shows that not a single variable loading is highest on component 2 – so are there really two *meaningful* components?

In Figure 5b the component loadings are depicted graphically, and you can see that they fall into two separate groups. There are in fact *two* components, the upper depicting the last four variables and the lower one the first four. However, our coordinate system is not able to disclose this unless we resort to a graph.

It is easily seen that a rotation of the coordinate system could bring the axes to pass nearer the two point clusters. By doing so, you obtain a simpler component structure, in that each variable has a large loading on one of the components and only a small loading on the other (or the others if there are more than two components). The result of this so-called *varimax rotation* is shown in Figure 6. You could name the first component 'bone structure' and the second 'flesh structure' (or 'height' and 'breadth').

It is possible, however, to let the axes go right through the point clusters of Figure 6, if we relax the restriction of orthogonal *Y*-axes. Such an *oblique rotation* is shown in Figure 7.

	component 1	component 2
1. Height	0.86	−0.37
2. Arm span	0.84	−0.44
3. Forearm length	0.81	−0.46
4. Lower leg length	0.84	−0.40
5. Weight	0.76	0.52
6. Bitrochanteric diameter	0.67	0.53
7. Chest girth	0.62	0.58
8. Chest width	0.67	0.42

(a)

(b)

Figure 5   Example 2: original component structure

An oblique rotation means that the two components are no longer un-correlated. In this case the correlation is 0.50. Whether to prefer an orthogonal or an oblique structure is not just a question of fit and figures, but a substantive question: 'Is it more reasonable to assume "bone structure" and "flesh structure" to be correlated, or is the opposite assumption more reasonable?'

In more complex cases there could be more than one among the infinite number of rotations that had meaningful but different substantive interpretations.

It is worth noting that SPSS (unfortunately!) does not allow you to use a covariance or correlation matrix as input when using roll-down menus. You have to write a command syntax. You can see how to do that on pages 421–422 of Norušis (2005).

Part of the output from the analysis is given in Table 2:

Table 2   Example 3: part of output from component analysis extracting one component (SPSS)

Communalities

	Raw		Rescaled	
	Initial	Extraction	Initial	Extraction
forb35	7.086	4.882	1.000	.689
forb36r	6.023	4.412	1.000	.733
forb37	4.681	1.283	1.000	.274
forb38	4.631	1.045	1.000	.226
forb39	4.650	2.864	1.000	.616
forb40	4.997	2.474	1.000	.495
forb41	3.013	.175	1.000	.058
forb42	6.988	4.382	1.000	.627

Extraction Method: Principal Component Analysis.

Total Variance Explained

	Component	Initial Eigenvalues(a)			Extraction Sums of Squared Loadings		
		Total	% of Variance	Cumulative %	Total	% of Variance	Cumulative %
Raw	1	21.517	51.148	51.148	21.517	51.148	51.148
	2	5.825	13.847	64.995			
	3	4.276	10.164	75.158			
	4	3.106	7.382	82.541			
	5	2.535	6.025	88.566			
	6	2.165	5.145	93.711			
	7	1.459	3.468	97.179			
	8	1.187	2.821	100.000			

Extraction Method: Principal Component Analysis.

Component Matrix[a]

	Raw Component	Rescaled Component
	1	1
forb35	2.210	.830
forb36r	2.101	.856
forb37	1.133	.524
forb38	1.022	.475
forb39	1.692	.785
forb40	1.573	.704
forb41	.418	.241
forb42	2.093	.792

Extraction Method: Principal Component Analysis.
[a] 1 components extracted.

Component Score Coefficient Matrix[a]

	Component
	1
forb35	.273
forb36r	.240
forb37	.114
forb38	.102
forb39	.170
forb40	.163
forb41	.034
forb42	.257

Extraction Method: Principal Component Analysis.
[a] Coefficients are standardized.

1. First in the output are the communalities. Recall that the communality is that part of the variance of a measurement that it has in common with the latent variables – or in this case the one latent variable – it is supposed to measure (and thus with all other variables supposed to measure that same latent variable). In principal components analysis, there is neither specific variance nor error variance as opposed the model in (2.21). Consequently *all* variance is common variance if all components are extracted, and the raw initial communalities are just the variances of the various items, while the extracted communalities are the variances shared with the extracted component(s).

   The rescaled communalities are the same variances, after rescaling the initial communalities to have the value 1.00 (e.g. for the first item, 4.882/7.086 = 0.689).

   The item forb41 catches the eye, because it shares only 6% of its variance with the extracted component. This item is therefore a candidate for exclusion and so are forb37 and forb38, the communalities of which are also much lower than the majority of items.

2. Then comes a listing of the principal components with their respective variances followed by an elbow plot that confirms the existence of only one component. You should compare this part of the output with Figure 4.

   Note that the variances of the principal components are called *eigenvalues*. Every symmetric $p \times p$ matrix (and that includes covariance matrices) has associated with it p eigenvalues. An eigenvalue is a function of the matrix. It is a mathematical concept, which in this case is interpreted as the variance of a principal component.

   The first component extracts 51% of the variance, which is more than the 40% often recommended as a rule of thumb. Also the following components extract about the same amount of variance. So, the two conditions mentioned above are fulfilled.

3. Next come the so-called component loadings, the covariances and correlations between the original variables and the component scores – compare this part of the output with Figure 5. We see that the loading of forb41 is extremely small and therefore measures a different concept, and the loadings forb37 and forb38 are also smaller than the rest.

4. We could therefore expect forb41 to have a very small influence on the component score. Looking at the component score coefficients – or weights – our expectation is confirmed. This item should be left out, as should forb37 and forb38. Running another component analysis after having left out these three items results in the output in Table 3.

The first component now extracts 66% of the variance (not shown). All rescaled loadings are above the often-recommended minimum value of 0.40, and the set of items would now be considered unidimensional according to that rule.

This is the same result we obtained in Example 2.1 based on traditional item analysis. From this, it is tempting to conclude that Cronbach's α is a measure of unidimensionality, but this is not the case: rather, *unidimensionality is a precondition for α.*

Unidimensionality means that correlations among items assumed to measure the same concept are only due to that concept, i.e. controlling for the effect of the concept, there should be no excess correlation among the items: Equation (2.6c) is assumed to hold, whether the measurements are parallel, tau-equivalent or congeneric.

Table 3   Example 3: components analysis (second run)

Component Matrix[a]

	Raw Component	Rescaled Component
	1	1
forb35	2.264	.850
forb36r	2.088	.851
forb39	1.723	.799
forb40	1.560	.698
forb42	2.182	.825

Extraction Method: Principal Component Analysis.
[a] 1 components extracted.

Component Score Coefficient Matrix[a]

	Component
	1
forb35	.307
forb36r	.261
forb39	.189
forb40	.177
forb42	.294

Extraction Method: Principal Component Analysis.
[a] Coefficients are standardized.

Furthermore, we can see from Table 3 that the component score coefficients are roughly located in the interval 0.20–0.30, and consequently a simple summation of item scores could be used as an adequate approximation to the 'optimal' component scores

While nowadays – where we do not use hand calculation – it is just as easy to calculate a component score as a summated score, one strong point against using component scores could be put forward. If the scale is expected to be used repeatedly in several studies, or if you are comparing your research with that of others, you could argue that the simple summated scale is a more robust instrument than a weighted scale, because the weights (the component score coefficients) could vary across studies.

Mapping and interpreting multidimensional item sets

The more items you consider for the measurement of a concept, the larger the risk that more than one dimension will be revealed when you take a closer look at your data.

If that should happen, you also have to decide whether the various dimensions describe several aspects of the same concept, or whether in fact you are measuring several distinct concepts.

As will be demonstrated in Chapter 6, SEM can be used to that end, but the 'quick and dirty tool' is principal components analysis.

Example 4
Finding the dimensionality in a scale

In the same study (as the one in Example 3), measurement of the respondents' 'involvement in procuring and serving fish' was also required. The items used in a Likert scale are shown in Table 4 and the data (Fish2) can be found on the book's website.

Table 4 Example 4: extract from the questionnaire

1. Fish is something I can talk about at length:	❑
2. I know so much about fish that I am able to evaluate the suitability of various types of fish for various dishes and various occasions:	❑
3. Fish is a product that interests me:	❑
4. I prefer some kinds of fish to others:	❑
5. Fish is a product or food product category which I don't believe that I have any use for:	❑
6. On the whole I don't know anything about fish:	❑
7. When I buy fish I usually buy the same kind every time:	❑
8. If I have decided to buy a certain type of fish, it is very possible that I change my mind if I have to go out of my way to get it:	❑
9. If somebody told me that the type of fish I have decided to buy was full of bones or maybe difficult to cook, I would stick to my decision no matter what:	❑
10. If I cannot get my favourite kind of fish where I usually shop, I don't mind buying another kind:	❑
11. Eating and serving fish add to the picture of me that I find ideal:	❑
12. Eating fish helps me live the life I strive for:	❑
13. There are many occasions and experiences in my life that I some way or another can connect to fish or eating fish:	❑
14. Fish is clearly something that I like:	❑
15. When I look at (fresh) fish or dishes made from (fresh) fish, there is a whole bunch of properties that I match them against:	❑
16. Eating fish is to a high degree something I do to express my 'ego':	❑
17. Personally it is of great importance to me to eat fish:	❑
18. On the basis of my personal values, I feel that I must eat fish:	❑
19. Eating and serving fish help me to expressing a way of life that I want:	❑
20. On the basis of what other people think, I feel that fish and eating fish is something I ought to be interested in:	❑
21. There is not much difference in the various types of fish that can be bought:	❑

Mean and standard deviations are – after reversing items 5–7, 10 and 21 – given in Table 5. If we require the standard deviation to be at least 1.5 and the mean to be in the interval 2.5–5.5, the following items are candidates for exclusion: 4, 5r, 16, 20 and 21r.

Items having extreme means should be reformulated in order to bring the mean towards the middle of the scale; this will usually also increase the variance.

Table 5 Example 4: average and standard deviation for the 21 items

	Mean	Std. Deviation		Mean	Std. Deviation
involv1	4.45	2.06	involv12	4.67	2.25
involv2	4.18	2.26	involv13	4.25	2.39
involv3	3.85	2.13	involv14	2.22	1.86
involv4	1.45	.99	involv15	3.69	2.20
involv5r	1.44	1.22	involv16	6.02	1.46
involv6r	2.34	1.86	involv17	4.10	2.08
involv7r	4.75	2.22	involv18	3.61	2.17
involv8	3.70	2.49	involv19	4.89	2.31
involv9	4.03	2.50	involv20	5.68	1.82
involv10r	5.16	2.14	involv21r	1.66	1.36
involv11	5.40	1.97			

The inter-item correlations – after deletion of items 4, 5r, 16, 20 and 21r – are as shown in Table 6.

The correlations vary in size from nearly 0.00 to nearly 0.80, which is a bad sign. Furthermore, it is possible to find clusters of items with satisfying intra-cluster correlations but with very small correlations to other clusters. For example, items 1, 2 and 3 seem to form a cluster, which is only very weakly linked to another cluster consisting of items 11, 12, 17 and 19. So, perhaps these two parts of the scale measure two different latent variables – and maybe there are more than two?

If so, the scale is not unidimensional and it might be a good idea to perform a principal components analysis in order to find out whether the items really make up a unidimensional scale, and, if not, how many dimensions it contains.

As in the previous example, choose 'Analyze/Data Reduction/Factor' and select the variables. In the 'Extraction' window choose to base your analysis on the covariance matrix, check the 'Scree plot' box, and leave everything else at the default values, because at present you are only interested in finding out how many dimensions are present in your data. Then click 'Continue', return to the dialog box in Figure 8b, and click 'OK'.

In Figure 9 you can see the scree plot, which indicates the existence of three dimensions. So, let us try a three-component solution.

You start all over again, and when the dialog box shown in Figure 8c appears you choose to extract 3 factors, click 'Continue' and when you return to the dialog box in Figure 8b, click 'Rotation'. In the dialog box in Figure 10a check 'Varimax' (the default method) and 'Display rotated solution', and click 'Continue'.

When you again return to the box in Figure 8b, open the dialog box in Figure 10b by clicking 'Options', and check 'Sorted by size'. Then click 'Continue', and after returning to the 'Factor Analysis' dialog box click 'OK'.

Taken together the first three principal components account for 56% of the variance in the data (output not shown).

Table 6 Example 4: inter-item correlations (decimal point not shown)

	1	2	3	6r	7r	8	9	10r	11	12	13	14	15	17	18
2	65														
3	77	69													
6r	47	56	56												
7r	24	42	32	23											
8	06	06	10	11	-18										
9	20	18	22	12	24	-04									
10r	17	20	23	22	14	47	01								
11	37	29	40	33	05	16	-05	16							
12	43	35	44	34	15	08	-01	15	61						
13	44	42	42	25	12	03	17	09	36	34					
14	49	45	59	43	30	03	38	23	37	46	26				
15	51	61	57	48	20	08	22	25	21	27	44	45			
17	35	40	44	34	10	16	18	10	31	49	26	56	26		
18	13	02	14	-04	03	-07	04	-08	12	36	13	24	-12	40	
19	26	21	23	26	05	-01	03	05	53	47	29	36	12	45	38

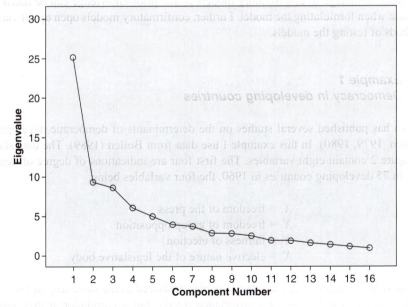

Figure 9 Example 4: principal components analysis, first run, elbow plot (SPSS)

(a)   (b)

Figure 10   Example 4: principal components analysis, dialog boxes for second run

The rotated component matrix in Table 7 shows the relations between the various items and each of the three components in raw (covariances) and in rescaled (correlations) form.

Table 7   Example 4: principal components analysis (selected output from second run)

Rotated Component Matrix[a]

	Raw			Rescaled		
	Component			Component		
	1	2	3	1	2	3
involv2	1.806	.444	.337	.800	.197	.149
involv3	1.629	.694	.395	.766	.326	.186
involv15	1.635	.120	.522	.742	.054	.237
involv1	1.448	.675	.280	.703	.328	.136
involv14	1.124	.791	.039	.605	.425	.021
involv6r	1.092	.419	.444	.586	.225	.238
involv7r	1.261	-.116	-.534	.567	-.052	-.240
involv9	1.348	-.311	-.689	.539	-.124	-.275
involv13	1.164	.845	.154	.486	.353	.064
involv19	.190	1.834	-.107	.082	.795	-.046
involv12	.585	1.701	.290	.260	.757	.129
involv18	-.207	1.429	-.575	-.096	.659	-.265
involv11	.375	1.295	.510	.191	.658	.259
involv17	.672	1.312	.174	.322	.630	.084
involv8	-.140	.086	2.167	-.056	.034	.870
involv10	.478	-.021	1.461	.224	-.010	.683

Extraction Method: Principal Component Analysis.
Rotation Method: Varimax with Kaiser Normalization.

[a] Rotation converged in 4 iterations.

The first component is an expression of personal knowledge, interests and behavior while the second is some sort of lifestyle dimension incorporating psychological and social elements such as consumption of fish as a signal to other people. The third component includes only two nearly identical items expressing the respondents' determination or the strength of their preferences.

Now, you have a choice between considering the three factors as three aspects of the same concept 'involvement' or considering them as three distinct concepts.

That choice must of course be based on substantive thinking taking into consideration all the information you have on the subject in the form of earlier research, discussions with colleagues, etc., and (not to forget) common sense.

However, since it is obvious that if the dimensions are just three aspects of the same concept, the correlations across dimensions should be larger than if they were best considered as three fundamentally different concepts. You can get a first impression of the picture by looking at the correlation matrix after having sorted the items by dimension as shown in Table 8.

It seems to me that the first two dimensions are closer together and that the third dimension is separated from the first two. So, dimension 3 is definitely a separate concept, while the question of whether the first two dimensions should be considered two separate concepts or two aspects of the same concept depends on the actual use of the measuring instrument. In the latter case be careful not to mix items from the two dimensions in the same parcel if you use parceling.

Table 8 Example 4: inter-item correlations sorted by dimension (decimal point not shown)

	Dimension 1									Dimension 2					Dim. 3	
	2	3	1	15	14	6r	7r	13	9	12	11	19	18	17	8	10
3	69															
1	65	77														
15	61	57	51													
14	45	59	49	45												
6r	56	56	47	48	43											
7r	42	32	24	20	30	23										
13	41	42	44	44	26	25	12									
9	18	22	20	22	38	12	24	17								
12	35	44	42	27	46	34	15	34	−01							
11	29	40	37	21	37	33	05	36	−05	61						
19	21	23	26	13	36	26	05	29	03	47	53					
18	02	14	13	−12	24	−04	03	13	04	36	12	38				
17	40	44	35	26	56	34	10	26	18	49	31	45	40			
8	06	10	06	08	03	11	−18	03	−04	08	16	−01	−07	16		
10	20	23	17	25	23	22	14	09	01	15	16	05	−08	10	47	

If you use oblique rotation, the correlations between the three dimensions will be shown in the output, and that gives a clearer expression of the data structure. They are

$$Corr(\text{Dim } 1, \text{Dim } 2) = 0.26$$
$$Corr(\text{Dim } 1, \text{Dim } 3) = 0.13$$
$$Corr(\text{Dim } 2, \text{Dim } 3) = 0.15$$

However, be warned that exploratory techniques such as principal components analysis or exploratory factor analysis are not always the most efficient way to uncover the structure of a data set. Confirmatory techniques will (as shown in Chapter 6) often do a better job.

If you plan to use the items in a simple summated scale, and therefore do a traditional item analysis, it is possible to obtain a Cronbach's α of about 0.90. This does not seem that bad, but as pointed out in Example 3, calculation of Cronbach's α across different dimensions is meaningless, and you should do an item analysis for each dimension. This is left to you as an exercise.

3   Exploratory Factor Analysis

The principal components Y_i are linear functions of the manifest variables X_j, as expressed in (9), which in a more compact form can be written as

$$Y_i = \sum_{j=1}^{p} a_{ij} X_j \text{ for } i = 1, 2, ..., p \tag{12}$$

This is an exact mathematical transformation with a one-to-one correspondence between the X- and Y-variables. Principal components analysis is therefore *not* a statistical model, the parameters of which have to be estimated. Therefore it is possible to isolate the X-variables on the left side of the equality sign, and consider them as functions of the Y-variables:

$$X_j = \sum_{i=1}^{p} b_{ji} Y_i \text{ for } j = 1, 2, ..., p \tag{13}$$

In this way the principal components are seen as latent variables, the values of which are mirrored in the manifest X-variables.

If there are theoretical reasons to assume that only $k < p$ Y-variables are 'significant', we can write

$$X_j = \sum_{i=1}^{k} \lambda_{ji} F_i + \lambda F_{j.spec} + \varepsilon_j \text{ for } j = 1, 2, ..., p \tag{14}$$

This is the so-called *factor model*, where the 'significant' Y-variables are designated F_i. The 'non-significant' Y-variables are then considered either to express that an X-variable apart from measuring the *common factors* F_i also measures a *specific factor* F_{spec} (i.e. a factor which is measured only by the X-variable in question), or to express purely stochastic uncertainty or noise ε_j.

It is not possible to isolate the specific factor in cross-sectional data and it will there-fore be included in the error term. This means that the error term will not be purely stochastic, even if it is usually treated as such and attributed the assumptions

$$E(\varepsilon_j) = 0$$
$$Cov(\varepsilon_j \varepsilon_l) = 0 \quad \text{for } j \neq l \tag{15}$$
$$Cov(\varepsilon_j F_{ji}) = 0 \quad \text{for all } i \text{ and } j$$

Contrary to (13), (14) is a hypothetical model, often based on theoretically founded a priori assumptions, e.g. regarding the number of common factors. Contrary to (13) it is also a *statistical* model, as it includes a stochastic error ε_j, and its parameters therefore need to be estimated.

Note that while we can go from (12) to (13) and vice versa, the same simple opera-tion is not possible on (14) because of the stochastic term ε_j. *Factor scores* can there-fore not be calculated in a simple way, but have to be estimated. Several estimation methods exist, but none of them are very satisfying. The reason is that the factor model contains more parameters than there are data points – a rare situation in statistics! As a consequence we can estimate an unlimited number of factor models (and factor scores) all having the same mathematical properties. This is the so-called 'factor indeterminacy problem', see e.g. Thurstone (1947) or McDonald and Mulaik (1979).

The variance of X_j is

$$Var(X_j) = \underbrace{\sum_{i=1}^{k} \lambda_{ij}^2 Var(F_i)}_{communality \ h^2} + \lambda_{spec}^2 Var(F_{spec}) + Var(\varepsilon) \tag{16}$$

Leaving out the specific factor, the exploratory factor model can be depicted as shown in Figure 11, where the principal components model is also shown for comparison.

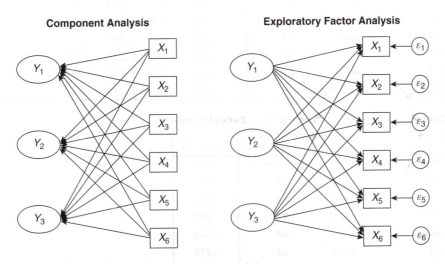

Figure 11 The exploratory factor analysis model

If you compare (14) with (2.21a) and (16) with (2.21c) it is obvious that the factor model is an extension of the traditional measurement model from Chapter 2 to the case of several factors.

It is also obvious that the exploratory factor model is more in accordance with the measurement models of SEM than the principal components model is. Indeed, it only differs from the ideal measurement model in that the various indicators are related to *all* the latent variables (factors) in the model – analogous to principal components.

Therefore it would have been more 'correct' to use factor analysis instead of component analysis in the examples above. However, as mentioned in the introductory part of this chapter, the two techniques will usually give nearly the same results (even if there is a tendency for factor analysis to extract fewer factors than component analysis), and component analysis is in many ways less complicated – for example, there is no 'factor indeterminacy problem'.

The factor model resembles the traditional regression model but differs from this in that the independent variables (the *F*-variables) are not directly measurable. The name 'factor analysis' covers a rather large number of different estimation and rotation techniques (and usually component analysis is included under the same hat). Consult Kim and Mueller (1978a, 1978b) for a short introduction and Harman (1976) or Mulaik (2009) for a deeper treatment of the subject.

As the main purpose of factor analysis is to connect the *X*-variables to the common factors, it is clear that you cannot base the analysis on the variances of the variables, as stated in the main diagonal of the covariance matrix. These variances must be reduced by that part of the variance caused by the specific factor and the random error ε_j, so that only the common variances (the communalities) form the basis of the calculations.

Usually factor analysis is based on standardized variables, i.e. on the correlation matrix, and the treatment here will follow that tradition. Analogous reasoning can, however, be used if the analysis is based on the covariance matrix.

In most estimation methods the communalities are estimated first, so that they can be substituted for the ones in the main diagonal of the correlation matrix. The estimation is usually done by an iterative process using as starting values R^2 from a regression of the variable in question on all other variables.

Usually this process will initially result in a matrix in which the smallest eigenvalues are negative. This is not very fortunate, as the eigenvalues are the variances of the factors (cf. the comments to Table 2). Therefore the correlations outside the diagonal have to be 'regulated' so as to secure non-negative eigenvalues. This is done 'automatically' by the computer program.

As mentioned several times, the name 'factor analysis' covers a suite of different algorithms varying in the ways that communalities and factor structure are estimated.

The most popular technique today is, perhaps, *maximum likelihood estimation*.

Maximum likelihood estimation is based on the calculation of the *likelihood function*, which expresses the probability of obtaining the present data (covariance or correlation matrix) as a function of the parameters of the model. Then the parameters are estimated as the values of the parameters that maximize the likelihood function. In other words, parameters estimated by maximum likelihood are the values that have the largest probability of producing the covariance or correlation matrix on which the estimation is based. In maximum likelihood estimation, invented by D. N. Lawley (see e.g. Lawley and Maxwell, 1971) in the 1940s, communalities are not estimated at the beginning of the process, but are a product of the estimation of the number of factors.

The likelihood function can be deduced from the assumption that the common factors and error terms are multivariate normally distributed. As maximum likelihood estimates (in addition to other nice properties, to be mentioned in the next chapter) are asymptotically normally distributed, this enables statistical testing to be carried out.

It is, however, only fair to mention that, for example, Morrison (2003) and Johnson and Wichern (2007) presented several examples of statistical testing in principal components analysis too.

As you will see, exploratory factor analysis is one step from classical measurement theory towards the measurement model of SEM, both with regard to introducing several common factors and with regard to estimation, as maximum likelihood estimation is also the preferred estimation method in SEM.

Component analysis or factor analysis?

Which should then be the preferred technique: component analysis or factor analysis?

The two techniques have had their followers, and it is not unreasonable to say that at times the arguments between the two groups have developed into 'wars' (Velicer & Jackson, 1990). However, a simple answer to the question can be found in the structure of the covariance matrix on which the analysis is based. In principal components analysis, the main diagonal contains variances and the components are extracted in decreasing order of variance. In factor analysis, the diagonal elements are the communalities, i.e. that part of each variable's variance that is shared with the common factors (and in that way with all other variables), and the factors are extracted in decreasing order of covariation with the other variables.

Therefore the answer is as follows:

- If you are interested in summarizing a number of correlating variables in a few new variables with the smallest possible loss of information, then component analysis is the answer.
- If you are interested in explaining the correlations in a data set as a result of a few underlying factors, then factor analysis is the answer.

In most situations component analysis and factor analysis will give nearly identical solutions, although factor analysis has a (very!) weak tendency to find a solution in fewer dimensions than component analysis. If you want to calculate scores, I would definitely recommend component analysis because of the unsatisfactory estimation methods offered by factor analysis.

In this chapter you met the following concepts:

- principal components analysis
- principal component
- component scores, component score coefficients
- component loading
- Kaiser criterion
- elbow plot and scree plot
- rotation
- pilot sample
- exploratory factor analysis
- maximum likelihood estimation

Questions

1. Explain the purpose and the principles of principal components analysis.

2. Define the following: principal component, component score, component score coefficient, component loading and communality.

3. What is the role of eigenvalues in component analysis?

4. Explain why and how you would employ rotation.

5. How do you use component analysis as item analysis?
   Compare component analysis and traditional item analysis. Discuss their vices and virtues.

6. What are the main differences between component analysis and (exploratory) factor analysis?

7. In many disciplines there are what we could call 'standard scales' (such as the SOP scale mentioned in Example 1.3). Select one from your own discipline and evaluate it using the techniques in this and the previous chapter. To get some inspiration take a look at Bearden, Netemeyer, and Haws (2011).

References

Bearden, W. O., Netemeyer, R. G., & Haws, K. L. (Eds.). (2011). *Handbook of marketing scales.* Thousand Oaks, CA: Sage.

Harman, H. (1976). *Modern factor analysis* (3rd ed.). Chicago: University of Chicago Press.

Johnson, R. A., & Wichern, D. W. (2007). *Applied multivariate statistical analysis* (6th ed.). Upper Saddle River, NJ: Prentice Hall.

Kim, J.-O., & Mueller, C. W. (1978a). *Introduction to factor analysis: What it is and how to do it*. Beverly Hills, CA: Sage.

Kim, J.-O., & Mueller, C. W. (1978b). *Factor analysis: Statistical methods and practical issues.* Beverly Hills, CA: Sage.

Lawley, D. N., & Maxwell, A. E. (1971). *Factor analysis as a statistical method* (2nd ed.). Sevenoaks: Butterworths.

McDonald, R., & Mulaik, S. A. (1979). Determinacy of common factors: A nontechnical review. *Psychological Bulletin, 86,* 297–306.

Morrison, D. F. (2003). *Multivariate statistical methods* (4th ed.). New York: McGraw-Hill.

Mulaik, S. A. (2009). *The foundations of factor analysis* (3rd ed.). New York: McGraw-Hill.

Norušis, M. J. (2005). *SPSS 14.00 Statistical procedures companion.* Upper Saddle River NJ: Prentice Hall.

Thurstone, L. L. (1947). *Multiple factor analysis.* Chicago: University of Chicago Press.

Velicer, W. F., & Jackson, D. N. (1990). Component analysis versus common factor analysis: Some issues in selecting an appropriate procedure. *Multivariate Behavioral Research, 25,* 1–28.

Further Reading

Child, D. (2006). *The essentials of factor analysis* (3rd ed.). London: Continuum.

Dunteman, G. H. (1989). *Principal components analysis.* Newbury Park, CA: Sage.

Mulaik, S. A. (2009). *The foundations of factor analysis* (3rd ed.). New York: McGraw-Hill.

The first two books are rather simple introductions to their subjects, while the third is more advanced.

Part 2

The Three Basic Models

4

Structural Equation Modeling with AMOS

In this chapter you are led through the various steps of structural equation modeling. On the way you will meet several problems that are connected with SEM.

Among the questions you will have to answer are: 'Are there enough data to estimate the model?' 'Which estimation method shall I use?' 'How do I get the computer to do what I want it to do?' 'How shall I react to error messages?' 'How do I interpret the computer output?'

As a soft introduction to AMOS, you will learn how to program a traditional multiple regression model and how to interpret the output from such an analysis.

All through the chapter a number of concepts, which will be used in the remainder of the book, will be introduced and defined.

1   How Do You Proceed?

SEM is usually done by going through the following steps:

1. Statement of research questions.
2. Formulation of a structural equation model, which (hopefully!) will answer the research questions.
3. Examination of whether the model can be estimated – the so-called identification problem, which was briefly mentioned in connection with the model in Figure 1.7c.
4. If necessary, a reformulation of the model in order to make it estimable.
5. Data collection and estimation of the model.
6. Examination of computer output.
7. If necessary, modification of the model based on interpretation of computer output.
8. Provisional acceptance of the model.
9. Test of the model on new data.
10. Acceptance or rejection of the model.

As should be clear from steps 4, 7 and 9, things are not always as simple as this list could lead you to believe. You must be prepared to run into problems at every step and therefore to go back and repeat earlier steps.

The first two steps above are problem specific and are therefore treated through various examples later on. The rest are taken up in this chapter, roughly following the sequence stated above.

Even if it is difficult to say much on model specification without referring to a specific problem, a warning is in order: always remember that SEM is not all about statistics and technicalities. When starting a new project, learn as much as possible from published theory and earlier research on the subject. If you start modeling too early, there is a great risk that you will end up with a misspecified model.

Read Example 1.6 once more – and think about it!

2   Identification

In relation to Bass's model (Figure 1.7c) in Section 1.4, the identification problem was briefly touched upon. We can formulate it as follows: is there enough data to estimate the parameters in the model?

Intuitively, the data should contain at least as many data points as there are parameters to estimate. A simple analogy will illustrate the idea.

Let β_1 and β_2 in the equation

$$\beta_1 + \beta_2 = 10 \tag{1}$$

be two parameters and let the number '10' be the collected data. It is clear that there are not enough data for estimation. The equation has an unlimited number of solutions for β_1 and β_2, and the model is *under-identified*. If we add another equation to get

$$\beta_1 + \beta_2 = 10$$
$$\beta_1 - \beta_2 = 2 \tag{2}$$

the two equations have one and only one solution:

$$\beta_1 = 6 \quad \text{and} \quad \beta_2 = 4 \tag{3}$$

and the model is *just-identified*. However, this model will agree with more than one data set, implying that it cannot be tested. If we add the equation

$$\beta_1 \times \beta_2 = c \tag{4}$$

we have 'one piece of information' left over for testing the model, which is now *over-identified*. If $c = 24$, the data are in agreement with the model, but if c is 'very' different from 24, the model is not supported by the data and should be rejected.

The number of surplus 'pieces of information' is called the *degrees of freedom* for the model. If the degrees of freedom are positive the model can be estimated and tested: the more degrees of freedom, the more precise the estimation and the more powerful the tests.

As – in most cases – the only data input needed is the sample covariance matrix, a model is identified if there are at least as many non-redundant elements in the covariance matrix as there are parameters to be estimated.

The so-called *t-rule*, that the number of 'pieces of information' shall be at least as large as the number of parameters to be estimated for the estimation to be possible, is, however, a necessary but *not* a sufficient condition. As was demonstrated in Section 1.7, a postulated model implies a special form of the covariance matrix, as the elements of this matrix are functions of the parameters of the model. This should make it possible to estimate the parameters from the covariance matrix, but even if the number of equations is at least as large as the number of unknowns, a system of equations can still have more than one solution.

In principle, it is possible to determine whether a model is identified or not by examining the structure of the implied covariance matrix and finding out whether the resultant system of equations has more than one solution for each and every parameter. This can be a very complicated process, so a general necessary and sufficient condition for identification would be very useful.

Such a condition does not exist. What we have is a series of conditions for special model types, but these are all either necessary or sufficient – but not both.

Two conditions must, however, always be satisfied for a model to be identified:

1. The *t*-rule must be met.
2. All latent variables must have assigned a scale. This is also true for the error terms (ε or δ). You cannot simultaneously estimate the coefficient and the variance of an error term. Usually (as in ordinary linear regression analysis) the coefficient is fixed at 1.00 and the variance is estimated. By fixing the coefficient at 1.00, the error term is measured in the same units as the dependent variable.

Remember: a model's parameters are regression coefficients – or *regression weights* as they are called in AMOS – and variances and covariances of the exogenous variables. An *exogenous variable* is a variable that does not appear as a dependent variable anywhere in the model. All other variables are called *endogenous variables*. Variances and covariances of endogenous variables are not parameters in the model, but consequences of the model.

What to do if a model is not identified

If a model is not identified, it must be made identifiable by increasing the number of manifest variables or by reducing the number of parameters to be estimated.

Reduction in the number of parameters to be estimated is done by *fixing* one or more parameters. Parameters are either *free* or *fixed*. A free parameter is a parameter that is 'free' to take on any value, and such a parameter is to be estimated. A fixed parameter is a parameter whose value is restricted in some way. In AMOS a parameter can be restricted in three ways:

1. The parameter can be restricted a priori to take on a certain value.
2. Two or more parameters can be restricted to have the same unspecified value.
3. The parameter can be missing in the model, because such a parameter is restricted to have the value 0.

I strongly recommend examination of the model in order to find out whether it is identified prior to data collection. One reason for this is that you can often attain identification by introducing more manifest variables.

Consider the measurement model in Figure 1a.

After having fixed the coefficients of the error terms to 1.00, the assignment of a scale to the latent variable F remains. We have two possibilities: (1) we can fix one of the coefficients (λ_1 or λ_2) at 1.00, in which case F will have the same scale as the X-variable in question; or (2) we can fix the variance of the latent variable at some arbitrary value – usually 1.00. Whatever we do, we have four parameters to estimate:

$$
\begin{array}{ccc}
\lambda_2 & \lambda_1 & \lambda_1 \\
Var(\varepsilon_1) & Var(\varepsilon_1) & \lambda_2 \\
Var(\varepsilon_2) \ \ \text{or} & Var(\varepsilon_2) \ \ \text{or} & Var(\varepsilon_1) \\
Var(F) & Var(F) & Var(\varepsilon_2)
\end{array}
$$

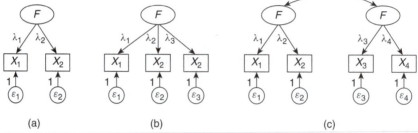

Figure 1   Identification

However, we have only three pieces of information, the variances of the two manifest variables and their covariance. Our model is under-identified.

Adding another indicator X_3 gives two further parameters to estimate, the coefficient λ_3 and the variance $Var(\varepsilon_3)$, but adds three new 'pieces of information': the variance of the new indicator and its covariances with the two other indicators – see panel (b). The model is just-identified.

In the model in panel (c), we have four indicators and consequently $(4 + 1)4/2 = 10$ pieces of information on which to base our estimation of the nine parameters:

$$
\begin{array}{lll}
\lambda_1 & Var(\varepsilon_1) & \phi_{12} \\
\lambda_2 & Var(\varepsilon_2) & \\
\lambda_3 & Var(\varepsilon_3) & \\
\lambda_4 & Var(\varepsilon_4) &
\end{array}
$$

assuming that the variances of the two latent variables are fixed. The model is over-identified with one degree of freedom.

However, suppose that ϕ_{12} is estimated to have a value near zero; then – because of rounding errors – you could end up in a situation similar to panel (a). This is an example of *empirical under-identification*. The problem is not with the model, but with the data, and is therefore more difficult to foresee. The lesson is always to have at least five indicators per latent variable in order to obtain an over-identified measurement model and avoid estimation problems. Do not underestimate the problems with formulating good items. It is not unusual for half of them not to pass item analysis!

Due to the lack of a general necessary and sufficient condition for identification of structural equation models, you will often have to fall back on empirical methods, i.e. try to estimate a proposed model and await AMOS's error messages.

You could say that this is a little too late to find out that a model is under-identified, but it is not impossible to use this method prior to data collection. Just sketch your model, construct one or more covariance matrices that are comparable with your model, run the model in AMOS and await the answer. If the model seems to be identified, run the analysis again with the implied covariance matrix as input. In your first run you order AMOS output to include the implied covariance matrix either by checking 'Implied moments' in 'Analysis Properties' (see Figure 8b) or by inserting the statement

```
Sem.ImpliedMoments
```

in the AMOS program (more on programming in AMOS in Section 4 below).

You could run the analyses several times with different *start values* (the values that the computer takes as initial 'guesstimates' of parameter values and steadily improves until the final solution – more about this below) and check that you obtain the same parameter estimates.

You will probably find it easier to construct a meaningful correlation matrix than a covariance matrix. Fortunately a correlation matrix will do, if you supplement it with standard deviations (take a look at Figure 6.2).

The identification problem is a consequence of the formulation of the model. However, sometimes the computer will tell you that the model is not identified even if all the sufficient conditions for identification are fulfilled. This could happen if computing problems arise. Because of rounding errors you could end up with calculations that are not defined, such as dividing by zero or taking the logarithm of zero. This is what I called above *empirical under-identification*.

3 Estimation

In Section 1.7 I wrote that the model is estimated in such a way that the difference between the empirical covariance matrix and the covariance matrix implied by the model is minimized. It is more correct to say that a function, F, of that difference is minimized:

$$F = f(S - \Sigma(\hat{\theta})) \tag{5}$$

where S is the empirical covariance matrix and $\Sigma(\hat{\theta})$ is an estimate of the covariance matrix implied by a model with the estimated parameters $\hat{\theta}$.

The fitting function F can have many forms, as each estimation method has its own special F-function. At present (version 19) AMOS offers the following estimation methods:

1. Maximum likelihood (ML)
2. Unweighted least squares (ULS)

3. Generalized least squares (GLS)
4. Scale-free least squares (SLS)
5. Asymptotically distribution-free (ADF) estimation.

The five estimation methods vary in distributional assumptions, but they all require the variables to be interval scaled.

All five estimation methods are so-called *full-information methods*, i.e. they estimate the parameters of the whole system in one go using all available data, while *limited-information methods* estimate one equation at a time. While full-information methods are generally more effective, they have two drawbacks:

1. There are sometimes difficulties in solving estimation problems, because specification problems in one corner of the model can have their roots in another corner of the model.
2. It is not possible to introduce non-identified relations into the model solely for the identification of other relations. The whole model must be identified for the estimation to work.

I shall say a few words about the various estimation methods. A deeper treatment can be found in Bollen (1989).

In addition to the above-mentioned estimation methods, AMOS also offers 'Bayesian estimation', a quite different estimation approach that I shall say a few words about below.

Maximum likelihood

As mentioned in Section 3.3, maximum likelihood estimation is the preferred estimation method in SEM. Parameters are estimated as the values that have the largest probability of producing the sample covariance matrix **S**.

The likelihood function can be deduced from an assumption of multivariate normality of the manifest variables (it can, however, also be deduced under less demanding assumptions (Browne, 1982; Bollen, 1989)).

ML estimation has a number of favourable qualities. First, it is consistent, i.e. the estimates $\hat{\theta}$ approach the parameter values θ asymptotically by increasing n. Furthermore, the ML estimator is asymptotically unbiased, asymptotically sufficient and asymptotically normally distributed. Also, $C = (n - 1)F_{ML}$, where n is the sample size, is asymptotically distributed as χ^2 with $p(p + 1)/2 - t$ degrees of freedom, where p is the number of manifest variables and t the number of free parameters. This makes it possible to test the model against the data.

Note that all these are asymptotic qualities, and therefore cannot be guaranteed to hold in small samples.

Finding the parameter values that maximize the likelihood function is too complicated to be done in an exact way. Instead the maximum is located by an iterative procedure, whereby the computer makes an initial 'guess' at the values of the parameters and then improves this initial guess step by step.

In a way you could compare this process with locating the top of a hill when you are blindfolded just by feeling with your feet.

From this picture it is obvious that the iterative process is not always successful in finding 'the top of the hill': An undulating landscape could have more than one hilltop, and perhaps the procedure does not find the highest one – or it does not find any top at all.

Unweighted least squares

ULS is analogous to ordinary least squares (OLS) in traditional regression: OLS minimizes the sum of squared errors and ULS minimizes the sum of squared values in the residual matrix. Like OLS, ULS does not make any distributional assumptions, and it is consistent (so are all the estimation methods listed above), but it is not asymptotically the most efficient.

Since you cannot be sure that $C = (n - 1)F_{ULS}$ is not even asymptotically distributed as χ^2, the output in AMOS does not contain the χ^2-test and other test statistics or measures of fit based on such statistics. For the same reason, neither standard deviations nor test statistics for the various parameters are reported. Browne (1982) discusses some possibilities for making various tests if ULS estimation has been used, but these are not at present implemented in AMOS.

ULS also uses an iterative procedure (as do all estimation methods in AMOS).

Generalized least squares

Just as ULS is analogous to OLS, GLS is analogous to weighted least squares (WLS) in traditional regression.

OLS gives equal weight to all observations in calculating the regression coefficients. This will result in inefficient estimates if all observations do not have approximately the same error variance. The solution to this problem is WLS, where each observation is given a weight proportional to the reciprocal of the error variance $Var(\varepsilon_i)$. In much the same way GLS weights all elements in the residual matrix taking variances and covariances of the elements into consideration.

GLS has the same asymptotic qualities as ML, and consequently the same tests can be performed. It is worth noting that GLS can be derived under less restrictive assumptions than ML (Bollen, 1989).

Scale-free least squares

You could say that SLS is ULS based on the correlation matrix (and not the covariance matrix), and the two algorithms will therefore give identical results if the correlation matrix is used for ULS estimation.

If used on the covariance matrix, SLS is scale invariant but ULS is not, i.e. if using ULS, linear transformations of scale for manifest variables will result in solutions that are not directly comparable.

I cannot think of any situation where SLS would be the natural choice.

Asymptotically distribution-free estimation

This heading seems promising because such an estimation method should be able to avoid building analysis and conclusions on doubtful assumptions.

Asymptotically distribution-free (ADF) estimation requires that the manifest variables have an eight-moment matrix, which requires a sample size measured in thousands.
Bootstrapping (treated in Chapter 9) could be a solution to the problem of ill-behaved
distributions if the sample is too small to allow for ADF estimation.

A few remarks on discrete (ordinal) variables

When ADF estimation makes such large demands on the sample size, how do we then
treat discrete (ordinal) data from the very popular five- or seven-point scales?

A special problem with ordinal scales is that the usual covariances cannot be used,
and therefore special measures of covariation must be calculated. These methods are
not implemented in AMOS at present, and, furthermore, they all assume that the ordinal
measurements cover underlying interval-scaled variables that fulfill the assumption of
multivariate normality – a rather strong assumption.

Alternatively you can treat the ordinal variables as if they are normally distributed
interval-scaled variables. This will be most realistic if:

1. The variables can take on 'many' values.
2. The variables are 'nearly normal', i.e. symmetric with kurtosis (see Appendix A)
   near zero.
3. Any possible (limited) skewness falls on the same side for all variables.

If a scale has at least five possible values, the first condition can usually be taken as
fulfilled. If your scale is shorter, you can use *parcelling* (see Section 2.2).

Unlike other SEM packages that use special correlation measures when variables are
ordinal or nominal, AMOS uses methods based on Bayesian estimation.

Bayesian estimation

Bayesian estimation – named after Thomas Bayes (1702–1761), who first suggested
this point of view on statistical inference (Bayes, 1763) – is an AMOS specialty. It has
a group all of its own, because it builds on a different view of the concept that is the
very foundation of statistics: namely, the concept of probability.

Probability can be seen either as an attribute of an element in the physical world (e.g.
the tendency of a dice to show a one in the next throw) or as a relation between you and
that element (e.g. how likely *you* think it is that the dice will show a one in the next throw).

Usually the two will be the same, namely one-sixth, but if the player is a notorious
cheat, you will probably not be willing to bet 1:5 on that outcome; that is, *your* (subjective) probability is different from one-sixth.

The two ways of looking at probability are usually called 'objective' and 'subjective'.

In the ordinary (the 'objective') statistical tradition, a parameter in a model is seen
as an *unknown constant*, the value of which you estimate.

From a 'subjective' Bayesian point of view, a parameter is an *uncertain quantity* the
size of which you have a – stronger or weaker – opinion about. You are not willing to
bet at even odds on every single possible value of that parameter!

Consequently the parameter is seen as a stochastic variable, which has a probability
distribution that matches your willingness to bet on the various values of the parameter,

and the empirical data are seen as a means for revising your prior opinion as expressed in your subjective probability distribution.

In that way Bayesian methods offer you a possibility of taking advantage of your prior knowledge, whereas traditional 'objective' methods in reality postulate that, prior to looking at the present data, every possible value of a parameter is equally likely. Of course this is not true. Are you really willing to place an even bet on every possible value of an unknown parameter?

Unfortunately Bayesian estimation is beyond the scope of this introduction, and I have to refer you to the AMOS User's Guide (Arbuckle, 2010) where Bayesian estimation takes up nearly 100 pages!

However, I would also like to draw your attention to one of my favourite articles, by Lindley and Phillips (1976), that should give you in a few pages an idea of the philosophy behind what is called Bayesian statistics.

4   Programming in AMOS

Having acquainted you with the various estimation methods available in AMOS, it is now time to show you how actually to estimate a model.

AMOS has one of the user-friendliest interfaces for this type of computer program. As in a few other programs the analysis can be done in two different ways:

1. You can write your program (in Visual Basic (VB) or C$^+$).
2. You can sketch your model in a user-friendly drawing environment (AMOS Graphics), where most of the drawing is done with a few mouse-clicks. AMOS then translates the drawing into a program and performs the necessary calculations.

In most of the examples in this and the following chapters, the programming is shown in both AMOS Graphics and VB, and you are strongly advised to compare the two.

If you are a beginner, you will probably prefer the graphic interface. However, I would advise you to become acquainted with the programming interface. My guess is that when you become more familiar with SEM, you will at some point switch to VB for the following reasons:

1. Programming usually takes less time than drawing.
2. Drawing the program could be problematic with complicated models, because the drawings easily become messy.
3. The exact model formulation is more precise – and uses less space – in a program, so that modifications to the model during the analysis are easier to follow, and require less explanation than would be the case with drawings.
4. The programming language is so simple that there is no reason not to use it.

AMOS has a nice feature that (apart from other uses) could help you transfer from the graphic to the programming interface. That is, when you have programmed using AMOS Graphics, you can ask AMOS to write (and save) the program in VB for later use (with the AMOS Graphics window open, choose 'Tools/Write a Program').

Example 1
Multiple regression analysis in AMOS

Bredahl (2001) used SEM in a cross-national study of factors influencing consumers' attitudes and buying intentions towards genetically modified food products.

I will use part of Bredahl's German data to illustrate the programming and estimation of a multiple regression model first using AMOS Graphics and then through VB. It must be emphasized, however, that this is not the way Bredahl analyzed her data.

The model is shown in Figure 2. The double-headed arrows indicate (possible) co-linearity among the independent variables.

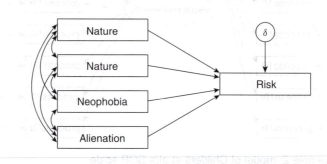

Variable name	Description	Measurement
Risk	Perceived risk by using genetically modified food	Six-item summated scale
Technology	Attitude to genetic modification in food production	Five-item summated scale
Nature	Attitude to nature	Six-item summated scale
Neophobia	Food neophobia	Five-item summated scale
Alienation	Alienation to the marketplace	Nine-item summated scale

Figure 2   Example 1: the model

As (in this case) we are only interested in relations between the variables and not in their values, the only input needed is the covariance matrix arranged as in Figure 3 (the means will not be used in this example). Remember to insert the underline after `row-type` and `varname`, otherwise AMOS will not read the file. As usual you can download the data from the book's website.

Programming in AMOS Graphics

Open AMOS Graphics (just as you did in Section 1.5). Choose the manifest variable symbol ▪, click where you want the first independent variable to be and drag the mouse until the rectangle has a suitable size. Then copy it four times, clicking and dragging the rectangle using the 'duplicate tool' 🖨 to look like Figure 4a. If by accident you drop a rectangle in the wrong position, you can – as mentioned in Section 1.5 – always pick it up using the 'removal van' 🚚.

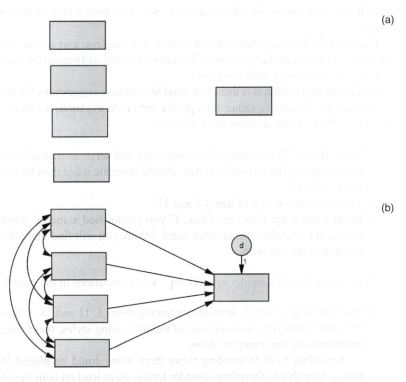

Figure 3   Example 1: the data

(a)

(b)

Figure 4   Example 1: drawing the model in AMOS Graphics

Figure 5   Example 1: entering your data

As the next step put in the arrows using the 'path tool' ← and the 'covariance tool' ↔ – again just as in Section 1.5.

The next step is to put in the disturbance. Select the error symbol ⌁ and click in the dependent variable. This makes your model look as shown in panel (b).

As you can see, the double-headed arrows indicating co-linearity make the picture a bit 'messy'. Now this model is very simple, so you can imagine how it could be almost impossible to get a clear view of a more complicated model. This is one of several reasons why I prefer to use the programming interface.

All that remains is to name the variables. Name the disturbance 'd' using the same procedure as in Section 1.5. Of course, you could name the manifest variables in the same way, but this would involve a lot of clicking, and there is an easier way. This necessitates that you enter your data, but, anyway, this has to be done at some point – so why not now?

Click the 'data file tool' ▥ (or choose 'File/Data Files' from the menu), and the window shown in Figure 5a will appear. Then click 'Group number 1 <working>', and the greyed-out buttons will become active as shown in panel (b).

When you click 'File Name', you will open up the documents file, where you can look for the data file you want to analyze. When you have found it, open it.

As you will recall (from Figure 3), the Excel file containing the data set had two tables, and therefore you have to choose 'Manifest' in the pop-up window in Figure 6a.

(a)

Select a Data Table

Latent
Manifest

View Data

OK   Cancel

(b)

Variables in Dat...   ?   X

Technology
Nature
Neophobia
Alienation
Risk

Figure 6   Example 1: choosing the right table in Excel and naming the variables

Now click the 'List variables in dataset tool' or choose 'View/Variables in Dataset', and when the window in Figure 6b pops up you choose the variables in the list one by one and, with the mouse button pressed down, move the mouse pointer to the corresponding manifest variable box in the drawing. Your model is now finished as shown in Figure 7.

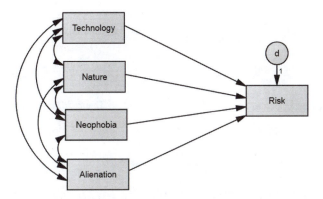

Figure 7   Example 1: the finished model

Figure 8   Example 1: choosing the estimation method and output

What is left is to estimate the parameters. In that connection you have some decisions to make:

1. You must decide which estimation method to use.
2. You must decide what information should be included in the output.
3. You must decide on the form of the output.

Click ▦ or choose 'View/Analysis Properties' and the menu in Figure 8a will appear. As you can see, ML estimation is already marked, i.e. the ML is the default estimation method – the method AMOS will use if not instructed otherwise.

Now click the 'Output' tab, and the window will change to the one in panel (b).

In addition to the standard output (including, for example, parameter estimates), this menu gives you the opportunity to choose from a variety of 'offers'. Choose the ones that are marked in the figure.

Now click ▦ or choose 'Analyze/Calculate Estimates' and AMOS will make the necessary calculations.

AMOS offers two forms of output. You can view the output in tabular form or it can be written into the pictorial model in Figure 7.

If you click ▦ or choose 'View/Text Output', the output is shown on the screen as in Figure 9. The panel to the left allows you to view portions of the output. As you can see, I have chosen to look at the estimates. We will have a closer look at the output below.

Note that what we usually call regression coefficients are called *regression weights* in AMOS.

Regression Weights: (Group number 1 - Model 1)

	Estimate	S.E.	C.R.	P	Label
Risk <--- Technology	-.240	.052	-4.636	***	
Risk <--- Nature	.371	.048	7.805	***	
Risk <--- Neophobia	.274	.043	6.328	***	
Risk <--- Alienation	.684	.082	8.324	***	

Standardized Regression Weights: (Group number 1 - Model 1)

	Estimate
Risk <--- Technology	-.175
Risk <--- Nature	.297
Risk <--- Neophobia	.240
Risk <--- Alienation	.318

Covariances: (Group number 1 - Model 1)

	Estimate	S.E.	C.R.	P	Label
Technology <--> Nature	-1.098	1.517	-.724	.469	
Technology <--> Neophobia	-10.865	1.738	-6.250	***	
Nature <--> Neophobia	1.488	1.825	.816	.415	
Technology <--> Alienation	.168	.881	.190	.849	

Figure 9 Example 1: text output as seen on the screen

At the top of the column to the left of your drawing area, you will see two icons:

At the moment, the left icon is highlighted, which means that the model in the right panel is your input model. If you click in the right icon, your screen will show your model with the parameter estimates.

As you can see, you can choose to view either the unstandardized or the standardized regression weights as shown in Figure 10.

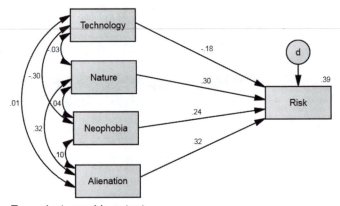

Figure 10   Example 1: graphic output

Now look at the output in Table 1:

1. First, information is given on the time and date for the run.
2. Then the title is shown.
3. Next is the number of the group. In this case there is only one group of respond-ents – the German one – though Bredahl in her cross-national study analyzed data from several groups (countries).
4. We are told that the model is recursive (roughly meaning that it has no 'loops' such as those in the model of Figure 1.7c) and that the sample size is 474.
5. Then comes a summary of the variables and parameters. The variables are listed and classified as exogenous (pre-determined) or endogenous (post-determined) and as observed (manifest) or unobserved (latent). The parameters are classified

as fixed (the regression weight of the error term) or labelled, i.e. provided with a name, which can be used when referred to. If AMOS needs labels for reference purposes, it will label the parameters itself.

6. Use of the name 'models' in the plural indicates that it is possible to estimate several models in the same run. In this case only one model, called 'default model', is estimated, but in Chapter 6 you will meet an example of multiple-model estimation.

7. Then follows the degrees of freedom account: there are 15 covariances in the input and 15 parameters to estimate. So the model has zero degrees of freedom. The model is just-identified and will fit any data set.

8. The χ^2-test cannot be carried out because no degrees of freedom are left over for testing.

9. Then follows the estimates of the parameters, their standard errors and *critical ratios* (C.R.). Critical ratios are the estimates divided by their standard errors and should be asymptotically standard normally distributed.

   The last column shows the *P*-values (see the subsections on statistical testing in Appendix A) of a two-sided test of the various parameters. The null hypothesis is the usual one: that the parameter in question is zero. *** means that the *P*-value is less than it is possible to express in the number of decimal places chosen for the output – in this case less than 0.001.

10. The coefficient of determination (multiple coefficient of correlation squared) follows.

We observe that even if all regression weights are highly significant, the four independent variables taken together explain less than 40% of the variation in 'Risk'.

As will be shown in Chapter 7, this is partly due to the fact that the measurements are not wholly reliable.

Table 1 Example 1: table output

Analysis Summary   (1)

Date and Time

Date: 7. januar 2011
Time: 15:27:46

Title   (2)

Example 4.1: 7. januar 2011 15:27

Groups   (3)

Group number 1 (Group number 1)

Notes for Group (Group number 1)   (4)

The model is recursive.
Sample size = 474

Variable Summary (Group number 1)   (5)

Your model contains the following variables (Group number 1)

Observed, endogenous variables
Risk
Observed, exogenous variables
Technology

(Continued)

(Continued)

```
Nature
Neophobia
Alienation
Unobserved, exogenous variables
d
```

Variable counts (Group number 1)

Number of variables in your model:	6
Number of observed variables:	5
Number of unobserved variables:	1
Number of exogenous variables:	5
Number of endogenous variables:	1

Parameter summary (Group number 1)

	Weights	Covariances	Variances	Means	Intercepts	Total
Fixed	1	0	0	0	0	1
Labeled	0	0	0	0	0	0
Unlabeled	4	6	5	0	0	15
Total	5	6	5	0	0	16

Models (6)

Default model (Default model)

Notes for Model (Default model)

Computation of degrees of freedom (Default model) (7)

```
        Number of distinct sample moments:    15
Number of distinct parameters to be estimated:    15
            Degrees of freedom (15 - 15):     0
```

Result (Default model) (8)

```
Minimum was achieved
Chi-square = .000
Degrees of freedom = 0
Probability level cannot be computed
```

Group number 1 (Group number 1 - Default model) (9)

Estimates (Group number 1 - Default model)

Scalar Estimates (Group number 1 - Default model)

Maximum Likelihood Estimates

Regression Weights: (Group number 1 - Default model)

			Estimate	S.E.	C.R.	P	Label
Risk	<---	Technology	-.240	.052	-4.636	***	
Risk	<---	Nature	.371	.048	7.805	***	
Risk	<---	Neophobia	.274	.043	6.328	***	
Risk	<---	Alienation	.684	.082	8.324	***	

**Standardized Regression Weights: (Group number 1 -
Default model)**

			Estimate
Risk	<---	Technology	-.175
Risk	<---	Nature	.297
Risk	<---	Neophobia	.240
Risk	<---	Alienation	.318

Covariances: (Group number 1 - Default model)

			Estimate	S.E.	C.R.	P	Label
Technology	<-->	Nature	-1.098	1.517	-.724	.469	
Nature	<-->	Neophobia	1.488	1.825	.816	.415	
Neophobia	<-->	Alienation	2.411	1.065	2.263	.024	
Technology	<-->	Neophobia	-10.865	1.738	-6.250	***	
Nature	<-->	Alienation	6.650	1.012	6.571	***	
Technology	<-->	Alienation	.168	.881	.190	.849	

Correlations: (Group number 1 - Default model)

			Estimate
Technology	<-->	Nature	-.033
Nature	<-->	Neophobia	.038
Neophobia	<-->	Alienation	.105
Technology	<-->	Neophobia	-.300
Nature	<-->	Alienation	.317
Technology	<-->	Alienation	.009

Variances: (Group number 1 - Default model)

	Estimate	S.E.	C.R.	P	Label
Technology	30.103	1.957	15.379	***	
Nature	36.103	2.348	15.379	***	
Neophobia	43.559	2.832	15.379	***	
Alienation	12.193	.793	15.379	***	
d	34.615	2.251	15.379	***	

Squared Multiple Correlations: (Group number 1 - Default model)   (10)

	Estimate
Risk	.387

Programming in VB

When you open the Program Editor, it looks like Figure 11a, and you write your program in place of the comment 'Your code goes here'. Observe that the comment begins with a single opening quote. This forces AMOS to skip that line and not consider it part of the program. You can therefore use single quotes to place comments in your programs, and you are advised to do so in order to keep track of various versions of the programs in your project. Figure 11b shows a VB program for estimation of the model.

Figure 11   Example 1: (a) new program editor and (b) program for first run

The program statement 'Sem.Dispose' releases resources used by the Sem object and 'Try/Finally/End Try' ensures that the Sem.Dispose statement will be executed even if the program runs into trouble. In a way you could say that the program is placed between 'Try' and 'Finally'.

The first line is a title, which will be printed in the output, and is followed by a comment.

The next line tells AMOS to find the data in the sheet 'Manifest' in the Excel file 'Bredahl.xls'. AMOS reads data from text files, and from various other formats such as Excel, SPSS, dBase, FoxPro, Lotus 1-2-3 and Access.

The line Sem.TextOutput forces AMOS to show the resulting output in a window on the screen after calculations. Otherwise, the calculations will be executed and saved to a temporary file but *not* shown on the screen.

As no estimation method has been specified, we estimate the model by ML (the default) and order the output to include standardized parameter values (Sem. Standardized) and the squared multiple correlation coefficient (Sem.Smc).

Then the model is described (Sem.AStructure). Note that every arrow in the program corresponds to an arrow in Figure 2, and thereby indicates that these regression coefficients – or regression weights – will be estimated. However, these five structure lines can be replaced by

```
Sem.AStructure ("Risk = Technology + Nature + Neophobia
                    + Alienation + d")
```

saving a good deal of writing, especially in more complicated models involving several regression functions.

Then the statement 'Sem.FitModel' fits the model.

As you can see, the correlations among the exogenous variables are not specified in the program because such correlations are defaults in AMOS when you use the programming interface. However, in the graphic interface the correlations must be specified, because here 'what you see is what you get'.

Also note that no constant is specified. This does not mean that AMOS cannot estimate models with explicit constant terms (as we shall see in Chapter 8) but usually the constant is of less interest and can be omitted.

Unfortunately the estimation could not be done. Part of the output is given in Table 2, from which you can see that the regression weight and the variance of the error term are both unidentified. The reason is that we have forgotten to set a scale for the latent variable *d*. Accordingly the last line in the program in Figure 11b is replaced by

```
Sem.AStructure ("Risk<--d (1)")
```

Or if you use the equation method

```
Sem.AStructure ("Risk = Technology + Nature
        + Neophobia + Alienation + (1)d")
```

and you have learned that in AMOS a parameter is fixed to have a certain value by writing that value in parentheses next to the variable. This change will result in the output in Table 1.

When you use the graphic interface, the regression weights of error terms are fixed at 1.00 by default (as you will see from Figure 4b). In Example 6.1 you will learn how to fix a parameter value if you use the graphic interface.

Table 2   Example 1: output first run (extract)

```
Number of distinct parameters to be estimated:   16
                  Degrees of freedom (15 - 16):   -1
```

Result (Model 1)

```
The model is probably unidentified. In order to achieve identifiability,
it will probably be necessary to impose 1 additional constraint.
The (probably) unidentified parameters are marked.
```

Regression Weights: (Group 1 - Model 1)

Risk	<---	Technology	
Risk	<---	Nature	
Risk	<---	Neophobia	
Risk	<---	Alienation	
Risk	<---	d	unidentified

Covariances: (Group 1 - Model 1)

Technology	<-->	Nature
Technology	<-->	Neophobia
Nature	<-->	Neophobia
Technology	<-->	Alienation
Nature	<-->	Alienation
Neophobia	<-->	Alienation

Variances: (Group 1 - Model 1)

Technology	
Nature	
Neophobia	
Alienation	
d	unidentified

5   Examining AMOS Output

Examination of AMOS output starts by looking for error messages, to see whether AMOS has encountered any trouble during the estimation process. Examples of such problems are the following:

1. The program fails to converge.
2. Parameters are (probably) not identified.
3. Negative variance estimates.
4. Covariance matrices that are not positive definite.

Point 2 was treated in Section 2 above; the other points in the list will be commented on below.

Convergence problems

If the program fails to converge, the cause most often is that the sample is too small, or that the model is extremely misspecified, so that correlations among indicators for different latent variables are larger than correlations among indicators for the same concept.

In both cases the cure is simple: collect more data and/or reformulate the model.

Another cause of failing convergence could be that the variances of the manifest variables are too different in size, e.g. a family's yearly income in dollars and family size. In this case the solution is just as simple: change the measurement scale from dollars to thousands of dollars or tens of thousands of dollars or to whatever is necessary to obtain nearly comparable variances for the variables.

Extreme non-normal data can also give rise to convergence problems.

Computer programs such as AMOS are generally very good in finding start values for the iterations, but if bad start values are the problem, you can supply your own start values for some or all of the parameters yourself. In AMOS, just label the parameter in question followed by a colon and the wanted start value: for example, to label the variable 'Nature' with the letter 'b' and specify the start value 0.5, you write

```
SEM.AStructure ("Risk = Technology + (b:0.5) Nature
          + Neophobia + Alienation + (1)d")
```

In Example 6.1 you will learn how to label a parameter if you use the graphic interface.

Convergence problems could also arise as a consequence of the sample covariance matrix not being positive definite, a subject that is dealt with below.

Negative variances

Negative variances are of course meaningless. Most often it is the estimated variances of error terms (ε and δ) that are negative. The reason could be a sample that is too small. Often the reason is that existing correlations among some of the indicators for the same latent variables have not been taken care of. Such correlations will emerge in situations where there have been problems in formulating items that are sufficiently different, but nevertheless similar enough to measure the same concept.

Reformulating the model by introducing the relevant correlations can solve the problem. The perfectionist will look at such correlations as a blemish, because the ideal is that the only cause for correlation among the items is the latent variable itself. If two correlating indicators are very similar, you can omit one of them.

If a negative variance is numerically small, you could fix it to have a small positive value.

Correlating the ε across latent variables in models based on cross-sectional data is difficult to defend, and should be avoided by reformulating the model.

Covariance matrices that are not positive definite

Every symmetric $p \times p$ matrix – and that includes covariance and correlation matrices – has associated with it p *eigenvalues* (some of which could be identical). If the eigenvalues are all positive, the matrix is said to be *positive definite* (if they are all negative, it is *negative definite*).

In component analysis (Chapter 3) we met a special interpretation of the eigenvalues of a covariance or correlation matrix, namely as variances of the principal components. Since a variance cannot be negative, covariance and correlation matrices cannot be negative definite.

But can they have one or more eigenvalues being zero (in which case the matrix is described as being *positive semi-definite*)? Yes, this is possible. It means that the data can be fully described in fewer than p dimensions. However, certain calculations, which could occur in the fitting function, are not defined for semi-definite matrices (because, for example, they lead to division by zero).

From (5) we can see that the fitting function F contains two covariance matrices $\mathbf{S}$ and $\Sigma(\hat{\theta})$ to which we can add a third matrix, namely a weight matrix $\mathbf{W}$ used for instance in ADF estimation. As $\mathbf{W}$ shall also be positive definite, all three matrices could cause problems for the estimation process, and lead to the error message.

If $\mathbf{S}$ is not positive definite, then either you have used pairwise deletion (see Chapter 9), or one or more of the variables is a linear function of one or more of the others.

If you cannot 'repair' the input and a positive semi-definite $\mathbf{S}$ makes sense in the situation, I recommend using ULS, as ML estimation then requires calculation of the logarithm of zero and GLS requires division by zero, both of which operations are of course undefined.

In this connection I must point out that, due to rounding errors, strong co-linearity among manifest variables will lead to the same problems as if this matrix was semi-definite, i.e. it will result in empirical under-identification as mentioned in Section 2. So be prepared to face problems if you have correlations larger than 0.80 among the manifest variables. However, there could also be more subtle co-linearities involving more than two variables at a time. A simple way to get an indication of such multivariate co-linearities is to calculate the multiple correlation coefficient for each variable when regressing it on the remaining variables. Large correlations signal co-linearity problems, but say nothing about their nature. Detecting such co-linearities can be a challenge. SPSS and other statistics packages have advanced output to assist you in such tasks. A simple explanation of the methods as implemented in SYSTAT (and SPSS!) can be found in Wilkinson, Grant, and Gruber (1996).

But what if the estimate $\Sigma(\hat{\theta})$ is not positive definite? It could be that the first guess for $\Sigma(\hat{\theta})$ is not positive definite. If this happens, AMOS will in most instances iterate to a positive definite $\Sigma(\hat{\theta})$ in a few steps. If this does not happen, there is a risk that the process will not find the global maximum of the fitting function. As you can imagine, most often problems with $\Sigma(\hat{\theta})$ can be traced back to problems with $\mathbf{S}$ – after all, the whole idea is to minimize the discrepancy between the two matrices. Another reason could be that your model is 'very wrong', and in that case you will have to respecify it.

If the problem arises with a matrix that emerges as a result of the calculations (i.e. covariance matrices of ε and δ), it can often be traced back to variances being estimated as negative (see above). Sometimes, however, a positive semi-definite covariance matrix is a natural (and meaningful!) consequence of the model. In such a case you can of course neglect the warning.

Last but not least, it should be pointed out that any of the three matrices could cause problems if the sample is too small.

Outliers and non-normality

Many of the problems discussed above can be traced back to the causes mentioned in the heading. Even if they do not result in error messages, estimates and the validity of the tests can, depending on the estimation method, be severely influenced by outliers and by data not being multivariate normal. Therefore it is advisable to examine the raw data very carefully before doing any calculation.

Outliers are observations which take on values that are very different from the main part of the data. As long as we consider each variable separately, it is not too difficult to locate outliers. A simple way to do so is to standardize all variables and then examine observations with one or more variables having values numerically larger than, say, 4.00. But when we look at two variables, we already encounter problems. Consider Figure 12 where the first two variables from Example 3.4 are depicted. A small amount of error is added to the values so that all observations can be seen, even if they take on the same values. A contour ellipse including about 68% of the observations is also shown.

Three observations (A, B and C) are marked. Observation C is farther from the centroid than A and B, but which is farthest from the centroid, A or B?

By traditional standards A is farther from the centroid than B, but B has a *combination* of the variable values that is more unusual than those of A. You could therefore argue that B is farther away from the centroid if we use a measure where the units are smaller in directions where the Euclidean distance from the centre to the 'limits' of the cluster of observations is small. Such a measure is the *Mahalanobis squared distance D^2*.

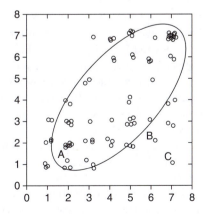

Figure 12 Example 4: identifying outliers

AMOS calculates D^2 for every observation as well as diagnostics to check normality assumptions.

Checking 'Tests for normality and outliers' in 'Analysis Properties' in Figure 8b or including the order

```
Sem.NormalityCheck
```

in the program in Figure 11 (and also basing the analysis on the raw data and not on the covariance matrix) will produce the additional output given in Table 3.

Table 3   Example 1: Checking for normality and outliers

Assessment of normality (Group 1)

Variable	min	max	skew	c.r.	kurtosis	c.r.
alienati	4	21	-.720	-6.447	.236	1.055
neophobi	5	35	.209	1.869	-.416	-1.863
nature	12	42	-.315	-2.820	-.485	-2.173
tech	7	35	-.359	-3.215	.028	.124
risk	7	42	-.553	-4.950	-.225	-1.008
Multivariate					4.021	5.270

Observations farthest from the centroid (Mahalanobis distance) (Group 1)

Observation number	Mahalanobis d-squared	p1	p2
185	27.719	.000	.020
354	22.608	.000	.016
198	22.103	.001	.002
473	20.868	.001	.001
206	18.293	.003	.009

(only first five observations shown)

As can be seen from the table, the following are shown for each variable: minimum value, maximum value, skewness and kurtosis; as far as the last two statistics are concerned, critical values (supposing the statistics to be standard normally distributed) are also presented. For a symmetric distribution, the skewness is zero. If the distribution has a long upper tail, the skewness is positive; if it has a long lower tail, it is negative. Kurtosis is a measure of the 'peakiness' of the distribution (see Appendix A). For a normal distribution the kurtosis is zero; if the distribution is flatter than a normal distribution with the same variance, the kurtosis is negative; and if it is peakier, the kurtosis is positive. In the last line in this section Mardia's measure of multivariate kurtosis (Mardia, 1970, 1974) is shown.

Note that severe non-normality biases parameter estimates, test results and fit measures.

Unfortunately, this section of the output is of limited value. The statistical significance depends on the sample size, and the null hypotheses of zero skewness and kurtosis are bound to be rejected with sample sizes relevant for SEM. Of course you could discard the critical values and just look at the statistics themselves, but it is difficult to judge from them whether the deviations from normality are serious enough to invalidate SEM estimation or testing.

I would rather recommend using graphical methods, such as histograms and normal probability plots, to judge whether it is necessary to transform a variable to obtain normality.

In the next panel the observations are shown in order of decreasing D^2 distance from the centroid. Column p1 shows that the probability that any arbitrary observation should have a larger distance from the centroid than 27.719 is 0.000, and in column p2 we see that the probability that the *largest* distance from the centroid exceeds 27.719 is 0.020. In the second line we see that the probability of any observation being farther away from the centroid than 22.608 is also 0.000, while the probability that the *second largest* distance exceeds 22.608 is 0.016, and so on.

You should expect small p1-values, whereas small p2-values indicate outliers.

It must be remembered, however, that the probability calculations are based on the assumption of multivariate normality, and in this case this assumption is far from fulfilled. As a consequence of this, most p2-values are small and cannot be used to locate outliers. However, observe that there is a rather large drop in d-squared from observation 185 to observation 354, so no doubt observation 185 is an outlier.

My advice would therefore be as follows:

1. Judge the univariate normality of the variables based on histograms and probability plots.
2. If necessary transform non-normal variables to (near) normality. Often this will also bring outliers nearer the main body of the data.
3. After transformations, use AMOS to detect outliers.

I am well aware that in theory normality of marginal distributions does not guarantee multivariate normality. However, in my experience, in practice you can in general assume multivariate normality if all marginal distributions are normal.

In addition, if the data are multivariate normal, all bivariate regression functions are linear. This could also be used as a check for multivariate normality – but note that it is also a necessary and not a sufficient condition.

Samples that are too small

As pointed out several times, small samples can generate a lot of problems, but when is a sample too small?

I mentioned that ADF estimation requires sample sizes measured in thousands, but apart from that, it is difficult to give precise guidelines – seldom will you have so large a data set at your disposal.

The problem is twofold:

1. The sample size plays a multiple role in SEM. It determines the precision and stability with which the model is estimated and the power of statistical tests, and, further, it influences the size of the various fit measures that are discussed in the next chapter.
2. The required sample size depends on lots of factors: the complexity of the model, the estimation method and the distributional qualities of the data – and what is more, these various factors interact in their demands.

The more complex the model, the larger the sample size required. As a rough rule of thumb it has been proposed that the sample size should be at least 10 times the number of free parameters, unless the model is *very* simple and the distribution of exogenous variables nearly multivariate normal.

Also, the more ill-behaved the distribution, the larger the sample size required. Remember: the arguments for using ML or GLS estimation are based on their asymptotic qualities.

As the decision on sample size is so complicated, many rules of thumb have emerged. Personally I think that a sample size about 100 would suffice for regression models like the one in this chapter, or for the development of a simple measurement model like the SOP scale mentioned in Example 1.3 and discussed in more detail in Chapter 6. In more complicated models like the one you will meet in Chapter 7, I usually demand 200–300 observations as a minimum.

The next steps

Having dealt with the problems that caused the error messages, you then move on to examine the output.

The first step is to look at the coefficients (and other parameters). Do they have the expected signs, and is their numerical magnitude in agreement with grounded theories, earlier empirical studies and common sense? Are any of the standard errors extremely large – causing uncertainties in the magnitude of the parameter estimates? Or are they perhaps extremely small, which could cause problems with the calculation of the test statistics?

Next, look at the global χ^2-test for the model as a whole and the long list of fit measures (not shown in Table 2). If the model fit is unsatisfactory you can try to improve it – usually by adding more parameters to the model – and if the fit is 'too good' the model can perhaps be simplified by fixing or deleting parameters. In both cases you can order output that can help with these modifications (you will see several examples on this in the following chapters).

In this step-by-step way you can reach a model which will give a satisfactory description of the data in as few parameters as possible, but at the same time is theoretically sound and substantively meaningful – a so-called *parsimonious* model.

I would like to emphasize the importance of simple models: the simpler the model, the more generalizable the model.

Exploratory use of SEM

This process is not without problems. The more revisions you go through, the larger the risk that you will profit from peculiarities in the sample at hand and that your model will not fit any other comparable data set.

In principle SEM is a confirmatory procedure, by which you test a model formulated a priori. However, the continual 'improvements' of the model is more exploratory and invalidates the 'testing': you test hypotheses on the same data that have given birth to them – a circular argument!

In this way the *P*-values lose their proper meaning and can only be used descriptively. This is the reason for including steps 9 and 10 in the list at the beginning of this chapter. Judging by published research, this cross-validation is very seldom done, and if you forgo it, it is extra important:

- that your original model is based on well-grounded substantive theory; and
- that stepwise alterations of the model are few in number and also based on substantive thinking.

Over the years AMOS has introduced a whole range of methods to automate revision of models and search for the 'best' one. No doubt this development will continue in future versions.

I will not treat these methods here, but remember that, the more you rely on automation, the greater the risk that you will neglect serious thinking based on substantive considerations. This is artificial intelligence in its worst form.

6   A Few Problems with SEM

I would like to end this chapter by pointing out three problems that you should always keep in mind when doing structural equation analysis: (1) the 'reverse' use of statistical tests; (2) the dependence of the χ^2-test on sample size; and (3) the existence of *equivalent models* that all have the same fit to the data.

The 'reverse' testing procedure

As is well known, the philosophy of traditional statistical testing goes as follows:

You formulate two hypotheses, a null hypothesis H_0 and an alternative hypothesis H_1. H_0 is the hypothesis that represents the status quo, while H_1 is the hypothesis you want to support. If the data do not support H_0, this hypothesis is rejected and H_1 is accepted – not as *true*, but as a *better* description of the data-generating process than H_0.

We accept H_1, not because we prove it is true but because we reject a competing hypothesis: statistical inference is 'the science of disproof'.

In SEM this logic is reversed: H_0 states that the model you actually want to support is true, and H_1 that it is not.

In a broader perspective this procedure conflicts with the basic philosophy of scientific discovery: that a new model proposed to explain an empirical phenomenon is only accepted if its explanation is better than the one taken to be 'true' hitherto. It is not 'true' in any absolute sense, only 'more true' than the old one, but it will in all probability give way to an even 'better' model at some point in the future.

R. A. Fisher (1890–1962) – whom many believe was the greatest statistician of all time – often quoted Thomas Fuller (1654–1734), 'Nothing is good or bad but by comparison', but this comparison very seldom takes place in SEM, except in implicit comparisons with the usually very unrealistic models that are the basis for fit measures.

There will in general be several processes that could be hypothesized to have generated the data at hand. It is therefore a good habit to start out with several models that are substantively meaningful (based on prior research, well-grounded theory or common sense), compare them and judge their relative ability to explain the data.

Based on published research this is very seldom done, in which case the researcher runs a risk of overlooking other plausible explanations of the data.

The example in Figure 1.7b is a positive exception to the usual way SEM is carried out.

The χ^2-test and the sample size

It is a well-known fact that the χ^2-test depends on sample size. In the case of SEM the test is based on $C = (n - 1)F$ where F is the fitting function. If the sample size is sufficiently small, you will always accept H_0, and if it is sufficiently large you will always reject H_0.

The combination of the 'reversed' test procedure and the dependence of χ^2 on sample size are therefore rather grotesque. Even if we know that our model is not literally 'true', we will accept it at small sample sizes and reject it at large sample sizes. This is the main reason for the invention of a long series of fit indices (some of them analogous to the well-known R^2) which you will meet in the next chapter.

Indeed, this is the problem with all two-sided tests, where a sharp null hypothesis is tested against a diffuse alternative. The null hypothesis is always false; it is only a matter of taking a sufficiently large sample to prove it is false!

This is one of several good reasons for using one-sided tests when testing estimated parameters – but remember to formulate your hypotheses before you look at the data! (Why?)

Equivalent models

If we estimate a simple regression model

$$y = \alpha_0 + \alpha_1 x + \delta_y \tag{6a}$$

we will obtain exactly the same fit as in

$$x = \beta_0 + \beta_1 y + \delta_x \tag{6b}$$

and in SEM where several equations and variables are involved, it will *always* be possible to find several different models with exactly the same fit but with different theoretical implications. While such *equivalent models* will include different parameters and different parameter values, they will show exactly the same values on all figures in the output used to measure the (global) 'goodness' of the model including the χ^2-test and fit measures.

Figure 13 shows a few of the models that will fit the data of a model with three manifest variables equally well: they are *equivalent*. In simple SEM models you might have only a limited number of equivalent models, but in larger models the number of

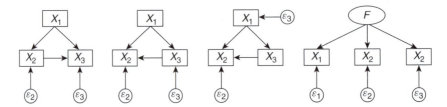

Figure 13   Equivalent models

equivalent models might be counted in hundreds or even thousands (in Figure 13 the models are just-identified, and all just-identified models are equivalent).

Even if most of the equivalent models are usually without any substantive meaning, there will in most cases exist a number of meaningful equivalent models. It is therefore the researcher's duty to explain why one meaningful equivalent model is preferred to others. Judging from published work this is very seldom done.

It can be a cumbersome job to specify all equivalent models (Lee, 1990; Herschberger, 1994), so the special computer program TETRAD was compiled to do this job (TETRAD Project homepage: http://www.phil.cmu.edu/projects/tetrad/).

The lesson learned is: an excellent fit guarantees that your model fits the data – but it does not prove that your model is a realistic picture of 'the real world'. Consequently, a bad fit is stronger evidence against the model than a good fit is evidence in support of it.

In this chapter you met the following concepts:

- identification
- *t*-rule
- fixed and free parameters
- maximum likelihood (ML)
- unweighted least squares (ULS)
- generalized least squares (GLS)
- scale-free least squares (SLS)

- asymptotically distribution-free (ADF) estimation
- Bayesian estimation
- convergence
- positive definite and positive semi-definite covariance matrices
- equivalent models

You learned how to use AMOS Graphics and VB in a simple regression model.

You also learned the following AMOS statements:

- Sem.Title
- Sem.Dispose
- Sem.FitModel
- Sem.TextOutput
- Sem.Standardized

- Sem.Smc
- Sem.AStructure
- Sem.NormalityCheck
- Sem.ImpliedMoments

Questions

1. Using an example from your own area of study or research, sketch out the various steps in a typical SEM project.

2. Explain the identification problem and what can be done with an under-identified model.

3. Give a short description of the estimation methods currently available in AMOS.

4. How would you go about examining AMOS output?

References

Arbuckle, J. L. (2010). *IBM SPSS© AMOS TM 19 User's Guide*. Crawfordville, FL: AMOS Development Corporation.

Bayes, T. (1763). An essay towards solving a problem in the doctrine of chances. *Philosophical Transactions of the Royal Society of London, 53*, 370–418.

Bollen, K. A. (1989). *Structural equation modeling with latent variables*. New York: Wiley.

Bredahl, L. (2001). Determinants of consumer attitudes and purchase intentions with regard to genetically modified foods – results of a cross-national survey. *Journal of Consumer Policy, 24*, 23–61.

Browne, M. W. (1982). Covariance structures. In D. M. Hawkins (Ed.), *Topics in multivariate analysis*. Cambridge: Cambridge University Press.

Herschberger, S. I. (1994). The specification of equivalent models before the collection of data. In A. E. von Eye & C. C. Clog (Eds.), *Latent variables analysis*. Thousand Oaks, CA: Sage.

Lee, S. (1990). A simple rule for generating equivalent models in covariance structure modeling. *Multivariate Behavioral Research, 25*, 313–334.

Lindley, D. V., & Phillips, L. D. (1976). Inference for a Bernoulli process (a Bayesian view). *The American Statistician, 30*, 112–119.

Mardia, K. V. (1970). Measures of multivariate skewness and kurtosis with applications. *Biometrika, 57*, 519–530.

Mardia, K. V. (1974). Applications of some measures of multivariate skewness and kurtosis in testing normality and robustness studies. *Sankhya, Series B, 36*, 115–128.

Wilkinson, L., Grant, B., & Gruber, C. (1996). *Desktop data analysis with SYSTAT*. Upper Saddle River, NJ: Prentice Hall.

Further Reading

In this chapter you have been introduced to lots of problems and methods to cope with these problems. No doubt you are also curious and looking for answers to the many questions you may have asked yourself during the reading – and to the many questions you will ask yourself when reading the following chapters. I will therefore mention three books that should be of help to you in further studies of structural equation models:

Bollen, K. A. (1989). *Structural equation modeling with latent variables*. New York: Wiley.

Hancock, G. R., & Mueller, R. O. (Eds.). (2006). *Structural equation modeling: A second course*. Charlotte, NC: Information Age Publishing.

Marcoulides, G. A., & Schumacker, R. A. (Eds.). (1996). *Advanced structural equation modeling: Issues and techniques*. Mahwah, NJ: Erlbaum.

The book by Bollen is still a cornerstone in the SEM literature (and we eagerly await a new edition). The next two are edited books which discuss newer developments in a not too advanced form.

5

Models with Only Manifest Variables

In this chapter you will be introduced to acyclic and cyclic models with only manifest variables.

As mentioned in Chapter 1, these models are commonly known as *path models* and in economics as *simultaneous equation models* or *econometric models*.

You will first learn how to analyze acyclic models. You will meet two sufficient rules for identification and then be led through a simple example through which you will learn how to interpret the very extensive output from AMOS, including the various fit measures you find in AMOS output.

Then we turn to cyclic models. The identification problem – which is much more of a problem in this kind of model – is illustrated using the cigarette-advertising example from Chapter 1.

The very meaning of 'two-way causation' is discussed, and final advice is given: Avoid cyclic models if at all possible!

1 Identifying and Estimating Acyclic Models

Of the few rules for identification in acyclic models with manifest variables only two are mentioned here.

The zero B-rule
A model with no variable that has both ingoing and outgoing arrows is always identified.

The recursive rule
If the regression weights can be arranged in a lower triangular matrix

$$X_1 = \delta_1$$
$$X_2 = \beta_{21}X_1 + \delta_2$$
$$X_3 = \beta_{31}X_1 + \beta_{32}X_2 + \delta_3 \qquad (1a)$$
$$X_4 = \beta_{41}X_1 + \beta_{42}X_2 + \beta_{43}X_3 + \delta_4$$
$$X_5 = \beta_{51}X_1 + \beta_{52}X_2 + \beta_{53}X_3 + \beta_{54}X_4 + \delta_5$$

and

$$Cov(\delta_i, \delta_j) = 0 \text{ for all } i \text{ and } j \tag{1b}$$

the model is said to be *recursive* and it is always identified. If some of the regression weights are zero, the model is over-identified.

The condition (1b) loosens any tie among the equations as far as estimation is concerned. Consequently, the equations can be estimated independently of each other, e.g. using OLS (Ordinary Least Squares), if the other conditions for that procedure are fulfilled.

It should be mentioned that all acyclic models are called recursive by AMOS, unless they include correlations between errors for endogenous variables that also have a direct causal connection.

Example 1
Is the buying of coffee a high- or a low-involvement action?

If in Aaker and Day's hierarchy-of-effects model (Aaker & Day, 1971), first met in Figure 1.7b, we let

$$X_1 = \text{exposure}$$
$$X_2 = \text{price}$$
$$X_3 = \text{awareness}$$
$$X_4 = \text{attitude}$$
$$X_5 = \text{market share}$$

then the model can be written as (1a), where

$$\beta_{21} = \beta_{32} = \beta_{42} = \beta_{51} = \beta_{53} = 0 \tag{2}$$

Figure 1   Example 1: acyclic causal models (from Figure 1.7b)

If the condition (1b) is met, the model is (over-)identified according to the recursive rule. It is left to the reader to verify whether the low-involvement model is identified. The models are shown in Figure 1.

Example 2
Examining the stability of alienation

Wheaton, Muthén, Alwin, and Summers (1977) conducted a panel study covering the years 1966–1971 in order to study the stability of alienation as measured on two summated scales called 'anomia' and 'powerlessness'. Like several others – for example, Jöreskog and Sörbom (1984), Bentler (1995) and Browne and Mels (2002) – I will use the Wheaton data to illustrate SEM analysis and to acquaint you with the extensive AMOS output.

The study included several background variables, but here I will concentrate on the two variables 'anomia' and 'powerlessness' and the two years 1967 and 1971.

Figure 2 from Bentler (1995) shows a so-called cross-lagged panel design with 932 respondents.

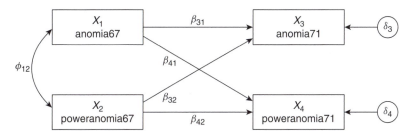

Figure 2   Example 2: the model (Reproduced with kind permission from Peter Bentler, Bentler 1995.)

With four variables there are $(4 \times 5)/2 = 10$ variances/covariances on which to base the estimation, and the number of parameters to be estimated is $4 + 4 + 1 = 9$ (number of coefficients + number of variances + number of covariances). The model is therefore possibly identified with one degree of freedom. The identification is confirmed by the zero-B-rule.

Table 1 contains the data and a program for estimation of the model.

We estimate the model by maximum likelihood (the default) and order the output to include standardized parameter values (Sem.Standardized) and the residual covariance matrix (Sem.ResidualMoments), mentioned in Section 1.7.

A few comments on the output in Table 2 are in order:

1. The global χ^2-test of the model has a P-value of 0.000. *The null hypothesis is that the model is correct.* This means that there is practically zero chance of getting a sample like ours, or one that is less consistent with the model, if the model is true. As mentioned in the previous chapter, in SEM the null

Table 1   Example 2: the program and data

	X_1	X_2	X_3	X_4
X_1	11.834			
X_2	6.947	9.364		
X_3	6.819	5.091	12.532	
X_4	4.783	5.028	7,495	9.986

```
Sub Main()
   Dim sem As New AmosEngine
   Try
      Sem.Title ("Example 5.2")
      'Data from Wheaton (1977)
      Sem.TextOutput
      Sem.Standardized
      Sem.ResidualMoments
      Sem.BeginGroup  ("C:\Users\Sony\Documents\Amos3  Chap  5\Wheaton.
xls","Sheet1")
         Sem.AStructure ("anomia71 = anomia67 + powerlessness67 + (1) d3")
         Sem.AStructure  ("powerlessness71 = anomia67 + powerlessness67 + (1) d4")
         Sem.FitModel
   Finally
      Sem.Dispose()
   End Try
End Sub
```

hypothesis is the hypothesis that we hope our data support, so we are interested in getting *large* values of P. On the other hand, very large P-values could be an indication of over-fitting, in which case the model should be simplified.

2. Then the parameter estimates follow in raw and standardized form. All parameters are statistically significant by traditional norms.

3. Next comes the residual covariance matrix in raw and standardized form. As mentioned earlier, the residual covariance matrix is the difference between the sample covariance matrix and the covariance matrix implied by the model. The smaller the elements in the residual covariance matrix, the more the model is supported by the data – and the smaller the χ^2-value.

   The standardized residual variances and covariances (the variances/covariances divided by their standard errors) are asymptotically distributed as standard normal.

4. Last in the output is a wide assortment of fit indices (not shown). I shall not comment on them here, but only point out that they are far from satisfying. I shall return to the fit measures in the next section.

Table 2   Example 2: output (to be continued in Table 3)

Result (Model 1)   (1)

```
Minimum was achieved
Chi-square = 341.863
Degrees of freedom = 1
Probability level = .000
```

Regression Weights: (Group number 1 - Model 1)   (2)

			Estimate	S.E.	C.R.	P	Label
anomia71	<--	anomia67	.455	.037	12.407	***	
anomia71	<--	powerlessness67	.206	.041	4.988	***	
powerlessness71	<--	anomia67	.158	.034	4.658	***	
powerlessness71	<--	powerlessness67	.420	.038	11.042	***	

Standardized Regression Weights: (Group number 1 - Model 1)

			Estimate
anomia71	<---	anomia67	.443
anomia71	<---	powerlessness67	.178
powerlessness71	<---	anomia67	.172
powerlessness71	<---	powerlessness67	.407

Covariances: (Group number 1 - Model 1)

			Estimate	S.E.	C.R.	P	Label
anomia67	<-->	powerlessness67	6.940	.413	16.806	***	

Correlations: (Group number 1 - Model 1)

			Estimate
anomia67	<-->	powerlessness67	.660

Variances: (Group number 1 - Model 1)

	Estimate	S.E.	C.R.	P	Label
anomia67	11.821	.548	21.575	***	
powerlessness67	9.354	.434	21.575	***	
d3	8.370	.388	21.575	***	
d4	7.113	.330	21.575	***	

Residual Covariances (Group number 1 - Model 1)   (3)

	powerlessness67	anomia67	powerlessness71	anomia71
powerlessness67	.000			
anomia67	.000	.000		
powerlessness71	.000	.000	.000	
anomia71	.000	.000	4.277	.000

Standardized Residual Covariances (Group number 1 - Model **1**)

	powerlessness67	anomia67	powerlessness71	anomia71
powerlessness67	.000			
anomia67	.000	.000		
powerlessness71	.000	.000	.000	
anomia71	.000	.000	11.255	.000

As is evident from Figure 2, our model states that the covariance between Anomia71 and Powerlessness71 can be explained as a result of Anomia67 and Powerlessness67.

This hypothesis cannot be maintained, as a χ^2-value of about 342 is significant by any reasonable criterion – even if the sample is 'large'.

The usual remedy in such a case, i.e. to introduce additional parameters, is not possible here. The only way to do so would be to allow δ_3 and δ_4 to correlate, and this would eat up our only degree of freedom, after which we would be left with a just-identified, i.e. a non-testable, model.

Nevertheless, let us take a look at the output.

All coefficients are statistically significant according to traditional criteria, and anomia seems to be slightly more stable than powerlessness. The two cross-effects are small and not very different in their standardized form. However, these conclusions must be taken with a grain of salt, as they are based on an incorrect model.

The residual matrix shows clearly where the problem is located. The model can reproduce the sample covariance matrix except the covariance between the two 71-variables.

As the residual covariance of Powerlessness71 and anomia71 is positive, the model underestimates the covariance between the two variables. As mentioned above, allowing the two variables to correlate more than caused by the exogenous variables would eat up our only degree of freedom.

As it is impossible to patch up the model, I will (in Chapter 7) construct a new one based on latent variables.

2 Fit Indices

As pointed out earlier, the χ^2-test has the weakness that if the sample is sufficiently small we will accept any model, and if it is sufficiently large any model will be rejected. To put it precisely, we test a hypothesis that we know a priori is false – and if the sample is large enough the test will show what we expect it to show.

In order to overcome this problem a large number of fit indices have been constructed to help evaluate the extent to which the model is supported by the data (see Table 3). Some of these indices take on values in the interval 0.00–1.00, just like a determination coefficient: the closer to 1.00, the better the fit. However, a coefficient of determination has the advantage of a certain interpretation, i.e. as the share of the variance of a dependent variable that can be 'explained' by one or more independent variables. Unfortunately most fit indices lack such an interpretation, so only experience will tell what is necessary for a specific fit index to show a good fit.

Table 3 Example 2: fit measures (continuation of output from Table 5.2)

Model Fit Summary

CMIN

Model	NPAR	CMIN	DF	P	CMIN/DF
Default model	9	341.863	1	.000	341.863
Saturated model	10	.000	0		
Independence model	4	1563.944	6	.000	260.657

RMR. GFI

Model	RMR	GFI	AGFI	PGFI
Default model	1.353	.867	-.332	.087
Saturated model	.000	1.000		
Independence model	4.738	.515	.192	.309

Baseline Comparisons

Model	NFI Delta1	RFI rho1	IFI Delta2	TLI rho2	CFI
Default model	.781	-.312	.782	-.313	.781
Saturated model	1.000		1.000		1.000
Independence model	.000	.000	.000	.000	.000

Parsimony-Adjusted Measures

Model	PRATIO	PNFI	PCFI
Default model	.167	.130	.130
Saturated model	.000	.000	.000
Independence model	1.000	.000	.000

NCP

Model	NCP	LO 90	HI 90
Default model	340.863	283.736	405.393
Saturated model	.000	.000	.000
Independence model	1557.944	1431.609	1691.640

FMIN

Model	FMIN	F0	LO 90	HI 90
Default model	.367	.366	.305	.435
Saturated model	.000	.000	.000	.000
Independence model	1.680	1.673	1.538	1.817

RMSEA

Model	RMSEA	LO 90	HI 90	PCLOSE
Default model	.605	.552	.660	.000
Independence model	.528	.506	.550	.000

(Continued)

(Continued)

AIC

Model	AIC	BCC	BIC	CAIC
Default model	359.863	359.960	403.399	412.399
Saturated model	20.000	20.108	68.373	78.373
Independence model	1571.944	1571.987	1591.294	1595.294

ECVI

Model	ECVI	LO 90	HI 90	MECVI
Default model	.387	.325	.456	.387
Saturated model	.021	.021	.021	.022
Independence model	1.688	1.553	1.832	1.688

HOELTER

Model	HOELTER .05	HOELTER .01
Default model	11	19
Independence model	8	11

Table 4   Fit measures in AMOS

Absolute Fit Measures	Relative Fit Measures	Parsimony Adjusted Measures	Fit Measures Based On The Non-Central Chi-Square Distribution	Information Theoretic Fit Measures	A Fit Measure Based On Sample Size
CMIN	NFI	PRATIO	NCP	AIC	Critical N
CMIN/DF	RFI	PNFI	FMIN	BCC	
RMR	IFI	PCFI	F0	BIC	
GFI	TLI	(PGFI)	RMSEA	CAIC	
AGFI	CFI			ECVI	
PGFI				MECVI	

Fit indices are different ways of expressing the 'distance' between the sample covariance matrix S and the estimated implied covariance matrix $\Sigma(\hat{\theta})$, i.e. they are functions of the residual matrix $S - \Sigma(\hat{\theta})$. But how do we measure this distance and express it in one number only?

As is evident from Table 3, this can be done in several ways. The many fit measures can be classified as in Table 4, where they are given in the same order as in the output.

Absolute fit measures judge the fit of a model per se without reference to other models that could be relevant in the situation. This means that there is no standard or basis relative to which the actual model could be judged, for, again, as Fisher says: 'Nothing is good or bad but by comparison'. In a way you could say that a model is judged relative to no model at all.

Relative fit measures introduce an explicit basis model, which usually is rather unrealistic, but which nevertheless serves the purpose of making it possible to judge the fit of different models on a common basis.

Parsimony adjusted measures introduce a 'punishment' for complicating the model by increasing the number of parameters in order to improve the fit.

Fit measures based on the non-central chi-square distribution have as their starting point the fact that no model is 'correct' – it can only be 'approximately correct'.

Information theoretic fit measures are not used for judging the fit of a single model, but are used in situations where you have to choose among several realistic but different models.

The *Critical N measure* – falling in a class of its own – pinpoints the connection between sample size and the significance of χ^2.

In Table 3 you will observe that most fit measures are shown for three different models:

1. The model at hand – called the *default model*.
2. The saturated model (with the maximum number of parameters).
3. The independence model (with zero correlation among the manifest variables).

For models estimated by other methods than maximum likelihood, AMOS will also state fit measures for the zero model, where all parameters take on the value 0.

Fit measures are stated for several models in order to make a basis for comparison – in line with the above quotation by Fisher.

Absolute fit measures

In the first row of Table 3 beneath 'Model Fit Summary' we first meet the number of parameters for the three models NPAR. Next to NPAR we find the minimum value of C, CMIN. As mentioned earlier, C is defined as $C = (n-1)F$, where F is the fitting function to be minimized, and CMIN is the minimum (the end result) of the minimization process. If ML or GLS estimation is used, CMIN is asymptotically distributed as χ^2, and we have already met the CMIN or χ^2-value of 341.863 in the output in Table 2. Next is the number of degrees of freedom DF, and, last in the row, CMIN divided by DF.

If the null hypothesis is true, $E(\chi^2) = DF$, so you could consider CMIN/DF to be a 'normalization' of χ^2. Usually a value of CMIN/DF near 1.00 is considered a sign of a good fit, and the value 341.863 for CMIN/DF confirms that our model fits extremely badly.

The fit is expressed in the residual covariance matrix. Analogous to the standard deviation, we could compute the *root mean-square residual*:

$$\text{RMR} = \sqrt{\frac{(sum)^2}{p(p+1)/2}} = \sqrt{\frac{2(sum)^2}{p(p+1)}} \tag{3}$$

Where '*sum*' represents the sum of all non-redundant elements in the residual covariance matrix.

Now, the size of this expression depends on the units of measurement for the various variables, so that it is more relevant to carry out an analogous calculation based on the residual correlation matrix. Unfortunately, this is not part of the output in AMOS, but is easily calculated by hand – which I leave to you as an exercise. Usually an RMR (based on correlations) of less than 0.05 is taken as a sign of a good fit.

Next to RMR we find GFI, the classical *goodness of fit index* introduced in LISREL many years ago. This index is calculated as

$$\text{GFI} = \frac{(\text{weighted sum of the variances in } \Sigma(\hat{\theta}))^2}{(\text{weighted sum of the variances in } \mathbf{S})^2} \tag{4}$$

where the weights depend on the estimation method. It has been proposed that GFI is analogous to R^2 in multiple regression (see Appendix A), and, just like R^2, GFI takes on values between 0 and 1.00.

If GFI is adjusted for the number of degrees of freedom compared with the number of parameters, this gives AGFI (*Adjusted Goodness of Fit Index*), which rewards models with fewer parameters.

In this case AGFI is negative, which should mean that not only is the model bad, but it is worse than no model at all! This of course is nonsense. Negative values of AGFI are rare, but the fact that they can occur is a weakness of this index.

A better way to take care of parsimony is to adjust GFI using the index of parsimony from James, Mulaik, and Brett (1982) (more on this below). This latter fit index is shown as PGFI.

Relative fit measures

As the saturated model has maximum fit and the independence model has the maximum number of constraints and consequently minimum fit, these two models indicate the limits between which 'your' model is placed.

You can therefore evaluate a model by looking at its 'location' between these two extremes.

You could, for example, calculate how far along the way from the independence model to the perfect fitting model 'your' model – the *default model* – has 'travelled':

$$\text{NFI} = \frac{\text{CMIN}_{indp} - \text{CMIN}_{deflt}}{\text{CMIN}_{indp}} = \frac{1563.944 - 341.863}{1563.944} = 0.781 \tag{5}$$

This is the so-called *normed fit index* (Bentler & Bonnett, 1980), which is bounded within the interval 0–1.00.

RFI (*Relative Fit Index*) and IFI (*Incremental Fit Index*) also include the degrees of freedom. RFI is derived from NFI by dividing CMIN_{indp} and CMIN_{deflt} in NFI by their degrees of freedom, and IFI by subtracting the degrees of freedom for the independence model in the denominator.

Just like GFI, NFI has been used as a standard for many years, but because it has shown a tendency to underestimate the fit in small samples, it has been modified into CFI (*Comparative Fit Index*; Bentler, 1990), which also takes the degrees of freedom into consideration:

$$\text{CFI} = \frac{(\text{CMIN}_{indp} - \text{DF}_{indp}) - (\text{CMIN}_{deflt} - \text{DF}_{deflt})}{(\text{CMIN}_{indp} - \text{DF}_{indp})}$$

$$= \frac{(1563.944 - 6) - (341.863 - 1)}{1563.944 - 6} = 0.781 \tag{6}$$

NFI- and CFI-values larger than 0.95 are usually taken as an indication of a good fit.

It is worth noting that if $\text{CMIN}_{deflt} < \text{DF}_{deflt}$ then $\text{CFI} > 1.000$, but CFI is reported as 1.000 in the output. Therefore $\text{CFI} = 1.000$ is not an indication of a perfect fit, but only indicates that $\text{CMIN}_{deflt} < \text{DF}_{deflt}$.

The *Tucker–Lewis* index (Tucker & Lewis, 1973)

$$TLI = \frac{(C_{indp} / DF_{indp}) - (C_{deflt} / DF_{deflt})}{(C_{indp} / DF_{indp}) - 1} \tag{7}$$

is another index, which (usually) takes on values in the 0–1.00 interval, values near 1.00 as usual being seen as a sign of good fit.

Parsimony-based fit measures

It is always possible to increase the fit by adding more parameters to a model. The saturated model has the maximum number of parameters and thus the maximum fit; the residual covariance matrix is a 0-matrix, i.e. it contains only zeros.

By uncritically adding parameters to the model you run the risk of profiting on peculiarities in the sample at hand, and thus ending up with a model that will not fit any comparable sample from the same population. This is one of the main reasons for preferring simple models with relatively few parameters: they are more generalizable.

The *parsimony ratio*, defined as

$$PRATIO = \frac{DF_{deflt}}{DF_{indp}} \tag{8}$$

is proposed by James et al. (1982) as a factor by which you can modify fit indices to take parsimony into consideration. In other words, you can introduce a penalty for complicating the model. In this way PNFI and PCFI result from NFI and CFI by multiplication with PRATIO. Analogously, PGFI is defined as

$$PGFI = GFI\left(\frac{DF_{deflt}}{DF_{sat}}\right) \tag{9}$$

GFI is an 'absolute' measure, so the basis model is not the independence model, but the saturated model, i.e. no model at all.

Usually parsimony-based fit indices are much lower than other normed fit measures. Values larger than 0.60 are generally considered satisfying.

Fit indices based on the non-central χ^2-distribution

As mentioned at the beginning of this section, the main reason for the introduction of the many fit measures is that the global χ^2-test is a test of a null hypothesis that we a priori know is false: that our model is 100% correct.

As any model is only 'approximately true', $C = (n-1)F$ is actually distributed according to *the non-central χ^2-distribution with non-centrality parameter*

$$\delta = \chi^2 - DF \tag{10a}$$

The ordinary χ^2-distribution (the central distribution) is thus a special variant of the non-central distribution with $\delta = 0$. The more 'wrong' our model, the larger the value of δ. Consequently, small values of δ are to be preferred. So δ is estimated as

$$NCP = max[CMIN - DF, 0] \tag{10b}$$

Therefore NCP = 0 does not indicate a perfect fit, but only that CMIN < DF (cf. the remarks in connection with (6)). This has similar consequences for the fit measures F0 and RMSEA mentioned below.

LO 90 and HI 90 are the lower and upper 90% confidence limits for NCP.

FMIN is the minimum value of the minimization function F, while F0 = NCP / n and is thus a 'normalization' of NCP. The lower the value of F0, the better. Next to F0 are the lower and upper 90% confidence limits. F0 will, however, never encourage parsimony, as it will never favor a simpler model with fewer parameters.

The *root mean square error of approximation* (Steiger & Lind, 1980) takes care of this problem by introducing the number of degrees of freedom:

$$\text{RMSEA} = \sqrt{\frac{\text{F0}}{\text{DF}}} \tag{11}$$

As usual in this group of fit measures, which could also be called 'population-based' fit indices, the lower and upper 90% confidence limits are also shown. Usually a RMSEA around 0.05 is considered a sign of a good fit and models with values larger than 0.10 should not be accepted. Last in this line are the *P*-values (PCLOSE) for testing the null hypothesis that RMSEA (in the population) is less than 0.05.

Information theoretic fit measures

This group of fit measures is based on the idea of expressing the extent to which the present model will cross-validate in future samples of the same size from the same population. Also it rewards parsimony. Another common feature is that small values are to be preferred, but that the measures have no upper limit and therefore these are primarily used as a basis for choosing among several substantively meaningful models.

I will not present formulae for these measures, since further information can be found in the references mentioned in Table 5.

A fit measure based on sample size

The last fit index is *Critical N* (Hoelter, 1983), indicating the largest sample size for which the actual model will be accepted as 'true' based on the traditional χ^2-test and the actual data.

In this case our model will be accepted as 'true' with a sample size of 11, if we set $\alpha = 0.05$, and it would be rejected if the sample size were 12. For $\alpha = 0.01$ the corresponding sample sizes are 19 and 20.

What indices shall I report?

With so many fit indices to choose from, this question is not irrelevant.

As indices that are placed in the same group in Table 4 measure about the same aspect of model fit, the question boils down to choosing the best fit index from each group. My suggestion is that you should report χ^2 with degrees of freedom and *P*-value, RMSEA with confidence interval and PCLOSE. If you compare *non-nested models* (see Example 6.1 for a definition of *nested* models) these indices can be supplemented with one of the information theoretic fit measures – the most used is perhaps AIC. Browne and Cudeck (1989, 1993) recommend reporting ECVI or, in the case of ML estimation, MECVI.

Table 5 Information theoretic fit measures

AIC	Akaike Information Criterion	(Akaike, 1973, 1987)	Has only a penalty for degrees of freedom, but not for sample size
BCC	Browne–Cudeck Criterion	(Browne & Cudeck, 1989)	As AIC, but carries a slightly harder penalty for introducing additional parameters
BIC	Bayes Information Criterion	(Raftery, 1993, 1995; Schwarz, 1978)	Assigns a greater penalty for introducing additional parameters than any of the other indices shown in this table
CAIC	Consistent AIC	(Bozdogan, 1987)	Reformulation of AIC, carrying a greater penalty for model complexity than AIC and BCC
ECVI	Expected Cross-Validation Index	(Browne & Cudeck, 1989)	Proportional to AIC
MECVI	Maximum likelihood ECVI	(Browne & Cudeck, 1989, 1993)	Proportional to BCC

If you want to report a relative fit measure I would suggest the use of CFI, but these measures have the common weakness that the baseline model is the very unrealistic independence model.

A common problem with most indices is that their sampling distribution is unknown. This means that decisions on whether the size of a fit index is 'satisfying' is based on rules of thumb obtained through experience and by computer simulations.

Also, always remember that fit measures are measures of the *average* fit of the model to the data. Even if this 'general' fit seems to be OK, the model could still have a bad fit in local places. Therefore be careful in checking the standard errors of the various parameters, and the coefficients of determination.

In this connection I should like to point out that in covariance-based SEM we are *not* predicting the dependent variables – we are predicting the covariance matrix. Therefore covariance-based SEM does not minimize the error variances. If you are more interested in making predictions than in explaining covariances, you should use another SEM methodology called *partial least squares* invented by Wold (1975). For an introduction, see Fornell and Cha (1994). A deeper treatment with many examples can be found in Vinzi, Chin, Henseler, and Wang (2010).

3   The Identification Problem in Cyclic Models

In cyclic models identification problems arise more often than in acyclic models, and it is generally more difficult to judge whether a model is identified or not by inspection or the use of simple rules.

This is easily demonstrated using the Bass example we met in Figure 1.7c, which is repeated in Figure 3 with the missing disturbance terms added. From the figure we see that sales of filter cigarettes (Y_1) depend on advertising for filter cigarettes (Y_3) – which

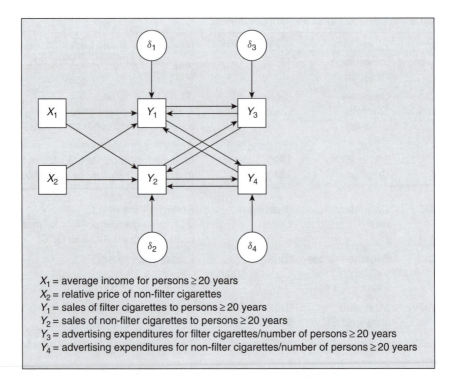

X_1 = average income for persons ≥ 20 years
X_2 = relative price of non-filter cigarettes
Y_1 = sales of filter cigarettes to persons ≥ 20 years
Y_2 = sales of non-filter cigarettes to persons ≥ 20 years
Y_3 = advertising expenditures for filter cigarettes/number of persons ≥ 20 years
Y_4 = advertising expenditures for non-filter cigarettes/number of persons ≥ 20 years

Figure 3   Cyclic causal model

is of course the very purpose of advertising – but at the same time (Y_3) could also depend on (Y_1) through advertising budgeting routines. How is it possible to map such relationships? Can we analytically separate the two functions and identify them?

Example 3
Mapping the effectiveness of advertising

Imagine you have collected data on sales and advertising over a longer period of time.

The time series data can be graphed as shown in Figure 4. The observations form a nearly straight line thus indicate a strong relationship between the two variables (for simplicity only four points are shown). The question, however, is: 'Is it the sales function or the budget function that is depicted in the figure?'

Now, any observation in Figure 4 must lie on both the sales curve and the advertising curve, which means that, except for 'noise', the observations must be placed at the intersections of the two curves.

Figure 5 shows four possible situations with the 'true' functions marked. In reality, of course, we never know the exact position of the 'true' curves, because then there would be no need to estimate them.

In Figure 5a both functions have been stable during the period covered by our data. Consequently, our observations are all clustered around the intersection of the curves, and they do not give us any information on the location of the two curves.

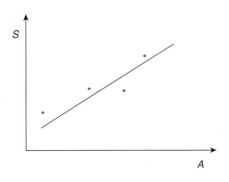

Figure 4   Example 3: scattergram of sales revenue S and advertising budget A

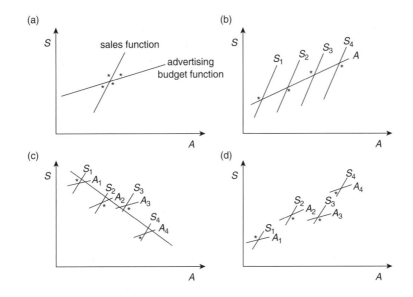

Figure 5   Example 3: the identification problem

In panel (b) of the figure the budget function has been stable in the period, while the sales function has moved around, influenced by variables other than advertising. As a result of this the budget function can be identified. If instead the budget function had moved while the sales function had been stable, the sales function would have been identified.

In panel (c) both curves have moved, and consequently the points depict only the intersections of the two functions and say nothing about their location. However, the points are placed from northwest to southeast, so the analyst could hardly believe that the sales function has been located – if that was the purpose.

In panel (d), however, such a misinterpretation is more likely. But as you will know by now, if there is a two-way causation, the points will only mirror the intersections of the curves and say nothing about their slopes.

To identify the functions in the model we must add to our model variables that can change the position of the functions, such as those shown in Figure 5b–d.

A necessary condition for identification: the order condition
Writing the sales function and the advertising budget function as

$$S = \beta_{S0} + \beta_{S1}A + \delta_S \tag{12a}$$

$$A = \beta_{A0} + \beta_{A1}S + \delta_A \tag{12b}$$

it is easy to see that the problem is that we have two linear functions with exactly the same variables. Such functions are impossible to separate (identify) empirically.

To identify a function we must add one or more variables to our model, the value of which is not determined within the model – that is, we must add exogenous variables.

If we add income, I, to (12a), we get

$$S = \beta_{S0} + \beta_{S1}A + \beta_{S2}I + \delta_S \tag{13a}$$

$$A = \beta_{A0} + \beta_{A1}S + \delta_A \tag{13b}$$

As variations in I will cause the function (12a) to move, it is natural to assume that including I in (13a) will lead to identification of (13b). This is actually the case (cf. Figure 5b).

The model (13) comprises three variables: two endogenous variables (S and A) and one exogenous variable (I). If the number of exogenous variables not included in an equation is one less than the number of endogenous variables in that equation, the equation is *just-identified*. If there are fewer, the equation is *under-identified* (*unidentified*), and if there are more, it is *over-identified*. This is the so-called *order condition*, which is necessary but not sufficient.

A sufficient condition for (13b) to be identified is that the coefficient β_{S2} is different from zero. This is the so-called rank condition, which for the two-equation model can be stated as follows: a necessary and sufficient condition for identification of an equation in a two-equation model is that the other equation contains at least one exogenous variable with a non-zero coefficient that is excluded from the equation in question. So identification depends not only on the structure of the model, but (unfortunately) also on parameter values.

Now, the sales function is probably of greater interest than the budget function, and to identify the former it is necessary to include in (13b) one or more exogenous variables that do not affect sales. This, however, is not as easy as it sounds, because most variables you could take into consideration when deciding how much to spend on advertising would also influence sales: namely, price of the product, degree of distribution, etc. A possible solution is to include the price of advertising.

The general order condition

If we have more than two equations in our model, the order condition is a little more complicated and can be stated as follows: a *necessary* condition for an equation to be identified is that the number of excluded *exogenous* variables is at least as large as the number of right-hand-side *endogenous* variables.

Let us use this rule on the model in Figure 3:

	Left-hand variable	Right-hand endogenous variables	Excluded exogenous variables	
Equation no. 1	Y_1	Y_3 Y_4	None	Under-identified
Equation no. 2	Y_2	Y_3 Y_4	None	Under-identified
Equation no. 3	Y_3	Y_1 Y_2	X_1 X_2	Just-identified
Equation no. 4	Y_4	Y_1 Y_2	X_1 X_2	Just-identified

We can see that only the budget functions are identified.

If these are the functions you are interested in, and equations 1 and 2 are only there to identify them, then of course that is OK and you can estimate functions 3 and 4 – but not using AMOS. Unfortunately, AMOS will not estimate part of a model. If just one parameter in a model is unidentified AMOS will give a warning and stop the calculation. Bass (partly) solved the identification problems by using two-stage least squares estimation – a limited information method not currently available in AMOS.

A warning

Recall the formulation of the error message in the output in Table 4.2:

```
The model is probably unidentified.
```

This formulation indicates that AMOS's identification check is not totally safe.

When I estimated the Bass model in Figure 3 using Bass's data I got no error message and AMOS estimated the total model even though it was only partially identified.

I must admit that this result was obtained using an earlier version of AMOS, and repeating the calculations using AMOS 19 gave the appropriate error message. However, as the formulation of the error message is still the same, it is only fair to warn the reader that he or she could run into the same problem.

If at all possible, you should examine the identification status of your model before you collect data, so that you can add the number of exogenous variables required to obtain identification.

It is possible to circumvent the warning and let AMOS try to fit a model that appears to be under-identified. However, this is usually not recommended – and for that reason I will not state the command!

A sufficient condition: the rank condition

As mentioned, the order condition is only necessary but not sufficient. The reason is that the variables introduced in order to obtain identification must be independent of each other. If we introduce a variable which covaries with another already in the model, the new one will to a larger or smaller degree repeat information that we already have.

An exact formulation of the (general) rank condition is beyond the scope of this book (but see e.g. Brown (1991) for a simple explanation) because it is based on matrix algebra, but fortunately it is rare in practice to find a model that meets the order condition but does not also meet the rank condition.

4   What Does Two-way Causation Really Mean?

In a model based on experimental data there is no doubt about the direction of the arrows: they depart from the manipulated variables, and it is absurd to think about letting them point in the opposite direction. In models based on non-experimental data you may sometimes have your doubts as to the causal direction. Unfortunately, this subject is rather poorly treated in the literature – but take a look at Davis (1985). However, some guidance can be found in the following two 'rules':

1. Cause is prior to effect.
2. Causes are often variables whose values are more stable than effects.

Nevertheless, you may often feel tempted to draw the arrows in both directions, and then end up with a cyclic model with all its complications.

What does two-way causation really mean? Is it not absurd to think of letting A have an effect on B, and at the same time letting B have an effect on A? At the very least you should expect some delay, so that A 'now' affects B 'a little later' and then B affects A again 'a bit later', because, as Hume formulated it, cause precedes effect.

If we accept this premise, the model in Figure 6b should be substituted for the model in 6a. All cyclic causal models are absurd and all realistic models are – or should be – acyclic!

Formally this is correct, but if the time period in Figure 6b is measured in months and we only have quarterly data, then both cause and effect will take place within one (data) time period. In other words, the length of the data time period compared with the reaction time will determine whether we end up with a cyclic or an acyclic model.

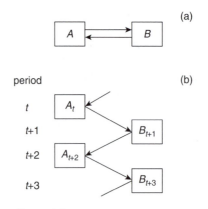

Figure 6   Cyclic and acyclic models

Example 3 (continued)
Mapping the effectiveness of advertising

If advertising affects sales in the same year while the budget is based on sales in the previous year, and we have yearly data, then (12) can be written as

$$S_t = \beta_{S0} + \beta_{S1} A_t + \delta_S \tag{14a}$$

$$A_t = \beta_{A0} + \beta_{A1} S_{t-1} + \delta_A \tag{14b}$$

If you assume the error terms to be uncorrelated across the two equations, you will have a recursive system: S_{t-1} is pre-determined in (14b), and A_t is pre-determined in (14a), where S_t is the only post-determined variable.

If you have data only for two-year periods, you have to fall back on a cyclic model.

A final piece of advice

In the large majority of cases you will build your model on cross-sectional data, and then of course a cyclic model will be the only possible choice if you have reciprocal causation.

Now, it is clear from Figure 6b that two-way causation is a *dynamic* process, and we can think of each of the two effects in Figure 6a as the sum of an infinite series of loops. Only in cases where the two sums are defined, i.e. where the corresponding series converge, is it possible to estimate the two effects.

However, such estimates only make sense if the process in reality has gone through the whole process and brought it to an end. This is a rather hard assumption that is difficult (if not impossible) to judge.

As you can see, cyclic models are much more complicated than non-cyclic models. This is true both as far as identification and estimation are concerned and when it comes to the substantive interpretation and recommendations based on the model.

Therefore, a final piece of advice would be: if at all possible, avoid cyclic models.

I will, however, present a single example of a cyclic model with only manifest variables in Chapter 8.

In this chapter you met the following concepts:

- the zero B-rule and the recursive rule for identification in acyclic models
- the order condition and the rank condition for identification in cyclic models

- a wide range of fit indices:
  - o absolute fit measures
  - o relative fit measures
  - o parsimony-based fit measures
  - o fit measures based on the non-central χ^2-distribution
  - o information theoretic fit measures

You also learned the following AMOS statement:
Sem.ResidualMoments

Questions

1. Explain the identification rules in your own words.

2. What characterizes each of the six groups of fit indices?

3. What are the numerical requirements usually used as rules of thumb in connection with the various indices?

4. Using examples from your own field of study or research, discuss the various problems raised by using cyclic models.

References

Aaker, D. A., & Day, D. A. (1971). A recursive model of communication processes. In D. A. Aaker (Ed.), *Multivariate analysis in marketing*. Belmont, CA: Wadsworth.

Akaike, H. (1973). Information theory and an extension of the maximum likelihood principle. Proceedings of the 2nd International Symposium on Information Theory, Budapest.

Akaike, H. (1987). Factor analysis and AIC. *Psychometrika, 52*, 317–332.

Bentler, P. M. (1990). Comparative fit indexes in structural models. *Psychological Bulletin, 107*, 238–246.

Bentler, P. M. (1995). *EQS structural equations program manual*. Encino, CA: Multivariate Software Inc.

Bentler, P. M., & Bonnett, D. G. (1980). Significance tests and goodness of fit in the analysis of covariance structures. *Psychological Bulletin, 88*, 588–606.

Bozdogan, H. (1987). Model selection and Akaike's information criterion (AIC): The general theory and its analytical extensions. *Psychometrika, 52*, 345–370.

Brown, W. S. (1991). *Introducing econometrics*. St Paul, MN: West Publishing.

Browne, M. W., & Cudeck, R. (1989). Single sample cross-validation indices for covariance structures. *Multivariate Behavioral Research, 24*, 445–455.

Browne, M. W., & Cudeck, R. (1993). Alternative ways of assessing model fit. In K. A. Bollen & J. S. Long (Eds.), *Testing structural equation models* (pp. 136–159). Newbury Park, CA: Sage.

Browne, M. W., & Mels, M. (2002). Path analysis (RAMONA) *SYSTAT 10.2 – Statistics II*. Richmond, CA: SYSTAT Software Inc.

Davis, J. A. (1985). *The logic of causal order*. Beverly Hills, CA: Sage.

Fornell, C., & Cha, J. (1994). Partial least squares. In P. Bagozzi (Ed.), *Advanced methods of marketing research*. Oxford: Blackwell.

Hoelter, J. W. (1983). The analysis of covariance structures: Goodness-of-fit indices. *Sociological Methods and Research, 11*, 325–344.

James, L. R., Mulaik, S. A., & Brett, J. M. (1982). *Causal analysis: Assumptions, models and data*. Beverly Hills, CA: Sage.

Jöreskog, K. G., & Sörbom, D. (1984). *LISREL 7: A guide to programs and applications* (3rd ed.). Chicago: SPSS Inc.

Raftery, A. (1993). Bayesian model selection in structural equation models. In K. Bollen & J. S. Long (Eds.), *Testing structural equation models* (pp. 163–180). Newbury Park, CA: Sage.

Raftery, A. (1995). Bayesian model selection in social research. In P. Marsden (Ed.), *Sociological methodology* (pp. 111–163). San Francisco: Jossey-Bass.

Schwarz, G. (1978). Estimating the dimension of a model. *Annals of Statistics, 6*, 461–464.

Steiger, J. H., & Lind, J. C. (1980). Statistically based tests for the number of common factors. Paper presented at the Annual Meeting of the Psychometric Society, Iowa City, IA.

Tucker, L. R., & Lewis, C. (1973). A reliability coefficient for maximun likelihood factor analysis. *Psychometrika, 38*, 1–10.

Vinzi, V. E., Chin, W. W., Henseler, J., & Wang, H. (2010). *Handbook of partial least squares: Concepts, methods and applications in marketing and related fields*. New York: Springer.

Wheaton, B., Muthén, B., Alwin, D. F., & Summers, G. F. (1977). Assessing reliability and stability in panel models. In D. R. Heise (Ed.), *Sociological methodology* (pp. 84–136). San Francisco: Jossey-Bass.

Wold, H. (1975). Path models with latent variables: The NIPALS approach. In H. M. Blalock et al. (Eds.), *Quantitative sociology: International perspectives on mathematical and statistical modeling*. New York: Academic Press.

6

The Measurement Model in SEM: Confirmatory Factor Analysis

We start by examining the differences between the three models, which are usually put under the common designation of factor analysis: namely, principal components analysis, exploratory factor analysis and confirmatory factor analysis – the latter being in fact the measurement model of SEM.

Next, you will learn two rules for identification in confirmatory factor models and you will explore estimation of confirmatory factor models through a classic example. You will also learn how AMOS can help you to obtain *parsimony*, i.e. to find as simple and uncomplicated (but still well-fitting) model as possible and how you can estimate several models in the same run.

Then you will learn how confirmatory factor analysis can be used to select items for inclusion in a measurement model or for use in a summated scale. You will also learn how to use SEM to measure reliability and validity in ways that are more in accordance with the theoretical definition of these concepts than those presented in Chapter 2.

The chapter ends with a short discussion of reflective and formative indicators, and points to a problem in item selection that has often led researchers astray.

1 The Three Factor Models

In component analysis the components are linear functions of the original variables, whereas in factor analysis – whether exploratory or confirmatory – the roles are reversed: the variables are considered functions of latent variables called factors.

However, there are a number of important differences between exploratory factor analysis and confirmatory factor analysis.

In exploratory factor analysis:

1. Every manifest variable is connected with every latent variable (as in component analysis).
2. Error terms are uncorrelated.
3. All parameters are estimated from the data.

In confirmatory factor analysis some or all of the above rules are violated:

1. Manifest variables are only connected with some pre-specified latent variables, the ideal being that every manifest variable is an indicator for one and only one factor.

2. Some error terms may be allowed to correlate.
3. Some of the parameters may be constrained to certain values or to have the same values as other parameters.

The differences among the three factor models are depicted in Figure 1 (it deserves mentioning that the component model and the exploratory factor model are shown prior to a possible rotation that could bring in correlations among the components or factors).

Comparing Figure 1 with Figure 1.5, it is obvious that the measurement model in SEM is a confirmatory factor model, and that it is this model that was the basis for the arguments against the classical methods of measuring reliability and validity in Chapter 2.

Remember that an indicator X_i can be:

- a single item in a many-item scale;
- a simple sum of several items, i.e. a summated scale; or
- a weighted sum of several items, e.g. a principal component.

Component Analysis

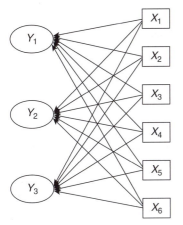

Exploratory Factor Analysis   **Confirmatory Factor Analysis**

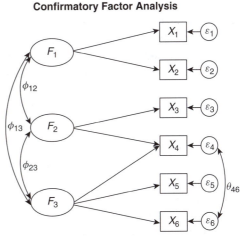

Figure 1   The three factor models

2   Identification and Estimation of Confirmatory Factor Models

In order to obtain identification every factor must be assigned a scale, either by fixing its variance or by fixing one of its regression weights; the same goes for the error terms. Further, the *t*-rule must be fulfilled, but as you have learned, this rule is only necessary, not sufficient.

Identification in confirmatory factor models

Two rules – both of which are sufficient but not necessary – are worth mentioning (cf. Figure 4.1):

1. *The three-indicator rule*: A confirmatory factor model is identified if:
   (a) Every factor has at least three indicators.
   (b) No manifest variable is an indicator for more than one factor.
   (c) The error terms are not correlated.

2. *The two-indicator rule*: A confirmatory factor model with at least two factors is identified if:
   (a) Every factor has at least two indicators.
   (b) No manifest variable is an indicator for more than one factor.
   (c) The error terms are not correlated.
   (d) The covariance matrix for the latent variables does not contain zeros.

The main advantage of confirmatory models is that prior knowledge can be taken into account when formulating the model. Further, confirmatory models open up for various methods of testing the models.

Example 1
Democracy in developing countries

Bollen has published several studies on the determinants of democratic development (Bollen, 1979, 1980). In this example I use data from Bollen (1989). The data shown in Figure 2 contain eight variables. The first four are indications of degree of democracy in 75 developing countries in 1960, the four variables being:

$$X_1 = \text{freedom of the press}$$
$$X_2 = \text{freedom of group opposition}$$
$$X_3 = \text{fairness of election}$$
$$X_4 = \text{elective nature of the legislative body}$$

The next four variables are the same variables measured in the same way in 1965.

As you can see, this is not a covariance matrix, but a correlation matrix supplemented with standard deviations. This is the kind of data summary you most often find in scientific journals, and it is just as good as a covariance matrix when used as input to SEM. Like other such programs, AMOS will use the data to construct a covariance

Figure 2   Example 1: the correlation/stddev matrix

matrix, which will then be used as input in the calculations. In Sheet 2 you will find the corresponding covariance matrix.

A component analysis of the covariance matrix (in Sheet 2) gives the first three eigenvalues as

$$57.17$$
$$8.47$$
$$5.26$$

and presents a strong case for a one-component solution, although we know that in fact there are two sets of measurements, one for 1960 and one for 1965.

If we insist on a two-component solution, the component loadings (covariances) are (after a varimax rotation)

	F_1	F_2
X_1	1.28	1.86
X_2	3.53	0.96
X_3	0.53	2.94
X_4	2.23	1.94
X_5	1.14	1.78
X_6	2.79	1.09
X_7	1.49	2.47
X_8	2.12	1.80

where we see that the two components in no way represent the two time periods.

Of course you can try an oblique rotation (which will give a correlation of 0.63 between the two components) or use exploratory factor analysis instead of component analysis, but none of these techniques will separate the two time periods.

This shows the danger of letting the automatic use of exploratory methods lead you astray without theoretical considerations.

Now, let us see how such considerations can guide us:

1. We must maintain two factors, one expressing the degree of democracy in 1960 and the other the degree of democracy in 1965.
2. It is reasonable to assume that error terms in the same (manifest) measurement in the two years will correlate.
3. In the same way we will assume that the error terms for X_2 and X_4 (and X_6 and X_8) correlate, as these measurements are based on the same written source.

A model along these lines is shown in Figure 3.

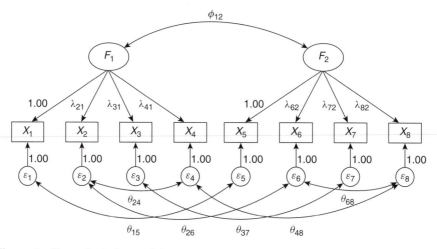

Figure 3   Example 1: the model

In order to estimate the model, two conditions must be satisfied:

1. We must create scales for the latent variables.
2. The model must be identified.

As mentioned earlier, the first condition can be met in two ways. The simpler way is to fix one of the λ for each factor to 1.00. This will transfer the scale of the indicator in question to its latent variable. Another possibility is to standardize the factors by fixing their variances to 1.00. I have chosen the first possibility, hence the ones on the arrows connecting F_1 with X_1 and F_2 with X_5 in Figure 3.

Regarding point 2 above, we have 23 parameters

6 coefficients
7 covariances
10 variances

to estimate. As input we have 8 variances and 28 covariances. We thus have 13 'pieces of information' or degrees of freedom left over for testing. The *t*-rule is satisfied.

However, the three-indicator rule cannot be used because of the correlated error terms. So the model is *possibly* identified.

You should be able to use AMOS Graphics to construct the graph in Figure 3 on your own.

As the model is wider than it is tall, it is perhaps a good idea to change the orientation of the paper from 'portrait' (the default) to 'landscape', just as you did in Section 1.5.

When you open 'Analysis properties' (by clicking ▦ or by choosing 'View/Analysis Properties'), mark 'Generalized least squares' (just for a change!) and when you have clicked the output tab, check the boxes as shown in Figure 4.

As in Example 4.2, click ▦ or choose 'Analyze/Calculate Estimates', after which clicking ▦ (or 'View/Text output') will produce the output given in Table 1.

Figure 4 Example 1: specifying output

Table 1 Example 1: output, first run

```
Result (Default model)
```

```
Minimum was achieved
Chi-square = 12.638
Degrees of freedom = 13
Probability level = .476
```

Scalar Estimates (Group number 1 - Default model)

Generalized Least Squares Estimates

(Continued)

(Continued)

Regression Weights: (Group number 1 - Default model)

			Estimate	S.E.	C.R.	P	Label
elect60	<---	Democracy60	1.250	.147	8.510	***	
fair60	<---	Democracy60	1.082	.142	7.643	***	
opp60	<---	Democracy60	1.251	.182	6.860	***	
press60	<---	Democracy60	1.000				
elect65	<---	Democracy65	1.304	.176	7.400	***	
fair65	<---	Democracy65	1.343	.170	7.911	***	
opp65	<---	Democracy65	1.235	.188	6.579	***	
press65	<---	Democracy65	1.000				

Standardized Regression Weights: (Group number 1 - Default model)

			Estimate
elect60	<---	Democracy60	.848
fair60	<---	Democracy60	.771
opp60	<---	Democracy60	.730
press60	<---	Democracy60	.871
elect65	<---	Democracy65	.838
fair65	<---	Democracy65	.845
opp65	<---	Democracy65	.789
press65	<---	Democracy65	.791

Covariances: (Group number 1 - Default model)

			Estimate	S.E.	C.R.	P	Label
Democracy60	<-->	Democracy65	4.422	.969	4.566	***	
e1	<-->	e5	.599	.356	1.684	.092	
e2	<-->	e6	1.548	.707	2.190	.028	
e3	<-->	e7	.705	.588	1.197	.231	
e4	<-->	e8	.495	.450	1.100	.271	
e4	<-->	e2	1.235	.708	1.745	.081	
e8	<-->	e6	.956	.560	1.708	.088	

Correlations: (Group number 1 - Default model)

			Estimate
Democracy60	<-->	Democracy65	.968
e1	<-->	e5	.300
e2	<-->	e6	.301
e3	<-->	e7	.203
e4	<-->	e8	.164
e4	<-->	e2	.270
e8	<-->	e6	.281

Variances: (Group number 1 - Default model)

	Estimate	S.E.	C.R.	P	Label
Democracy60	5.001	1.117	4.477	***	
Democracy65	4.176	1.067	3.913	***	
e4	3.050	.731	4.171	***	
e3	3.992	.896	4.456	***	
e2	6.849	1.382	4.956	***	
e1	1.594	.418	3.810	***	
e8	3.003	.714	4.206	***	
e7	3.005	.701	4.287	***	
e6	3.849	.871	4.421	***	
e5	2.502	.515	4.863	***	

1. We see that a χ^2-test of the model has a P-value of 0.476. This means that there is a probability of 0.476 of getting this result or one that is more against our model, if the model is correct. A P-value near 50% does not seem unsatisfying. We are, however, not interested in very large P-values, as this could be a sign of over-fitting, and therefore suggest that the model could be simplified.
2. Next are the parameter estimates, their standard errors and C.R. values. The only parameters that are not significant by traditional standards are e3 <--> e7 and e4 <--> e8 (one-sided tests, $\alpha = 0.05$). Remember that the P-values are for two-sided tests, but here one-sided tests seem more appropriate.
3. The χ^2-test indicated a good fit, and the standardized residual covariance matrix (not shown) confirms this: the three numerically largest values are -0.92, -0.61 and 0.51. The same goes for the various fit measures: they all show extremely good fit.

As the fit is so good, it should perhaps be possible to simplify the model. Generally, we want a parsimonious model with as few free parameters as possible. Not only will a simple model be easier to interpret, but also it will be easier to generalize.

So there is not much to gain by introducing more parameters. On the contrary, it is perhaps possible to simplify the model by placing restrictions on parameter values. Such restrictions could, for example, be that some parameters are fixed to have the same values.

You could therefore argue that the connection between a latent variable and its indicator is the same in the two years, i.e. that the measuring instrument itself does not change between the two measurements. If so, you could stipulate the conditions

$$\lambda_{21} = \lambda_{62}$$
$$\lambda_{31} = \lambda_{72} \tag{1}$$
$$\lambda_{41} = \lambda_{82}$$

To help judge whether the data are in accordance with such restrictions, you can ask for 'Critical ratios for differences between parameters' by selecting the appropriate option from the menu in Figure 4. These critical ratios are the differences between parameter estimates divided by the standard errors of the differences. Subject to the usual conditions, these are standard normally distributed. If you do so your output will include the table shown in Table 2.

As you may have guessed, AMOS will then label the free parameters (in Table 1) par_1, par_2, etc.

If you put in the labels in Table 2, you will see that the restrictions (1) are not inconsistent with the data. Consequently let us revise the model to include the restrictions.

Table 2   Example 6.1, first run: critical ratios for differences between parameters

Critical Ratios for Differences between Parameters (Default model)

	par_1	par_2	par_3	par_4	par_5	par_6	par_7	par_8
par_1	.000							
par_2	-1.014	.000						
par_3	.009	.799	.000					
par_4	.271	1.008	.229	.000				
par_5	.452	1.359	.402	.251	.000			
par_6	-.067	.629	-.075	-.488	-.602	.000		
par_7	3.091	3.298	3.074	2.948	2.919	3.029	.000	
par_8	-1.783	-1.336	-1.714	-1.906	-2.050	-1.693	-3.522	.000
par_9	.414	.644	.399	.337	.282	.423	-2.405	1.186
par_10	-.895	-.596	-.879	-.969	-.997	-.847	-3.370	.141
par_11	-1.544	-1.252	-1.567	-1.611	-1.777	-1.517	-3.696	-.180
par_12	-.020	.212	-.022	-.094	-.148	.000	-2.717	.779
par_13	-.506	-.218	-.501	-.568	-.660	-.452	-3.163	.515
par_14	3.137	3.340	3.133	3.186	3.148	3.274	1.040	3.638
par_15	2.670	2.830	2.650	2.435	2.413	2.496	-.527	3.052
par_16	2.325	2.654	2.348	2.296	2.274	2.401	-1.157	2.925
par_17	3.005	3.098	2.977	2.932	2.863	2.997	-.334	3.332
par_18	4.012	4.149	3.939	3.984	3.948	4.011	1.457	4.327
par_19	.831	1.255	.802	.661	.580	.809	-2.561	2.598
par_20	2.383	2.646	2.382	2.215	2.274	2.354	-1.199	2.947
par_21	2.449	2.642	2.411	2.355	2.197	2.427	-1.216	2.904
par_22	2.945	3.132	2.896	2.836	2.818	2.846	-.448	3.350
par_23	2.384	2.717	2.332	2.327	2.281	2.434	-1.671	4.237

	par_9	par_10	par_11	par_12	par_13	par_14	par_15	par_16
par_9	.000							
par_10	-.947	.000						
par_11	-1.128	-.267	.000					
par_12	-.330	.563	.866	.000				
par_13	-.655	.315	.675	-.290	.000			
par_14	2.631	3.489	3.763	2.858	3.256	.000		
par_15	2.057	2.916	3.198	2.302	2.697	-.833	.000	
par_16	1.396	2.380	3.633	2.579	2.217	-1.471	-.875	.000
par_17	2.164	4.027	3.412	2.381	2.899	-.727	-.134	.784
par_18	4.430	4.103	4.207	4.824	3.853	1.044	1.534	2.559
par_19	.054	1.132	1.784	.439	.886	-2.689	-2.196	-1.738
par_20	1.369	2.420	3.818	1.696	3.435	-1.518	-.922	-.048
par_21	1.487	3.358	2.850	1.783	2.233	-1.536	-.936	-.044
par_22	2.732	3.087	3.253	2.256	3.938	-.819	-.239	.672
par_23	1.088	2.163	2.895	1.448	2.020	-1.987	-1.330	-.606

	par_17	par_18	par_19	par_20	par_21	par_22	par_23
par_17	.000						
par_18	1.735	.000					
par_19	-2.230	-3.618	.000				
par_20	-.858	-2.401	1.684	.000			
par_21	-.926	-2.491	1.677	.002	.000		
par_22	-.116	-1.914	2.254	.808	.762	.000	
par_23	-1.394	-2.948	1.519	-.565	-.549	-1.326	.000

When you open your model (shown in Figure 5a) and double-click the arrow between 'Democracy60' and 'press60', the window in panel (b) appears.

As you can see in Figure 5a, the first regression weight for each factor is (by default) set at 1.00 in (b). As you might have guessed, you are free to delete the '1' and fix another regression path to have the value '1'. In fact, you can fix any parameter in the model to have any value you may want by double-clicking it and putting in the desired value.

With the menu still open, click at the arrows between 'Democracy60' and the other three indicators and set the regression weight to 'a', 'b' and 'c'. Repeat the procedure with 'Democracy65'. After that your model should look as in panel (c). This forces the estimates of model parameters with the same non-numeric 'value' to be equal, as can be seen from the output in Table 3.

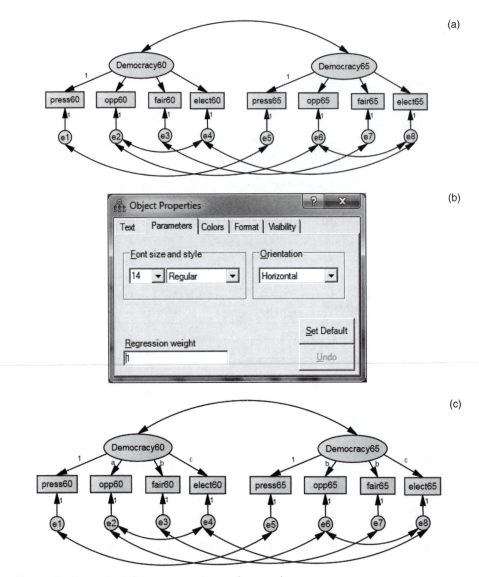

Figure 5   Example 1: fixing parameters to be equal

Table 3   Example 1: partial output, second run

Result (Default model)

Minimum was achieved
Chi-square = 14.633
Degrees of freedom = 16
Probability level = .552

Regression Weights: (Group number 1 - Default model)

			Estimate	S.E.	C.R.	P	Label
elect60	<---	Democracy60	1.214	.126	9.616	***	c
fair60	<---	Democracy60	1.216	.130	9.346	***	b
opp60	<---	Democracy60	1.122	.143	7.860	***	a
press60	<---	Democracy60	1.000				
elect65	<---	Democracy65	1.214	.126	9.616	***	c
fair65	<---	Democracy65	1.216	.130	9.346	***	b
opp65	<---	Democracy65	1.122	.143	7.860	***	a
press65	<---	Democracy65	1.000				

Covariances: (Group number 1 - Default model)

			Estimate	S.E.	C.R.	P	Label
Democracy60	<-->	Democracy65	4.318	.964	4.477	***	par_4
e1	<-->	e5	.591	.362	1.634	.102	par_5
e2	<-->	e6	1.568	.702	2.234	.025	par_6
e3	<-->	e7	.712	.600	1.188	.235	par_7
e4	<-->	e8	.498	.448	1.111	.266	par_8
e4	<-->	e2	1.293	.687	1.883	.060	par_9
e8	<-->	e6	.946	.553	1.712	.087	par_10

Variances: (Group number 1 - Default model)

	Estimate	S.E.	C.R.	P	Label
Democracy60	4.783	1.055	4.534	***	par_11
Democracy65	4.206	.996	4.225	***	par_12
e4	3.088	.715	4.316	***	par_13
e3	3.732	.935	3.993	***	par_14
e2	6.932	1.358	5.106	***	par_15
e1	1.618	.418	3.870	***	par_16
e8	2.990	.704	4.246	***	par_17
e7	3.087	.682	4.528	***	par_18
e6	3.857	.862	4.472	***	par_19
e5	2.438	.522	4.668	***	par_20

The χ^2-test results are:

$$\text{New model:} \quad \chi^2 = 14.633 \quad df = 16 \quad P = 0.552$$
$$\text{Old model:} \quad \chi^2 = 12.638 \quad df = 13 \quad P = 0.476$$

(2)

We compare the two models as follows:

	χ^2	f
New model	14.633	16
Old model	12.638	13
Difference	1.995	3

(3)

The difference is asymptotically distributed as χ^2 with three degrees of freedom. As a value of 1.995 with three degrees of freedom is not statistically significant according to traditional criteria, we prefer the new and simpler model.

This so-called χ^2-*difference test* is restricted to cases where one of the two models is nested under the other – that is, one model can be obtained by placing restrictions on the other.

In introducing these restrictions I had an eye on the output in Table 2, but my choice of restrictions was based on substantive reasoning. I was not fishing in the output. You can find lots of very small differences in this section of the output, but to restrict the corresponding parameters to be equal will in most cases be without meaning.

You are strongly advised not just to fish for small differences that are not theoretically defendable.

The revision of the original model was theory driven, but if model revision is more or less driven by empirical evidence the 'testing' is not meaningful, because you test on the same data that have formed the hypotheses. For example, if you drop non-significant parameters from a model you can be almost sure that the χ^2-difference test will also be non-significant.

Sample or population?

There is a problem with the analysis in Example 1: shall we consider the 75 developing countries as a random sample drawn from a larger population (and if so, how is that population defined?), or do they constitute the complete population? This is a fundamental question.

The basic idea in statistical estimation and testing is that you use a sample to draw conclusions about the *unknown* parameters of the population, taking the sampling error into consideration. But if your 'sample' is in reality the population, your 'parameter estimates' *are* the population parameters, and consequently there is no need for testing!

Even if the sample could be considered as drawn at random from some population, it is in all probability so large a fraction of that population that special formulae should be used to calculate the standard errors. Remember this if your analysis in based on macro data.

Programming in Visual Basic

As a newcomer you probably prefer the graphic interface, and one of the great things about AMOS is that it is possible to convert a path diagram to a VB program, save the program, print it out, etc. This is not only a convenient way to keep your programs for later use, but also a great way to learn the various commands used in VB.

In Table 4 you will find a VB program for the second run of Example 1. The program estimates parameters in the model shown in Figure 5c.

Table 4 Example 1: AMOS program for the second run

```
Sub Main
  Dim Sem As New AmosEngine
  Try
    Sem.Title ("Example 6.1")
    'Data from Bollen 1989
    Sem.TextOutput
    Sem.Gls
    Sem.Standardized
    Sem.ResidualMoments
    Sem.Crdiff
    Sem.BeginGroup ("C:\Users\Sony\Documents\Amos3 Chap 6\Bollen.
xls","sheet1")

    Sem.AStructure ("press60 = (1) Democracy60 + (1) e1")
    Sem.AStructure ("opp60   = (a) Democracy60 + (1) e2")
    Sem.AStructure ("fair60  = (b) Democracy60 + (1) e3")
    Sem.AStructure ("elect60 = (c) Democracy60 + (1) e4")

    Sem.AStructure ("press65 = (1) Democracy65 + (1) e5")
    Sem.AStructure ("opp65   = (a) Democracy65 + (1) e6")
    Sem.AStructure ("fair65  = (b) Democracy65 + (1) e7")
    Sem.AStructure ("elect65 = (c) Democracy65 + (1) e8")

    Sem.AStructure ("e1 <-> e5")
    Sem.AStructure ("e2 <-> e6")
    Sem.AStructure ("e3 <-> e7")
    Sem.AStructure ("e4 <-> e8")
    Sem.AStructure ("e2 <-> e4")
    Sem.AStructure ("e6 <-> e8 ")
    Sem.FitModel
  Finally
    Sem.Dispose
  End Try
End Sub
```

I use *generalized least squares* (Sem.Gls) and ask for *standardized parameters* (Sem.Standardized) and the *residual covariance matrix* (Sem.ResidualMoments), mentioned in Section 1.8. Furthermore, I ask for *Critical Ratios for Differences between Parameters* (Sem.Crdiff).

The next line states that data are to be found in the Excel file 'Bollen1.xls' in 'sheet1'. Then the model is formulated as a series of equations (Sem.AStructure), which the reader is recommended to compare with the model in Figure 5c.

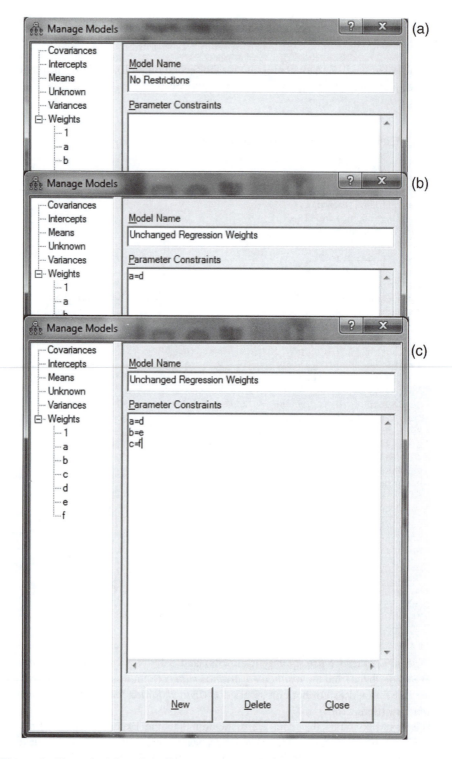

Figure 6 Example 1 (*continued*): managing several models

Placing the same letters in parentheses next to two variables forces them to have the same regression weight.

Note that the correlation between the two factors is not specified in the program, because such correlations are defaults in AMOS when the programming interface is used. However, in the graphic interface you must specify the correlation, because here 'what you see is what you get'.

Estimating several models in the same run

Sometimes you will be in a position where theoretical considerations lead you to consider several models, which a priori seem (nearly) equally likely. You met this situation in the models depicted in Figure 1.7b. In such situations it is not necessary to go through a long series of model formulations and estimations, because AMOS makes it possible to estimate all the considered models in one run.

In fact, the hypothesis of a stable measurement model was meaningful a priori, so given a little more thought I should have seen the two models as 'competitors' from the beginning. If I had, I could have estimated both models in one run.

Example 1 (continued)
Democracy in developing countries

Every parameter that you want to restrict in some way or another must be given its own name. In this case the three regression weights that I named a, b and c must have different names in the second model: d, e and f.

After you have done this renaming (and by now yould should know how to do it) you double-click 'Default Model' in the Models panel to the left of your path diagram, the window shown in Figure 6a will appear. In the Model Name box you write 'No Restrictions' and click 'New'.

A new empty 'Manage Models' box will appear. Name your second model 'Unchanged Regression Weights'.

Then double-click 'a' in the left panel, and 'a' will appear in the 'Parameter Constraints' box. Write a '=' and double-click 'd' – and the window will change to the one shown in panel (b).

Repeat the procedure with the remaining regression weights as shown in panel (c).

Now click 'Analyze/Calculate Estimates' and 'View/Text Output'.

As you may have guessed, there is a lot of output of which just a little is shown in Table 5. As you can see, all fit measures are shown for both models and you avoid hand-calculation of the χ^2-difference test.

The program in Table 6 demonstrates how to estimate several models in the same run using the programming interface:

1. All parameters that, in one model or another, are restricted are given a label in parentheses next to them.
2. The various restrictions are expressed in the lines Sem.Model ("Model A"), Sem.Model ("Model B"), etc.

Table 5   Example 1 (continued): extract of output

CMIN

Model	NPAR	CMIN	DF	P	CMIN/DF
No Restrictions	23	12.638	13	.476	.972
Unchanged Regression Weights	20	14.633	16	.552	.915
Saturated model	36	.000	0		
Independence model	8	70.446	28	.000	2.516
Zero model	0	296.000	36	.000	8.222

Nested Model Comparisons

Assuming model No Restrictions to be correct:

Model	DF	CMIN	P	NFI Delta-1	IFI Delta-2	RFI rho-1	TLI rho2
Unchanged Regression Weights	3	1.994	.574	.028	.035	-.023	-.038

Remember to use 'FitAllModels' instead of 'FitModel' when using the 'Model method', otherwise AMOS will only estimate the first model.

It is a good idea to spend some time familiarizing yourself with this example and the use of VB – you will need it in the following.

Compare the program in Table 6 with the one in Table 4.

Table 6   Example 1 (*continued*): VB program for fitting multiple models

```
Dim Sem As New AmosEngine
Try
   Sem.Title ("Example 6.1")
   'Data from Bollen 1989
   Sem.TextOutput
   Sem.Gls
   Sem.Standardized
   Sem.Crdiff
   Sem.BeginGroup ("C:\Users\Sony\Documents\Amos3 Chap 6\Bollen.
   xls","sheet1")

   Sem.AStructure ("press60 = (1) Democracy60 + (1) e1")
   Sem.AStructure ("opp60   = (a) Democracy60 + (1) e2")
   Sem.AStructure ("fair60  = (b) Democracy60 + (1) e3")
   Sem.AStructure ("elect60 = (c) Democracy60 + (1) e4")

   Sem.AStructure ("press65 = (1) Democracy65 + (1) e5")
   Sem.AStructure ("opp65   = (d) Democracy65 + (1) e6")
   Sem.AStructure ("fair65  = (e) Democracy65 + (1) e7")
   Sem.AStructure ("elect65 = (f) Democracy65 + (1) e8")
```

```
      Sem.AStructure ("e1 <-> e5")
      Sem.AStructure ("e2 <-> e6")
      Sem.AStructure ("e3 <-> e7")
      Sem.AStructure ("e4 <-> e8")
      Sem.AStructure ("e2 <-> e4")
      Sem.AStructure ("e6 <-> e8")

      Sem.Model ("No Restrictions")
      Sem.Model ("Unchanged Regression Weights", "a=d","b=e","c=f")
      Sem.FitAllModels
    Finally
      Sem.Dispose
    End Try
End Sub
```

3   Item Selection and Scale Construction

Very often confirmatory factor analysis will give a more differentiated picture of a scale's characteristics than traditional item analysis or exploratory factor analysis.

In Example 2.1 an item analysis in SPSS reduced the scale with three items and increased Cronbach's α from 0.831 to 0.866. In Example 3.3 we reached the same conclusion using principal components analysis.

These are the two 'classical' techniques for item analysis, but they are not without drawbacks:

1. A large Cronbach's α and/or large item–rest correlation is no guarantee of unidimensionality.
2. In component analysis (and exploratory factor analysis) every manifest variable is connected to every latent variable, whereas in the ideal scale, every manifest variable is connected to only one factor. This blurs the picture (cf. Figure 1).
3. In both cases the possibilities for statistical testing are limited.

Example 2
Constructing a scale to measure 'Style of Processing'

Childers, Houston, and Heckler (1985) constructed a summated scale for measuring 'Style of Processing' (SOP), i.e. a person's preference to engage in a verbal and/or visual modality of processing information about their environment.

You met this scale in Example 1.3.

The SOP scale is a 22-item, four-point scale, of which 11 items are assumed to reflect a verbal processing style, and 11 a visual processing style. Childers et al. proposed the two sub-scales to be used either separately or in combination as one scale – although they preferred using the combined scale.

The items are shown in Table 7.

The scale was used by Sørensen (2001) in a project on consumer behavior, the respondents being 88 randomly selected Danish housewives. The scale used was a

Table 7 Example 2: style of processing (SOP) scale

1. I enjoy work that requires the use of words.
2. There are some special times in my life that I like to relive by mentally 'picturing' just how everything looked.*
3. I can never seem to find the right word when I need it.*
4. I do a lot of reading.
5. When I'm trying to learn something new, I'd rather watch a demonstration than read how to do it.*
6. I think I often use words in the wrong way.*
7. I enjoy learning new words.
8. I like to picture how I could fix up my apartment or a room if I could buy anything I wanted.*
9. I often make written notes to myself.
10. I like to daydream.*
11. I generally prefer to use a diagram rather than a written set of instructions.*
12. I like to 'doodle'.*
13. I find it helps to think in terms of mental pictures when doing many things.*
14. After I meet someone for the first time, I can usually remember what they look like, but not much about them.*
15. I like to think in synonyms of words.
16. When I have forgotten something I frequently try to form a mental 'picture' to remember it.*
17. I like learning new words.
18. I prefer to read instructions about how to do something rather than have someone show me.
19. I prefer activities that don't require a lot of reading.*
20. I seldom daydream.
21. I spend very little time trying to increase my vocabulary.*
22. My thinking often consists of mental 'pictures' or images.*

NOTES: *Denotes items that are reverse scored. Items 1, 3, 4, 6, 7, 9, 15, 17, 18, 19, and 21 compose the verbal component. Items 2, 5, 8, 10 through 14, 16, 20, and 22 compose the visual component.

seven-point scale and not a four-point scale as in the original one. You can find Sørensen's data on the book's website.

Cronbach's α was 0.76 for the verbal sub-scale and 0.71 for the visual sub-scale, while for the combined scale it was 0.74. In their original paper Childers et al. stated the same α to be 0.81, 0.86 and 0.88 respectively. In most circumstances, values of α of this size will lead to acceptance of the scales as reliable and *unidimensional*.

Here I will use Sørensen's data in order to evaluate the scale; the measurement model is shown in Figure 7.

The program and output are given in Table 8.

Note that I ask for *modification indices larger than four* (Sem.Mods (4)). A modification index is attached to a fixed parameter and states by how much the χ^2-value will be reduced if the parameter is set free (cf. the χ^2-difference test mentioned in connection with Example 1). In the output you will see that there are eight covariances

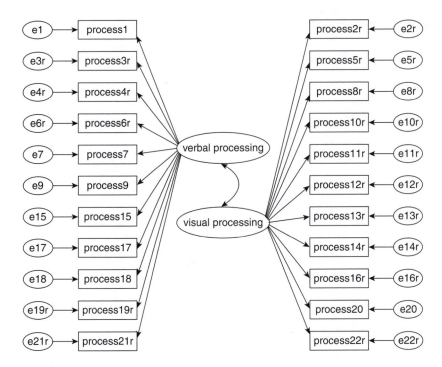

Figure 7   Example 2: model of Childers et al.'s SOP scale

and six regression weights that can be expected to reduce χ^2 by at least 4.00 if they are set free.

Next to the modification indices (M.I.) you will see the expected change in parameter values (Par Change). At present these parameters are not in the model, i.e. they are fixed at zero. Consequently the expected parameter changes are the expected parameter values.

However, always remember that these figures are indications of marginal changes, and do not say anything about what would happen if more than one parameter were set free simultaneously.

If you include the covariance between e11r and e13r as suggested by the output, you can expect χ^2 to be reduced by 6.103.

Four is also the default value for the threshold value, so I could just as well have omitted the '4' (cf. Figure 4).

You may wonder why the inventors of AMOS chose that value as the default, but the simple reason is that 4 is the integer nearest to 3.841, the critical *P*-value of a χ^2-difference test with one degree of freedom.

The reason for my choice of a rather modest threshold value is that I expect the inventors of the SOP scale to have done their homework, and consequently the possibilities of dramatic improvements in fit should be limited.

The last two structure lines in the program fix the variances of the two factors at 1.00 in order to identify the model.

Table 8 Example 2: program and output of first run (extract)

```
Sub Main
  Dim Sem As New AmosEngine
  Try
    Sem.Title (Example 6.2
    'SOP scale, 1st run. Data from Sørensen (2001)
    Sem.TextOutput
    Sem.Gls
    Sem.Standardized
    Sem.Mods (4)
    Sem.BeginGroup ((C:\Users\Sony\Documents\Amos3\SOP.xls","SOP")

    Sem.AStructure ("process1    = verbal + (1) e1")
    Sem.AStructure ("process3r   = verbal + (1) e3r")
    Sem.AStructure ("process4    = verbal + (1) e4")
    Sem.AStructure ("process6r   = verbal + (1) e6r")
    Sem.AStructure ("process7    = verbal + (1) e7")
    Sem.AStructure ("process9    = verbal + (1) e9")
    Sem.AStructure ("process15   = verbal + (1) e15")
    Sem.AStructure ("process17   = verbal + (1) e17")
    Sem.AStructure ("process18   = verbal + (1) e18")
    Sem.AStructure ("process19r  = verbal + (1) e19r")
    Sem.AStructure ("process21r  = verbal + (1) e21r")

    Sem.AStructure ("process2r  = visual  + (1) e2r")
    Sem.AStructure ("process5r  = visual  + (1) e5r")
    Sem.AStructure ("process8r  = visual  + (1) e8r")
    Sem.AStructure ("process10r = visual  + (1) e10r")
    Sem.AStructure ("process11r = visual  + (1) e11r")
    Sem.AStructure ("process12r = visual  + (1) e12r")
    Sem.AStructure ("process13r = visual  + (1) e13r")
    Sem.AStructure ("process14r = visual  + (1) e14r)
    Sem.AStructure ("process16r = visual  + (1) e16r")
    Sem.AStructure ("process20  = visual  + (1) e20")
    Sem.AStructure ("process22r = visual  + (1) e22r")

    Sem.AStructure ("verbal (1)")
    Sem.AStructure ("visual (1)")
    Sem.FitModel
  Finally
    Sem.Dispose
  End Try
End Sub
```

Result (Model 1)

```
Minimum was achieved
Chi-square = 242.238
Degrees of freedom = 208
Probability level = .052
```

Scalar Estimates (Group number 1 - Model 1)

Generalized Least Squares Estimates

Regression Weights: (Group number 1 - Model 1)

			Estimate	S.E.	C.R.	P	Label
process1	<---	verbal	.817	.150	5.453	***	
process3r	<---	verbal	-.379	.198	-1.908	.056	
process4	<---	verbal	.366	.209	1.749	.080	
process6r	<---	verbal	.150	.166	.902	.367	
process7	<---	verbal	.949	.114	8.293	***	
process9	<---	verbal	.129	.256	.504	.614	
process15	<---	verbal	.570	.222	2.566	.010	
process17	<---	verbal	.994	.112	8.890	***	
process18	<---	verbal	.059	.167	.353	.724	
process19r	<---	verbal	.292	.187	1.559	.119	
process21r	<---	verbal	.580	.198	2.936	.003	
process2r	<---	visual	.871	.185	4.704	***	
process5r	<---	visual	.151	.182	.827	.408	
process8r	<---	visual	.462	.146	3.170	.002	
process10r	<---	visual	1.513	.181	8.380	***	
process11r	<---	visual	-.070	.198	-.352	.725	
process12r	<---	visual	-.224	.234	-.957	.339	
process13r	<---	visual	.414	.224	1.847	.065	
process14r	<---	visual	.224	.225	.999	.318	
process16r	<---	visual	.178	.207	.861	.390	
process20	<---	visual	1.747	.194	8.990	***	
process22r	<---	visual	.428	.203	2.105	.035	

Covariances: (Group number 1 - Model 1)

			Estimate	S.E.	C.R.	P	Label
verbal	<-->	visual	-.366	.117	-3.117	.002	

Modification Indices (Group number 1 - Model 1)

Covariances: (Group number 1 - Model 1)

			M.I.	Par Change
e11r	<-->	e13r	6.103	.541
e18	<-->	e8r	4.461	-.320
e17	<-->	e8r	4.467	.174
e15	<-->	e5r	4.843	-.552
e7	<-->	e8r	4.874	-.178
e6r	<-->	e8r	5.757	-.294
e3r	<-->	e8r	4.916	.343
e3r	<-->	e2r	4.030	-.379

(Continued)

(Continued)

Variances: (Group number 1 - Model 1)

	M.I. Par Change

Regression Weights: (Group number 1 - Model 1)

			M.I.	Par Change
process13r	<---	process11r	6.088	.278
process11r	<---	process13r	4.907	.432
Process8r	<---	process18r	4.406	-.342
process8r	<---	process6r	5.471	-.413
Process5r	<---	Process15	4.391	-.237
process15	<---	Process5r	4.954	-.372

A Chi-square of 242.236 with 208 degrees of freedom giving a *P*-value of 0.052 is a little on the low side. What is more serious is that the fit indices are not quite satisfactory:

CMIN/DF	CFI	RMSEA	LO 90	HI 90	PCLOSE
1.165	0.531	0.043	0.000	0.065	0.665

CFIs below 0.80 should be taken seriously. So let us take a look at the modification indices.

Causal paths between items are of course meaningless, and so are the suggested covariances (although the covariance between e11r and e13r could be taken as a sign that the two items are a little too close).

As I advocated earlier, it is usually a good idea to base suggestions for modifications to a model on substantive rather than purely empirical evidence, so let us look at the items in Table 8. A few of them catch the eye:

1. Items 10 and 20 say nearly the same thing and serve as mutual controls on the consistency of the answers, so they should correlate more than by their common cause: 'visual'.
2. The same can be said of items 7 and 17.
3. Items 3 and 6 are also very close. If you cannot find a special word when you need it and therefore use another word, I think you will find that other word less suitable in the situation.

At least you should consider introducing these correlations in the model.

4. You should also expect correlations among items 5, 11 and 18. Whereas most of the other items only mention one of the processing styles, these three explicitly mention both, and compare them.

   According to their wording these three items could be placed in both sub-scales. You should therefore consider letting them load on both factors.

If you substitute the three lines:

```
Sem.AStructure ("process18  = verbal +visual + (1) e18")
Sem.AStructure ("process5r  = visual  + verbal + (1) e5r")
Sem.AStructure ("process11r = visual  + verbal + (1) e11r")
```

for the corresponding ones in Table 8, and add

```
Sem.AStructure ("e10r<-->e20")
Sem.AStructure ("e7 <-->e17")
Sem.AStructure ("e3r<-->e6r")
```

you will get the output shown in Table 9.

Table 9 Example 2: output for the second run

Result (Model 1)

```
Minimum was achieved
Chi-square = 216.288
Degrees of freedom = 202
Probability level = .233
```

Regression Weights: (Group number 1 – Model 1)

			Estimate	S.E.	C.R.	P	Label
process1	<---	verbal	.505	.177	2.858	.004	
process3r	<---	verbal	.760	.202	3.756	***	
process4	<---	verbal	.262	.218	1.204	.229	
process6r	<---	verbal	.529	.169	3.131	.002	
process7	<---	verbal	.225	.137	1.646	.100	
process9	<---	verbal	.768	.265	2.892	.004	
process15	<---	verbal	.314	.235	1.335	.182	
process17	<---	verbal	.198	.136	1.456	.145	
process18	<---	verbal	1.858	.386	4.808	***	
process18	<---	visual	-.996	.425	-2.343	.019	
process19r	<---	verbal	1.247	.203	6.155	***	
process21r	<---	verbal	.085	.209	.405	.685	
process2r	<---	visual	.802	.197	4.065	***	
process5r	<---	visual	-.430	.380	-1.131	.258	
process5r	<---	verbal	1.745	.355	4.915	***	
process8r	<---	visual	.874	.160	5.474	***	
process10r	<---	visual	.571	.210	2.718	.007	
process11r	<---	visual	-.212	.343	-.620	.535	
process11r	<---	verbal	1.232	.321	3.834	***	
process12r	<---	visual	.318	.243	1.310	.190	
process13r	<---	visual	1.282	.216	5.930	***	
process14r	<---	visual	.701	.231	3.035	.002	
process16r	<---	visual	.684	.212	3.225	.001	
process20	<---	visual	.649	.228	2.848	.004	
process22r	<---	visual	1.285	.197	6.524	***	

(Continued)

(Continued)

Covariances: (Group number 1 - Model 1)

			Estimate	S.E.	C.R.	P	Label
verbal	<-->	visual	.680	.124	5.469	***	
e10r	<-->	e20	1.409	.355	3.968	***	
e7	<-->	e17	.349	.105	3.335	***	
e3r	<-->	e6r	.456	.211	2.161	.031	

With a Chi-square of 216.288 with 202 degrees of freedom giving a *P*-value of 0.233, the model seems satisfactory, and a look at the fit indices confirms this:

CMIN/DF	CFI	RMSEA	LO 90	HI 90	PCLOSE
1.071	0.804	0.029	0.000	0.055	0.895

Although CFI is not quite up to standard (> 0.90–0.95), it is considerably larger than in the first run, and the other indices are all fine.

By studying the parameters of the model, you can observe the following:

1. Item 18 has significant loadings on both factors whereas items 5 and 11, which were supposed to measure visual processing style, actually both have significant loadings on 'verbal' and non-significant loadings on 'visual'. However, all coefficients have the expected signs.
2. The following regression weights are non-significant (one-sided test, $\alpha = 0.05$): 15, 17, 21r, 5r, 11r and 12r.
3. All the covariances are significant, and the correlation between the two factors is 0.680 (as the two factors are standardized, the correlation equals the covariance).

What, then, can we conclude?

1. The SOP scale has two dimensions as suggested by Childers et al. In fact it has *more* than two dimensions showing up as highly significant correlations between items in the same 'main dimension'.
2. Some of the items have very little loading on the factor they are supposed to measure. A reformulation or exclusion should be considered.
3. Although the two sub-scales correlate, there are in fact *two* dimensions, and treating them as one scale could – depending on the research question – cause problems, because it assumes that the two ways of processing are alternatives.
4. In fact it has long been known that verbal and visual processes take place in functionally separate cognitive systems and thus are not alternatives (Paivio, 1971).

From the last point above you will learn that it is of the utmost importance to spend a good deal of time making clear the nature of the concepts you intend to measure. This preliminary step is all too often not given the necessary care.

Now, in light of point 4 above, you may wonder: why do the two factors correlate at all?

A possible explanation is that the correlation is caused by item 18 loading on both factors, and that the correlation would disappear if this item (together with items 5 and 11) were removed.

This line of reasoning immediately gives birth to another question: the SOP scale is intended to measure preference, but do all items really measure preference? It seems to me that items 3, 6 and 14 measure ability rather than preference. Of course preference and ability must be expected to correlate, because we generally prefer activities where we feel we have the largest potential – but is ability not exogenous, and should the arrows connecting items 3, 6 and 14 to their latent variables not point in the opposite direction?

These two last points have taught us an important lesson: that serious thinking about the subject area is much preferred to thoughtless dependence on computer output.

If we delete items 5, 11 and 18 together with the three 'ability questions' we get the output in Table 10.

Also observe that the modifications to the original model were *not* based on the modification indices, but on substantive reasoning.

Table 10   Example 2: output from third run

```
Minimum was achieved
Chi-square = 108.185
Degrees of freedom = 101
Probability level = .294
```

Group number 1 (Group number 1 - Model 1)

Estimates (Group number 1 - Model 1)

Scalar Estimates (Group number 1 - Model 1)

Generalized Least Squares Estimates

Regression Weights: (Group number 1 - Model 1)

			Estimate	S.E.	C.R.	P	Label
process1	<---	verbal	1.024	.176	5.809	***	
process4	<---	verbal	.785	.230	3.407	***	
process7	<---	verbal	.846	.140	6.026	***	
process9	<---	verbal	.386	.291	1.326	.185	
process15	<---	verbal	.572	.241	2.376	.018	
process17	<---	verbal	.766	.141	5.422	***	
process19r	<---	verbal	.559	.230	2.434	.015	
process21r	<---	verbal	.742	.214	3.477	***	
process2r	<---	visual	.605	.207	2.917	.004	
process8r	<---	visual	.492	.163	3.018	.003	
process10r	<---	visual	.439	.228	1.923	.055	
process12r	<---	visual	.243	.253	.959	.338	
process13r	<---	visual	1.494	.220	6.798	***	
process16r	<---	visual	.796	.217	3.664	***	
process20	<---	visual	.921	.251	3.675	***	
process22r	<---	visual	1.252	.197	6.365	***	

(Continued)

(Continued)

Covariances: (Group number 1 - Model 1)

			Estimate	S.E.	C.R.	P	Label
verbal	<-->	visual	-.066	.163	-.408	.684	
e10r	<-->	e20	1.974	.418	4.722	***	
e7	<-->	e17	.275	.142	1.940	.052	

The fit of this model is not too bad:

CMIN/DF	CFI	RMSEA	LO 90	HI 90	PCLOSE
1.071	0.893	0.029	0.000	0.064	0.805

Of the three models, the third one is the best fitting. However, the most striking support for this model is found using the decision theoretic measures:

	Model 1	Model 2	Model 3
AIC	332	318	178
BCC	365	355	195
BIC	444	445	265
CAIC	489	496	300

Looking at the parameter estimates, we can see the following:

1. The correlation between the two factors disappeared, as it should according to theory.
2. The other two correlations are significant (remember: one-sided tests!).
3. Items 9 and 12 are not significant.

The purist would remove items 7 and 20 in order to get rid of the remaining correlations. However, as these correlations would probably be (nearly) constant and repeat themselves in future uses of the scale, they would not reduce its reliability. You could also consider removing or rephrasing the non-significant items.

If your research demands that you compare your study with others that used the SOP scale, it will perhaps be necessary for you to use the items as a summated scale (or scales). If that is not a demand, I would prefer to use the items un-summated. You could consider parcelling if you need to keep down the number of parameters.

4 Reliability and Validity

The classical methods of judging the reliability and validity of a measuring instrument all have their shortcomings in the fact that none of them take the latent variables explicitly into account as part of the measurement model.

Therefore the theoretical definitions of reliability and validity as coefficients of determination when regressing the measurement on the theoretical constructs cannot be used as a basis for calculations. However, using SEM as the basis for judging reliability and validity should open up this possibility.

Reliability

In Equation (2.3a) the reliability coefficient was defined as the coefficient of determination when a measurement (an indicator, a manifest variable) is regressed on its latent variable(s). Using SEM, you can use this definition to calculate reliability coefficients.

Example 2 (continued)
Constructing a scale to measure 'Style of Processing'
Evaluating Reliability

If you include the statement

Sem.Smc

(Smc = squared multiple correlation) in the program for the third run, the output will include the estimates in Table 11.

Table 11 Example 2 (continued): calculation of reliabilities

Squared Multiple Correlations: (Group number 1 - Model 1)

	Estimate
process22r	.559
process20	.224
process16r	.225
process13r	.656
process12r	.019
process10r	.079
process8r	.217
process2r	.170
process21r	.225
process19r	.132
process17	.493
process15	.122
process9	.039
process7	.595
process4	.220
process1	.552

It comes as no surprise that the two items with the smallest reliabilities are the ones that have non-significant regression weights. However, a few of the highly significant items have rather small reliabilities and should be discarded or reformulated.

Anyway, if apart from measuring SOP you also want to measure several other concepts in order to construct a causal model, 16 (not to mention 22!) items are quite a lot. If the other latent variables require a similar number of items your questionnaire will easily grow to a length that could cause messy data, because respondents might refuse to participate, not answer all the questions, or fill out the questionnaire more or less at random in order to get the job done as quickly as possible.

Very often scale constructors in their efforts to obtain perfection end up with scales that are too long for practical use. The SOP scale is perhaps an example of this.

This way of calculating a reliability coefficient has at least five advantages:

1. It is based on the very definition of reliability.
2. It is possible to calculate the reliability of every single item and not just a sum of them.
3. It can be used whether the measurements are parallel, tau-equivalent or congeneric.
4. It does not assume errors to be uncorrelated across items.
5. It can be used when an item is an indicator for more than just one latent variable.

If you have only cross-sectional data it is in general not possible to estimate the specific variance, which is then absorbed into the error variance. In this case you must either assume that the specific variance is zero or consider the estimated reliabilities to be lower bounds.

Validity

Calculation of a suitable measure for the validity is more complicated.

Let us assume that we have a manifest variable X, which is an indicator of more than one latent variable in our model. If as our starting point we take the validity of X to be the extent to which X is connected to each concept it is assumed to measure, then the most straightforward measures of validity are the coefficients λ in raw or standardized form. Each of these measures has the same advantages and drawbacks that we know from traditional regression analysis. One advantage of the standardized coefficients is that they are independent of the measurement units. This is very important in the case of SEM, where the measurement scales of the variables and especially those of the latent variables are often more or less arbitrary. On the other hand, standardized coefficients depend on the variances in the populations, and if we wish to compare several groups from different populations this could be a problem.

Another way is to start with the reliability coefficient as the coefficient of determination when regressing the variable X on all variables that have a direct effect on it. This is of course the Smc as defined in the section above on reliability.

If we want the validity coefficient to measure that part of the variance in X attributable to for example F_1, we must deduce from the squared multiple correlation coefficient the variation caused by all other factors influencing X.

We can then define the validity coefficient of X with regard to F_1 as

$$U_{XF_1} = R_X^2 - R_{X(F_1)}^2 \tag{2}$$

where R_X^2 is the coefficient of determination obtained by regressing X on all variables that have a direct influence on X, while $R_{X(F_1)}^2$ is the coefficient of determination obtained by regressing X on the same variables except F_1. The symbols in (6.4) are taken from Bollen (1989), who proposed the measure, to designate *unique validity variance*.

Example 2 (continued)
Constructing a scale to measure 'Style of Processing'

Let us estimate the unique validity variance of *process18* with regard to *verbal* in the model for the second run.

We have

$$U_{process18verbal_1} = R_{process18}^2 - R_{process18(verbal)}^2 \tag{3}$$

$R_{process18}^2$ is estimated including the statement Sem.Smc in the program, and $R_{process18(verbal)}^2$ by regressing *process18* only on 'visual':

$$U_{process18verbal_1} = 0.728 - 0.095 = 0.633 \tag{4}$$

While the reliable share of the variance of process18 is 0.728, only a share of 0.633 is valid.

As pointed out several times, the concept of validity is much more problematic both to define and to measure than reliability. The reader is referred to Bollen (1989) for further reading.

5   Reflexive and Formative Indicators

In a confirmatory factor model (and also in an exploratory factor model), the arrows point *from* the latent variable to its manifest indicators. As a consequence, indicators of the same latent variable must correlate (cf. Figure 8a).

It is a very common mistake among newcomers to SEM to overlook this simple fact, and to use indicators that are not *necessarily* correlated.

The classic example is that you want to measure a person's consumption of alcoholic beverages, and to that end you use a series of questions each measuring the consumption of one single beverage. That is, indicators such as:

Consumption of beer
Consumption of wine
Consumption of whisky
Consumption of cognac
etc.

While a (weighted) sum of these variables is a measure of total consumption of alcohol, there is no reason to believe that all these indicators should be correlated.

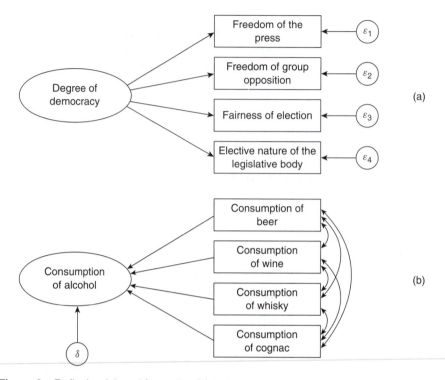

Figure 8   Reflexive (a) and formative (b) indicators

In a graphic illustration of this situation, the arrows should point *from* the indicators and *to* the latent variable (cf. Figure 8b).

The indicators in panel (a) of the figure are called *reflexive*: they reflect the underlying latent variable. In contrast the indicators in panel (b) are called *formative*: they *form* or define the latent variable, which in this case is not latent at all, as it is a function of manifest variables.

While a certain amount of correlation should exist among reflexive indicators for the same latent variable, correlations among formative indicators are not a necessity.

It is important to be aware that classical test theory and concepts like reliability and validity assume indicators to be reflexive. Using formative indicators in SEM programs like AMOS is rather complicated. Apart from identification problems (that can be very tricky to solve) you can see from the figure that making the indicators exogenous means that they lose their error terms, and that measurement errors will instead be absorbed in the disturbance of the latent variable together with other sources of unexplained variance if the latent variable is affected by other variables in a larger model.

In fact, you have already met examples of indicators that could perhaps be considered formative, namely the three problematic items forb38, forb39 and forb41 in the fish example (Example 2.1).

In many applications of SEM, socio-economic variables are used to characterize a person. The various indicators used are most realistically seen as formative, but it is not uncommon to see them treated as reflexive.

The many problems with using formative indicators in traditional SEM are given an excellent treatment by Kline (2006).

If your model includes several latent variables with formative indicators, you should try using another SEM technique, namely *partial least squares* (PLS) invented by Herman Wold (1975). An introduction to this technique can be found in Fornell and Cha (1994). A deeper treatment with many examples is given by Vinzi, Chin, Henseler, and Wang (2010).

You could say that PLS relates to covariance-based SEM like component analysis relates to factor analysis (see Figure 1).

In this chapter you met the following concepts:

- confirmatory factor analysis
- three-indicator rule
- two-indicator rule

- smc as a measure of reliability
- unique variance as a measure of validity
- χ^2-difference test

You also learned the following AMOS statements

- Sem.Gls
- Sem.Crdiff
- Sem.FitAllModels

- Sem.Model
- Sem.Mods (–)

Questions

1. State the differences among the three (main) factor models, and discuss their virtues and vices.

2. Can you suggest further modifications to the model in Figure 3?

3. Reflecting on your own studies or research, comment on the various instruments AMOS offers for helping you with model modifications. Discuss their virtues and vices.

4. Comment on the differences between reflective and formative indicators. Why is this distinction important?

5. Why does it matter which item is used as a reference (with its regression weight set at 1.00)?

References

Bollen, K. A. (1979). Political democracy and the timing of development. *American Sociological Review, 44*, 572–587.

Bollen, K. A. (1980). Issues in the comparative measurement of political democracy. *American Sociological Review, 45*, 370–390.

Bollen, K. A. (1989). *Structural equation modeling with latent variables*. New York: Wiley.

Childers, T. L., Houston, M. J., & Heckler, S. (1985). Measurement of individual differences in visual versus verbal information processing. *Journal of Consumer Research, 12*, 124–134.

Fornell, C., & Cha, J. (1994). Partial least squares. In P. Bagozzi (Ed.), *Advanced methods of marketing research*. Oxford: Blackwell.

Kline, R. B. (2006). Reverse arrow dynamics: Formative measurement and feedback loops. In G.R. Hancock & R.O. Mueller (Eds.), *Structural equation modeling: A second course* (pp. 43–68). Charlotte, NC: Information Age Publishing.

Paivio, A. (1971). *Imagery and verbal processes*. New York: Holt, Rinehart & Winston.

Sørensen, E. (2001). Means-end chains og laddering i et kognitivt perspektiv. PhD thesis, Aarhus School of Business, Aarhus.

Vinzi, V. E., Chin, W. W., Henseler, J., & Wang, H. (2010). *Handbook of partial least squares: Concepts, methods and applications in marketing and related fields*. New York: Springer.

Wold, H. (1975). Path models with latent variables: The NIPALS approach. In H. M. Blalock et al. (Ed.), *Quantitative Sociology: International perspectives on mathematical and statistical modeling*. New York: Academic Press.

7
The General Model

In this chapter the structural model (Chapter 5) and the measurement model (Chapter 6) are brought together to form the general structural equation model.

This model is introduced by way of Example 4.1, which is modified by letting the structural variables be latent instead of manifest. After this simple example has demonstrated the advantages of basing your analyses on latent variable models, we move on to a larger example.

In this example you will learn the two-step strategy: separate analyses of the measurement and structural models. Among other things, you will also learn how to analyze indirect effects, i.e. effects that are mediated by other variables.

Next you will look at a time series model, which has one real advantage compared with cross-section models: there is no doubt about the causal directions.

1 Combining the Structural and Measurement Model

As you will probably have guessed, combining the structural and the measurement model into one model complicates the analysis. Among the questions to be answered are the following:

1. If I have problems with model fit, is the problem then with the measurement model or the structural model?
2. Combining the two models into one makes them dependent on each other. Therefore the parameter estimates in one sub-model could depend on the parameter estimates in the other. What are the consequences for the substantive interpretation if that happens?

Before answering these questions, let us examine what happens when we transform a model with only manifest variables into one with latent variables.

Example 1 (continued from Example 4.1)
Mapping European consumers' willingness to buy genetically modified food: from manifest to latent variables

In Example 4.1 you were introduced to AMOS programming by way of a simple multiple regression example (you may wish to look back at this before moving on) using only manifest variables – in this case summated scales. This presupposes that measurement

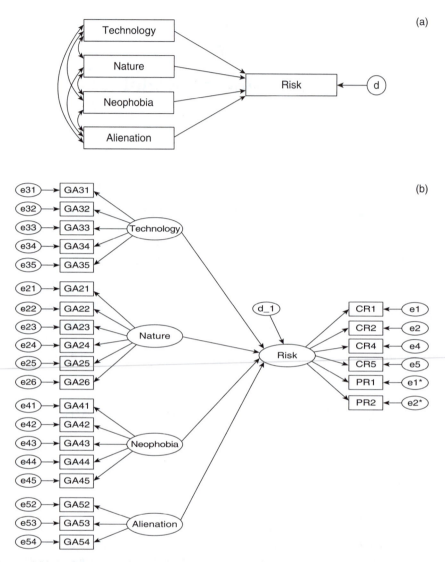

In panel (b) the four exogenous variables should be connected by six double-headed arrows, but these are not shown in order to make the illustration clearer.

Figure 1   Example 1: a regression model (a) without and (b) with latent variables

error is absent – that the measurements are totally reliable. This is of course a very unrealistic assumption, but we can lose it by introducing latent variables. In Figure 1 you can compare the original regression model in panel (a) with the model in panel (b), obtained by splitting the various summated scales into their separate items.

Identification: the two-step rule
As already mentioned, there is no general necessary and sufficient condition for identification, so often you have to rely on the computer's messages about 'probably non-identified' parameters.

As the general model consists of two sub-models, intuitively the total model must be identified if its two parts are identified when considered separately. This can in fact be proved to be the case, and can be formulated in the so-called *two-step rule*.

First you look at the model in Figure 1b as a confirmatory factor analysis model (i.e. you let the one-headed arrows in the structural model be substituted by two-headed arrows depicting covariances) and make sure that it is identified. Then you regard the structural part of the model as consisting of only manifest variables, and you make sure that this model is identified too. If both conditions are fulfilled this is *sufficient* (but not necessary) to secure identification of the original model.

The first condition is met according to the three-indicator rule (mentioned in Section 6.2), and the second follows from the zero B-rule (mentioned in Section 5.1).

Estimation

A program for estimating the model is given in Table 1 and part of the output in Table 2. The data can be found on the book's website.

Table 1 Example 1: the program

```
Sub Main
        Dim Sem As New AmosEngine
        Sem.TextOutput
        Sem.Standardized
        Sem.Smc

        Sem.BeginGroup ("C:\Users\Sony\Documents\Amos3\Bredahl.xls","Latent")
        Sem.GroupName "Germany"

        Sem.AStructure "GA31 = (1) Technology + (1)e31"
        Sem.AStructure "GA32 =     Technology + (1)e32"
        Sem.AStructure "GA33 =     Technology + (1)e33"
        Sem.AStructure "GA34 =     Technology + (1)e34"
        Sem.AStructure "GA35 =     Technology + (1)e35"

        Sem.AStructure "GA21 = (1) Nature + (1)e21"
        Sem.AStructure "GA22 =     Nature + (1)e22"
        Sem.AStructure "GA23 =     Nature + (1)e23"
        Sem.AStructure "GA24 =     Nature + (1)e24"
        Sem.AStructure "GA25 =     Nature + (1)e25"
        Sem.AStructure "GA26 =     Nature + (1)e26"

        Sem.AStructure "GA41 = (1) Neophobia + (1)e41"
        Sem.AStructure "GA42 =     Neophobia + (1)e42"
        Sem.AStructure "GA43 =     Neophobia + (1)e43"
        Sem.AStructure "GA44 =     Neophobia + (1)e44"
        Sem.AStructure "GA45 =     Neophobia + (1)e45"

        Sem.AStructure "GA52 = (1) Alienation + (1)e52"
        Sem.AStructure "GA53 =     Alienation + (1)e53"
        Sem.AStructure "GA54 =     Alienation + (1)e54"

        Sem.AStructure "CR1 = (1) Risks + (1)e1"
        Sem.AStructure "CR2 =     Risks + (1)e2"
        Sem.AStructure "CR4 =     Risks + (1)e4"
```

(Continued)

(Continued)

```
            Sem.AStructure "CR5 =        Risks + (1)e5"
            Sem.AStructure "PR1 =        Risks + (1)e1*"
            Sem.AStructure "PR2 =        Risks + (1)e2*"

            Sem.AStructure "Risks = Technology + Nature + Neophobia + Alienation
            + (1)d_1
End Sub
```

Table 2 Example 1: output

Regression Weights: (Germany - Model 1)

			Estimate	S.E.	C.R.	P
Risks	<---	Technology	-.327	.067	-4.878	***
Risks	<---	Nature	.617	.090	6.824	***
Risks	<---	Neophobia	.378	.080	4.712	***
Risks	<---	Alienation	.341	.079	4.329	***
GA31	<---	Technology	1.000			
GA32	<---	Technology	.979	.080	12.212	***
GA33	<---	Technology	.933	.077	12.064	***
GA34	<---	Technology	.880	.079	11.192	***
GA35	<---	Technology	.888	.078	11.373	***
GA21	<---	Nature	1.000			
GA22	<---	Nature	.830	.089	9.322	***
GA23	<---	Nature	.658	.090	7.331	***
GA24	<---	Nature	.736	.102	7.226	***
GA25	<---	Nature	.554	.097	5.696	***
GA26	<---	Nature	.690	.093	7.412	***
GA41	<---	Neophobia	1.000			
GA42	<---	Neophobia	1.306	.132	9.902	***
GA43	<---	Neophobia	1.319	.138	9.567	***
GA44	<---	Neophobia	1.505	.143	10.510	***
GA45	<---	Neophobia	1.308	.137	9.570	***
GA52	<---	Alienation	1.000			
GA53	<---	Alienation	1.097	.085	12.971	***
GA54	<---	Alienation	.899	.082	10.988	***
CR1	<---	Risks	1.000			
CR2	<---	Risks	.696	.059	11.881	***
CR4	<---	Risks	.662	.051	13.058	***
CR5	<---	Risks	.851	.059	14.467	***
PR1	<---	Risks	.815	.063	12.986	***
PR2	<---	Risks	1.073	.066	16.203	***

Squared Multiple Correlations: (Germany - Model 1)

	Estimate
Risks	.584

The main results from the analysis in Example 4.1 and the present analysis are most easily compared in Table 3.

Table 3 Example 1: comparing the results of the two analyses. Estimated regression weights (standard errors in parentheses) and coefficients of determination

	Manifest variables	Latent variables
Technology	−.240	−.327
	(.052)	(.067)
Nature	.371	.617
	(.048)	(.090)
Neophobia	.274	.378
	(.043)	(.079)
Alienation	.684	.341
	(.082)	(.079)
R^2	.387	.584

What first catches the eye is the increase in the coefficient of determination caused by introducing latent variables: from 0.387 to 0.584 – an increase of no less than 50 pct. So part of the reason for the apparently low overall explanatory power in the original regression model is the low reliability of the measurements.

Also observe that rather dramatic changes in regression weights have taken place, and that neglecting the measurement errors underestimates most of the standard errors.

The effects of introducing latent variables

From the above example, you will see that neglecting the inevitable measurement error ε has the following consequences:

1. Unreliable measurement of the dependent variable deflates the coefficient of determination and increases the standard error of the estimated regression weights.
2. Unreliable measurements of independent variables bias the estimated regression weights and the coefficient of determination.

Both problems can be solved by regarding the variables in question as latent.

2 Analysis of the General Model

In the above example the measurement model is over-identified and the structural model is just-identified (cf. Table 4.1). This means that the χ^2-test is a test of the measurement model only and that all the fit indices only measure the fit of the measure-ment part of the model. If you substitute unexplained covariances for the one-headed arrows in the structural part of the model, you end up with exactly the same fit meas-ures. The two models are equivalent.

Therefore the only measure of 'fit' for the structural part of the model is R^2.

Often the measurement model and the structural model are estimated in one go – the so-called *one-step strategy*. However, this could raise problems, one of which is that if the (complete) model does not fit the data, it can sometimes be complicated to find out whether the structural model depicting your theory is wrong, or the bad fit is due to unreliable measurements.

Therefore, a two-step rule should also be applied to the analysis of the model. First analyze the model as a confirmatory factor analysis model and then put in the one-headed arrows and analyze the full model. This is the so-called *two-step strategy*. Anyway, it is meaningless to analyze the structural part of the model if the measure-ment model does not show satisfactory reliabilities.

Another problem is this: if the model fits the data, and a measurement model shows a satisfactory reliability, can we then be sure that it will show the same excellent qualities if used in connection with another structural model? In other words, a measuring instru-ment should ideally work in the same way whenever it is used, irrespective of the struc-tural model. Therefore the regression weights in the measurement model should not change significantly when making modifications to the structural part of the model.

The two-step strategy could therefore easily be expanded to a many-step procedure. One example is given by Mulaik and Millsap (2000) who proposed a four-step strategy starting with an exploratory factor analysis. However, using an exploratory technique as the first step could be a bit dangerous if no more than two samples are used for cross-validation – and if you forgo substantive thinking.

Another point to consider is whether the measuring instruments also generalize to other populations, other points in time, etc. – a subject I shall take up in the next chapter.

Example 2
Does mental condition influence the immune system?

Using Danish data, Thomsen et al. (2004) mapped the relationships between rumination (negative recurrent thoughts), immune parameters and health care utilization for two samples, one of young and one of elderly people. I will use only the elderly sample. The data (Thomsen1) can be found on the book's website.

The model that seems to be the basis for their analysis is shown in Figure 2.

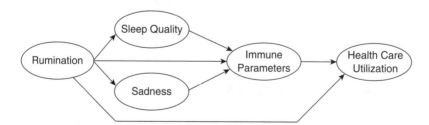

Figure 2   Example 2: the structural model

Rumination was measured using the rehearsal sub-scale from the *Emotional Control Questionnaire version 2* (Roger & Narajian, 1989), sadness by the depression-dejection sub-scale from the short version of the *Profile of Moods Scale* (McNair, Lorr, & Dopplemann, 1981; Shacham, 1983) and sleep quality by the one item on subjective sleep quality from the *Pittsburgh Sleep Quality Index* (Buysse, Reynolds, Monk, Berman, & Kupfer, 1989). The items used are shown in Table 4.

Table 4 Example 2: scales used for measuring the psychological constructs

Rumination	
ecq 1	I remember things that upset me or make me angry for a long time afterwards
ecq 2	I generally don't bear a grudge – when something is over, it's over, and I don't think about it again
ecq 3	I get 'worked up' just thinking about things that have upset me in the past
ecq 4	I often find myself thinking over and over about things that have made me angry
ecq 5	I can usually settle things quickly and be friendly again after an argument
ecq 6	If I see or hear about an accident, I find myself thinking about something similar happening to me or to people close to me
ecq 7	I think about ways of getting back on people who have made me angry a long time after the event has happened
ecq 8	I never forget people making me angry or upset, even about small things
ecq 9	I find it hard to get thoughts about things that have upset me out of my mind
ecq 10	I often daydream about situations where I'm getting my own back on people
ecq 11	If I see something that frightens or upsets me, the image of it stays in my mind for a long time afterwards
ecq 12	Thinking about upsetting things just seems to keep them going, so I try to put them out of my mind
ecq 13	If I lose out on something, I get over it quickly
ecq 14	If I have to confront someone, I try not to think too much about it beforehand
Sadness	(5-point scale, scaled 'not at all' to 'extremely')
poms4d	Unhappy
poms8d	Sad
poms12d	Blue
poms14d	Hopeless
poms20d	Discouraged
poms23d	Miserable
poms28d	Helpless
poms33d	Worthless
Subjective sleep Quality: psqik1	During the past month, how would you rate your sleep quality overall (scaled 0 – 4, the smaller, the better)?

Looking at the items in Table 4, it is noticeable that items ecq 7, ecq 8, ecq 9 and ecq 10 are very similar, so I would expect them to correlate more than due to their common factor ruminations. Furthermore, they are placed together, which could strengthen the correlations. This is not the only example of similar items being placed together. I really hope that the researchers randomized the order of items in the questionnaire they used!

The following immune parameters were measured: number of leukocytes, number of lymphocytes, number of CD19$^+$ lymphocytes and PHA-stimulated T-cell proliferation. Data on health care utilization were extracted from the country's central register where the following two variables were used: number of personal consultations with GP during follow-up period and number of telephone consultations during the same period. In the following analysis both these variables are divided by five in order to put their variances on a level with the other manifest variables (cf. the comments in Section 4.5).

Thomsen et al. analyzed the various effects on immune parameters and on health care utilization in two separate sets of stepwise regressions, one with immune parameters as dependent variables and one with health care utilization as a dependent variable.

I will reanalyze their data using SEM, taking as my point of departure the model sketched in Figure 2.

There are a rather large number of missing values in the data, which means that only two of the four immune parameters will be used. Furthermore, I will use only respondents who have no missing values on any measurement.

This limits the sample to 247 respondents and is of course not the most efficient use of the data. However, this choice is taken for pedagogical reasons, which should become clear when you read Chapter 9 on the 'missing value problem'.

As a first step, I will analyze the model as a confirmatory factor model as shown in Figure 3.

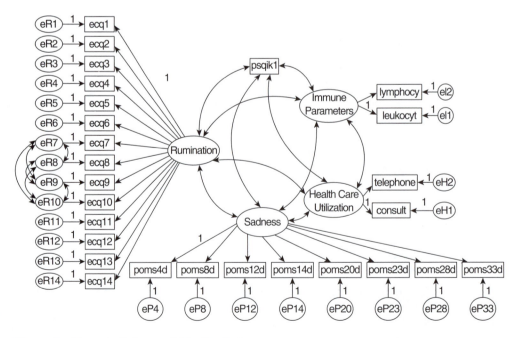

Figure 3   Example 2: the model for the first run

Figure 4   Example 2: specifying output for the first run

As you can see, the one item that measures sleep quality has been included in the model as a 'factor'.

When you bring in your data using the 'List variables in dataset' tool ▦ or by choosing 'View/Variables in Dataset', remember to choose the 'elder' sample.

If you choose output as shown in Figure 4, you will obtain the results given in Table 5.

As this is a new area in which I have no experience, I do not expect my first model to fit very well. That is why I have chosen a rather large threshold for the modification indices.

Table 5   Example 2: output of the first run (confirmatory factor analysis)

```
Chi-square = 752.935
Degrees of freedom = 309
Probability level = .000
```

Regression Weights: (Group number 1 - Default model)

			Estimate	S.E.	C.R.	P	Label
ecq14	<---	Rumination	-.020	.088	-.223	.823	
ecq13	<---	Rumination	.366	.096	3.802	***	
ecq12	<---	Rumination	.129	.093	1.384	.166	
ecq11	<---	Rumination	.607	.076	8.038	***	

(Continued)

(Continued)

			Estimate	S.E.	C.R.	P	Label
ecq10	<---	Rumination	.193	.035	5.448	***	
ecq9	<---	Rumination	.874	.079	11.005	***	
ecq8	<---	Rumination	.529	.069	7.699	***	
ecq7	<---	Rumination	.364	.051	7.084	***	
ecq6	<---	Rumination	.501	.086	5.857	***	
ecq5	<---	Rumination	.404	.088	4.582	***	
ecq4	<---	Rumination	.805	.071	11.322	***	
ecq3	<---	Rumination	.820	.075	10.884	***	
ecq2	<---	Rumination	.334	.099	3.363	***	
ecq1	<---	Rumination	1.000				
poms33d	<---	Sadness	.596	.065	9.168	***	
poms28d	<---	Sadness	.529	.058	9.088	***	
poms23d	<---	Sadness	.597	.057	10.456	***	
poms20d	<---	Sadness	.941	.069	13.692	***	
poms14d	<---	Sadness	.655	.070	9.300	***	
poms12d	<---	Sadness	.859	.066	13.015	***	
poms8d	<---	Sadness	.933	.068	13.709	***	
poms4d	<---	Sadness	1.000				
lymphocy	<---	Immunity	.329	.104	3.170	.002	
leukocyt	<---	Immunity	1.000				
telephone	<---	Health	1.684	.539	3.122	.002	
consult	<---	Health	1.000				

Covariances: (Group number 1 - Default model)

			Estimate	S.E.	C.R.	P	Label
Rumination	<-->	psqik1	.158	.044	3.618	***	
Rumination	<-->	Sadness	.212	.041	5.148	***	
Rumination	<-->	Immunity	.284	.102	2.794	.005	
Rumination	<-->	Health	.106	.046	2.277	.023	
Immunity	<-->	psqik1	.165	.077	2.140	.032	
Immunity	<-->	Health	.047	.064	.732	.464	
Sadness	<-->	Immunity	-.007	.063	-.107	.915	
Health	<-->	psqik1	.108	.041	2.620	.009	
Sadness	<-->	Health	.096	.036	2.626	.009	
Sadness	<-->	psqik1	.188	.032	5.824	***	
eR8	<-->	eR7	.028	.027	1.050	.294	
eR9	<-->	eR7	-.122	.028	-4.408	***	
eR10	<-->	eR7	.093	.016	5.824	***	
eR9	<-->	eR8	.123	.038	3.247	.001	
eR10	<-->	eR8	.046	.020	2.347	.019	
eR10	<-->	eR9	-.014	.019	-.727	.467	

Squared Multiple Correlations: (Group number 1 - Default model)

	Estimate
consult	.263
telephone	.637
leukocyt	.434
lymphocy	.392
poms4d	.663
poms8d	.624
poms12d	.576
poms14d	.333
poms20d	.622
poms23d	.406
poms28d	.320
poms33d	.325
ecq1	.572
ecq2	.052
ecq3	.512
ecq4	.553
ecq5	.096
ecq6	.156
ecq7	.237
ecq8	.278
ecq9	.540
ecq10	.142
ecq11	.288
ecq12	.009
ecq13	.067
ecq14	.000

Modification Indices (Group number 1 - Default model)

Covariances: (Group number 1 - Default model)

			M.I.	Par Change
eP28	<-->	eP14	21.435	.078
eP33	<-->	eP14	31.244	.105
eR5	<-->	eR2	50.601	.567
eR12	<-->	eR5	35.219	.450
eR13	<-->	eR2	23.254	.424
eR13	<-->	eR5	55.915	.574
eR13	<-->	eR12	75.312	.727
eR14	<-->	eR12	26.008	.398
eR14	<-->	eR13	25.720	.401

The fit could be better (CFI = 0.797, RMSEA = 0.076, LO 90 = 0.070, HI 90 = 0.083, PCLOSE = 0.000).

A glance at the squared multiple correlations shows that some of the indicators have very small reliabilities – and what is more eye-catching, the five items with the lowest reliabilities (items ecq2, ecq5, ecq12, ecq13 and ecq14) are exactly the five items that are worded in the opposite direction to the rest.

A look at the modification indices shows quite a few suggestions for letting items ecq2, ecq5, ecq12, ecq13 and ecq14 inter-correlate. This is no surprise, since the inter-correlations signal that these items have something in common that they do not share with the other items – and we know what it is: they are oppositely worded.

A preliminary component analysis of the ecq scale would have shown the scale to be two dimensional, the two dimensions being made up of items worded positively and negatively respectively (and an item analysis on the complete scale would have eliminated the dimension with fewest items).

A glance at the wording of the items poms14d and poms33d shows that introduction of the correlation

$$eP14<-->eP33$$

is defendable. Putting in the correlations results in the output in Table 6. The new model is shown in Figure 5.

Table 6 Example 2: output for second run

```
Minimum was achieved
Chi-square = 454.780
Degrees of freedom = 298
Probability level = .000
```

Regression Weights: (Group number 1 - Default model)

			Estimate	S.E.	C.R.	P	Label
ecq14	<---	Rumination	-.067	.088	-.767	.443	
ecq13	<---	Rumination	.307	.096	3.183	.001	
ecq12	<---	Rumination	.060	.093	.644	.520	
ecq11	<---	Rumination	.597	.075	7.918	***	
ecq10	<---	Rumination	.190	.035	5.355	***	
ecq9	<---	Rumination	.874	.079	11.026	***	
ecq8	<---	Rumination	.527	.069	7.674	***	
ecq7	<---	Rumination	.369	.051	7.183	***	
ecq6	<---	Rumination	.513	.085	6.001	***	
ecq5	<---	Rumination	.349	.088	3.956	***	
ecq4	<---	Rumination	.814	.071	11.488	***	
ecq3	<---	Rumination	.823	.075	10.960	***	
ecq2	<---	Rumination	.277	.099	2.780	.005	
ecq1	<---	Rumination	1.000				
poms33d	<---	Sadness	.562	.065	8.678	***	

			Estimate	S.E.	C.R.	P	Label
poms28d	<---	Sadness	.512	.058	8.864	***	
poms23d	<---	Sadness	.594	.056	10.544	***	
poms20d	<---	Sadness	.933	.068	13.814	***	
poms14d	<---	Sadness	.618	.070	8.807	***	
poms12d	<---	Sadness	.858	.065	13.252	***	
poms8d	<---	Sadness	.932	.067	13.960	***	
poms4d	<---	Sadness	1.000				
lymphocy	<---	Immunity	.328	.104	3.154	.002	
leukocyt	<---	Immunity	1.000				
telephone	<---	Health	1.720	.557	3.087	.002	
consult	<---	Health	1.000				

Covariances: (Group number 1 - Default model)

			Estimate	S.E.	C.R.	P	Label
Rumination	<-->	psqik1	.151	.043	3.471	***	
Rumination	<-->	Sadness	.212	.041	5.124	***	
Rumination	<-->	Immunity	.280	.101	2.763	.006	
Rumination	<-->	Health	.106	.046	2.280	.023	
Immunity	<-->	psqik1	.165	.077	2.141	.032	
Immunity	<-->	Health	.047	.063	.737	.461	
Sadness	<-->	Immunity	-.007	.063	-.117	.907	
Health	<-->	psqik1	.106	.041	2.582	.010	
Sadness	<-->	Health	.094	.036	2.587	.010	
Sadness	<-->	psqik1	.189	.033	5.799	***	
eR5	<-->	eR2	.582	.090	6.495	***	
eR12	<-->	eR2	.390	.091	4.270	***	
eR13	<-->	eR2	.444	.094	4.717	***	
eR14	<-->	eR2	.336	.085	3.937	***	
eR12	<-->	eR5	.465	.083	5.636	***	
eR13	<-->	eR5	.590	.087	6.754	***	
eR14	<-->	eR5	.246	.074	3.321	***	
eR13	<-->	eR12	.740	.097	7.617	***	
eR14	<-->	eR12	.399	.082	4.848	***	
eR14	<-->	eR13	.407	.084	4.854	***	
eR8	<-->	eR7	.027	.027	1.000	.317	
eR9	<-->	eR7	-.125	.028	-4.534	***	
eR10	<-->	eR7	.093	.016	5.836	***	
eR9	<-->	eR8	.124	.038	3.259	.001	
eR10	<-->	eR8	.047	.020	2.409	.016	
eR10	<-->	eR9	-.012	.020	-.633	.527	
eP33	<-->	eP14	.108	.021	5.110	***	

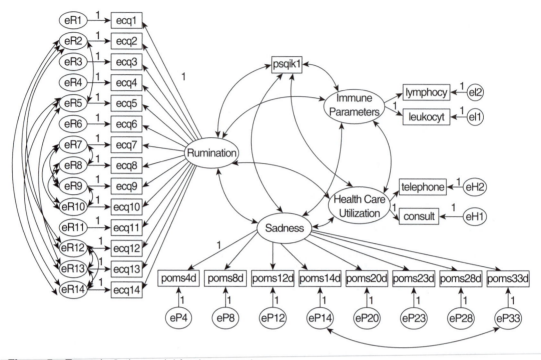

Figure 5 Example 2: the model for the second run

The fit is excellent (CFI = 0.928, RMSEA = 0.046, LO 90 = 0.038, HI 90 = 0.055, PCLOSE = 0.763). I am sure that if I lowered the threshold for modification indices, many suggestions would come up, but there seems to be no reason for 'improving' the model – that would only result in over-fitting and reduce the chances for getting the same result if the analysis was repeated on a comparable sample.

It is now time to move on to the analysis of the hypothesized causal model. The model we are going to analyze is shown in Figure 6 (cf. Figure 2).

Now, however, I must decide how to handle the sleep quality factor. The 'one-indicator problem' is most often dealt with by fixing the error variance at 0.00. In most cases it is of course unrealistic to assume that measurement error is wholly absent, so I will deal with the problem in another way.

The average reliability of the items in the two ecq sub-scales is about 0.40 and the average reliability of the poms items is about 0.50. As the psqik1 question seems rather unproblematic, I will assume that the reliability of psqik1 is 0.50, and consequently fix the error variance of psqik1 at 50% of the total variance of psqik1 (cf. Equation (2.3b)).

Double-click the error term eSl, and when the 'Object Properties' menu appears, click the 'Parameters' tab and set the variance at 0.262 as shown in Figure 7. The result of this is that the number 0.262 is shown next to the eSl error term in Figure 6.

Unfortunately I got an error message:

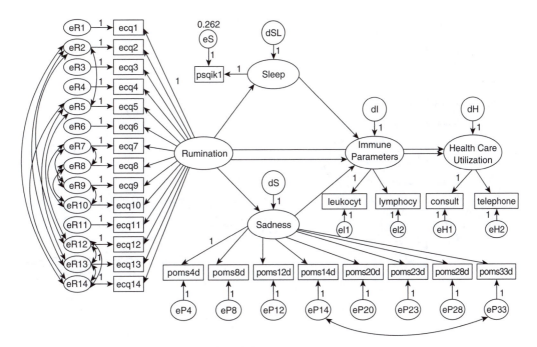

Figure 6   Example 2: the first 'causal' model

Figure 7   Example 2: fixing the variance of an error variable

The following variances are negative. (Group number 1 –
                    Default model)

	eH2
	-1.783

Notes for Group/Model (Group number 1 – Default model)
               This solution is not admissible.

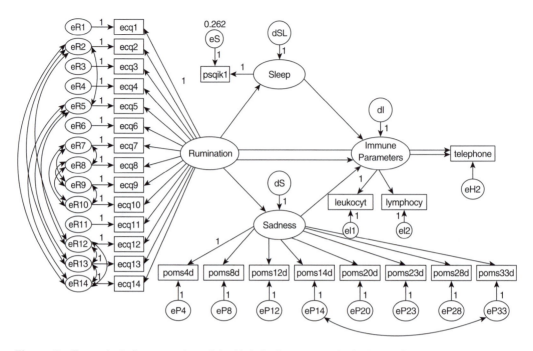

Figure 8   Example 2: first causal model with 'telephone consultation' as only
health care variable

How could that be? A possible explanation is that the explanatory variables predict
health care use with varying success, depending on whether consultations are face-to-
face or by telephone.

It could be argued that perhaps rumination, sleeping problems and the like are problems that could be cleared up without taking the trouble of going to the doctor. If I am
right, the model should have greater success in predicting the number of telephone
consultations than personal consultations.

From this point of view, the two indicators of health care utilization are *formative*
(cf. Section 6.5). To avoid complications from working with a model with formative
indicators, I choose a more simple procedure: to do two separate analyses. Or (nearer
to the truth) I will proceed with the analysis with 'telephone consultation' as the only
health care variable, and leave the analysis of personal consultation to you as an
exercise.

My model is shown in Figure 8 and output in Table 7.

Table 7   Example 2: output for first causal model with 'telephone consultation' as only
health care variable

```
Chi-square = 473.426
Degrees of freedom = 277
Probability level = .000
```

Regression Weights: (Group number 1 - Default model)

			Estimate	S.E.	C.R.	P	Label
Sadness	<---	Rumination	.318	.052	6.066	***	
Sleep	<---	Rumination	.242	.058	4.146	***	
Immunity	<---	Sleep	.680	.325	2.094	.036	
Immunity	<---	Sadness	-.485	.206	-2.359	.018	
Immunity	<---	Rumination	.390	.173	2.249	.025	
ecq14	<---	Rumination	-.066	.087	-.758	.448	
ecq13	<---	Rumination	.313	.096	3.256	.001	
ecq12	<---	Rumination	.065	.093	.700	.484	
ecq11	<---	Rumination	.602	.075	8.010	***	
ecq10	<---	Rumination	.190	.035	5.374	***	
ecq9	<---	Rumination	.875	.079	11.126	***	
ecq8	<---	Rumination	.516	.068	7.552	***	
ecq7	<---	Rumination	.362	.051	7.076	***	
ecq6	<---	Rumination	.505	.085	5.935	***	
ecq5	<---	Rumination	.356	.088	4.040	***	
ecq4	<---	Rumination	.801	.071	11.352	***	
ecq3	<---	Rumination	.821	.075	10.993	***	
ecq2	<---	Rumination	.281	.099	2.835	.005	
ecq1	<---	Rumination	1.000				
poms33d	<---	Sadness	.558	.065	8.648	***	
poms28d	<---	Sadness	.501	.058	8.684	***	
poms23d	<---	Sadness	.592	.056	10.563	***	
poms20d	<---	Sadness	.919	.067	13.618	***	
poms14d	<---	Sadness	.608	.070	8.684	***	
poms12d	<---	Sadness	.865	.064	13.495	***	
poms8d	<---	Sadness	.933	.066	14.079	***	
poms4d	<---	Sadness	1.000				
psqik1	<---	Sleep	1.000				
leukocyt	<---	Immunity	1.000				
lymphocy	<---	Immunity	.335	.096	3.491	***	
telephone	<---	Rumination	.327	.094	3.494	***	
telephone	<---	Immunity	-.009	.076	-.112	.911	

Covariances: (Group number 1 - Default model)

			Estimate	S.E.	C.R.	P	Label
eR5	<-->	eR2	.580	.089	6.481	***	
eR12	<-->	eR2	.389	.091	4.260	***	
eR13	<-->	eR2	.441	.094	4.700	***	
eR14	<-->	eR2	.336	.085	3.940	***	
eR12	<-->	eR5	.464	.082	5.626	***	
eR13	<-->	eR5	.587	.087	6.737	***	
eR14	<-->	eR5	.246	.074	3.327	***	
eR13	<-->	eR12	.738	.097	7.612	***	
eR14	<-->	eR12	.399	.082	4.851	***	
eR14	<-->	eR13	.407	.084	4.860	***	

(Continued)

(Continued)

			Estimate	S.E.	C.R.	P	Label
eR8	<-->	eR7	.032	.027	1.167	.243	
eR9	<-->	eR7	-.122	.028	-4.439	***	
eR10	<-->	eR7	.094	.016	5.867	***	
eR9	<-->	eR8	.128	.038	3.380	***	
eR10	<-->	eR8	.048	.020	2.460	.014	
eR10	<-->	eR9	-.013	.019	-.667	.505	
eP33	<-->	eP14	.110	.021	5.162	***	

Modification Indices (Group number 1 - Default model)

Covariances: (Group number 1 - Default model)

			M.I.	Par Change
dS	<-->	dSL	27.751	.135
dt	<-->	dSL	6.090	.115
dt	<-->	dS	5.255	.090
eSl	<-->	dS	27.832	.135
eSl	<-->	dt	6.075	.115
eP4	<-->	dt	9.485	.096
eR12	<-->	eP20	5.574	-.067
eR13	<-->	eP28	6.858	-.071
eR13	<-->	eP33	4.135	.056
eR14	<-->	eR6	7.994	-.176

Regression Weights: (Group number 1 - Default model)

			M.I.	Par Change
Sleep	<---	Sadness	21.097	.354
Sadness	<---	Sleep	19.738	.435
telephone	<---	Sleep	4.330	.369
telephone	<---	psqik1	5.680	.222
telephone	<---	poms4d	9.650	.287
telephone	<---	ecq8	4.845	-.176
psqik1	<---	Sadness	21.149	.355
psqik1	<---	telephone	5.693	.097
psqik1	<---	poms4d	12.968	.218
psqik1	<---	poms8d	13.958	.235
psqik1	<---	poms14d	12.565	.232

The model is not too bad, but could be better (CFI = 0.909, RMSEA = 0.054, LO 90 = 0.045, HI 90 = 0.062, PCLOSE = 0.226). Sadness and low sleeping quality go together, but it is obvious that this could be due to causes other than rumination. Introducing the covariance between dS and dSl as suggested by the output would be expected to reduce χ^2 by 27.751. I will leave it to the experts to consider the suggestions about a causal link between 'Sleep quality' and 'Sadness'.

For this run I also set the threshold for modification indices at its default value, i.e. 4.

As mentioned earlier, the modification indices (and the implied χ^2-difference tests) are marginal. They say nothing about what would happen if several parameters were added at the same time. For example, there are several suggestions on connections between psiq1 and the poms items, but most of them would probably disappear if you introduced a covariance between dS and dSl.

However, the suggestion in the output

```
         telephone   <---   Sleep
```

also deserves some consideration.

So, I have two options:

1. To add parameters one by one.
2. To add several parameters at the same time and use a χ^2-difference test.

I choose the first option, and put in the covariance between dS and dSl. When I run that model, the output comes up with the following suggestions:

```
                            M.I.   Par Change
     telephone  <---   Sleep    6.854         .437
     telephone  <---   Sadness  4.808         .261
```

I included the first suggestion in the final model, which is shown in Figure 9. The second suggestion above did not show up in the final output.

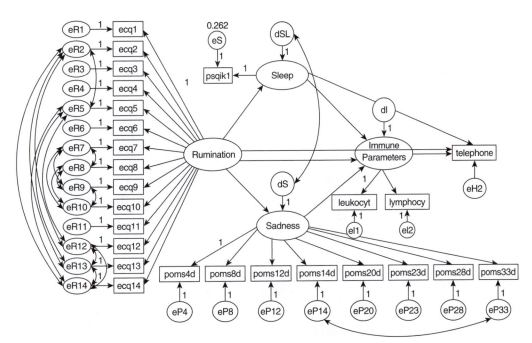

Figure 9   Example 2: the final model

Modification indices offered lots of suggestions on introducing parameters that would increase fit, but none of them could be substantiated.

Table 8   Example 2: output, final model

```
Chi-square = 433.375
Degrees of freedom = 275
Probability level = .000
```

Regression Weights: (Group number 1 - Default model)

			Estimate	S.E.	C.R.	P	Label
Sadness	<---	Rumination	.302	.052	5.761	***	
Sleep	<---	Rumination	.214	.059	3.653	***	
Immunity	<---	Sleep	.943	.441	2.140	.032	
Immunity	<---	Sadness	-.776	.315	-2.466	.014	
Immunity	<---	Rumination	.427	.161	2.656	.008	
ecq14	<---	Rumination	-.068	.088	-.781	.435	
ecq13	<---	Rumination	.308	.096	3.191	.001	
ecq12	<---	Rumination	.060	.093	.643	.520	
ecq11	<---	Rumination	.599	.075	7.935	***	
ecq10	<---	Rumination	.190	.035	5.343	***	
ecq9	<---	Rumination	.874	.079	11.031	***	
ecq8	<---	Rumination	.526	.069	7.660	***	
ecq7	<---	Rumination	.368	.051	7.174	***	
ecq6	<---	Rumination	.512	.085	5.999	***	
ecq5	<---	Rumination	.349	.088	3.951	***	
ecq4	<---	Rumination	.814	.071	11.477	***	
ecq3	<---	Rumination	.824	.075	10.970	***	
ecq2	<---	Rumination	.276	.099	2.770	.006	
ecq1	<---	Rumination	1.000				
poms33d	<---	Sadness	.563	.065	8.676	***	
poms28d	<---	Sadness	.513	.058	8.878	***	
poms23d	<---	Sadness	.594	.056	10.530	***	
poms20d	<---	Sadness	.934	.068	13.810	***	
poms14d	<---	Sadness	.618	.070	8.797	***	
poms12d	<---	Sadness	.858	.065	13.242	***	
poms8d	<---	Sadness	.932	.067	13.946	***	
poms4d	<---	Sadness	1.000				
psqik1	<---	Sleep	1.000				
leukocyt	<---	Immunity	1.000				
lymphocy	<---	Immunity	.336	.106	3.172	.002	
telephone	<---	Rumination	.195	.102	1.910	.056	
telephone	<---	Immunity	-.052	.081	-.642	.521	
telephone	<---	Sleep	.590	.197	2.998	.003	

Covariances: (Group number 1 - Default model)

			Estimate	S.E.	C.R.	P	Label
dS	<-->	dSL	.144	.029	5.059	***	
eR5	<-->	eR2	.583	.090	6.498	***	
eR12	<-->	eR2	.390	.091	4.270	***	
eR13	<-->	eR2	.444	.094	4.718	***	
eR14	<-->	eR2	.336	.085	3.939	***	
eR12	<-->	eR5	.465	.083	5.636	***	
eR13	<-->	eR5	.590	.087	6.754	***	
eR14	<-->	eR5	.246	.074	3.325	***	
eR13	<-->	eR12	.740	.097	7.617	***	
eR14	<-->	eR12	.399	.082	4.849	***	
eR14	<-->	eR13	.407	.084	4.858	***	
eR8	<-->	eR7	.027	.027	1.017	.309	
eR9	<-->	eR7	-.125	.028	-4.525	***	
eR10	<-->	eR7	.094	.016	5.844	***	
eR9	<-->	eR8	.124	.038	3.275	.001	
eR10	<-->	eR8	.048	.020	2.423	.015	
eR10	<-->	eR9	-.012	.020	-.619	.536	
eP33	<-->	eP14	.108	.021	5.111	***	

The fit is excellent (CFI = 0.926, RMSEA = 0.048, LO 90 = 0.040, HI 90 = 0.057, PCLOSE = 0.612), but as mentioned several times, it takes more to accept a model: it must also be substantively meaningful.

In short, the model says that rumination raises the defense system of your body, both through a direct effect and by reducing sleep quality and causing depression. Also rumination has a direct effect on health care utilization, whereas the rise in the immune parameters does not seem to have an effect on health care utilization.

However, rumination could have a larger influence on the immune parameters than seen at first sight. For example, rumination has indirect effects on the immune parameters, both via sleep quality and via sadness – and, furthermore, we can measure that effect.

The effect of rumination on sleep quality is measured by the regression weight 0.214 and the effect of sleep quality on immunity is measured by the regression weight 0.943. So, from the rumination 'carried' to sleep quality (0.214) a share of 0.943, i.e. 0.214 × 0.943 = 0.202, is 'carried' through to immunity.

In the same way the indirect effect of rumination on immunity via sadness can be calculated as $0.302 \times (-0.776) = -0.234$. So the indirect effect of rumination on immunity is 0.202 −0.234 =−0.032, which, added to the direct effect (0.427), gives a total effect of 0.395.

If you check 'Indirect, direct & total effects' in 'Analysis Properties/Output' or put in the statement 'Sem.TotalEffects' if using the programming interface, AMOS will calculate direct, indirect and total effects for all regression functions. As you may have guessed, this takes up a lot of space in the output, and thus for space considerations here I show only a small part of the output in Table 9.

Table 9 Example 2: total, direct and indirect effects

Total Effects (Group number 1 - Default model)

	Rumination	Sleep	Sadness	Immunity
Sleep	.214	.000	.000	.000
Sadness	.302	.000	.000	.000
Immunity	.395	.943	-.776	.000
telephone	.300	.541	.040	-.052

Direct Effects (Group number 1 - Default model)

	Rumination	Sleep	Sadness	Immunity
Sleep	.214	.000	.000	.000
Sadness	.302	.000	.000	.000
Immunity	.427	.943	-.776	.000
telephone	.195	.590	.000	-.052

Indirect Effects (Group number 1 - Default model)

	Rumination	Sleep	Sadness	Immunity
Sleep	.000	.000	.000	.000
Sadness	.000	.000	.000	.000
Immunity	-.032	.000	.000	.000
telephone	.106	-.049	.040	.000

From the table you can see for example that even if sadness does not have a direct effect on telephone, it could have an indirect effect.

However, two things about AMOS must be kept in mind:

1. AMOS does not calculate standard errors on the indirect and total effects, but these can be estimated by bootstrapping – a subject to be discussed in Chapter 9.
2. AMOS does not calculate separate indirect effects via each of the mediating factors – they must be calculated by hand if you need them.

I will leave it to the specialists to defend the direction of the arrows. However, if an amateur in the field is allowed to speculate, then is it not possible that depression – as measured by 'sadness' – influences rumination and not the other way round?

A last word of warning. Even if modifications to the model were guided by substantive thinking, I would feel safer if the same model could be shown to fit comparable data. If it is not possible to take another sample from the same population you could split your sample into two or more parts, and cross-validate between sub-samples. But remember: you still have to assume that your original sample is representative of the population!

3 Time Series Models

Models where the measurements are taken at various points in time have at least two characteristics that differentiate them from models based on cross-sectional data:

1. The problem of direction as far as causal influences are concerned is less problematic because future events cannot affect the present.
2. Such models will often include correlations among error terms in measurement models across latent variables describing the same concept at different points in time (cf. Example 6.1).

Example 3 (continued from Example 5.2)
Examining the stability of alienation

Recall that the model I proposed in Figure 5.2 had a very bad fit. That model was a path model; it had only manifest variables. However, the structure of the model in Figure 5.2 is very similar to the model in Figure 6.3. In both cases the same variables are measured at two points in time. A reformulation of the model in Figure 5.2 incorporating latent variables as in the model in Figure 6.3 is shown in Figure 10a.

A quick look will show that the model is not identified. It has 11 parameters to be estimated – three regression weights, two covariances and six variances – but we have only 10 data points. Consequently the model must be simplified. If we assume that the

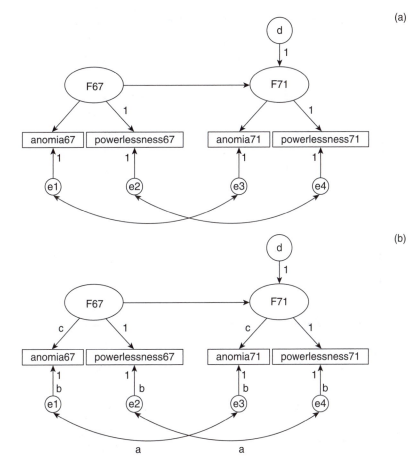

Figure 10   Example 3: the model

two covariances are of the same magnitude, and that the same apply to the four ε-variances and the two 'free' regression weights (if the regression weights are not the same in the two years, it is meaningless to compare F67 and F71), we have four degrees of freedom left over for testing.

You impose these restrictions in the usual way by double-clicking the parameters in question and filling in the letters a, b and c in the 'parameter' box in the 'Object Properties' pop-up window (see e.g. Figure 6.5b). Your model will change to the one shown in Figure 10b.

If you check the output boxes as shown in Figure 11, you will get the output given in Table 10.

Figure 11 Example 3: choosing the output

As is obvious from the standardized residual covariance matrix, the fit is extremely good, and the various fit indices (not shown) confirm this. With a P-value of 0.834 you would usually look for possibilities of simplifying the model by introducing more parameter restrictions. But that is not possible here. It seems impossible to find a better model.

Table 10   Example 3: output

```
Minimum was achieved
Chi-square = 1.458
Degrees of freedom = 4
Probability level = .834
```

Regression Weights: (Group number 1 - Default model)

			Estimate	S.E.	C.R.	P	Label
F71	<---	F67	.714	.035	20.175	***	
powerlessness67	<---	F67	1.000				
anomia67	<---	F67	1.188	.033	35.952	***	c
powerlessness71	<---	F71	1.000				
anomia71	<---	F71	1.188	.033	35.952	***	c

Standardized Regression Weights: (Group number 1 - Default model)

			Estimate
F71	<---	F67	.685
powerlessness67	<---	F67	.786
anomia67	<---	F67	.834
powerlessness71	<---	F71	.798
anomia71	<---	F71	.844

Covariances: (Group number 1 - Default model)

			Estimate	S.E.	C.R.	P	Label
e1	<-->	e3	.905	.122	7.448	***	a
e2	<-->	e4	.905	.122	7.448	***	a

Correlations: (Group number 1 - Default model)

			Estimate
e1	<-->	e3	.252
e2	<-->	e4	.252

Variances: (Group number 1 - Default model)

	Estimate	S.E.	C.R.	P	Label
F67	5.823	.392	14.867	***	
d	3.355	.270	12.421	***	
e2	3.596	.122	29.589	***	b
e1	3.596	.122	29.589	***	b
e4	3.596	.122	29.589	***	b
e3	3.596	.122	29.589	***	b

(Continued)

(Continued)

Residual Covariances (Group number 1 - Default model)

	anomia71	powerlessness71	anomia67	powerlessness67
anomia71	.001			
powerlessness71	-.024	.056		
anomia67	.040	-.161	.009	
powerlessness67	.147	-.040	.022	-.066

Standardized Residual Covariances (Group number 1 - Default model)

	anomia71	powerlessness71	anomia67	powerlessness67
anomia71	.001			
powerlessness71	-.055	.122		
anomia67	.088	-.412	.016	
powerlessness67	.376	-.113	.054	-.150

In this chapter you met the following concepts:

- the two-step rule
- the two- and four-step strategy

- direct, indirect and total effects

You also learned the following AMOS statement:

- Sem.TotalEffects

Questions

1. State the consequences of measurement error in the dependent and independent variables in (traditional) regression analysis.

2. Comment on the various strategies for analyzing structural (causal) models.

3. Go through the various outputs in Example 2 and comment on the changes in the measurement part of the model.

4. Define direct, indirect and total effects, and explain how to calculate (by hand) the latter two.

5. Discuss the two-factor problem that could emerge from oppositely worded items. Can you suggest other ways to cope with it than the one used in the example?

References

Buysse, D. J., Reynolds, C. F., Monk, T. H., Berman, S. R., & Kupfer, D. J. (1989). The Pittsburgh Sleep Quality Index: A new instrument for psychiatric practice and research. *Psychiatry Research, 28*(2), 305–306.

McNair, P. M., Lorr, M., & Dopplemann, L. F. (1981). *POMS Manual* (2nd ed.). San Diego, CA: Educational and Industrial Testing Service.

Mulaik, S. A., & Millsap, R. E. (2000). Doing the four-step right. *Structural Equation Modeling, 7*, 36–73.

Roger, D., & Narajian, R. D. (1989). The construction and validation of a new scale for measuring emotion control. *Personality and Individual Differences, 10*, 845–853.

Shacham, S. (1983). A shortened version of the Profile of Moods Scale. *Journal of Personality Assessment, 47*, 305–306.

Thomsen, D. K., Mehlsen, Y. M., Hokland, M., Viidik, A., Olesen, F., Avlund, K., et al. (2004). Negative thoughts and health: Associations among rumination, immunity and health care utilization in a young and elderly sample. *Psychosomatic Medicine, 66*, 363–371.

Part 3

Advanced Models and Techniques

8

Mean Structures and Multi-group Analysis

We have hitherto analyzed only *relations* among variables, but not been very interested in the *values* of the variables. In this chapter you will learn how to estimate means of latent variables and compare means across groups.

As this necessitates estimation of intercepts in addition to regression weights, the chapter will start with an introduction to the analysis of *mean structures*. Therefore the input covariance matrix must be supplemented by the means of the manifest variables.

It is also time to look at how to estimate SEM in several groups at the same time and how to examine the degree to which models are equivalent across groups. You will learn how to judge the equivalence of a model across several samples through a systematic sequence of tests.

Then you will move on to a larger model involving only manifest variables, although it has a complication: namely, two-way causation.

1 Identifying and Estimating Mean Structures

Until now we have only estimated covariance structures. We were only interested in *relations* between variables – be they manifest or latent – but not in the *values* of the variables.

As long as we are working only with manifest variables, hypotheses about means can be tested by traditional statistical techniques such as *t*-test, analysis of variance, multivariate analysis of variance and the like, but these techniques cannot treat means of *latent* variables.

Now, let us look at the simple measurement model

$$X = \lambda_0 + \lambda_1 F + \varepsilon \tag{1a}$$

Taking the expectation we get

$$\mu_X = \lambda_0 + \lambda_1 \mu_F \tag{1b}$$

It is this decomposition of the means of dependent variables that has given rise to the name *analysis of mean structures*. As is evident from (1b), this necessitates the estimation of regression intercepts and consequently the input sample covariance matrix has to be supplemented by the sample means.

In one-group analysis means and intercepts are in most cases of no interest. Nevertheless I will introduce mean structure analysis by estimating the intercept in the regression model from Example 4.1.

Example 1 (continued from Example 4.1)
Mapping European consumers' willingness to buy genetically modified food: estimating means and intercepts

Once again you will have to access the companion website and download the data 'Bredahl.xls/Manifest' (if it is not already on your computer). The analysis is done as in Example 4.1. The only difference is that when you open the dialog box shown in Figure 4.8a, check 'Estimate means and intercepts'.

The output is the same as the output given in Table 4.1, but with the addition of the estimates given in Table 1.

Table 1 Example 1: additional output[C8Q1]

Means: (Group number 1 - Default model)

	Estimate	S.E.	C.R.	P	Label
Technology	25.002	.252	99.106	***	
Nature	32.357	.276	117.118	***	
Neophobia	18.985	.303	62.562	***	
Alienation	16.578	.161	103.253	***	

Intercepts: (Group number 1 - Default model)

	Estimate	S.E.	C.R.	P	Label
Risk	7.289	2.388	3.052	.002	

A VB program for estimation of the regression model without intercept (from Figure 4.11) is shown in panel (a) in Table 2, and a program for estimating the same model including an intercept term is shown in panel (b). Both cases are based on the data from Figure 4.3, but this time the means in the input are used.

Table 2 Example 1: program for regression analysis (a) without and (b) with intercept

```
Sub Main()                                              (a)
    Dim sem As New AmosEngine
    Try
        Sem.Title ("Example 4.1")
        'Traditional regression analysis using data from Bredahl (2001)
        Sem.TextOutput
        Sem.Standardized
        Sem.Smc

        Sem.BeginGroup    ("C:\Users\Sony\Documents\Amos3\Chap4\Bredahl.
        xls","Manifest")
```

```
      Sem.GroupName ("Germany")
        Sem.AStructure ("Risk = Tech + Nature + Neophobia + Alienation + (1)d")
        Sem.FitModel
    Finally
        Sem.Dispose
    End Try
End Sub


Sub Main()                                                          (b)
    Dim sem As New AmosEngine
    Try
        Sem.Title ("Example 8.1")
        'Regression with intercept. Data from Bredahl (2001)
        Sem.TextOutput
        Sem.Standardized
        Sem.Smc
        Sem.ModelMeansAndIntercepts

        Sem.BeginGroup    ("C:\Users\Sony\Documents\Amos3\Chap4\Bredahl.
        xls","Manifest")
        Sem.AStructure ("Risk  =  ()+Technology  +  Nature  +  Neophobia  +
        Alienation + (1)d")
        Sem.Mean ("Technology")
        Sem.Mean ("Nature")
        Sem.Mean ("Neophobia")
        Sem.Mean ("Alienation")

        Sem.FitModel()
    Finally
        Sem.Dispose()
    End Try
End Sub
```

The program in panel (b) differs from that in panel (a) in two respects:

1. The line Sem.ModelMeansAndIntercepts tells AMOS that it should consider means and intercept parameters in the model.
2. The empty paranthesis in the line Sem.AStructure tells AMOS that the intercept should be freely estimated. If this paranthesis is not there, AMOS will fix the intercept at zero, even if you have ordered AMOS to 'Model Means And Intercepts'.
3. The same goes for the four 'Sem.Mean' statements. If one of these statements is missing, the mean will be fixed at zero.

In Example 4.1 we had 15 'pieces of information' (5 variances and 10 covariances) on which to estimate 15 parameters (4 regression weights, 6 covariances and 5 variances), which left us with zero degrees of freedom. Now, we could add to our input information 5 means, but as the number of parameters to be estimated also grew by 5 (4 means and 1 intercept), we still have zero degrees of freedom and a just-identified model.

As you may have guessed from this example, degrees of freedom are rare goods in mean structure modeling. The problem is that the mean structure and the covariance structure must be identified *separately* – and it is obvious that identification of the mean structure is generally very problematic.

Mean structures in multi-group studies

We easily run out of degrees of freedom when trying to estimate mean structures in single-group studies and the same is the case in multi-group studies. If such a study is done in order to compare means of latent variables across groups, it is not possible to estimate the means in all groups in one go. However, if we fix the means of the latent variables in one group at zero, it is possible to estimate the means in the other groups, and these means will then express the *differences* in means between the various groups and the reference group.

In Examples 2 and 3, you will need the input given in Table 3. The data are also available from the companion website.

Table 3   Input for Examples 2 and 3

France 1994 (F94)

rowtype_	varname_	v10	v65	v23	v27	v45	v42
n		991	991	991	991	991	991
cov	v10	3.547					
cov	v65	1.707	4.038				
cov	v23	1.219	1.131	2.131			
cov	v27	0.149	0.426	0.541	3.837		
cov	v45	0.131	0.362	0.173	1.528	4.561	
cov	v42	0.118	0.072	0.071	1.183	0.959	4.793
mean		2.501	2.996	1.873	3.066	4.358	4.215

France 1998 (F98)

rowtype_	varname_	v10	v65	v23	v27	v45	v42
n		995	995	995	995	995	995
cov	v10	2.751					
cov	v65	1.385	3.430				
cov	v23	1.178	1.195	2.301			
cov	v27	0.498	0.391	0.667	3.485		
cov	v45	0.359	0.348	0.356	1.429	3.932	
cov	v42	0.207	0.241	0.200	1.068	0.661	3.888
mean		2.366	3.039	2.005	3.119	4.378	4.520

UK 1998 (UK98)

rowtype_	varname_	v10	v65	v23	v27	v45	v42
n		1000	1000	1000	1000	1000	1000
cov	v10	3.370					
cov	v65	0.990	3.719				
cov	v23	0.881	1.155	3.368			
cov	v27	0.236	0.204	0.347	3.990		
cov	v45	0.167	-0.067	0.202	1.579	4.435	
cov	v42	-0.061	-0.029	0.154	1.205	0.787	4.988
mean		2.894	3.520	2.413	3.159	3.501	3.872

Example 2
Comparing food-related lifestyle in France in 1994 and 1998

The *Food-Related Lifestyle* (FRL) instrument is a 69-item battery, measuring 23 dimensions in 5 major domains (ways of shopping, cooking methods, quality aspects, consumption situations and buying motives). Since its invention (Brunsø & Grunert, 1995), it has been widely used in several European countries. I use data from Scholderer, Brunsø, Bredahl, and Grunert (2004).

In order to keep things simple I will only use data from the two-factor dimension 'consumption situations', whose items are listed in Table 4.

Table 4   Example 2: items used in the analysis

How are meals spread over the day? (snacks versus meals)

> (v10) I eat before I get hungry, which means that I am never hungry at meal time

> (v65) I eat whenever I feel the slightest bit hungry

> (v23) In our house, nibbling has taken over and replaced set eating hours

How important is eating-out? (social event)

> (v27) Going out for dinner is a regular part of our eating habits

> (v45) We often get together with friends to enjoy an easy-to-cook, casual dinner

> (v42) I do not consider it a luxury to go out with my family to have dinner in a restaurant

We will test the hypothesis that the two-factor means in this dimension have not changed in France from 1994 to 1998.

In order to do so, we must make sure that the measures are comparable, i.e. that the measuring instrument functions in the same way at the two points in time. Otherwise, there is no sense in comparing the factor means (cf. Example 6.1).

So, we must demand that regression weights and regression intercepts are equal across groups – and of course also that the same general two-factor structure exists in both groups. A model along these lines is shown in Figure 1.

As you can see, the parameters have been labeled in accordance with the remarks above:

1. The corresponding regression weights and intercepts in the two models have the same non-numerical label to ensure that the estimates are fixed to have the same values.
2. The means of the errors are fixed at zero in both models.
3. The means of 'Snacks' and 'Social' are fixed at zero in 'France 1994', but freely estimated in 'France 1998'.

The model is similar to the one in Example 6.1, and you should have no problems as far as the drawing is concerned.

When conducting a multi-group study, you start as if it was a single-group analysis. After the drawing work is done, you bring in your data using the 'Data File' tool as described in connection with Figures 4.5 and 4.6 – and remember to select the F94 data from the Scholderer file.

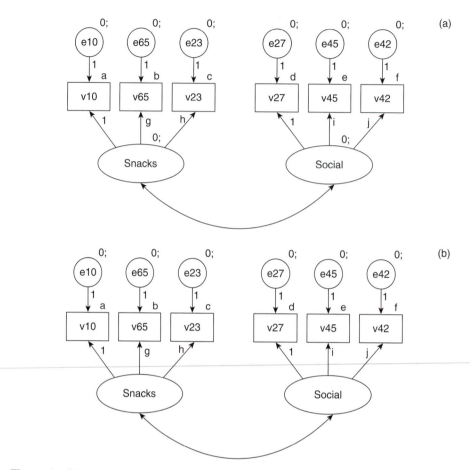

Figure 1   Example 2: (a) model for France 1994; (b) model for France 1998

Figure 2   Example 2: bringing in the second group

Figure 3 Example 8.2: (a) the 'Data Files' window showing the two groups; (b) the model (France 1998)

Then it is time to tell AMOS that there is more than one group.

Select 'Analyze/Manage Groups' and the window in Figure 2a will appear. Now change the name 'Group number 1' to 'France 1994', click 'New' and the window will change to (b). Change the group name to 'France 1998' as shown in panel (c) and close the window.

What remains is to bring in data for 'France 1998'. The procedure is of course the same as hitherto, only now the 'Data Files' window has two groups as shown in Figure 3a. Observe that you can toggle between the two models (France 1994 and France 1998) by clicking the group name in the panel to the left of your drawing.

In panel (b) you can see the result of your efforts. Note that France 1998 is highlighted, so it is this model you are looking at.

The next step is to fix the parameters as mentioned above. As usual, double-click each of the parameters to open up the 'Object Properties' window. When you open it up, 'All groups' is checked. Remember to uncheck it when you fix the factor means in 'France 1994' at zero – see Figure 4.

Figure 4 Example 2: fixing the factor mean of 'France 1994'

Part of the output is given in Table 5. For space considerations regression weights and intercepts are shown for the year 1994 only.

Table 5   Example 2: output

```
Minimum was achieved
Chi-square = 76.490
Degrees of freedom = 24
Probability level = .000
```

Regression Weights: (France 1994 - Unconstrained)

			Estimate	S.E.	C.R.	P	Label
v10	<---	Snacks	1.000				
v65	<---	Snacks	.992	.054	18.491	***	g
v23	<---	Snacks	.800	.043	18.465	***	h
v27	<---	Social	1.000				
v45	<---	Social	.674	.070	9.640	***	i
v42	<---	Social	.514	.056	9.138	***	j

Intercepts: (France 1994 - Unconstrained)

	Estimate	S.E.	C.R.	P	Label
v10	2.413	.053	45.467	***	a
v65	3.012	.055	54.563	***	b
v23	1.931	.043	45.212	***	c
v27	3.045	.061	50.135	***	d
v45	4.335	.055	79.410	***	e
v42	4.358	.052	84.201	***	f

Covariances: (France 1994 - Unconstrained)

			Estimate	S.E.	C.R.	P	Label
Social	<-->	Snacks	.389	.091	4.280	***	

cMeans: (France 1998 - Unconstrained)

	Estimate	S.E.	C.R.	P	Label
Snacks	.014	.066	.209	.834	
Social	.091	.082	1.118	.264	

Covariances: (France 1998 - Unconstrained)

			Estimate	S.E.	C.R.	P	Label
Snacks	<-->	Social	.554	.084	6.577	***	

Model Fit Summary

CMIN

Model	NPAR	CMIN	DF	P	CMIN/DF
Unconstrained	30	76.490	24	.000	3.187

Model	NPAR	CMIN	DF	P	CMIN/DF
Saturated model	54	.000	0		
Independence model	24	1644.099	30	.000	54.803

Baseline Comparisons

Model	NFI Delta1	RFI rho1	IFI Delta2	TLI rho2	CFI
Unconstrained	.953	.942	.968	.959	.967
Saturated model	1.000		1.000		1.000
Independence model	.000	.000	.000	.000	.000

RMSEA

Model	RMSEA	LO 90	HI 90	PCLOSE
Unconstrained	.033	.025	.042	1.000
Independence model	.165	.158	.171	.000

With a χ^2 of 76.490 with 24 degrees of freedom giving a P-value of 0.000, the model seems not to hold. However, such a conclusion is perhaps a little too hasty, because with a sample size of about 2×1000 the dependence of χ^2 on sample size becomes a problem.

Therefore I will (like Scholderer et al.) fall back on RMSEA as my main measure of model fit.

In this case RMSEA is 0.033, and the hypotheses of *configural invariance*, equal regression weights and equal intercepts are accepted.

As the factor means in 1994 are fixed at zero, the 1998 means should estimate the *differences* between the 1994 and the 1998 factor means.

From the output we can see that none of factor means are significantly different across the two measurements.

These, however, are marginal tests. In order to test the hypothesis that the two factor means *taken together* are equal, we must fix the 1994 factor means to be equal to the 1998 means, i.e. fix them both at zero.

As 'France 1994' is already fixed at zero, just open the model for 'France 1994', do the necessary clicks to get the window in Figure 4, and check 'All groups'.

I will not show the output from estimating this model (let us call it model B), but I can assure you that if it were the only model tested, it would be accepted based on the same measures as the model in Table 5 (model A).

You could also ask the question: 'If we accept model A as "true", is the fit of model B then significantly worse?'

You can test this with the χ^2-difference test:

	χ^2	f
Model B	77.728	26
Model A	76.490	24
Difference	1.238	2

This is not significant at any reasonable significance level, and we conclude that the two factor means *together* have not changed from 1994 to 1998.

Another possibility is to use the 'model method' as in Example 6.2. I will illustrate this method in the next example.

The output in Table 5 could also be obtained by using the VB program in Table 6. For programming model B, just exclude the two 'Sem.Mean' statements from the program or just place a single opening quote at the beginning of the two lines.

Table 6   Example 2: the program

```
Sub Main()
  Dim sem As New AmosEngine
  Try
    Sem.Title ("Example 8.4")
    'Data from Scholderer et al. 2004
    Sem.TextOutput
    Sem.Standardized
    Sem.Smc
    Sem.ModelMeansAndIntercepts

    Sem.BeginGroup ("Scholderer.xls", "F94")
    Sem.GroupName ("France")
    Sem.GroupName ("France 1994")
    Sem.AStructure ("v10 =  (a) + (1) snacks + (1) e_10")
    Sem.AStructure ("v65 =  (b) + (g) snacks + (1) e_65")
    Sem.AStructure ("v23 =  (c) + (h) snacks + (1) e_23")
    Sem.AStructure ("v27 =  (d) + (1) social + (1) e_27")
    Sem.AStructure ("v45 =  (e) + (i) social + (1) e_45")
    Sem.AStructure ("v42 =  (f) + (j) social + (1) e_42")

    Sem.BeginGroup ("Scholderer.xls", "F98")
    Sem.GroupName ("France 1998")
    Sem.AStructure ("v10 =  (a) + (1) snacks + (1) e_10")
    Sem.AStructure ("v65 =  (b) + (g) snacks + (1) e_65")
    Sem.AStructure ("v23 =  (c) + (h) snacks + (1) e_23")
    Sem.AStructure ("v27 =  (d) + (1) social + (1) e_27")
    Sem.AStructure ("v45 =  (e) + (i) social + (1) e_45")
    Sem.AStructure ("v42 =  (f) + (j) social + (1) e_42")
    Sem.Mean ("snacks")
    Sem.Mean ("social")

    Sem.FitModel
  Finally
    Sem.Dispose
  End Try
End Sub
```

You should by now be familiar with the way regression weights are constrained, so I will not comment on that. Note that I ask for estimation of the two factor means in 1998, but not in 1994, because – as mentioned in Example 1 – if this is not requested, AMOS assumes zero means.

2   Comparing Covariance Structures Across Groups

You will often want to fit a model to more than one data set, e.g. for comparing two or more populations or for cross-validating within the same population.

Of course you can do separate analyses of the various samples, but there are several advantages in doing a simultaneous analysis in which the parameters in the various samples are estimated in one go.

You can test whether it is reasonable to assume that some or all parameters in the model are equal across samples, and that estimation of parameters that (based on such tests) are considered equal can then be based on the combined data from all samples.

Often such analyses begin with a global test of equality of the covariance matrices for the various data sets. The argument is that if the same model describes the data equally well across groups, then the matrices are bound to be equal.

I cannot recommend the procedure. One problem is that the test does not build on a model of the data-generating process. With small or moderate sample sizes you run the risk that you will accept the null hypothesis of equal covariance matrices even if it is not possible to find a meaningful model that describes the data. Besides, the earlier mentioned problem of two-sided tests depending on sample size is itself a good reason for quitting this procedure altogether.

Testing a measuring instrument for cross-group equivalence

In the previous example we were very lucky in that the FRL scale showed intra-country stability to a degree that made it possible for us to compare the factor means. We will not always be that lucky.

In order to compare research results across groups it is of course important to make sure that the measurements are comparable.

Cross-group validity of a measuring instrument is usually checked by going through a series of tests, where the demands for the equivalence of the measuring instrument are increased step by step, as we ask the following questions:

1. *Configural invariance*: Is the model structure the same across groups? That is, is the graphic picture of the measurement model the same across groups?
2. *Metric invariance*: Are the regression weights ($X \leftarrow F$) equal across groups? If so, the manifest variables are measured in the same scale units across groups.
3. *Scale invariance*: Are the item intercepts equal across groups? If so, the manifest variables are measured on common interval scales.
4. *Factor covariance invariance*: Are the factors interrelated in the same way across groups?
5. *Factor variance invariance*: Do the factors exhibit the same variation across groups?
6. *Error variance (and covariance) invariance*: Are the error variances (and covariances) equal across groups?

The last two questions secure equal reliabilities for the items and the complete measuring instrument across groups.

Example 3
Does the FRL instrument work in the same way in the
UK and in France?

Let us test the inter-cultural validity of the FRL instrument across UK and French consumers in 1998 with data from Scholderer et al. (2004). Again I will (in order to save space) only use the 'Consumption Situation Dimension'.

The models are shown in Figure 5.

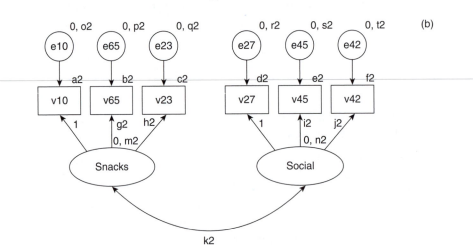

	UK 1998		France 1998	
	Labelled	Fixed at	Labelled	Fixed at
Regression intercepts	a1–f1		a2–f2	
Regression weights	g1–j1		g2–j2	
Covariance	k1		k2	
Variances	m1–t1		m2–t2	
Error means and factor means		0		0

Figure 5   Example 3: the models: (a) UK 1998; (b) France 1998

I have used the 'model method' introduced in Example 6.1, which you first met in Figure 6.6, to estimate six models, placing increasing restrictions on the invariance of the measuring instrument in the two populations:

1. Configural invariance: Basis model: the same structure is assumed
2. Metric invariance: As 1 + regressions weights are assumed equal
3. Scale invariance: As 2 + the intercepts are assumed equal
4. Factor covariance invariance: As 3 + the factor covariances are assumed equal
5. Factor variance invariance: As 4 + factor variances are assumed equal
6. Error variance invariance: As 5 + error variances are assumed equal

As is evident from Figure 6, this demands a lot of 'clicking around'.

From Table 7 we can see that models 1 and 2 are accepted at any conventional significance level, while all other models are rejected, As the χ^2-test has excessive power

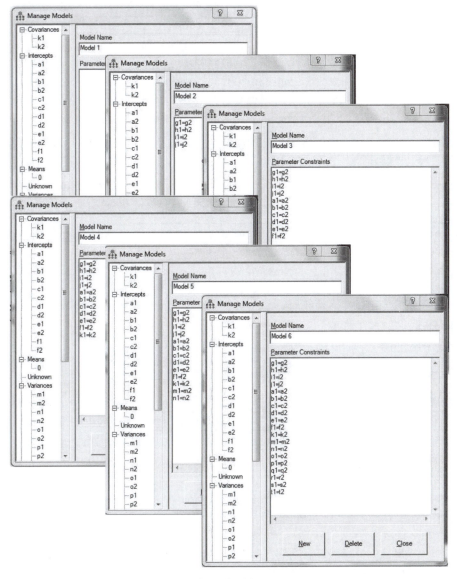

Figure 6   Example 3: managing multiple models

in large samples, this is a very good argument for the measurement model having *at least* metric invariance.

As in Example 2 – and for the same reason – I will forgo testing and use RMSEA as the main fit measure. From Table 8 you can see that although RMSEA is generally rather small, it has a marked increase from model 2 to model 3, which could cast doubt on the hypothesis of scale invariance across the two populations. Also observe that the null hypothesis that RMSEA in the population is less than 0.05 is rejected for all models except 2 and 3. The information theoretic criteria point at model 2 as the 'best'.

Table 7 Example 3: output (extract)

CMIN

Model	NPAR	CMIN	DF	P	CMIN/DF
Model 1	38	22.994	16	.114	1.437
Model 2	34	27.219	20	.129	1.361
Model 3	28	249.464	26	.000	9.595
Model 4	27	257.216	27	.000	9.527
Model 5	25	261.057	29	.000	9.002
Model 6	19	413.438	35	.000	11.813
Saturated model	54	.000	0		
Independence model	24	1344.395	30	.000	44.813

RMSEA

Model	RMSEA	LO 90	HI 90	PCLOSE
Model 1	.015	.000	.027	1.000
Model 2	.013	.000	.025	1.000
Model 3	.066	.058	.073	.000
Model 4	.065	.058	.073	.000
Model 5	.063	.056	.071	.001
Model 6	.074	.067	.080	.000
Independence model	.148	.142	.155	.000

AIC

Model	AIC	BCC	BIC	CAIC
Model 1	98.994	99.532		
Model 2	95.219	95.700		
Model 3	305.464	305.861		
Model 4	311.216	311.598		
Model 5	311.057	311.411		
Model 6	451.438	451.707		
Saturated model	108.000	108.764		
Independence model	1392.395	1392.735		

Another way to judge the fit of the various models is to look at the incremental fit measures as given in Table 8. The table is constructed from several tables of marginal χ^2-test for hierarchical models.

Table 8 Example 3: output, marginal analysis

`Assuming prior model to be correct:`

Model	DF	CMIN	P	NFI Delta-1	IFI Delta-2	RFI rho-1	TLI rho2
Model 2	4	4.225	.376	.003	.003	-.002	-.002
Model 3	6	222.245	.000	.165	.168	.184	.188
Model 4	1	7.752	.005	.006	.006	-.002	-.002
Model 5	2	3.841	.147	.003	.003	-.012	-.012
Model 6	6	152.381	.000	.113	.116	.063	.064

As mentioned several times, the χ^2-difference test is of little value in such large samples, but in the NFI column we can see that the value of NFI (which for model 1 is 0.983) only drops to 0.003 when we impose the restriction of metric invariance, whereas the (marginal) drop when we also impose scale invariance is not less than 0.165. Adding restrictions on factor covariances and factor variances (in that order) only makes NFI drop by 0.006 and 0.003 respectively, whereas adding the last restriction of equal error variances once more causes NFI to drop by a considerable amount. The other fit indices show the same tendencies, as do the RMSEA and the information theoretic fit measures in Table 7.

Our conclusion then is that the measuring instrument shows configural, metric, factor covariance and factor variance invariances, whereas scale invariance and error variance invariance are not supported by the data.

Table 9 contains a VB program for this analysis. You should compare it with the process you went through using AMOS Graphics and with Figure 6. You will find it useful when you come to Example 4!

As in the program in Table 6.6,

1. All parameters that, in one model or another, are restricted are given a label in parentheses next to it:
2. The various restrictions are expressed in the lines Sem.Model ("Model 1"), Sem.Model ("Model 2"), etc.
3. Use 'FitAllModels' instead of 'FitModel', otherwise AMOS will only estimate the first model.

Table 9 Example 3: the program

```
Public Sub Main()
  Dim Sem As New AmosEngine
  Try
     Sem.TextOutput
     Sem.Standardized
     Sem.ResidualMoments
     Sem.Smc
     Sem.ModelMeansAndIntercepts
```

```
Sem.BeginGroup ("Scholderer.xls", "UK98")
Sem.GroupName ("UK 1998")
Sem.AStructure ("v10 =   (a1) +   (1) snacks + (1) e_10")
Sem.AStructure ("v65 =   (b1) + (g1) snacks + (1) e_65")
Sem.AStructure ("v23 =   (c1) + (h1) snacks + (1) e_23")
Sem.AStructure ("v27 =   (d1) +   (1) social + (1) e_27")
Sem.AStructure ("v45 =   (e1) + (i1) social + (1) e_45")
Sem.AStructure ("v42 =   (f1) + (j1) social + (1) e_42")
Sem.AStructure ("snacks<-->social (k1)")
Sem.AStructure ("snacks (m1)")
Sem.AStructure ("social (n1)")
Sem.AStructure ("e_10 (o1)")
Sem.AStructure ("e_65 (p1)")
Sem.AStructure ("e_23 (q1)")
Sem.AStructure ("e_27 (r1)")
Sem.AStructure ("e_45 (s1)")
Sem.AStructure ("e_42 (t1)")

Sem.BeginGroup ("Scholderer.xls", "F98")
Sem.GroupName ("France 1998")
Sem.AStructure ("v10 =   (a2) +   (1) snacks + (1) e_10")
Sem.AStructure ("v65 =   (b2) + (g2) snacks + (1) e_65")
Sem.AStructure ("v23 =   (c2) + (h2) snacks + (1) e_23")
Sem.AStructure ("v27 =   (d2) +   (1) social + (1) e_27")
Sem.AStructure ("v45 =   (e2) + (i2) social + (1) e_45")
Sem.AStructure ("v42 =   (f2) + (j2) social + (1) e_42")
Sem.AStructure ("snacks<-->social (k2)")
Sem.AStructure ("snacks (m2)")
Sem.AStructure ("social (n2)")
Sem.AStructure ("e_10 (o2)")
Sem.AStructure ("e_65 (p2)")
Sem.AStructure ("e_23 (q2)")
Sem.AStructure ("e_27 (r2)")
Sem.AStructure ("e_45 (s2)")
Sem.AStructure ("e_42 (t2)")

Sem.Model ("Model 1")
Sem.Model ("Model 2", "g1=g2","h1=h2","i1=i2","j1=j2")
Sem.Model ("Model 3", "g1=g2","h1=h2","i1=i2","j1=j2",
          "a1=a2","b1=b2","c1=c2","d1=d2","e1=e2","f1=f2")
Sem.Model ("Model 4", "g1=g2","h1=h2","i1=i2","j1=j2"
          ,"a1=a2","b1=b2","c1=c2","d1=d2","e1=e2","f1=f2","k1=k2")
Sem.Model («Model 5», «g1=g2»,»h1=h2»,»i1=i2»,»j1=j2»,
          "a1=a2","b1=b2","c1=c2","d1=d2","e1=e2","f1=f2","k1=k2",
          «m1=m2»,»n1=n2»)
Sem.Model («Model 6», «g1=g2»,»h1=h2»,»i1=i2»,»j1=j2»,
          "a1=a2","b1=b2","c1=c2","d1=d2","e1=e2","f1=f2","k1=k2",
          «m1=m2»,»n1=n2»,»o1=o2»,»p1=p2»,»q1=q2»,»r1=r2»,»s1=s2»,»t1=t2»)

Sem.FitAllModels

  Finally
    Sem.Dispose
  End Try
End Sub

End Module
```

If you use AMOS Graphics, you can automate the process.

Example 3 (continued)
Does the FRL instrument work in the same way in the UK and in
France? Automating multi-group analysis

If you choose 'Analyze/Multiple-Group Analysis', the window in Figure 7a will appear.

The eight columns of checkboxes each represent a model where each check mark represents a set of parameters that are constrained to be equal across groups. The default checks (in Figure 5a) are as follows:

Model 1:   Regression weights are assumed equal

Model 2:   Model 1 + the intercepts are assumed equal

Model 3:   Model 2 + factor means are assumed equal across groups

Model 4:   Model 3 + factor variances and covariances are assumed equal
            across groups

Model 5:   All parameters are assumed equal across groups

As you can see, this is not the same strategy as the one used by Scholderer et al., so I have to make a few changes. For example, it is obvious that model 3 above is irrelevant when the purpose is to judge the quality of a measuring instrument across groups where the measured concepts may or may not have the same value.

(a)

(b)

Figure 7   Example 3: managing multiple groups

The solution in panel (b) is the nearest I could come to repeating Scholderer et al.'s analysis, the only difference being that they analyzed factor variances and factor covariances in two steps.

The effect of using the 'automated' method is that AMOS fills out the necessary 'Manage Models' windows (see Figure 6).

As we do not intend to estimate the means, all six (two factor and four error means) must be fixed at zero.

Multi-group analysis of causal models with latent variables

For multi-group analysis of causal models things become a little more complicated, because in addition to analyzing the measurement model you must also analyze the causal model.

As in all other cases, it is very important to make sure that the measurement model is valid before trying to analyze the structural model. So, I recommend using the two-step strategy mentioned in Chapter 7 and starting the analysis by going through the same sequence of steps as in Example 8.3.

Then you should continue with the structural model, first testing for the equivalence of the regression weights (and intercepts if this is relevant) and then the variances and covariances of the disturbances.

Usually error and disturbance variances (and covariances) are of the least interest, so you can put error variances (and covariances) last in the sequence together with the disturbance variances.

3   AMOS Graphics or VB?

While the graphic interface is convenient when you do 'standard analyses', i.e. more or less follow the same analysis strategy as everyone else (doing the same things in the same order), it is less convenient in complicated projects where you experiment with many different model formulations. The reason is simple.

The various pop-up menus are shaped to suit the majority. Therefore, if you go off the beaten track the programming interface is much more preferable for the following reasons:

1. It is flexible.
2. It is less time consuming.
3. It gives a much clearer picture of the various model modifications because you have all the information you need on one piece of paper, so you do not need to click around. Therefore it is easier to keep track of various models in your project.

The next example will illustrate this.

Example 4
Are the good beautiful or the beautiful good?

It is generally agreed that a person's appearance affects other people's impressions of the person. A long line of evidence supports the view that physically attractive people are often attributed more positive qualities, and quite a few studies suggest that physically attractive people are more often seen as more intelligent than people that are less physically attractive (Byrne, London, & Reeves, 1968; Clifford & Walster, 1973; Landy & Sigall, 1974; Sarty, 1975). However, there are also quite a few studies that point the other way: that persons with an attractive personality are perceived as more physically attractive (Gross & Crafton, 1977; Owens & Ford, 1978)

Felson and Bohrnstedt (1979) studied 209 girls and 207 boys from the sixth to the eighth grade (approximately 11–14 years of age) in order to find the direction of a (possible) causal effect between physical attractiveness and perceived academic ability – or if there perhaps exists a two-way causation. (Felson and Bohrnstedt in a single passage in their article write that the number of girls is 207 and the number of boys 209. However, the two figures are so close that whichever is correct, it will not affect the conclusions.)

Felson and Bohrnstedt measured the following variables:

academic: Perceived academic ability, based on the item: Name who you think are the three smartest classmates.
attract: Perceived attractiveness based on the item: Name the three girls (boys) in the classroom who you think are the most good-looking (excluding yourself).
GPA: Grade point average.
height: Deviation of height from the mean for a subject's grade and sex.
weight: Weight, adjusted for height.
rating: Ratings of physical attractiveness obtained by having children from another city rate photographs of subjects.

Their model is shown in Figure 8.

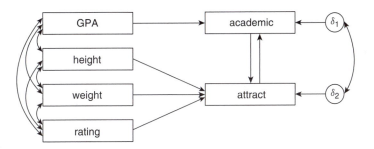

Figure 8   Example 4: Felson and Bohrnstedt's model

The reason why the model includes height and weight is that Felson and Bohrnstedt also wanted to test the following two hypotheses:

1. *Height* has a positive effect on *attract* for boys, but a negative or no effect for girls.
2. *Weight* has a negative effect on *attract* for both girls and boys.

Formulating the two regression equations as

$$academic = attract + GPA + \delta_1$$
$$attract = academic + height + weight + rating + \delta_2$$

(2)

it is evident that the model is identified as the two functions have no exogenous variables in common.

Note the two opposed arrows that depict the hypothesized effects between *academic*
and *attract*. While the possible correlations among the exogenous variables only
express traditional multicollinearity, the inclusion of a correlation between the error
terms is more doubtful. The only reason Felson and Bohrnstedt give is that 'it is unrealistic in a simultaneous equation model to assume they are uncorrelated'. I would have
preferred a substantive argument.

The data given in Table 10 can also be found on the book's website. Note that as the
input consists of correlation coefficients and not covariances, the standard deviations
have been added so that AMOS can calculate the covariance matrix as a basis for estimating the model parameters. The means are also included in the data file but will not
be used in this example.

You should have no problems in estimating the model separately for the two groups
in AMOS Graphics, using the same procedure as in Example 2.

Table 10 Example 4: data input

Fels_fem

rowtype_	varname_	academic	athletic	attract	GPA	height	weight	rating
n		209	209	209	209	209	209	209
corr	academic	1.000						
corr	athletic	0.430	1.000					
corr	attract	0.500	0.180	1.000				
corr	GPA	0.490	0.220	0.320	1.000			
corr	height	0.100	-0.040	-0.030	0.180	1.000		
corr	weight	0.040	0.020	-0.160	-0.100	0.340	1.000	
corr	rating	0.090	0.140	0.430	0.150	-0.160	-0.270	1.000
stddev		0.160	0.070	0.490	3.490	2.910	19.320	1.010
mean		0.120	0.050	0.420	10.340	0.000	94.130	2.650

Fels_mal

rowtype_	varname_	academic	athletic	attract	GPA	height	weight	rating
n		207	207	207	207	207	207	207
corr	academic	1.000						
corr	athletic	0.470	1.000					
corr	attract	0.490	0.720	1.000				
corr	GPA	0.580	0.270	0.300	1.000			
corr	height	-0.020	0.150	0.040	-0.110	1.000		
corr	weight	-0.110	-0.010	-0.190	-0.160	0.510	1.000	
corr	rating	0.110	0.240	0.280	0.130	0.060	-0.180	1.000
stddev	stddev	0.160	0.210	0.490	4.040	3.410	24.320	0.970
mean	mean	0.100	0.170	0.440	8.630	0.000	101.910	2.590

The output is given in Table 11. As can be seen from the χ^2-test, the fit is extremely good, and the various fit indices, which are not shown in order to save space, confirm this. As the fit is excellent it should be possible to simplify the model.

Table 11 Example 4: output for model A

Result (Model 1)

```
Minimum was achieved
Chi-square = 3.183
Degrees of freedom = 4
Probability level = .528
```

Regression Weights: (Girls - Model 1)

			Estimate	S.E.	C.R.	P	Label
academic	<---	GPA	.023	.004	6.241	***	
attract	<---	height	.000	.010	.050	.960	
attract	<---	weight	-.002	.001	-1.321	.186	
attract	<---	rating	.176	.027	6.444	***	
academic	<---	attract	-.002	.051	-.039	.969	
attract	<---	academic	1.607	.350	4.599	***	

Covariances: (Girls - Model 1)

			Estimate	S.E.	C.R.	P	Label
GPA	<-->	height	1.819	.712	2.555	.011	
GPA	<-->	weight	-6.710	4.676	-1.435	.151	
height	<-->	weight	19.024	4.098	4.642	***	
GPA	<-->	rating	.526	.246	2.139	.032	
height	<-->	rating	-.468	.205	-2.279	.023	
weight	<-->	rating	-5.243	1.395	-3.759	***	
error1	<-->	error2	-.004	.010	-.382	.702	

Squared Multiple Correlations: (Girls - Model 1)

	Estimate
attract	.402
academic	.236

Notes for Group/Model (Girls - Model 1)

```
Stability index for the following variables is .003
attract
academic
```

Regression Weights: (Boys - Model 1)

			Estimate	S.E.	C.R.	P	Label
academic	<---	GPA	.021	.003	6.927	***	
attract	<---	height	.019	.010	1.967	.049	
attract	<---	weight	-.003	.001	-2.484	.013	

			Estimate	S.E.	C.R.	P	Label
attract	<---	rating	.095	.030	3.150	.002	
academic	<---	attract	.063	.059	1.071	.284	
attract	<---	academic	1.386	.315	4.398	***	

Covariances: (Boys - Model 1)

			Estimate	S.E.	C.R.	P	Label
GPA	<-->	height	-1.508	.961	-1.569	.117	
GPA	<-->	weight	-15.645	6.899	-2.268	.023	
height	<-->	weight	42.091	6.455	6.521	***	
GPA	<-->	rating	.507	.274	1.850	.064	
height	<-->	rating	.198	.230	.860	.390	
weight	<-->	rating	-4.226	1.662	-2.543	.011	
error1	<-->	error2	-.010	.011	-.898	.369	

Squared Multiple Correlations: (Boys - Model 1)

	Estimate
attract	.313
academic	.424

Notes for Group/Model (Boys - Model 1)

Stability index for the following variables is .087
attract
academic

The estimates of the coefficients seem partly to support Felson and Bohrnstedt's hypotheses (level of significance 0.05, one-sided test, region of rejection $|C.R.| > 1.65$ – in the relevant direction!). That is:

1. Perceived academic ability does not depend on attractiveness (C.R. $= - 0.039$ for girls and 1.071 for boys), whereas the opposite effect seems to exist (C.R. $= 4.599$ and 4.398).
2. *Height* has nearly no effect on attractiveness for girls (C.R. $= 0.050$) but has a positive effect for boys (C.R. $= 1.967$).
3. Attractiveness does not depend on weight for girls (C.R. $= -1.321$) but does for boys (C.R. $= -2.484$).
4. Error1 and error2 are not correlated (C.R. $= -0.382$ and -0.898, two-sided test). Felson and Bohrnstedt should have foreseen this result. It is difficult to imagine that *academic* and *attract* should have correlations that are not fully explained by their possible two-way causation.
5. *Weight* and *GPA* are not correlated (C.R. $= - 1.435$).

Point 1 above answered the main research question, point 2 supports hypothesis 1 and point 3 partly supports hypothesis 2.

However, just as in traditional regression analysis these are marginal tests, and you cannot use such tests to argue that several parameters should be removed at the same time.

We could of course exclude one parameter at a time, but due to co-linearity this is perhaps not the most preferable procedure. Instead we can formulate a few reasonable models and compare them.

No doubt the effect from *attract* to *academic* and the correlations between the error terms should be excluded, while all correlations among exogenous variables should be maintained. These correlations are not given by the model but more or less by 'nature', and there would be no sense in restricting them to zero, even if they were not significant.

Having said this, there are still quite a few models that could all be substantively grounded and are also supported to a certain extent by the data, as follows.

Model B: One of Felson and Bohrnstedt's hypotheses was that *height* had a positive effect on *attract* for boys but a negative or no effect for girls. As the effect for girls was not significant by traditional standards I will exclude this effect in model B.

Model C: Even if *weight* is not significant for the girls but is significant for the boys, you could argue that the two regression weights are so close (-0.02 and -0.03) that for all practical purposes they could be considered equal. The same argument goes for the regression weights for *GPA*.

Model D: The regression weights attract<--academic are nearly identical, and could be restricted to be equal.

Model E: Even if it could be argued that rating as a measure of *attract* is possibly more 'sex-dependent' than *GPA* is as a measure of *academic*, I will tentatively restrict attract<--rating to have the same value in the two groups.

Model F: Finally I will test a model where all regression weights are assumed equal across the two groups.

The program in Table 12 will do the job.

Table 12 Example 4: the program for estimating models A–F

```
Sub Main
' A reciprocal causation model of
' perceived academic ability, using
' both female and male samples of the
' Felson and Bohrnstedt (1979) data set.
'

  Dim Sem As New AmosEngine
  Try
    Sem.TextOutput
    Sem.BeginGroup ("Felson.xls","Fels_fem")
    Sem.GroupName ("girls")
    Sem.Structure ("academic = (g1)GPA + (g2)attract + error1 (1)")

    Sem.Structure ("attract   = (g3)height + (g4)weight + (g5)rating
        + (g6)academic + error2 (1)")
    Sem.Structure ("(g7)error2 <--> error1")

    Sem.BeginGroup ("Felson","Fels_mal")
    Sem.GroupName ("boys")
    Sem.AStructure ("academic = (b1)GPA + (b2)attract + error1 (1)")
```

```
   Sem.AStructure ("attract   = (b3)height + (b4)weight + (b5)rating
      + (b6)academic + error2 (1)")
   Sem.AStructure ("(b7)error2 <--> error1")

   Sem.Model ("Model A)"
   Sem.Model ("Model B", "g2=0","g3=0", "g7=0","b2=0","b7=0")
   Sem.Model ("Model C", "g2=b2=0","g3=0", "g7=b7=0","g4=b4","g1=b1")
   Sem.Model ("Model D", "g2=b2=0","g3=0", "g7=b7=0","g4=b4","g1=b1","g6=b6")
   Sem.Model ("Model E","g2=b2=0","g3=0","g7=b7=0","g4=b4","g1=b1","g6=b6", «g5=b5»)
   Sem.Model («Model F», «g2=b2»,»g3=b3»,»g4=b4»,»g1=b1»,»g6=b6»,»g5=b5»)
   Sem.FitAllModels
 Finally
   Sem.Dispose
 End Try
End Sub
```

As you can imagine, there is a tremendous amount of output. Therefore I will show only a very small portion of it.

Towards the end of the output all the fit measures are given for the various models. For space considerations only the first table appears in Table 13. We can see that, *judged by themselves*, all six models are acceptable, and would have been accepted if only the same single model were under consideration. The various fit measures (not shown) exhibit the same picture: the six models all have acceptable fit, so how do we choose among them?

Table 13 Example 4: fit measures for the various models

CMIN

Model	NPAR	CMIN	DF	P	CMIN/DF
Model A	38	3.183	4	.528	.796
Model B	33	4.503	9	.875	.500
Model C	31	4.996	11	.931	.454
Model D	30	5.039	12	.957	.420
Model E	29	8.618	13	.801	.663
Model F	32	9.493	10	.486	.949
Saturated model	42	.000	0		
Independence model	12	475.682	30	.000	15.856

One possibility is to use the χ^2-difference test for hierarchical models that you met in Example 6.1. The very last part of the output shows the results of a series of such tests, as in Table 14.

The last four columns show changes in the fit indices relative to the basis model. None of the models are significantly different according to traditional norms, and changes in fit measures seem insignificant.

Table 14 Example 4: marginal χ^2-test for hierarchical models

```
Nested Model Comparisons
```

```
Assuming model Model_A to be correct:
```

Model	DF	CMIN	P	NFI Delta-1	IFI Delta-2	RFI rho-1	TLI rho2
Model B	5	1.320	.933	.003	.003	-.019	-.020
Model C	7	1.812	.970	.004	.004	-.022	-.023
Model D	8	1.856	.985	.004	.004	-.024	-.025
Model E	9	5.434	.795	.011	.012	-.008	-.009
Model F	6	6.310	.389	.013	.013	.010	.010

```
Assuming model Model_B to be correct:
```

Model	DF	CMIN	P	NFI Delta-1	IFI Delta-2	RFI rho-1	TLI rho2
Model C	2	.492	.782	.001	.001	-.003	-.003
Model D	3	.536	.911	.001	.001	-.005	-.005
Model E	4	4.114	.391	.009	.009	.010	.011

```
Assuming model Model_C to be correct:
```

Model	DF	CMIN	P	NFI Delta-1	IFI Delta-2	RFI rho-1	TLI rho2
Model D	1	.044	.834	.000	.000	-.002	-.002
Model E	2	3.622	.163	.008	.008	.013	.014

```
Assuming model Model_D to be correct:
```

Model	DF	CMIN	P	NFI Delta-1	IFI Delta-2	RFI rho-1	TLI rho2
Model E	1	3.578	.059	.008	.008	.015	.016

It could be argued that as the models are not significantly different, parsimony should lead us to accept model F, the simplest of the six. On the other hand, the first table shows a rather dramatic drop in *P*-value for model F.

In a situation like this where one has to choose among several defendable models, it is reasonable to base the choice on information theoretic fit measures as given in Table 15. Note that BIC and CAIC are not stated in multi-sample analysis.

Based on the output in Table 15, it is evident that the initial model A as well as model F must be rejected. Model D seems most in accordance with the data and model E is not much worse. Table 16 gives the regression weights of the two models.

In model E the regression weight of *height* for boys (italicized) is *not* significant. All other regression weights in the table are significant, $P < 0.01$ (one-sided).

As the model formulations B–F were partly data driven, the results of the analysis should be cross-validated on a new independent sample from the same population.

Table 15 Example 4: information theoretic fit measures

AIC

Model	AIC	BCC	BIC	CAIC
Model A	79.183	81.843		
Model B	70.503	72.813		
Model C	66.996	69.166		
Model D	65.039	67.139		
Model E	66.618	68.648		
Model F	73.493	75.733		
Saturated model	84.000	86.940		
Independence model	499.682	500.522		

Table 16 Example 4: regression weights for models D and E

REGRESSION WEIGHT FOR	MODEL D		MODEL E	
	Girls	Boys	Girls	Boys
GPA	0.023	0.023	0.023	0.023
Height	–	0.015	–	*0.014*
Weight	-0.003	-0.003	-0.003	-0.003
Rating	0.174	0.100	0.142	0.142
Attract	–	–	–	–
Academic	1.422	1.422	1.419	0.419

A short remark on two-way causation

This is the first (and only) worked example of a cyclic model, so a few remarks are in order.

Recall from the last subsection of Chapter 5 that two conditions must be met to give a meaningful substantive interpretation of model parameters in a cyclic model:

1. As the regression weights in a loop are interpreted as the result of an infinite sum of loops, it is necessary that the sum is defined.
2. It is assumed that the whole process has come to an end.

AMOS calculates a *stability index* for each two-way causation. If this index is numerically *less than* 1.00, the first condition can be considered fulfilled. A stability index that is numerically larger than 1.00 is meaningless in the same sense as a negative variance. As you can see from Table 4, stability indices in model A are 0.003 for girls and 0.087 for boys.

However, a stability index numerically larger than 1.00 could also indicate that the sample is too small to estimate the effects with any degree of precision.

It is a common misunderstanding that a stability index having a numerical value less than 1.00 guarantees that the second condition is met. It does *not*!

Time series data are required to judge the second condition – and if such data were at hand you would probably specify a time series model.

In this chapter you met the following concepts:

- stability index
- mean structure
- configural invariance
- metric invariance

- scale invariance
- factor covariance invariance
- factor variance invariance
- error variance invariance

You also learned the following AMOS statements:

- Sem.ModelMeansAndIntercepts
- Sem.Mean

Questions

1. List the various steps in testing a measuring instrument for cross-group equivalence. Comment on the rationale behind the procedure.

2. Comment on the problems of cyclical models using examples from your own area of study or research.

References

Bredahl, L. (2001). Determinants of consumer attitudes and purchase intentions with regard to genetically modified foods – results of a cross-national survey. *Journal of Consumer Policy, 24*, 23–61.

Brunsø, K., & Grunert, K. G. (1995). Development and testing of a cross-cultural valid instrument: Food-related lifestyle. *Advances in Consumer Research, 22*, 475–480.

Byrne, D. O., London, O., & Reeves, K. (1968). The effects of physical attractiveness, sex and attitude similarity on interpersonal attraction. *Journal of Personality, 36*, 259–271.

Clifford, M. M., & Walster, E. (1973). The affect of physical attractiveness on teacher expectations. *Sociology of Education, 46*, 248–258.

Felson, R. B., & Bohrnstedt, G. W. (1979). Are the good beautiful or the beautiful good? *Social Psychology Quarterly, 42*, 386–392.

Gross, A. E., & Crafton, C. (1977). What is good is beautiful. *Sociometry, 40*, 85–90.

Landy, D., & Sigall, H. (1974). Beauty is talent: Task evaluation is a function of the performer's physical attractiveness. *Journal of Personality and Social Psychology, 29*, 229–304.

Owens, G., & Ford, J. G. (1978). Further considerations of the 'what is good is beautiful' finding. *Social Psychology, 41*, 73–75.

Sarty, M. (1975). The 'pretty girl' as a sexual and reproductive stereotype. Paper presented at the Western Psychology Association, summary from Department of Human Behavior, University of Southern California School of Medicine.

Scholderer, J., Brunsø, K., Bredahl, L., & Grunert, K. G. (2004). Cross-cultural validity of the food-related lifestyle instrument (FRL) within Western Europe. *Appetite, 42*, 197–211.

9

Incomplete and Non-normal Data

Missing data are more the rule than the exception in empirical research, and several solutions to the problem have been suggested. As will be argued in the opening paragraphs of this chapter, the most widespread ones are not wholly satisfactory.

Then you will learn about the two more satisfying methods implemented in AMOS, the first of which is a special maximum likelihood procedure that makes it possible to estimate a model using all the data at hand even if some observations are missing. However, it turns out that this technique is not without its drawbacks, the most serious being that you can easily run out of degrees of freedom, because it is necessary to estimate means and intercepts.

Unfortunately this is also the problem with the other technique *multiple imputation* (as implemented in AMOS), which has grown in popularity during the last few years. However, SPSS makes it possible to do multiple imputation independently of model estimation and thereby to solve this little problem.

Another common problem is the non-normality of data. No variable is strictly normal, and more often than not deviations from normality are so serious that they cannot be ignored. We take a look at the consequences of non-normality and the remedies used most often.

You will learn to use *bootstrapping*, which is an estimation procedure that makes no distributional demands at all.

Bootstrapping is some sort of Swiss Army knife, capable of solving a lot of different problems in and outside of SEM – but as with all statistical methods, it has its shortcomings.

1 Incomplete Data

It is very unlikely that you will undertake a large research project without meeting the problem mentioned in this heading. The most obvious consequence of incomplete data is that it could – depending on how you choose to handle the problem – reduce your sample. What is more serious is that it biases the estimation.

Of the many ways of coping with the missing data problem, the following seem to be the most popular:

1. *Listwise deletion* (LD for short): Delete all observations that have missing values on any variable.

2. *Pairwise deletion* (PD): Use LD for all pairs of variables.
3. *Mean imputation* (MI): Replace the missing value with the mean of the variable.
4. *Regression imputation* (RI): Estimate the value of the missing observation by regressing the variable on other variables.

It is obvious that the first method, which is the default in many computer programs (including SPSS), could easily reduce the sample size to an unacceptable level, and might also bias your estimates depending on the mechanism that produces the missing data.

If you use PD, the calculation of variances and covariances in the input matrix is based on all observations where the one or two variables involved are not missing. One problem with this procedure is that the various sample moments are based on different sample sizes. What sample size should then go into the calculation of test statistics and the like?

No doubt some rough rules of thumb could be put forward, but what is more serious is: if separate parts of the covariance matrix are based on different observations you run the risk that the matrix will not be positive definite.

It is obvious that MI will reduce the sample variances and covariances, and as SEM is based on variances and covariances this too seems to be a bad solution to the problem.

RI also reduces estimates of variances and covariances, but to a lesser degree than MI.

None of these methods are very satisfying and none of them are implemented in AMOS. Instead, AMOS gives you the choice between *full information maximum likelihood* (FIML) and *multiple imputation* (MUI) – two methods that are much more preferable to the four listed above.

A few things are worth noting when working with incomplete data using FIML or MUI:

1. Calculations must be based on raw data – a matrix summary will not function.
2. You must estimate means and intercepts.
3. AMOS cannot calculate modification indices.
4. AMOS could run into difficulties when trying to estimate the saturated and the independence model.
5. If AMOS does not succeed in estimating the saturated model, the χ^2-statistic cannot be calculated, and if the independence model cannot be estimated, some fit measures (e.g. CFI) cannot be calculated.

Full information maximum likelihood

In general the FIML procedure as implemented in AMOS is the natural choice, because it allows maximum likelihood estimation to be based on a data set with missing values and still make use of all available data without any form of imputation.

There is, however, one situation in which none of the above-mentioned methods including FIML will give consistent estimates. This is when the fact that a value is missing conveys information about its value. An example is when the probability that a respondent will not report his or her income is larger for higher incomes. In that case an empty cell in the data matrix indicates that the respondent may belong to the higher income classes. Even in this situation, however, FIML is less biased than any of the methods mentioned above.

Example 1
Analyzing incomplete data using FIML

I will use the Thomsen et al. (2004) data (from Example 7.2) to illustrate FIML estimation with incomplete data, estimating the measurement model in Figure 7.3 after having deleted 20 pct. of the measurements by simple random sampling. As usual, you can find the data ('missing 20') on the book's website.

The analysis is done just as in Example 7.2, but remember to check 'Estimate means and intercept' in the 'Analysis Properties' window (see Figure 4.8a).

Part of the output is given in Table 1 for comparison with Table 7.5.

Table 1   Example 1: output from analysis of incomplete data file

Result (Default model)

```
Minimum was achieved
Chi-square = 697.669
Degrees of freedom = 315
Probability level = .000
```

Regression Weights: (Group number 1 - Default model)

			Estimate	S.E.	C.R.	P	Label
ecq14	<---	Rumination	.066	.100	.665	.506	
ecq13	<---	Rumination	.363	.111	3.253	.001	
ecq12	<---	Rumination	.184	.103	1.793	.073	
ecq11	<---	Rumination	.651	.088	7.379	***	
ecq10	<---	Rumination	.168	.039	4.357	***	
ecq9	<---	Rumination	.880	.095	9.283	***	
ecq8	<---	Rumination	.623	.082	7.608	***	
ecq7	<---	Rumination	.326	.057	5.748	***	
ecq6	<---	Rumination	.399	.103	3.876	***	
ecq5	<---	Rumination	.436	.100	4.357	***	
ecq4	<---	Rumination	.819	.092	8.938	***	
ecq3	<---	Rumination	.799	.087	9.189	***	
ecq2	<---	Rumination	.313	.113	2.780	.005	
ecq1	<---	Rumination	1.000				
poms33d	<---	Sadness	.635	.073	8.724	***	
poms28d	<---	Sadness	.494	.058	8.531	***	
poms23d	<---	Sadness	.572	.061	9.333	***	
poms20d	<---	Sadness	.779	.067	11.645	***	
poms14d	<---	Sadness	.614	.081	7.614	***	
poms12d	<---	Sadness	.786	.069	11.320	***	
poms8d	<---	Sadness	.925	.076	12.128	***	
poms4d	<---	Sadness	1.000				
lymphocy	<---	Immunity	.290	.084	3.455	***	

			Estimate	S.E.	C.R.	P	Label
leukocyt	<---	Immunity	1.000				
telephone	<---	Health	1.103	.329	3.356	***	
consult	<---	Health	1.000				

Covariances: (Group number 1 - Default model)

			Estimate	S.E.	C.R.	P	Label
Rumination	<-->	Sadness	.205	.043	4.730	***	
Rumination	<-->	Immunity	.252	.106	2.370	.018	
Health	<-->	Rumination	.094	.056	1.689	.091	
Health	<-->	Immunity	.117	.104	1.128	.260	
Sadness	<-->	Immunity	-.070	.073	-.963	.336	
Health	<-->	Sadness	.130	.044	2.956	.003	
psqik1	<-->	Rumination	.150	.049	3.078	.002	
psqik1	<-->	Immunity	.267	.094	2.827	.005	
psqik1	<-->	Health	.170	.055	3.113	.002	
psqik1	<-->	Sadness	.186	.037	5.080	***	

Programming in VB

If you use the program in Table 2, you will (of course!) get exactly the same estimates as in Table 1, but instead of

```
Minimum was achieved
Chi-square = 697.669
Degrees of freedom = 315
Probability level = .000
```

you will get

```
Minimum was achieved
Function of log likelihood = 2455.278
Number of parameters = 90
```

Table 2 Example 1: program

```
Public Sub Main()
  Dim Sem As New AmosEngine
  Try
    Sem.TextOutput
    Sem.Smc
    Sem.Standardized
    Sem.ModelMeansAndIntercepts
    'Sem.Mods(20)
    Sem.BeginGroup("Missing20.sav")
```

(Continued)

(Continued)

```
Sem.AStructure("ecq1   = () + (1) Rumination + (1) e_ecq1")
Sem.AStructure("ecq2   = () +     Rumination + (1) e_ecq2")
Sem.AStructure("ecq3   = () +     Rumination + (1) e_ecq3")
Sem.AStructure("ecq4   = () +     Rumination + (1) e_ecq4")
Sem.AStructure("ecq5   = () +     Rumination + (1) e_ecq5")
Sem.AStructure("ecq6   = () +     Rumination + (1) e_ecq6")
Sem.AStructure("ecq7   = () +     Rumination + (1) e_ecq7")
Sem.AStructure("ecq8   = () +     Rumination + (1) e_ecq8")
Sem.AStructure("ecq9   = () +     Rumination + (1) e_ecq9")
Sem.AStructure("ecq10 = () +     Rumination + (1) e_ecq10")
Sem.AStructure("ecq11 = () +     Rumination + (1) e_ecq11")
Sem.AStructure("ecq12 = () +     Rumination + (1) e_ecq12")
Sem.AStructure("ecq13 = () +     Rumination + (1) e_ecq13")
Sem.AStructure("ecq14 = () +     Rumination + (1) e_ecq14")

Sem.AStructure("poms4d  = () + (1) Sadness + (1) e_poms4d")
Sem.AStructure("poms8d  = () +     Sadness + (1) e_poms8d")
Sem.AStructure("poms12d = () +     Sadness + (1) e_poms12d")
Sem.AStructure("poms14d = () +     Sadness + (1) e_poms14d")
Sem.AStructure("poms20d = () +     Sadness + (1) e_poms20d")
Sem.AStructure("poms23d = () +     Sadness + (1) e_poms28d")
Sem.AStructure("poms33d = () +     Sadness + (1) e_poms33d")

Sem.AStructure("psqik1 = () + (1) Sleep Quality + (1) e_psqik1")

Sem.AStructure("leukocyt = () + (1) Immunity + (1) e_Imm1")
Sem.AStructure("lymphocy = () +     Immunity + (1) e_Imm2")

Sem.AStructure ("consult   = () + (1) Health care + (1) e_health1")
Sem.AStructure ("telephone = () +     Health care + (1) e_health2")

Sem.AStructure("Sleep Quality <-->Rumination")
Sem.AStructure("Sleep Quality <--> Sadness")
Sem.AStructure("Sleep Quality <--> Immunity")
Sem.AStructure("Sleep Quality <--> Health care")

Sem.AStructure("e_psqik1 (0)")

    Sem.FitModel
  Finally
    Sem.Dispose
  End Try
End Sub
```

The reason is that when you use the programming interface, AMOS does not estimate the saturated model and the independence model. Consequently the χ^2-statistic cannot be calculated, and for the same reason most of the fit measures are also missing. Instead you get the message:

Model Fit Summary

```
The saturated model was not fitted to the data of at least one group. For
this reason. only the 'function of log likelihood'. AIC and BCC are
reported. The likelihood ratio chi square statistic and other fit measures
are not reported.
```

Since AMOS does not automatically estimate the saturated model when you use the programming interface, you have to do it yourself.

Now, there are many saturated models (all equivalent) so why not choose the simplest one? The program for this is given in Table 3.

Table 3 Example 1: program for estimation of a saturated model

```
Public Sub Main()
  Dim Sem As New AmosEngine
  Try
    Sem.TextOutput
    Sem.Smc
    Sem.Standardized
    Sem.ModelMeansAndIntercepts
    Sem.AllImpliedMoments
    Sem.BeginGroup("Missing20.sav")

    Sem.Mean("ecq1")
    Sem.Mean("ecq2")
    Sem.Mean("ecq3")
    Sem.Mean("ecq4")
    Sem.Mean("ecq5")
    Sem.Mean("ecq6")
    Sem.Mean("ecq7")
    Sem.Mean("ecq8")
    Sem.Mean("ecq9")
    Sem.Mean("ecq10")
    Sem.Mean("ecq11")
    Sem.Mean("ecq12")
    Sem.Mean("ecq13")
    Sem.Mean("ecq14")


    Sem.Mean("poms4d")
    Sem.Mean("poms8d")
    Sem.Mean("poms12d")
    Sem.Mean("poms14d")
    Sem.Mean("poms20d")
    Sem.Mean("poms23d")
    Sem.Mean("poms28d")
    Sem.Mean("poms33d")

    Sem.Mean("psqik1")

    Sem.Mean("leukocyt")
    Sem.Mean("lymphocy")

    Sem.Mean ("consult")
    Sem.Mean ("telephone")

    Sem.FitModel
  Finally
    Sem.Dispose
  End Try
End Sub
```

Even if the model specification only demands that means are estimated, AMOS estimates variances and covariances too. However, there is no reason to show the complete output, as the only output you need are the few lines

```
Minimum was achieved
Function of log likelihood = 1757.609
Number of parameters = 405
```

found at the beginning of the output at the place where you would expect to find the χ^2-test.

These figures and the corresponding ones from the output obtained from running the program in Table 2 can be used to calculate a χ^2-value for your model in the following way. Subtract the function of log likelihood for the saturated model from the one for 'your' model and the number of parameters for 'your' model from that of the saturated model:

	Function of log likelihood	Number of parameters
Your model	2455.278	90
Saturated model	1757.609	405
	697.669	315

The difference between the values of log likelihood is then distributed as χ^2 with degrees of freedom equal to the differences in number of parameters.

If you consult a statistical table, you will find this to be highly significant ($P < 0.000$ as in the analysis based on complete data). The χ^2-value and degrees of freedom are of course exactly the same as those in Table 1.

Of course you can use another model (than the saturated model) as the basis model for comparison with 'your' model.

For the calculation of χ^2 you need a basis model that fulfills the following demands:

1. It fits the data better than your 'default model'.
2. Your model is nested under your basis model.
3. The basis model should in fact be accepted as 'true'.

In that way you are in fact doing a χ^2-difference test.

As mentioned several times, it is often better to base the judgment of model fit on fit indices rather than on the χ^2-test because of the latter's dependence on sample size. Unfortunately you must compute your preferred fit indices by hand (using the formulae in Chapter 5). This, however, necessitates estimation of the independence model in addition to the saturated model.

If you use the graphic interface you will avoid most of the calculation problems connected with missing data, as all these calculations are then done automatically, and you get the usual output you know so well. But as mentioned in the beginning of this section, AMOS Graphics could run into trouble when trying to estimate the saturated and independence models.

Multiple imputation

Remember that the problem with mean imputation and regression imputation is that they underestimate the variation in the data, because: (1) the spread in the data is reduced; and (2) the 'noise' in the regression estimation is not taken care of.

The solution to this problem is to use several imputations for estimating each of the variables that have missing values – the various imputations only differentiate themselves by the addition of a small amount of 'random noise'. In that way you end up with several imputed data sets.

Each of these is now analyzed as if they are a 'normal' complete data set, and – as a last step – the various model estimates are combined taking the above-mentioned 'regression noise' into consideration.

This is by far the best imputation method and it is a good alternative to FIML.

So, multiple imputation (MUI) goes through the following three steps:

1. Create several complete data sets using MUI.
2. Perform the desired analysis on each of the data sets.
3. Combine the various analyses into one.

Only the first step is at present fully implemented in AMOS; the last two steps must be done by hand. According to the *User's Guide* (Arbuckle, 2010) a calculator for doing these two steps should be available for download from http://www.amosdevelopment.com/ bayes/calculator. However, this calculator was not available as this book went to press.

All MUI methods build on predicting the missing values conditional on the non-missing variables – as does the simpler regression imputation mentioned at the beginning of this chapter. This could of course be done in many ways. AMOS gives you three options (see Figure 1).

Concerning regression imputation, it is obvious that you must be very careful in choosing your regressors. As the purpose is to maintain the interrelations in the data, you choose regressor variables that correlate with the variables having missing values and regressors that covary with the reasons for the missing values. This means that you could run into difficulties if you use regressor variables that are not included in the model that is the basis of your later statistical analysis.

It could be said that AMOS takes full consequence of this, basing the imputation on the very structural equation model you want to estimate. This of course means that AMOS's first step is to estimate the model using FIML.

For comparison, I will demonstrate MUI using the same model and data as in Example 1.

Example 2
Analyzing incomplete data using MUI

Using the same data, you do the analysis as in Example 1, except that you choose 'Analyze/Data Imputation' and the window shown in Figure 1 will appear.

As you can see, AMOS gives you the choice of three imputation methods:

1. *Regression imputation*: After the model parameters are estimated, the missing values are predicted using non-missing values of manifest variables from the same observation.

2. *Stochastic regression imputation* (Little & Rubin, 2002): After the model parameters are estimated, the missing values are estimated by drawing at random from
the distribution of the missing values conditional on the manifest variables.
3. *Bayesian imputation*: This is the same as stochastic regression imputation, but
considers model parameters as stochastic variables and not single estimates of
unknown constants (cf. Section 4.3).

Figure 1   Example 2: data imputation

Choose 'Stochastic regression imputation' and 'Multiple output files', and let the
'Number of completed datasets' remain at the default value (10). Usually only very few
(5–10) imputed data sets are necessary to obtain a satisfactory result (SPSS has five as
the default).

As you will see, you can choose to save each imputed data file as a separate file, or
put them all into one file. This last option is practical if you choose to work in SPSS,
because SPSS can then split the file during analysis, while AMOS cannot.

When you click 'File Names' a 'Save as' box is shown that gives you the choice
between saving the imputed files as text files or as SPSS data files. As you can see, I
have chosen SPSS data files.

When you click 'Impute' AMOS starts imputation and saves the original file and the
imputed files, numbering them as in Figure 2.

Part of the first imputed file is shown in Figure 3. Note that AMOS adds the four factors (Immunity, Sadness, Rumination and Health) as variables, the values being the estimated factor scores. Two more variables are added: case number and imputation number.

You can now run your model as a 10-group analysis just as you learned in Chapter
8. However, you will have to delete the latent variables from the data before you can
run your model; if not, you will get the error message shown in Figure 4. I suggest you

Figure 2   Example 2: list of imputed data files

Figure 3   Example 2: first imputation (extract)

save your revised data files under new names if you expect to use the estimated factor means in future analyses.

What now remains is to combine the 10 estimated models (output can be found on the book's website) to form the final output. As mentioned above, this must (at present) be done by hand.

If we let

$$m = \text{number of imputed data sets}$$

$$\hat{Q}^{(t)} = \text{parameter estimate based on sample } t$$

$$\sqrt{\hat{U}^{(t)}} = \text{estimated standard error based on sample } t$$

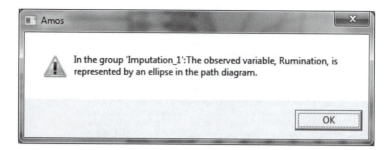

Figure 4 Example 2: error message

then the MUI estimate of a model parameter (e.g. a regression weight) is simply the mean of the m (= 10) estimates of that parameter:

$$\bar{Q} = m^{-1} \sum_{i=1}^{m} \hat{Q}^{(t)} \tag{1}$$

To obtain the standard errors is a bit more complicated. The average within-imputation variance is computed analogously with the average regression weight:

$$\bar{U} = m^{-1} \sum_{i=1}^{m} \hat{U}^{(t)} \tag{2}$$

You must, however, also compute the between-imputation variance:

$$B = (m-1)^{-1} \sum_{i=1}^{m} \left(\hat{Q}^{(t)} - \bar{Q} \right)^{2} \tag{3}$$

Now, you combine (2) and (3) to obtain the total variance:

$$T = \bar{U} + \left(1 + m^{-1}\right) B \tag{4}$$

and of course the standard error is then

$$SE = \sqrt{T} \tag{5}$$

and the critical ratio is

$$CR = \frac{\bar{Q}}{\sqrt{T}} \tag{6}$$

This means lots of calculations by hand, but while we are waiting for the promised calculator (mentioned above) the calculations can be easily done in a spreadsheet. The FIML and MUI estimates are given in Table 4 together with estimates based on the full data set (and in the last column results obtained by using SPSS as demonstrated in Example 3 below). Estimates that are not statistically significant are in boldface ($\alpha = 0.05$, one-sided).

Table 4 Example 2: model estimates based on full data set, FIML and MUI

`Regression Weights: (Group number 1 - Default model)`

			Non-Missing	FIML	MUI	SPSS
ecq14	<---	Rumination	**-.006**	**.066**	**0.102**	**0.089**
ecq13	<---	Rumination	.372	.363	0.370	0.381
ecq12	<---	Rumination	**.136**	.184	**0.158**	**0.161**
ecq11	<---	Rumination	.608	.651	0.666	0.639
ecq10	<---	Rumination	.215	.168	0.173	0.182
ecq9	<---	Rumination	.866	.880	0.889	0.880
ecq8	<---	Rumination	.583	.623	0.620	0.636
ecq7	<---	Rumination	.350	.326	0.321	0.352
ecq6	<---	Rumination	.493	.399	0.384	0.364
ecq5	<---	Rumination	.426	.436	0.466	0.419
ecq4	<---	Rumination	.786	.819	0.800	0.838
ecq3	<---	Rumination	.807	.799	0.800	0.811
ecq2	<---	Rumination	.358	.313	0.311	0.354
ecq1	<---	Rumination	1.000	1.000	1.000	1.000
poms33d	<---	Sadness	.596	.635	0.633	0.614
poms28d	<---	Sadness	.530	.494	0.481	0.448
poms23d	<---	Sadness	.598	.572	0.563	0.514
poms20d	<---	Sadness	.941	.779	0.774	0.760
poms14d	<---	Sadness	.656	.614	0.612	0.637
poms12d	<---	Sadness	.859	.786	0.781	0.698
poms8d	<---	Sadness	.934	.925	0.927	0.905
poms4d	<---	Sadness	1.000	1.000	1.000	1.000
lymphocy	<---	Immunity	.331	.290	0.304	0.320
leukocyt	<---	Immunity	1.000	1.000	1.000	1.000
telephone	<---	Health	1.580	1.103	1.139	1.017
consult	<---	Health	1.000	1.000	1.000	1.000

`Covariances: (Group number 1 - Default model)`

			Non-missing	FIML	MUI	SPSS
Rumination	<-->	psqik1	.156	.205	0.207	0.211
Rumination	<-->	Sadness	.212	.252	0.236	0.249
Rumination	<-->	Immunity	.287	.094	**0.091**	**0.102**
Rumination	<-->	Health	.098	**.117**	**0.100**	**0.116**
Immunity	<-->	psqik1	.164	-.070	-0.077	-0.087
Immunity	<-->	Health	**.048**	.130	0.127	0.148
Sadness	<-->	Immunity	**-.007**	.150	0.150	0.154
Health	<-->	psqik1	.115	.267	0.250	0.244
Sadness	<-->	Health	.101	.170	0.164	0.177
Sadness	<-->	psqik1	.188	.186	0.187	0.201

Missing data patterns

In this case the missing values were chosen by simple random sampling from all the measurements: the data were *missing completely at random* or *MCAR* (Rubin, 1976). This means that the probability that a value is missing is independent of one and every variable missing or not missing. Under this condition all the methods for dealing with missing data mentioned so far give consistent estimates, although of course only FIML is efficient in the statistical sense, because it uses all available information in the data.

In all probability such a simple 'selection model' is very rare in practice. It is more realistic to assume that the probability that a measurement is missing is independent of its value *conditional* on the values of the non-missing variables. Even in this situation – called *missing at random* or *MAR* by Rubin – FIML estimation as implemented in AMOS will give efficient and consistent estimates, while other methods will be inefficient and (in most cases) also lack consistency.

As mentioned earlier, FIML estimation will not be consistent if the MAR condition is not met, but FIML will still be less biased than other solutions to the missing data problem. This situation is called *non-ignorable* by Rubin.

MUI using SPSS

You may have wondered why I have chosen the factor model and not the causal model from Figure 7.6 to demonstrate FIML estimation with missing data. The reason is simple: it is not possible to estimate the causal model if you have missing data, because the need for estimating means and intercepts eats up your degrees of freedom. This is not apparent from a calculation of variances, covariances, means and the number of parameters to be estimated. The crucial point is that the covariance structure and the means structure must be identified *separately*. In this case the covariance structure is over-identified while the means structure is under-identified – and the extra degrees of freedom in the covariance structure cannot save the identification of the means structure. This is a real limitation of this method if you have only a single sample.

Since MUI as implemented in AMOS builds on FIML, we still have to answer the question: 'How do I estimate the causal model in Figure 7.6 if I have missing data?' The answer is that you have to use a model-independent imputation method. Fortunately SPSS has several options at your disposal.

The 'Missing Values' module in SPSS is a rather large one that has its own manual of nearly 100 pages (SPSS Inc., 2010), so I will barely scratch the surface.

The module is roughly divided into two sections that deal with:

1. A description and analysis of missing data patterns.
2. Imputation.

Although no imputation should be performed without a prior analysis of the patterns in the missing values, I will (for space reasons) leave it to you to explore the tools and go directly to imputation.

Example 3
Analyzing incomplete data using MUI

Once again, open the SPSS data set 'Missing 20' from the book's website and from the top menu choose 'Transform/Random Number Generators'. When the window in Figure 5 appears, be sure to check:

'Set Active Generator'
'Set Starting Point'
'Fixed Value'

and set a starting point for generating 'random noise' in the imputation, so that you (if necessary) can replicate the analysis.

Next, choose 'Analyze/Multiple Imputation/Impute Missing Data Values', and the window in Figure 6 will appear. As is now routine, move the variables – all of them except 'id' and 'køn' (for the curious, this means 'sex' in Danish) – to the right panel. As you can see, the default number of imputations is 5, but change it to 10 for comparison with the results obtained in Examples 1 and 2. Save the imputed data as 'Imputed.sav'. SPSS saves imputed data to one file and therefore puts in a variable 'Imputation'. The original data are saved in the same file as 'Imputation 0'.

As you can guess, clicking the various tabs in the window in Figure 6 gives you a rich palette of choices so that you can make a tailor-made imputation, based on a serious analysis of the pattern of missing values.

If you click the 'Method' tab in the window shown in Figure 6, the window in Figure 7 appears. To keep things simple I chose 'Automatic'.

As mentioned above, the imputed data sets are saved in a single file (see Figure 8). The reason is that most of the statistical procedures in SPSS can be carried out directly on this data file, because SPSS automatically splits the file using the variable 'Imputation' as the split variable.

However, AMOS is not that clever, so you must manually split the file, and then do the analysis as a multi-group analysis – as in Example 2. The estimated regression weights and covariances are shown in the last column in Table 4.

Figure 5   Example 3: choosing a starting point for random generation of 'noise'

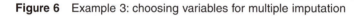

Figure 6   Example 3: choosing variables for multiple imputation

Figure 7   Example 3: choosing imputation method

Figure 8   Example 3: saved imputed data sets

2   Bootstrapping as an Aid to Deal with Non-normal Data

Maximum likelihood estimation is based on an assumption of multivariate normality of the manifest variables, and so are the large-sample properties of generalized least squares. If the data fail to meet this assumption, it could have serious consequences:

1. The program could run into convergence problems.
2. The asymptotic χ^2-values become excessively large.
3. The standard errors of parameter estimates are underestimated.

Even if you do not run into convergence problems, the last two problems could easily lead you astray in the interpretation of the output.

Now, there are several ways to cope with non-normality:

1. You can transform variables to (near-)normality.
2. You can use an estimation method that makes no distributional assumptions such as ULS or ADF. However, as mentioned earlier, testing in ULS is somewhat complicated, and ADF makes large demands on the sample size.
3. Since the consequences generally lie more with test statistics than with parameter values, you can use GLS or ML, and then regulate the test statistics using so-called *robust statistics* (see e.g. Chou, Bentler, & Satorra, 1991). This may in many cases be the best way to solve the problem, but it is not available in the present version (19) of AMOS.
4. You can use bootstrapping – the topic of the rest of this chapter.

What then is bootstrapping?

Most statistical inference is based on the concept of a *sampling distribution* of a sample statistic, i.e. the distribution of a sample statistic taken across repeated samples of the same size from the same population. Now, we usually take only one sample, and consequently we do not have an actual empirical sampling distribution on which to base our inference. Instead we have to *derive* the sampling distribution from assumptions about the population from which the only sample was taken, e.g. an assumption of multivariate normality.

The idea behind bootstrapping is that you consider your sample to be your population. From this 'population' you take, say, 500 samples *with replacement*. From each sample you then calculate the required sample statistic. This gives you an empirical sampling distribution, and averaging the various sample statistics, you get an estimate of the parameter and an empirical standard error of the estimates.

This in short is the principle of bootstrapping, and it can be used to obtain empirical standard errors of whatever statistic you may want, including various fit indices, squared correlation coefficients, etc.

It is tempting also to use bootstrapping as a remedy for samples that are too small to give meaningful test results based on the asymptotic properties of ML or GLS. However, as the whole process is based on considering the original sample to represent the population from which it was taken, the sample should be large enough to guarantee stable estimates – and of course the sample selection should also be based on simple random sampling.

As you will probably have guessed, bootstrapping demands that the original data file is used as input – a covariance and mean summary of the data are not enough.

Example 4
Bootstrapping severely non-normal data

Once again we will return to the FRL scale (see Example 8.2). The quality domain of the FRL scale refers to health, price/quality relation, novelty seeking, preference for organic food, taste and freshness, and thus is a six-factor domain, each factor being measured by three items.

As you may expect everyone to prefer quality for money and good-tasting food, it is no surprise that the distributions of answers to the items measuring these two factors are severely skewed. The items used to measure these two dimensions are given in Table 5. As usual, you can find the data on the book's website.

Table 5 Example 4: items used in the analysis

Price/quality relation	
	v64: I always try to get the best quality for the best price.
	v13: I compare prices between product variants in order to get the best value for money.
	v7: It is important for me to know that I get quality for all my money.
Taste	
	v5: I find taste in food products important.
	v21: When cooking, I first and foremost consider the taste.
	v50: It is important to choose food products for their nutritional value rather than for their taste.

When you have constructed the model shown in Figure 9, select 'View/Analysis Properties/Output' and check 'Standardized estimates', 'Squared multiple correlations', 'Residual moments' and 'tests for normality and outliers'. Then click the 'Bootstrap' tab, and fill in the checkboxes as shown in Figure 10. I will explain the meaning of 'Bias-corrected confidence intervals' when I comment on the output.

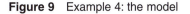

Figure 9 Example 4: the model

Figure 10 Example 4: ordering bootstrapping

Part of the output is given in Table 6.

The first part of the output is the traditional one, with χ^2-test and parameter estimates. A χ^2 of 85.088 with eight degrees of freedom is significant according to any traditional criteria (but remember that χ^2 is inflated with non-normal data), but, as mentioned previously, this test is of limited value with such a large sample. In order to save space I have not reported the variance estimates. For the same reason I have not shown the residual moments and the tests for normality and outliers. You can find the complete output on the book's website, and rest assured that the variables are indeed far from normally distributed.

Then comes the bootstrapping part of the output, starting with a report on the bootstrapping process itself. In this case everything went well, but if a considerable share of the bootstrap samples turn out to be useless because of the problems mentioned in the output, then perhaps you should look for another solution to your problem.

The bootstrapping parameter estimates follow. The first column (SE) shows the estimates of the standard errors of the various parameter estimates, while the second (SE-SE) shows the standard errors of the standard errors themselves. Then comes the mean of the parameter estimates calculated across the 1000 samples and the difference (Bias) between the bootstrap mean and the maximum likelihood estimated parameter value. Perhaps you may be surprised that the two sets of parameter estimates are so different given the large sample, but this happens quite often. The last column shows the standard error of the bias estimate.

Table 6 Example 4: partial output from bootstrapping

```
Minimum was achieved
Chi-square = 85.088
Degrees of freedom = 8
Probability level = .000
```

Maximum Likelihood Estimates

Regression Weights: (France 1994 - Model 1)

			Estimate	S.E.	C.R.	P	Label
v64	<---	quality	1.000				
v13	<---	quality	.938	.132	7.126	***	
v7	<---	quality	.322	.053	6.044	***	
v5	<---	taste	1.000				
v21	<---	taste	1.482	.169	8.788	***	
v50	<---	taste	.853	.111	7.706	***	

Standardized Regression Weights: (France 1994 - Model 1)

			Estimate
v64	<---	quality	.729
v13	<---	quality	.511
v7	<---	quality	.302
v5	<---	taste	.611
v21	<---	taste	.755
v50	<---	taste	.324

Covariances: (France 1994 - Model 1)

			Estimate	S.E.	C.R.	P	Label
taste	<-->	quality	.290	.044	6.555	***	

Correlations: (France 1994 - Model 1)

			Estimate
taste	<-->	quality	.405

Squared Multiple Correlations: (France 1994 - Model 1)

	Estimate
v50	.105
v21	.570
v5	.374
v7	.091
v13	.261
v64	.532

0 bootstrap samples were unused because of a singular covariance matrix.
0 bootstrap samples were unused because a solution was not found.
1000 usable bootstrap samples were obtained.

Regression Weights: (France 1994 - Model 1)

Parameter			SE	SE-SE	Mean	Bias	SE-Bias
v64	<---	quality	.000	.000	1.000	.000	.000
v13	<---	quality	.147	.003	.931	-.007	.005
v7	<---	quality	.137	.003	.339	.017	.004
v5	<---	taste	.000	.000	1.000	.000	.000
v21	<---	taste	.214	.005	1.500	.018	.007
v50	<---	taste	.144	.003	.861	.008	.005

Standardized Regression Weights: (France 1994 - Model 1)

Parameter			SE	SE-SE	Mean	Bias	SE-Bias
v64	<---	quality	.088	.002	.733	.004	.003
v13	<---	quality	.051	.001	.501	-.009	.002
v7	<---	quality	.075	.002	.306	.004	.002
v5	<---	taste	.052	.001	.611	.000	.002
v21	<---	taste	.054	.001	.755	-.001	.002
v50	<---	taste	.039	.001	.323	-.001	.001

Covariances: (France 1994 - Model 1)

Parameter			SE	SE-SE	Mean	Bias	SE-Bias
taste	<-->	quality	.062	.001	.292	.002	.002

(Continued)

(Continued)

Correlations: (France 1994 - Model 1)

Parameter			SE	SE-SE	Mean	Bias	SE-Bias
taste	<-->	quality	.088	.002	.411	.007	.003

Squared Multiple Correlations: (France 1994 - Model 1)

Parameter	SE	SE-SE	Mean	Bias	SE-Bias
v50	.025	.001	.106	.001	.001
v21	.082	.002	.572	.002	.003
v5	.064	.001	.376	.003	.002
v7	.050	.001	.099	.008	.002
v13	.049	.001	.254	-.007	.002
v64	.128	.003	.545	.013	.004

As you can see from Table 7, the bootstrap estimates of standard errors are generally much larger than the ML estimates – and in two cases at least 100% larger.

Table 7 Example 4: comparison of ML and bootstrap estimates of standard errors

Parameter	ML estimate	Bootstrap estimate	Difference	Difference in pct.
v13<---quality	0.132	0.147	0.015	11
v7 <---quality	0.053	0.137	0.084	158
v21<---taste	0.169	0.214	0.045	27
v50<---taste	0.111	0.144	0.033	30
taste<--->quality	0.044	0.088	0.044	100

You will observe that you can obtain bootstrap estimates of standard errors of standardized parameter estimates, coefficients of determination and the various fit indices.

Now, it is one thing to obtain bootstrapped estimates, but something else to test the significance of the various parameters as well as of the whole model.

You will have observed that in the bootstrapping part of the output in Table 6 there are no standard errors or critical ratios and *P*-values. Instead we ordered bias-corrected (empirical) confidence intervals. This part of the output is given in Table 8.

The interval can be used to test the hypothesis that the parameter is zero against the two-sided alternative that it is not – exactly the same test as the traditional *P*-values refer to. If a confidence interval contains zero, the hypothesis that the parameter is zero cannot be rejected at $\alpha = (100 - 95)\%$.

The last column can be interpreted as a traditional *P*-value of the two-sided test. For example, $P = 0.002$ in the last column of the covariance table means that a $(1.000 - 0.002)100\% = 99.8\%$ confidence interval would have 0.000 as its lower limit. Note that in this way you can also test hypotheses about standardized estimates etc.

Table 8 Example 4: bias-corrected confidence intervals

Regression Weights: (France 1994 - Model 1)

Parameter			Estimate	Lower	Upper	P
v64	<---	quality	1.000	1.000	1.000	...
v13	<---	quality	.938	.671	1.236	.001
v7	<---	quality	.322	.164	.766	.001
v5	<---	taste	1.000	1.000	1.000	...
v21	<---	taste	1.482	1.136	1.971	.002
v50	<---	taste	.853	.579	1.142	.002

Standardized Regression Weights: (France 1994 - Model 1)

Parameter			Estimate	Lower	Upper	P
v64	<---	quality	.729	.559	.921	.002
v13	<---	quality	.511	.417	.602	.001
v7	<---	quality	.302	.179	.479	.002
v5	<---	taste	.611	.511	.718	.002
v21	<---	taste	.755	.658	.874	.001
v50	<---	taste	.324	.248	.404	.002

Covariances: (France 1994 - Model 1)

Parameter			Estimate	Lower	Upper	P
taste	<-->	quality	.290	.178	.428	.002

Correlations: (France 1994 - Model 1)

Parameter			Estimate	Lower	Upper	P
taste	<-->	quality	.405	.266	.628	.002

Squared Multiple Correlations: (France 1994 - Model 1)

Parameter	Estimate	Lower	Upper	P
v50	.105	.061	.164	.002
v21	.570	.433	.763	.001
v5	.374	.261	.515	.002
v7	.091	.032	.229	.002
v13	.261	.174	.362	.001
v64	.532	.313	.848	.002

What remains is a test of the model as a whole, i.e. a bootstrapped χ^2-test.

In fact Bollen and Stine (1993) have invented an 'empirical χ^2-test' to be used in judging a model when using bootstrapping. The idea is as follows.

As the χ^2-test is a test of the (very unlikely!) hypothesis that your model is totally correct, the Bollen–Stine approach is to transform your input data so that the model fits the (transformed) data exactly and then to obtain an empirical distribution of the χ^2-statistic across bootstrap samples taken from this 'population'. This distribution is then taken to be the distribution under the hypothesis of a correct model.

AMOS then calculates the 'empirical *P*-value' as the share of the bootstrap samples having χ^2-values larger than the χ^2 obtained from the ML estimation (85.088).

In order to use this test, you must run another bootstrapping, where you check the 'Bollen-Stine bootstrap' box in Figure 10. The output is given in Table 9.

Table 9   Example 4 : Bollen–Stine output

Notes

Bootstrap confidence intervals are not available when the Bollen-Stine bootstrap is performed.

Bollen-Stine Bootstrap (Model 1)

The model fits better in 1000 bootstrap samples.
It fits about equally well in 0 bootstrap samples.
It fits worse or failed to fit in 0 bootstrap samples.
Testing the null hypothesis that the model is correct, Bollen-Stine boot-
strap p = .001

Bootstrap Distributions (Model 1)

ML discrepancy (implied vs sample) (Model 1)

```
                           |--------------------
                  1.333    |**
                  3.375    |***********
                  5.417    |***************
                  7.458    |*******************
                  9.500    |****************
                 11.542    |***************
                 13.584    |*********
N = 1000         15.625    |********
Mean = 9.678     17.667    |****
S. e. = .152     19.709    |***
                 21.751    |*
                 23.792    |*
                 25.834    |*
                 27.876    |*
                 29.917    |*
                           |--------------------
```

As is apparent from the note, this bootstrapping procedure is *only* for calculation of the Bollen–Stine statistic, and no standard errors or confidence intervals can be calcu-lated in the same run. The first part of the output is just as in Table 6, but when you reach the bootstrapping part of the output you will see the output shown in Table 9. The *P*-value is small, as might be expected with a sample of nearly 1000. Together with the *P*-value, the empirical distribution of the *C*-statistic is also shown.

By comparing the ML χ^2 (85.088) with the B–S χ^2 (9.678) you will observe that the latter is much nearer to its expected value – which is the number of degrees of freedom (8). You can also see from the distribution of χ^2 that the bootstrapped χ^2-values cluster around this value, even if some of the samples have values that are up to four times larger.

A VB program for the analysis of Example 4 is given in Table 10.

Table 10   Example 4: the VB program

```
Public Sub Main()
   Dim Sem As New AmosEngine
   Try
      Sem.TextOutput
      Sem.Bootstrap (1000)
      Sem.ConfidenceBC (95)
      Sem.ResidualMoments
      Sem.NormalityCheck
      Sem.BeginGroup ("France94Quality.sav")
      Sem.GroupName ("France 1994")
      Sem.AStructure ("v64 = (1) quality + (1) e_64")
      Sem.AStructure ("v13 =     quality + (1) e_13")
      Sem.AStructure ("v7  =     quality + (1) e_7")
      Sem.AStructure ("v5  = (1) taste   + (1) e_5")
      Sem.AStructure ("v21 =     taste   + (1) e_21")
      Sem.AStructure ("v50 =     taste   + (1) e_50")
      Sem.FitModel
   Finally
      Sem.Dispose
   End Try
End Sub
```

Two new statements are: 'Sem.Bootstrap (1000)', which orders AMOS to draw 1000 random samples of size 994 with replacement from the original sample of 994; and 'Sem.ConfidenceBC', which orders AMOS to calculate bias-corrected 95% confidence intervals.

To do the B–S test, the line

```
Sem.BootBS
```

is substituted for the three lines

```
Sem.ConfidenceBC (95)
Sem.ResidualMoments
Sem.NormalityCheck
```

Other uses of bootstrapping

Even if bootstrapping cannot cure all problems, it has other uses than for the analysis of non-normal data. You can use bootstrapping to compare the merits of different estimation methods and different models, and on the book's website, you are given the opportunity to use it to test the significance of indirect and total effects.

A final note!

After having read this chapter – and especially after having struggled with the exercises on the website – you will be well aware that a covariance or correlation summary of your data can hide a lot of problems in the raw data, such as non-normality, non-linearities, outliers, etc. Give this some thought next time you read a journal article in which a covariance or correlation matrix is the only kind of data published.

In this chapter you met the following concepts:

- listwise and pairwise deletion
- mean imputation
- regression imputation full information maximum likelihood(FIML) estimation

- multiple imputation (MUI)
- function of log likelihood
- bootstrapping
- Bollen–Stine χ^2-test

You also learned the following AMOS statements:

- Sem.Bootstrap()
- Sem.ConfidenceBC()

- Sem.BootBS

Questions

1. Judge the virtues and vices of various imputation methods.

2. State the characteristics of the three missing data concepts: 'missing completely at random', 'missing at random' and 'non-ignorable', and comment on the various methods for coping with the problem in each of the three situations.

3. Consider how bootstrapping could help solve problems that you might encounter, or have already encountered, in your own area of study or research.

References

Arbuckle, J. L. (2010). *IBM SPSS© AMOS TM 19 User's Guide*. Crawfordville, FL: AMOS Development Corporation.

Bollen, K. A., & Stine, R. A. (1993). Bootstrapping goodness-of-fit measures in structural equation modeling. In K. A. Bollen & J. S. Long (Eds.), *Testing structural equation models* (pp. 111–135). Newbury Park, CA: Sage.

Chou, C.-P., Bentler, P. M., & Satorra, A. (1991). Scaled test statistics and robust standard errors for nonnormal data in covariance structure analysis: A Monte Carlo study. *British Journal of Mathematical and Statistical Psychology, 4*, 21–37.

Little, R. J. A., & Rubin, D. B. (2002). *Statistical analysis with missing data*. New York: Wiley.

Rubin, D. B. (1976). Inference and missing data. *Biometrika, 63*, 581–592.

SPSS Inc. (2010). IBM SPSS Missing Values 19.

Thomsen, D. K., Mehlsen, Y. M., Hokland, M., Viidik, A., Olesen, F., Avlund, K., et al. (2004). Negative thoughts and health: Associations among rumination, immunity and health care utilization in a young and elderly sample. *Psychosomatic Medicine, 66*, 363–371.

10

Latent Curve Models

The last few decades have seen rapid growth in the amount of longitudinal data – both public (government) data and commercial data (e.g. panel data in marketing research) – and a growing interest in methods for the analysis of such data. SEM has much to offer in that context.

The idea is that the repeated measurements are considered as manifestations of an underlying process that generates their so-called *trajectory* in much the same way as a latent variable generates the answers to items in a scale. This is the so-called *latent curve model*.

You will learn the subject through a simple example. As is now (I hope) your habit, you start the analysis with the measurement model and then introduce the structural model.

After this simple introduction to the subject, the last part of the chapter brings in more complicated methods: how to deal with metrics of time, how to interpret indirect effects and how to expand the simple model in more elaborate directions.

1 What is a Latent Curve Model?

Sometimes your research problem demands that you follow your 'respondents' (be they people, companies, geographic areas) over a shorter or longer period, taking measurements at various intervals in order to map the development through time.

Until now you have met two examples where data were collected in two waves. In Examples 5.2 and 7.3 information on a group of patients was collected over an interval of four years to study the stability of alienation, and in Example 6.1 the degree of democracy in developing countries was measured in 1960 and again in 1965. But what if you want to follow these up, continuing to collect data in order to find answers to questions such as:

1. Is there a general trend in the data? Does a patient's feeling of alienation generally speaking increase, decrease or remain stable over time? Is democracy gaining or losing terrain in developing countries or are things not changing?
2. Does every member (patient/country) of the group follow the same trend, or are there variations?
3. If the trend varies across group members, is it then possible to locate variables that could account for such variations?

A simple way to analyze such data is to use regression analysis (Appendix A), regressing the measure of interest on a time variable. To make things simple, I use a linear model:

$$y_{it} = \alpha_i + \beta_i \lambda_t + \varepsilon_{it}$$

where

y_{it} = the value of the variable of interest

for 'respondent' i at time λ_t, (1)

and ε_{it}, is an error terms fulfilling

the usual conditions

You can carry out a regression for each and every 'respondent' as well as for the group as a whole. However, this is perhaps not the most efficient way to analyze the data, e.g. in testing and comparing the various regression functions you have to do a lot of testing. In each test, you can control the risk α of making a type 1 error (i.e. the maximum probability of rejecting H_0, if H_0 is true; see Appendix A), but how large is α for the whole set of tests combined? Also, there is no way to judge the fit of the total model. These are not the only inconveniences in this choice of analysis strategy (Bollen & Curran, 2006).

So let us look at a more effective way to analyze these sorts of data. As a start we could assume that the parameters α_i and β_i are stochastic variables:

$$y_{it} = \alpha_i + \beta_i \lambda_t + \varepsilon_{it}$$
$$\alpha_i = \mu_a + \delta_{\alpha i}$$
$$\beta_i = \mu_\beta + \delta_{\beta i}$$

where

y_{it} = the value of the variable of interest (2)

for the respondent i at time λ_t

$\mu_a = E(\alpha_i)$

$\mu_\beta = E(\beta_i)$

and ε_{it}, $\delta_{\alpha i}$ and $\delta_{\beta i}$ are error terms

fulfilling the usual conditions

In this way we take care of the possibility that the intercept and the slope may vary across respondents.

It is obvious that the model could also be interpreted as a confirmatory factor model as first proposed by Meredith and Tisak (1984, 1990) building on the work of Tucker (1958). Usually a factor model is used to model the connection between a series of questions in a questionnaire and some underlying construct that the questions are supposed to measure, e.g. a series of questions intended to measure depression or some other psychological variable of interest.

In this use of the factor analysis approach, we let a series of repeated measurements $y_1, y_2, \ldots, y_k$ on a variable take the place of the test questions in the above-mentioned example. These measurements are then regarded as indicators of the parameters in a model describing the trajectory generating the observations – for example, a curve

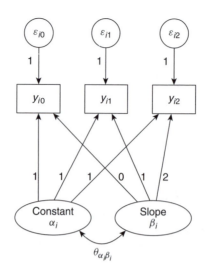

Figure 1   Linear latent curve model

describing the development in patients of feelings of alienation or the development of democracy in a selection of countries. Our model (2) can then be depicted as shown in Figure 1, where, in order to keep things simple, I assume that the measurements are taken three times at one-year intervals.

As read from the model

$$y_{i0} = \alpha_i + \varepsilon_{i0}$$
$$y_{i1} = \alpha_i + 1\beta_i + \varepsilon_{i1} \tag{3}$$
$$y_{i2} = \alpha_i + 2\beta_i + \varepsilon_{i2}$$

cf. (2).

What first catches the eye is that the regression weights that are usually at the center of interest in factor models are all fixed, and therefore not to be estimated. Also apparent is that the arrow from 'Slope' to y_{i0} is fixed at zero. I could just as well have excluded it from the drawing, but it has become common practice to include it.

In a way the scaling of time is somewhat arbitrary, but letting the first regression weight have the value 0 means that α_i represents the value of y_i at the time of the first measurement.

Since we are interested in the means of intercepts and slope, remember to check 'Estimate means and intercepts' when using AMOS Graphics or include the statement 'Sem.ModelMeansAndIntercepts' if you are using VB. However, as these are the only means we are interested in, we fix all other means and intercepts at zero.

2   The Two-step Strategy in Latent Curve Modeling

In latent curve modeling (LCM) we follow a two-step strategy (introduced in Section 7.2). First we analyze the measurement model and then we bring in the causal model. But there is a difference.

If you compare the first step in Figure 7.5 with the second step in Figure 7.6, you will see that *all* variables in the second step (the 'causal model') are also included in the first step ('the factor model').

This is not the case in LCM. Here the first step is to *describe* the trajectory without including any of the variables that are brought in during the second step to 'explain' the trajectory. So what we have in Figure 1 is the first step in any LCM.

Example 1
Does union negotiation raise wages?

Vella and Veerbek (1998), in a project on the influence of union membership on wages, interviewed 545 young men yearly over eight years. If we let 'lwage' be the logarithm of the wage, we will try to answer the first two questions mentioned above: (1) is there a trend in wages during the eight years; and (2) do all respondents follow the same trend or are there differences?

Now a trend could have many forms – it is not necessarily linear – so, as a first step, we will use SPSS to plot 'lwage' against 'year'. (Remember: it is always a good habit 'to draw before you calculate'!)

However, as is evident from Figure 2, the trend is as linear as you could ever demand.

This also answers the first question raised above: there is a strong (linear) trend in wages at group level.

So, I will use the model shown in Figure 3 as the basis for the analysis. As you will observe, the means of the error terms are fixed at zero, and the same goes for the intercepts in the measurement part of the model.

You should have no problems in formulating the model and estimating it using the data 'wagepanX' from the book's website.

Part of the output is given in Table 1.

Figure 2   Example 1: linear trend at group level

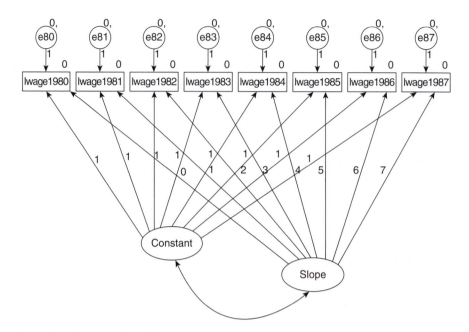

Figure 3 Example 1: the first model

Table 1 Example 1: output, first run

Result (Default model)

```
Minimum was achieved
Chi-square = 126.598
Degrees of freedom = 31
Probability level = .000
```

Means: (Group number 1 - Default model)

	Estimate	S.E.	C.R.	P	Label
Constant	1.436	.020	70.429	***	
Slope	.061	.003	19.588	***	

Covariances: (Group number 1 - Default model)

	Estimate	S.E.	C.R.	P	Label
Constant <--> Slope	-.010	.002	-5.585	***	

Correlations: (Group number 1 - Default model)

	Estimate
Constant <--> Slope	-.431

Variances: (Group number 1 - Default model)

	Estimate	S.E.	C.R.	P	Label
Constant	.175	.014	12.641	***	
Slope	.003	.000	8.587	***	

	Estimate	S.E.	C.R.	P	Label
e80	.214	.015	13.931	***	
e81	.127	.009	13.425	***	
e82	.084	.006	13.248	***	
e83	.078	.006	13.854	***	
e84	.110	.007	14.825	***	
e85	.097	.007	14.349	***	
e86	.101	.007	13.717	***	
e87	.057	.006	9.312	***	

Modification Indices (Group number 1 - Default model)

Covariances: (Group number 1 - Default model)

			M.I.	Par Change
e87	<-->	Slope	5.730	-.002
e87	<-->	Constant	10.402	-.017
e85	<-->	Slope	5.996	.002
e85	<-->	Constant	6.120	.014
e84	<-->	Constant	4.584	.013
e84	<-->	e87	7.395	-.012
e84	<-->	e85	12.102	.017
e83	<-->	e87	7.059	-.011
e83	<-->	e84	14.205	.017
e82	<-->	e87	12.178	-.015
e82	<-->	e83	8.051	.012
e81	<-->	e87	15.786	.021
e81	<-->	e85	5.794	-.014
e80	<-->	Constant	24.375	-.042
e80	<-->	e87	6.723	.017
e80	<-->	e84	15.416	-.029
e80	<-->	e83	4.989	-.014
e80	<-->	e82	4.547	-.015

Regression Weights: (Group number 1 - Default model)

			M.I.	Par Change
lwage1980	<---	Constant	13.555	-.053
lwage1980	<---	lwage1987	7.715	-.031
lwage1980	<---	lwage1986	8.875	-.034
lwage1980	<---	lwage1985	10.219	-.038
lwage1980	<---	lwage1984	15.534	-.048
lwage1980	<---	lwage1983	13.538	-.047
lwage1980	<---	lwage1982	14.183	-.050
lwage1980	<---	lwage1981	10.405	-.044

Chi-square is highly significant, but that seems to say as much about the sample size as about the model fit: CFI = 0.96, RMSEA = 0.075, LO 90 = 0.062, HI 90 = 0.089, PCLOSE = 0.001.

Although CFI is above the often-recommended limit of 0.95, RMSEA indicates that there is room for improvement. Correlations between error terms as suggested by the modification indices are defendable (cf. Example 6.1).

Letting only neighboring error terms correlate has only a marginal effect on fit, while letting all error terms correlate will result in an under-identified model. As a compromise (and not to make the example too complicated) I will put in correlations between error terms that are at most three periods away. Part of the output is given in Table 2.

The fit is excellent: CFI = 0.992, RMSA = 0.051, LO 90 = 0.028, HI 90 = 0.074, PCLOSE = 0.446.

The analysis answers the second question raised above. Since the variances are statistically significant for both 'Constant' and 'Slope', these two parameters vary across respondents.

So let us try to answer the third question, and put in variables that could perhaps account for the individual differences in trajectories.

Table 2   Example 10.1: output, second run

Result (Default model)

```
Minimum was achieved
Chi-square = 31.117
Degrees of freedom = 13
Probability level = .003
```

Means: (Group number 1 - Default model)

	Estimate	S.E.	C.R.	P	Label
Constant	1.428	.020	72.102	***	
Slope	.063	.003	20.246	***	

Covariances: (Group number 1 - Default model)

			Estimate	S.E.	C.R.	P	Label
Constant	<-->	Slope	-.005	.003	-1.548	.122	
e80	<-->	e81	.013	.018	.713	.476	
e81	<-->	e82	.032	.013	2.485	.013	
e82	<-->	e83	.042	.010	4.193	***	
e83	<-->	e84	.048	.008	5.791	***	
e84	<-->	e85	.044	.010	4.409	***	
e85	<-->	e86	.013	.012	1.122	.262	
e86	<-->	e87	.000	.016	.009	.993	
e80	<-->	e82	.006	.014	.429	.668	
e82	<-->	e84	.042	.008	5.127	***	
e83	<-->	e85	.025	.006	3.922	***	
e85	<-->	e87	.009	.012	.689	.491	
e81	<-->	e83	.025	.011	2.283	.022	
e84	<-->	e86	.011	.010	1.101	.271	
e80	<-->	e83	.005	.011	.453	.651	
e81	<-->	e84	.020	.008	2.511	.012	
e82	<-->	e85	.024	.006	3.835	***	
e83	<-->	e86	.004	.005	.746	.456	
e84	<-->	e87	.006	.009	.620	.536	

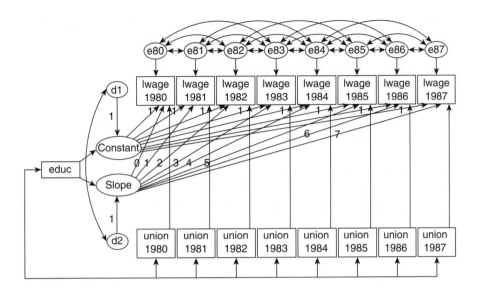

Figure 4   Example 1: conditional model, first run

A conditional latent curve model

The model in Figure 3 is often called an *unconditional curve model*. It describes the trajectory *unconditional* on any variable that could have shaped it. If we put in independent variables that we think account for individual differences in trajectories, we obtain a so-called *conditional curve model*, which is the second step in our two-step strategy.

In their original article Vella and Veerbek included 16 variables and a number of dummy variables to indicate industry and occupation. Since the purpose here is to illustrate a technique and not to solve a substantive research problem, I will include only two exogenous variables, 'years of schooling' and 'union membership', i.e. a dummy variable indicating whether the wage was negotiated with a union. See Figure 4.

Whereas 'years of schooling' is time independent, 'union' is time dependent.

Note that the two latent variables 'Constant' and 'Slope' are now endogenous variables. This means that they have disturbance terms, and that the covariance is now between these two disturbances.

You may wonder why I have not used AMOS Graphics when drawing the figure; an explanation follows below.

The output is given in Table 3.

As my a priori expectation is that union-negotiated wages are higher, and that longer education has a positive effect on start wages as well as on the wage rises one can expect, one-sided tests are appropriate when testing regression weights.

From Table 3 we can see that union-negotiated wages have had a positive effect on the wage level during the period, but that this effect seems to have followed a negative trend from 1980 to 1987.

Longer education has a positive effect on the start wage as well as on the rate of increase in wage one can expect. However, the effect on rate of increase is much smaller than the effect on the start wage. Perhaps, as time goes by, other factors such as work experience play an increasing role.

Even if the model fit is excellent (CFI = 0.982, RMSEA = 0.046, LO 90 = 0.037, HI 90 = 0.056, PCLOSE = 0.732), the modification indices suggest several things.

However, what most strikes the eye is that none of the covariances involving 'educ' is significant, while most other covariances are highly significant.

Table 3 Example 1: output, first conditional model

Result (Default model)

```
Minimum was achieved
Chi-square = 166.394
Degrees of freedom = 77
Probability level = .000
```

Regression Weights: (Group number 1 - Default model)

			Estimate	S.E.	C.R.	P	Label
Constant	<---	educ	.117	.002	67.575	***	
Slope	<---	educ	.006	.000	19.506	***	
lwage1980	<---	Constant	1.000				
lwage1983	<---	Constant	1.000				
lwage1987	<---	Constant	1.000				
lwage1983	<---	Slope	3.000				
lwage1982	<---	Slope	2.000				
lwage1981	<---	Slope	1.000				
lwage1987	<---	Slope	7.000				
lwage1986	<---	Slope	6.000				
lwage1985	<---	Slope	5.000				
lwage1984	<---	Slope	4.000				
lwage1980	<---	Slope	.000				
lwage1984	<---	Constant	1.000				
lwage1985	<---	Constant	1.000				
lwage1986	<---	Constant	1.000				
lwage1982	<---	Constant	1.000				
lwage1981	<---	Constant	1.000				
lwage1980	<---	union1980	.148	.044	3.355	***	
lwage1981	<---	union1981	.158	.036	4.320	***	
lwage1982	<---	union1982	.121	.030	4.008	***	
lwage1983	<---	union1983	.085	.029	2.933	.003	
lwage1984	<---	union1984	.103	.032	3.208	.001	
lwage1985	<---	union1985	.105	.033	3.177	.001	
lwage1987	<---	union1987	.042	.029	1.421	.155	
lwage1986	<---	union1986	.052	.036	1.449	.147	

Means: (Group number 1 - Default model)

	Estimate	S.E.	C.R.	P	Label
educ	11.767	.075	157.190	***	
union1981	.250	.019	13.450	***	
union1987	.262	.019	13.911	***	

	Estimate	S.E.	C.R.	P	Label
union1986	.211	.017	12.062	***	
union1985	.224	.018	12.526	***	
union1984	.251	.019	13.515	***	
union1983	.246	.018	13.318	***	
union1982	.257	.019	13.713	***	
union1980	.251	.019	13.515	***	

Covariances: (Group number 1 - Default model)

			Estimate	S.E.	C.R.	P	Label
union1987	<-->	union1986	.108	.009	12.019	***	
union1985	<-->	union1986	.122	.009	13.563	***	
union1984	<-->	union1985	.127	.009	13.421	***	
union1983	<-->	union1984	.131	.010	13.382	***	
union1982	<-->	union1983	.124	.010	12.835	***	
union1981	<-->	union1982	.103	.009	11.147	***	
union1980	<-->	union1981	.104	.009	11.323	***	
union1985	<-->	union1987	.108	.009	11.856	***	
union1984	<-->	union1986	.114	.009	12.624	***	
union1982	<-->	union1984	.119	.010	12.396	***	
union1981	<-->	union1983	.107	.009	11.651	***	
union1980	<-->	union1982	.082	.009	9.282	***	
union1984	<-->	union1987	.107	.009	11.367	***	
union1983	<-->	union1986	.100	.009	11.573	***	
union1982	<-->	union1985	.102	.009	11.408	***	
union1981	<-->	union1984	.097	.009	10.698	***	
union1980	<-->	union1983	.083	.009	9.485	***	
union1983	<-->	union1987	.093	.009	10.304	***	
union1982	<-->	union1986	.091	.009	10.581	***	
union1981	<-->	union1985	.091	.009	10.499	***	
union1980	<-->	union1984	.074	.009	8.578	***	
union1982	<-->	union1987	.081	.009	9.079	***	
union1981	<-->	union1987	.074	.009	8.447	***	
union1980	<-->	union1987	.062	.009	7.257	***	
d1	<-->	d2	-.005	.003	-1.517	.129	
union1981	<-->	union1986	.087	.008	10.289	***	
union1983	<-->	union1985	.114	.009	12.487	***	
union1980	<-->	union1985	.068	.008	8.263	***	
union1980	<-->	union1986	.055	.008	6.946	***	
union1987	<-->	educ	-.014	.033	-.428	.669	
union1986	<-->	educ	.016	.031	.528	.597	

(Continued)

(Continued)

			Estimate	S.E.	C.R.	P	Label
union1985	<-->	educ	.001	.031	.025	.980	
union1984	<-->	educ	-.031	.033	-.964	.335	
union1983	<-->	educ	-.007	.032	-.215	.830	
union1982	<-->	educ	.005	.033	.147	.883	
union1981	<-->	educ	.016	.032	.492	.623	
union1980	<-->	educ	-.022	.032	-.682	.495	
e80	<-->	e81	.012	.018	.664	.507	
e80	<-->	e82	.007	.013	.532	.595	
e80	<-->	e83	.005	.011	.449	.653	
e81	<-->	e82	.031	.013	2.444	.015	
e81	<-->	e83	.024	.010	2.245	.025	
e81	<-->	e84	.019	.008	2.401	.016	
e82	<-->	e83	.040	.010	4.111	***	
e82	<-->	e84	.042	.008	5.196	***	
e82	<-->	e85	.022	.006	3.670	***	
e83	<-->	e84	.048	.008	5.901	***	
e83	<-->	e85	.024	.006	3.805	***	
e83	<-->	e86	.003	.005	.585	.559	
e84	<-->	e85	.043	.010	4.474	***	
e84	<-->	e86	.012	.010	1.205	.228	
e84	<-->	e87	.008	.009	.890	.374	
e85	<-->	e86	.012	.012	1.062	.288	
e85	<-->	e87	.008	.012	.690	.490	
e86	<-->	e87	.000	.016	.021	.984	

Modification Indices (Group number 1 - Default model)Covariances: (Group number 1 - Default model)

			M.I.	Par Change
d2	<-->	educ	21.262	-.020
d1	<-->	educ	43.867	-.182
e87	<-->	educ	4.535	-.047
e85	<-->	union1987	4.843	-.010
e82	<-->	union1986	7.952	-.010
e82	<-->	union1985	5.344	.008
e82	<-->	union1983	5.345	.008
e82	<-->	e87	4.225	-.008
e82	<-->	e86	8.094	.014
e81	<-->	union1985	6.292	-.010
e81	<-->	e87	5.045	.011
e81	<-->	e86	6.239	-.015

It is tempting as a first step to exclude the insignificant covariances involving 'educ'. None of the correlations (not shown) are numerically larger than 0.04.

However, this conflicts with one of my long-established rules: 'Never leave out correlations among exogenous variables.' So, I decided to keep the insignificant covariances. Remember that correlations among exogenous variables are 'acts of nature' and, so to speak, outside your modeling.

Looking at the modification indices, the most striking suggestions are to incorporate d1 <--> educ and/or d2 <--> educ.

A substantiated reason for this is that omitted variables that are incorporated in the disturbances and thus affect 'Constant' and 'Slope' also influence a respondent's schooling. There is a long list of such variables: parents' economic condition, and education and race, to mention just a few. I will, however, leave further modifications to you as an exercise.

Instead I will use the limited space at my disposal to discuss (in the next section) some general problems. But first a few words about AMOS Graphics versus VB in programming of latent curve models.

AMOS Graphics or VB?

It is apparent from Figure 5 that when modeling LCM in AMOS Graphics the model easily becomes 'messy'. Recall that this model is a very simple one; I only included two explanatory variables. Think about what the model would look like if I included a few more explanatory variables – or if I included all 16 variables and the various dummies in Vella and Veerbek's original work!

This messiness has two consequences:

1. Drawing the covariances is time consuming and you could very easily miss some of them.
2. If you need a graph of your model for publication, you will need a drawing program, so that you can depict your model in a way similar to the one I have used in Figure 4. Also observe that a large part of the model in Figure 5 is outside the printing area, and will be lost if you copy your model to a word processing program.

You can of course try to solve the second problem by using the 'touch-up tool' ✎ or the 'fit-to-page tool' ⊡ to improve the drawing. You can use the 'touch-up tool' to change individual arrows and the 'fit-to-page tool' will expand or compress a diagram to fit a page exactly. You are welcome to experiment with the tools, but I can assure you that none of them can save the model in Figure 5.

Perhaps it is time for you to get acquainted with VB?

The program in Table 4 is very quick to compile because you can use 'copy & paste' frequently.

3 Some Special Problems and Extensions

In this section I will deal with two problems: (1) what to do if the trajectory is not linear and alternative coding of time; and (2) how to interpret the estimated parameters. Lastly in the chapter I will sketch a few extensions of the basic model.

Figure 5 Example 1: the conditional model as drawn in AMOS Graphics

Table 4 Example 1: VB program for the conditional model

```
Public Sub Main()
  Dim Sem As New AmosEngine
  Try
    Sem.TextOutput
    Sem.Standardized
    Sem.TotalEffects
    Sem.Mods( 4)
    Sem.ModelMeansAndIntercepts
    Sem.BeginGroup("C:\Users\Sony\Documents\Wagepan.sav")
    Sem.AStructure("Constant =(0)+educ+(1)d1")
    Sem.AStructure("Slope    =(0)+educ+(1)d2")
    Sem.AStructure("lwage1980=(0)+(1)Constant+(0)Slope+union1980+(1)e80")
    Sem.AStructure("lwage1981=(0)+(1)Constant+(1)Slope+union1981+(1)e81")
    Sem.AStructure("lwage1982=(0)+(1)Constant+(2)Slope+union1982+(1)e82")
    Sem.AStructure("lwage1983=(0)+(1)Constant+(3)Slope+union1983+(1)e83")
    Sem.AStructure("lwage1984=(0)+(1)Constant+(4)Slope+union1984+(1)e84")
    Sem.AStructure("lwage1985=(0)+(1)Constant+(5)Slope+union1985+(1)e85")
    Sem.AStructure("lwage1986=(0)+(1)Constant+(6)Slope+union1986+(1)e86")
    Sem.AStructure("lwage1987=(0)+(1)Constant+(7)Slope+union1987+(1)e87")

    Sem.AStructure("d1 <--> d2")

    Sem.Mean("educ")
    Sem.Mean("union1981")
    Sem.Mean("union1987")
    Sem.Mean("union1986")
    Sem.Mean("union1985")
    Sem.Mean("union1984")
    Sem.Mean("union1983")
    Sem.Mean("union1982")
    Sem.Mean("union1980")
  Finally
    Sem.Dispose
  End Try
End Sub
```

Alternative codings of time

What will you do if an unconditional linear model does not seem to fit?

In other applications of SEM, the natural answer to this question is: let us free some fixed parameters. You can 'unfix' all regression weights for the slope parameter except two. The most common thing is to fix the first at zero and the second at one. In this way you use the growth from the first to the second time period as your unit of measurement.

However, if you choose to 'unfix' the regression weights it is perhaps a better idea to fix the last regression weight at one. If you do that, the regression weights are interpreted as the cumulative proportion of total (positive or negative) growth from the first measurement. Consequently, differences between regression weights reflect the proportion of total growth between the two measurements. This is the default coding in AMOS's LCM plug-in.

Freeing model parameters in order to improve the fit has one virtue: it maximizes fit with the lowest demands for observations.

It has, however, one serious drawback: making the coding of time dependent on the data is not very practical if you want to compare your results with other studies.

Instead you could try a quadratic trajectory as shown in Figure 6.

As you may have guessed, you need three waves to estimate a linear trend, four waves to estimate a quadratic trend, etc.

It is almost impossible to imagine a linear trend going on for ever – a digressive trend is much more likely in practice. However, the quadratic trend has a drawback in many situations: it will at some point in time reach its point of return and begin to decrease. What is needed in many situations is a digressive function with an upper asymptote. The exponential function could be the answer. This would, however, take us too far for an introductory text; instead, the reader is referred to du Toit and Cudeck (2001).

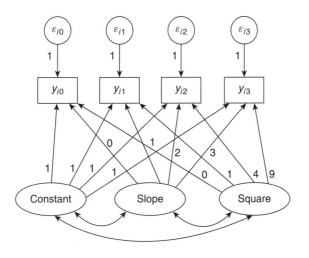

$$y_{it} = \alpha_i + \beta_{1i}\lambda_t + \beta_{2i}^2\lambda_t + \varepsilon_{it}$$

Figure 6 Quadratic trajectory

Sometimes you will find that the variable that defines the time dimension is not the best one, when you consider the purpose of your research. Then you have to redefine the time variable.

As an example, consider an analysis of development in children's reading ability, where you collect data in three waves (i.e. at three points in time). If in any wave there are children of different ages, it might perhaps be better to use age as a time metric.

If children in the first wave are aged 6, 7 and 8 we have in fact three age cohorts. Following these three cohorts through three waves will result in a time variable having values 6, 7, 8, 9, and 10. However, we have only three observations on each child and consequently a lot of missing data: the first cohort will have missing values at 'time' 9 and 10, the second at 'time' 1 and 10, and the third at 'time' 1 and 2. It might perhaps also be a problem that the observations on children of the same age are not collected at the same time. For an extensive treatment of these problems see Bollen and Curran (2006).

Interpreting the model parameters

Following Curran, Bauer, and Willoughby (2004, 2006), the regression weights linking the exogenous variables to the latent factors and to the growth variable ('lwage' in our example) are the parameters of main interest in the conditional model.

Until now we have looked only at the time-invariant variable's influence on the constant and the slope parameters in our trajectory, and in this case the influences were both highly significant. But does that mean that the time-invariant variable also has the same significant influence on our growth variable (lwage) at all points in time? Not necessarily.

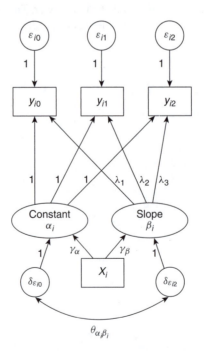

Figure 7   Conditional latent curve model based on the model in Figure 1

   To keep things simple and in general terms, I have added in Figure 7 a time-invariant variable to the model in Figure 1, and at the same time introduced a few λ-terms to underpin that the following arguments are independent of the coding of time
The following equations are just a repetition of (2) stating the *unconditional* model:

$$y_{it} = \alpha_i + \beta_{1i}\lambda_t + \varepsilon_{it}$$
$$\alpha_i = \mu_\alpha + \delta_{\alpha i} \tag{3}$$
$$\beta_i = \mu_\beta + \delta_{\beta i}$$

with the same conditions. I now modify this model as follows to represent the conditional model in Figure 7:

$$y_{it} = \alpha_i + \beta_i\lambda_t + \varepsilon_{it} \tag{4a}$$

$$\alpha_i = \mu_\alpha + \gamma_\alpha x_i + \delta_{\alpha_i} \tag{4b}$$

$$\beta_i = \mu_\beta + \gamma_\beta x_i + \delta_{\beta_i} \tag{4c}$$

By inserting (4b) and (4c) in (4a) we obtain

$$y_{it} = \mu_\alpha + \gamma_\alpha x_i + \delta_{\alpha_i} + \left(\mu_\beta + \gamma_\beta x_i + \delta_{\beta_i}\right)\lambda_t + \varepsilon_{it}$$
$$= \left(\mu_\alpha + \mu_\beta\lambda_t + \gamma_\alpha x_i + \gamma_\beta\lambda_t x_i\right) + \left(\delta_{\alpha_i} + \delta_{\beta_i}\lambda_t + \varepsilon_{it}\right) \tag{5}$$

Looking at the first paranthesis, $\mu_\beta\lambda_t$ depicts the main effect of time on the repeated measure, $\gamma_\alpha x_i$ is the main effect of the time-invariant variable x_i and the last term $\gamma_\beta\lambda_t x_i$ is the interaction effect between the two. However, this interaction is also the indirect effect of x_i via the slope variable.
   All this boils down to the simple conclusion that the effect of the regressor x on the repeated measure depends on time λ_t and vice versa.
   Often one of the two conditional effects on the repeated measurement (i.e. the effect of time conditional on a time-invariant regressor, or the effect of a time-invariant regressor conditional on time) is the main interest in a study, but most often an analysis stops short of that way of thinking.
   Taking the expectation of (5b), we get

$$\mu_{y_t} = \mu_\alpha + \mu_\beta\lambda_t + \gamma_\alpha x_i + \gamma_\beta\lambda_t x_i \tag{6a}$$

and after rearrangement

$$\mu_{y_t} = \underbrace{\left(\mu_\alpha + \gamma_\alpha x_i\right)}_{\text{constant}} + \underbrace{\left(\mu_\beta + \gamma_\beta x_i\right)}_{\text{slope}}\lambda_t \tag{6b}$$

which clearly shows that, while the expected value of the repeated measurement is a linear function of time, this linear function depends on the value of the time-invariant variable x_i.

From the symmetry in (6a) you can get an analogous equation expressing μ_{y_t} as a linear function of x_i, conditional on λ_t.

Example 1 (continued)

Let us look at the effect of time on 'lwage' conditional on years of education.

In order to use (6b), we need estimates of μ_α and μ_β. So, go back to your program for the model in Figure 4 and check 'All implied moments' in 'Analysis Properties/Output' (or add the statement 'Sem.AllImpliedMoments' to the program in Table 4 if you used VB).

We insert our estimates $\hat{\mu}_\alpha = 1.383$ and $\hat{\mu}_\beta = 0.065$ in (6b):

$$\hat{\mu}_{y_t} = \left(1.383 + 0.118x_i\right) + \left(0.065 + 0.005x_i\right)\lambda_t \tag{7}$$

Let us compare the trajectories for young men with 8 years of education and 14 years of education:

$$\hat{\mu}_{y_t|8} = (1.383 + 0.118 \times 8) + (0.065 + 0.005 \times 8)\lambda_t \tag{8a}$$

$$\hat{\mu}_{y_t|14} = (1.383 + 0.118 \times 14) + (0.065 + 0.005 \times 14)\lambda_t \tag{8b}$$

which give

$$\hat{\mu}_{y_t|8} = 2.327 + 0.105\lambda_t \tag{8c}$$

$$\hat{\mu}_{y_t|14} = 3.035 + 0.135\lambda_t \tag{8d}$$

From this we can see that not only is the start wage higher for young men with 14 years of education, but while the yearly growth rate in wage is about 10.5% if they have 8 years of education, it is about 13.5% if they have 14 years of education.

That was a lot of calculations you had to do without much help from AMOS, and in a serious analysis of this kind you also need to estimate variances and standard errors, but fortunately there is a calculator available at http://quantpsy.org/calc.htm that will assist you (Preacher, Curran, & Bauer, 2006).

Some extensions of the latent curve model

In this chapter I have barely scratched the surface of the subject, and to give you some idea of the many possibilities that SEM offers in the analysis of panel-like data, I will sketch a couple of examples.

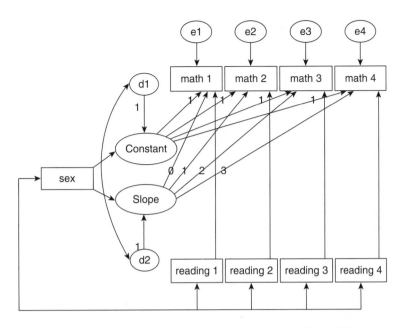

Figure 8   Example 2: Math ability as a function of sex and reading ability

Example 2
Development of mathematical skills

Imagine we want to analyze the progress in math ability of a group of students measured once a year over four years. The model in Figure 8 is parallel to the one in Figure 4, with sex as the time-invariant variable and reading ability as the time-dependent variable.

However, perhaps it would be a better foundation for the analysis to start by getting a feel for the trajectories of both math and reading ability as shown in Figure 9.

Introducing reading ability as a 'cause' for math ability can be done in several ways. You could substitute one-headed arrows for one or more correlations between the disturbances in Figure 9, or – if you wish to keep year-by-year connections between math and reading abilities as in Figure 8 – you could analyze the data as a four-period cross-lagged panel design as in Figure 5.2. You could even combine the cross-lagged panel design with a linear curve model (Bollen & Curran, 2004, pp. 210ff.).

Example 3
Democracy in developing countries

Imagine that you want to follow up the analysis of democracy in developing countries in Example 6.1 to find out whether democracy is gaining or losing ground over time. So you perform a third wave of data collection and construct the model in Figure 10.

You should compare this model with the one in Figure 6.3.

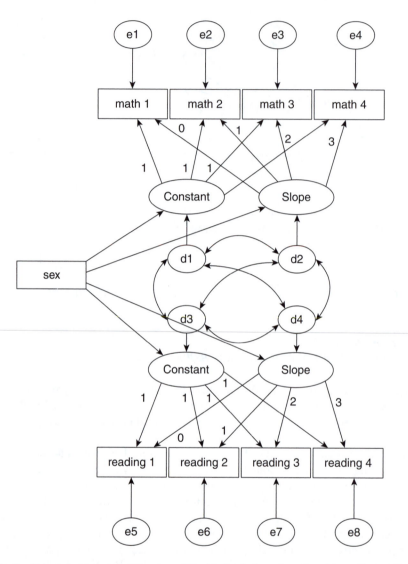

Figure 9 Example 2: unconditional model of trajectories of math and reading ability

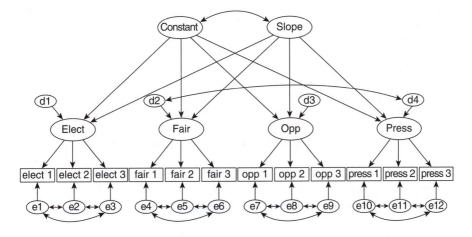

Figure 10   Example 3: latent curve factor model

In this chapter you met the following concepts:

- latent curve model
- trajectory
- unconditional and conditional LCM

time-dependent and
timeindependentregressors

You also learned the following AMOS statements: Sem.AllImpliedMoments

---

Question

1. Compare LCM with other techniques for the analysis of longitudinal data. Discuss the virtues and drawbacks of the various techniques using examples from your own field of study or research.

References

Bollen, K. A., & Curran, P. J. (2004). Autoregressive latent trajectory (ALT) models: A synthesis of two traditions. *Sociological Methods and Research, 32,* 336–383.

Bollen, K. A., & Curran, P. J. (2006). *Latent curve models: A structural equation perspective.* Hoboken, NJ: Wiley.

Curran, P. J., Bauer, D. J., & Willoughby, M. T. (2004). Testing and probing main effects and interactions in latent curve analysis. *Psychological Methods, 9,* 220–237.

Curran, P. J., Bauer, D. J., & Willoughby, M. T. (2006). Testing and probing interactions in hierarchical linear growth models. In C. S. Bergeman & S. M. Boker (Eds.), *Methodological issues in aging research* (Vol. 1, pp. 99–129). Mahwah, NJ: Erlbaum.

du Toit, S. H., & Cudeck, R. (2001). The analysis of nonlinear random coefficient regression models wwith LISREL using constraints. In S. du Toit & D. S. R. Cudeck (Ed.), *Structural equation modeling: Present and future.* Lincolnwood, IL: Scientific Software.

Meredith, W., & Tisak, J. (1984). On "Tuckerizing" curves. Paper presented at the Annual Meeting of the Psychometric Society, Santa Barbara, CA.

Meredith, W., & Tisak, J. (1990). Latent curve analysis. *Psychometrika, 55*(1), 107–122.

Preacher, D. J., Curran, P. J., & Bauer, D. J. (2006). Computational tools for probing interactions in multiple linear regression, multilevel modeling, and latent curve analysis. *Journal of Educational and Behavioral Statistics, 31*, 437–448.

Tucker, L. R. (1958). Determination of parameters of a functional relation by factor analysis. *Psychometrika, 23*, 19–23.

Vella, F., & Veerbek, M. (1998). Whose wages do unions raise? A dynamic model of unionism and wage rate determinination for young men. *Journal of Applied Econometrics, 61*, 783–820.

Further Reading

Bollen, K. A., & Curran, P. J. (2006). Latent curve models: A structural equation perspective. Hoboken, NJ: Wiley.

Duncan, T. E., Duncan, S. C., & Strycker, L. A. (2006). An introduction to latent variable growth curve modeling: Concepts, issues, and application (2nd edn). Mahwah, NJ: Erlbaum.

Appendices

A

Statistical Prerequisites

This appendix is intended as a statistical refresher, and can be read as an introduction to the book or consulted when necessary during reading of the main text.

The appendix contains the following sections:

1. Probability and Probability Distributions
2. Describing Your Data
3. Sample and Population (Including Estimation and Testing)
4. Correlation and Regression

1 Probability and Probability Distributions

If A_i for $i = 1, 2, 3, \ldots$ is a series of mutual exclusive and collective exhaustive *events*, having probabilities $P(A_i)$ of occurring, then X is called a *random variable*, if the value of X depends on A.

A *probability function* is a function $f(X)$ that assigns a probability to every possible value of X. If $f(X)$ is a probability function, then

$$\sum_i X_i = 1.00 \tag{1}$$

if X is discrete, i.e. can only take on a countable number of values, and

$$\int_i X_i = 1.00 \tag{2}$$

if X is continuous, i.e. can take on all values (possibly only in one or more intervals).

In this book, most often the event is that respondent i is included in a random sample from some population, and X_i is the value of some measurement taken on this respondent, e.g. his or her answer to a question in a questionnaire.

The normal distribution

The probability function you will most often meet in this book is the *normal distribution*. The normal distribution is a symmetrical, bell-shaped distribution, as can be seen from Figure 1. The normal distribution is continuous with probability function

$$f(x \mid \mu, \sigma^2) = \left(\sigma\sqrt{2\pi}\right)^{-1} e^{-(x-\mu)^2/2\sigma^2} \tag{3}$$

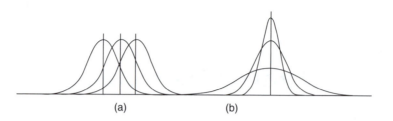

Figure 1   Normal distributions: (a) with the same σ but different μ; (b) with the same μ but different σ

The distribution has two *parameters* μ and σ^2. μ is the so-called *expected value* (the 'mean') of the distribution, and σ^2 is the *variance* (a measure of the 'spread'). I will have more to say on expected value and variance later on.

If for example you want to calculate the probability that a normally distributed random variable with $\mu = 20$ and $\sigma^2 = 4$ takes on values less than or equal to 25, you *standardize* the variable to have $\mu = 0$ and $\sigma^2 = 1$, by subtracting μ and dividing by σ:

$$P\left(X \leq 25 \big| \mu = 20;\ \sigma^2 = 4\right) = P\left(\frac{X - \mu}{\sigma} \leq \frac{25 - 20}{2}\right) = P(Z \leq 2.5) = 0.994$$

The value 0.994 can be read from a table of the *standard normal distribution*.

The chi-square distribution
The chi-square distribution – usually denoted by χ^2 – is a continuous one-parameter distribution. Its parameter is usually denoted by ν (the Greek letter nu), which can take on all positive integer values. The distribution is right-skewed, the skewness declining with increasing values of ν. For $\nu \to \infty$ the chi-square distribution approaches a normal distribution. See Figure 2.

The main purpose of χ^2 is as a measure of a model's accordance with the same data.

2   Describing Your Data

The most obvious way to describe your sample data is to depict the distribution in a histogram, but often you need only to summarize the characteristics of the distribution in a few figures.

The central tendency in a distribution of a variable X is most often summarized in the *mean* of the observations

$$\overline{X} = \frac{\sum\limits_{i=1}^{n} X_i}{n} \tag{4}$$

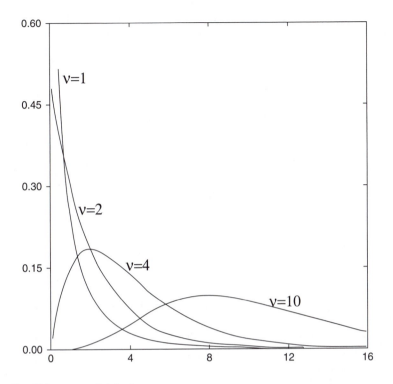

Figure 2 Chi-square distributions

where n is the sample size. Likewise the spread of the data is most often measured by the *variance*, the mean of the squared deviations around the mean

$$s^2 = \frac{\sum_{i=1}^{n}(X_i - \bar{X})^2}{n-1} \tag{5}$$

In defining the variance as the *mean* of the squared deviations around the mean, you may wonder why I divided by $n-1$ and not n in the expression (5). An explanation follows in Section 3.

Now, the variance is measured in other units than the data, which could be a little annoying, e.g. in dealing with people's heights measured in centimeters, the spread would be measured in square centimeters! To solve this problem we take the square root of the variance in order to obtain the *standard deviation*

$$s = \sqrt{s^2} = \sqrt{\frac{(X - \bar{X})^2}{n-1}} \tag{6}$$

and thus return to the original measurement units.

The mean and variance (or standard deviation) say nothing (or little) about the shape of the distribution. We need a measure for describing the skewness. In AMOS skewness is measured by

$$M_3 = \frac{\sum_{i=1}^{n}\left(X_i - \bar{X}\right)^3}{ns^2} \tag{7}$$

If $M_3 = 0$, the distribution is symmetric, if $M_3 > 0$, it has a long upper tail, and if $M_3 < 0$, it has a long lower tail.

The last descriptor of univariate distributions is the *kurtosis*

$$M_4 = \frac{\sum_{i=1}^{n}\left(X_i - \bar{X}\right)^4}{ns^4} \tag{8a}$$

Most often kurtosis is interpreted as a measure of 'peakiness' but in fact this descriptor is a bit more complicated (DeCarlo, 1997).

If you have a symmetric distribution – such as the normal in Figure 1 – you can think of it as consisting of three parts: the peak, the shoulders (in the normal case located around $\bar{X} - s$ and $\bar{X} + s$) and the tails.

For a normal distribution $M_4 = 3$. If $M_4 > 3$ the distribution is 'peakier' and has thicker tails than a normal distribution *with the same variance*. In other words, you can imagine that weight is pushed from the shoulders towards the peak and – in order to preserve variance – also towards the tails. If $M_4 < 3$, the weight is pushed from the peak and the tails towards the shoulders: the distribution gets flatter with thinner tails.

In AMOS Equation (8a) is normalized by subtracting 3, so that a normal distribution gets a kurtosis of zero:

$$M_4 = \frac{\sum_{i=1}^{n}\left(X_i - \bar{X}\right)^4}{ns^4} - 3 \tag{8b}$$

3   Sample and Population

Usually your interest is not in the sample itself, but in making inferences about the population from which the sample was drawn. Then the sample statistics defined in (4)–(8) are considered *estimators* of the equivalent population parameters as shown in Table 1, where N is the size of the population.

For continuous variables integrals should be substituted for the summations. I have chosen to forego the complications of distinguishing between finite and infinite populations – so in the following think about a finite population being large enough to consider it infinite!

Table 1 Sample statistics and population parameters

Sample	Population
$\bar{X} = \dfrac{\sum\limits_{i=1}^{n} X_i}{n}$	$\mu = \dfrac{\sum\limits_{j=1}^{N} X_j}{N}$
$s^2 = \dfrac{\sum\limits_{i=1}^{n}\left(X_i - \bar{X}\right)^2}{n-1}$	$\sigma^2 = \dfrac{\sum\limits_{j=1}^{N}\left(X_i - \mu\right)^2}{N}$
$M_3 = \dfrac{\sum\limits_{i=1}^{n}\left(X_i - \bar{X}\right)^3}{ns^2}$	$\mu_3 = \dfrac{\sum\limits_{j=1}^{N}\left(X_j - \mu\right)^3}{N\sigma^2}$
$M_4 = \dfrac{\sum\limits_{i=1}^{n}\left(X_i - \bar{X}\right)^4}{ns^4}$	$\mu_4 = \dfrac{\sum\limits_{j=1}^{N}\left(X_j - \mu\right)^4}{N\sigma^4}$

Estimation and degrees of freedom

It seems reasonable to use

$$\hat{\sigma}^2 = \frac{\sum\limits_{i=1}^{n}\left(X_i - \bar{X}\right)^2}{n} \tag{9}$$

as an estimator of σ^2. In fact it can be shown that $\bar{X}$ and $\hat{\sigma}^2$ are *maximum likelihood estimators* of the corresponding population parameters – that is, they give the values of the parameters that have the largest probability of producing the sample statistics.

However, it can be shown that (9) has a tendency to underestimate the population variance. This is no surprise, because ideally the unknown μ should be used in the numerator of (9), and the sample will of course cluster more around $\bar{X}$ than around μ. In order to correct for this the denominator is reduced by one in (5). Of course this is no proof that reducing the denominator by one is the right thing to do, but it is!

Looking at the numerator, it consists of a sum of squares of n terms. However, these n terms are not independent. If you know the values of the first $n-1$ terms, you also know the last term because of the restriction

$$\sum_{i=1}^{n}(X_i - \bar{X}) = 0 \tag{10}$$

so you could say that in a way s^2 is the 'mean' of *independent* squared deviations around the sample mean.

s^2 is an *unbiased* estimator of σ^2. This means that if you take a 'large' number of samples from the population and calculate s^2 for every sample, then the average of s^2 across the samples – the expected value of the *sampling distribution* of the mean – will equal σ^2.

The denominator $n-1$ in (5) is called the *degrees of freedom*, and the general rule is that for each estimate based on sample information that is substituted for a parameter value, you lose one degree of freedom.

It is worth mentioning that as estimation in SEM is generally based on maximum likelihood estimation or other estimation methods with similar large-sample properties, all variances and covariances in the output are maximum likelihood estimates using n as the denominator, while the entries in the input covariance matrix are supposed to be unbiased estimates (of course you can override these defaults).

The standard deviation of a sampling distribution is called the *standard error* of that particular estimator. In the case of the sample mean, the standard error is

$$\sigma_{\bar{X}} = \frac{\sigma}{\sqrt{n}} \tag{11a}$$

and is estimated as

$$s_{\bar{X}} = \frac{s}{\sqrt{n}} \tag{11b}$$

If the sample is sufficiently large – or if the population from which it is drawn is normal – the sampling distribution of the mean is normal. This means that a 95% *confidence interval* for the mean can be constructed as

$$\mu \approx \bar{X} \pm 1.96 s \tag{12}$$

Meaning that there is a probability of 0.95 that the actual interval contains the (unknown) parameter μ.

Interval estimates for other parameters are constructed in similar ways.

Properties of estimators

The quality of estimators is judged on several criteria, of which the most important are as follows:

1. An estimator $\hat{\theta}$ is *unbiased* if $E(\hat{\theta}) = \theta$.
2. An estimator $\hat{\theta}$ is *efficient* if its sampling distribution has a small variance.
3. An estimator is *consistent* if it tends to be near the population parameter as the sample becomes larger. If an estimator is biased, consistency assures that the bias becomes smaller as the sample size increases.

4. An estimator is *sufficient* if it contains all information from the sample that bears on the unknown parameter. For example, $\bar{X}$ is a sufficient estimator of μ: once you have computed $\bar{X}$, no other sample statistic can add to the information about μ.

It can be shown that $\bar{X}$ is unbiased, consistent and sufficient. Further, $\bar{X}$ is the most efficient of all unbiased estimators of μ.

The central limit theorem

This theorem states that if X_i $(i = 1, 2, 3, \ldots, n)$ is a sequence of random observations from a population and $f(X_i)$ has a finite variance, then under fairly general conditions

$$\hat{\theta} = \sum_i \alpha_i X_i \qquad (13)$$

converges towards a normal distribution as $n \to \infty$.

This in fact means that most of the estimators you will meet in this book are asymptotically normally distributed.

Statistical testing

Often you will want to test a hypothesis about the population from which the sample is taken. The idea is that you make all calculations on the assumption that the hypothesis you want to support is false and if you then end up with an unlikely result, either a miracle has happened or your starting point, that your hypothesis is wrong, must be rejected. Usually the last interpretation is the more realistic of the two.

You go through the following steps:

1. Formulation of *null hypothesis* H_0 and *alternative hypothesis* H_1. H_1 is the hypothesis you want to support, and H_0 is the opposite hypothesis.
2. Determination of *significance level* α. α is the maximum probability for rejecting H_0 if H_0 is true; α is most often (arbitrarily) set at 0.05.
3. Choice of a *test statistic* (e.g. $\bar{X}$), the sampling distribution of which is known if H_0 is true.
4. Calculation of the value of the test statistic.
5. Calculation of the *P*-value, the probability of observing the actual value of the test statistic, or a value that casts even more doubt on H_0, assuming that H_0 is true.
6. Conclusion: if $P < \alpha$, reject H_0 (and accept H_1), otherwise accept H_0.

Example 1

Say you want to test the hypothesis that the mean length of a certain component in a large production batch is at least 25 cm, and you have drawn a simple random sample of 50 components from the batch.

Let us now go through the six steps above:

1. $H_0 : \mu \le 25$

   $H_1 : \mu > 25$

2. α is (traditionally!) set at 0.05.

3. I choose to base my conclusion on the value of $\overline{X}$, which is normally distributed here with largest mean $\mu = 25$ and variance given by (11) if H_0 is true.

4. $\overline{X}$ is calculated at 26.5 cm with a standard error of 0.83.

5. $P(\overline{X} \ge 26.5 | \mu = 25) = P\left(Z \ge \dfrac{26.5 - 25}{0.83}\right) = P(Z \ge 1.81)$ where Z is standard normally distributed. This probability is read from a table of the standard normal distribution to be 0.035.

6. As the probability of getting a sample mean equal to or larger than the one observed is so small (smaller than α) if H_0 is true, we reject H_0, and conclude that (in all probability) $\mu > 25$.

One- and two-sided tests

The example above was a one-sided test. You will also meet two-sided alternative hypotheses such as

$$H_0 : \mu = 25$$
$$H_1 : \mu \ne 25$$

In this situation you will be interested in both positive and negative deviations.

The trouble with this formulation is that you know beforehand that H_0 is false. It is not very likely that $\mu = 25.000000000000\ldots$ and so on to infinity. If your sample is large enough you will reject H_0. So what is the rationale behind this sort of test?

You will meet this situation whenever you have a 'sharp' null hypothesis and a 'soft' alternative.

The chi-square test

I shall not go deeply into the actual calculations involved, but just point out that χ^2 is used to test the fit of a model to the data at hand. The model could have many forms, but whatever it is, the null and alternative hypotheses are

H_0: the model fits the data exactly

H_1: the model does not fit the data

Observe that when testing for model fit in SEM, the roles of the two hypotheses are interchanged. Now H_0 is the hypothesis you want the data to support, and as no model fits the data exactly, H_0 is false a priori with the consequences mentioned above.

4 Correlation and Regression

SEM is about mapping relations between variables, so traditional correlation and regression analysis is a natural primer for SEM.

You can calculate the means and the variances of two variables (call them X and Y), but you also need a measure of the interdependence of the two. To that end you can compute their covariance

$$s_{XY} = \frac{\sum_{i=1}^{n}\left(X_i - \bar{X}\right)\left(Y_i - \bar{Y}\right)}{n-1} \tag{14}$$

which is an unbiased estimator of the population covariance

$$\sigma_{XY} = \frac{\sum_{i=1}^{N}\left(X_i - \mu_X\right)\left(Y_i - \mu_Y\right)}{N} \tag{15}$$

The covariance is a sort of 'mix' of the two variances (a variable's covariance with itself is its variance).

If $s_{XY} = 0$, the two variables are *linearly* independent; if $s_{XY} > 0$, the two variables are *positively correlated*, i.e. they covary *linearly* in the way that if one goes up, the other does too; and if $s_{XY} < 0$, they covary linearly in the opposite direction.

A problem with the covariance as a measure of correlation (linear interdependence) is that it has no upper or lower limit because its size depends on the units of measurement. So, how large numerically should a covariance be, before we accept that a (positive or negative) correlation is present?

If we standardize both variables

$$X_i^* = \frac{X_i - \bar{X}}{s_X} \text{ and } Y_i^* = \frac{Y_i - \bar{Y}}{s_Y} \tag{16}$$

to have mean 0 and variance 1, and then calculate the covariance between the two

$$r = \frac{\sum\left(X_i^*\right)\left(Y_i^*\right)}{n-1} = \frac{\sum\left(X_i - \bar{X}\right)\left(Y_i - \bar{Y}\right)}{(n-1)s_X s_Y} = \frac{\sum\left(X_i - \bar{X}\right)\left(Y_i - \bar{Y}\right)}{\sqrt{\sum\left(X_i - \bar{X}\right)^2 \sum\left(Y_i - \bar{Y}\right)^2}} \tag{17}$$

we obtain the so-called (*simple*) *correlation coefficient*, which is scale independent and bounded within the limits $-1 \le r \le 1$. Further, r^2 (*the coefficient of determination*) indicates the proportion of the variance that one variable has in common with the other.

Equation (17) is a biased estimate of the population parameter, which is defined as

$$\rho = \left.\sum_{i=1}^{n}\left(\frac{X - \mu_X}{\sigma_X}\right)\left(\frac{Y - \mu_Y}{\sigma_Y}\right)\right/ N \tag{18}$$

Example 2
Estimating covariance and correlation coefficient

Bredahl (2001) used SEM in a cross-national study of factors influencing consumers' attitudes and buying intentions towards genetically modified food products (Example 4.1).

As an illustration I will use the first 20 observations on the variables 'tech' (attitude to genetic modification in food production) and 'risk' (perceived risk by using genetically modified food) from Example 4.1, as shown in Figure 3.

You can download the complete data set as an SPSS file from the book's website.

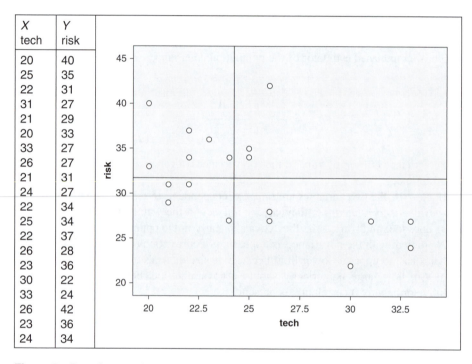

X tech	Y risk
20	40
25	35
22	31
31	27
21	29
20	33
33	27
26	27
21	31
24	27
22	34
25	34
22	37
26	28
23	36
30	22
33	24
26	42
23	36
24	34

Figure 3   Data for correlation and regression analysis

Means, variances, standard deviations and covariance are calculated as shown in Table 2. In this case we have

$$r = \frac{-243.9000}{\sqrt{310.5500 \times 532.2000}} = -0.6000 \tag{19}$$

which gives $r^2 = 0.36$. The two variables have 36% of their variance in common.

Simple regression analysis

While the covariances and correlation coefficients are measures of covariation, and as such measures of what we could call a symmetric relationship, in (simple) regression

Table 2 Calculation of sample statistics

	X = tech	Y = tech	$(X_i - \bar{X})^2$	$(Y_i - \bar{Y})^2$	$(X_i - \bar{X})(Y_i - \bar{Y})$
	20	40	23.5225	68.8900	−40.2550
	25	35	0.0225	10.8900	0.4950
	22	31	8.1225	0.4900	1.9950
	31	27	37.8225	22.0900	−28.9050
	21	29	14.8225	7.2900	10.3950
	20	33	23.5225	1.6900	−6.3050
	33	27	66.4225	22.0900	−38.3050
	26	27	1.3225	22.0900	−5.4050
	21	31	14.8225	0.4900	2.6950
	24	27	0.7225	22.0900	3.9950
	22	34	8.1225	5.2900	−6.5550
	25	34	0.0225	5.2900	0.3450
	22	37	8.1225	28.0900	−15.1050
	26	28	1.3225	13.6900	−4.2550
	23	36	3.4225	18.4900	−7.9550
	30	22	26.5225	94.0900	−49.9550
	33	24	66.4225	59.2900	−62.7550
	26	42	1.3225	106.0900	11.8450
	23	36	3.4225	18.4900	−7.9550
	24	34	0.7225	5.2900	−1.9550
Σ	497	634	310.5500	532.2000	−243.9000
$\Sigma/20$	24.85	31.70			
$\Sigma/19$			16.3447	28.0105	−12.8368
$\Sigma/19$			4.04	5.29	
	↑	↑	↑	↑	↑
	$\bar{X}$	$\bar{Y}$	s_X^2	s_Y^2	s_{XY}

analysis one variable (e.g. X) is called the *independent* variable or *predictor* or *regressor* and the other (Y) is called the *dependent* or *criterion* variable, and the purpose is to estimate the parameters in the model

$$Y_i = \beta_0 + \beta_1 X_i + \varepsilon_i \tag{20}$$

with the aim of predicting the value of Y from knowledge of the value of X.
    It is assumed that:

1(a) the values of X are known and fixed a priori (e.g. through an experimental design); or

1(b) X is a stochastic variable that is uncorrelated with ε and whose distribution is independent of the regression coefficients.

In addition we assume that:

2. the error terms ε_i that depict the combined effects of all other factors having an effect on Y are uncorrelated and all have expected value 0 and the same variance.

Under these conditions the parameters of (20) can be estimated using least squares minimizing of the variance of ε_i.

The estimated *regression coefficients* b_0 and b_1 are called *regression weights* in AMOS. If the error terms can be assumed to be normally distributed, you can calculate confidence intervals for the population parameters and test various hypotheses about them.

If the variables are standardized before the analysis, the regression coefficients are usually called *beta coefficients* or, in AMOS, *standardized regression weights*.

Example 3
Simple regression analysis using SPSS

You use the same data set as in the previous example. After opening the data set in SPSS, choose 'Analyze/Regression/Linear' as shown in Figure 4a, and the window in Figure 4b will appear. Select the variable *risk*, and by clicking the top little arrow, move the variable from the left panel to the box marked 'Dependent'. Then select the variable *tech* and move it to the box marked 'Independent' by clicking the appropriate little arrow. When you click 'OK', the output in Table 3 will be shown.

(a)

(b)

Figure 4   Example 3: the first steps in regression analysis in SPSS

In the first table, note that (in connection with regression analysis) SPSS calculates the correlation coefficient as positive, although we know from (18) that, in this case, it is negative! This is because SPSS uses the same algorithm as in the calculation of the multiple correlation coefficient – see next section. I will postpone commenting on the output in the second table to the next section on multiple regression.

In the third table you will find estimates of the parameters making up the line shown in Figure 5. The equation for the estimated regression line is

$$\hat{Y} = 51.217 - 0.785X \tag{21}$$

Table 3   Example 3: output from SPSS

Model Summary

Model	R	R Square	Adjusted R Square	Std. Error of the Estimate
1	.600(a)	.360	.324	4.350

a   Predictors: (Constant), tech

ANOVA(b)

Model		Sum of Squares	df	Mean Square	F	Sig.
1	Regression	191.554	1	191.554	10.122	.005(a)
	Residual	340.646	18	18.925		
	Total	532.200	19			

a Predictors: (Constant), tech
b Dependent Variable: risk

Coefficients(a)

Model		Unstandardized Coefficients		Standardized Coefficients	t	Sig.
		B	Std. Error	Beta		
1	(Constant)	51.217	6.211		8.246	.000
	tech	-.785	.247	-.600	-3.181	.005

a Dependent Variable: risk

and the standard deviation of the error term ε is estimated at 4.350. It is found in the first table, where it is called *Std. Error of the Estimate*.

Next to the estimates 51.217 and $-.785$ are the standard errors of the two estimates. If ε_i (for $i = 1, 2, ..., n$) follow the same normal distribution with mean 0, then $t = b_j / std(b_j)$ has a t-distribution with $n-2$ degrees of freedom (because we have estimated two parameters in the regression line, β_0 and β_1; the degrees of freedom are a parameter in the t-distribution). The t-distribution resembles the normal distribution, but has fatter tails. However, the more degrees of freedom, the more the t-distribution approaches the normal distribution.

Even if ε_i is not normally distributed, the sampling distributions of β_0 and β_1 are asymptotically normally distributed – by the central limit theorem – which makes testing possible if the sample is sufficiently large.

Next to the standardized coefficients (Beta), we find the t-values for the two (unstandardized) regression coefficients, and in the last column are the *significance probabilities* or *P*-values of a test of $H_0: \beta_j = 0$ against $H_0: \beta_j \neq 0$. As is evident, this null hypothesis is rejected for both coefficients at any reasonable level of significance.

Multiple regression
Introducing another predictor, using

$$Y_i = \beta_0 + \beta_1 X_{1i} + \beta_2 X_{2i} + \varepsilon_i \qquad (22)$$

does not make any principal difference but adds to the calculations and opens up problems associated with *co-linearity*. Co-linearity is the correlation among regressors. If the regressors covary, it is easy to see that it could be difficult to measure their

Figure 5   Example 3: regression line

individual effects on the criterion variable – and consequently the standard errors of the regression coefficients are increased.

The correlation coefficient between the actual Y-values and the values $\hat{Y}_i$ predicted by the estimated regression function is called the *multiple correlation coefficient*, usually designated R. The square of R is called the *multiple coefficient of determination*, and as you will have guessed it shows how large a proportion of its variance Y shares with the regressors taken as a whole, or as is usually expressed: how large a proportion of the variation in Y that is 'explained' by variation in the regressors.

R^2 is upward biased – especially if the number of regressors is large compared with the number of observations. The *adjusted* R^2, defined as

$$R^2_{adjusted} = 1 - \left(1 - R^2\right)\frac{df}{n - k} \tag{23}$$

where *df* is the degrees of freedom and k the number of regressors, adjusts R^2 downwards in order to compensate for this.

Perhaps you might expect the sum of the simple correlation coefficients squared to equal R^2, i.e.

$$R^2 = r^2_{X_1 Y} + r^2_{X_2 Y} \tag{24}$$

but this is only true in the absence of co-linearity.

Example 4
Multiple regression analysis using SPSS

If in addition to 'tech' we use 'alienation' (alienation to the marketplace) from the same data set as the regressor, we get the output given in Table 4.

Table 4 Example 4: output from multiple regression analysis

Model Summary

Model	R	R Square	Adjusted R Square	Std. Error of the Estimate
1	.818(a)	.669	.630	3.219

a   Predictors: (Constant), alienati, tech

ANOVA(b)

Model		Sum of Squares	df	Mean Square	F	Sig.
1	Regression	356.002	2	178.001	17.174	.000(a)
	Residual	176.198	17	10.365		
	Total	532.200	19			

a   Predictors: (Constant), alienati, tech
b   Dependent Variable: risk

Coefficients(a)

Model		Unstandardized Coefficients		Standardized Coefficients	t	Sig.
		B	Std. Error	Beta		
1	(Constant)	23.856	8.265		2.886	.010
	tech	-.344	.214	-.263	-1.609	.126
	alienati	1.041	.261	.650	3.983	.001

a   Dependent Variable: risk

In the first table you will find the multiple correlation coefficient R, the (multiple) coefficient of determination R^2, the adjusted R^2 and the standard error of estimate, i.e. the standard deviation of ε.

The sum of squares in the second table is defined as follows:

Regression sum of squares: $$\sum_i \left(\hat{Y}_i - \bar{Y} \right)^2 \qquad (25a)$$

Residual sum of squares: $$\sum_i \left(Y_i - \hat{Y} \right)^2 \qquad (25b)$$

Total sum of squares: $$\sum_i \left(Y_i - \bar{Y} \right)^2 \qquad (25c)$$

The regression sum of squares is that part of the sum of squares for Y that is 'explained' by the regression function, while the residual sum of squares is the 'unexplained' sum of squares measuring the deviations of the observations from the regression line – or in the case of multiple regression, the regression plane.

As you may have guessed (and as you can easily verify)

$$R^2 = \frac{\sum_i \left(\hat{Y}_i - \bar{Y} \right)^2}{\sum_i \left(Y_i - \bar{Y} \right)^2} \tag{26}$$

The F-test is a traditional analysis of variance F-test of the hypothesis

$$H_0 : \beta_j = 0 \text{ for all values of } j \text{ or } H_0 : R^2 = 0 \tag{27}$$

and is then a test of the regression function taken as a whole.

As can be seen from the second table, the regression function is highly significant, and from the third table it appears that only alienation is significant. But remember: these are two-sided tests. The one-sided P-value for 'tech' is 0.063, so if you have formulated a one-sided hypotheses *before* observing the data, 'tech' is nearly significant at the traditional significance level of 0.05.

References

Bredahl, L. (2001). Determinants of consumer attitudes and purchase intentions with regard to genetically modified foods – results of a cross-national survey. *Journal of Consumer Policy, 24*, 23–61.

DeCarlo, L. T. (1997). On the meaning and use of kurtosis. *Psychological Methods, 2*(3), 292–307.

Further Reading

Kutner, M., Nachtsheim, C., & Neter, J. (2004). *Applied linear regression models* (rev. edn). New York: McGraw-Hill.

B
Glossary

acyclic model Consider the graphical picture of a model with variables (manifest or latent) connected by one- and two-headed arrows. If it is not possible by following one-headed arrows to return to the variable where you started, the model is *acyclic*, otherwise it is *cyclic*

ADF estimation Short for 'asymptotically distribution-free estimation', one of the estimation methods available in AMOS

AMOS Graphics The graphic interface that makes it possible to compile programs in AMOS by drawing the model (as opposed to writing the program in VB or C+)

asymptotically distribution-free estimation One of the estimation methods available in AMOS

Bayesian estimation One of the estimation methods available in AMOS. It is beyond the scope of this book

binary variable A variable that can have only one of two values, e.g. the variable 'sex'

Bollen–Stine χ^2-test When using bootstrapping with non-normal data, the 'traditional' χ^2-test will be misleading, and instead you use the Bollen–Stine χ^2-test, which is based on an 'empirical' χ^2-distribution calculated across the bootstrapped samples

bootstrapping A resampling method, where you construct a sampling distribution of a *statistic* by drawing a large number of simple random samples with replacement from your original sample (which serves as a 'population'), all samples having the same size as your original one

causal relation Although the word is used in everyday language without causing misunderstandings, the concept of causality is rather dim and a more stringent definition can only be given within a scientific *model*. A causal relation can be seen as a 'force' from one event or concept – the 'cause' – to another event or concept – the 'effect'. Since we cannot observe this 'force', the definition is an *operational definition* that allows listing of the criteria that a relationship must fulfill in order to be called 'causal'. Most often three criteria are used: (1) a co-occurrence or covariation; (2) a time difference between the two, the cause coming before the effect; and (3) the grounded exclusion of other possible explanations of the fulfilling of the other two conditions than that of a 'causal relation' (whatever that means!)

coefficient of determination	This is the same as the correlation coefficient squared, R^2. It can be interpreted as the fraction of variance in the dependent variable that is 'explained' by an equation
component loading	The correlation or covariance between a variable and a *principal component*. Factor loading is defined analogously
component score	The value of a principal component. Factor score is defined analogously
component score coefficient	The coefficient of a variable when a *component score* is expressed as a linear function of the variables involved. Factor score coefficient is defined analogously
conceptual definition	As you would find in a maths book or in an encyclopedia, new concepts are defined with reference to concepts defined earlier or (in the case of an encyclopedia) to concepts that are assumed to be better known. An *operational definition* defines a concept through the method used to measure it: 'temperature' is what you measure using *this* thermometer, 'intelligence' is what you measure using *this* test
conditional latent curve modelling	Latent curve modeling (LCM) that includes variables that are supposed to influence the trajectory of the LCM
confirmatory analysis	Verification (confirmation) of a model (theory) formulated a priori, e.g. before you look at the present data. If the analysis is not confirmatory it is *exploratory*, i.e. you explore your data in order to find some meaning in them and perhaps be able to formulate a model without having very precise ideas in mind. The distinction is, however, not as absolute in practice as in theory
confirmatory factor model	A factor model with parameter restrictions
constraint	See *parameter constraint*
construct	Same as *latent variable*
convergent and discriminating validity	Criteria for judging the validity of a measuring instrument
correlation matrix	A *matrix* whose element in the i, j position is the correlation between the ith and jth variable
covariance matrix	A *matrix* whose element in the i, j position is the covariance between the ith and jth variable
critical ratio (CR)	A parameter estimate divided by its *standard error*
Cronbach's α	A commonly used measure of reliability for *summated scales*
cyclic model	Consider the graphical picture of a model with variables (manifest or latent) connected with one- and two-headed arrows. If it is possible by following one-headed arrows to return to the variable where you started, the model is *cyclic*, otherwise it is *acyclic*

data matrix	A *matrix* whose element in the *i*, *j* position is the *i*th respondent's (or whatever the analytical unit may be) value on the *j*th variable
default	The method the computer program would choose if not instructed otherwise, e.g. MLmaximum likelihood is the default estimation method in AMOS
default model	(In AMOS) The actual model you are working on
degrees of freedom	In general, the degrees of freedom (df) of an estimate of a parameter is equal to the number of independent 'pieces of information' that go into the estimate minus the number of parameters used as intermediate steps in the estimation of the parameter itself (e.g. in estimating a variance, df is the sample size minus one, since the sample mean is the only intermediate step). In the case of SEM, the df is (in most cases) the number of non-redundant entries in the sample covariance matrix ('pieces of information') minus the number of parameters to be estimated
direct effect	See *total effect*
disturbance	The combined effects of all omitted variables on a dependent variable in a structural model. Usually called δ, but in AMOS most times called 'd'
eigenvalue	Every symmetric $p \times p$ matrix – and that includes covariance and correlation matrices – has associated with it *p eigenvalues* (some of which could be identical). If the eigenvalues are all positive, the matrix is said to be *positive definite* (if they are all negative, it is *negative definite*). If they are non-negative, the matrix is *positive semi-definite*. As the eigenvalues can be interpreted as the variances of the *principal components* of the matrix, covariance and correlation matrices must necessarily be (at least) positive semi-definite. However, some calculations used in the estimation process are not defined for positive semi-definite covariance matrices, so you have a problem if your sample covariance matrix is not (at least) positive semi-definite
elbow plot	A graphic depiction of the variances of the *principal components* or factors in decreasing order. Also called *scree plot*
endogenous variable	A variable whose value is determined by other variables in the model
equivalent models	It is always possible to construct at least two different models that are equally good in 'explaining' the data. Such models are called equivalent
error	See *measurement error*
estimation method	The method by which the parameters in a model are estimated. In AMOS the following estimation methods are available: (1) ML or maximum likelihood estimation (2) ULS or unweighted least squares (3) GLS or generalized least squares (4) SLS or scale-free least squares (5) ADF or asymptotically distribution-free estimation (6) Bayesian estimation (not treated)

estimator | A sample statistic that is used to estimate a parameter

exogenous variable | A variable whose value is only determined by variables not included in the model

exploratory factor model | A factor model without parameter restrictions

FIML | Short for 'full information maximum likelihood' estimation. An estimation method used to estimate a model in the case of missing data

fit measure | A fit measure (or fit index) is a measure of a model's agreement with the data. It is, however worth noting that a good fit does not guarantee that the model is in agreement with the 'real world', i.e. that it is 'correct' (see also *equivalent model*). Fit measures are classified as 'absolute', 'relative', 'parsimony based', 'non-central chi-square based', 'information theoretic' and 'sample-size based'

fixed parameter | See *parameter constraint*

free parameter | See *parameter constraint*

generalized least squares | One of the estimation methods available in AMOS

GLS | Short for 'generalized least squares', one of the estimation methods available in AMOS

goodness of fit | The degree to which a model is in agreement with the empirical data. It is, however, worth noting that a good fit does not guarantee that the model is in agreement with the 'real world', i.e. that it is 'correct'. See also *fit measure* and *equivalent model*

identification | The process of finding out whether there are enough data to estimate a model

implied covariance matrix | Every model formulation implies a certain pattern in the covariances between the various variables in the model. This pattern is summed up in the implied covariance matrix. If the model is in good agreement with the data, the difference between the sample covariance matrix on which the estimation is based and the implied covariance matrix should be small. This difference is called the *residual covariance matrix*

imputation | Replacing missing values in your data with other data. In mean imputation you replace missing values with the mean of the variable in question; in regression imputation you regress the variable with missing values on other variables in the data set and use the regression function to estimate the missing value; in multiple imputation you make several imputations, each resulting in a separate data set, and then you estimate your model for every data set. Finally the various models are combined to be your final model

independence model	A model with zero correlation between all manifest variables
indicator	A manifest variable that is used as a measuring instrument for a latent variable
indirect effects	See *total effect*
information theoretic fit measure	See *fit measure*
interval scale, interval-scaled variable	A scale with a zero point and a unit of measurement, but both are arbitrary, i.e. chosen and agreed upon. Examples are temperature scales (Celsius and Fahrenheit). Standard methods in SEM require (at least) interval scaled data. See also *nominal, ordinal* and *ratio scale*
item analysis	The process of selecting the best items for a (summated or non-summated) measuring instrument. It can be done using 'reliability analysis' (for summated scales) or exploratory factor analysis in SPSS or confirmatory factor analysis in AMOS
iterative	All estimation methods in AMOS are iterative, i.e. they start with some values for the parameters to be estimated and then gradually improve the fit step by step until a satisfactory fit is obtained
just-identified	A *model* is just-identified if it has zero *degrees of freedom*
Kaiser criterion	A criterion used to decide how many *principal components* or factors to keep for further analysis
latent curve model	A model describing and perhaps also 'explaining' the change over time in some variable of interest
latent growth model	Same as *latent curve model*
latent variable	A variable for which no generally agreed measuring instrument exists. Examples are intelligence, preference and satisfaction (cf. *manifest variable*)
LCM	Short for 'latent curve modeling'
listwise deletion	Deletion of any observation with missing values on any variable that goes into the analysis, i.e. using only complete cases
manifest variable	A variable that is measurable, i.e. there is a well-defined and usually generally agreed way of measuring it. Examples of such variables are temperature, length, number of cigarettes sold
matrix	A rectangular arrangement of numbers in rows and columns. An example is the data matrix where X_{ji} is the value of variable j on observation i. In this book the observation is most often a person, and the variable an answer to a question in a questionnaire

maximum likelihood estimation   One of the estimation methods available in AMOS

mean imputation   See *imputation*

mean structure   In SEM you most often analyze covariance structures, i.e. you analyze the covariances and try to 'explain' them. In doing so, AMOS fixes all means and intercepts at zero. Sometimes you are also interested in estimating means and intercepts, and want to 'explain' them too. So, your covariance structure must be supplemented with a mean structure, and the sample means must be added to the sample covariances in the input

measurement error   The error of a measuring instrument. The error involved in using an indicator for a latent variable. Traditionally called ε but in AMOS usually called 'e'

measurement model   A model that describes the connection between a latent variable and its (manifest) indicators

ML estimation   Short for maximum likelihood estimation, one of the estimation methods available in AMOS

model   A simplified 'picture' of the phenomenon you want to study. The 'picture' could be an informal 'mental' one, a graphic model, a set of mathematical equations or whatever you find most practical to get an overview of a complicated world. Scientific work is characterized by the use of formal models

modification index   A measure of the increase in fit you could obtain in setting a parameter free

multiple imputation   See *imputation*

nested model   A model is nested under another model if it can be obtained by placing restrictions on the latter model

non-central chi-square distribution   A generalization of the 'normal' chi-square distribution. In connection with SEM the non-central chi-square distribution can be considered as the distribution that the test statistic will follow if the null hypothesis is wrong

non-cyclic models   See *cyclic model*

non-recursive   Roughly the same as cyclic. See *cyclic model*

non-summated scale   The use of the separate items as measures for a construct without summing them

operational definition   See *conceptual definition*

order condition   A necessary condition for the identification of cyclic models

ordinal scale, ordinal variable	A scale that indicates a rank (e.g. measuring preference by ranking)
over-identified	A *model* is over-identified if its *degrees of freedom* are positive
***P*-value**	In statistical testing, the probability of observing the actual value of a statistic or one that casts even more doubt on the null-hypothesis, assuming it is true
pairwise deletion	*Listwise deletion* on any pair of variables
parallel measurements	Two measurements are called parallel if (1) they have the same 'connection' with the concept they are supposed to measure and (2) their measurement errors are equal
parameter	A measure that describes a population or a model
parameter constraint	A constraint placed on the estimated values of a parameter. A parameter is unconstrained or *free*, if it is to be estimated from the data with no restrictions on the estimated values. If it is not free it is *fixed*, i.e. there are restrictions placed on the estimated values. In AMOS a parameter can be fixed to have a certain value, two or more parameters can be fixed to have the same (estimated) value, or the parameter can be missing, i.e. it can be fixed at zero
parceling	Grouping indicators and using summaries of the groups (parcels) as manifest variables
parsimony	In connection with SEM, the word means 'simple' or 'uncomplicated'. We usually look for simple models with as few parameters as possible
parsimony-based fit measure	See *fit measure*
path model	A model with no latent variables
pilot sample	A smaller sample taken prior to the main sample, e.g. in order to test a questionnaire
positive definite matrix	See *eigenvalue*
positive semi-definite matrix	See *eigenvalue*
principal component	Principal components are linear functions of the data. The first principal component is the linear function with the largest variance, the second principal component is the linear component with the second largest variance under the condition that it is uncorrelated with the first etc. There are as many (non-correlated) principal components as there are variables in your data set. However, some of them could be identical. The variances of the principal components are the *eigenvalues* of the *covariance* or *correlation matrix*

principal components analysis	A method for summarizing data in fewer variables (the first few *principal components*) with minimum loss of information or for determining the number of dimensions in a data set
rank condition	A sufficient condition for the identification of cyclic models
ratio scale, ratio-scaled variable	An interval scale with a fixed zero point (e.g. scales measuring weight and length). See also *interval scale*
recursive model	Roughly the same as non-cyclic. See *cyclic model*
recursive rule	A recursive model is always identified
regression imputation	See *imputation*
regression weight	AMOS's designation of regression coefficient
relative fit measure	See *fit measure*
reliability	A measuring instrument has (large) reliability if it has a small amount of measurement error
reliability coefficient	A measure of reliability having values in the interval 0.00 to 1.00; the higher, the better
residual covariance matrix	See *implied covariance matrix*
rotation	A transformation of component axes or factor axes to obtain a simpler factor structure that is easier to interpret
sampling distribution	The probability distribution of a *statistic* across an infinite number of samples of the same size as the one at hand and from the same population
saturated model	A model with the maximum number of parameters and therefore exact fit to the data
scale-free least squares	One of the estimation methods available in AMOS
scree plot	Also called *elbow plot*
SEM	Short for 'structural equation modelling'
SLS	Short for 'scale-free least squares'. One of the estimation methods available in AMOS
SSCP matrix	Short for 'sum of squares and cross-products matrix'
stability index	A measure of the bias of the estimation effects in *cyclic models*
standard deviation	A measure of the spread in the distribution of a statistical variable or in a data set
standard error	The *standard deviation* in the *sampling distribution* for a *parameter*

standardized coefficient	Also called beta coefficient. A regression coefficient based on standardized variables. Called *standardized regression weight* in AMOS
standardized regression weight	The same as *standardized coefficient*
standardized variable	A variable with a mean of 0.00 and a variance of 1.00
start value	The initial parameter value used in *iterative* estimation methods
statistic	A measure that describes a sample. Sometimes a statistic is used as an *estimator* for the corresponding *parameter*
structural model	A model describing the (suggested) 'causal' connections among the variables, as opposed to the measurement model that describes the connection between *latent variables* and their (*manifest*) indicators. If a model includes latent variables the structural model describes 'causal' relations between latent variables. If the model only includes manifest variables the whole model is structural
summated scale	A summated scale is obtained by adding scores obtained by answering a series of questions. One of the most popular is the Likert scale: the respondents are asked to indicate their agreement with each of a series of statements by checking a scale from, for example, 1 (strongly disagree) to 5 (strongly agree) and the scores are then added to make up the scale
t-rule	A necessary (but not sufficient) condition for identification: the number of data points should be at least as large as the number of parameters to be estimated
theory	See *model*
three-indicator rule	A sufficient condition for identification of a confirmatory factor model
total effect	The effect of one variable on another variable. It is the sum of the *direct effect* and the *indirect effect*, i.e. the effects that are mediated by one or more other variables
trajectory	The path that a moving object follows through space as a function of time. The object might be a projectile or a satellite. In SEM a trajectory is used in connection with *latent curve models* as a description of the change over time in some variable of interest
two-indicator rule	A sufficient condition for identification of a confirmatory factor model
two-step rule	A model with latent variables is identified if: (1) it is identified if modeled as a confirmatory factor model (if all one-headed arrows are replaced by two-headed arrows); and (2) the structural model is identified if all latent variables were seen as manifest

two-step strategy	When your model includes latent variables and 'causal' relations, it is preferable to analyze the model in two steps. First the model is analyzed as if it was a measurement model (a confirmatory factor model) and then the total model is analyzed. One reason for this is that if your measurement model does not have a satisfactory fit, it is meaningless analyzing the structural part of the model. A four-step strategy has also been proposed, starting with an explorative factor model
ULS	Short for unweighted least squares. One of the estimation methods available in AMOS
unconditional latent curve modeling	LCM that describes the trajectory of a latent curve model, but does not include variables that are supposed to influence the trajectory
under-identified, not identified	A *model* is under-identified if its *degrees of freedom* are negative
unique variance	An expression of validity
unweighted least squares	One of the estimation methods available in AMOS
validity	A measuring instrument has (large) validity if it measures exactly the concept it is supposed to measure and nothing else
zero B-rule	A sufficient condition for identification. If a path model has no variable with both incoming and outgoing arrows, it is always identified
zero model	A model where all parameters have the value 0
χ^2-**distribution**	The distribution of the χ^2-statistic used to test the model fit
χ^2-**difference test**	A test for the difference in fit between two *nested models*

C

AMOS Statements

AMOS statement	Example no.	Page
Sem.ImpliedMoments	4.1	81
Sem.Title	4.1	96–97
Sem.Dispose	4.1	96–97
Sem.FitModel	4.1	96–97
Sem.TextOutput	4.1	96–97
Sem.Standardized	4.1	96–97
Sem.Smc	4.1	96–97
Sem.BeginGroup	4.1	96–97
Sem.GroupName	4.1	96–97
Sem.AStructure	4.1	96–97
Sem.NormalityCheck	4.1	102
Sem.ResidualMoments	5.2	111
Sem.Crdiff	6.1	143
Sem.Gls	6.1	143
Sem.Model	6.1	145
Sem.FitAllModels	6.1	146
Sem.Mods	6.2	148
Sem.TotalEffects	7.2	183
Sem.ModelMeansAndIntercepts	8.1	195
Sem.Mean	8.1	202
Bootstrap	9.4	243
Sem.ConfidenceBC	9.4	243
BootBS	9.4	243
Sem.AllImpliedMoments	10.1	262

Author Index

Subject Index

Sports, Virtues and Vices

Morality plays

Mike McNamee

Routledge
Taylor & Francis Group

LONDON AND NEW YORK

First published 2008
by Routledge
2 Park Square, Milton Park, Abingdon, Oxon OX14 4RN

Simultaneously published in the USA and Canada
by Routledge
270 Madison Ave, New York, NY 10016

*Routledge is an imprint of the Taylor & Francis Group,
an informa business*

© 2008 Mike McNamee

Typeset in Sabon
by Swales and Willis Ltd, Exeter, Devon
Printed and bound in Great Britain by Antony Rowe Ltd,
Chippenham, Wiltshire

British Library Cataloguing in Publication Data
A catalogue record for this book is available
from the British Library

Library of Congress Cataloging in Publication Data
A catalog record has been requested for this book

ISBN 10: 0–415–19408–3 (hbk)
ISBN 10: 0–415–19409–1 (pbk)
ISBN 10: 0–203–09010–1 (ebk)

ISBN 13: 978–0–415–19408–2 (hbk)
ISBN 13: 978–0–415–19409–9 (pbk)
ISBN 13: 978–0–203–09010–7 (ebk)

To the girls: Cheryl, Megan and Ffion, with love

Contents

Preface

The book is comprised of essays, many of which were presented or published between 1992 and 2007. While some of them are unpublished in their present form, all of them, bar the final chapter of this book, have undergone significant revisions from their earlier forms as papers and articles.

In Part I, I set out the groundwork for the book. Some remarks from Chapter 1 were collected in a conference proceedings of the International Association for the Philosophy of Sport (1995b) under the title 'Sport: relativism, commonality and essential contestability' though I have substantially changed my understanding of conceptual analysis since then and limited the scope of my ambitions as a result. An early version of Chapter 2 was published under the heading 'Physical education and the development of personhood' in the *Physical Education Review* (1992). I have removed all discussion of educational and physical educational relevance from the paper and indeed I have softened up the cognitive-linguistic emphasis a little in relation to work that was published later in moral psychology and philosophical anthropology. Chapter 3 is adapted from "Sporting practices, institutions and virtues" published in the *Journal of the Philosophy of Sport* (1995a) while Chapter 4 is a significantly revised version of 'Ethics, psychology and sports: back to an Aristotelian "museum of normalcy"' which appeared in the *International Journal of Sport and Health Science* (2003) and was written with Carwyn Jones and Joan Duda. I have removed portions of the empirical psychology of the original article and have adapted the chapter to fit specifically with the virtue-ethical framework of the book, and I happily record my appreciation for their earlier collaboration.

In Part II, on the virtues and vices of sports, I gather together and revise various chapters that deal specifically with the virtue ethics of sports. Chapter 5, 'Celebrating trust: virtues and rules in the ethical conduct of sports coaches' (1998) was published in *Ethics and Sport* edited by myself and Jim Parry, the first book in our series of the same name. The essay has been revised in a number of ways showing the continuity between modern codes and the ancient sixth-century BC Hippocratic Oath and third-century BC Beroia Law for *gymnasiarchos* in Ancient Greece. A version of Chapter 6, like Chapter 4, was published jointly as 'The moral economy of racism and racist rationalisations in sport' with Jonathon Long in the *International Review for the Sociology of Sport* (2004) whom I thank here. Originally the paper was split along methodological lines: half articulation of conceptual and ethical aspects of racism, and half comment on rationalisations sportspersons used for their racism based on empirical research he had conducted with colleagues over a decade. I have omitted direct reference to that substantial body of empirical research and have developed the virtue-ethical aspects of racism with respect to the racist act/racist character distinction and also included discussion of role modelling in relation to racism and racial stereotypes.

The following chapters (7 and 8) appeared first in the *Journal of the Philosophy of Sport* (2002, 2003a respectively). While 'Hubris, humility and humiliation' remains fairly intact, the subsequent chapter '*Schadenfreude* in sport' underwent very substantial revision when I published another version of the ethics of *schadenfreude* in healthcare contexts in *Medicine, Healthcare and Philosophy* (2007b). A perceptive and helpful reviewer forced me to give a much more sympathetic account of Kant's conception of the emotions than I had done originally in the former article and I have included those revisions in the chapter here.

The final part of the book (III), rather like the final chapter of Part II, reflects work over the last few years where I have attempted to explore the interfaces between medical ethics and sports ethics. Chapter 9, 'Suffering in and for sport' (2005a) appeared first in an anthology from the 'Ethics and Sports Series' entitled *Pain and Injury in Sport* and is only slightly altered. While Chapter 10 has not been previously published, I draw upon some portions of an essay on slippery slopes that was published jointly with Steve Edwards as 'Transhumanism, medical technology, and slippery slopes', in the *Journal of Medical Ethics* (2006) and a report written for the UK Parliament Select Committee on Science and Technology entitled "Ethical issues regarding human enhancement technologies" (2006) (www.publications.parliament. uk/pa/cm/200607/cmselect/cmsctech/67/67we16.htm; accessed 1.1.08). The final essay deals with a subject that strikes to the very heart of ethics more generally and the future of sports specifically: the uses and abuses of biotechnology to transfigure our very conception of the human. I draw from some remarks from the former essay and also a talk I gave at the Thomas More Institute (2006) in the writing of Chapter 11: 'Whose Prometheus?: Transhumanism, biotechnology and the moral topography of sports medicine' (2007a), which was published in the journal that I launched as editor in 2007: *Sport, Ethics and Philosophy*.

I thank the various Editors for their kindness in allowing the part reproduction of those papers and the many reviewers who gave freely and generously of their wisdom. Naturally, all mistakes remain of my own making and responsibility.

Acknowledgements

Like any book that has been a long time in the writing (and like this book that is considerably late in the making) I have many people that I wish wholeheartedly to thank. Sadly, there are simply too many of them to list without descending into a sentimental Oscar-winning-style appreciation speech. Those friends not specified here I hope will content themselves with my unfailing, though unspecified, appreciation.

Perhaps the first place to start is with thanks to two Editors I have worked with at Routledge, Samantha Grant and Simon Whitmore, whose patience and support have been considerable. I am immensely grateful too, for what I learnt in the supervision of many Doctoral students it has been my pleasure to work with. Among them Andrew Bloodworth, Carwyn Jones and Heather Sheridan deserve special mention. Equally, I have to thank Jim Parry with whom I have enjoyably worked for many years as the Series Editor of 'Ethics and Sport'.

My colleagues in the Centre for Philosophy, Law and Healthcare at Swansea University – Steven Edwards, Thomas Schramme and Hugh Upton – have been both a source of intellectual stimulation and exemplary collegiality. I have learnt from all of them and enjoyed every minute in their insightful and warm company.

Sigmund Loland, Rektor of the Norwegian School of Sport Sciences, kindly afforded me the opportunity to gather a draft of the whole book while on a sabbatical there in 2006. I also happily record my gratitude to Graham McFee with whom I have shared much of the book, in different stages of its development as individual papers or chapters. His genial company has, as the Irish poet Seamus Heaney once remarked, always seemed like a cure one never noticed happening.

Finally, it is a pleasure to record my love and appreciation to my wife, Cheryl, and our beautiful daughters, Megan and Ffion, without whose forbearance the book would never have been finished and without whom it would not have been worthwhile.

Introduction

Ancient rituals and modern morality plays

In Medieval Europe, the Roman Catholic Church was the dominant social and political institution as well as the seat of learning. The vast majority of the populace, however, were illiterate and the possibility of their understanding or even following its principal ceremony, Holy Mass, conducted in Latin, was unthinkable. One fairly widespread way of reducing the mysteriousness of religious morality was the enactment of morality plays. The precise details of this cultural practice is unknown, so I offer here the merest sketch to make the point I wish to at the beginning of this book on the ethics of sports. Around this time, travelling circuses not only brought entertainment to the masses, but typically included in their show a morality play. Here good and evil were played out on a stage where what was at stake was the very soul of the principal character: Everyman. Though crudely analogous, it is my contention that sports, among other things, now fulfil this role or function on a global scale. In a world where the Enlightenment myth of shared morality is assaulted on every side by anthropologists, cultural commentators and philosophers alike, sports offer a cognitively simple canvas of good and evil writ large in the everyday contexts of the arena, the court, the field and, of course, the back pages of our newspapers and the screens of our televisions. Just as the moralising point of the medieval plays was not dramatically dense, one needs neither complex cognitive nor moral vocabularies to understand cheating and courage, nor fair and foul play in the varied forums of sport. Indeed, sports, I will argue, offer our best vehicles for moral education in the light of the clash of moral cultures that the present world throws up.

While different philosophical approaches have been developed in sports ethics, the aim of this book is to situate ethics at the heart of sports and to do it via virtue-ethical considerations derived in large measure from the gymnasia of Ancient Greece.

Book synopsis

The book comprises three parts. The first provides a foundation. It sets out an account of what we need to understand about sports and sports ethics to develop a virtue-ethical account. The second part develops an account of why rules and rule books do not supplant virtues and opens the way for a close consideration of a family of vices and virtues that are to be found in sport throughout all levels of competition. The final part links the virtues and vices that attend the pursuit of excellence with respect to suffering and the harm that elite sports foster. I discuss the greed and shame that attend those who cheat by doping, and finally the future of sports and how this may be undermined by recent advances in biomedical technology aligned to the vices that have traditionally attended sports' limited focus on a technical excellence. I offer below a thumbnail sketch of each chapter.

In Chapter 1, I give an account of the nature of sports. I highlight the ethical core of sport and relate it to its gratuitous logic (Suits, 1978), the very fact that in engaging in sports we undertake activities, the pursuit of which are rendered more difficult by the rules that define the activity and which we agree to be governed by in pursuit of athletic victory. I offer a critique of those essentialists who seek to find some kind of closure to the analysis of the concept of sport simply by defining it in terms of necessary and sufficient conditions. I offer an account of sports as an open concept that nonetheless has a form of rule-governed gratuitous activities demanding and developing embodied capacities in the ethically defensible pursuit of the ends of victory in a shared contest.

In Chapter 2, I argue that we cannot have a substantive normative account of sportspersonship without a theory of personhood. Charles Taylor's work on the philosophy of agency is used to articulate personhood as the capacity for strong evaluation – or qualitative discrimination – among one's ends, goals and identities, arising partly from our ethically informed emotional lives. Contrary to the everyday understanding of sportspersonship where one plays with ruthless efficiency to reach the goal while bending all possible rules to one's advantage, I hold that sportspersonship is crucially related to this normative capacity of distinguishing between goals that are desirable, noble, valuable and worthy from those which are not.

Developing on from the account of sports and sportspersons, in Chapter 3 I situate the ethics of sports within a critical account of social practices first developed in the work of Alisdair MacIntyre. It is in sports, conceived historically as social practices, that the virtues can be developed and sustained by sportspersons, administrators, coaches and officials, in pursuit of the internal goods of sports and their institutional promotion and protection. In the last chapter of this section, Chapter 4, I give a more fine-grained account of ethical development in and through sport that pays close attention to the emotions in harmony with our considered perceptions and judgements of right and wrong, good and bad, and that are formed first by habitualised training and emulation. This paves the way for more detailed discussion of particular vices and virtues.

In Chapter 5, which initiates Part II, I argue that rule-based moralities underdetermine moral action. In particular I show how they can foster an attitude of moral minimalism, the like of which is often crystallised in codes of conduct. This institutionalised response to ethical difficulty and the attitude it often spawns are not new. Indeed it is to be found in third-century BC Greek Beroia Law for the *Gymnasarchoi* who had authority over the conduct of athletes and instructors in the gymnasium. In considering more contemporary examples of rule-based codes, I show how the fetish for codes of conduct can in fact undermine the very trust in human character and conduct that they were supposed to foster. I close the chapter with a consideration of the virtue of trust which, though it does not replace institutional needs for rules and sanctions, can better underscore the types of action the rule book attempts crudely to foster.

In Chapter 6, I offer an account of racism as a vice. While the sociological and political anti-racist literatures often present us with a simplistic dichotomy (either one is racist or not racist) I offer a dispositional account that holds that one cannot typically be considered a racist on the basis of a one-off act or utterance. Developing this account I present a richer catalogue of the vices that attend our attitudes towards otherness and reinforce the idea of a responsibility for feelings of dominance over and antipathy to racialised others in sports. Focusing on the fact that the ethos of certain sports may still harbour racist sentiments, I offer an example of moral courage of two cricketers who risked limb and livelihood in their public denunciation of racist norms outside the sub-cultures of sports.

In Chapter 7, I develop the theme of feelings of superiority over others that are often thought to be a precondition of success in elite sports. I offer a critical revision journalistic idea that teams and athletes who lose in certain ways are thereby humiliated. Against the hubris typical of certain sports stars, I argue for greater humility and empathy in sports winning and losing. In Chapter 8 I continue this train of thought in relation to our attitudes towards losers whom we may think deserve their humiliation and whose suffering is somehow merited. I attempt to render problematic the celebration of the suffering of those who are humiliated despite their responsibility for it, as in cases of doping and other forms of cheating or poor conduct.

These chapters culminate in what I take to be a deep and serious problem in sports, its relation to suffering. A common picture of the logic of sports is twofold: winners rejoice, losers suffer. In Chapter 9 I give an account of the ethical nature and significance of suffering by exploring the common ground between the experience of losing in sports and undergoing serious illness. It seems to me that considering an applying scholarship from medical ethics may, with the appropriate changes, help us better understand our responses to vulnerability and promote shared understanding of our humanness in and outside sport.

In Chapter 10, I offer an original line of discussion in an often tired debate. I first sketch the typical arguments regarding the im/permissibility of doping (e.g. fairness, harm, paternalism, and so on). Due to the inherent conceptual vagueness of un/acceptability of illicit means of preparation and performance in sports it seems that we cannot logically determine a point at which we can say doping is wrong. In contrast, I argue in defence of the bans on certain pharmacological means of performing enhancement via the notion of slippery slopes. Moreover, developing the aretaic position in sports ethics, I offer two vices that characterise cheats who dope and which underwrite our perception of the undesirability of those who cheat thus. I return, as I do throughout the book, to the Greek catalogue of vices and virtues. We can understand the wrongness, or baseness, of the character of those who dope, as an example of what the ancient Greeks called '*pleonexia*' (loosely understood as greed aligned to the desire for more than is one's due) and the loss of '*aidos*' (shame) to be understood literally as the shamelessness of athletes who, on being caught, are merely embarrassed or fretful over their loss of external goods (salary, sponsorship, status and other financial rewards). I argue that although the World Anti-Doping Association is inevitably based in a catch up game, their task, although analogous to the struggle of Sisyphus, is both admirable and necessary.

In Chapter 11, I present two versions of the myth of Prometheus in order to consider the normativity of elite sports and what is becoming ever more closely aligned to it, the practice of sports medicine. It is often said that those who would promote genetic engineering in and out of sports are engaged in a Promethean enterprise. I present two contrasting accounts of the myth (Hesiod v Aeschylos) to bring to light dispositions favourable and unfavourable to those who seek to challenge and revise the very nature of humans themselves in order to gain excellence whether in or beyond sports. I then argue that these human-enhancing ideologues may well use elite sports as the vehicle for legitimating otherwise unacceptable technological libertarianism and how their pursuit is contrary to the spirit of sports and the flourishing of sportspersons therein.

Sport, ethics and Ancient Greece: a methodological note

Although the title of this book indicates a Christian context, I argue throughout the book that the context of the virtues in Ancient Greece offers us instructive examples for our conduct and character in sport in (post)modernity. True, there is much overlap between Aristotelian ethics and, via St Thomas Aquinas, later Christian ethics. A critic might well latch on to Woody Allen's remark that my posture in this book is predicated on the belief that "nostalgia ain't what it used to be". Some methodological notes are therefore required in order at least to forestall this objection.

It seems to me that there is sufficient continuity in the human condition that certain vices and virtues are historically present irrespective of the age in which they are commented upon. They are so deeply embedded within our language and social life as to be unavoidable. I take the spirit of this posture directly from Peter Strawson who writes:

> [H]uman commitment to participation in ordinary interpersonal relationships is, I think, too thoroughgoing and deeply rooted for us to take

seriously the thought that a general theoretical conviction might so change our world that in it, there were no longer any such things as interpersonal relationships as we normally understand them.

(Strawson, 1968: 86)

The position presented is close to that of Hart (1961) who once remarked that human society is not a suicide club. Our present concern with a given aspect of the continuation of social existence – ethical action in sports – is also embedded in our very thought and language. Consider the metaphors that derive from sport which find wider application in our daily lives: "playing with a straight bat"; "keeping one's eye on the ball"; "a level playing field"; "moving the goalposts"; or the widespread usages of a "slam-dunk", "home-run" or "strike out" and so on. Reaching deeper, one need only look to generalisations concerning human nature to derive certain necessary ideals of character and conduct that any society must seek to uphold.

Notions such as blame, praise, responsibility, courage, cowardice, vice and so on, are likely to occur in all modern societies by virtue of the sorts of social creatures that human beings are and the forms of social organization they construct. The language of human action presupposes their import; but what exactly they mean and how they are interpreted will of course be instantiated differently over time within and between cultures, classes and sexes. Bringing complex and incomplete notions such as justice, freedom, politics, power, education and those of which the wholesale term "social concepts" has been applied into some meaningful characterisation of human nature and association has the effect of allowing an objective grounding for the inevitable disputes as to their meanings whilst appreciating the great significance of variability in their interpretation. Sports do not enjoy this complexity though their sophistication is often underplayed.

Of course the caveat has also to be made that the precise contours of ethical ideals and the virtues – wise and particular patterns of action, feeling, judgement and perception – that shape them and are shaped by them in their pursuit, are nuanced in ways that must be understood within a historical frame. Thus regret and responsibility, trust and truthfulness, these are not historically conditioned social constructions that could be swept away in any particular historical epoch or cultural settings. They are not mere social constructions but presuppositions of the very idea of a community or society.

So the power of Hampshire's view that there should be a "no shopping principle" when it comes to adopting and adapting moral notions from various cultures and historical epochs, should not, I think, take as its target those historical ideas and ideals that I have drawn from the settings of Ancient Greece. I hope that in drawing deeply and frequently from the quarry (though not the supermarket) of Ancient Greek culture I have resisted the idea that all we need in sport, as elsewhere, is the simple reincarnation of an earlier epoch when all was well. All was palpably not well. It takes no prescience to rebuke the naive memory makers, the reactionaries, that ancient Greek life was very often elitist, sexist and xenophobic among its many unethical postures. Much of what has motivated the book has been a task of reconstructing the point of ancient virtues, myths and models, not merely reviving them.

In this book, I have been guided, though perhaps not enough or not subtly enough, by philosophers who have challenged the liberal paradigm of moral progress. The point is made by moderns, as Williams (1985) points out, that the word "morality", that peculiar institution as he called it, with its universalising scope of duties owed to all humankind was not present in Ancient Greek times. And though he is sceptical of this claim, he argues that progress was indeed made even in the epoch of Ancient Greece. Although MacIntyre brilliantly captures the more limited role of morality of the time, where what one is defines what one ought to be and do, Williams claims that the notion of aretē, or excellence, was not strictly determined by social position, that there existed some possibility to achieve this state irrespective of the perception that only certain classes of persons could attain it.

It is not, then, that there are no differences between these historical cultural junctures nor that they are insignificant, yet it still is true, I believe, that we have much to learn from them in order to make our sports better, our sportspersons more excellent in the ethical and technical senses of that word, and thus possible that our lives may go better too. Williams puts the general point eloquently:

> Still more there are differences, differences we must approve, between ourselves and the ancient Greeks. The question is how these differences are to be understood. My claim is that they cannot best be understood in terms of a basic shift in ethical conceptions of agency, responsibility, shame, or freedom. Rather, by better grasping these conceptions themselves and the extent to which we share them with antiquity, we may be helped to recognize some of our illusions about the modern world, and through this gain a firmer hold on the differences that we value between ourselves and the Greeks. It is not a question of reviving anything. What is dead is dead, and in many important respects we would not want to revive it even if we knew what that could mean. What is alive from the Greek world is already alive and is helping (often in hidden ways) to keep us alive.
>
> (Williams, 1993: 7)

I am conscious that I have not come anywhere near exhausting the ethics of sports even from an aretaic perspective. I hope only to have sown the seeds of doubt that all sports ethics should be conceived of either in deontological or consequentialist frameworks. I hope also to have shown that there is much to be gained from considering the value of sports from within a perspective informed critically by the contestual nature of Ancient Greek life, and in doing so to have offered a better understanding of the characters that perform nightly on our screens in the modern morality plays.

Part I

Sports, persons and ethical sport

1   What is this thing called sport?

Introduction

In a book devoted to the ethics of sports, one might properly expect a clear account of what sports are, what ethics is and how – if at all – they are related. What form those clarifications take, however, is a matter of some dispute. While I will develop a virtue-ethical account of sports that unfolds throughout the course of the book, this chapter focuses on what sport is taken to mean. I will argue that attempting to locate some transhistorical essence of the concept sport simply by reducing its complexity and variety to a set of necessary and sufficient conditions is not a helpful way to proceed. I conclude the chapter with an account of sports that I hope is sufficiently uncontentious (at least) for the purposes of the book. I understand sports in a rather more open-ended way than many authors who have attempted to circumscribe the concept. I argue that sports are best understood ritually as rule-governed contests with a gratuitous logic, and which necessarily embody an ethical dimension.

Defining sports as games

On the national holiday that occurs each year at the end of August, the World Championships for a not very well-known sport is hosted in the smallest town in Great Britain: Llanwrtyd.[1] In the heart of rural Wales, the smallest of the nations that comprise Great Britain, the championships take place in a stretch of water in the middle of a dense peat bog (Waen Rhydd) on the outskirts of the town. It is that much heralded sport called 'Bog Snorkelling'. For those of you unfamiliar with the activity, the following account is offered on their web site (see Llanwrtyd Well Coming Events, 2007):

> Competitors have to complete two lengths of a 60 yard [50m] trench cut through the peat bog in the quickest time possible, wearing snorkels and flippers (wet suits optional but advisable) but without using any conventional swimming strokes.

One can imagine addicts of baseball, devotees of basketball and aficionados of cricket arise in shared outrage. You cannot 'call that a sport' they surely will protest. Well, 'why ever not?' the bog snorkellers might respond. One common way of settling this matter, or the host of similar conceptual border disputes that are vented frequently in the media (such as the sporting status of darts, ice-dance, pool, river-swimming, synchronised swimming and so on) is by defining what sports essentially are and then applying that definition to the disputed activity. The problem at the heart of the definitional project is almost as old as philosophy itself. Aristotle thought that a definition was a phrase signifying a thing's essence. This common approach allows us to think of a definition then as a kind of conceptual abbreviation. Defining might be thought of as an activity where the complex (or at least many similar) things are analysed into simpler (constitutive) elements. Consider the following simple examples: a bachelor is an unmarried male; a mother is a female parent; a fortnight is fourteen days; a triangle is a plane three-sided object whose internal angles add up to 180 degrees.

Technical terms such as these, possessed of a certain determinacy, present us with a definitional task that seems straightforward. On first inspection at least, other concepts such as 'art', 'democracy' and 'education'[2] seem considerably less promising candidates for definitions. For our present purpose, understanding sport by way of defining it will take us to consider its conceptual cousin 'game' of which Wittgenstein (1953) famously remarked there was no essence. In order to test out the value of each of any definition we might look for tests of inclusion and exclusion. Does the definition allow things other than those properly belonging to the class to be defined or does it fail, in the opposing direction, by ruling out cases which it is agreed should fall in the class? In each of the conceptually simple cases above (bachelor, mother, fortnight, triangle) what is being defined corresponds to the thing falling under the definition. This activity seems reasonable enough, one might think, therefore the application of it to sport should not trouble us too much.

While most adults would have little difficulty in recognising as sports those commercialised activities that appear regularly on the back pages of newspapers or on prime time weekend viewing such as baseball, football or tennis, others might be less clear. Consider the example above: should bog snorkelling be properly classified as a sport? Well, if we looked at what these examples had in common we could attempt to see whether there was anything by way of necessary conditions (conditions that were necessary for the ascription of the term sport properly to the activity in question) which jointly would be sufficient (for the proper ascription). Working through such an example as this might lead us to a position, often attributed to Wittgenstein, and loosely labelled 'anti-essentialism'. Here is what Wittgenstein famously had to say:

> Consider for example the proceedings that we call "games." I mean board-games, card-games, ball-games, Olympic games, and so on. What

is common to them all?-Don't say: 'There must be something common or they would not be called "games"' – but look and see whether there is anything common to all. – For if you look at them you will not see something that is common to all, but similarities, relationships and a whole series of them at that. To repeat: don't think, but look! . . .

And the result of this examination is: we see a complicated network of similarities overlapping and criss-crossing: sometimes overall similarities, sometimes similarities of detail.

(Wittgenstein, 1967: §66–7)

The idea of recognising family resemblances rather than attempting forlornly to locate a conceptual essence is often accorded great status within the thought of the later Wittgenstein. In contrast to the picture theory of meaning which he advocated in the *Tractatus Logico Philosophicus*, where words supposedly stood for some *thing* in external reality, Wittgenstein begins to develop a more subtle and complex appreciation for the complexity of the relations between language, thought and the world. The earlier picture theory of meaning was based upon the idea that the sum world was the sum of all facts that could be captured in propositions. Facts represented the world and did so in a pictorial way. Coming to understand these propositions, how words captured the world, meant that philosophers were required to grasp the meaning of words by analysing what was essential to them. The idea of generality and diversity in language is brought about in his posthumously collected lectures *Philosophical Investigations* by several variations of the family metaphor such as 'family of meaning' (1953: §77), 'family of structures' (§108), 'family of cases' (§168) and 'family of language games' (§179), and most famously 'family resemblances' (McFee, 2003a). What lay behind the deployment of the familial metaphor was Wittgenstein's foil against those who craved such generality in meaning. This notion, after Bambrough (1968: 189), is commonly illustrated in the following manner where numbers 1–6 are the names of certain games and the letters beneath them are their observable features or characteristics:

1	2	3	4	5	6
abcde	bcdef	cdefg	defgh	efghi	fghij

It can be seen from this representation of the family resemblance idea that there is a very strong set of resemblances between one grouping and the next (i.e. between 1 and 2, 2 and 3 and so forth) but that there is no single common element that holds all groups together. So Wittgenstein tells us to consider things we call games that are as diverse as chess, football, patience, the Olympic Games and children's games. Contra the idea set out in the *Tractatus Logico Philosophicus* Wittgenstein does not accept that a definition can be given for the essence of language. Rather, the metaphor shows us that of words in general, and 'games' in particular, 'these phenomena have no one thing in common which makes us use the same word for all, – but they are related to one another in many different ways' (1953: §65). Wittgenstein uses the analogy that the concept of 'games' is held together by the similarities that hold between members of a family; build, features, colour of eyes, gait, temperament and the like. One member of the family may share the same colour eyes as his brother, yet have the build of his father, the gait of his mother and so forth. Wittgenstein offers, perhaps, a better analogy by asking us to consider a thread; the thread is held together not by a single fibre that runs the entire length, but by the criss-crossing, overlapping and inter-twining of many fibres.

Many critics have, however, latched on to what appears to be a throw-away line of Wittgenstein in §66: 'don't think, but look!' For if we do not think how are we to know what to look at, where to look for it, and how do we recognise whatever it is when we see it? Or, as Baker and Hacker put it most philosophers criticising Wittgenstein on this point have found his answers 'either non existent or inadequate' (Baker and Hacker, 1980: 332 cited in McFee, 2003a: 21).

This simple line of criticism belies a more fundamental objection to the idea of family resemblances as a family of meanings for a given concept. If this artificial construction of Wittgenstein's suggestion is followed through one could conceivably end up with the following:

7	8	9	10	11	12
ghijk	hijkl	ijklm	jklmn	klmno	lmnop

While it is clear that 7 is closely related to 8 and, likewise, 8 to 9, it is not immediately apparent what resemblances 1 has in common with 9, 10, 11 or 12? It can be seen that 1, 2, 3, 4, 5 and 6 are clearly related to each other. But what similarities have these in common with 9 other than empirical traits shared with other groups that might ordinarily be considered quite disparate? Kovesi puts the point less abstractly:

> The similarities are connected like threads in a rope. The family resemblances between games illustrate this picture well. But I do not see any foundation for a claim that we call both football and chess games because football is played with a ball, and so is tennis, while tennis is played by two people, and so is chess.
>
> (Kovesi, 1972: 22)

One might anticipate the following response: 'It is only when we know that these individuals *are* members of a family that we test them to see if they have empirical similarities.' On this reading the resemblances themselves do not make them members of the family. Rather it should be said that they *are* members of the family *and* they have resemblances. The 'family resemblances' idea is simply an analogy to prove that there is no single essence or essential characteristic within a given concept.

Within the philosophy of sport literature, a celebrated attempt to define sports by way of a definition of games was given by Bernard Suits.[3] Suits argued for a definition of game that met the demands of inclusivity and exclusivity without remainder. He conceived of his thesis as a direct response to Wittgenstein's challenge to 'look and see' and a refutation of his anti-essentialist line of thinking. It was argued by Suits that all sports were a type of game. His account was not circular for he also argued that there were certain games that were not sports. This looks like a strong contender to establish whether, for our purposes, bog snorkelling should indeed be classified a sport. The elements of his definition act as individually necessary and jointly sufficient conditions of the concept 'sport'. This is the very thing that Wittgenstein had denied. That is to say, that for any X to count as a sport it must contain all necessary elements and that, moreover, any activity that contained them was sufficient to be classified a sport.

Suits argued that for an activity to be called a game it must have (1) a *pre-lusory goal* (that is to say a goal specified prior to the contest such as scoring more goals, jumping the furthest, and so on); (2) a set of *means* that limited the ways in which the goal could be legitimately achieved; (3) *rules* that define the activity and specify permissible and impermissible means in the achievement of the pre-lusory goal; and (4) a disposition that the game player must adopt in their attempt to achieve the pre-lusory goal.

This disposition to achieve the pre-lusory goal (as opposed to any further goals the sportsperson may individually hold) is called the 'lusory attitude': 'the knowing acceptance of constitutive rules just so the activity made possible by such rules can occur' (Suits, 1998). Anyone failing to hold such a disposition is simply not *playing* sport even where they share the same field, or court, or track with others so engaged. In a wonderfully pithy summary Suits (1978) holds: 'Playing a game is the voluntary attempt to overcome unnecessary obstacles.' Now all this seems apposite for sports. It seems, if we take paradigmatic examples such as football or hockey they certainly fit the bill.

How are we to know that the definition offered is authoritative in the settling of the conceptual dispute? One difficulty with the idea, that is to say the whole enterprise, is to consider the idea of conceptual revision. Suits, like so many others in different contexts, offers an analysis of the concept in a way that is ahistorical. It is as if the concept has been crystallised in time by the analysis. One way of challenging the thesis, then, will be to look back at examples of activities we might recognise as games but that do not fit the features of the activity thus defined.

No one, I think, would call an activity a game were it not rule-governed. And games typically have a purpose or a goal that is specified in the game. And not any means could constitute a legitimate way of achieving the ends of the activity lest we have mayhem. And games may be manic, but not mayhem. Could we not, it might be said, imagine players making up rules as they go along, and deciding on the precise goal and its manner of achievement as they went along their merry way? It is unlikely to be sure, but it is not logically impossible. Consider now a much stronger objection. Suits argues that the lusory attitude is a necessary condition for a game. That is to say, for any X to be a game it must be played and played in a certain way. Contrast this lusory attitude with an account from (not a philosopher but a classicist) David Young who criticises Harris's account of Ancient Greek athletics:

> The glaring difference between Harris' ideal amateur sport and Greek athletics lies in the seriousness of the latter. They were not a diversion or recreation. They were not play. The Greek verb *paizen*, "to play" in Greek comes from the word *pais*, "child." Etymologically, at least, "to play" means to act like a child and in a sportive way. The Greeks some-times apply the verb to playing music, to dancing and playing games (such as board games or drinking games) to playing ball, to jesting and to what we call mere "horseplay." Yet I know of no text that uses the verb *paizen*, "play", for athletic contests. They were not associated with child-hood behaviour. [. . .] a boy athlete was acting like a man, not the other way around. Neither game nor play, Greek athletics were a serious busi-ness and an organized adult activity.
>
> (Young, 1984: 171–2)

Here then, we have at least a plausible candidate for an exception to what should be an exceptionless class: that is after all the point of developing nec-essary and sufficient conditions. Of course, one can just say if these activities were not play-like then they cannot have been games. But to stipulate such a meaning is itself like offering a prescriptive definition. Why should one not offer a definition that bore no reference to the motivations of the gamewrights? Analysis is supposed to offer more than mere prescriptive def-initions. Might it not be the case that modern sports, in the Western world at least (for I have said nothing of similar activities whether in antiquity or the present[4]), have come to embrace the lusory attitude? Young (1984) is highly critical of the romantic writings of De Coubertin that try to link the aristo-cratic amateur sensibility of playing the game for its own sake to a con-structed tradition that harked back to Ancient Greece.

Well, *if* this is the case then we have to acknowledge not some timeless essence but a meaning that is shared *and* revised over time. I will develop this idea below. Another move might be to say that Greek athletics is not the same as sports. But that would beg another argument: what kinds of activities are sports?

Suits' definition of 'sports'

Suits' original argument has it that all sports are games but that they are games of a particular kind. He argues that in addition to being games, there are four necessary conditions for sports that, taken together, are sufficient:

1   That the game be a game of skill;
2   That the skill be physical;
3   That the game have a wide following;
4   That the following achieve a wide level of stability.

The first condition rules out games that are entirely based on, say, luck or chance such as lotteries. By holding that the skill is physical Suits attempts to rule out card games or board games such as chess. It is interesting to note, however that in Cuba, for example, chess is considered a sport. So that necessary condition appears not to hold or else the relevant Cuban institutions are ill-conceived in designating it thus. For the moment let us set this aside for it is true of certainly most sports that we think of them as requiring and cultivating physical skills. How does our example of bog snorkelling fare? Let us say that bog snorkelling is a game. And it certainly fits the condition of being physical. Does it further satisfy these conditions in order for it to fall under the definition, or within the class of sports?

Suits' final two necessary conditions have a vagueness about them which is not apparent in the first two. It is true that one could argue for chess players the skills involved do entail moving the pieces around the board according to its constitutive rules but one can easily imagine a disabled chess player who was physically unable to so move the pieces and had someone else to move them without this negating the general claim. One can imagine a tightening up of this condition to the effect of specifying the relation of physical skill to the achievement of the pre-lusory goal where the skill of the player was internally related to the achievement. Yet here we can imagine that the champion bog snorkeller will have to have efficient techniques (though not those recognised in swimming) to transport themselves efficiently up the bog. What does it mean to say that activities without a wide following are not sports, or that those without a wide level of stability cannot so be classified?

Suits makes it clear that what he is ruling out are mere fads. But what is logically improper about imagining a sport that does not persist substantially over time? There is considerable dispute now over what was once called 'blood sports' or 'field sports' or 'country sports' such as fox hunting or badger baiting or cock fighting. And then of course there is bull fighting. Now of the former there is considerable dispute as to whether these activities should be called sports by some who feel that the designation sport somehow legitimates otherwise barbarous activities. Fox hunting has now been made illegal in the UK: does that mean it is not a sport?; can sport be only legally permissible activities? And this is to say nothing of boxing. What about the idea that bull fighting, being confined to the Iberian cultures, has an insufficiently wide following to enable it to be classified a sport? One can imagine bog snorkelling enthusiasts arguing that the rules of the activity have been laid down for a given number of years. Its World Championships include over one hundred participants from places as far flung from Great Britain as Australia and Russia. Its spectators attend in significant numbers and it is sponsored commercially.[5] All these simple criticisms seem legitimate objections to the idea of a once-and-for-all crystallising of the essence of sport in any way, not merely the manner in which Suits has.

What is to be gained then from a definition of sport which apparently captures its transhistorical essence? Very little it seems to me.

Sport, language and conceptual revision

So, what is this thing called sport? Part of this answer must be historically specific; part not. Let us be clear that, consistent with the above, in offering an account of sport for the purposes of this book, I am not setting out a timeless account, an ahistorical core or essence. What is formal to my account, as any other, is always open to revision. And to reconfirm, part of this openness is that the practitioners themselves will reflexively conceive and re-conceive the particularities of sports in the light of new circumstances. A cursory etymological examination shows how this is so. In English the word sport appears in the fifth century while many languages have no word for 'sport' and many languages simply used slightly modified versions of the English word 'sport' (Sansone, 1988): *spòrs* (Gaelic); *supōtsu* (Japanese); *spor* (Turkish). The archaic English word disport which in turn comes from the Old French *desport* (Sansone, 1988).

If Greek athletics were considered deadly serious attempts to attract glory to one's name and honour to oneself and family, it seems clear that the Anglo-French usage is linked to something less serious and more diversionary or recreational. This is attested to in various places from the King James's translation of the Bible (Proverbs, 10.23: 'It is as sport to a fool to do mischief' and in Judges, 16.25: 'And it came to pass, when their hearts were merry, that they said, Call for Samson out of the prison house; and he made them sport; and they set him between the pillars') (cited in Sansone, 1988: 4). Does this mean that we have different concepts in operation? I think not. It is more simply the case that activities we can recognise as sports have a long and varied history though the specific designation is less antique. It is also widely suggested that in its current form sport refers to a family of activities that is closely associated with the industrial revolution (Eichberg, 1990; Guttman, 1978; Holt, 1989; Mangan, 1986).

One way of distinguishing these activities is to refer to them as 'modern sports'. While this does help to clarify the genesis of certain activities codified largely in seventeenth- and eighteenth-century Britain (think of Association Football (that is, soccer), field hockey, rugby, tennis and so on), there are sufficient similarities with wrestling contests in Ancient Greece, or in the footraces of the Apache Indians, or even in Mayan ball games for us to recognise their family resemblances and talk about them in the same breath. We may, moreover, see their codification as a particularly important conceptual revision. Or, to take a more local example, consider Connolly's discussion of the formation of a concept of foul in basketball:

> Suppose a friendly group of Americans compete together each week in a game something like our game of basketball. The rules governing the game differ from ours in one significant respect: it is permissible for the offense to block, tackle or push members of the defense while trying to score a basket, and the defense can reply in kind. In fact, short of maiming or injuring opposing players, 'anything goes' in this game of basketball. . . .
>
> Suppose, now, a British gentleman of high character and charismatic personality, invited to join the weekly game, begins to describe as "foul play" various practices of holding, hacking, bumping and pushing opposing players. Overwhelmed by his reasonableness and character – he himself never indulges in "foul play" – the American players gradually begin to reciprocate. They incorporate into their play the precept, "Try to avoid, bumping, pushing . . . opposing players" and they characterize a player as indulging in "foul play" when he stoops to such conduct.
>
> The term "foul play" gradually comes to be a means of describing a certain open-ended range of behavior within the game *and* an expression of reproach in the light of that description. Gradually the concept is refined and sharpened through the accumulation of shared experience.
>
> (Connolly, 1993: 181–2)

What Connolly describes in his artificial example is meant to show how conduct in politics is altered by the reflexive understandings of the political actors themselves. And so it is with sports. Conceptual revisions must be understood historically too. But there must be a limit to the range of revisions possible for the social activity to retain its referent: sport.

We could recognise a given activity to be a sport without this condition while we could not recognise as a sport an activity that enshrined a problem, in a rule-governed manner that was in some way inefficient and artificial and to be pursued by inefficient means. And this understanding or self-understanding of the activity so conceived represents a shift from traditional folk activities to which the label sports might be withheld (see Eichberg, 1990). Of course, in light of the example above, it is possible that this trend towards codification, seriousness of intent within a playful structure, and morally limited means of securing the goal, might be reversed. After all, it was not merely some lofty goal of British aristocrats that wrought the change to a more codified and ethical pursuit of excellence but the needs of the gambling economy for relatively fair contests whose outcomes might be reasonably guessed upon and where chance or "foul play" ought not to be too influential in the determination of the outcome.

It seems moreover that Morgan (1994), following Suits (1978), may best have captured this notion of accepting morally limited means by the term 'gratuitous logic'. This term felicitously brings out not merely the artificiality of sporting actions, their non-necessity we might say, and the instrumental inefficiency that is characteristic of them too. It extends beyond this to the normative dimension of sports and sporting acts. That this is historically specific need not be denied. It is clear that such a notion is woven into certain prevailing morals of Victorian Britain (harking back *mistakenly* to an aristocratic Greece[6]) where it was canonized in one form or another as 'muscular Christianity'. But to move much further in that direction would not be to cash out what is minimally central to the concept but to give a full-blown account of sport and that is not my aim here.

Nevertheless, the notion of gratuitous logic is not sufficient for the account of sport I want to deploy as the context for the ethical discussion that follows. I want to add three further specifications; first the nature of the gratuitous act must involve physicality centrally in the achievement of the gratuitous act. Think of the ways in which we admire the touch of the golfer as they weight their stroke to coincide with the topography of the putting green surface; the strength of the gymnast as they move gracefully in and out of the crucifix position on the rings; the subtlety of the badminton player who alters their wrist to contact the shuttlecock earlier in order to deceive their opponent with a drop shot instead of a high clear to the back court that was feinted; and so on. Second, there is a sense in which the act is ritualistic (this is of course not new, several authors have talked about non-necessitated action) but I think that this feature in some sense belies the gratuitous logic. This is part of Sansone's (1988) slightly incredible but original thesis that sport is the ritual sacrifice of energy. For while we may trace back the proto-movement vocabulary in running, jumping, throwing and so on to paleolithic hunters, and while their history is importantly tied to functional activities such as hunting, we need some explanation as to why (when rendered unnecessary to survival) these forms became celebrated in agonal contexts. It is not accidental that the ancient Greek word 'agon' meaning contest or struggle is the etymological root of agony and that sports are often called agonistic after Caillois (1955).

In contests we struggle variously to overcome nature, or others, and always the self, in myriad ways. And this is my third point: the gratuitous acts are in some way agonal in a socially structured way. I do not mean this in the sense that sports are necessarily competitive; that competition is *the* defining element of sport. What I mean, rather, is that sports engage their participants in a conversation with the past and the present whereby they strive towards standards, both technical and ethical, of past, current and future. This requires acknowledgement of the social and historical dimensions of their logic that is irreducible. I shall attempt to develop this notion in Chapter 3 but for the moment I wish merely to acknowledge that the forms of movement canonised in sports are part of a vocabulary that were born of very different motives where efficiency and necessity drove the honing of embodied capacities such as speed, strength and stamina, along with associated skills and strategic thinking (and maybe even proto-virtues such as bravery or daring).

Conclusion

I have tried in this chapter to sketch an account of sport that is sufficiently open but also sufficiently familiar with the family of activities that go by that name in schools and stadia, as well as in the media reporting of such. For my purposes, what typically allows us to recognise a sport is the arrangement of many of the following features: sports are activities characterised by a gratuitous logic involving, centrally, physical skills, and agonal qualities to which both technical and ethical standards pertain that are ritually derived. And I shall develop this account further, emphasising a particular account of the virtue-ethical nature of sports, in Chapter 4. For now I am content to note that the debates over whether certain characteristics are necessary and sufficient, or whether certain features are ineliminably bound to the concept itself or the social and economic climate are themselves part of a broader terrain of contested philosophies of sport. While there is no original exemplar of sport, we can see its genesis in play, historically developed into the variety of forms that the activity can take and for which no final or determinate shape can ever be captured once and for all in a definition; there is a certain openness to the concept that precludes such finality. Nonetheless, the account of conceptual characteristics sketched above resists its characterisation as either relativistic or essentialist and provides sufficient grounding of the concept of sport for me to embark on an ethical exploration of its nature and significance.

2 Sports, persons and sportspersonship

As a matter of grammar, the terms 'sportsman' and 'sportswoman' are genus of the species 'sportsperson'. As a matter of linguistic politics, 'sportsperson' is the gender neutral term to designate anyone who plays sport, despite the tendency of coaches and journalists alike in using the grammatically correct masculine designation for the collective noun. The term 'sportsperson' is, I suggest, deceptively simple. We use it all too unproblematically. Sports sociologists often peddle talk of 'sporting bodies' and sports psychologists often refer to 'sporting minds'. At one level it is neither difficult to understand nor complain about their language. On another this body–mind bifurcation, despite its long and reputable history in Western philosophy, is deeply regrettable. It clearly reduces the complex wholes that are persons into separable elements and does this in such a fashion, as Marx noted so well, of leaving minds to dominate dumb muscle.

I want in this chapter to uncover some of that undesirable philosophical history and refocus our attention from *sports*persons to sports*persons*. I do not wish to commit the fallacy of composition by simply bringing together the meanings of the two separable terms and then adding them to get to a composite meaning. Nevertheless, coming to an appreciation of a richer sense of the term 'sportsperson' requires an analysis of the complex concept of personhood and its ethical significance, not least of all for sport.

To do that I shall attempt to articulate the importance of persons as animals of a particular kind: with the capacity to interpret themselves and what matters to them, in part, out of their emotional life. This will set the ground of much of the later chapters that deal with specific virtues and their emotional content.

Persons as self-interpreting animals

Before diving deep into treacherous metaphysical waters, where sportsmen and women have often metaphorically drowned, I offer the following caveat. Given that this is not a project solely in philosophical anthropology there will be no substantive discussion concerning the possibility and/or nature of non-human persons. It may well be the case that aliens, machines and monkeys may come to be regarded as persons, but these issues do not affect, in any substantive way, the concern of this book.[1] Though the idea of men and women competing with machines is not a new one it is not one I wish to delve into here though I will have something to say of the promises and perils of biotechnology in sport in the final chapter.[2] Second, it should be noted that the substantive account I am going to develop is clearly not value neutral. The idea that such important questions about person could generate entirely uncommitted answers is something of a non-starter.

The account of personhood developed here draws initially upon parts of Charles Taylor's work in philosophical anthropology.[3] After a critical and selective appraisal of his work on personhood an account will be developed towards an inherently social and ethical account of sports and sportspersons enabled to live full and valuable lives in and through sports thus conceived.

Taylor argued that a person's self-interpretations and the experience of them are partly constitutive of the sorts of beings that persons are. Briefly put, this means that our self-understanding cannot be considered as an epiphenomenon. Instead this capacity is placed at the heart of our conception of what it is to be a person. His argument can be summarised in five propositions:

1   some of our emotions involve import-ascriptions;
2   some of these imports are subject-referring;
3   that our subject-referring feelings are the basis of our understanding of what it is to be human;
4   that those feelings are constituted by the articulations we come to accept of them; and
5   that these articulations, which we can think of as interpretations require language.[4]

It is necessary to examine each of these claims in some detail.

First, it is commonly held that the feelings, emotions and desires that are experienced are essentially related to certain objects. When someone is frightened, they are frightened of some thing, or some person or situation, that scares them; they experience shame when they are confronted by a situation that makes explicit the breaking of a confidence, and so on. But this characterisation of our experiences becomes difficult in the face of examples where an experience is not related to a specific object. It is not that there is *no* object in respect of which persons are, for example, anxious, it is rather that their unfocused anxiety is in relation to something that they cannot articulate fully. That is to say, there is a felt absence of an object; a gap where something ought to be. Furthermore, this inability to focus is part of the experience of the situation. The person must, of course, have some apprehension of threat or possible impending harm, it is just that they cannot articulate what it is in respect of. In consequence, then, one speaks more accurately of desires, motivations and feelings involving a sense of our situation rather than in terms of an essential relation to an object.

When, for example, someone says they are disgraced, elated, ashamed or humiliated they are clearly moved in certain ways. These adjectives describe what Taylor calls an 'import'. To make an import ascription is to say that in some way a thing can be relevant, i.e. of importance, to the desires, aspirations, feelings or purposes of a human being. Put succinctly, an import ascription is a property of some thing or situation that is a matter of non-indifference to a given person. In identifying this relevance or import, one depicts what it is in that situation that gives the grounds for those feelings, desires or motivations. It is this that enables us to recognise an emotion as one of shame, or fear, or pride. In such situations it is not the case that one is simply stating (in other terms) that a given feeling is experienced in a certain situation; it is much stronger than that. It is the point of our experiencing *that* feeling in *this* situation. The idea of an import is that there are certain standards within our sense of a given situation that relate to the feeling in a manner that constitutes it. That is to say, the emotion is internally related to the situation. This position has elsewhere been called a 'judgmental' view of emotion (Solomon, 1976). To experience an emotion is in part to have made a judgement about ourselves and the world.

Of course, one could imagine situations where the motivation for action could be conceived of in an experience-independent way. One can think of reflex actions; shuddering at someone scratching a blackboard or pulling away from a hot iron. The important point is, however, that where the situation calls for an import ascription it cannot be done without reference to the experiencing subject. Second, one might ask who, or what, could interpret the significance and sophistication of these import ascriptions? It appears that such imports could only be meaningful to a being who could be the subject of such (emotional) meanings, since they could only be explicated by and to such beings. Terms such as 'dignity' or 'shame' only have sense in a world in which there are beings who can experience its import. But there is a categorical difference between, for example, concepts such as 'shame' and 'pain'. The feeling of being ashamed, of doing something that failed to live up to the standard of the coach, or a parent or community, could be experienced by a being who could make sense of it.[5] By contrast, experiencing pain may go on independently of the awareness of its potential import. This is not to say that experiencing fear or pain is necessarily pre-linguistic – we need to teach infants not to put their hands in the fire after all. When we try to get to the ethical and emotional significance of more sophisticated notions such as guilt or shame and suffering (as I shall do in Chapters 8, 9 and 10) this sort of explanation is found wanting. Taylor refers to those properties whereby the import must in part refer to an experiencing subject as 'subject-referring'. This then explains claims (1) and (2) of the argument; some imports are experience dependent and subject referring.

The third stage of the argument focuses on the idea that by exploring our subject-referring emotions, our sense of shame, dignity, joy, remorse and the like, an insight into the life of such a subject qua person may be gained. Some of our seemingly immediate desires and feelings are 'partially constituted by a skein of subject-referring imports' (C. Taylor, 1985a: 60) that offer potential insights into our lives as subjects; what is of value, what matters to us. Our awareness of these things is central to us as reflexive animals. This point is pregnant with possibilities for virtue ethics and highlights the kind of critical reflection for sportspersons that the label "dumb jock" denies. I spend considerable time and attention in Part II of the book attempting to articulate the contents of this critical reflection in the virtues and vices of sports and related practices such as coaching and sports medicine.

Fourth, the issue of imports and their attribution is closely associated to arguments concerning the nature of feeling and reason.[6] Taylor argues that there is no such thing as brute data where feelings are concerned for they are always mediated by our consciousness. And the interpretation is part of the feeling (C. Taylor, 1985a: 60):

> [T]he feeling is what it is in virtue of the sense of the situation it incorporates. But a given sense may presuppose a certain level of articulacy, that the subject understand certain terms or distinctions. For example, a feeling cannot be one of remorse unless there is a sense of having done wrong. Some understanding of right/wrong is built into remorse to its attributing the import that it does.

Here one can say that the negative normativity is conceptually central of the notion of remorse. It is not as if one experiences X or Y feelings upon which is layered later the judgement that one had done wrong. If someone did not understand that they had done something wrong how could they be said (or indeed expected) to be remorseful? Or, put another way, if they failed to grasp that a subject must be a wrong-doer prior to feeling remorse it could be said that they have failed to understand what the concept 'remorse' meant and would be unable to attribute it to other cases. In short, they would be unable to follow the rule.

Feelings, therefore, incorporate an articulation of a given situation and, as has been argued, may sometimes be incomplete. One is thus enabled to attach import to them; if they were inarticulable this would not be possible.[7] These feelings attribute imports that open up the domain of what it is to be a person. The imports give a form to what matters to creatures such as ourselves. In offering a characterisation of our feelings and desires, therefore, questions are raised concerning adequacy, appropriateness, completeness and distortion: 'whether we have properly explicated what the feeling gives us a sense of' (C. Taylor, 1985a: 64).

Where subject-referring imports are concerned the articulation of these emotions must be self-validating. This is the fourth claim: feelings are bound up with the process of articulation. This is of course precisely the problematic junction of mind and matter and its relationship is notoriously difficult to articulate. What has been typical of Western thought however is a division of labour where rationality is assigned to an executive role over the body – here in the form of felt emotions. But to set out feeling and reason in this fashion is highly questionable, even if the idea does have a long and respectable history. Setting them out in the fashion of employer/employed is, as Midgley points out, hopelessly crude.[8]

Finally, the idea of articulation brings with it questions concerning the role of language. Taylor's strong claim is that our emotions open us up to the possibility of the good life; the ability to make discriminations, entertain desires and pursue goals. These fine discriminations among our mental states are only made possible because they can be articulated through language. These discriminations are referred to as 'strong evaluations' (C. Taylor, 1985a: 16).[9] Unlike weak evaluations, which merely consider whether some action will be a successful means to some desired end state, strong evaluation is of a different character. Some acts are considered to be good or bad, desirable or undesirable, and articulate it accordingly as praiseworthy or blameworthy. These evaluations consider the motivations for the action, which are laudable or repugnant. That is to say, qualitative discriminations are made among motivations, and they arise, so to speak, out of our feelings, emotions and aspirations. To make a strong evaluation is to render articulate the import to which the feeling relates. Our revulsion at an act of cheating is only possible when we are aware of the import of moral baseness.[10] Taylor summarises:

> This drawing a moral map of the subject is an intrinsic part of [. . .] discerning the good or higher life, or the shape of our aspirations, or the shape of our life as a subject. It involves entering the problematic area of our self-understanding and self-interpretation.
>
> (C. Taylor, 1985a: 68)

These strong evaluations attach to us in a very important sense. Thus, Taylor writes: 'Our identity is therefore defined by certain evaluations which are inseparable from ourselves as agents. Shorn of these we would cease to be ourselves' (C. Taylor, 1985a: 34).

The way in which the good life is related to our self-understanding (and hence the notion of language) can be represented thus; the subject-referring imports that are attributed to persons are shaped by the agent's interpretation of them. This in turn is shaped by the language through which he or she learns to express such ideas. Therefore language shapes these emotions.[11] It needs to be noted that, as was argued above in point (1), it is only subject-referring import attributes that are of concern here. Thus fear, shame, remorse and the like are considered but *not* the feelings that are experienced when, for example, someone runs their fingernails down the blackboard or someone pulling their hand from the hot saucepan. Such pains are language-independent and there is no difficulty imagining non-human agents performing them. However, as agents articulate the import in a situation, the emotions change as they become increasingly aware of themselves and their situation. This, or at least a very close relation of this idea, is sometimes known as the hermeneutical circle: what is understood is inevitably coloured by an agent's preconceptions and those preconceptions are in turn modified by what the agent comes to understand. Persons, therefore, characterise things differently; language transforms their experiences and the way they characterise these experiences. From this there is no turning back.[12] Only a language animal could have a person's emotions and thus entertain strong evaluations that come to frame a vision of the good life and an orientation to it.

In summary, it might be said that human language and linguistically constituted emotions are the prerequisite of qualitative discriminations that constitute any vision of the good life. It is not simply the means by which the question of what constitutes the good life is answered. The attempted definition of what matters to persons, their interpretations, are an ongoing affair that is part of why subjects such as ourselves are called persons:

> The paradox of human emotions is that although only an articulated emotional life is properly human, all our articulations are open to challenge from our inarticulate sense of what is important, that is, we recognize that they ought to be faithful articulations of something of which we have only fragmentary intimations. If one focuses only on the first point, one can believe that human beings are formed arbitrarily by the language they have accepted. If one focuses only on the second, one can think that we ought to be able to isolate scientifically the uninterpreted basis of human emotion that all these languages are about. But neither of these is true. There is no human emotion which is not embodied in an interpretive language; and yet all interpretations can be judged more or less inadequate, more or less distortive. What a given human life is an interpretation of cannot exist uninterpreted; for a human emotion is only what is refracted as in human language.
>
> (C. Taylor, 1985a: 75)

Thus far the idea of subject-referring imports has been discussed and a little has been said about the way in which these come to be shaped by the language one comes to deploy. The notions of emotions, feelings, aspirations and self-understanding were placed at the centre of the account as was the ability to discriminate qualitatively between them. It was also intimated that there was some direct relation between these two ideas and the opening up of a vision of the good life. Strong evaluations are not fleeting acts like deciding to buy this packet of sweets rather than that because one has, at that moment, a taste for sugar rather than bran. Rather, they are closely related to styles of action and, indeed, of life. By strong evaluation persons shape their commitments and thus reinforce ideas about the sort of person they are or the sort of person they wish to become.

Persons, minds and bodies

Central to Taylor's task in articulating his conception of person is to distinguish it from another conception that is inspired by the seventeenth-century, epistemologically grounded notion of the subject derivative of Descartes whose celebrated phrase '*cogito ergo sum*' supposedly captures our essential nature: persons are conscious beings. But consciousness on the Cartesian conception refers only to the capacity to frame representations of things, such as understanding complex cause–effect relationships or forming strategic action over time. According to Taylor this view of persons fails to attend adequately to the nature of agency. If persons are to be characterised by their performances in framing representations of things then this leaves us with the problem of relating the performances of physical objects to consciousness. Taylor's conception of person, in contrast, focuses on the nature of agency. Rather than identifying agents by their performances, what is crucial to personal agency is that things can matter; can possess significance. This means that we can, and of course do, attribute purposes, desires, motivations, preferences and aversions to agents in a strong, original sense. Importantly, it must be noted that the capacity to frame representations is not rejected. It is simply that our notion of consciousness is impoverished if we see it only as the capacity to frame representations. It is for this reason that I find repugnant the seemingly constant references by sports commentators to consistent sports performers via machinistic metaphors. One might ask probing questions as to the role of sports scientists, here, in their aim to continually push forward the frontiers of performance. Hoberman remarks pointedly:

> Sport science does not physically hybridize humans and machines; as of today there is no sportive equivalent to Dr. Frankenstein's monster. Instead sport science treats the human organism as though it were a machine, or as though it ought to be a machine. This technologized human organism comprises of both mind and body, for which there are distinct sets of strategies, in my view is a streamlined and decomplexified image of the human being.
>
> (Hoberman, 1988: 323)

The machine metaphor is inappropriate but it is easily adopted when persons become thought of as simply the centres from which representations are framed and strategic action formed. What is wrong with this picture is the palpable fact that things just do not matter to machines in the strong and original sense in which they do to humans. It is precisely because they do matter to humans that we engage wholeheartedly in such activities (as both spectator and participant) as sports. And it is in this point that our joy and fascination with them reside. Mary Midgley's (1974) remarks are apposite here. In attempting to articulate what is meant by a game (i.e. why we call games 'games') she brings into question one of the chief shibboleths regarding games and their supposed non-seriousness. She points out that when people say things such as 'Relax man, calm down, remember it's only a game' (Midgley, 1974: 237) we need to consider the motives the person has for playing in the first place, for they will be crucial to our understanding of their actions. Now the first point, of course, is that there is no machine analogue possible here. Second, this is the sort of remark that I sometimes make when playing rugby or soccer at the weekend in the seventh team or whatever. I have no great desires to push my playing limits any further than they are currently at and so my motivations may be, one might say, weak. I enjoy the social aspect of meeting with friends, the exposition of (albeit limited) skill, the aerobic and anaerobic workout, the competitive and fair striving for victory and so on. But my allegiance to neither game is total or totalising. I enjoy a whole range of ludic activities and often for similar though differing reasons. If a team-mate says to me 'calm down – it's only a game' when I start to question the referee's parentage the force of his point is palpably clear: 'get a grip', 'take a reality check', 'sort out your priorities' and so on. Imagine saying the same thing to Paula Radcliffe toiling in the Athens heat of the 2004 Olympics marathon as the pre-race favourite broke down at the roadside, outside of medal contention with perhaps her last realistic chance of a Gold medal gone and with world titles and a world record as scant consolation in her eyes.[13] Many British readers will also call to mind the famous photograph of a weeping 'Gazza' (Paul Gascoigne) during the semi-final of the 1990 Football World Cup after he had just been cautioned and *ipso facto* precluded from playing in the final of the competition.[14] Football is his game but the mention of non-seriousness in this context would be bizarre. Whether apocryphal or not, the legendary Liverpool football manager Bill Shankly is alleged to have said: 'Some people talk about football as if it were life or death itself, but it's much more serious than that.' What is typically called the ethos of games (though some philosophers have referred to this as the institution of games[15]) captures the way in which each ought to be played but it also responds to ritualised and historical practices. What is acceptable by way of conduct in rugby or ice hockey is scarcely appropriate in softball or cricket. But we do not even need to cross game types to find this particularity; nowhere near the same level of physical contact and aggression is allowed in soccer in the United States by comparison with Northern Europe. Games thus become important vehicles for certain forms of expression, central among which are emotional.

The sorts of emotions experienced in game playing give us further reason to distance persons from machines and non-human animals. In considering further the idea of agency we find that non-human agents do not have open to them the rich and varied emotional life that human agents who are also persons do. Notions such as praise, blame, shame, dignity, moral goodness and evil have no analogue in the non-human animal world, 'when we consider these human emotions, we can see that the ends which make up a human life are *sui generis*' (C. Taylor, 1985a: 102).

Such emotions as characteristic of humans are, of course, *not* divorced from matters of consciousness (or to use the familiar terminology, reason). Indeed, these emotions are only available to linguistic animals since they require the marking of distinctions either by the formulation of language or some expressive ceremonial that would have higher prerequisite demands than could be fulfilled by non-human agents. The problems of morality, so it seems, can only arise for us through the medium of a language.

By way of summary, then, the first conception of a person bases itself on the power to plan and it is this ability that I have to respect. In contrast, Taylor's preferred conception sees as problematic the notion of agency and human ends. Therefore, agents are centres of significance; beings for whom things matter. This is what enables them to have their point of view on the world. Persons, as opposed to other agents, have qualitatively different concerns. Taylor summarises thus:

> Consciousness is indeed essential to us. But this cannot be understood simply as the power to frame representations, but also what enables us to be open to these human concerns. Our consciousness is somehow constitutive of these matters of significance, and does not just enable us to depict them. This supports a quite different reading of the essentially personal capacities. The essence of evaluation no longer consists in assessment in the light of fixed goals, but also and even more in the sensitivity to certain standards, those involved in peculiarly human goals . . . The centre of gravity thus shifts in our interpretation of the personal capacities. The centre is no longer the power to plan, but rather the openness to matters of certain significance. This is now what is essential to personal agency.
>
> (C. Taylor, 1985a: 104–5)

Finally, in recognising this ability to focus on the significance things can have for us and our ability to apprehend and transform them through language, new areas are opened up for the characterisation of morality above and beyond the path to rights duties and obligations that are often thought to be at the heart of personhood.

Sports, persons and play

It might reasonably be objected at this point that the account offered is only one (albeit large) step in the right direction. What are often thought of as the mindless bodies of sportspersons, or captured in machine metaphors, is wildly wrong. Two particular objections might be made: first, is it true that language plays so dominant a role in the identity of persons seeking to live good lives; and, second, what has happened to that aspect of sports that is both visceral and visible? In emphasising the emotions and their linguistic/judgemental features I seem to have lost sight of the essentially corporeal nature of human persons. Of course it could be said that we feel our emotions and embodiment is a precondition of this: they are not merely cognitive judgements. This much must be conceded. But it is not enough.

One reason why we cannot simply disestablish sports, why they are central to our lives, is that they draw from the wellspring of play and that is not something we can do without. As human persons we are inherently embodied animals. And animals play. Indeed, as Huizinga (1970) noted, play is older than culture itself.

More than that, Huizinga tells us that play adorns culture. A considerable body of opinion in anthropology is inclined to support his conjecture. Sutton-Smith (1974/1981) notes the following cross-cultural generalizations. First, play and games playing are functionally related to culture and are not trivial, essential or random. This generalization provides support for the positions of both proponents and sceptics of play. Sceptics of play may draw attention to the fact that two major studies support the idea that play is not always and everywhere to be found in abundance in the early years of childhood. Sutton-Smith cites the work of Whiting (1963) in agrarian cultures in Kenya and Feitelson[16] in carpet-weaving cultures in the Middle East, which suggests that where children are vital links in a fragile economic framework there will be little scope for play. The important feature, however, is not necessarily the pre-industrial nature of the society (there are extensive records of Aboriginal play) but the direct and immediate economic necessities of the situation that require children to be initiated into adult, work-like activities. Supporters of play, on the other hand, will point to the fact that forms of play are neither trivial nor randomly occurring in cultures. The differences of the structure of play relative to its function within that culture is interesting too. It is suggested that Aboriginal play involves exploration and testing that would immediately be valuable in a functional sense to inhabitants of that culture, whereas in symbolic and achievement-oriented cultures most play involves make-believe and contest. Second, Sutton-Smith notes that persons in more complex cultures (howsoever defined) not only play more complex games but also play a greater variety of them. A point very much like this is capture in Rawls "Aristotelian Principle":

> [O]ther things equal, human beings enjoy the exercise of their realized capacities (their innate or trained abilities), and this enjoyment increases the more the capacity is realized, or the greater its complexity. The intuitive idea here is that human beings take more pleasure in doing something the more they become proficient at it, and of two activities they do equally well, they prefer the one calling on larger and more intricate and subtle discriminations.
>
> (Rawls, 1972: 435)

This point bears directly on the appreciation of Western sports, which form the bulk of my examples in this book. And it follows directly from the idea of a gratuitous logic that we entertain in sports so that the challenge they offer us is neither too simple nor too difficult. Nor should it be too open to chance or luck, but tied closely to merit and thereby encapsulating the idea of responsibility.

Third, and closely related to the above, there are structural relationships between games playing and patterns of association within a culture. Strategy is linked with obedience, training and the complexity of the social systems; chance is linked with responsibility, divination, nomadic habits and economic uncertainty; physical skill is linked with the tropics and hunting; central person games are linked with independence, training and marriage. What these generalizations alert us to is the hazardous enterprise of conceptualizing play in a manner that is insensitive to rich contextual factors.

The forms that sports take bear relationality to our particular animal nature, which is tied to some basic biological facts as well as the anthropological ones noted above. It is tied to the basic motor actions: running, throwing, jumping, gliding, catching, striking and so on. Although sports give form to play, they are dependent on it. And these forms are themselves dependent on our typically bi-pedal nature, forward looking eyes, sideways ears, developed central nervous system and so much more.[17] All these valuable remarks about the ubiquity of play remind us that our nature is as rational animals. When we remember this we can avoid the lopsided evaluation and exaltation of rationality.

Is there still, however, a rationalist predilection in the concept of strong evaluation? The weak and strong evaluators are set out thus: weak evaluators can only reason between means to ends: which is the most efficient, the quickest, and the most productive. It is this capacity that is often called technical or instrumental rationality or means–ends reasoning according to the discipline in which the form of thought is being presented. By contrast, strong evaluation entails the contrasting of worth among our chosen means and ends: actions, choices, habits, predilections and values. The contrast is an important and a seductive one. And Taylor gives a rich account of how we come to better understand ourselves and our place in the world both by emotion and reason that are well ordered. But a nagging doubt remains: need this capacity be so strongly linked to articulacy?

Sports journalists often mock the "dumb jock" who apparently fails to account for the excellence of their performances; the well-timed run for home by the middle distance runner; the perceptive interception of the handball player; the fake pass by the quarterback; the deft flick of the striker who lifts the ball or puck over the advancing goalkeeper. They exhibit in their action performances to be marvelled at yet seem incapable of articulating the 'why' of the action in the post-contest interview. Now this may not trouble so many philosophers beyond the sphere of sport, but in ethics can we cauterise morality from the inarticulate – those who cannot specify the 'why' of their actions of benevolence, or courage, or indeed love? This leads Flanagan (1991), among others, to question the role of articulation as basis of the distinction between strong and weak evaluation and hence of non-persons. It seems to render problematic the knowing of the body that phenomenologists have often talked of: the non-linguistic acquaintance with things and persons that seems important to us. On Taylor's account, the concept of personhood seems to be loaded with a weight it cannot bear.

We can begin to explore this intuitive response in relation to Frankfurt's (1988) work on personhood and the structure of the will. Taylor follows Frankfurt's lead by developing the distinction between first and second order desires. Frankfurt notes that we not only desire certain things (let's say a beer) but we can also have desires of a second order that relate to the first (let's say the desire not to give into my desire and instead get on with some writing). So the distinction is in the hierarchy of desires, where the latter have an executive function over the former. Imagine the following sporting scenario. Anyone who has played basketball, or football, or hockey has engaged in what physiologists characterise as a multiple sprint activity. And those with the experience of these activities will know the dreaded devil lactic acid. This is the necessary by-product of anaerobiosis. In lay language, this means the energy system(s) that deliver(s) quick bursts of energy of approximately 40–50 seconds. The first 10 seconds or so are delivered by the breakdown of phosphocreatine, which is limited in supply but which, luckily, has no nasty side effects. One simply runs out of energy stores that can contribute to short duration intense activity. The demand of energy may not abate though and the body draws unconsciously upon stores of glycogen (from carbohydrates), which produces lactic acid that inhibits muscular contraction and can range from the mildly irritating to the excruciating. So the first few sprints – with a little recovery time – go well but as we increase frequency, duration, repetition, our legs feel like they are wading through treacle, our calf muscles turn into knotted sinews, the legs and lungs feel like they will burst, the sickening dryness at the back of the throat reaches the front and (to anyone who has done multiple 400m training), wretching soon follows.

It is easy to think of this intense physical performance as merely that: 'physical' or worse 'mindless'. Yet short of hypnotic training, this is a grossly inadequate description. Each step of the way is mindful even though we need not think of the reflection in action as intellectual. Consider an attenuated catalogue of judgements that inform my emotionally laden experiences as I run: how quick should I go in the first repetitions?; do I burst into or ease into it?; can I keep up with my superior running partner?; will I try to establish my preferred tempo in the first set?; will I save myself for the latter?; how full is my foot plant?; am I running too much on the outside of my feet and reducing power output?; am I relaxed in my neck and shoulders and allowing for the smooth transition of power from the arms and torso?; is my stride shortening as the lactic acid bites into my thighs?; will I stick to the schedule and do my full sets of ten repetitions or will I steer clear of the final repetition like a coward? If anyone thinks of the performance of the training schedule as mindless or machinistic they are clearly mistaken. Yet the catalogue of interior dialogue I have included is multi-faceted and heterogeneous.

Applying Frankfurt's analysis one can readily find oneself questioning one's commitment to the training plan. Sure I had the first order desire to complete the 3 × 3 × 400m session but can I really face the last set? My legs feel like they will knot up in cramp and my lungs feel like they are outside of my body.[18] Sooner rather than later the second order desire to give up early overtakes the first order desire to complete the session and supplants itself with a desire not to have the desire to complete it (which itself driven by guilt may be overtaken by a third order and so on) until such time as I act to end the series. This is all straightforward enough. But does the account of weak evaluation exhaust the description?

Taylor's account analogously distinguishes between levels of evaluation. Both may decry the moral status of the mere wanton: the one who cannot regulate their desires but must give into them or bow to their superior weight over an inferior or diminished will. On Taylor's account, the weak evaluator is the one who can only come to consider the technical merits of different courses of action, from the person proper: one capable of determining between the ignoble and the noble; the admirable and the contemptible; the fat ego from the generous soul. Of my thin catalogue of some phenomenological aspects of 400m training, only once have I asked the kind of question that looks like contrastive, strong, evaluation. How will I conceive of myself if I give up? Ought I interpret my actions as cowardice or prudence? How will I understand the emotional flurry inside my suffering body and soul? Recognition of this categorical distinction certainly seems to take us into a conceptual terrain beyond Frankfurt's framework.

To see whether the distinction holds up in relation to difficult cases, consider another example. Elite sport is often said to be young man's/woman's game. This is a fact saturated with ethical import with respect to the vulnerability of those with less developed modes of self-critique and reflection. As a top level swimmer, teenagers are often expected to train twice a day for five or six days of the week; one can easily imagine their devising training strategies that combine water and land-based regimes. Maybe the coach scours recent physiological research to most effectively combine training modes, muscle recovery times, co-ordinate their peaks and troughs in training intensity to match the yearly competitions cycle and so on. They present the plan to the swimmer who may (or more likely, may not) evaluate the new plan. The ends of athletic excellence – that which above all the elite athlete properly desires – are assumed and what are contrasted are the most effective means. Such a person is already disciplined and focused. They are scarcely wantons: incapable of controlling their desires. But their conception of the ends aimed at may have been arrived at (to use Bertrand Russell's beautiful phrase) without the consent of their deliberate reason. Many elite swimmers have been training since the age of 5 or 6 and the source of their self-esteem and even identity is often deeply interwoven with their athletic status. Few may be able to conceive of themselves outside of the role of swimmer. In this role-immersion, to invent a term of art, they are incapable under Taylor's account of strong evaluation. When, then, they are confronted with new techniques for performance enhancement they are limited in their evaluative capacities to considerations of effectiveness: how quickly will my performance gains arrive?; how long will they last?; with how much effort?; with what health side effects, if any?; is there a positive outcome from risk or cost–benefit analysis? The strong evaluator asks themselves: is this technique ethically defensible?; even if it is, is it admirable?; is it the action of one who is worthy of esteem and respect?; does it represent an unfair advantage?; would my parents and those whose values I aspire to think it wise or foolish?; would I be proud to win on the basis of the type of preparation it allows me?; will I feel guilty if I use it?; would I be ashamed if it became public knowledge?; and so on. I have set out the weak from the strong evaluator in stark terms; it is fairer, however, to recognise that the weak and strong evaluator categories as housing persons of varying depth and breadth (Flanagan, 1991).[19] Yet these latter questions certainly seem to take us to the heart of sports when they are engaged in and envisaged as ethically significant practices for persons. I will elaborate this conception in the chapter that follows, but although I have now cast off the misperception of the mere physicality or animality (so to speak) of sportspersons, I appear to have reinforced the cognitive or judgemental aspect of sports engagement as ethically significant. This requires further comment.

Taylor's thesis demands that persons and their identity are bound up in strong evaluation. Flanagan (1990) among others argues that this is, to use a sporting metaphor, setting the bar too high. How many human agents will satisfy this strong demand ethically to evaluate the means and ends of their actions, character, choices, habits, reflections in the course of planning and enacting their life plans? Should we deny the descriptor of the 400m athlete 'sportsperson' on the grounds he or she cannot evaluate him or herself ethically in the dominant social sphere of his life? It is certainly counter-intuitive to consider those who are not deep in the required sense somehow not persons given that we typically think that those belonging to that category enjoy widespread rights and are obliged to respect equally widespread duties too. Flanagan's less linguistic thesis coheres in large parts with key features of Taylor's account. He agrees that the persons must be created in intersubjective contexts, that they must be self-comprehending and that this must have normative force. Flanagan insists, however, that the capacity for comprehending normativity is not merely to be found in developed linguistic competence but in the activities of living, which may admit of dim and inchoate self-awareness. In the last two points we see a subtle shift away from Taylor's linguistic abilities to comprehend the way in which emotions open persons' conceptions of the good life. He argues that persons can satisfy these conditions without being obliged to reach the heights of Taylor's strong evaluation. He summarises thus:

> If firm, self-respecting identity is possible for persons who are both inarticulate and (let us suppose) unaware of contrastive possibilities, and if

both these things are necessary for strong evaluation then it follows that strong evaluation is not a necessary foundation and indispensable font of identity and motivation.

(Flanagan, 1990: 47)

He goes on to critique the demands of articulacy in Taylor by arguing that although it is necessary for strong evaluation it is not sufficient since one can very well imagine weak evaluators who are articulate just as we can imagine strong evaluators who are capricious or vicious. To be fair to Taylor, Flanagan's alternative proposal is somewhat sketchy. He tentatively proposes an alternative anthropological scheme whereby persons that are 'relatively impoverished linguistically' (1990: 52) can develop means of self-comprehension. This might comprise normative feedback by gesture, body language, feelings of co-ordination and integration and so on. Oddly enough, Flanagan chooses an example, rather than a sustained argument to push his point home and it is taken from sports (or as is typical in US English, 'athletics'):

> Great athletes often cannot coach, because they cannot say how they do what they do. It is not that they linguistically know how they do what they do but simply cannot get at the module that contains the relevant linguistic description. Often, if they were not coached in certain ways, there was never cause to linguistically formulate the relevant skills. But surely what such athletes are able to do involves highly developed know-how, reflexive comprehension and self-control.

(Flanagan, 1990: 53)

I want largely to agree with Flanagan here but correct his perception in two ways. The first is a problem with generalisation. It is a mistake made too often that people generalise about the conditions and character of sports in ways that lump all the activities in one category. For analytical purposes we can do this. In ethical evaluation it is at best infelicitous. For the cultures and sub-cultures of sport, their ethos(es) so to speak, are highly particular. The variation is not merely between sports but among them. Ice hockey in Sweden is played, coached and observed according to social rules notably different from those of the USA and Canada where not infrequently naked violence can be a key variable in the determination of victories. But the differentia are not merely geo-cultural. Contrast elite women's football (soccer) with its male counterpart in Western Europe at least. Note how skill is more pervasive and power and aggression less dominant. Mountaineers and orienteers often attract sportspersons from middle-class backgrounds. Competitive boxers (by which I exclude health clubs and their sanitised 'boxercise' conceptions) are typically drawn from the most disadvantaged of our societies while polo players are drawn from the social elite of the world who have more in common with their economic equals than almost any of their national brothers and sisters. Equally Nilsson (1993) argues that there are different perceptions of the good player and the good game in the eyes of rather young players. So my point here is that to imagine that there were some particular coaching style (linguistically driven or otherwise) is to make a weak empirical claim. Sometimes coaches will use demonstrations with no language, at other times they will provide lots of information, sometimes verbal, sometimes visual, sometimes aural, and so on. Much will depend not merely upon the coach's education but their sport, the age of the population, their skill levels, their experience of the game, their own abilities and disabilities, the preferences of their learning styles and so on.[20] I shall say a lot more about the significance of these facts in the chapters that follow and a little more after the final critical point. Flanagan's analogy is a weak one for the similarities between linguistic and motor-skill (henceforth motoric) are somewhat strained. One might argue that what disabled these would-be coaches was their inarticulacy, but one might just as easily argue that their ability had been such that they rarely experienced clumsiness, lack of balance or co-ordination in skill acquisitions. Equally, they may never have experienced what their charges were feeling in acute and distressing self-awareness at the all-too-public display of their ineptitude: embarrassment, ignominy, even humiliation. Equally, they might never have felt the contempt being signalled by the ex-great athlete significantly in their own career. All these things, and many more, might explain the deficiency of the would-be coaches and what really let them down was a distinct lack of empathy, not diminished articulacy.

I am not trying to deny here Flanagan's excellent point that Taylor has overstated the role that articulacy plays in the assignation of personhood,[21] or the construction of our identities of those struggling to conceive of and enact the living of good lives. My point is simply that (1) the apparent inarticulacy of certain performers and coaches may be a more heterogeneous phenomenon than he conceives of it; and (2) there seems to be something awry in *his* example of motoric learning as an analogy for moral development.[22]

Another of Flanagan's examples is that of peasants in Tolstoy's writings. The idea of simple peasants leading good but unreflective lives seems at least a logical possibility. Mackinnon (1999) challenges this example by pointing out the seduction of a simple life lived close to nature, free from the stresses of complex modern life. Nonetheless, she argues that this freedom has its price: '[T]hese peasants cannot understand themselves and the kinds of beings they are in ways which more consciously self-interpreting beings can. They cannot lead fully human lives. They cannot be fully autonomous agents' (1999: 88–9).

I have some sympathy with this view. There is something ethically significant missing in the lives of those whose critical self-awareness is attenuated. There is something absent that demands a mode of response that is neither nostalgia nor pity. To be sure pre-articulate choices and responses in and to the world can be made, but only in response to a limited mode of being. Living in complex, multilayered societies the spaces for these agents is limited as are the possibilities of their flourishing therein. For my purposes at least, the ethical character of strong evaluation opens up the possibility of a greater scope of good living. Of course spelling out what this demands requires a full account of practical reasoning the like of which is not possible here. For our purposes relate to developing a richer sense of sportsperson than the mere descriptor: those who play sports. And there is no denying the inarticulacy of so many who play sports excellently.

For the sake of clarity I will offer a brief summary before passing on to the notion of sportspersonship. Taylor seems to set the bar too high in arguing that strong evaluation is necessary for his conception of personhood and identity. Flanagan seems to lower it perhaps too generously to include those agents with 'dim and inchoate' (1990: 44) self-awareness. There is something to be admired though in the capacity for deeper, contrastive, evaluation that resonates with our emotional responses and vocabularies that open up the possibility of good living which is undeniable. It can set an ideal for those who love sport to develop something a little deeper, ethically admirable and more meaningful to the self-striving to attain excellence in sports and that will lead us a good way down the path to articulacy. As Mackinnon puts it:

> While it need not be denied that some good behaviours that contribute to an agents' well-being are pre-articulate, the more self-conscious and articulate an agent is about the kinds of choices she is making and the kinds of lives she admires, the more fulfilling and meaningful she will find her life. If excellence in practical reasoning underpins the best kinds of choices humans can make in the questions to lead good human lives, and if this kind of reasoning requires agents to recognize ends as more or less worthy for humans, as more or less suited to human nature, then we would expect humans to have to be cognisant about human nature and the fittingness of human ends. It is difficult to see how this would be possible without the kind of conceptual richness made possible by linguistic categories.
>
> (Mackinnon, 1999: 89)

Yet in conclusion she echoes a point made by Flanagan about the insufficiency of the strong evaluators' capacity to lead full and valuable lives:

> A richer vocabulary increases the chances of identifying optimal choices, but it does not ensure it. Being articulate about one's options will not, on its own, guarantee that the right kinds of choices will be recognised or made.
>
> (Mackinnon, 1999: 90)

What does assure that the right kinds of choices are made, other things being equal, is a good character and nothing less than that. How this is formed is necessarily a developmental story about emulation, habit, initiation, instruction and so on: in short the virtue-ethical position I wish to develop in this book.

Sportspersonship is not simply *a* virtue

I openly confess to the reader that it seems to have taken an age to get to this point. What then is the picture of a sportsperson I wish to commend? Having said that I wanted to avoid the fallacy of composition, simply adding the concepts of sports to persons,[23] I want also to avoid the idea of sportspersonship being thought of as a single virtue; a mistake made by psychologists and philosophers alike.[24]

Before offering an account of 'sportspersonship' it is necessary to ask the questions: 'what use is the concept of sportspersonship for?'; 'why do we need a concept such as sportspersonship?'; and 'what role does the concept play in our playing, spectating and teaching of sports?'. Given the account of sports in the previous chapter, it seems reasonable to say that the answers to these questions will be made in the context of certain standards of athletic excellence in persons striving mutually for exclusive goals by admirable standards of conduct and character. With the devotion to the *telos* or ends of sports being so focused we understand the temptations to behave in ways that might be described as moral minimalism. Such engagement with the practices of sport, as we shall consider them in the next chapter, ought to aim above mere rule keeping in order to satisfy the proper motives for engagement. In this context, sportspersonship is an ideal: a set of standards, without precise specification in the modes of attainment, that might be aimed for so that they elicit and ramify the best in our conduct and character as persons in the strong sense that I have developed, via Taylor and Flanagan above.

What are the contours of this conception of 'sportspersonship'? I want to say that sportspersonship is exemplified by the athlete, player, contestant, who is able to act in ways that either are (1) the effects of strong evaluation; or (2) illustrative of the product of strong evaluation. I have expressed it in this manner in order that I do not make sportspersonship *necessarily* a hostage to developed ethical articulacy though clearly that is the more mature reflection of sportspersonship. Expressing it in this manner leaves open the possibility of the assignation of sportspersonship to young children who have been properly habituated in the best standards of human excellence in their sports, or indeed those who lack moral maturity but are nonetheless uncritically reflective but good, or even those incapable of self-critical reflection, or with severely diminished capacities for self-critical awareness, are nonetheless good. In 2006 I spent a short sabbatical at the Norwegian University of Sport Sciences. During my stay my host invited me to an international competition-festival (Ridderenet) for disability skiers at Beitostolen in the West of Norway. I found myself lost in admiration (among a welter of other emotions) for those from the entire spectrum of disability who simply flew down mountains and across terrains with courage and élan assisted by the athletic elite of the University's students. Of course, that admiration is itself a strong evaluation. It was a recognition that here was a sporting community richly deserving of respect and support. Many of the skiers were amputees, blind, deaf or suffering from other debilitating conditions. They represent an alternative to the paradigmatic sports communities we typically think of and those which sports philosophers write about.

In the welter of emotional experience during that visit, I learnt later that part of my emotional response was untoward. I certainly pitied the athletes who were, by virtue of their impairments, forced to struggle with everyday acts (such as getting out of their wheelchair or mobility apparatuses), putting on equipment and clothing, holding equipment with a difficulty that able-bodied persons have, for the most part, no inkling of. In discussion with disability sport colleagues later I was instructed as to the inappropriateness of that emotion since it implied a wrongly privileged position of myself as able-bodied. Here then, the emotions are educated by better judgements and the subsequent experience was patterned both in feeling and perception as well as cognitive judgement. Yet it is for such people that Flanagan's critique may well prove to be auspicious in a way that he had not intended. Might not sports communities for the severely disabled be offended by the failure to incorporate them into the categories (sports)persons? It is absolutely clear that they are capable of sportspersonship – that they may have appreciated, recognised, taken on board the exemplars of courageous, honest, tenacious competitors and imitated their conduct so as to make it their own. I want to say then that strong evaluation is still a valuable heuristic tool for sports ethics despite the dominance of linguistic articulacy in Taylor's earlier writing if we allow it to depict an ideal to which all can and should strive in their pursuit of athletic excellence.

I shall now offer a paradigmatic example of what I consider sportspersonship. When Australia play England at cricket in the traditional 5-day contest format, they play for a symbolic urn referred to as The Ashes. The name refers to the ashes of the burnt bails of wood which sit on top of the stumps of wickets that the batsmen defend against the bowlers. Upon losing their first series of matches ("tests") against Australia in 1882, the Ashes – symbolically the remains of English cricket – were presented to Australia and became the unofficial trophy for all ensuing tests. The rivalry between the two teams is the stuff of legend and in recent years the Australians have been so dominant that many tests have been rather one-sided affairs. In the 2005 Ashes series of five tests, Australia beat England easily in the first test but were on the receiving end of a rejuvenated England in the second. Going into the final day the Australians had only two wickets remaining (two batsmen to be got out) and were nearly 100 runs behind. After losing their last recognised batsman, Australia were left with two batters attempting to score around 60 runs: an all but impossible situation for what are really specialist bowlers (ie pitchers). Little by little, however (and by luck and guts as much as technique or skill), they kept scoring runs. One of them, Brett Lee, was repeatedly struck by the ball travelling from England's lead bowler at around 80–90 miles per hour. With only three runs to win, the other batsman Kasprowicz was caught out and all hell broke loose around the Edgbaston ground. English relief-fuelled jubilation was tangible as players jumped for joy, hugged each other, screamed, and so on. Nevertheless, the most poignant picture in all the papers had escaped the TV crew though not the photo-journalists. Amid the mayhem, England's man of the match, Andrew Flintoff, had gone to console Lee whom he had struck so many times with sickening blows. Both were crouched on their haunches, heads bent toward each other in mutual recognition of suffering and success. To have borne in mind the suffering of his competitor in such a way, while all around were losing their heads, speaks volumes for the ethical capacity of Flintoff to rise above the egoistic triumphalism of the masses and show what really counted. Flintoff's actions displayed a range of virtues including empathy and fairness, and dominant among those virtues was the rare one of compassion. This was as forceful an example of the capacity of strong evaluation one could wish for – acting for the sake of the fine and noble as Aristotle would have put it. And it stands out in the minds of many as the defining picture of that great summer of cricket.

(Sports) persons and the scope of (sports) ethics

Throughout this chapter I have drawn heavily from the resources of Charles Taylor's writings. His general standpoint in ethics in many ways coheres largely with that of Alisdair MacIntyre whose work in moral philosophy has influenced sports philosophers widely and will be the object of critical discussion in the next chapter on sport as a social practice. The third philosopher I wish to draw into the debate is Bernard Williams. While many and various aspects of their philosophical thinking separate these celebrated figures in philosophy, I draw upon them as sources since their philosophical concerns go well beyond the avoidable battles of twentieth-century philosophy, which was often concerned exclusively with the articulation of the meanings of concepts. Of course no philosopher worth their salt is unconcerned with conceptual clarity. But there is much more to philosophy and especially philosophical ethics, in and out of sports talk, than the elaboration of concepts such as cheating, deception, doping, fairness and fair play, promising, rules and rule-following. Despite the valuable task of enunciating the various and sometimes competing concepts and conceptions, the primary task for applied philosophers will be to move people in the world to conceive of the good and to act in accordance with it. That means, very often, getting off and well clear of the fence of mere clarification.

MacIntyre, Taylor and Williams are prominent among the philosophers who have attempted to chart the moral topography of contemporary Western culture. Some commonality can be found in their insistence that morality and moral theory is incomplete if it focuses solely on the nature of our obligations. And just as mainstream philosophical thinking in ethics had followed the linguistic turn and reified a special moral language, so too sports philosophers had largely focused on their counterparts in sports. Like others, this triumvirate has decried the manner in which much contemporary moral philosophy in the Anglo-American tradition has narrowly conceived its direction, importance and responsibility. Modern moral philosophy for at least two hundred years had tended to focus on what it is right to do rather than what it is good to be. This focus either led philosophers to rule that the currency of moral thought was moral action whether this was inspired by a recognition of one's rational moral duties or the moral imperative to maximise happiness in the world. As with many dualisms this simple dichotomy between moral action and moral being, what it is right to do or good to be, is somewhat misleading.

Many accounts of personhood are woven into an account of morality in the language of rules as duties or obligations or some other principle such as the maximisation of good consequences. In discussing the nature of morality many philosophers have adopted the stance that acting morally is related to certain principles about what we should and should not do that could be universalised, that is, to be done by all people in all places at all times where the situation was appropriately similar. They have argued, in a manner characteristic of the time that acting morally requires sticking to principles rather than responding to moods and feelings. This axis between universalised moral demands and rationality is one that will be the object of considerable discussion when I try to articulate a virtue-ethical account of sports and sportspersons in later chapters. For the moment I want to signal the sources of discontent in writers such as MacIntyre, Taylor and Williams.

Williams, against the grain of universalistic moral demands, argued that obligations ought to be viewed as merely one type of ethical consideration among others. MacIntyre, following Aristotle's lead, argues that we should return to the ethical ideal of living well as opposed to acting right. Both offer an account of the good life and of moral philosophy which was greater in scope than the 'peculiar institution' of morality. This moral language was cauterised from daily living: *moral* rules became rather special rules. Their properties could be teased out with linguistic care: they were universal in scope, impartial in application, and prescriptive or action guiding in nature. People in all walks of life became familiar in conversation with the idea that somehow *moral* decisions are categorically superior to, more important than and more demanding of, other kinds of decisions. A dominant belief was that how one should conduct oneself generally and how one should *morally* conduct oneself were somehow separate. Morality had a special and overriding 'demandingness' in contrast to other practical reasons encountered in the course of living. It is no accident that Williams began his powerful book *Ethics and the Limits of Philosophy* with the words Plato recalls of Socrates: it is no trivial matter how one is to live their life. This is no simple project of ethical nostalgia, but a complex attempt to widen the focus of ethics, and to understand the life of moral agents that are persons, to a wider vocabulary of living well.

Taylor too addresses himself to the question 'what is it that makes life worth living?' He outlines a cluster of notions that are central to ethical life: the respect for life, integrity, well-being and the flourishing of others. These concerns, indeed Taylor calls them 'demands' (1989: 4), are so deep-rooted that one could be forgiven for considering them instinctual. Examples of such demands might, specifically, be the compunction to inflict death or injury on others as well as the inclination to help those in injury or danger. Culture helps define 'relevant' other demands but not the basic reaction itself. Even if the notions of duty, obligation and rights were constitutive of morality then we must also recognise that there are other demands upon us that bring in strong evaluations that are also of central concern to us:

> These are questions about how I am going to live my life which touch on the issue of what kind of life is worth living, or what kind of life would fulfil the promise implicit in my particular talents, or the demands of someone with my endowment, or of what constitutes a rich, meaningful life.
>
> (Taylor, 1989: 14)

More precisely, Taylor articulates three axes for moral thinking in its most general sense: (1) our sense of respect for and obligation to others; (2) our understanding of what makes life full; and (3) the range of notions concerned with dignity (Taylor, 1989: 15).

In an important qualification, Taylor states that the meaning of 'respect' in (1) is not the usual respect for rights but rather the respect we have for someone we look up to or admire such as is affirmed when we say that someone 'has our respect'. Taylor demarcates this special sense by calling it 'attitudinal'. Similarly, he refers to as 'attitudinal' the notion of dignity in (3) whereby it represents our sense of ourselves commanding the above sense of respect.

Setting these axes in the contexts of sports ethics it seems fair to say that the majority of writings have thus far followed the dominant traditions of modern moral philosophy as deontology (duty ethics) or consequentalism (usually some form of utilitarianism). A considerable body of knowledge on rule-keeping and rule-breaking emerged for example in early debates about formalism within games (Leamon, 1988; Lehman, 1981) and more recently with respect to moral realism and the moral authority of the rules within sports (Dixon, 2003; McFee, 2003b; Morgan, 2004; Roberts, 1998; Russell, 1999, 2004; Simon, 2000, 2004a, 2004b[25]). The classic statement of a strict deontological sports ethics duties of sports contestants and coaches alike is in Fraleigh (1984) while other authors focus on issues of justice and (in)equality (especially Loland, 2002). Occasionally a representative of utilitarianism has promoted that particular moral rationalism to problems such as cheating, doping, and the morality of sports technology (most notably Tamburrini, 2000, 2006). Less frequently has there been any extended and systematic treatment of sports ethics within the second axis (with the exception of Arnold, 1994; Gibson, 1993; Reid, 2002).

Conclusion

The questions that turn around the meanings our life can possess, fragmented and conflicting as they are, are the very stuff of persons. I have followed Charles Taylor here in arguing that a capacity to evaluate among our goals and the means by which we pursue them is definitive of persons. This sets the bar rather high with respect to personhood, namely foetuses or those with severe intellectual disabilities. I am aware that his account is not without its regrettable consequences. The consequences of the account, however, are nowhere near as corrosive in the vast majority of adult populations who at least attempt to conceive of their activities and goals in a critical way. And this is the manner in which I wish to promote the proper understanding of sportspersonship.

It is the case that in 'all' times there has been a framework regardless of how poorly articulated it has been, that enabled people to define the demands by which their lives are judged as less or more full. These pictures, or 'narratives' as MacIntyre calls them, are never so dominant that they can command universal assent. Moreover, he has forcefully argued that modernity is characterised partly by the fragmentation of competing traditions. His argument rests upon a proper recognition of the practices, goods and virtues to be found in historically formed social traditions. Into this idea the account of sportspersonship I have developed here is to be insinuated. To be a sportsperson, in the normative sense that I have struggled to articulate, is to engage wholeheartedly with the actions of sport as one's own, at first by training and emulation and then by critical reflection until the choices one makes are fully one's own and no longer in need of constant intentionality. To this idea, instantiated in sports, I now turn.

3   Sports as practices

In the previous chapters I have sketched an initial account of sport and presented a critical account of personhood that will serve as the foundation of the argument that good sports and sportspersons are to be conceived in virtue-ethical terms. The basis of the explicitly ethical conception of sports I want now to develop is based on another philosopher who has attacked the modern liberal worldview: Alasdair MacIntyre. Like Taylor, he is uncomfortable being labelled a communitarian but many of his writings sit comfortably under that banner. Discussion of MacIntyre's arguments surrounding his notions of 'practices', 'institutions,' and 'virtues' have been taken up by many philosophers of sport[1] who have used them to articulate the inherently ethical nature of sports and their apparent recent decline. While I am persuaded by much that is central to MacIntyre's brilliant analysis of morals in modernity, I argue that applying his general account to the particular case of modern sports is not without difficulty.

The chapter is based around four such difficulties (1) the clarity of the distinction between practices and institutions and the methodological limits of his analysis; (2) the manner in which the individual is transposed to the social; (3) the apparent reductivism of his account of virtues and their function in practices; and finally (4) the characterisation of internality and externality of goods to practices. This will pave the way for a critical discussion of particular vices and virtues in sports in Part II of the book.

After MacIntyre: sports as practices

One of the chief reasons for the influence MacIntyre's account has had over the philosophy of sport, I suggest, is due to the sterility of analytical accounts of sports with respect to their ethical nature. It would, however, be futile to offer an extended description of MacIntyre's position as set out in his classic *After Virtue* (1986) since critical commentaries of the work are now legion. I therefore offer only the briefest of overviews sufficient for the purpose at hand before illuminating some difficulties for philosophers of sport wishing to utilise his account. And I attempt in the remainder of the book to make good on some of these criticisms by developing an account that builds upon them.

In his rejection of modern morality with its individualism, fragmented incoherence and interminable disagreements of modern societies, MacIntyre sets out by contrast the richness and coherence of conceptions of ethics in Ancient Greece, notably those found in the works of Aristotle. The picture of the good life MacIntyre focuses on is one lived in accordance with virtue against a background of a proper nature of 'man' [sic]. The virtues are excellences that enable us to achieve our goal (telos) of flourishing and are also an ingredient of the attainment of that goal at the same time. What MacIntyre attempts to supply is a revised Aristotelianism with its focus on a narrative self, situated in place and time, who is possessed of a core of virtues that are acquired, displayed and produced in a variety of shared social practices that are themselves constitutive of broader cultural traditions.

With something approaching litigious precision, MacIntyre sets out his account of practices and their internal goods in the following way. A practice is defined as:

> Any coherent and complex socially established co-operative human activity through which goods internal to that form of activity are realised in the course of trying to achieve those standards of excellence which are appropriate to, and partially definitive of, that form of activity, with the result that human powers to achieve excellence and human conceptions of the ends and goods involved are systematically extended.
>
> (MacIntyre, 1985: 187)

While the account is far from easy at first sight, in his examples of what are and are not practices, MacIntyre brings further light and shows the ready application of the idea to modern living. MacIntyre first distinguishes between technical skills and the institutions that give them their context and allow us to make sense of them. Tic-tac-toe (hopscotch) is not a practice in this sense nor is the throwing or catching of a football. The game of football, however, is. Similarly bricklaying is not a practice, but architecture is. Other examples of practices are arts, games, sciences, and the making and sustaining of family life. In his later book, *Whose Justice, Which Rationality* (1998), MacIntyre offers a more variegated list, the elements of which he argues are the sites of the production in which human excellences are instantiated:

> [W]arfare and combat, seamanship, athletic and gymnastic activity; epic, lyric and dramatic poetry; farming both arable and the management of animals; rhetoric and the making and sustaining of the communities of kinship and the household and later of the city-state. To this list architecture, sculpture and painting were to be added, as were the intellectual enquiries of mathematics, philosophy and theology.
>
> (MacIntyre, 1998: 30)

None of these practices can be reduced to the various skills that are required to exemplify and sustain them without remainder. Nor can they simply be thought of as the institutions that give rise to them. Football/soccer cannot be reduced to its technical skills or the various clubs and administrative structures, though these are important in our understanding of, and successful participation in, football/soccer as a practice.

The notion of goods internal to a practice is central to MacIntyre's account. What they are, in Brown's words, is far from easy to say. Indeed Brown (1991) goes as far as to comment that his account of internal goods is almost hopelessly vague.[2] They are most readily comprehended by distinguishing them from those goods that are external. MacIntyre considers the example of teaching an intelligent young child how to play chess. The child is motivated to learn the game only in so far as he or she is offered a given amount of candy to play, and even more upon winning, a game. When candy is the primary motivation, the child has every reason to cheat and no reason not to cheat since the game is irrelevant (or at the very least secondary) in his or her motivational hierarchy. Over time, however, the child may come to recognise and value the achievement of a certain kind of analytical skill, strategic imagination, competitive intensity and so forth. These are internal goods and are specific to the practice of chess. MacIntyre then holds that if the child cheats after recognising these internal goods, this will not constitute defeating the tutor but his or herself. This example is supposed to show that there are goods that are externally or contingently related to the practice of chess, and, alternatively, that there are those goods that are internal to that practice. It is fairly clear here that the candy is an external good in MacIntyre's example. In other areas of life, power, prestige, status or wealth are external goods. These goods can, by definition, be isolated and achieved by alternative means that are not exclusively tied to engagement in a particular practice. External goods stand, therefore, in an instrumental relation to practices. Where external goods are the locus of value and motivation for the practitioner, it should be noted that they may be brought about by a variety of means that are more or less successful in that task. This explains the disinterestedness with which some approach practices; only as a means to secure external goods. On the other hand, there are goods internal to (or inherent within) a practice that cannot be had except by engagement in that practice. These goods can only be gained by first-hand experience of them in the relevant practice, and those who lack this experience are not competent to judge those practices.

With the game of chess, MacIntyre says that the internal goods cannot be had except by playing chess or 'some other game of that specific kind', but it is not clear just what this latitude opens up. In what follows this point will briefly be addressed. Perhaps this exclusivity is in any case a little too strong. Many philosophers may find more defensible the idea that Stout suggests, against MacIntyre's scepticism, that the requisite experience and competence to judge a practice, and therefore its internal goods, may come second-hand 'through a skilful reporter's thick descriptions' (Stout, 1988: 267).

More convincing is the idea that these goods can only be specified in the language of such practices and through examples of them. Brown captures this point well:

> One of the good things to be achieved by participating in a practice is the development of human capacities in the manner dictated by a given practice, its goals, skills, styles and procedures insofar as they promote the flourishing of human powers and potential.
>
> (Brown, 1991: 73)

When we move on to consider the relationship between institutions and practices we find an apparent paradox. For not only is it the case that the respective institutions are corruptive of their practices, they are also essential to them. Thus:

> Institutions are characteristically and necessarily concerned with what I have called external goods. They are involved in acquiring money and other material goods; they are structured in terms of power and status, and they distribute money and power and status as rewards. Nor could they do otherwise if they are to sustain not only themselves, but also the practices of which they are the bearers. For no practices can survive any length of time unsustained by institutions. Indeed so intimate is the relationship of practices to institution – and consequently of the goods external to the goods internal to the practice in question – that institutions and practices characteristically form a single causal order in which the ideals and the creativity of the practice are always vulnerable to the acquisitiveness of the institutions, in which the co-operative care for common goods of the practice is always vulnerable to the competitiveness of the institution. In this context the essential function of the virtues is clear. Without them, without justice, courage and truthfulness, practices could not resist the corrupting power of institutions.
>
> (MacIntyre, 1985: 194)

There are several points of importance here that will form the substance of what follows. In the first instance, the celebrated distinction between practices and institution, though intimate,[3] is one that allows MacIntyre to celebrate the characteristic features of the former while deriding particular corruptive influences upon them by the latter in the context of 'contemporary emotivist cultures' as he calls them.[4] MacIntyre's selective emphasis upon the deleterious effects of the latter are worthy of note, as is the sharpness with which the further distinction between internal and external goods is drawn and the respective virtues and vices that enable the agent to secure them. First, however, I wish to discuss one of the ramifications of MacIntyre's communitarian stance and the manner in which it operates in relation to the notion of internal goods in sporting practices.

Practices and virtues: personal and/or social

MacIntyre sets store by three virtues to ward off the corruptive influences of institutions: justice, courage and honesty. It has been suggested that his justi-fication for this lies in the essentially social nature of these virtues.[5] This coheres with MacIntyre's moral, social and political polemic against liberal individualism. By locating the virtues in practices in which social co-operation is essential, the virtues become irreducibly social. Seung (1991) argued that by restricting his conception of a practice to the domain of social co-operation, MacIntyre excluded from consideration those activities that do not require social co-operation. It would follow, then, that mountain climbing would be a practice if performed co-operatively but not if performed individually. This interpretation misconstrues MacIntyre's position. He is nowhere so exclusive about practices. Indeed, his historical layering of practices allows precisely for such cases. Here individuals toil only in apparent isolation. Alternatively, they may be viewed as participants who co-operate over time in a tradition according to the canons developed over time between other participants. This would apply just as much to Van Gogh developing postimpressionism in seeming isolation at Arles as it would to a mountain climber attempting some new technique while on an ascent of Mount Everest. Their activities may only be understood in the light of the ongoing practice. To label them 'individual activities' as Seung does (1991: 207–8) is to ignore the purpose of MacIntyre's third tier of practices, which requires that the understanding of (practitioners') actions ought not to be wrenched from their social and historical context. Such a move, dubbed the 'ontogenetic fallacy' by Gellner (1967: 53), misses the mark somewhat as a criticism of MacIntyre's thesis.

What can be rescued from this line of criticism is the idea that MacIntyre's emphasis on the social aspects of virtues and practices effectively obscures the notion of personal achievement. While it is true that rules and standards structure the public nature of the achievements and set goals for future prac-titioners, they also attach to the individual in a strong and important way. MacIntyre argued that external goods are characteristically someone's prop-erty or possession. They are exclusive such that, for example, your having X denies my having it. Now although internal goods may be the object of com-petition, it is characteristic of their achievement that the good of the whole community of practitioners is advanced. He cites as an exemplar W. G. Grace who advanced the art of batting in cricket. As with the example above, how-ever, the achievement attaches to the individual in a strong and original way. Though other practitioners are indebted to these individuals and may emu-late their achievements, they are not esteemed in the same way. Those who have broken new ground are thereby rewarded and esteemed. Athletes remember, with propriety, the fact that Dick Fosbury introduced the 'flop' to the world of track and field. They will not know, nor ought they to, that you or I acquired the skill and displayed it with considerably more modest competence. After the 1974 Football (Soccer) World Cup every school boy was imitating the Cruyff turn where the ball was played behind the non-playing leg of the player in possession so as to put off-balance the defender. Yet their achievement of this technical trick is of course secondary to its progenitor. In a similar vein, Geoff Hurst is written deep into English football folklore by scoring a hat-trick in the 1966 World Cup final, and Martina Navratilova is credited with raising women's tennis to new heights of athleticism and competitive intensity. It is true that the whole community has been advanced by their achievements but not in the manner in which the individual is heralded. In one of the earliest texts in the sociology of sport, Inglis entitles a chapter 'The name of the game' with insight 'The memory of a people – now let us praise famous men [*sic*]'. It is the celebration of such people that correspondingly is the celebration of the practice. MacIntyre recognises this point at the level of tradition while failing to acknowledge the disjunction between the individual and the practice. Inglis writes with insight:

> Sporting photographs are like the snapshots of a national photograph album. They bring back memories of what has been lost, and is irrecoverable. And just because it is irrecoverable, the men and women who stir up those lost hopes become special heroes, whose like we shall not look upon again. So it is forever that old men forever tell young boys, "You ought to have seen Victor Trumper or Bobby Jones."
>
> A queer use of "ought really"; the young boys could hardly have seen Victor Trumper or Bobby Jones. Yet the young boys in their turn will say the same sort of thing when they themselves become old men, and the young boys of the future will shuffle their feet, and yawn inwardly, and wonder when the old men will fall silent. This is how society makes its history. How its imagination continues and makes a tradition: an assembly of names and occasions, great victories and defeats, of ways of seeing and celebrating these things.
>
> (Inglis, 1977: 5)

The function of such stories and their relationship to the sustaining of practices through narrative raises important questions in relation to practices generally and sporting practices specifically. More will be said of the nature of rewards and their relation to the goods of practices below. Yet before moving on we should note that the idea of rewards, remembered and venerated in such narratives, is neither as pernicious nor as contemporary as MacIntyre appears to suggest. As was noted earlier, it is not the case that MacIntyre's monsters of modernity have brought about a new (over-)emphasis on rewards to the detriment of practices. There is ample evidence of such customs from Ancient Greece onwards (Kyle, 2007). In this historical vein, Santayana, writing at the end of the nineteenth century, concurred with the view that sports have their own integrity that can be diminished with emphasis on external goods, yet he reminds us:

> Athletic sports are not children's games; they are public spectacles. . . . Spectators are indispensable, since without them the victory, which should be the only reward, would lose half its power. For as Pindar, who knew, tells us:
> Success
> Is half the prize, the other half renown.
> Who achieves both, he hath the perfect crown.
> (Santayana, 1894: 185)

It is clear that, in relation to their celebrative character, sports (especially elite sports) are public affairs, while performances still flow from, and are properly regarded as, the products of the exercise of individual agency. The just distribution of such rewards depends precisely upon this recognition. It would be wrong, however, to focus on elite sport only, for to do so might reinforce the framing of success, reward or the achievement of goods in sport at that level and in so doing over-emphasise the public aspect of achievement. On a larger scale, there is a real danger of losing sight of the personal dimension in adopting or employing uncritically MacIntyre's conception of practices in the contexts of sports. I am suggesting that sporting heroes do exist and ought still to be celebrated. Though it is often the case that those who are called 'sporting heroes' are mere celebrities whose fame and/or notoriety rests upon reasons other than desert; it is still the case that we may properly celebrate individual excellence within a particular practice without slipping into romantic individualism. Without the context that makes meaningful their excellence of course, they cannot be so understood. Such an account need not be a new one. Homer's *Iliad* is just such an account of heroes within tightly knit communities with shared evaluations as to the good life and its constituents. But the notion of local heroes, even in modernity, is not unheard of. From any objective standpoint it may well be inconsequential that the standards of a practice are advanced by any particular person. But from the personal viewpoint it is not.

When MacIntyre uses examples such as W. G. Grace and Turner he is talking of performances at the outer edges of practices. And this emphasis is not only apparent in *After Virtue* but also in his later *Whose Justice, Which Rationality* where, in properly recognising the subordinacy of novices or initiates in a practice to those more authoritative therein, he writes:

> The concept of the best, of the perfected, provides each of these forms of activity with the good toward which those who participate in it move. What directs them toward that goal is both the history of successive attempts to transcend the limitations of the best achievement in that

particular area so far and the acknowledgement of certain achievements as permanently defining aspects of the perfection toward which that particular form of activity is directed. Those achievements are assigned a canonical status within the practice of each type of activity. Learning what they teach is central to apprenticeship in each particular form of activity.

(1998: 31)

While I am in agreement with the general point being made here, a corrective needs to be made about this emphasis. Most persons engage in practices at the humdrum level of mediocrity against this absolute standard of excellence. Few will ever become a Beethoven or a Pelé; 'ordinary mortals' very often do not possess the potential in terms of natural capacities, tendencies or capabilities to justify the pursuit of a single calling to such absolute excellence. Nonetheless, anyone can pursue excellence in various activities where this is interpreted in relation to their own particular circumstances: their own previous best performances, or comparisons among standards of contemporaries in terms of age, body composition, years of training or education, and so on. Here the individual may make advances that are utterly unimportant to the practice as a whole but that are of enormous personal significance. Nowhere is this more the case than with beginners whose abilities may, at the initial stages, increase rapidly in range and sophistication. Yet MacIntyre's over-emphasis on the public or the social nature of recognition and inclusive achievement in practices stands in need of a counter-balance of the phenomenological character of achievement.

The British philosopher of education, Ray Elliot, once gave a beautiful account of the phenomenological character of initiation and personal development within a practice (that could as easily be applied to any of MacIntyre's post-Homeric practices whether athletics or mathematics) which is richly suggestive:

> [A] child at school finds a subject attractive, takes delight in it, and begins to look forward to the lessons in which it is taught. The subject seems to welcome his [*sic*] attention, his work pleases his teacher, and he comes to think of himself as "good at" the subject. It becomes "his subject." During its lessons time passes with a strange swiftness. He believes it to be "better" than other subjects, and is prepared to give up other pleasures because absorption in his subject pleases him still more. Perhaps he develops a passion for it, and begrudges time spent on anything else. In due course it dawns on the student that his enthusiastic interest in his subject is not enough. There are standards which have to be met, and to meet them he has to develop skills and abilities which he did not originally associate with his subject. He also has to do a good deal of work which seems to be commonly like drudgery. Pleasures do not come easily now, but he finds fulfilment in trying to satisfy the demands his subject makes

upon him. He has become devoted to its disciplines and feels at times that he has been enlisted in its service.

(Elliot, 1974: 6)

There is every reason to believe that this account of initiation is precisely what MacIntyre was driving towards both in terms of the non-egoistic engagement with practices and a non-hedonistic account of the way in which success in practices enriches our lives. Moreover, it gives a corrective to the exemplars whose achievements are to be understood as belonging to the practice as a whole. Now it might be argued that this stress on the quasi-individual character of achievement highlighted by Elliot, along with esteem that attaches to the absolutely excellent practitioners, is antithetical to MacIntyre's overall project. It would appear to be an attempt to incorporate a quasi-individualistic ethos into the broader communitarian worldview. To this the response must be that there are communitarians and there are communitarians. MacIntyre is never as staunch as Sandel (1982), who in his earlier writings appears to transpose the individual entirely to the social so that the individual appears to be no more than the nexus of situated narratives.[6] Yet by arguing for the objective status of internal goods, against the idea that they can also be felt- satisfactions of a personal kind, MacIntyre effectively closes the door on the personal dimension. He is so concerned to eschew subjectivism that he rides roughshod over the phenomenological aspects of internal goods as experienced by the agent.

The distinction between practices and institutions and its methodological status

A central motivating factor behind the virtues MacIntyre wishes to attribute to his practitioners and their relationship to those practices is something more deep than what is typified in the phrase 'the three minute culture'.[7] He expresses distaste for the acquisitiveness and fleeting disengagement that is often thought to be a defining characteristic of liberal capitalism in late modernity. A significant partner in the establishment of such a shallow culture is the rise of institutions that treat the ends that practices embody with indifference, ignore the authority invested in them over time, and usurp them with mere subjective preferences represented by the economic demand of a not necessarily educated, but consuming, public. Examples of such sporting corruption are legion. Athletes who competed in the marathon in the Seoul and Barcelona Olympics were told to their dismay that they would be competing in the noon-day sun. This posed a serious threat to their health. The apparent justification for such a potential hazard was the maximization of media revenue; a consideration external to the logic of the practice.[8] Likewise, professional tennis players have regularly complained at being forced to compete in the New York Tennis Open tournament in the twilight hours under floodlights with the incessant noise of John F. Kennedy airport traffic overhead. While undermining the players' attempt to personify the best of their abilities such a move made more random the outcomes of contests that more properly should be settled by the defining excellences of the activity: skill, strength, speed, co-ordination of hand and eye, anticipation of one's opponent's actions and so forth – not the ability to see the ball under floodlit conditions or to concentrate on one's game through the noise of peak flying times from the nearby New York airport.

Despite acknowledging the supportive role that institutions play in organising, regulating and promoting practices, MacIntyre emphatically wrote of the institutions' corruptive powers and emphasised the fact that the practice is always vulnerable to the acquisitiveness of the institution. It is to save practices from such perversion that the nature and functions of the virtues are located, by contrast, in practices. He reinforces this view by setting out institutions as the agencies that organise and distribute external goods or rewards, such as power, wealth and status, while passing over their supportive role. Arnold (1992, 1994), Brown (1991) and Schneider and Butcher (1993, 1994) do not equivocate on this matter. Morgan (1994)[9] has given an extended and less one-sided treatment of the institutions related to sport, though he is no less scathing in his criticism.

If practices are coherent and complex forms of socially established co-operative activities, and institutions are the mechanisms through which external goods are distributed, where do we place sportspersons, coaches, officials, parents of young sports players and so forth? Imagine a scenario at the end of a successful season of Little League baseball. There is of course an annual meeting to celebrate the team's successes, to thank the parents who faithfully drove the kids around to the various venues, encouraged them to perform to (and often beyond) the best of their abilities, maybe even to playfully admonish those who too often abused the umpires. Here the team committee functions precisely like an institution in MacIntyre's sense by distributing external rewards such as medals, trophies, acclamations, maybe even monetary or token rewards. But given that the self-same people may have been the guardians of various traditions upheld in the club, given that they too are the initiates and initiators to the various skills, strategies and standards of excellence and modes of conduct as are characteristics of all that is good in the activity, they appear to be part of the practice also. The lack of clarity of the distinction once pushed shows a certain ambiguity. Perhaps it is the case that they can at one time be a member of both the practice and the institution.

It should be clear that such ambiguities, as are present on the borderline, scarcely undermine the entire MacIntyrean position. A distinction need not be watertight to be valuable. It does raise, however, some questions about the 'empirical content' of the thesis. While it is clear that, in sports at least, when MacIntyre talks of the institution, we unproblematically instantiate the idea with names such as the IAAF (International Amateur Athletics Federation), the IOC (International Olympic Committee), the

FIFA (Fédération Internationale de Football Association), the NBA (National Basketball Association), and so on. It is easy to see how the distinction operates. Lower down the order things are less clear.

Morgan, in his characterisation of the relationship in a sporting context, is more careful than other philosophers of sports have been. He takes time, even though he focuses on large-scale organisations, to adumbrate the varieties of functions of institutions from distributing external goods to the nurturing, regulating, normalising and legitimating of various aspects of the practice. Like MacIntyre, however, it is not long before Morgan moves to strong critique. The main target for his detailed and penetrating analysis is the fact that institutions necessarily operate in the economic marketplace with an unsophisticated and inadequate qualitative vocabulary that is inimical to the practice. Morgan approvingly quotes Nozick to the effect that money is not 'a vehicle for nuanced expression' (Morgan,1994: 143) and that the institution, in Walzer's phrase, issues 'scandalous couplings between people and goods' (Morgan, 1994: 141).

There are two respects in which this interpretation is selective. Following Lasch, Morgan argues that (1) there is a specific historical juncture (the late 1940s and 1950s) where we can mark out the importantly deleterious effects of sports' institutionalisation; and (2) contemporary institutions have wrought new havoc to the internal logic of practices by attempting to replace them with their own institutional logic. At the heart of this critique are the notions of corruption and distortion – the notion that institutions have moved well beyond their functions of nurturing practices by de-emphasising the internal goods of practices via the domination of goods external to the practice. Morgan quotes Walzer effectively: 'To convert one good into another, when there is no intrinsic connection is to invade the sphere' (Morgan,1994: 146).

First, then, we must ask the question, 'Why select this historical juncture?' Would not a cursory glance at Greek and Roman sports (or any other epoch for that matter) offer us a not dissimilar picture of the usurpation of the internal goods of sports by external goods wielded by the institution?[10] Similarly, as MacIntyre wrote: 'Where the notion of engagement in a practice was once socially central, the notion of aesthetic consumption now is, at least for the majority' (1985: 228). MacIntyre offers no evidence for his claim; given the fact that his examples of practices are so varied, perhaps he could not. In our specific case, it is not clear if such a shift has ever taken place because it is not known what levels and kinds of performer–spectator relationship have existed hitherto. With elite sport, however, by definition it will be representation of specialist labour, and it might not be unreasonable to expect the same for any elite instrumental practice that is wedded to economic consumption. Furthermore, while it is of course true analytically that there is no logically necessary connection between sports and external goods by definition (that is to say if they were not extrinsic why should we call them 'external' goods?), we can at least meaningfully ask when sports were ever present without their existence. This relates strongly to whether we use the distinction between practices and institutions as descriptive or merely heuristic. Just to be clear, though, I am not denying the corruptive influences of external goods promoted and distributed by institutions. It is just that it is not clear how we are to conceive of them on strictly MacIntyrean lines. A much better case seems to be articulated by Walsh and Giulianotti when they argue that there is a need to identify the point at which the institutional commodification of sports becomes pathological. They write:

> Commodification is ethically undesirable when it leads to an elimination or significant limitation of the epistemic space available for the pursuit of non-commercial internal goals that supervene on sport and which are an essential element of the moral value that sports generate.
>
> (Walsh and Giulianotti, 2007: 63)

Secondly just as examples of usurpation are legion, so too are examples in which the institution has chided players, coaches and spectators alike for poor ethical standards in their chosen activities. Most recently the Tour De France, one of the greatest spectacles in all sports, has thrown up precisely such a case. The event, organised since 1903, is a monumental challenge of human (some would say "superhuman") capabilities. Cyclists travel over 3000km during 22 days of relentless back-to-back competition. Of course the reputation of the Tour has been sullied by year upon year exposure of doping-related offences to the point that the general public is entirely sceptical as to there being honest winners. Recently Barne Riis, the winner from 1996, bowed to pressure and confessed (as several of his team mates had done earlier) to taking banned stimulants during the race. One of his colleagues proclaimed that he took amphetamines only when it was strictly necessary to help him recover and get through the next day's cycling – which was just about every day! So guilt-ridden indeed has Riis felt that he says he left his famous winner's yellow jersey in a plastic bag in his house. Many commentators have argued in the past that the world body for the sport, the International Cycling Union (UCI), is partly to blame since it turned a blind eye for so many years to the systematic approach to doping that was endemic in the sport. Doping in professional cycling was an open secret.

Whether motivated for reasons of a financial kind, or for the love of their sport (or most likely for both, but in that order) the UCI enacted, with the support of the French legislature, tougher measures to catch and sanction doping cheats. The race in 2007 saw the expulsion of not one yellow jersey rider, but two. On the 24 July the Russian cyclist Alexandr Vinokourov tested positive for blood doping having performed a near miraculous comeback from a previous days exhausted and below par performance. The pattern followed that of Floyd Landis last year whose dramatic recovery between stages had first raised eyebrows and then headlines. The very next day, however, Danish cyclist Michael Rasmussen was expelled for violating internal "whereabouts" rules of his team by missing two random tests. These out-of-season tests are thought to be essential to catch doping cheats in their out-of-competition training cycles where they can enhance their physical capacities with illicit substances or procedures while not under the watchful eye of doping agencies. Rasmussen claimed to be in Mexico visiting relatives when it turns out that a journalist had in fact seen him training in Italy. All this might seem an unacceptable case of guilty until proven innocent until one thinks of the veritable litany of doping offences that have surrounded the Tour in the recent past. Mistrust, it seems, begets itself.

As if this were not enough, on 20 September 2007 there was confirmation of the fact that last year's disgraced winner Floyd Landis had his challenge to the efficacy of the doping results rebutted and now finds his claim to fame has transformed from being winner of the Tour to first winner to lose the much coveted title.

It is not a coincidence that the leading team, Channel Discovery, who has won the Tour team event for eight of the last nine years, has been forced to disband because it cannot find sufficient sponsorship. Here it seems we have the clearest of examples of the paradoxical influence of corruption/support by a sporting institution.

What is unclear throughout the text of *After Virtue* is just how the distinction between a practice and its simultaneously supporting/corrupting institution is to be interpreted. This problem may well be paradigmatic of certain methodological queries about MacIntyre's conception of philosophy itself. Having charted MacIntyre's long-standing commitment to ethical theory and practice with one eye on both historical and sociological factors, one might ask whether his distinction between practices and institutions (indeed any part of his critique and positive thesis) is best to be seen as either a (quasi) factual account of contemporary ethical life or a heuristic philosophical device. It is worth quoting MacIntyre at length for the purpose of accurate exposition:

> It is Ferguson's type of sociology which is the empirical counterpart of the conceptual account of the virtues which I have given, a sociology which aspires to lay bare the empirical, causal connection between virtues, practices and institutions. For this kind of conceptual account has strong empirical implications; it provides an explanatory scheme which can be tested in particular cases. Moreover, my thesis has empirical content in another way; it does entail that without the virtues there could be a recognition only of what I have called external goods and not at all of internal goods in the context of practices. And in any society which recognized only external goods competitiveness would be the dominant and even exclusive feature. We have a brilliant portrait of such a society in Hobbes's account of the state of nature; and Professor Turnbull's report of the fate of the Ik suggest that social reality does in the most horrifying way confirm both my thesis and Hobbes's.
>
> (MacIntyre, 1985: 195–6)

Of course one of the great problems of skating the thin line between proto-description and ideal typical analysis is the selectivity of social facts marshalled in favour of one's adopted position. MacIntyre is acutely aware of this. Midgley (1983) gives short shrift to Turnbull's interpretation of the Ik's unfortunate state. The Ik are a desperately unfortunate tribe who have lost their traditional hunting and gathering grounds after the redrawing of political frontiers. In consequence, the tribe are literally starving and the traditional culture is effectively disintegrated. They act toward each other in horrific brutality. This does not prove, as Turnbull asserts, that society is some kind of luxury to be dispensed with since the Ik are (just) coping with-out it. Midgley (1983: 299–300) argued that social animals such as humans cannot live a life that they are fitted for without particular forms of society. She writes:

> Turnbull found little or no altruism among the Ik, which is not surprising when you consider that they have already been in their present desperate situation for quite long enough to ensure a steady selection of those inter-ested solely in surviving. They are a dying society. But what does it mean to suggest that everything else in their lives was a luxury? Is the idea that only extreme situations are real and serious? If so, most of life is unreal: what sort of unreality is this?
>
> (Midgley, 1983: 300)

It may well be the case that in any society that recognises only external goods, competitiveness may become the dominant factor. But citing the Ik as confir-mation of MacIntyre's thesis is question-begging to say the least. In what sense can we still describe this poor unfortunate existence as a 'society'? In what sense do they 'recognise' external goods? The verb seems wholly out of place when it appears there are virtually no goods of any sort on offer; one can scarcely choose (recognise) options (goods) not on offer. Such are the problems of selectivity when philosophy meets social description. Now the point at hand is whether the distinction is supposed to be accurate descrip-tion or heuristic device. More specifically, it would be helpful to unpack precisely what MacIntyre means by the term "empirical content", since it is far from clear. Morgan (1994: 128–75) adopts the latter stance. Indeed the point may be viewed as the central and strongest stance in his excellent book. He charges the 'Leftists' with failing to offer a description of sporting prac-tices aside from their institutional character. The logic of the critique is pre-cisely what the anti-emotivist moral philosopher Kovesi (1972), among others, offers: no evaluation without description. One can only proceed to evaluate a given object or activity when one has offered a description of its proper nature. Whether such latitude should be given, however, is another matter.

The problems, as with any institution that seeks to preserve a practice and its tradition, are twofold: what criteria are chosen to justify changes that will benefit the practice while at the same time preserving its integrity, and who will decide them? Perhaps, the general problems here are conceptual: how should we understand the notion 'integrity' in instances such as these and what virtues are to be developed in our practice communities if that integrity is to be maintained?[11] I want to suggest a vague and very probably unsatisfactory answer to this question after addressing the notion of the virtues within MacIntyre's account of practices with specific reference to sport.

The nature and function of the virtues

I want now to draw attention to the manner in which MacIntyre sets his account of virtues to work in his overall thesis about the role and importance of practices. This is separable from the issue of whether it is the only true, or merely the best, definition of a virtue for it is clear that there are many and competing definitions of virtue. MacIntyre sets a first, partial and tentative definition of a virtue thus:

> A virtue is an acquired human quality the possession and exercise of which tends to enable us to achieve those goods which are internal to practices and the lack of which effectively prevents us from achieving any such goods. . . . For it is not difficult to show for a whole range of key virtues that without them the goods internal to practices are barred to us, but not just barred to us generally, but barred in a very particular way.
>
> (MacIntyre, 1985: 191)

I want partly to stall a discussion of the relationship between the virtues and the different types of goods until I have discussed more fully the nature, range and functions of the virtues. What is noteworthy here, however, is that MacIntyre's subtle three-tiered thesis of the virtues is incomplete without reference to practices, the narrative unity of a human life and authority of tradition:

> I have suggested so far that unless there is a *telos* which transcends the limited goods of practices by constituting the good of a whole human life, the good of a human life conceived as a unity, it will both be the case that a certain subversive arbitrariness will invade the moral life and that we shall be unable to specify the context of certain virtues adequately. These two considerations are reinforced by a third: there is at least one virtue recognised by the tradition which cannot be specified at all except with reference to the wholeness of human life – the virtue of integrity or constancy. "Purity of heart" said Kirkegaard, "is to will one thing." This notion of singleness of purpose in a whole life can have no application unless that of a whole life does.
>
> (MacIntyre, 1985: 203)

I shall not enter into a discussion of the notion of the narrative unity of a whole human life here. Brown (1991) gives that dimension of MacIntyre's thesis an interesting application elsewhere. Furthermore, problems concerning the relationship between practices and who is to contribute to the maintenance of their integrity were discussed in the last section. In the penultimate section I shall deal briefly with the notion of integrity or purity in respect of the narrative unity of a human life and internal goods. It is commonplace to note the conservative strand in MacIntyre's thought whereby he invests the *de jure* authority of what is to count as purity or integrity within the tradition and those who are already committed to its constitutive practices. This notion of internality prioritised over externality runs right through MacIntyre's whole account and is closely related to the means–ends relation characterised by modern morality.

MacIntyre points out that it is a feature of modern theories of morality and reason that means and ends be clearly distinguished. But MacIntyre's theory of the virtues is one that denies such a classification. His virtue-based theory of the good is one in which 'being a causal condition of the good does not rule out being constitutive of it' (Taylor, 1989: 25). For MacIntyre the virtues are functionally valuable; they help us to secure internal goods, and without them we simply cannot attain them. But the relationship is not one of simple means and ends. The term 'virtue', as Taylor points out, can refer to two kinds of qualities: either facets of the good life or properties that have the effect of bringing about and preserving the good life. What is central to Aristotelian ethics, and which MacIntyre re-invigorates, is the notion that the latter class also forms part of the former. The virtues are not only constituents of the good life but also the means by which it is secured and maintained. The distinction between internal and external means must be drawn, MacIntyre argues, if we are to understand what Aristotle intended.

The virtues, then, stand in an internal relation to practices, the narrative unity of a human life and the concept of a tradition. They can be interpreted as goods-securing and practice/tradition-sustaining, as most philosophers of sport have interpreted them. It is interesting that few have noted their crucial role as institutional correctives. They may function both within the practice and/or inside the institutions. While quick to applaud sports as potentially valuable sites for the cultivation of virtue, it is easy to ignore (1) the fact that, as MacIntyre notes, where the virtues flourish so too may the vices, and (2) that sports administrators need no less to ally themselves to the practice, and just as any other persons must seek the good life no less through their employment in institutions as in their leisure time. Virtues are needed more than ever to stall their wayward and acquisitive nature. Is it that institutions, because of their logic, can never be co-operative enterprises? Can we not conceive, for example, of sports administration as a practice with its own excellences, or would that undermine the whole point of applying the distinction between the institutions and practices of sports?

But there is another dimension in MacIntyre's account of the virtues that is important to note. Pincoffs (1986) argued that several of the most notable moral philosophers, including MacIntyre, have been involved in a form of reductivism. The purported reductivism has taken more than one shape. On the one hand there are philosophers such as Kant and Mill who have celebrated single virtues such as conscientiousness and benevolence, respectively. Then there are cardinal virtues of courage, honesty, justice and temperance, which the Church fathers accepted and to which Aquinas added three theological virtues (faith, hope and love). To avoid this reductivism Pincoffs generated a list of the moral and non-moral virtues. Like MacIntyre, he locates the virtues in a functional setting but not the setting of practices that MacIntyre does. Instead he argued that virtues are dispositional qualities of persons that give us reasons for our preference or avoidance of them. He describes the virtues as the natural language of categories in terms of which we justify our choice, not of acts or lifestyles but of persons.[12] Whether or not we accept this picture of the virtues, what is more important is that it will generate a more heterogeneous account of the virtues than MacIntyre offered us:

> If we understand virtues and vices as dispositional properties that provide grounds for preference or avoidance of persons, the list will be indefinitely long, and it will be functionally various. There can be many different sorts of reason for preference [. . .] and a definition of virtue that picks out one or a very few dispositions as constituting the whole of virtue must shoulder the burden of showing that it is not unjustifiably reductive.
>
> (Pincoffs, 1986: 82)

Pincoffs set out two broad classes of virtues that are instrumental and non-instrumental. The former is subdivided into aesthetic, meliorating and moral, while the latter is divided into agent and group instrumental virtues. MacIntyre's analysis, Pincoffs argued, has an uncomfortably reductivist appearance in the sense that he limits his list of virtues to those that stand in a particular relationship to the internal goods of practices. There is another sense in which MacIntyre's account appears reductivist that is not mentioned by Pincoffs. Without the virtues of courage, honesty and justice, the practices could not resist the corrupting influences of the institutions. MacIntyre, however, does not state that the virtues are only gained in and through practices (1985: 187, 201) nor that these are the only three that secure internal goods, sustain the practice, and deter its institutional corruption. Though he does say that they are necessary, he does not commit himself to the view that they are sufficient (1985: 191–2). Nevertheless, his consistent emphasis upon the location of the virtues within practices and his exemplification of only those three at least give grounds for interpreting him as involved in an apparent double reduction.

Why is this long excursion into the location of the virtues, their nature, functions and extent important for philosophers of sport? There are several answers to this question. First, if the virtues are not merely exhibited in practices, how should we view those people who engage in activities on the borders of sporting practices such as weight training, keep fit, aerobics and step classes. While these sports-related activities are not practices in the MacIntyrean sense, they often engage many of the embodied dispositions that we value in sports and may contribute to what may be called an 'athletic way of life' or perhaps, in a phrase that has been barbarously abused by a range of ideological forces, a 'healthy lifestyle'. It seems clear that they require similar commitments and dedication even if the range of internal goods they encapsulate is somewhat etiolated. Second, we may come to evaluate more even-handedly the role of institutions, which, like practices, require of their members a whole range of virtues in order for their nurturing and distributive functions to be carried out effectively and morally so that practices flourish.[13] Third, there is much mileage in the notion of considering a virtue to be the basis of evaluating persons, and it is, I surmise, at the heart of the discussion of sportsmen and sportswomen as role models. It has often been said of sports and their excellent practitioners that we esteem them as ideals; they offer us pictures of what we may become if we immerse ourselves in the practice and become committed to the socially and historically embedded achievements they instantiate. Finally, most philosophers of sport have taken MacIntyre literally on the exultation of justice, courage and honesty as the primary virtues required by and developed in sport. To be sure these are three of the four cardinal virtues (temperance notwithstanding) and it may be the case that justice, courage and honesty are our best travelling companions in that quest for narrative unity in our lives. But sports are after all highly instrumental endeavours and the range of virtues they encapsulate, like any other instrumental practice, is much richer than this. Sports exalt instrumental action. Indeed we invent sports and games for their 'gratuitous difficulties', as Lasch (1979: 181) put it, in order to devise arenas for instrumentality (or purposive action as Best (1978) put it), albeit of a non-utilitarian kind.

Pincoffs (1986) listed the following agent instrumental virtues: alertness, carefulness, cool-headedness, courage, determination, energy, persistence, prudence and resourcefulness. It would not be difficult to contextualise each of the virtues in a sporting context. For example, what sports coach would not desire that his or her athletes were cool-headed in moments of intense pressure and would never give up until the final whistle was blown. By contrast, who would favour as team-mates the arrogant, callow, docile, fickle or merely selfish? This is not to say that in any and all circumstances, each of the agent instrumental virtues would apply but that in situations where instrumental action is required specifically, those virtues become prominent.

In his briefer list of group instrumental virtues, Pincoffs (1986) listed co-operativeness, practical wisdom and the virtues of followers and leaders. The list is not conclusive and consideration of specific practices may illuminate other, more fruitful, additions. Moreover, to think in that direction might well lead us to ask why some virtues are categorised as they are. I will offer only brief comments regarding this point in the following section.

Before turning to that discussion, and by way of linking themes, we should consider a remark made by Pincoffs (1986) that remains undeveloped. One of the strengths and, paradoxically, one of its weaknesses is the great generality of MacIntyre's application of the notion of practices, which are everywhere around us (law, education, medicine, sports, the arts, and so forth). And while it is certainly true that practices require the exercise of virtues to secure their internal goods and also for their continuance, we need not only ask, as we have already, precisely which virtues are required but also what sort of practice is it in relation to which the virtues are functional. Yet it is worth noting with Pincoffs that, given his fairly broad definition, there appear to be practices in which the external goods appear to be a 'kind of barbarian intrusion', whereas there are others in which the internal goods 'are at least arguably secondary to those gained from the consequences of successfully engaging in it' (1986: 97). Part of the problem of ascertaining whether such intrusions are, as it were, 'barbaric' rests upon a further discussion of what is to count as internal to practices.

Internality and externality re-examined

Much of MacIntyre's thesis, by his own admission, trades upon the idea of internal and external goods. And this distinction is not without its problems. Earlier I argued how the notion of internality should be interpreted partly as the felt-satisfactions of personal achievement derived from various performances. This accords with the idea that intrinsic value is subject-dependent. MacIntyre, however, wanted the notion of internality to have objective status, in the sense that the internal goods exist independent of any particular subject (i.e. person). The chess-playing example is supposed to secure this by the objective or public demarcation of goods that are internal and external to the practice. The selective example, however, wins the point without requiring vigorous defence. To be sure, his candy-seeking child exemplifies an instance in which the subject is motivated by something external to the practice. The child is extrinsically motivated; their reasons for playing are derived from the candy and not the chess. Here the means are neutral to securing the valued ends.

Not all relationships between goods are so straightforward. One can imagine the child playing chess for enjoyment, not because it is simply one means among many of being entertained, but because it is the exercise of their capabilities in that discipline that they desire. Furthermore, chess may well be the activity in which they are known by others to excel and is so esteemed. It is not only for the internal goods they seek to play the game but also for the external goods that they may, otherwise, be unable to secure. The playing of chess is, then, not merely instrumental to their securing entertainment, it is itself a specification of the very thing that is sought.[14] MacIntyre recognised the existence of such a relationship as we have seen but failed, implicitly or explicitly, to apply it in this manner. Because MacIntyre wanted to specify the internal goods as objective characteristics of the practice, he failed to apply the notion of internal means to those instances in which the personal satisfactions and their attendant motivations mean that a given activity is a valued (by a particular subject) and valuable (independent of my particular subject) means to securing external goods. Relying on the traditional vocabulary of intrinsic and extrinsic valuing is unhelpful here and to convey more clearly the subtlety and complexity of the activity and/or the attitudinal stance of the person, I shall use the term 'relational value' or 'relational valuing' to cover these ranges of meaning.

Certain activities may fulfil several aims for the participant at one and the same time and may be open to even greater variation in description. This is one aspect of those activities that prevents their complete explanation in simple means–ends terms. The individual's aims in playing sports (catharsis, esteem, fun, health, social affiliation and so on), may be sought through other activities if they are isolated into atomistic entities. It may be the case that one participates in a given practice because, empirically speaking, one could nowhere else secure that particular range of goods in that particular manner. For instance, MacIntyre argued that strategic imagination and competitive intensity are goods internal to the practice of chess and that internal goods can be sought only within their respective practices. He wrote: 'There are goods internal to the practice of chess which cannot be had in any way but by playing chess or some other game of that specific kind' (1985: 188). It could be argued, however, that strategic imagination might be developed in activities such as war, and competitive intensity might be promoted at least as well through sales marketing. Neither of these are what might be described reasonably as 'games of that specific kind'. Moreover, the development of strategic imagination and competitive intensity may be no part of my motivation to play chess but may be the consequence of my playing. How are these aims to be reconciled? Which refer to internal and which to external goods? And if no one actually valued such things as competitive intensity and strategic imagination, would this make them internal goods?

Philosophers have sometimes argued that some goods are valued in their own right, irrespective of consequences, and that others are valued exclusively for their consequences.[15] It seems difficult to cash out these two extremes. What would an activity look like that was valued for its internal goods but produced no valuable consequences? What sort of activity could yield valuable consequences but was, itself, of no value? Where the value of an activity is situated between these polar extremes it is often overlooked. These goods are, as Plato called them, 'mixed goods' (1974: 102–4), which he conceived to be the highest category of good. The motivation for considering mixed goods as higher lies in the fact that all actions have consequences even if those consequences are not the prime feature in the motivational hierarchy of the agent. For an agent to conceive of an activity in its wholeness is to include both its internal features and the direct consequences it produces as a product of that participation.

Chess is an example, like all sophisticated games, which belongs to the category of mixed goods; it is of relational value and may be valued thus. It can be valued for its own sake due to its internal features as one project among many to which persons become committed. At the same time, it may bring about external goods such as prestige, esteem among contemporaries, or wealth. Further, these external goods (if this is indeed what they are) also contribute significantly towards the living of valuable lives. Finally, there are those activities that have been called relationally valuable because they have internal goods and are at the same time specifically valuable ways of achieving (what have otherwise been called) external goods. One ought not ignore the consequences a practice may bring just because those goods might be secured alternatively. We should avoid the 'isolationism' entailed in considering activities apart from their direct consequences and consequences apart from the activity that wrought them. This enables us to see that if a good is valuable for its internal features and for the consequences it secures then it may be seen to confer greater benefit than that which is 'simply' valued for its own sake and that which is valued merely for its consequences. Yet ought sporting practices be offered as exemplars of activities that may be valued relationally as mixed goods? Part of the problem here is that MacIntyre is not prepared to concede the relationship between the participant who is at one and the same time fully committed to the practice (1) for both the internal goods that are intrinsically rewarding and (2) for the value of his or her commitments to the athletic form of life and the external rewards that he or she can only gain from that particular practice. From the first-person perspective, this or that practice need not be a neutral means to the securing of external goods. Even in his second edition of *After Virtue*, MacIntyre ran roughshod over this distinction in his negative evaluation of a 'grandmaster' in chess by describing an altogether different example. Instead of describing the example previously mentioned, he went back to the clean cut internal/external (pure/impure) characterisation of his earlier chess example. He asks us to consider the great chess grandmaster who cares only about winning. MacIntyre asserts that such a player

> could have achieved precisely the same good, that of winning and its contingent rewards, in any other field in which there is competition and there are victors, had he been able to achieve a comparable level of skill in those fields.
>
> (MacIntyre, 1985: 274)

There are two points to make here. First, reducing sophisticated practices to a single feature (their competitive logic) is spurious since the ranges of goods they encapsulate go far beyond the truism that practices with competitive logic will throw up winners and losers. Second, MacIntyre, in order to give force to his remark, begs two empirical questions: Could that person with particular capacities, potentialities, and environmental situation have achieved 'precisely the same good' elsewhere?; and are these goods really so practice-neutral? Is winning in chess really the same as winning in football or winning a violin competition or presenting the most cogent argument in a philosophical debate?

An answer to this question is closely related to the very question with which the previous section was concluded. Does the focus on external goods represent a barbarian intrusion in or of the practice? It seems reasonable to argue that there will be no satisfactory universal answer to that question, not even for the category of sports. While it is clear that the range of practices to which MacIntyre alludes are sufficiently diverse to warrant diverse answers it is less than clear that it ought to spawn such diversity within a single category such as sports. If business and the making of war (perhaps even politics) are to be seen as practices then it would seem peculiar to use MacIntyre's list of external goods as indeed external. The making of money in business, or so it seems at least, is a partially definitive internal good. Likewise, the ascertaining of power is to the excellent politician as esteem is to the excellent academic.

Part of the question of whether, say, the payment to professional sportspersons is the importing of an external logic rests upon the manner in which MacIntyre has drawn the distinction between internal and external goods. This same terminological distinction has been differently characterised by John Kekes[16] who broadly agreed with MacIntyre that 'internal goods are the satisfactions involved in the successful exercise of some of our dispositions in the context of a way of life to which we have committed ourselves'. But Kekes set out a different interpretation of external goods and their relationship to practices and persons as they are recast as 'satisfactions involved in possessing the means to their exercise and in receiving various forms of recognition for doing well' (1989: 187).

One may anticipate that a MacIntyrean might have little difficulty with the idea of external goods as forms of recognition (this is the point argued in earlier that elite sports are partially related to 'esteem' when justly conferred in an internal, not external relation) but might still want to dispute the propriety of receiving external forms of recognition that are inimical to the internal logic of the practice. What they could further argue, as Morgan has done so thoroughly, is that the sporting institutions have typically executed their distributive duties unjustly. While this may be the case, it does not force us to abandon Kekes' position.

It is the source of this reinterpretation, and the position against which it sets itself, that is most interesting. There seems to be implicit in MacIntyre's work (and hence in Arnold (1992, 1994), Brown (1991), Schneider and Butcher (1993, 1994) and Morgan (1994) by implication) the notion that the goods of our lives ought properly flow from the successful exercise of our own agency and not from considerations that we have not merited. This is one of the points at which MacIntyre sets himself against Nozick (1974) and Rawls

(1972). Kekes traces this line of argument to Socrates' position that the good man [sic] cannot be harmed since those harms and injustices the world heaps upon us may not be of our making and that the goodness of good lives depends upon what we do and not what is done to us. Kekes sharply criticised this conception of the purity or integrity of a practice since it falsely presupposed that 'moral purity requires turning inward, working for one's salvation while ignoring as much as possible the soiling, corrupting influence of the world' (1989: 188).

By contrast Taylor, in tracing the historical landmarks of moral sources, discusses the turn to 'inwardness' in his remarks on Plato. In using the language of 'inside/outside' he remarks:

> Thus if we think of the external as the realm of action in the polis, and the internal as that of the soul's disposition, then we could express the doctrine of the hegemony of reason in contrast to that of glorious action as an exaltation of the internal over the external.
>
> (Taylor, 1989: 120)

Taylor argues that this is the central point of Plato's *Republic*, that irrespective of external success the truly wise person will live a life of virtue irrespective of the pains he or she suffers for it. This is the crucial turn inward to reason as Taylor sees it and is related to the myth for example of Gyges' ring which I will discuss in relation to doping and its attendant vices in sport. What is more interesting perhaps for present purposes is that 'an ethic of reason and reflection gains dominance over one of action and glory' (Taylor, 1989: 117). This is exalted in Homeric times as celebrative of the physical and moral prowess of the warrior-cum-sporting ethic.[17] This difference of view was one of the reasons why I laboured over the issues of articulacy and critical self-awareness in the good life in the previous chapter.

The disdain that MacIntyre appears to reserve for external goods in contrast to internal goods may well be the product of a latent evaluation; practices would be pure but for the corrupting institutions they are vulnerable to.[18] But to think in terms of mixed goods may allow us to defuse at least part of the normative cutting edge of this distinction.

Internal goods are the products of my own agency justly conferred since no one can deny that my securing them was primarily my responsibility with the obvious caveats regarding the importance of persons of standing and authority in the practice to whom I submit my skills and judgements. So when I feel the delight at getting a back somersault just right, the feeling of exhilaration at achieving significant vertical elevation, allowing time for a tight tuck and patient, controlled, opening to landing, I feel (commensurate with that display of relative excellence) a partially defining good of gymnastics; I deserve it and no one may deprive me of it. External goods, however, require individual effort neither as a necessary nor sufficient condition. Status, prestige or wealth may always be accorded to those undeserving of it through the caprice of the institution just as the deserving may not be so rewarded upon such contingency.

It is important to be clear of what does not follow from this. It does not follow from this that external goods are necessarily randomly conferred; just as it does not follow that internal goods are solely the product of the successful exercise of some of our dispositions within a sporting form of life. When the institution conducts its distributional role properly it will be neither fortuitous nor incidental. Likewise it might be said that securing internal goods is not entirely due to one's own merit since, as Peter Singer[19] argued, we deserve no merit for coming up trumps in the genetic lottery. In a sporting context the acclaimed Scandinavian physiologist Per Åstrand (Åstrand and Rodahl, 1986) once said that if one wishes to maximise his or her chances of becoming an Olympic champion, one must be selective in choosing one's parents. While such successful choosing may not be a sufficient condition of securing the internal goods of sporting practice it may well be necessary.

The emphasis present in Kekes and absent in MacIntyre is the awareness that external goods such as esteem, security, status and respect can be valued intrinsically as public recognitions, when properly conferred, that our achievements are valued:

> They are intrinsically satisfying in two ways. First, as justly earned rewards they are public confirmations that we are doing well at our ways of life. . . . And second, external goods are intrinsically good also as specific contents that forms of appreciation have. They confer privilege because their recipients receive a greater share of scarce good than others. If the system of distribution is just and if the goods received enhance the enjoyment of their lives without injuring others, then there is nothing objectionable about such privilege.
>
> (Kekes, 1989: 192)

What this implies for practices such as sport is that the presence of external goods as rewards for achievement is not inherently bad except that their corrupt and distorted systems of distribution make them so. Of course paying a sports coach much more than the nation's prime minister or president is absurd. To be sure, external goods are competitive; we cannot all have as much as the other, but this scarcity points to them as rewards. Internal goods may be had by us all to the same degree, ability, motivation and context, notwithstanding. They are shared, social or public goods in this sense, but this does not exclude them from being private, felt satisfactions, as MacIntyre seemed to imply. Although offering public forms of recognition for sporting excellence does not seem inherently bad, I am uncertain as to how far this latitude should be extended. I have argued that at least some of the things that MacIntyre has called external goods appear not to be a barbarian intrusion in sport, at least not elite sport. I have mentioned, albeit briefly, that monetary rewards have been with us so long that they are only by heuristic analysis distinguishable from elite sport and that esteem is tied to the internal logic of practices such as sport since they are public celebrations of ludic capacities.

I am unclear whether the philosophers of sport who have utilised MacIntyre's thesis want to take his *Weltanschauung* on wholesale. His idea that the good life takes the shape of a narrative quest seeking itself, the good life always requiring and displaying the virtues in practices, is both challenging and noble. I am, however, less certain about the underlying picture of purity it seems to incorporate. I am happier with the following notion:

> The ultimate test of the goodness of our lives is whether they involve lasting possession of external and internal goods and whether the satisfactions derived from their possession outweigh, in quantity and quality, such hardship and suffering as we experience.
>
> (Kekes, 1989: 202)

This proper balancing of internal and external goods gained from our engagement in shared practices such as sport depends of course on their existence as the morally situated endeavours that MacIntyre so eloquently described. But their purity or integrity must be actively supported not merely by the practice and its best practitioners but also by those committed in other ways to the practice or institution. Given that sports, at least elite sports, have been historically, though contingently, associated with some external rewards, it seems preposterous that we abuse them so thoroughly. Even MacIntyre accedes to the necessity of their presence. And given that public recognition, in at least some forms, is central to the celebrative character of sport, we should perhaps focus more on the kinds of hierarchically organised moral perspectives in order to sustain the practices in the best kinds of ways we can. Of course, anyone who thinks only of external goods abuses the practices that afford them; and a life lived only in their pursuit will be shallow and meaningless. Because practices offer us the variety of goods that sports do and a range of public recognitions for our relative excellence in them, in proper part and justly conferred, we have all the more reason to value them. This will not be done by denying the place of external goods in those practices and in our lives but by ensuring their subordination to our prior commitments to the internal goods but by keeping them in their place.

Conclusion

I have attempted in this chapter to develop a minor though critical revision of MacIntyre's account of institutions, practices, virtues and their relationships in order to make better senses of the ethics of sports. I have tried to show that the generality of his application opens MacIntyre up to the charge that his ideological commitments focus on the shared social aspect of goods, practices and virtues to the detriment of the individual counterparts therein.

Furthermore, the diversity of applications to which MacIntyre puts the idea of a practice to work, glosses over what appears to be salient differences between practices and therefore the virtues that sustain them and preserve their integrity. I presented a less reductionist account of the virtues which hopefully displayed greater phenomenological fidelity than is suggested by MacIntyre. Finally, this move towards greater complexity was made manifest when considering the relationship between the practitioners, the practices and the goods, both definitive of and secured by the practice. I have retained MacIntyre's overarching framework while attempting to rework, in small and specific areas, some limited ideas in order for that framework more successfully to catch the nature of sports as practices. In the following chapters I hope to illuminate a broader range of vices and virtues that are to be found widely in sport and which cash out the value of the reductionist account originally given by MacIntyre and adopted widely in the philosophy of sport.

4 Sport and ethical development

Introduction

In the previous chapters I have begun to build a case for a particular vision of the ethical status and potential of sports. Of course, the arguments over whether sports build or merely reveal character is probably as old as sport itself. The aim of this chapter is to further develop an account of the moral educational potential of sports from a virtue-ethical perspective. While this may seem straightforward enough, it is not. In recent years social scientific research has denied the possibility of ethical development in sport. Indeed, it has typically argued that sport arrests development at an egoistic stage.

In an attempt to better understand the problem, certain philosophers (see Carr, 1998; Gough, 1998) have attempted to undercut the validity of that research and have argued for the impossibility *in principle* of any kind of science of ethical development. While I am in substantial agreement with these philosophers, my position here is more open to the aims of the dominant psychological approaches to moral education (which is necessarily conceived of as narrower than ethical development as I shall discuss later) in sport, and I attempt to bring out certain aspects of agreement that might be reached by philosophers and psychologists in their attempt to explore this contested and important matter. Of course, the translation of theoretical frameworks and conceptual revisions is a hazardous affair. I am mindful of the particular pitfalls of operationalisation when researchers attempt to go out into the field and assess carefully a range of controversial and complex issues such as are involved in the moral dimensions of sporting participation and performance. This chapter attempts to critique both the theoretical assumptions of that social scientific research and its methodologies and to consider more carefully the museums of normalcy as they have been called,[1] where sports may significantly build, shape, test and challenge the virtuous sportsperson.

Moral personality and the emergence of the moral development tradition

In current psychological research into sport and morality, cognitive developmentalism has been the dominant theoretical approach. To understand this dominance it is necessary to appreciate how early researches into the psychology of moral development, notably Jean Piaget, Lawrence Kohlberg and Norma Haan committed themselves to various theoretical positions regarding human agency and morality itself. Subsequent research design and analysis in sports that denies the moral educational potential of sports is a hostage to these commitments, which I criticize and reject in this chapter.

Although moral philosophising in the West has been with us since the Ancient Greeks, empirical moral psychology has twentieth-century roots. Hartshorne and May (1928) were the first to investigate the link between personality traits and moral action. They compared hundreds of children's behaviour in certain contexts with their self-attribution of moral traits including dishonesty and deceit. In keeping with the dominant behaviourist Zeitgeist, their findings pointed towards situational factors rather than personality traits of the children as the primary causal explanation for behaviour. These early findings raised a number of questions about the existence of moral character and personality, and more specifically about which psychological theories, concepts and methods have the most heuristic force and predictive potential. In particular, the 'thought–action' problem highlighted by Hartshorne and May, the unreliable relations between what people believe to be right and what in fact they do, is a ubiquitous and perplexing conundrum for moral psychology and undermines much research in the area of moral psychology in sport. In his account of *akrasia* or weakness of the will we find that Aristotle had already said much about that particular problem but in that positivistic time in the history of psychology, philosophizing was pejoratively thought to be beyond the realm of fact and thus epistemologically unreliable.

In his important book in moral psychology, Flanagan (1991) argues that Hartshorne and May's results are mistakenly taken as evidence against the existence of moral personality seen as a collection of traits. It would follow then that their critique need not consign the virtue-ethical account of character to the pre-scientific dustbin. Rather than abandon the idea of moral traits altogether, Flanagan (1991: 291) argued that the results can be read as evidence for the existence of traits 'albeit not traits of unrestricted globality or totally context – independent ones'. Reports, therefore, of the death of traits was premature. Rather, it is a particular conception of a character trait – the idea that it was a simple disposition enacted every time a person found himself or herself in a given situation – that should be rejected. The development of a more sophisticated account of moral traits and their role in moral character is the appropriate response to this research, and other studies such as Stanley Milgram's (1964) (in)famous research into obedience to perceived authority, which lends weight to the plasticity – though not complete malleability – of moral character and traits.[2] What is important to recognise in the non-trait globality issue from the perspective of current sport-related research, is the primary influence of Hartshorne and May's studies on alternative theoretical and methodological foci.

Piaget (1932) later conducted extensive studies focused on moral aspects of children's interactions. Describing himself as a genetic epistemologist he was interested in the growth of knowledge or cognition and conceptions of ethics based solely upon powers of reason. In keeping with the times he largely ignored the development of emotion that was thought to be antithetical both to reason and ethics. Piaget believed that rationality was the normative end point of cognitive development because rationality itself was the primary adaptive capacity of human agency. He argued that the development of human rational powers occurred in stages, each of which represented a particular logical-cognitive structure. The stages were progressive; each subsequent stage accommodated its predecessor in a more complex cognitive structure. The development of cognitive powers was therefore linear and unidirectional. His studies of morality, groundbreaking as they were, are necessarily a hostage to a narrowly focused conception of human rationality. As a hostage to the spirit of the then 'new' scientific age he wrote:

> Readers will find in this book no direct analysis of child morality as it is practiced in home and school life or in children's societies. It is the moral judgment that we propose to investigate, not moral behaviour or sentiments.
>
> (Piaget, 1932: 8)

Piaget makes it clear that his interest is narrowly focused on the moral judgement – its structure and form – since it is this that is a scientific indicator of the child's stage of development. The focus takes explanatory priority over affective and behavioural considerations. Although Piaget explicitly denies the reduction of moral development to the development of moral judgement, there has been a de facto reduction of moral development to the development of moral cognition (moral judgement) in subsequent moral psychology. I will argue in subsequent chapters that this posture has important consequences for the consideration of the role of emotions in ethics generally, and sports ethics specifically (see Chapters 7, 8 and 9 in particular).

Another important feature of Piaget's groundbreaking work was the introduction of explicit normative criteria for the stages of cognitive and, therefore, moral development. The child's development is seen in the adaptation to the natural and social environment. The development of moral judgement, therefore, is an adaptation to the moral world. Given Piaget's elevation of rationality, it is no surprise to philosophers that Kant's moral theory provides the normative criteria to evaluate these moral judgements. Kant also provides the conception of the moral world in the Piagetian scheme of thought. 'All morality', he wrote 'consists in a system of rules, and the essence of morality is to be sought for in the respect which the individual acquires for these rules' (Piaget, 1932: 9).

In order to study the moral development of the child Piaget focused on their understanding of rules in games. Notwithstanding methodological criticism, Piaget concluded that there were two stages to the development of the child's understanding of the obligatory (i.e. prescriptive) nature of rules. The first is a heteronymous understanding of morally right action wherein the child believes that it is subject to an external law that ought universally to be followed. The second stage is characterised by an autonomous understanding of the obligatory nature of rules. Following Kant, rules are obligatory if they are the result of rational deliberation. All moral rules, being at the same time rational rules, have such weight as they compel all rational beings to comply with them. It is worth reiterating that Piaget did not study rule–compliance, but rather examined the ways in which children understood the rules. The form of the judgement, whether it is heteronymous or autonomous, is more important than the content. Two children may follow the same rule thus visibly performing the same behaviour, yet only one may have a proper understanding of the rules' obligatory requirement. Only the latter may be said to be acting autonomously and therefore morally. The context and the content of moral rules, therefore, became largely unimportant for his project compared to the understanding of the source and grounds of legitimate obligation. In light of these factors Piaget's work marks the beginning of the methodological focus on what people *say* rather than what people *do* that came to dominate much moral psychology in general and the moral psychology of sport in particular.

The most important development after Piaget was the work of Kohlberg (1981) who embraced his central theoretical commitments, and constructed a more complex six-stage developmental sequence. His research design utilised a dilemma-based questionnaire to gather data on moral reasoning and judgement. Crucially he argued that people reason consistently according to their stage of moral development. This element of consistency of moral agency went some way to countering the situationism suggested by Hartshorne and May's (1928) studies. Although sharing significant common ground, Kohlberg made significant philosophical and psychological revisions to Piaget's work. First, he further embraced Kantian moral theory and argued that the moral world was governed by universal moral principles. Kohlberg (1981) believed that 'justice' was the overarching moral principle and the end point of moral development, or 'moral maturity', which itself was characterised by consistent judgements that embodied this principle. Second, departing from Piaget, he explicitly advocated the causal role that cognition played in moral agency and action. So although cognition, and its embodiment in judgement remains central, Kohlberg believed that moral cognition and moral action are more or less synonymous.[3] He argued that mature moral character was unified and consistent just as the rules in a moral theory. In its ideal form moral reasoning (and therefore moral action) is always in accordance with principles of justice. This rationalist picture of morality, driven very much by both Ancient Greek (Plato) and modern European (Kant) thought, holds that those who know the good choose the good. Therefore, those who are said truly to know the right thing to do will always act correspondingly. The guiding belief here then is one of a normative account of morality grounded in rational and universal moral principles. The impartial application of principles, not the plasticity of situations, should dictate moral action, which can be assessed through the reasoned judgements of agents.

Within this theorised picture of morality, moral judgements based on moral rules ought to be consistent and not contextually variable. The right thing to do is always the right thing to do; the wrong thing to do is always the wrong thing to do. The fact that other features of the situation (oneself, one's close relations or one's friends) might find their way into some children's reasoning was a sign of moral immaturity since these features necessarily compromise the impartial character of morality. Based upon such apparently secure foundations children can therefore be classified and ranked according to the stage of their moral maturity; their ability to reason about the right thing to do – which follow moral rules that were universal in scope, prescriptive in nature and impartial in application.

Kohlberg's theory is reductive in a number of problematic ways. First, (im)moral action is reduced to (un)principled action, and moral agency or moral character is reduced to a mature grasp of moral duty.[4] The emotions and other character traits are devoid of intrinsic moral worth. They are morally significant only in so far as they function in the impartial application of universal moral principles. Critics of Kohlberg's theory are legion[5] despite the continued propagation of his theory and method in education and sport research. Gilligan (1982) objected to the reduction of moral concerns to those of justice. Kohlbergian findings typically evaluated girls and women on a lower level than boys and men who reasoned more impartially. Gilligan argued convincingly that this picture of the moral reasoner as an independent rational chooser ignored the complex of rationality and affect in our estimations of moral judgements. She argued that moral concepts such as care, which was set aside because of its emotional character, might be equally important in evaluating moral maturity.

From a psychological perspective, the main weakness of Kohlberg's theory is the extent to which moral maturity is predictive of action across different settings. Paradoxically, situation, or context variation, was the very criticism aimed at Hartshorne and May (1928) and the very issue his theory aimed to avoid. Kohlberg (1984) himself recognised this problem and argued that people did not always take responsibility for moral action even though they might know what ought to be done. Moreover, he also thought that the prevailing moral atmosphere of the context might inhibit moral reasoning (Power *et al.*, 1989). Flanagan (1991) argued that a defence of Hartshorne and May's (1928) findings could be constructed on similar grounds.

In light of some of the problems with the theory, a former research collaborator of Kohlberg, Norma Haan developed an important revision to the Kohlbergian tradition that attempted to move away from his rationalistic preconceptions both of human agency and morality. Haan (1978) argued that morality was not to be narrowly characterised as a set of universal principles but rather a socially constructed set of norms, values, rules and solutions that could not be exclusively deduced from the principle of justice. Rather they must be constructed in a process called 'moral dialogue'. Moral dialogues, according to Haan, can result in moral balance and/or moral truth. The former refers to a mutually acceptable agreement in dialogue. The latter, moral truth, refers to solutions achieved under the procedural conditions of fairness. Moral truth is most likely to occur, therefore, in dialogues between those most capable of fair negotiation, or in dialogues heavily influenced by those who possess such egalitarian instincts. Haan assesses the maturity of moral agents based on the legitimacy of their strategies in moral dialogue. Most importantly, she proposes five stages that although similar to Kohlberg's do *not* represent a linear developmental sequence but rather provide normative criteria for evaluating the quality of moral interaction.

Haan partly avoids the 'thought–action' problem by observing moral interaction rather than merely evaluating moral judgements. Scores are then assigned to individuals based on the conduct of the subjects observed. This combination of a humanistic conception of morality and the observation of *actual* behaviour is supposed to deliver greater ecological validity. Some of the purported methodological advantage is lost, however, because the moral dialogues are constructed role-play situations that are themselves artificially constructed.

That factors extraneous to a person's cognitive capacities often influence the way one behaves may not come as a great surprise to those of a less cognitive persuasion. In addition to her important advances in methodology and operationalisation of the concept of morality, Haan looks to the psychoanalytic concept of ego-processing to explain these inter-test inconsistencies in moral action. Many children and adults as they play sport know that breaking the rules is wrong, they simply fail to carry that understanding through to action for a variety of personal (e.g. contingent self-worth (Duda, 2001; Duda and Hall, 2001), egoism, the untrammelled desire to win) and environmental (e.g. the motivational climate (Duda, 2001; Roberts, 2001), coach-induced norms (Stornes, 2001)) reasons. Haan argues that consistent moral engagement requires that a person remains 'coping'. A person who is coping remains in control of thought and action. If a person is suffering stress in the situation and fails to cope effectively, or employs defending processes, inconsistent moral action is likely to ensue (Roth and Cohen, 1986; Weinberger *et al.*, 1979). Although Haan refers to the importance of coping processes, her perspective does not readily account for spontaneous, or 'heat of the moment', rule violations.

What most of us know through our own experience in and out of sport is, as I noted earlier, the phenomena Aristotle called *akrasia*: the weakness of the will. We do not always and everywhere exhibit the consistency of belief and action that a moral theory – when conceived of as a scientific theory – exhibits. Thus in Haan's scheme there is an expectation that systematic discrepancies will sometimes occur among the moral levels that people use when they think about what a hypothetical person should do, what they should do, and when they act. Further, it is assumed that these discrepancies will not only be associated with people's moral capacity but also with their more general ability to cope with the complexity, intensity and content of particular situations (Haan, 1975). Having charted the normative development of the cognitive-moral developmental psychology we are now in a position to critically situate our evaluation of more recent psychological research, which is particularly damning of the ethics of sports.

Sport psychological and ethical development

Early studies of morality in sport seemingly confirmed what Kohlberg himself wrestled with, namely that moral judgements were contextually sensitive and that the 'moral atmosphere' of given contexts had a role to play (Power *et al.*, 1989). Bredemeier and Shields (1984a) found that individual moral judgement gravitated towards the prevailing level of moral judgement in the researched context. They introduced the term 'game frame' to refer to the particular 'atmosphere' of sports contests. In philosophical literatures this concept is often referred to as the 'ethos of sports'.[6] Sports contests are widely taken to be rule-governed instrumental activities hived off from other aspects of life by their peculiar gratuitous logic and their temporal and spatial boundaries. As such participants are characteristically instrumentally orientated. Bredemeier and Shields (1984a) suggest that this collective instrumental orientation or the 'game frame' is usually detrimental to what they call "optimal moral functioning".[7] It frequently promotes and rewards moral judgements of a lesser maturity than one might expect to find in non-athletic situations. Bredemeier and Shields (1986a) argued that 'game reasoning' is characteristically egocentric and suggested that the structure of competitive games locate moral responsibility with the official or the rules consequently encouraging the abdication of responsibility by the competitors. Moral autonomy under such a conception cannot be attained and this results in retardation of moral growth it is said. More recent studies, for example Guivernau and Duda (2002), provide further empirical support for the important influence of the 'moral atmosphere' of sports activities. Moreover, they found that the players' beliefs regarding their team, coaches and parents significantly shaped the moral atmosphere. Moral atmosphere (as perceived to be manifested on the team and at home) predicted self-reported moral behaviour of individuals.

Irrespective of gender, or the particular scenario involved, the athletes perceived the coach as the most influential figure. Of course, in Greek ethics the

idea of the *phronimos* (the wise practical chooser) is an important consideration in our considerations of role modelling and the selection of the right sorts
of persons we choose to emulate when we reflect on difficult choices. I will
develop the salience of this point with regard to both critical habituation and
role modelling below. Another closely related and significant early finding
was that moral reasoning correlated significantly with other moral indicators. Bredemeier and Shields (1984b) found a significant inverse relationship
between high moral reasoning scores and aggression.[8] Bredemeier (1994)
argued that moral reasoning is predictive of both aggressive and assertive tendencies in sport. In addition Bredemeier (1985) found an inverse relationship
between the numbers of potentially injurious acts respondents found
acceptable, and their level of moral maturity. These findings offer empirical
endorsement of the Kohlbergian belief that moral reasoning is a significant
determinant of moral action.

This sustained research programme also proposed that other important
factors demanded consideration. Consequently, a model of moral action
(Shields and Bredemeier, 1995) and a measure of "moral functioning"
(Stephens *et al.*, 1997) that integrate their main conclusions were formulated.[9] Informed by Piaget (1932), Kohlberg (1981, 1984) and Haan (1978,
1983), and their own discoveries (Bredemeier and Shields, 1984a, 1984b,
1986a, 1986b), Bredemeier (1985, 1994), Bredemeier *et al.* (1986, 1987),
Shields *et al.* (1995), and other research, Duda *et al.* (1991), their model
represents a more complex and holistic account of moral agency or moral
functioning.

Drawing on Rest (1984) they argued that moral action is rooted
not just through judgement but also through additional processes central
to the foundation of their model of moral action. The first process is
interpretative consisting in the identification and recognition of situational
cues. The second process consists in the making of a moral judgement,
which coheres with Kohlberg's account. The third process is the choice of
a value that will guide moral action. The final process is the actual implementation of action (irrespective of the action chosen). In a further development they offer a brief account of the virtues that might operationalise
their model.

At first sight, the model distances itself from the excessive reductionism of
Kohlberg's original formula. The model describes moral agents as more than
just stage-specific moral reasoners recognising that values, attitudes, beliefs
and motivational orientation are important constituents of moral agency.
The import of the additional processes, however, gives rise to some related
problems. For Kohlberg, moral maturity was considered significantly, if not
exclusively, to be predictive of moral action on Socratic lines: 'who knows the
good chooses the good'. Yet folk psychology and common sense tell us that
those who know the good also need to interpret well, choose the right value
and implement appropriate action in conjunction with formulating a mature
moral judgement.

The recognition that "moral functioning" involves more than moral reasoning is borne out in the sports psychology literature. The construct that has received the most recent attention is that of achievement-goals. In sport in particular, research suggests that an over-emphasis on winning, conceived as concerns relating to the demonstration of superiority, leads to poor "moral functioning".[10]

Notwithstanding the complexity of Shields and Bredemeier's model and the subsequent attempts to investigate the value-dominance problem for athletes, two problems persist. First, the methods only measure cognitive components of morality: what people say rather than what people do is what counts. This problem is rooted in the belief that moral behaviour is intentional and that intention must be characterised, and driven by, appropriate moral motives. Moral motives cannot be seen or inferred; they must therefore be accessed in speech acts:[11]

> One difficulty with direct behavioural observation, however, is that the meaning of specific behaviors is never transparent and the researcher who observes a behavior must invariably interpret the meaning of that behavior if the observation is to be meaningful.
>
> (Stephens *et al.*, 1997: 374)

Within this research programme, then, researchers must therefore interrogate the motivating values and principles in order to make a judgement about the moral status vis à vis their reflective values or moral maturity. A morally praiseworthy action in this scheme requires that the intentions and motives behind it are themselves morally praiseworthy.[12] Still, as I will argue below, the model remains at best a thin account of how (sports)persons come to act qua moral agents. Although the idea of moral functioning is an expanded one, it lacks what we consider to be a substantive account of the qualities (and their development), above and beyond moral reasoning, that a person requires to function. Moral rules still dominate the picture, but are supplanted by certain virtues that are highly selective, and without an extensive rationale.[13]

In a gesture towards virtue ethics Shields and Bredemeier (1995) briefly present four qualities of character, or virtues, that are important for the model. They define character as 'the possession of those personal qualities or virtues that facilitate the consistent display of moral action' (Shields and Bredemeier, 1995: 193). Like MacIntyre they too opt for a reduced catalogue of virtues but, it seems, for very different reasons. It seems to me that their catalogue is driven by operational expediency. The four virtues, considered sufficient for this task, in Bredemeier and Shields' model are (1) compassion; (2) fairness; (3) sportspersonship; and (4) integrity.

Each of these virtues supports an allegedly specific component of the model of moral action. First, compassion, they argue, facilitates interpretation of the situation in order to decide upon a course of moral action. Second, having interpreted a situation compassionately, fairness facilitates the right judgement and, third, sportspersonship facilitates choosing values. Finally, the virtue of integrity is necessary to facilitate implementation of action. The four virtues selected appear, however, to raise more questions than they answer. Why should compassion merely drive interpretation and not action? Why could a perception of the fair thing to do not move us straight to action? We should keep in mind the most significant lesson of Kohlberg's research programme, from a meta-ethical viewpoint, that sometimes compassion and fairness clash violently. As was argued in Chapter 2, sportspersonship is not a singular virtue but rather an internally complex amalgam of values, attitudes and beliefs that hang together in a more or less loose way. In the same vein we can ask whether integrity is a singular virtue or does it suffuse all other virtues in order that the moral agent comes to the right choice? This, in particular, is a classic problem in Aristotelian and Platonic scholarship. Is virtue one or many? Do the virtues combine to form a mutually supportive network in an integrated character or are they at times in conflict? Rorty (1988: 314–29) offers an elaboration of this thorny issue and a proposed resolution (I subscribe to) in favour of a conflict-model where the more-or-less integrated character seeks to hold itself together while always in tension. Two points need to be made here. First, one could not reasonably expect a group of psychological researchers to have final answers to problems that have dogged moral philosophers since Plato. The desirability of multi-disciplinary scholarship (between philosophy and the social sciences) should be clear. Second, meta-ethical questions are present from the start in all such research whether they are theoretically (e.g. philosophical and/or grounded in a conceptualisation of moral motivation or moral functioning) or empirically (i.e. data) driven. A point of the deepest import attaches to whether indeed morality is to be seen as a quasi-scientific theory of rules and axioms or whether it is both more piecemeal and conflict-ridden from the beginning. While I favour the latter position, time and space do not permit an elaboration of such.[14]

A further and more general criticism attaches to their conception not of individual virtues per se but of the idea of virtue in itself. In the model, virtues, following Erikson (1964), are described as strengths that animate moral ideals. This picture of virtue is found most famously in the writings of Immanuel Kant, whom many consider to be the founding father of modern deontological (duty theory) ethics that have underwritten most modern moral developmentalism.[15] For Kant, the virtues are subordinate to the concept of duty and were important only in so far as they facilitated the exercise of duty. The virtues are defined primarily, therefore, in terms of their executive function, which in this case is the achievement of mature and consistent moral action. The deontological commitment to rationally grounded moral principles, initially taken by Piaget (1932) and adopted by Kohlberg (1981) and Haan (1978), remains a cornerstone of Shields and Bredemeier's (1995) model. The adjective 'moral' is exclusive and is reserved for the cognitive capacities of the agent, namely their moral reasoning ability. As for Kant, other capacities are only moral in an instrumental sense if they are exercised in the service, and facilitate the achievement, of an a priori standard of morality. Concepts such as care, consequence, courage and duty must play a role in any adequate moral theory. The precise shape that they play must be subject to coherence of course. One cannot just add and stir components. As Hampshire remarks:

> Ways of life are sharply coherent and have their own unity in the trained dispositions that support them, and in the manners and observances and prescriptions which as children we are taught to see as normal. [. . .] At some time we may be introduced to a museum of normalcies which have accumulated in history. But still we cannot pick and choose bits of one picture to put besides bits of another: the coherence of the pictures comes from their distinct histories: this may be called the no shopping principle.
> (Hampshire, 1983: 148)

There are a number of reasons why Bredemeier and Shields' model is problematic. Before proceeding to the critique of the model it is important to stress again that their model represents an important advance of previous research attempting to accommodate a more complex and multi-dimensional model of moral action than had been present in previous research. Part of my critique rests upon theoretical controversies in moral philosophy that do not appear in the operation of the model while others pertain to the robustness of individual stages of the model, or furthermore to the internal coherence of those features.

The ongoing debate between various forms of virtue or (agent) centred ethics, and rule (or act) centred ethics is clearly important in the evaluation of the model. Shields and Bredemeier's model seems to be a psychological hybrid that attempts to draw on the strengths of both camps. The firm footing that deontology boasts gives the model a universalist flavour. From virtue ethics comes the ability to explain contextual variation and a sense of embodied agency. In one sense the model is a concerted attempt to rectify a particular criticism made of Kohlberg's work concerning its inflation of the cognitive capacities of reasoning. Flanagan (1991) argues that any moral theory must be more than an abstract philosophical or psychological model and must adhere to a principle of minimal psychological realism. It must be 'possible, or perceived to be possible, for creatures like us' (Flanagan, 1991: 32).

Although there are some reservations about the normative commitments and the methodological strategy of much of the psychological research, what emerges is a body of empirical evidence that points towards a more complex picture of moral development and education. The Piaget/Kohlbergian account of development prioritised the reorganisation and increasing adaptation of cognitive capacities. Cognitive dissonance or disequilibria drives development. The primary goal of the educator is to provide the stimulus, the disequilibria, that necessitate the reorganisation and adaptation of perception, emotion and judgement. Given that empirical research in sport undermines the exclusively cognitive antecedents of moral functioning, a different account of moral education is also required. Evidence suggests that the moral atmosphere is a strong mediating factor, and the influence of the coach, as a 'moral exemplar' seems crucial.[16] Moral education should therefore take into account the moral climate of sport, particularly the example set by the coach, if the moral behaviour of individuals in sport is to improve. The qualities at which education aims must also be wider in scope than the exclusively cognitive capacities that Piaget and Kohlberg focused upon. Haan's (1978) ego-processes, and Shields and Bredemeier's (1995) four virtues, point towards the need for a more expansive focus. Although I welcome a move towards concepts of virtue and character, a more faithful approach is required. I shall now consider the contours of an Aristotelian account that is also developmental in character, yet gives a greater emphasis on the emotions, a more considered view of deliberation, and exults the necessary non-cognitively saturated account of moral training that is the basis of praiseworthy conduct and character.

Back to Aristotle: character, emotion and judgement

Baechler (1992) describes how, nearly 30 years ago, the Académie Française (French Academy) ceased the performance of its annual ritual wherein one of its established members gave a public lecture on virtue. It was indeed a sign of the times. On the one hand, as we have observed above, the scientific academy had apparently debunked its folk psychology. While on the other, as Baechler observed, the 1960s were in full swing and the idea that good and bad could not be objective but were rather relative to each and every culture became ever more fashionable. Both trends worked against the middle, each assaulting the very idea of virtue. One group of scholars (usually sociologists and historians) thought it too fixed and insufficiently attentive to cultural differences, the other (usually psychologists) thought it too loose and yearned for a scientifically valid measure based on a single more concrete concept: justice.

In contrast to the moral reasoning model of Kohlberg, the Aristotelian model appears antiquated to psychologists. To social scientists and historians, Aristotelian thought represents a 'brave' leap back to antiquity an inappropriate and ill-considered revival. What merits might there still be in a scheme of Aristotelian moral development? Recently, and perhaps especially in applied ethics, there has been a move back towards a virtue-theoretical approach to moral philosophical thinking and practice inspired by (though not hostage to) the seminal work by Alasdair MacIntyre whose ideas were presented and, to a limited extent, revised in the previous chapter. Agreeing largely with this Aristotelian scheme of thought and living which celebrated the virtues as essential travelling companions in our search for a good life, I now turn to the idea of what a theory of ethical development, inspired by Aristotle, might look like in the contexts of sport.

In the first instance we should say that an Aristotelian theory of ethical development would be aretaic. This concept derives from the ancient Greek word *Arēte* (usually translated as 'virtue' but denoting any form of personal excellence and not merely those that are widely recognised as moral). So an aretaic conception of ethics focuses first and foremost on excellent character; on being a certain kind of person. This picture is essentially distinct from the deontological picture of the rational moral agent disposed to follow certain kinds of rules and performing correspondingly obligatory acts. This focus is often captured in ethics in the idea that virtue ethics is more concerned with being rather than doing, with goodness rather than simply rightness. The right kind of person (i.e. a good one, a virtuous one) is one who does the right thing, for the right reason, at the right time, feeling the right way about it as they do it. Having said that explanatory primacy must go to personal character rather than rules, we must acknowledge the situated nature of character, of vices as well as virtues.[17]

Kohlberg's famous jibe, that the problem with aretaic ethics was that everyone had his or her own bag of virtues, contains an important criticism despite its rhetorical style. The kinds of persons that are celebrated as paradigms of human excellence do change somewhat over time and between cultures. It does not follow, however, that goodness is merely a hostage to relativism. There are certain human excellences that span time and place. As we saw, MacIntyre cites justice, courage and honesty as key among the virtues of any civilised community. And in addition to that we might also cite respectfulness, responsibility, integrity and a host of others, some of which I explore in the following chapters. Are humans not all better for these traits as opposed to disrespectfulness, irresponsibility and wantonness? Of course, precisely which actions these virtues issue in, and when, will be a thorny problem. But that does not mean we should throw the baby out with the bath water.

If we agree then upon the importance of character, some other things will follow. First, we should eschew simple reductionism for the reasons set out in the previous chapter. Whether in philosophical accounts such as MacIntyre's or psychological ones such as Bredemeier and Shields', we must be careful to give robust psychological accounts of human being and action so that our experiments into sports ethics are not predicated upon diaphanous apparitions, thinly operationalised human agency, in order merely to facilitate empirical research.[18] Second, as noted above, we have to acknowledge the important contribution of context, for as Rorty observes, 'community is the context of character' (1988: 324) and MacIntyre's practice-communities thesis is a robust articulation of such a context, even if it is not the only one. A recognition of context-sensitivity is one place where Bredemeier and Shields have notably made ground in describing the role and influence of the moral atmosphere of sports and how these alter according to age, gender, playing level, sport-type and so on.

One of the ways in which our accounts of action in sport can become more ethically robust is by attending to the tripartite account offered by Aristotle.

Action typically issues from relatively settled dispositions to see, feel and think, and is the product of our habituation. This requires an emphasis on the concept and importance of childhood learning, imitation, emulation and so on that is rather more powerful than is commonly acknowledged. This requires an examination of the patterns of normalcy as a complex of perception, emotion and deliberation. Of course, reasoning and judgement are critical to our moral development but crucially they will be a product of a habituation into modes of perception and feeling that are not simply precursors to, but rather constitutive of, mature moral action and reflection.

Thus, in the Golden Age, as Freud referred to it, 'hooked up securely to the sources of nourishment and comfort, the infant is indeed in a state of blissful totality' (Nussbaum, 2001: 185). Then, of course, the child is born into the world of objects and beings and things start to get more complex and confounding. Birth through infancy can be called the initial stage of Aristotelian moral development.[19] As Nussbaum (2001)[20] argues, psychoanalysts typically focus on the gratification of physical needs and basic desires while ignoring how the world is itself an object of interest and pleasure, fear and anxiety. Notwithstanding this, emotions and proto-cognitive mastery are there pretty much from the beginning. It is the centrality of these features of early experience that are frequently ignored or diminished in cognitivist accounts of moral development. It is as if childhood can be thought of as a necessary evil rather than a complex and emotionally charged view of the world. A crucial part of that world is the connectedness of the infant and the carer. It is precisely this essential connectedness that the Kohlbergian picture eschews in its desire to put an autonomous judger at the apex of moral development. And, it must be noted, this too is gendered from the beginning:

> Taught that dependence on the mother is bad and that maturity requires separation and self sufficiency, males frequently learn to have shame about their own human capacities for receptivity and play, whereas females are more likely to get the message from their parents that maturity involves a continued relation of interdependence, and that emotionally expressing need is appropriate.
>
> (Nussbaum, 2001: 219–20)[21]

Along with the growing awareness of language, the inchoate emotions emerge, and with them the growth of ethical sensibility, however limited throughout infancy. Even at this stage, there is means–ends reasoning related to wants and needs (ice cream is preferable to fruit) but also to relations (jealousy arises at the carer's attention to siblings; a sense of unfairness is felt when deprived of what was before given without qualification).

In the intermediate stage, habit formation is critical to the development of moral sense. Practice does not make perfect, as sports psychologists are fond of telling us. Rather, it makes things permanent, as Aristotle (1980) observed long before the psychologist's remark became a commonplace: 'It makes no small difference then, whether we form habits of one kind or of another from our very youth; it makes a very great difference, or rather *all* the difference' (Bk. II.I; 1103b22–5).

It is, therefore, the acquisition of good habits that we are crucially after in general and in particular in sport. The moral educational potential rests precariously on sports as a moral laboratory in which habituation can be first enlisted and only later reflected upon and, if necessary, problematised. In the intermediate stage the character is in transition. Children and youths learn to adopt attitudes less egoistically driven and come to care as well as to reason for others' interests and needs. But crucially it is also a time for the formation of reflexive emotional attitudes that are cognitively grounded. In this stage, moral emotions such as regret, shame and guilt, as well as pride and loyalty, come to be conceived of as appropriate responses to situations and acts. These are the fare of strong evaluation as I set it out in the context of sportspersonship in Chapter 2. Typically, these responses come to form patterns of more or less stable perception, emotion and deliberation. But they must be struck upon the right reasons of course. To act virtuously is indeed to act from a settled character that sees and feels and judges things properly.

Moral instruction, in its various forms, will be critical in this stage in addition to the more informal modes of learning. Two are particularly noteworthy. The first relates to the powerful though old-fashioned notion of a role model. In Aristotelian thought, understanding the right thing to do, feel and see is a product of our learning from wiser souls than ourselves:

> Actions, then, are called just and temperate when they are such as the just or the temperate man would do; but it is not the man who does these that is just and temperate, but the man who also does them *as* just and temperate men do. It is well said, then, that it is by doing just acts that the just man is produced, and by doing temperate acts the temperate man; without doing these no-one would have a prospect of becoming good.
>
> But most people do not do these, but take refuge in theory and think they are being philosophers and will become good in this way, behaving somewhat like patients who listen attentively to their doctors, but do none of the things they are ordered to do. As the latter will not be made well in body by such a course of treatment, the former will not be made well in soul by such a course of philosophy.
>
> (Bk. II.V; 1105–21)

Several points need to be made here. First, we must acknowledge the situatedness of Aristotelian thought. It is clear that the practices of Ancient Greece would be misogynistic by modern lights. As I noted in the methodological note in the introduction, a revival project is not needed. Indeed, Aristotle talks of the good and wise 'man' and often of the 'great-souled man' when he is referring to acts of manly courage and nobility. Of course, our interpretation needs to be revisionist in this regard. Nonetheless, this notion of habituated action is still apposite. Aristotle's beautiful remark that we will come to the palace of reason only through the courtyard of habit and tradition is well made. For in times of uncertainty, we literally act according to our early habituation and only thereafter according to our appreciation of what good people would do in such situations. This is how we learn to perceive the rule (how properly to proceed when faced with competing claims on our motivations) and to follow it with cognisance. Merely blind rule-following observance is in a clear sense not the same thing as following a rule wholeheartedly, where one's actions are predicated on a conception and dedication to do the right thing by being the right kind of person.[22] Nonetheless, this stage is characterised by uncertainty and unreliability. True, one comes to begin to resist one's motivations and values that belong to and persist from the earlier more egoistic stage, but developing mature reflexive attitudes and developing these self-critical attitudes in relation to their evolving value-scheme is still an undertaking in the process of becoming.

Character training[23] in the intermediate phase helps our evolving moral agent to reliably (re)produce the right acts at the right times while coming to feel appropriately about them. It is a mistake, however, to think of this habituation as mere rote learning in the way that early skill-psychologists believed. It is as if we need, in moral learning, to replace this arcane way of thinking with a more open-ended framework to understand and explain action. One learns the generalised responses and then one must refine them, becoming ever more sensible to the particularities of each situation.

This stage is often summed up by the phrase that one has learnt the 'that' of moral action. One appreciates that one must act according to the dictates of virtue. In order to fully mature, to reach the final stage of Aristotelian moral development, moral agents must also comprehend the 'why'. As Tobin puts it: 'Acquiring the why in ethics will help [those in the intermediate stage] to overcome the gaps, unclarities, and straightforward mistakes in his moral awareness' (1989: 203).

Fully, to act virtuously, which as always at the same time to act wisely, is a matter of hitting a mean between acts that are lacking in some regard, or excessive in others. It is here that Aristotle's celebrated 'Doctrine of the Mean' gives guidance as to how moral training and education, with appropriate exemplars, gives rise to our feeling, judging and acting virtuously. Here again we have a critical point of contrast with both Kohlbergian and Haanian thinking.

On the one hand, doing the right thing and being the right kind of person in a Kantian-inspired Kohlbergian scheme is about deducing action-guiding conclusions from general principles. On a Haanian scheme it is about coming to uncoerced and fair agreements that we can simply be comfortable with. So the operationalisations of these ideas in sports psychology has meant one of two problematic methodological and theoretical paths are followed. First, we can use a universal measure of morality (as in Kohlberg's universal principle of reasoned justice) and then we see the extent to which our sportspersons can approximate it in action. Or alternatively (in Haanian fashion) we measure the extent to which the moral balance that has been struck between competitors' clashes of interests (I want to win. OK, so too do you) has been fairly made. There are correspondingly two points of theoretical contrast I wish to make here. On the one hand one can come to fair agreements that are not ethically defensible. It seems in professional North American ice hockey that 'everyone' agrees to be violent. No problem of unfairness there then. Equally, for the Kohlbergians, there is no appreciation that ethics is *to a certain extent* situational. And the appreciation of this point – that morality is not some special sphere of universal obligations but a matter of trying to live good lives – is central to the Aristotelian scheme I am trying to develop in this book. In our guidance as moral educators whether as coaches, parents or pedagogues we must hit the mean between vices of cowardice (a deficiency) and rashness (an excess) if we are to act courageously in the face of danger or things that we are properly afraid of. Consider those who over-conform to violent norms of sports sub-cultures (Coakley, 2001). This is not courage as a virtue, but rashness, a failure to see what dangers are properly to be faced; failure emotionally to attach significance to the respect owed to the health and well-being of an opponent. As Sherman (1989: 35) puts it:

> Action which hits the mean is directed towards the right persons, for the right reasons, on the right occasions, and in the right manner. The overwhelming sense is that virtue must fit the case. But, as Aristotle insists above, the formula of the mean itself seems to offer little concrete guidance.

This last point, that ethical perception, affection and decision are open-ended is critical to the final stage of moral development. We can only go so far in our moral training in sports as elsewhere. There will be no formulaic application of principles that are necessarily to be adapted to circumstance and context. This philosophical point, crucially, must be amplified by political strictures. Which of us will operate in Kohlberg's level six or Haan's level five? Which of us will be the perfect practical and moral reasoners? None of us that are human, that much is for sure. While the final stage is what we aim for, we commonly fail and we can do so just as easily by failures of perception (or moral blindness we might say), of emotion (we become unfeeling automata, conditioned to blot out our affectivity) or of judgement (we simply apply the rule wrongly, select an inappropriate value) and of course we may do all things right, but fail to move ourselves to action in one or all of these ways.

Thus, after good and critical habituation, there will always be the matter of institutionally and politically creating the strong and supportive structures that will incentivise and punish those whose perception is blinded, whose affections have withered under the calluses of indifference and whose reasoning has been thwarted by continued and robotic observance to their tribal attachments whether as team or school or college or nation.

Conclusion

In this chapter I have tried to show how a critical appreciation of the historical and theoretical antecedents of moral philosophy and moral psychology place us in a stronger position to present a critique of current sports psychological research into the ethics of sporting participation and performance. It has enabled us to reach back to a richer tradition of moral thought, itself arising from a competitive social culture, that offers a better 'museum of normalcy' from which to situate moral character and conduct in sport.

Whether such a scheme can offer anything that would yield a moral barometer with which to test the atmosphere of sport is yet to be revealed. While Carr (1998) and Gough (1998) argue that it cannot do this in principle, I prefer to leave the door ajar. What Carr and Gough properly object to, and what I have illustrated and amplified here, is that a positivistic science in the area of ethics is a logical non-starter. Science proceeds by observation and experiment. And as I have argued, our observations of sports ethics are already saturated with normative commitments in the concepts of 'duty', 'respect', 'rule-following', 'virtue' and so on. Second, any empirical research in these fields must itself make theoretical assumptions about the very nature of morality, which is then presented as the standard against which behaviours are described and evaluated. What I do know is that moral learning, development and maturing can occur. I have attempted to set out a richer conceptual scheme in which to consider such learning and development. I have shown how that must take childhood patterns of perception, emotion and deliberation more seriously along with modes of increasingly critical habituation in a strongly supportive community. Whether this can yield anything approximating a scientific programme must itself be the object of further research. In developing a picture of particular vices and virtues in the following chapters I want to take seriously both MacIntyre and Rorty's view that community is the context of character and to situate the moral psychology of sportspersons within an aretaic scheme.

Part II

Vicious and virtuous sport

5 Codes of conduct and trustworthy coaches

Introduction

During the 1980s and 1990s considerable discussion was generated concerning the regulatory checks and balances for a number of occupations. Perhaps the key drivers for the development of social responsibility were the excesses of stock market traders or CEOs who toiled happily under the leitmotif 'greed is good', affording themselves huge financial salaries and bonuses unchecked by the market or their own corporate structures. What followed thereafter was the development of a serious debate about the loss of personal virtues such as responsibility and organisational values such as accountability and trust. This very general atmosphere was compounded in sports, at least in the UK, by two other factors. The first was a process of professionalisation where what had ruled in sport hitherto, whether in terms of administration or coaching, was distinctly unregulated. The voluntary nature of most sports labour (from youth sport and even up to national sports federations) seemed to lack structure, efficiency, accountability and control. Second, coupled with this awakening was a plethora of child abuse cases where the lack of organisational checks and balances allowed paedophiles to move freely within the structures of sports and similar youth movements under voluntary labour. The response both within and outside of sports was the development of rule-based codes of conduct. Into these codes of conduct can be read a moral conservatism; a flight back to the language of moral certainty, of duties, obligations, principles and rules. The task of how we should understand these codes of conduct and what may properly be expected of them in the context of sports coaching is explored in this chapter. In order to effect this task I set out a caricature of professionalism that is partly at odds with the rule-based conceptions of ethics and, utilising the concept of 'trust', I attempt to underwrite the notion of sports coach as professional.

Professions and professionals

The clergy, medicine and law are often referred to as the 'liberal professions'. They represent paradigmatic examples of professions in which persons ply their occupation's knowledge and skills in a very particular way. The list, though traditional, is somewhat incomplete and based upon historical contingencies that have much to do with the manner in which the labour employed in these spheres was monopolistically constructed. This feature was surely the motivation for George Bernard Shaw's quip that all professions are conspiracies against the laity. There is already, however, a significant literature in sports regarding the ideas of 'professional' and 'professionalism' though it is typically centred around the payment of athletes and the apparent contrast with the idea and ideal of amateurs and their motivational sets. I do not intend to review those arguments here[1] and instead focus on the idea of coaching as an emergent or aspiring profession. Instead, I take the spirit of Daryl Koehn's analysis of the liberal professions and situate it in the context of sports coaching.

Koehn argues that the concept of 'professional' is inherently normative since any attempt to describe the boundaries of the concept is at the same time to recommend a particular version of the powers of a person under that description. Koehn sets to ground the *moral* authority of professionals in contradistinction to two alternative models that are not uncommonly characteristic of relationships in sporting contexts: (1) the professional as expert; and (2) the professional as service-provider for fee. Neither of these conceptions, it is said, can underwrite the trust we place in professionals. Koehn draws upon Baier's work in feminist ethics to argue that trust is the heart and soul of professions and professionalism.[2] And it is in this vein that I want to recast the ways of working of sports coaches.

The notion of professional as possessor of expertise deals only with techniques or means and is not tied to proper ends among which is the client's good; in this conception the expert pursues their own private agenda which may or may not coincide with their client. The professional as service provider for fee is similarly untrustworthy. This contractual understanding of the relations between professional and client, although placing the client's agenda in the foreground, can serve to obscure the proper end of the profession. The caricature is the defence lawyer unconcerned with justice but hell-bent on achieving a result of not guilty for their client. The professional, placed in the service of the client, becomes little more than a (more or less expensively) hired hand.

Koehn begins her account by drawing upon interesting etymological support. The word 'profess' comes from the Greek verb *prophaino* meaning 'to declare publicly'. The Greek *prophaino* became the Latin *professio*, a term applied to the public statement made by persons who sought to accompany a position of public trust (Koehn, 1993: 59). Developing the idea of a public profession of trustworthiness, Koehn (1993) sets out seven conditions, which I elaborate in square brackets, that are intended to ground the moral authority of the professions and thus professionalism:

1 the professional must aim at the client's good [whose desires do not simply entail that good];

2   the professional must exhibit a willingness to act toward this aim;
3   such willingness to act thus must continue for as long as is necessary to reach a determination;
4   the professional must be competent [in the appropriate knowledge and skills];
5   the professional must be able to demand from the client [specific appropriate knowledge and performances];
6   the profession must be free to serve the client with discretion [which, as with (1) above, need not be consistent with their desires];
7   the professional must have a highly internalized sense of responsibility.

From these conditions, the grounds for trusting the professional are given moral authority the like of which enables a fairly open-ended definition that, at least on the face of it, does not disqualify sports coaching. As professionals, sports coaches aim towards the production of relative and absolute excellence of their performers; this is the proper end of sports and what is to be aimed for within the framework of the relevant practices. Moreover, the coaches have been initiated into a body of knowledge and skills in areas ranging from the physiology of conditioning, efficient techniques of skill acquisition, performance motivation, goal setting and so on. Further, and reciprocally, the coaches demand from their athletes appropriate performances. At least in most cases, the 'client' is not the master of the entire agenda. Finally, some authority, often paternalistic (with old and especially with young athletes), is invested in coaches whose powers are effected with discretion in a framework of responsibilities to self, performer and sport. Not in reference to sports, but applicable to them, Koehn summarises:

> A professional is an agent who freely makes a public promise to serve persons [. . .] who are distinguished by a specific desire for a particular good [. . .] and who have come into the presence of the professional with or on the expectation that the professional will promote that particular good. In other words, agents become professionals by virtue of what they profess or publicly proclaim before persons lacking particular goods.
>
> (Koehn, 1993: 59)

She later states that 'professionals must have some way of establishing that they are worthy of the client's continuing trust. Adherence to the professional pledge in each and every interaction with the client constitutes a solution to this problem' (1993: 68). The notion of a public pledge is one that finds no home in contemporary sporting practices just as medical professionals too have eschewed the Hippocratic Oath. But oaths there were in antiquity and were not merely sworn by the forerunners of medical physicians but sports coaches too.

Swearing public oaths in sports and medicine

In Ancient Greece the *gymnasiarchos*, literally the leader of the *gymnasion* or school, held official roles to oversee the tutelage of young educands (those to be educated) (Miller, 1991). The *gymnasiarchos* were responsible for the education of youths from 15–17 of wealthy families. Their training was not just in gymnastics as the name implies, but also in music, literature and philosophy. The *gymnasiarchos* not only supervised training, but also directed the activities of the pedagogues and even acted at times as their benefactor, and were empowered to make judgements where the law was unclear or unspecific (Harris, 2007). And, given the separate careers, so markedly different in public prestige and payment, the proximity between their oath and the Hippocratic Oath (fourth century BC) is quite striking. Although commonly and wrongly confused with the Latin dictum *primum non nocere* (first, do no harm), the oath to the Greek God Hippocrates runs as follows:

> I swear by Apollo the physician, by Asclepius, Hygeia, and Panacea, and I take to witness all the gods, all the goddesses, to keep according to my ability and my judgment, the following Oath.
>
> To consider dear to me as my parents him who taught me this art; to live in common with him and if necessary to share my goods with him; To look upon his children as my own brothers, to teach them this art if they so desire without fee or written promise; to impart to my sons and the sons of the master who taught me and the disciples who have enrolled themselves and have agreed to the rules of the profession, but to these alone the precepts and the instruction.
>
> I will prescribe regimens for the good of my patients according to my ability and my judgment and never do harm to anyone.
>
> To please no one will I prescribe a deadly drug nor give advice which may cause his death.
>
> Nor will I give a woman a pessary to procure abortion.
>
> But I will preserve the purity of my life and my art.
>
> I will not cut for stone, even for patients in whom the disease is manifest; I will leave this operation to be performed by practitioners, specialists in this art.
>
> In every house where I come I will enter only for the good of my patients, keeping myself far from all intentional ill-doing and all seduction and especially from the pleasures of love with women or with men, be they free or slaves.
>
> All that may come to my knowledge in the exercise of my profession or in daily commerce with men, which ought not to be spread abroad, I will keep secret and will never reveal.
>
> If I keep this oath faithfully, may I enjoy my life and practice my art, respected by all men and in all times; but if I swerve from it or violate it, may the reverse be my lot.

Not restricted to the avoidance of harming the patient the bar is set much higher. In pursuit of the goals of healthy living, the avoidance of the procurement of death whether by abortion or euthanasia, the physician publicly declares himself to a range of virtues such as his trustworthiness, the binding-ness of his confidence to the patient, but also to the 'purity' of his profession. While no one knows for sure the precise historical origin of the oath it is thought to emerge around the fourth century BC.

While not quite as ancient we might think of the first sports code of conduct, the Beroia Law for the *gymnasiarchos* which dates back to the third century BC. One particularly noteworthy feature of the Law is the specificity of the behaviours that it demands, permits and proscribes and the penalties to be exacted upon their transgression. Modern codes might well learn from its precision irrespective of the fact that only fragments remain of it.

The Beroia Gymnasiarchy Law

No one under the age of thirty shall take off his clothes when the signal is lowered, unless the leader should give his permission. When the signal is raised, no one else shall do so, unless the leader should give his permission, and no one should anoint himself in another wrestling-ground in this city, and if he does, the gymnasiarch shall prevent him and fine him 50 drachmas.

All those who come to the gymnasium shall obey the person whom the gymnasiarch appoints as leader, as is prescribed by the gymnasiarch. The gymnasiarch will flog whoever does not obey (the leader) with a rod, and fine the others.

The ephebes and those who are under twenty-two years old shall practice javelin throwing and archery every day, when the boys have anointed themselves, and, equally they should do anything else that it appears necessary for them to learn.

Concerning the Boys

None of the young men may enter among the boys, nor talk to the boys, and if someone should do this, the gymnasiarch will fine him and prevent him from doing any of these things.

The physical trainers of the boys shall present themselves twice a day in the gymnasium, at hours that the gymnasiarch shall set, except in case of illness or some other trouble that compels it; otherwise, they shall report to the gymnasiarch.

If one of the physical trainers of the boys should neglect his duties, and not appear before the boys at the appointed hour, the gymnasiarch shall fine him five drachmas each day.

The gymnasiarch shall have the power to flog the boys and their paedagogoi who are disobedient, if they are not free, and to fine those who are.

He shall order the physical trainers of the boys to make an inspection of the boys three times a year, once every four months, and appoint judges for them, and crown the victor with an olive crown.

Those who may not participate in the Gymnasium

(A person) may not take off his clothes in the gymnasium if he is a slave, or a freedman, or the son of one of these, or *apalaistros*, or a prostitute, or works at a trade in the agora, or is drunk, or mad. If the gymnasiarch knowingly allows one of the people indicated above to anoint himself, or if someone has revealed and pointed this out, he will pay a fine of 1000 drachmas. To ensure that the fine will be paid, the person making the denunciation will give a written statement to the city auditors so that they will place his name with the city praktor. [If] they do not lodge his name, or the praktor does not act, they will also be fined the equal amount, and give a third of the sum to the person making the denunciation.

If the gymnasiarch has been written up unjustly, he shall respond within [t]en days, and be judged before the appropriate court.

Future gymnasiarchs shall prevent those who act against the law from anointing themselves. [If] they do not do this they will be subject to the same fines.

No one may verbally abuse the gymnasiarch in the gymnasium. If a person does, he will be fined 50 drachmas. If anyone should move to strike the gymnasiarch in the gymnasium, those present should prevent and not allow him to do so, and (the gymnasiarch) shall fine the person who sought to strike him 100 drachmas, and he shall be liable to prosecution according to the common laws. Any of those present who, although able, did not come to the aid of the gymnasiarch, shall be fined 50 drachmas.

> http: //www.umich.edu/~classics/programs/class/cc/372/B015.html;
> accessed 9.4.06

Now it might be said that the time when one might autocratically flog one's charges is long gone and good riddance. But this is not exactly true as Koukouris (2000) points out the practice is alive and "well" in rural Greece to this day. So perhaps we should not assume that democracies are respectful of basic human rights across Europe let alone the rest of the world (David, 2005). Moreover, having a rule and a fine to attach to those who verbally abuse sports coaches or commit acts of violence against them might well be worth reconsidering as would the idea of fining those who fail to prevent them from so doing.

In modern times it is simply presumed that the coach always acts in the interest of their performer and, indeed, of the sport. Where the paradigmatic professions have been thought to be related to essential social goods (justice, health and salvation) their import might be such that the public pledge was a strong normative lever. Sport seems by comparison to be trivial. Why would such a pledge be necessary? Well, the preparation of athletes must begin at a young age. Athletes stand before coaches in need of their sporting wisdom. It may be the case that to trust them requires not merely that they are, qua professional, virtuous but perhaps that they have been legitimised by the appropriate authority *and* are regulated in proper ways by that authority. It is in this lacuna then that codes of conduct in sport may find their *raison d'être*.

Codes of ethical and professional conduct

Why should professionals adopt a code of practice to govern their conduct? It is commonplace in moral philosophical circles at least, to search for authoritative support for ethical commitments in order to avoid caprice or arbitrariness. Likewise it is often thought that moral rules allow us to point up most clearly the clashes between permissible and impermissible conduct. We can still ask, though, why we need a *code* of rules to guide ethical conduct in professional life?

In answer to this question a number of reasons recommend themselves: first, they offer *apparent* clarity and simplicity in a confusing world; second, they set out standards and criteria to evaluate provision and expectation in relationships that are consistent over time; third, they offer a neutral framework for resolving conflict or ambiguity to those under the authority of the organisation; and fourth, in constraining certain actions they allow exclusion from that organisation anyone who will not conform to the code.[3] In short we might say that codes of conduct franchise 'blameability' and consequently 'punishability' to their respective organisations. The closeness of these ethical objectives to a legal mindset is apparent. 'Blame', as Williams reminds us, 'is the characteristic reaction of the morality system' (1985: 177); it invites us to think of the whole of ethical life in terms of a series of obligations of increasing power that must be met for fear of incurring blame and possible retribution.

Characteristic of these guides to professional conduct is the codification of a set of rules that describe, prescribe and, more commonly, proscribe the actions of professionals. The codes are a pastiche of eclectic ethical notions. But one particular portion of the picture dominates: a 'common sense' view of morality as a set of rules or principles that stops people from acting *purely* in the pursuit of their interests to the detriment of others. The sums of these rules or principles, both negative and positive, constitute the moral code enshrined in ideals, duties, rights and obligations. To what extent does this common sense picture recommend itself above others?

The sheer range of ethical theories in this pastiche makes the task of summarising difficult. In keeping with the brevity of this argument, albeit following many philosophers before, we may separate ethical theories into two categories: those that concern themselves with actions and those that concern themselves with agents, or, put another way, those that focus on what it is right to do and those that focus on what sort of agent it is good to be. In keeping with the above, I will eschew felicity for the sake of brevity and generalise further by naming them rule-based and virtue-based theories of ethics. I will now consider how these caricatured positions underwrite codes of conduct.

Rules, rule-following and rule-based ethical theories

My compass here is necessarily broad and the targets I aim at are less than well focused. The name 'rule-based ethical theories' is not intended to be definitive. Rather, what it captures is the fact that the ethical considerations that belong to a theory under this description are centred around considerations to do with actions that are governed by something like a set of rules that is designed to frustrate the worst of people's desires and that is grounded in reason (such that they have an authoritative voice). These were the moral foundations that bolstered social scientific research into sports and ethical development that I criticised in the previous chapter. In rule-based theories, being largely modern, there is no appeal to a deity; the rules are human constructions. Given that professionals are faced with problems of how to decide between competing courses of action in a way that is not merely capricious nor God-given, the rules are supposed to point us towards what any reasonable person would agree is right.

Perhaps the most well-known theories of right actions are deontological in character and the most celebrated of these belongs to Kant.[4] To act rightly is to refrain from things that can be known, before the fact, to be wrong. The rules are effectively negative, whether as constraints, proscriptions, prohibitions or norms. They prevent us from doing, with good conscience, things that are known before the fact to be wrong, irrespective of all consequences, including good ones. Characteristic of deontological theories is the prioritisation of the right over the good. The fact that my harming one person may save the lives of several others does not weigh with the strict deontologist; the rules guide my conduct that is good or bad *in itself*, and not in respect of other considerations. A deontologist writing a code of conduct would not be directly concerned with maximising happiness or minimising pain or indeed with any of the range of considerations that an emotivist, intuitionist or virtue-based theorist would necessarily appeal to. Instead what would inform the rules of conduct is the distinction between that which is and is not permissible. This distinction enables agents to perceive what is the right thing to do. Again, this may be stated negatively: I am obliged *not* to do that which is not permissible. This negative characterisation of morality is captured well in Mill's 'Essay on Liberty':

> Its ideal is negative rather than positive; passive rather than active; Innocence rather than Nobleness; Abstinence from evil, rather than the energetic Pursuit of the Good; in its precepts (as has been well said) "Thou shalt not" predominates unduly over "thou shalt".
>
> (Mill, 1859 cited in Mill, 1962: 177)

Deontological constraints are paradigmatic of such rules. Three considerations show their nature and structure.[5] First, though it is possible to formulate these rules or constraints positively (for example one might say 'never lie' can be translated into 'always tell the truth'), they are negatively formulated and there is neither entailment nor equivalence between them. Additionally, the rules are narrowly framed and directed. One is not permitted to act in ways that are wrong. Not only does this give them a form of specificity to the rule but it also puts into context the distinction between actions intended to bring about certain outcomes intentionally and those where, for example, bad outcomes result from foreseen and unforeseen consequences from our prima facie permissible action. For the deontologist writing or indeed enforcing a code of conduct, wrong action (rule-breaking) is necessarily intentional action.

In many ways the moral value of games and sports has resided in rather opaque accounts of rule-responsibility. It is thought that if we can develop children (or coaches for that matter) who follow the rules (moral and non-moral) then we will thereby develop moral maturity (or professional conduct). But all this is still a far cry from the idea of a moral *code*, a systematised set of principles, not merely aggregated and ultimately reducible to one. Thus we often find reductions from many rules to the 'Golden Rule', and this is instanced in more than one type of ethico-religious system and, perhaps, most famously in philosophical terms by Kant's Categorical Imperative 'act so as to treat rational beings always as ends and never as means only'.[6] Yet the elegance of Kant's formulation of moral actions motivated by impartial duty with universality of application under the assent of practical reason is not mirrored in codes of conduct. Where Kant attempted to achieve a non-conflicting order of moral principles (notwithstanding the distinction between perfect duties that oblige to all rational beings to act in specific ways that observe the rights of all rational beings, and imperfect duties that are not categorical but are selective and do not have corresponding rights), codes of conduct tend to be more eclectic. They have maintained, perhaps implicitly, the idea that rule-responsibility is at the heart of ethical conduct.

From here it is a short step to the assertion that the heart of the rule-based ethics, especially deontological ones, is negative; moral behaviour consists in the avoidance of wrong acts.[7] This is one reason why codes of conduct are framed explicitly or implicitly in rule-like ways but also because of their legalistic nature and the blameability they offer. Where there are rules we should be able to distinguish right from wrongdoing and wrongdoers.

There are, however, weaknesses in this way of thinking. I shall take, for the purpose of exposition, merely one principle from the code of conduct of the most important coaching organisation in the United Kingdom, the National Coaching Foundation (NCF)/Sports Coach UK[8]. The code displays a wide variety of rules, principles, duties and general exhortations the type of which are likely to be familiar to the reader and, therefore, the one exemplar is chosen merely as representative of the kind of analyses that might be made of the remainder of the code and, indeed, any other code of its kind. Consider, then, principle 3.3 in the Code of Practice for Sports Coaches:

PRINCIPLE OF PRACTICE 3.3

Coaches should not condone or engage in sexual harassment [. . .] with performers or colleagues. It is considered that sexual relationships with performers are *generally* inappropriate to the professional conduct of coaches.

(emphasis added)

There is no reasonable person who would not want to say that sexual harassment is wrong. Surely part of what 'harassment' actually means is the negative evaluation; 'wrongful' (in the same way that someone could not condone murder which is *defined* as 'wrongful killing'; if it were not wrongful it would have to be an act that fell under some other description). Surely this principle is heading in the right direction at least; it sets out wrongful conduct and allows us to blame would-be wrongdoers and enable sanctions to be taken against them.

What, though, are we to think of this principle? First, let us be clear that it is an odd principle that admits of exceptions.[9] What is the function of the word 'generally' in its midst? Isn't a principle something that is absolute? Consider some classic deontological principles that are commonplace to those in a Judaeo-Christian tradition at least: 'thou shalt not kill' or 'thou shalt not steal'. Imagine now, then, 'thou shalt not lie, generally speaking'. This would appear an odd commandment were Moses to have brought it down from Mount Sinai. This might appear a trivial point but it is not. It kicks out at the very idea of establishing principles that are designed to function as universal rules not mere guidelines.[10] This is, again, a very general difficulty with the universalisation of moral rules. Perhaps it would be better to follow Hart's (1955) jurisprudential idea that we have rules that are defeasible. In special circumstances, things that we might normally disapprove of or even abhor may become permissible. This is the function of the word 'generally'; perhaps it could be stronger put. By contrast, the American Psychological Association's (APA) code is less equivocal. It forbids sexual intimacies with existing clients or patients for a minimum of two years after professional contact. Of course, the client or patient relationship is of a different kind than that of coach and athlete yet the potential for abuse is also there. What is significant about the APA's code regarding sexual harassment is the further, explicit rule that its members shall accord the complainant dignity and respect. The idea that the victim of sexual harassment should be taken seriously, morally seriously that is, is an interesting one. What it points to is the institutional recognition of norms of acceptable and unacceptable practice in areas that can be ignored or ridden roughshod over because of the sometimes macho ethoses of sporting practices. Stories are legion in sports of sexual harassment being ignored, not taken seriously or considered as part and parcel of the whole package of elite sport (Brackenridge, 2001). Again, there are salient differences between coaching and psychology not least of all in respect of the control exercised over its members by a governing legislature. So much of sports coaching is carried out on a voluntary basis and there is little hope of exercising such a degree of control as could be exercised by the APA or the British Medical Council or the Law Society in Great Britain. Perhaps codes of conduct in sport are best viewed as forms of institutional posturing; important but without real bite.[11] I shall return to this point later.

Second, let us also be clear, as Wittgenstein points out in the *Philosophical Investigations*, that a rule cannot determine its own application. The sophistication of this insight is one that will be underdeveloped here.[12] I will explicate a little of the import of this remark by way of discussion of the scope, application and interpretation of rules and also by noting the different aspects of rule-following as distinct from merely acting in accordance with a rule.

How should I conceive of the scope of any given rule that I am supposed to follow? Is it properly the place of a code of conduct to govern the conduct of its members outside the role of coach given the many related and unrelated roles that a coach has to play? These roles range from parent, friend and counsellor merely in the coaching relationship; there are a plethora of others. Would it really be unethical, or 'inappropriate professional conduct' for someone to have sexual relations with a colleague? This is one of the points at which there is a salient distinction between coaching and psychology; we refer to those who seek their service as clients yet the service they offer, though conceivably similar in certain contexts, *is* clearly different. So then, let us agree that sexual harassment is wrong, but how did the formulation of the 'rule' concerning sexual harassment lead us here?

Perhaps we should ask 'what is the concept of "rule"?' or 'what does "rule" actually mean?' in order to begin. Fortunately, that question has already been asked. Baker and Hacker make the Wittgensteinian point that the concept of a rule does not adequately allow for an essentialist analysis; there are no common features to all the things we call 'rules' in virtue of which we call them 'rules'. The recognition of such need not paralyse us though, for even if it opens up a certain generality, that generality is of a specific kind, as Baker and Hacker write:

> The generality of a rule lies in its *use*, not (or not necessarily) in its form. We *guide* our actions by reference to rules: we teach and explain rule-governed activities by citing the rules that govern it. When in doubt as to how to proceed we consult the rules. [. . .] *But the forms of guidance by a rule are most varied.*
>
> (Baker and Hacker, 1985: 45; emphasis added)

An important cautionary note is embodied in the final sentence regarding the variability of the forms of guidance that rules take. A cursory glance at the types of rules in any particular code of conduct would make this evident. That the rules refer to so many different types of activities and interests from confidentiality and safety to informed consent makes this inevitable. For present purposes let us take the type of rule that is of direct concern to codes of conduct: moral rules. This theme has been taken up by Edmund Pincoffs, in his tirade against reductivism in ethics that I observed in the previous chapters. He warns us to be wary of asking of moral rules what they cannot deliver by attending to their divergent powers:

> Rules may be like general standing commands or like general standing orders; analogously they may be like general standing specific and non-specific prescriptions. They may allow no leeway in compliance or they may allow a great deal of compliance.
>
> Some moral rules are more like general standing orders than like general standing commands: for example, "Love thy neighbor" or "Do not cause suffering." They say what is wanted but do not say what to do. If, however, we concentrate upon rules that are like commands, such as "Do not kill" or "Never break promises," we are likely to think of moral rules much like criminal laws, in that they will consist for us, largely of specific injunctions and directions. But if we recognize that they can also be like orders, we will be more aware of the discretion they sometimes allow. They do not tell us exactly what to do so much as they indicate what we should struggle toward in our own way.
>
> (Pincoffs, 1986: 25)

We can see now, perhaps, the unavoidable disparity of the *kinds* of rules that are on offer in codes of conduct. For not only must attention be paid to their differing roles, but also the comparative directness and ambiguity of their application.

Third, following one of Wittgenstein's major theses against the 'private language' argument, Baker and Hacker offer exegesis on the distinction between rule-following and acting merely in accordance with the rule. (It will repay attention for my present purpose even if I attend only to the consequences of this point, though its original target is significantly different, and significantly more profound in philosophical terms, than that which I aim at.) The distinction is apposite; it points to the discontinuity between the vogue for codes of professional (and therefore ethical) conduct and much current practice in elite sports that is characteristic of behavioural accordance rather than rule-following proper. Baker and Hacker write:

> [I]t is not at all necessary that for an activity to be guided by a rule the rule should enter into the activity or even cross the minds of those engaged in it (chess players do not think about the rules of chess as they play; they know them too well) [. . .]. But neither is it enough that the behaviour of someone following a rule merely conforms with the rule (a chess computer follows no rules). Nor is it sufficient that he once learned the

rule – for that is past history [. . .] and the issue here is his present possession of an ability, not its genesis. Nor would it suffice that the rule might
be encoded in his brain (whatever that might mean); for being caused to
act by the encoding of a rule is precisely *not* to follow a rule [. . .]. That a
person's action is normative, that he is following a rule, that he is guided
by a rule (or better, guides himself by reference to a rule) is manifest in the
manner in which he uses rules, invokes rule-formulations, refers to rules
explaining what he did, *justifying* what he did in the face of criticism,
evaluating what he did and *correcting* what he did, *criticizing* his mistakes, and so forth.

(Baker and Hacker, 1985: 45)

As with the actions of our sports coaches, so with codes of conduct. Why do
we need a *rule* like that concerning sexual harassment? Well, let us be clear
that such actions are wrong and that we scarcely need a code to tell us this.
We can no more sexually harass our colleagues or athletes than we can any
other person in the street. So the rule, in this sense tells us nothing new. No,
to follow the rule with regard to sexual harassment is to understand the psychology of the situation: its thick, substantial richness. But rule-based theories do not work that way. What is the point then? Well, as an organisation,
the NCF/Sports Coach UK recognises clearly and properly that situations in
which coaches and athletes find themselves can introduce temptations into
human relationships. Such vicious behaviours as exploitation, domination,
extortion or bribery can and do occur. And with specific reference to sexual
harassment, oftentimes athletes are scantily clad and situations where the
coach is required to physically manipulate body positions are not rare.[13] The
rules are *intended* to preserve proper human relationships in the coaching situation. We use them for a variety of purposes as Baker and Hacker note; to
explain, justify, evaluate, correct and criticise. An example will better illuminate this point.

Consider the following scenario. I am the coach of some elite female ado-
lescent gymnasts. You are one of these gymnasts, aspiring to a full-time sporting career. Mine is a privileged position. The children are with me two or
three hours nearly every day of the week. They respond to me. I am a power
figure. I know my sport: its history; its techniques and skills; its hierarchy. I
hold a privileged position within that hierarchy. I am the gate through which
the successful gymnast must go first. I am esteemed in the community. I am
strong physically; I can catch you, literally, when you fall; I can lift you up
psychologically or I can destroy you and your career by various means; you
need me; above all perhaps, you trust me; your parents trust me. The sexual
harassment of you by me through the powers of my station violates that trust.
We do not need the rule book to guide our actions; we do not consult it to see
whether we do right or wrong, good or bad nor to explain, criticise or justify
those actions. (Though here again we must ask how, even when rules are clear
and unambiguous, such as that for sexual harassment, there are difficulties: 'it

wasn't harassment' says the coach 'of course that's wrong. But she gave me the come-on, she wanted it; that's not harassment' as the unfortunate script too often goes.) Instead we enquire as to what sort of person the coach is (we often ask for character witnesses); what his or her motivations might have been; whether he or she was disposed to other kinds of abuses; what his or her biography or institutional affiliations point towards and so on. The rules may allow us to blame, but they do not fully do the job of determining the context or evaluating the person; other considerations must come into play.

To consider the actual abuses that codes of professional conduct seek to highlight enables us to see the laudable work that the word 'generally' was trying to perform in our principle above. No rule book can anticipate all actions, nor can they describe, or predict, all possible actions that may be considered professional and unprofessional. Rule books just cannot do that sort of thing. And so what we have is an eclectic mix: some rules we make can perform specific tasks, others have more general application. We cannot expect them to be like a calculus table to be consulted prior to performance nor is this how they work in real life. And to capture coaches who are unprofessional in their conduct, we may very well wish to distinguish those who are genuinely following the rules (of course, not in the calculus-like parody) from those whose behaviour merely *appears* not to break the rule while appearing to act in accordance with it.

What becomes clear from this brief consideration of rules in codes of conduct, in addition to the diversity of rules and their action-guiding implications, is the need for something beyond mere rule-observance where this means the avoidance of rule-breaking actions. We can imagine, quite wrongly, that rule-responsibility is at the centre of ethical life. This is why Koehn's condition that a professional must have a highly developed sense of responsibility, though true, falls short of the mark. It is clear that it is not merely an important professional virtue, but that it is an essential social virtue; how could we get along if there were social anarchy or mere unpredictability and randomness of behaviour? What, of course, does not follow is the idea that ethics and ethical conduct can be simply *reduced* to the idea of rule-responsibility. To see why this is the case, we need to return to our earlier distinction of being and doing; of agency and acts. By turning to a non-reductivist vocabulary of the virtues we can prise open the reasons why such unprofessional conduct is reproachable; for the coach in our scenario is left in the care, or striking distance, of someone who is valuable in and of his or herself, and that trust has been violated by the coach. I shall develop this point in relation to the virtue of trust in the sections that follow.

One of the central reasons why we need either to replace or augment the notion of rules as exhaustively descriptive of ethical theory and conduct is, so to speak, their underdetermination. Put simply though they commonly tell us what not to do, often what to aim towards and, occasionally, what to do, they leave so much else in the void. Fried captures this point well: 'One cannot live one's life by the demands of the domain of the right. After having avoided wrong and doing one's duty, an infinity of choices is left to be made' (Fried, 1978: 13).

When, therefore, we consult the rules, to examine conduct that is under question, just as when we wish to commend conduct, the rule book will not do the work for us. The rule cannot determine its own application; we must do that from within the forms of life we inhabit. And in so doing we must try to work our way through the unavoidable pitfalls and fallibility of character evaluation in a spirit devoid of capriciousness or any of the forms of bias. But such actions as we will attempt to inspect and label 'professional' and 'unprofessional' will admit various, perhaps conflicting, interpretations. We are left to ask 'how we can possibly ground our interpretations, to know we have seen a situation aright?' and 'what underwrites our confidence?' to avoid the vertigo of subjectivity. These particular questions must be left for another day, but one thing is certain: if we are to discuss more fully such conduct as is to be characterised 'professional' and 'unprofessional', we must move to the language of virtues.

Virtue, virtues and virtue ethics

Let it be clear, however, that in making transparent some of the difficulties of rule-based ethics and in commending virtue-based ethics, at least with respect to my present concern with the theoretical and practical limitations codes of conduct, I must make similar caveats. First, the term 'virtue-based ethics' is itself a label for diverse modern and pre-modern theories of virtue and the good life. And I have only scratched the surface of these thus far while committing myself to a modified version of MacIntyre's conception of them. Second, I am not in any way committed to the thesis that rule-based considerations are always and everywhere either inferior, or reducible, to virtue considerations. It will be one of my conclusions that they may happily co-exist for the purposes of guiding professional conduct. I hold, instead, to the rather weaker claim that rules, principles and their like are not exhaustive of the basic facts of moral life, a picture of which is incomplete without reference to the virtues.

I shall argue that the pursuit of *eudaimonia* (human well-being or flourishing) is better served by certain sorts of characters rather than others. We prefer the just to the unjust, the courageous to the cowardly, the honest to the dishonest, and so forth. It is these virtue-based considerations that guide my conduct, not the moral rule book. In a sporting context there is a clear analogy. Are we not to prefer those who merely keep the rules for fear of being punished but those who keep them in order that the contest is a fair and equal test of relevant abilities and powers? And if sports are to flourish too, must we not have trustworthy coaches and wise administrators as well as honest performers all of whom keep the sporting faith; the spirit of the game?

The picture of the good life is one that is lived in accordance with virtue against a given background, for example, of the proper nature of human being (as in the pre-modern work of Aristotle) or the cultural and historical traditions I am heir to (as in the modern works of MacIntyre). *Aretē* (excellence) is that which enable persons to achieve their *telos* (proper end) of flourishing, yet *aretē* is also an ingredient of the attainment of that goal at the same time. As we have seen what constitutes the good life is socially and historically located, yet it will be achieved by persons who are possessed of a core of virtues that are acquired, displayed and produced in a variety of shared social practices that are themselves constitutive of broader cultural traditions.

When I am faced with a quandary, on a virtue-based account, it is not that I can simply consult a moral rule book that tells everyone, irrespective of context, not to do this and not to do that. I cannot write off the particularity of quandary. It is 'me', a grounded self, with particular goals, desires, needs, habits and roles. What will *I* do here in the light of what I conceive myself to be: just, cowardly, arrogant, sensitive, untrustworthy.

One of the key points in such a scheme is the notion of a virtue conceived not as an isolated act but as part of a narrative that is my life. This consideration points us toward the psycho-social aspects of my agency because the virtues or vices I display in this or that situation flow from relatively settled dispositions in qualitatively different ways. Virtues and vices are displayed in the *manner* in which I am disposed to act in regular and interrelated ways. This point is usually developed by remarking first that one cannot simply possess a virtue in isolation and second that the moral sphere is thereby extended to include a wider range of acts and appraisals that are found in rule-based accounts. MacDowell develops the point:

> Thus the particular virtues are not a batch of independent sensitivities. Rather, we use the concepts of the particular virtues to mark similarities and dissimilarities among the manifestations of a single sensitivity which is what virtue, in general, is: an ability to recognise requirements which situations impose on one's behaviour. It is a single complex sensitivity of this sort which we are aiming to instil when we aim to inculcate a moral outlook.
>
> (McDowell, 1981: 332–3)

But if there is no rule to guide us, how do we know which virtue, which sensitivity, ought properly to be triggered by this or that situation? One resort, analogous to the reduction to the 'master rule', is to pick out a 'master virtue' such as the disposition to be just. What can assure that my acts tend towards the appropriate amount of each virtue and fail not in excess or deficiency? Time and space do not allow further elaboration but a second example will show the more complete range of ethical considerations that virtue accounts would raise to the surface over and above mere rule-responsibility.

Trust and the virtuous coach

To enact and to evaluate trusting relationships necessarily requires a range of dispositions from courage to wickedness, spite, generosity, foolhardiness, benevolence and beyond. To dislocate trusting from the fuller gamut of dispositions and the contexts in which they are triggered is to focus on a partial aspect of the picture and thus to distort the grasp we have of it. There are, therefore, two reductive temptations that are to be avoided. We should neither consider isolated acts in our evaluation of the professional conduct of coaches nor should we focus too resolutely on single dispositions in evaluations thereof.

What is it then for the parent and performer to trust a coach? Social scientists have often talked about trust merely as reliance on another person or thing to perform some kind of act or function under conditions of limited knowledge.[14] But this understanding of trust is economistic; it lacks an explicit moral dimension. Sisela Bok was one of the first philosophers to recognise this dimension when she wrote: '*Whatever* matters to human beings, trust is the atmosphere in which it thrives' (Bok, 1978: 31). It is precisely because activities such as sport are inherently social that virtues such as trust are ineliminable. Developing this point Baier has offered a developed account of the moral concept of trust and its close conceptual relations.[15] Among other things, she highlights the importance of considering the notions of value and vulnerability in addition to reliance:

> [L]ook at the variety of sorts of goods or things one values or cares about, which can be left or put within the striking powers of others, and the variety of ways we can let or leave others "close" enough to what we value to be able to harm it. Then we can look at various reasons we might have for wanting or accepting such closeness of those with power to harm us, and for confidence that they will not use this power.
>
> (Baier, 1994: 100)

Now the coach is someone in whom discretion is invested. Parents value their children more than just about anything in the world. When they entrust the coach with their children they place within his or her sphere of influence a vulnerable person, one who can be damaged in a variety of ways. Yet they necessarily trust the coach as a professional. Expectations issue from the status of coach *as* professional as we have seen. Parents properly expect the coach not merely to be the bearer of expertise either with or without a fee. Loaded into the coaching situation are a set of normative expectations whereby the coach, implicitly at least, aims towards the good of the performer with appropriate knowledge and skills utilised in a framework of accumulated wisdom generated within the practice.

Consider, then, another scenario. My young gymnast, Johnny, shows great promise. He has the potential to be an Olympian. His parents are exceptionally keen. Perhaps their zealous guidance is motivated by their lowly socio-economic status (this would be a route to a good college scholarship, a lucrative career and so forth), perhaps it is vicarious success that makes them want their child to succeed. Whatever the motivation, I am told in no uncertain terms that I am to do whatever it takes to make Johnny the best gymnast that he can be. He is struggling with his flares on the pommel horse; he cannot perform sufficient repetitions and their quality is lacking owing to his own deficient amplitude in the adductors. And this afternoon he is tired after a heavy conditioning session this morning. Various options compete in my mind: shall I make him try that routine one more time?; is he too tired?; have I succeeded in achieving all I wanted to this session?; have I done enough for next week's championship? All these questions are invoked in everyday contexts that commonly fall well outside the rule-governed jurisdiction of the code of conduct (or perhaps better, beyond even the most comprehensive rule book), yet in each, as coach, I may have to ask myself 'what sort of person am I/would I be to act in this way or that?' And the spectrum of replies may range from considerate, sympathetic and supportive, to insensitive, myopic, arrogant, intolerant, vindictive and spiteful. How could any rule book cover such a range without tearing down all the rainforests in order to attempt to write rules for every possible occasion or eventuality? And yet the exaltation of the rule book mentality, 'moral minimalism' to invent a term of art for the occasion, is precisely that mentality whose character is raised by the exclamation 'we have done nothing wrong or immoral; we have broken no rules' as if the latter were synonymous with the former.

I decide that the only way Johnny will succeed is if I 'help' him gain the amplitude by further stretching exercises. I ask Johnny to go down into the splits and to get his chest as close to the floor as possible. He fails to get close. I continue to urge him with greater vociferousness. He complies, he utters no words of complaint. Then, while he is unaware I come behind him and with all my strength, force his chest down to the floor and hold him down. I prove to him his body's capabilities; I chastise him for his laziness and lack of willpower; I rebuke him for the ingratitude for his parent's sacrifices for his kit, travel expenses, coaching fees and so forth. And all the time I *may* have broken no rule. I may have complied with every consenting wish of his parents (perhaps even Jonny himself, after he has recovered his tearful fit) and I have reinforced the 'no pain, no gain' ethic in him. Yet on the way home I reflect: what sort of person am I that I should do such a thing; shall I convince myself that I have done nothing wrong since I have broken no rules and in any case it is all in the child's long-term financial and performative interests; his parents sanctioned it; without my intervention there is no way he would have . . . and so on. Such a view *may* be underwritten by our rule-based ethic. I am comforted. But perhaps I reflect upon considerations that perhaps should have weighed with me as the boy's coach, a figure esteemed in the community, a role model. I think to myself 'Johnny trusted me, and his parents trusted me with a son whose respect I have complied with only under the auspices of potential star performer.'

What are we to think of this not uncommon scenario? Let us accept that there is no clear application of a rule that will help us unequivocally here. The situation, if not a moral dilemma, is deeply ambiguous. Given that we impart to the trusted coach a valued child, within limits of discretionary power we run the risks of verbal, physical or psychological abuse. Anyone who has been engaged with elite sport knows how cruel it can be. Yet this is not something that can be avoided lest we attempt to live in a bubble or indeed to wrap our children in cotton wool; it comes part and parcel both of sports and of trust itself:

> To understand the moral risks of trust, it is important to see the special sort of vulnerability it introduces. Yet the discretionary element which introduces this special danger is essential to that which trust at its best makes possible. To elaborate Hume: "'Tis impossible to separate the chance of good from the risk of ill."
>
> (Baier, 1994: 104)

Trust, then, on Baier's analysis is characterised as letting persons take care of something that is cared for or valued, where such caring involves the use of discretionary powers about the reliance and competence of the trusted. Risk, as she reminds us, is of the very essence in trusting. But there are good and bad bets. In accepting this Baier builds in a normative dimension that inescapably requires good judgement. To leave your baby with the nearest passer by while you go into a store to buy some provisions while on a shopping trip to London or New York is not trusting but *ceteris paribus* foolishness. We should be wary of jumping to the conclusion that the proper attitude to adopt in such a situation is to distrust. The consequences of distrust are dire; it is, as Baier reminds us, a fragile plant that does not long survive the inspection of its roots. This point is reinforced that we must view trust, as any other disposition, in the context of the person as a whole and the community in which they reside.

We do not, of course, expect to read in any code of ethics a rule confirming the trustworthiness of the coach. Under the cloak of moral minimalism coaches may sell themselves the story that where no rules are broken there is no moral difficulty. Yet, as we have seen, the rules underdetermine the ethical sphere in everyday life as well as in professional interactions. There is no rule to trust; it is almost a matter of volitional necessity. We have no choice in the matter most of the time. Like our health, which is foregrounded as a concern only when we are ill, so we attend to trust only when it is broken. And what would be the cost of continual distrust? Is not paranoia the name for such a condition?

The latter considerations are brought before us *only* under the aspect of a proper consideration of the place and role of virtue in ethical situations, whether everyday or climactic. And these considerations are to be prioritised not simply by asking whether I have broken any rules, but by asking what a person in my situation might do in the light of the kind of life that they consider 'good'. And this cannot be done by the methodological trick of making dispositions generalisable under principled propositions, though this is, I think, precisely what codes of conduct illicitly do; code writers attempt to make rules do the work of virtue requirements by replacing the need for particularity. They attempt to relegate context-sensitive judgement to the rule of law.

One needn't throw the baby out with the bath water. What we might say by way of temporary conclusion is, first, that the scope of rule-based ethics is underdetermining; there is still oftentimes a wide range of options and corresponding dispositions to fill the void after the rules have been laid out. Second, the rules do not specify their own scope and interpretation; agents who are variously virtuous and vicious do. Likewise, third, even after the rule is specified it will only be *followed*, in the strong sense, by the virtuous agent. Mere robot-like rule-observance is an inappropriate point of departure for our description of ethical lives, professional and otherwise. And worse, it can lead to the further entrenchment of the ethos of rule-bending in its extreme as is characteristic of so much conduct in modern sports.

This is precisely the case of our gym coach whose actions are those of the technocrat. His reasoning is instrumental. He sets out his ends unreflectively in accordance with the relevant dominant ethoses and chants slogans around his workhouse: 'no guts, no glory'; 'just do it'; 'nobody remembers who came second'. What justifies the selection of means is technical efficiency and economy. Ethical discourse is suspended under various guises such as 'nice guys come last'. Bend the rules as much as you can but don't break them or if you do, whatever else, don't get caught. Here the professional as craftsman/woman finds no home; their dedication, care and commitment to the defining excellences of the practice, moral *and* technical, are relegated to the sole, justifying, end: winning performance whose services have been bought and paid for, whose contractual labour measured only against that reductivist end.

Conclusion

What kind of communities are developed in professional sports practices is a question insufficiently asked in the education of coaches whose typical agendas are narrowly conceived in instrumental and technicist terms. Two witticisms spring to mind. First, I think it was Samuel Becket who once said that, at 50, we get the face we deserve. Perhaps, at the beginning of the twenty-first century we are getting the sporting milieu we deserve too. Too readily, journalists, administrators, performers and coaches refer to sports and athletes as professionals merely by virtue of their grossly inflated remuneration or their expert knowledge, without recognising what by virtue of that normative description is entrusted to them; the demands that the term places upon them. Their mien is too often characteristic of Molière's remark about writing, a profession 'like prostitution: First you do it because you enjoy it; then you do

6 Racism, racist acts and courageous role models

Racism and responsibility

Having argued the case for the possibility of ethical development in and through sports, I now want to argue further what this development does and does not consist in. One obvious challenge to such a claim is the sheer ubiquity of vicious behaviours in sports. Social scientific research abounds that shows how sports can be a vehicle for child abuse, misogyny, sexism and of course racism. To my knowledge, however, despite the voluminous literature on racism and sport, there has been no attempt to give an aretaic account of it: that is to say, of racism as a vice. This chapter attempts to articulate a clearer picture of the repugnance of racism as it manifests itself in sport and to develop a virtue-ethical perspective by considering racism as a vice. In particular, I explore questions of responsibility and culpability for both committed and less-entrenched racism in sports.

I argue against the binary understanding of persons as either racist/not racist which brings with it an undifferentiated moral response. Thus understood, the almost universal acceptance that racism is wrong somewhat ironically brings its own problems. It is sometimes suggested by anti-racist scholars that there is an unwillingness to acknowledge certain practices, within and outside sport, as racist because that might require us to recognise, at least potentially, the racism within ourselves. More importantly, for my purposes at least, the homogeneity of moral opprobrium attached to racist attitudes, policies or utterances effectively carries disproportionate sanctions and thereby threatens to jeopardise more considered, and perhaps more productive, ethical responses to it. I explore here the desirability of imagining a scale of severity rather than the more common but analytically crude binary categories of racist/non racist. In an attempt to do justice to the complexities of the debate I offer what I hope is a more nuanced appreciation of racism, taking account of context, intentionality and the centrality of the trait to the identity of the person alleged to be racist. To do this I consider the case of a high-profile football commentator and former manager, Ron Atkinson, whose racist remarks lost him his job in 2004. In arguing for an ethically salient distinction between a racist act and a racist character I offer a clearer it for a few friends, then you do it for money.'[16] We must remind ourselves continuously that professionalism demands *much* more.

I am conscious that the burden of my argument has rested on the explication of theoretical weaknesses as applied to a single principle for professional conduct. Ironically enough my argument requires that it be taken on that trust which I have briefly argued is definitive of professionalism; that, indeed, extrapolation can further be made to other principles, rules and codes.[17] This is one of the areas that needs far greater explication in the same way as we need to explicate more fully the relationships that exist between rules and virtues themselves. There is, of course, no use in philosophers who favour rule-based ethics castigating their otherwise inclined colleagues as 'allergic to principles', or in virtue theorists characterising rule-reliant adversaries disparagingly as 'psychologically phobic'. The debate must instead focus on the complexity of their unavoidable relations. I have not eschewed rules altogether from codes of conduct but have instead focused on their variety, the difficulties necessarily entailed in their interpretation and application as well as their characteristic underdetermination. Codes of conduct are indeed indispensable to the safety-net task of catching those who will be unprofessional in their conduct and enabling their punishment and/or expulsion. What they cannot do, and what they should not be expected to do, is to have any great effect in ensuring ethical behaviour per se. In highlighting this shortfall, I have focused positively on the role that virtues play in professional life and ethical explanation and have argued the necessary incompleteness of ethical evaluation and motivation in their absence. I have hinted at difficulties entailed in conceiving professionals as technocrats, whether merely as hired hands or providers of expertise and how, following Koehn, we might more profitably look to the notion of trust as characteristic of the basis of professionalism rather than to mere rule-responsibility and the legally inspired 'moral minimalism' that so often accompanies it. In the particularity and richness of personal relationships such as that exists most commonly between coach and performer, the rules, I fancy, play very little motivating or explanatory roles.[18]

conceptual schema for evaluating beliefs and behaviour in this highly charged arena. I conclude the chapter with one of the finest examples of role modelling by sportspersons, the Zimbabwean cricketers Andrew Flower and Henry Olonga, who were prepared to forego their participation in the Cricket World Cup of 2003 in order to declare objectionable the racism of their own nation's political policies.

Understanding racism

Among social scientific scholars the concept of 'race' is a discredited biological concept. Hence in sociological writings 'race' commonly appears within inverted commas, and is taken to refer to the antipathy that people experience because of their appearance/inheritance, which arises from other people's designation of them as 'others'. But this discredit has a longer history than might be assumed. The invidious tendency to consider racial characteristics as scientifically endorsed rather than as the product of a merely convenient biological classification as Darwin had intended (Appiah, 1996) often goes unnoticed even in modern times. Yet Ralph Waldo Emerson had challenged and discredited the convenient race classification well over a century ago:

> An ingenious anatomist has written a book to prove that races are imperishable, but nations are pliant constructions, easily changed or destroyed. But this write did not found his assumed races on any necessary law, disclosing their idea or metaphysical necessity; nor did he on the other hand count with precision the existing races and settle the true bounds; a point of nicety, and the popular test of his theory. The individuals at the extremes of divergence in one race of men are as unalike as the wolf to the lapdog. Yet each variety shades down imperceptibly into the next, and you cannot draw the line where one race begins or ends. Hence every writer makes a different count. Blumenbach reckons five races; Humboldt three; and Mr Pickering, who lately in our Exploring Expedition thinks he saw all kinds of men that can be on the planet, makes eleven.
>
> (cited in Appiah, 1996: 68–9)

The emergence of genetic discoveries threw into the dustbin of scientific anachronism the idea of there existing separate races in nature. Nevertheless, despite its redundancy the continuing significance of racism as a social process and lived experienced still resonates today and shows no ready signs of giving way. Wieviorka (1995) draws on Guillaumin's (1972: 63) explanation that 'imaginary and real races play the same role in the social processes and are therefore identical as regards their social function'. As a falsehood or product of bad science Massara (2007: 498–9) argues that race is ontologically false. Although, in opposition to the ideas put forward here, he neatly captures their stance: 'race cannot tell us anything about who we really are as individuals – it does not function, that is as a causal explanation of behaviour – however strategically necessary in the short term the concept may prove for political resistance'. The use of the concept of 'racism' has been extended to a consideration of the treatment of ethnic groups and a range of signifiers that may or may not include skin colour (e.g. Miles, 1989). Whether or not it can legitimately be applied to the treatment of religious groups is a matter of some dispute in the literature (Hall, 1992; Modood, 1997; Solomos and Back, 1996).

In other writings the term 'racism' has been re-labelled to as the 'new racism' or 'cultural racism' (e.g. Back, 1996; Barker, 1981; Gilroy, 1987; Parekh, 1995). The terminology is designed to indicate a more defensive mode of racism that seeks (allegedly) more to preserve a given way of life against the incursions of those labelled 'outsiders' rather than a direct assault on those so labelled. This can raise uncomfortable issues around the difference between asserting one's identity as a statement of difference, and racism. Paradoxically, as Solomos and Back (1996: 27) put it, this line of argument 'can produce a racist effect while denying that this effect is the result of racism'.

Some writers, such as Connolly (2000), suggest it is not just direct actions, but all those beliefs, behaviours, practices and processes that contribute either directly or indirectly to the racialisation of certain groups that can be designated as racist. Connolly also notes that this is seen to arise because of the way in which the signification of certain groups comes to 'shape the development of future social relations, institutions and processes' (2000: 503). Similarly, in a passage where it is easy to draw parallels with sport, Macpherson (1999: 17) noted:

> Unwitting racism can arise because of lack of understanding, ignorance or mistaken beliefs. It can arise from well intentioned but patronising words or actions. It can arise from unfamiliarity with the behaviour or cultural traditions of people or families from minority ethnic communities. It can arise from racist stereotyping of black people as potential criminals or troublemakers. Often this arises out of uncritical self-understanding born out of an inflexible police ethos of the 'traditional' way of doing things. Furthermore such attitudes can thrive in a tightly knit community, so that there can be a collective failure to detect and to outlaw this breed of racism.

In keeping with these anti-racist positions, it is necessary to hold on to the ideas of 'race' and 'racism' despite their having no genuine ontology because they function wrongly to privilege or derogate social groups. Within the broad framework that this represents, the basis for prejudice and discrimination is multidimensional, embracing culture, ethnicity and nationality.

D'Souza (1995: 27) presents an account of racism as 'an ideology of intellectual or moral superiority based upon the biological characteristics of race'.

This hierarchical portrayal of superior and inferior races is obviously central to white supremacists, but offers an incomplete definition of racism. This can be seen particularly clearly in the sporting arena where the apparent and widespread celebration of black sporting prowess has failed to eradicate racism.

More subtle variations of racism play along the borders of ethnocentrism. It is not always clear where to draw the line when what is perceived as benign ethnocentrism may be perceived as more exclusionary and properly deserving of the label racism. In an effort to counteract protestations of innocence it has been suggested that an action should be deemed to be racist if it is perceived as such by the person subjected to that action (see, for example, the report of the inquiry into the police investigation into the murder of the British African-Caribbean schoolboy, Stephen Lawrence: Macpherson, 1999). This position effectively embodies a relativistic argument (typical of some social constructivists) that reflects an inadequate way of conceptualizing the phenomenon of racism. If it is desirable to argue that people may be being racist even when they protest their innocence (as I do), then it is necessary to argue that people may not be being racist when others believe they are. Racism, to corrupt a well-known phrase, cannot therefore merely be 'in the eye of the beholder'.

Other writers have sought to dismantle conceptions of what they see as falsely unified accounts of racism, drawing attention to its variegated nature, its different forms and levels. Carrington and McDonald (2001), for example, illustrate dimensions of racism in cricket that extend beyond the immediate form of crude racial abuse. They see two further levels evidenced through racial stereotyping of cultural essentialisms that discriminate against black and Asian people, and racial exclusion based on a conception of white Englishness that creates a form of institutional racism serving to limit access to socially valued opportunities. Others have stressed the importance of analysing racism within the triplex of concepts: 'race', 'class' and 'nation' (e.g. Balibar and Wallerstein, 1991).

Wellman attempts to demonstrate that racism is not simply reducible to the concepts of 'bigotry' or 'prejudice'. Instead he sees racism as 'culturally acceptable beliefs that defend social advantages that are based on race' (Wellman, 1993: 4). I have considerable sympathy with the proposition that we all have embedded racial constructions affecting the way we think and behave towards each other, and that most, if not all, of us in the West at least, operate within social structures that favour certain ethnic groups. Indeed, it is important that people recognise this before they become too free in their criticism of others.

Without gainsaying the possibility of institutional racism, or the defence of social advantage, there is an important distinction to be noted between sometimes behaving in a way that reflects thinking grounded in racially prejudicial thought and being 'a committed racist'. Note this distinction is not backsliding. Nor is it intended to exculpate those whose racism is simply not as strong as others'. The distinction is clearly put in Aristotle's *Nichomachean Ethics* between an act and a character (see Williams, 1980: 190). It is important to uphold in order to not treat as equals those who behave in a racist manner unknowingly and those who do so characteristically and reflectively as part of a chosen way of life.

To examine whether one might exhibit racist behaviour without properly being a racist, consider a paradigmatic case of racist language. In his discussion of the use of the word 'nigger' in the context of the legacy of white supremacy, Blum (2002: 19) notes that its use by certain young blacks as a term of affection and bonding is a context-bound use that has confused many whites, and is objected to by many, especially older, blacks. This leads to the point that our evaluations of racism, though not relativistic, are deeply context-sensitive (cf. Wellman, 1993). To treat them otherwise is not (socio)logical. True, there are actions that require little understanding of context to be appreciated, but some knowledge of context is always necessary to evaluate social action.

In order to appreciate the intentionality of racism we need to appreciate historically the shifting attitudes towards racism. Nonetheless, as Blum (2002: 18) argues:

> In general, people beyond a certain age should recognise what is racist; their moral responsibility for perpetrating racism when they do not recognise it is analogous to the fault of citizens who cause injury through negligence rather than direct intent. They could be reasonably expected to recognise or anticipate the moral damage. Except for people with extraordinarily sheltered lives and upbringings, ignorance of racism does not absolve one from responsibility, although, everything else being equal, intentionally demeaning a racial group is morally more blameworthy than unintentionally doing so.

To some the possibility of racist actions or attitudes being 'innocent' or 'ignorant' is politically indefensible. Nevertheless, it *is* logically possible. And if we find those to whom it might apply, however unlikely, our position is that we should not treat it in the same way as fully conscious or premeditated racism. In estimating the potential grounds for latitude the following questions might be useful:

1   Can racist beliefs be held, or racist acts be performed, by persons we *ought* not to label 'racists'?
2   Is it helpful to articulate an underlying scale of racism?
3   When does racist thought, feeling or action genuinely form a part of one's character *as* racist?

There are those who will reject (1) the logical possibility, and/or (2) the normative justification that such questions attempt to create a space for. I believe, however, that the preservation of these possibilities is both logically possible and morally desirable.

If sociological understandings of action are always to be context-sensitive, then our moral responses should be the same. Children raised in a racist family who merely mouth racist sentiments are, however, less culpable than their elders. If it is true that our moral responses to racism should be sensitive to these features, perhaps we can extend that list. Consider the level of entrenchment of racist beliefs. Some, who though prejudiced (and thus deserving of moral opprobrium), when challenged might concede that their views are based on ignorance or prejudice born of reprehensible socialisation. To what extent ought we to treat such a person *in the same way* as an otherwise intelligent white supremacist? In such a case might it not be better to think of them as 'ethically disabled' (Jacobs, 2001) and therefore not fully responsible for their agency? The level of awareness of one's racism appears to be an important contextual feature to be taken into account in the moral register of racism presented below.

The level of premeditation or reflective awareness should also be considered. Contrast the deliberate use of racist language to antagonise an opponent (e.g. 'sledging' in cricket or 'trash talking' in basketball) with an abusive racial remark blurted out in the heat of the moment. It might be appropriate to ask to what extent the racist remark is characteristic of the person's other conduct or 'merely a lapse'. This is not an apology for the equivalent of racist Freudian slips. Yet if we acknowledge that, for the sake of argument, anyone over 50 years old (in Britain or the USA at least) was brought up in a society that harboured deep and widespread racist prejudices, then it is reasonable to suspect that their early socialisation contained at least some pernicious social and moral views based improperly on racialised characteristics.

While modern moral theories in some sense mirror the rationalist idea of universal reason – and hence universal moral registers (impartiality, universality, prescriptivity) – virtue-theoretical evaluations of moral character and agency, as we have seen, pay significant attention to the forces of habituation in the learning of our im/moral responses as patterns of thought, feeling and action. Of course the questions remain open as to what we should do with our knowledge of such habituation in and outside sport; how it is that people come to hold racist views, feel racist emotions and act in racist ways. We need to consider this properly in our evaluation of persons, but not to use it as a ready excuse for racists proper, whose acts and attitudes are not merely 'disabled' but self-consciously vicious. Of the latter, the more vicious end of the racist register, there are others for whom such abuse is not out of character in time of stress, but reveals their 'true' character.

Such non-benign contextual features require moral responses to racism to be classified in a more subtle manner than the in/out, yes/no binary divide of racist/not-racist. We need a vocabulary that qualitatively discriminates appropriately and does so in an ethically self-conscious way. The philosophical task as I see it is to set out the moral scales of racism from innocence, ignorance and ambivalence on to outright bigotry, and show why this more conceptually and morally nuanced vocabulary is important. Only after this is done can we consider the extent to which racist actions or utterances genuinely form part of the character of the person labelled 'racist'.

Articulating the moral repugnance of racism

To help resolve these questions I draw heavily on the work of Lawrence Blum (2002). Blum draws upon the widely used distinctions of personal, social and institutional racism, and we concur with his suggestion that merely to consider racism individualistically (Allport, 1987) or socially (Ture and Hamilton, 1992) is to replace one partial definition with another. However, we focus here on the individual while being aware that, in its ontology, racism can never in reality be separated from other levels. Blum (2002: 9–10) writes:

> We do better to accept the plurality of items that can be racist (beliefs, institutions, systems, attitudes, acts and so on), without thinking that one of these needs to be the foundation of all the others. Personal, social and institutional racism are each morally problematic, in at least partially distinct ways.

His starting point is a categorisation of racial discrimination/differentiation derived from his assertion that all forms of racism relate to two general themes or paradigms: *inferiorisation* and *antipathy*. Blum's inferiorising racism is expressed in attitudes and actions that variously show disrespect, contempt, derision, derogation or are demeaning. While an inferiorising racist generally thinks that the racial other is inferior, sometimes people believe their own group to be inferior. In sport we have witnessed interesting reversals in this process. For example, the previous common presumption of the inferiority of black athletes has been inverted in many events. The populist position has become one that asserts that black athletes are 'naturally' better equipped to run the 100 metres and other power-based activities involved in, for example, American football. But even on its own terms this prejudice is limited since one cannot ignore how many more Olympic and World Championship medals are won over 800 and 1500 metres by Sudanese and Moroccan athletes, nor the complete dominance of Kenyan long-distance runners on the track. The implication is that black athletes have an unfair advantage so there is no point in 'our' valiant men and women trying to compete. In the 1990s there was even discussion of limiting athletes from African nations on the televised American running circuit.

In Blum's construction, inferiorising and antipathy racists are distinct because the former do not necessarily hate the target of their beliefs. It is quite possible for them to have a paternalistic concern for people they regard as their inferiors. So not every race-hater is supremacist, nor is every supremacist a race-hater. Moreover, antipathy might be based on feelings of inferiority as well as superiority. Blum argues that 'racial prejudice' is illustrative of the antipathy theme. Although the linguistic root suggests a prejudging of something precipitously, racial prejudice, he suggests, is a generalised antipathy towards another racial group, or members thereof, merely in virtue of that membership. He draws upon Allport's (1987) definition that prejudice is antipathy based on erroneous generalisation, but argues in addition that all antipathy to a racial group must be considered prejudicial since the variegated nature of the group would deny the validity of grounds for antipathy to the entire group based on race-founded suppositions. The notion of racial prejudice, as we have noted, can cut across the conscious/unconscious division. One may have prejudices towards others and be unaware of it. Much racism falls into the category of racist views without the people holding them necessarily identifying self-consciously with those views. A reasonable anti-racist expectation in those circumstances is that, when made aware of the damaging consequences of such prejudice, those who do not on reflection subscribe to racist values ought to seek to instigate change in themselves. Blum (2002: 13) modifies Allport's definition:

> [P]rejudice is a kind of antipathy, toward a race-defined group and would by my definition appear to count as a form of 'racism'. Indeed racial prejudice is often called 'racism'. But, 'prejudice' often implies dislike or antipathy, but not necessarily hatred or strong antipathy. . . . Because prejudice is, in general, a less malevolent attitude than hatred and intense hostility, it is less morally evil. It is not clear whether we should call weaker forms of racial prejudice 'racism'. These forms should, in any case, evoke opprobrium in their own right.

Thus, someone who might typically be considered as racist may yet have grounds for less than total moral condemnation. There are a few cases where a lack of moral agency (e.g. the very young, the severely intellectually challenged) may to a certain extent yield cases where there cannot be ascription of responsibility. There are also clear-cut cases of vicious racists whose attitudes may be the result of inferiorising or antipathy or both. While the former may be racial supremacists in less corrosive ways, still heavy moral opprobrium attaches to them while antipathy-based racists appear to be *ceteris paribus* the group to be most morally reviled. There is a rather grey area, then, involving those who hold racist views, beliefs or attitudes, or who commit racist acts on a non-regular basis, that we need to consider more fully. If vice is typically the opposite of virtue, what grounds are there for thinking that a certain person exhibits the vice of racism? Which beliefs mould it? What language evidences this? Which acts typify it?

Racism and a vice

While the dominant moral theories of utilitarianism and deontology are diametrically opposed to each other in the direction of their moral schemes, they are similar in form. Just as deontological concerns direct our moral salience to universal rights and duties that we 'know' to be true before we act (don't harm people, don't disrespect them, allow free speech and movement to all, etc.), utilitarianism pushes us to maximise good outcomes while at the same time treating all persons as equal in our calculations. As guides to the moral life deontology, or duty-based ethics, is thought of as an ethics of the 'right action', whereas utilitarianism is a teleological theory of the 'good living'.[1] It may at first be difficult to see how utilitarianism can make sense of the idea of racial wrongs. One of the foundational premises of utilitarianism is that everyone must be treated as equals so racism is ruled out *ab initio*. Beyond arguing that maximising the good entails the calculation of pleasures/utility of all relevant persons, utilitarianism offers little in the way of theoretical resources to understand the wrongness of racism, though its consistent application (the impartial treatment of all, considered equally, in order to maximize happiness in the world) might help significantly to remove racism.

Deontology fares better. Sharing the principle of impartial treatment of all persons, and the universalisation of rights and duties, it illuminates proper guides to conduct in its foundational ideas such as equal treatment, respect and autonomy among others. Nevertheless, deontology with its resolute focus on moral *reasons* is commonly held to be inadequate in terms of moral psychology. It holds, in the classic form of moral cognitivism from Kant and Plato, that merely by knowing the right thing to do one will act in accordance with the dictates of moral reason; moral reasoning and moral action are one. Such a theory holds no space for either weakness of will or for inconsistencies of thought and action. In Chapter 8 I attempt, in some small way, to defend Kant against this pernicious characterisation by considering some remarks within his theory of virtue as opposed to his overall moral philosophy of duties. Virtue ethics is more hospitable to social and psychological factors, attempting to take seriously the agency of embedded and embodied agents in the particularity of time and place.

To think of someone as a racist is a particular way of conceiving someone as possessed of a vicious character. A racist character is not typically revealed in a one-time activation, but through a complex and interrelated pattern of thoughts, feelings and acts relating to inferiorising and/or antipathy racism over time. The particular configuration of this patterning will be person-specific and derivative of the usual catalogue of social indexicals: age, embodiment, class, gender, intelligence, sexual orientation, wealth and so on. It may range, as we have seen, from unacceptable paternalism to wicked subjugation and violence. Equally, contrast the disaffected youth for whom overtly racist political parties become a source of self-esteem with the controlling mind of the organisation; or with the international sportsmen who were apologists for apartheid sport. All are racists, but surely of different depth and intensity. Racists are not a 'natural kind'; they do not form a homogeneous class. What can be said more generally though, is that to ascribe the condemnatory title 'racist' to a person, like any other aspect of their character, it should be one that typically informs their modes of being in the world in relatively consistent ways that they understand to be part of their identity:

> A racist *person* is not merely someone who commits one racist act or acts on a racist motive on a small number of occasions. Motives and attitudes such as bigotry, antipathy, and contempt must be embedded in the person's psychological makeup as traits of character. In this sense being a racist is like being hateful, dishonest, or cruel, in implying an ingrained pattern of thought and feeling as well as action.
>
> (Blum, 2002: 14–15)

Rather than a binary thing, perhaps it is better to think of racism in subtle gradations, and/or subtle inflections activated by particular contexts. This is why the question 'When is a racist a racist?' is unhelpful. There may be cases when one act is sufficiently malevolent, but more typically there will not be. Blum argues that holding one racist view, or making one racist remark, or telling one racist joke ought not necessarily induce the label racist:

> The beliefs themselves were genuinely racist, but belief in them had not been deeply enough rooted in her psychological makeup to make her 'a racist'. She must be *genuinely committed* to and invested in racist beliefs in order to be a racist.
>
> (Blum, 2002: 21; emphasis added)

Of course, everything hangs on what is meant by the elliptical phrase 'genuinely committed' here. The committed racist in his or her actions is ethically inexcusable. No one would seriously dispute that (except, presumably, a racist). However, defining a person as 'racist' may not require so strict a condition as 'genuine commitment'; reserving the term only for 'genuinely committed' racists may be to 'throw the baby out with the bathwater':

> Calling the belief in question, or the believing of it, racist, emotionally overloads a discussion of the validity or worthiness of the belief and leads us to think that because a view may have undesirable racial implications, it should be dismissed prior to discussion.
>
> (Blum, 2002: 22).

The point is well made, but fails to accord fully with some of the more subtle ways in which racist attitudes move from embryo to actuality. We need to attend to the processes of racialisation that are present in contextualised evaluations of those we consider more or less racists. These are captured well by Connolly (2000: 503) who, following Miles, notes:

> The signification of certain groups is not only grounded in the specific social relations that exist, but will also come to inform and shape the

Sources and degrees of race-related actions/feelings/thoughts		
Ethically excusable	⟵ ⟶	Ethically inexcusable
↕		↕
ethically disabled	ethically immature	committed racist
ignorance	misperception/misrecognition	evil
one-off racist remark (out of character)	occasional	typical (in character)
unintentional	negligent	pre-meditated
incapable of change	amenable to change/education	entrenched

Figure 6.1 A racist register

> development of future social relations, institutions and processes. As such . . . all those beliefs, behaviours practices and processes that contribute, either directly or indirectly, to the racialisation of certain groups can be designated as racist . . . [I]t is not just overt racist attitudes and discriminatory and exclusionary practices that constitute racism, but all of the more subtle ideas and processes, however indirect and unintentional, that tend to maintain and reproduce the racialisation.

There can be no sharp distinctions here that will be conceptually felicitous, though those more politically inclined may say that the price of greater subtlety is simply not worth paying given the scope of the problem. A register of race as a vice would need to pay attention at least to the factors outlined in Figure 6.1.

What no typology can achieve is a complex grasp of the relationality of agency, context and structure. Nor should it aim to. In articulating this register I am merely trying in a preliminary way to draw attention to the degrees of viciousness that are often unhelpfully lumped together under the label 'racist'. Yet the moral economy of racism must be more differentiated than this. By contrast, I am suggesting that there exist degrees of culpability that allow us to differentiate the viciousness of different kinds of characters labelled racist. Consider the following example:

Cricketers and baseball players commonly rail against the decisions of umpires. In a recent study of cricketers in the north of England, Long *et al.* (1997) report that one of the Asian batters in the study protested that he had been the victim of a bad decision by an umpire, protesting: 'I was never "out". He gave me out because I'm Asian . . . and he did that for three others.' The perception of racist behaviour makes it a racial issue, but does not mean that any racism has necessarily been committed. That is to say, a perception of racism by an apparently maltreated other is neither a necessary nor sufficient condition of its existence. In this case, the umpire may indeed have been racist, but he may also have been an incompetent umpire judging them incorrectly out (or struck out in baseball). Or he may not be racist in any way shape or form and the batter is merely using the racist slur to bring pressure to bear on the umpire for future decisions or to mask their own incompetence. There is also the possibility that the umpire is indeed a repugnant racist but feels bound in this situation by the ethos and laws of cricket to make impartial decisions.

Just as the belief that one is the subject of racist sentiments does not automatically mean that another is a racist, so another's denial that they are being racist is insufficient to deny the truth of the assertion. The remark or behaviour does not stand alone. Consider a circumstance in which a player or official has told a racist joke, used racial abuse or made a decision on the basis of some racial presumption. Interpretation of the significance of that might vary depending upon whether the perpetrator: says sorry (then or later) or shakes hands with a 'Well played mate' at the end of the game; insists it was 'just in the heat of the moment'; does so in a team founded on the principles of cultural pluralism; or elsewhere engages in actions to counter racism. Even then there are other contextual layers that those involved will use to arrive at their interpretation of meaning. It was clear that the black players in Long *et al.* (2000) viewed and responded to incidents in a differentiated manner depending upon the context. Quite properly, it seems to me, they attached varying degrees of moral opprobrium to those whom they perceived had acted in the 'heat of the moment incidents' to those whose behaviours displayed a clearer pattern of consistency.

If virtues and vices are enduring traits of character, it should mean that the idea of a one-off racist would be an oxymoron. To be a racist it must be part of one's character; one's relatively settled dispositions to think, feel and act in regular and interrelated ways. As I have said above, this makes judging whether a person is a racist, in the light of the register above, a more complex matter than some allow.

In their discussion of identity and agency, Rorty and Wong (1997: 20) attempt to explore the questions one might ask in order to judge whether a given trait is central to one's character. Their questions have salience for a more nuanced understanding of racism as a vice. They list seven ways in which a trait may be central in virtue of:

- the degree of its objective ramification, the extent to which other traits (that is dispositions to beliefs, desires, habits, attitudes and actions) are dependent on it;
- the degree of its contextual or regional ramification, that is, the extent to which a trait is exemplified across distinctive spheres (e.g. public and private domains, work and leisure) and across different types of

relationships (as they are differentiated by gender, status, class, age, etc.);

- the degree for which it is difficult for a person to change the trait (which is often a function of its temporal persistence);
- the degree of its social ramification, the extent to which the trait affects the way the person is categorized and treated by others;
- the extent to which it is dominant in situations that require coping with stress or conflict;
- the extent to which it is dominant when it conflicts with other traits (e.g. when generosity conflicts with vengefulness); and
- the degree to which it is appropriated as important in that the person regards herself as radically changed if the trait is lost or strongly modified. Such appropriations may, but need not be, explicitly articulated; they can be sporadic or contextualized; a person can appropriate a trait without succeeding in acting from it habitually. Sometimes what matters to a person's identity is that she centrally strives to strengthen and exercise a trait. Important traits are often also the focus of self-evaluation and self-esteem.

It is useful to illustrate the power of these questions in the context of a real example from sports. In 2004 the veteran English football manager, commentator and pundit, Ron Atkinson, resigned from his job immediately upon hearing that remarks he had made about the lacklustre performance of Chelsea's French defender Marcel Desailly in the European Champions League had in fact not been completely "off-air" but had been broadcast to several international audiences. Big Ron (as he was affectionately referred to) remarked: 'He's what is known in some schools as a fucking lazy thick nigger.' Naturally, and properly, the media frenzy that followed was immediate and severe. But where ought we to place Atkinson on the racist register above?

At first sight it appears to be a one-off racist remark that was not premeditated. But does this make him merely ethically disabled? His immediate resignation shows some level of remorse and recognition of the wrong committed. Much will hang on whether the remark was the product on an entrenched disposition or whether it was "out of character" so to speak. This is where things get philosophically interesting. To go further down this road we need to ask some conceptual questions about the centrality of the disposition to this attitude/remark and some empirical ones about his biography. Rorty and Wong's questions become particularly helpful here and I want to situate them in the Atkinson case along with the remarks of other media commentators from within and outside of sport.

Atkinson's remarks seem to be without objective ramification. That is to say, the racist trait does not appear to form a central part of his identity. After his resignation and the widespread condemnation of his comments, Atkinson made several protestations about his career being one that had been supportive of players of colour. During the 1970s, as a manager Atkinson had helped to develop several British African-Caribbean players not only to top division football but also the point where they represented their national team: England. This is one reason why so many people were shocked. Atkinson remarked himself: 'What I said is racist, I understand that, but I'm not a racist.' Moreover, he insisted in an interview with the editor of *New Nation* (a leading newspaper of the black community): 'I've offended nobody more than me at the moment. Christ almighty it's cost me roughly a million quid. I've done my penance.' Beyond the blasphemy that some might take offence at, one must ask whether Atkinson has the conceptual wherewithal to distinguish between penance and sanction. It's clear he has lost out financially and that, to his credit, he did not wait to be sacked. What is there to be said of the contextual ramification of the trait? Is Big Ron a racist in private but not in public (or at least not normally in public)? Critics have suggested that this is not the first such slip he has made. I shall discuss them further below. The point seems ambiguous but resonates with the idea of the social ramification of the trait. Clearly Atkinson's capital has fallen through the floor with nearly all sports fans and the wider public. He has not been associated with racist remarks and they hitherto formed no part of his social standing – unlike those whose standing, say, in a white supremacist movement is predicated on their racist credentials, Atkinson's certainly is not. Moreover, in his interview, Atkinson inadvertently displayed all of his non-politically correct credentials in his casual acceptance of the historical use of derisory language (queer, nigger etc.). One thing in Atkinson's defence is the clear idea that his remark is at odds with his promotion of black players within the football teams he has managed. Whether this is equity or expediency (it might be argued, though I think unfairly, that the black players were simply the only ones of any quality he could afford or attract) is open to question though certain black players who played for him appear to give support to his testimony. He has succeeded in his career without the trait; he does not depend on it for his success or self-esteem. It seems clear that the trait of racism is not central to his identity. Though the opprobrium that flew his way was well deserved, and though his utterance was utterly repugnant, it seems fair to conclude that despite his racist act(s) he himself is not possessed of a committed racist character.

Ron's racism, sports reporting and other courageous role models

Some media colleagues offered levels of support for Atkinson's person though not his remarks. A fellow football TV pundit, the septuagenarian[2] Jimmy Hill, offered the quasi defence that the remarks were no more than 'fun' between footballers. Hill, a former anchor man of the most popular British football programme of the last 30 or so years is reported to have said the following on the web site for Football Against Racism in Europe (2004):

> In that context, you wouldn't think that words like 'n****r' were particularly insulting: it would be funny. Without meaning to insult any black

men, it's us having fun. What about people who make jokes about my long chin? I mean, n****r is black – so we have jokes where we call them n****rs because they're black. Why should that be any more of an offence than someone calling me chinny?

Now Hill is well known in the UK to have a pronounced chin but to equate his facial characteristic with the use of a word so historically loaded with disrespect and the fundamental denial of human rights, coupled with abusive derogation of Desailly's character, seems not so much bizarre but the product of a limited intellect. Despite Hill's being in his seventies, and Atkinson in his sixties, it seems clear that both person's character have been forged in racist times and neither has been able to break free of those limiting shackles.

On the basis that racial groups have been historically subjected to destructive forms of prejudice, stigma, exclusion and discrimination, Blum (2002: 96) notes that 'a somewhat greater wrongfulness attaches to racial differentiations than to others. Race *is* an especially invidious category, both uniquely inferiorising and uniquely divisive'. In a similar vein, Muhammad Ali taunted Joe Frazier before their first fight for the Heavyweight Championship of the World. This was in response to Frazier's refuse to call Ali by his adopted Islamic name and, instead, by his former name Cassius Clay Ali had called Frazier an 'Uncle Tom' meaning to demean Frazier whom he mocked as a gorilla; an unthinking beast, a person of colour insufficiently intelligent or articulate enough to challenge the hegemonic racial order, one happy (and with complicity) to preserve the racially based social hierarchies. Moreover, in the one-sided and bitter fight that followed, Ali berated Frazier 'what's my name? . . . what's my name?' repeatedly whilst brutally beating him. In 2001 Ali offered an apology in the *New York Times* but Frazier, though appearing to accept it, later remarked that the apology had been made to the paper rather than him. In Atkinson's case, the instant apology might incline us to move Atkinson to the centre of the register in Figure 6.1, but if subsequent events confirm that this is representative of an underlying trait we would return him to the right of the register.

If Hill's remarks are those of denial, how much better are the inflammatory remarks of the columnist Darcus Howe?:

Football managers tend to be dictatorial brutes. They treat their charges with a paternal brutality that would have any father hauled up in court for child abuse. These men, almost all of them white, behave in a way that would not be tolerated in any other area of modern society. They infect the players with the brutishness they dispense. As a consequence, women and blacks – perceived as the weaker sections of society – are deemed the lowest of the low. Gang sex and racial barracking are the stock-in-trade of players. The game has become a sewer containing all sorts of filth not permitted elsewhere.

Atkinson is up to his neck in it. He pleaded a lapse in an otherwise unblemished career, which included signing several black players when he was manager of West Bromwich Albion. Yet Atkinson once alluded to a Cameroonian player's mother who, he claimed, lived up a tree in Africa. He boasted about how he had made Cyrille Regis, one of the blacks he signed while at West Brom, travel to away games at the back of the bus, as blacks were once forced to travel in the American South. Ian Wright, the Arsenal and England player, once asked a players' representative to warn Atkinson about his racial jibes.

(Howe, 2004)

It appears then that, given the truth of the claims above, Atkinson was no one-off racist. The trait had surfaced elsewhere in public but was clearly at odds with others in his character. But having made his point, Howe then descends into a diatribe of disrespect that robs him of the moral high ground. He continued:

So steeped is football in racist muck that nobody thought Atkinson's behaviour exceptional. Even black people accepted it. He demanded from them, and got, gratitude for letting darkies into the game. Hence several black players were at the front of the queue saying that, though his remarks on Desailly were wrong, he is no racist.

Then what is he? A leader in the vanguard of anti-racism? All I have to say to Atkinson is: "Get thee hence." In case he doesn't know what that means, I'll translate into dressing-room jargon: "Fuck off."

(Howe, 2004)

But if we are to understand racism in sport in the round, it is appropriate to ask what kind of response is ethically called for to such situations; what is the virtuous response to racist sports journalism or reporting? At first sight it appears that Howe's diatribe has some provenance from no lesser figure than Aristotle, who argued that anger was the virtuous response to injustice. As we read on though, we find that it is not simply the angry response that is just:

[A]nyone can be angry – that is easy – or give or spend money; but to do this to the right person, to the right extent, at the right time, with the right motive, and in the right way, *that* is not for everyone, nor is it easy; wherefore goodness is both rare and laudable and noble.

(*NE* II Bk. 9; 1109a25–30)

And later, in a slightly different context, Aristotle notes: 'It is not easy to determine both how and with whom and on what provocation and how long one should be angry . . .' (*NE* II Bk. 9; 1109b14–16).

Of course there is some irony in quoting Aristotle here. For like other great philosophers he too was a hostage to the times. He had a conception of aristocratic nobility that appeared to influence heavily his conception of the good life for 'man'. Slaves and women were distinctly second class.

The idea of racism in sports has a long history. Though shorter, there is also a history of defiance against racial barriers, which perhaps achieved its epitome when in front of the Aryan supremacist Adolf Hitler, Jesse Owens won his Olympic sprint title in 1936 in Berlin. More recently, and against the racially segregated and vengeful backlash against white imperial rule in Zimbabwe, one black and one white cricketer stood together in defiance of the widespread racially motivated violent repatriation of land, and unlawful acquisition of property under the acquiescence (and some would say active support of) President Mugabe. On the eve of the Cricket World Cup, to be hosted by Zimbabwe for the first time, Andrew Flower and Henry Olonga, two of their leading players, wore black arm bands during a World Cup match to protest at their nation's racist policies. Not since the 'black power' protest of Tommy Smith and his fellow American athlete John Carlos in the Mexico Olympics had sportsmen or women put their head above the parapet to enter the political arena. Flower and Olonga jointly made the following pronouncement to the media:

> It is a great honour for us to take the field today to play for Zimbabwe in the World Cup.
>
> We feel privileged and proud to have been able to represent our country.
>
> We are, however, deeply distressed about what is taking place in Zimbabwe in the midst of the World Cup and do not feel that we can take the field without indicating our feelings in a dignified manner and in keeping with the spirit of cricket.
>
> We cannot in good conscience take to the field and ignore the fact that millions of our compatriots are starving, unemployed and oppressed.
>
> We are aware that hundreds of thousands of Zimbabweans may even die in the coming months through a combination of starvation, poverty and Aids.
>
> We are aware that many people have been unjustly imprisoned and tortured simply for expressing their opinions about what is happening in the country.
>
> We have heard a torrent of racist hate speech directed at minority groups.
>
> We are aware that thousands of Zimbabweans are routinely denied their right to freedom of expression.
>
> We are aware that people have been murdered, raped, beaten and had their homes destroyed because of their beliefs and that many of those responsible have not been prosecuted.
>
> We are also aware that many patriotic Zimbabweans oppose us even playing in the World Cup because of what is happening.

It is impossible to ignore what is happening in Zimbabwe. Although we are just professional cricketers, we do have a conscience and feelings.

We believe that if we remain silent that will be taken as a sign that either we do not care or we condone what is happening in Zimbabwe.

We believe that it is important to stand up for what is right.

We have struggled to think of an action that would be appropriate and that would not demean the game we love so much.

We have decided that we should act alone without other members of the team being involved because our decision is deeply personal and we did not want to use our senior status to unfairly influence more junior members of the squad.

We would like to stress that we greatly respect the ICC (International Cricket Council) and are grateful for all the hard work it has done in bringing the World Cup to Zimbabwe.

In all the circumstances we have decided that we will each wear a black armband for the duration of the World Cup.

In doing so we are mourning the death of democracy in our beloved Zimbabwe.

In doing so we are making a silent plea to those responsible to stop the abuse of human rights in Zimbabwe.

In doing so we pray that our small action may help to restore sanity and dignity to our nation.

Andrew Flower, Henry Olonga
(http: //news.bbc.co.uk/sport3/cwc2003/hi/newsid_2740000/newsid_
2744700/2744795.stm; accessed 10.4.06)

It seems to me this is as moving and powerful an example of a virtuous response to racism in society through the equally powerful medium of commercialised sports. Their act was courageous. They knew in publicly articulating the racism of the ruling regime they not merely ended their international sporting careers but would in all likelihood face retribution from the governmental security forces, not known for their polite treatment of political dissenters. And it did. The proclamation led to a warrant for the arrest of Olonga on the grounds of treason and the pair were forced into hiding and then to move from the country. Finally, their statement expresses the anger and indignation that is apt in response to injustice even if others will merely see it as a small corrective of the vicious historical white domination of that continent. It also shows how sport, far from standing outside of the ordinary business of living, can seek to act as a powerful agent for social change.

On a final note, I am conscious that the examples mentioned here are both males and I certainly do not wish to give the impression, perhaps suggested by Rorty (1980) that courage as bravery needs detoxifying. Rather these examples of courage show its fortitudinal aspect and not merely its risk-engendering aspects. Some examples to counter this tendency would include Julie Krone who, in 2004, won the Wilma Rudolph Courage Award recognising her

18-year career as a top-flight female jockey fighting both injury and prejudice alike. Equally, Hassiba Boulmerka had to overcome considerable sexist prejudice and threats against her performing in immodest Western athletics clothing in order to represent her country and eventually win the 1991 1500m gold medal at the World Championships (see Morgan, 1998). It is a sad fact indeed, then, that the less noble role models who so often attract the media's attention, such as Mike Tyson and Michael Vick, regrettably endure as racially stereotyped role models. Whether this is indicative of some unacknowledged racism in sports journalism is itself a moot point.

Conclusion

Research on racism in sport has tended to adopt an on/off conceptualisation of racism: either that person is a racist or they are not; that it was a racist incident or it was not. Such certitude is enviable, but does scant justice to a complex phenomenon. I recognise the problem with facilitating the nuanced appreciation of racism set out here, with its degrees of severity. Nonetheless, an appreciation of the register suggests the need for more subtly differentiated anti-racism campaigns and targeted actions in the playing, administering and reporting of sport. Of course, there is the danger that it may give succour to those not inclined to act to counter racism if they can justify inaction on the basis that there are others who are worse than they are. It might, however, be counter-productive to alienate potential allies in campaigns against racism in sport by berating them for what they consider to be minor indiscretions. In presenting this register of racism I have tried to open up a space for an appreciation of the significance of context, the possibility of a dynamic process of alignment on racial issues and the moral opprobrium that ought differentially to attach according to these factors.

7 Hubris, humility and humiliation

Vice and virtue in sporting communities

Introduction

In this chapter I extend the virtue-ethical discussion into a much talked of vice. In modern parlance it is typically, though with a certain loss of meaning, called arrogance. In the popular psychology of sports, some even go as far as to say it is a necessary condition of athletic success. In the Ancient Greek catalogue of virtues and vices it was known as hubris. In its moral gravitational field is its opposite, humility, and the emotion of humiliation, which is often spoken of in sports journalism. I argue that humiliation felt as a response to sporting defeat may indeed be rational. In distinguishing weak from strong humiliation I show that while the latter is reserved to those cases where one's moral status as a person has been assaulted, the former may be experienced by sportspersons who fail to observe certain standards of character and conduct. To make this case I argue that it is necessary to locate the felt humiliation against the hierarchical nature of sports identities and practice communities where the notion of honour still resonates. This context makes the idea of a highly committed sportsperson's humiliation more plausible than the idea that a heavy or unsuspected defeat necessarily occasions a mere blow to their self-esteem. I develop an account of humiliation in close relation to its conceptual cousins: shame, embarrassment, dignity and humility. I show how, paradigmatically, those who display the vice of hubris are predisposed to weak humiliation and illustrate such in a case study of the boxing contest between two of the greatest ever welterweight boxers, (Sugar) Ray Leonard and Roberto Duran.

Sports as practices: hierarchy and honour

I discussed in Chapter 3 the relevance of MacIntyre's thesis that modernity has loosened the bonds between fact and value, role and identity to the contexts of sports. Who we are and what we ought and ought not to do and be are commonly supposed to occupy separate realms. Unlike many other cultural practices, however, sports retain a strong vestige of the view that our roles still issue in clear directives for personal action and life-commitments.

Sports, with their structural exultation of the heroic, still offer a partial vision of what is honourable. While it may be the case that we are less clear of our role-related expectations in our everyday (post)modern lives, sports by contrast offer themselves as a bastion of social conservatism. How is this so? First, at an individual level, there is a strong explicitness surrounding the specified roles we occupy in the sports arenas. As goalkeeper, or umpire, or coach, the expectations attached to our positions are relatively circumscribed. Second, sports' ethoses too can be tightly bracketed in an explicit system of social structure that is notably hierarchical. It is in these structures, and the expectations that flow from the roles we occupy within them, that sports share many similarities with honour-based heroic societies.

I have noted how it has become commonplace in the literature to eschew previously dominant analytical accounts of sports and instead consider them under some social aspect as a 'practice'. One aspect commonly ignored in the application of a MacIntyrean account of social practices is the notion of ritual. I have argued in Chapter 1, following Sansone's (1988) anthropological thesis of sports as the sacrifice of energy, that the conceptualisation of sport as *inherently* social urges upon us a picture of elite sports at least as forms of public ceremonies and all forms of sports as partly both play and display. So I simply assert here that sports are the object of practice communities and that they are essentially forms of ritual and ceremony in and through, and for, those communities. The shared background presupposed in the very idea of sporting communities is essential. In more abstract political debates it can be difficult to make much sense of communitarian ideas such as 'shared ideals', 'shared goals' and 'shared purposes'. In the less diverse and less complex worlds of sports one scarcely has to work hard to conceptualise their contents and contexts. And it is in this idea, coupled with the Western heritage of sports as play and display, where spectators are thought to be part and parcel of the activity and not mere adornments, that the crucial structural context to the moral psychology of sports is given. Here individualised evaluations of winning and losing, of bragging and moaning about lost opportunities or refereeing incompetence are seen in the life of an evolving tradition of each and every sport, told and re-told by deed of print or word of mouth, of hard-earned success and undeserved 'tragedies', of hollow victories and glorious defeats.

It is often difficult to dislocate talk of ungracious or hollow victories, humbling defeats, or of moral winners and losers from our self-evaluations regarding winning and defeat.[1] The idea that Western sports have emerged from a civilization that made pre-eminent the honour ethic is one that I will not sufficiently analyse here.[2] Nevertheless, conceptions of honourable conduct are always in the background, with attendant virtues and vices displayed by the winner and loser. What I wish to do is draw on Miller's quasi anthropological theses about shame and humiliation. This, at least, will help to gain some conceptual clarity concerning humiliation and hubris in sports. So, just as the Greek myths and legends give birth to an agonal context that allowed sports to flourish, so the agonal warrior ethic can be found in Norse sagas such as Beowulf too. And these can help to illuminate a modern sense of emotions such as shame and humiliation in sport. It will repay attention if we bear in mind the structural similarities of honour societies and elite competitive sports, especially those that involve direct competition involving physical contact (such as football, boxing, rugby, hockey). So we might say that the concept of 'honour' is deeply intertwined with hierarchical societies. Thus Miller writes:

> Honor was more than just a set of rules for governing behavior. Honor permeated every aspect of consciousness: how you thought about yourself and others, how you held your body, the expectations you could reasonably have and the demands you could make on others [. . .]. It was your very being. For in an honor based culture there was no self-respect independent of the respect of others, no private sense of 'hey, I'm quite something' unless it was confirmed publicly. Honor was then not just a matter of the individual; it necessarily involved a group, and the group included all those people worthy of competing with you for honor. For the most part, people acted as if the mechanics of honor had the structure of a zero-sum game or less-than-zero-sum game. The shortest road to honor was thus to take someone else's [. . .].
>
> (1993: 116–17)

Nowhere is this better exemplified in late modernity than in the zero-sum structure of sports. And it is almost deified in sports such as boxing, where the language of the 'champion' and 'contender' is most obvious, where the claims to be 'the greatest' are the strongest. Honour though is not merely to be thought of as representing oneself appropriately in a social structure. It is noteworthy that, like other dispositions, honour predisposes us to feel and act in regular and interrelated ways. Those who value honour necessarily value reputation and above all the appearance of that reputation. A 'loss of face' is the modern vernacular for loss of honour. It follows then that how others see us is critical to our standing in the scheme of things. This is why in premodern societies (among other reasons of course) the social concept of shame is the powerful regulator of our thoughts and deeds. Lest it appear that I have some nostalgic view of honour, it is worth acknowledging the dangers to the powerful social structures that weave our identities and actions so tightly. Characteristically such structures function to preclude critical self and other reflection and comment. Moreover, in sports as in academic lives, shame is commonly the fruit of envy. Academics covet the positions and status held by colleagues who get tenure first, or publish most prolifically, or who attract prestigious national funds. Individual sportspersons are characteristically thought to covet the number one slot in leagues or drafts. Responses to that shame in tight social structures can be equally problematic to (post)modern minds. Falling on one's sword (perhaps the ultimate act of masculine honour in shame-cultures) is widely thought unacceptable now, though retiring gracefully after a drunken fall at a party is not. Emotional economies scarcely stand still. How we match social failings and their analogue feelings and subjective judgements are themselves subject to cultural change.

The ancient warrior ethic, if you like, operates tightly since the background beliefs, the framework or supporting structure, is itself tight; there are no gaps or interstices. Nowhere is the tightness of roles and their expectations developed so effectively than in the conflicts of Greek tragedy such as in King Creone who, to execute his role-duties, must execute his daughter for her defiance of the law. Creone knows what he must do because he knows who he is. As MacIntyre puts it:

> Every individual has a given role and status within a well-defined and highly determinate system of roles and statuses. [. . .] In such a society a man knows who he is by knowing his role in these structures; and in knowing this he knows also what he owes and what is owed him by the occupant of every other role and status. [. . .]
>
> But it is not just that there is for each status a prescribed set of duties and privileges. There is a clear understanding of actions that are required to perform these and what actions fall short of what is required. For what are required are actions. A man in heroic society is what he does.
>
> (MacIntyre, 1985: 122)

What is so interesting about these role-related commitments is how an appreciation of them can illuminate our understanding of the moral psychology of winning and losing in sports. Both Dixon (1992) and Hardman *et al.* (1996) highlight the ranking function in sportspersons' self-evaluations in terms of comparative measurements of athletic ability. But there is more to it than this. I have proposed that attention be paid not merely to the fact that certain sports (though surely not all – compare the ethoses of heavyweight boxing and ice-skating) still retain a vestige of honour codes. But more importantly I think the relation between differentia – how players are ranked in that structure (favourites, no-hopers, new-stars, fading stars and so on) – need to be apprehended. What merit is accorded to sportspersons and their sporting status rests partly on how they themselves evaluate their worth within the scheme. The expectations of how they comport themselves alter according to the places they register in the social scales of sports. Tolerance may be given to the new kids on the block who shout their mouths off a little too quickly; it is less easily afforded to those who are old enough, or experienced enough, to know better. What will be termed 'structural pretension' within a system of rankings will be crucial to understand felt-humiliation in sports I will argue. The idea that one judges oneself worthy of esteem beyond that which one merits makes one easy prey to the emotion. In sporting practices, as I have said, we come to know who we are, not merely as athletic performers, in our understandings of what we stand for and where we stand in the catalogue of those who come before us and are the canons of excellence in that activity. And proof of that standing comes not in verbal forms but as action. If we are first or twenty-first we come to know our place, which is verified in the public forum of sporting competition. Virtuosity and incompetence are there for all to see, and esteem and derision follow hard on their heels. Sports are not intellectually complex. They are scarcely comparable to the high arts in terms of their (im)penetrability by the masses. And this brings me to speak of recognition and esteem; for both notions lie close to an understanding of honour and expectations of conduct in the execution of role-related behaviour.

I want to re-affirm why, as I argued in Chapter 3, what MacIntyre sets out generically as external goods (e.g. wealth, status and social esteem) are not simply to be thought of as the necessarily corrupting components of modern commercialised sports. I argued there that external goods *justly conferred* are proper signifiers that our (sporting) lives are going well. A better way to talk of this relation is not to slip into the old intrinsic/extrinsic dichotomy but to think of the sportsperson who relationally values the sport for the esteem it brings him or her. To be sure, esteem can be wrought from a range of activities beyond sports, but it is a clear (and for some people, perhaps, the only) means to that particular end. Talk of esteem as an external good of sports, one that is merely extrinsically valuable, is too crude. Moreover, given that elite sports have historically been associated with certain of what are called external goods, there comes a point when one wants to ask the role that the word 'external' is playing here. In ancient schemes death or glory was the chant of virtuous soldiers and clearly was intrinsic to their motivational set. I see no reason why this need not still be part of the ethical-emotional stance of many elite athletes, and particularly in those sports in which there is considerable physical contact where putting bodies on the line is not so much metaphor as reality.

Of course there are ways of pursuing these ends, such as esteem, that are more and less morally acceptable. Tony Skillen's discussion of Rousseau and the fall of 'social man' captures important points about competitive status ranking and the proper means of their pursuit:

> This is the sort of thing we find in Thrasymachus, Glaucon and Adeimantus' defence of injustice in Plato's *Republic*. They argue that the reputation of virtue is desirable because it brings material rewards. [. . .] But this is not what Rousseau is on about. He is not primarily concerned with people's pursuing social reputation as a means to materialistic, asocial ends, but rather with their quest for esteem as a confirmation of their social identities. [. . .] And without shared 'recognition' of superiority, such distinction is worth-less.

(Skillen, 1985: 114)

What I think we have in sports then is the demonstration of who we are *in the way* that we play sports and the myriad of ways in which we make comparisons of athletic excellence. And when our sports are played and officiated properly, when we develop our talents and capacities, when we pit them against others, we visit an inner sporting oracle; we come to know the limits of our sporting world, and the sporting world comes to know our limits too. That is the central function of ranking systems such as leagues and titles, demotions, promotions and so on. But *how* we win and lose speaks crucially of who we are. Keeping a close eye on the relations between ends and means is critical; perceptions of their natures are an inherent part of the context. But we also have to reflect upon the self-conceptions of performers (how, for example, they saw themselves win or lose) if we are to understand properly the weak humiliation visited on or felt by them. Below I argue that, in cases of strong humiliation, the context is relatively unimportant. I will argue that strong humiliation entails an awareness of the violation of basic respect of a person, not the deflation of their self-esteem. I will then show how weak humiliation may be the proper emotional corollary of defeat.

'Strong' and 'weak' humiliation and structural pretension

It has been argued by Dixon (1992, 1998) that humiliation is not a proper emotional response to a sporting defeat, since it conflates humiliation with a mere loss of self-esteem, which is the appropriate emotional response. Since the defeat itself does not *morally reduce* the opposition as persons, it cannot therefore be considered as an example of strong humiliation:

> In general, a loss of self-esteem is a regrettable but morally acceptable consequence of many legitimate actions in the pursuit of legitimate goals. In contrast, inflicting strong humiliation, which brings moral shame and disgrace on a person, is a more serious harm that requires a more substantial justification.
>
> (Dixon, 1998: 67)

This is not quite right. Dixon persuasively distinguishes between a loss of self-esteem and strong humiliation. But he pays little attention to what might be called 'weak humiliation', whose conceptual territory is different from the individualistic evaluation entailed in 'self-esteem'. Furthermore, he fails to clarify sufficiently what 'strong humiliation' actually is and presupposes that justification thereof is possible. By way of extending this discussion I will begin with the distinction between loss of self-esteem and strong humiliation. Dixon argues that not all lowerings of self-esteem are strongly humiliating. Yet the difference between a lowering of self-esteem and weak humiliation should not be thought of merely as a matter of degree. Dixon fails throughout to distinguish strong humiliation from shame and disgrace and merely says that strong humiliation is a 'different beast' (1998: 67) from weak humiliation. It essentially involves a lowering of moral standing that is not a necessary condition of weak humiliation:

> An athlete who competes fairly and with dignity, who prepares assiduously and performs to the best of her ability, and who has a decent minimal level of competence at the game, is absolutely not shamed or disgraced (i.e. strongly humiliated) by a lop-sided defeat.
>
> (Dixon, 1998: 67)

Dixon is absolutely right that the lop-sidedness of the defeat is independent of the humiliation felt, justifiably or unjustifiably, by the humiliated. Nevertheless, the criteria relate only to the loser and not the quality of defeat nor the broader social context that is necessarily to be understood if the actions themselves are properly to be characterised. In all acts of strong humiliation, the context is relatively unimportant for the actions to be understood as humiliating. In Margalit's (1996) discussion of the decent society, 'humiliation' is tied to the most basic respect for persons. It is indeed the kind of thing a torturer seeks to inflict on a victim. We need to know little of the context to appreciate the humiliation of the torturer/tortured variety. In such strong humiliation the humiliated are passive at the hands of the tormentor, whereas in weaker cases the power balance is not as dramatic. So clear is the denial of the status of personhood to the subject of strong humiliation that the imposition of powerless degradation requires little or no awareness of a moral and conceptual vocabulary to modern minds.[3] In contrast, sports require at least a minimal conceptual background to be understood before winning and losing, and the deflation of recognised status, can be perceived. Moreover, in terms of the violence done to one's status as a person in strong humiliation, we may say that sports never reach this depth. But are there instances of 'weak humiliation' to the serious sportsperson (amateur or professional) rather than merely a loss of self-esteem?

To explore this question requires further attention to the nature of humiliation and related concepts. One's self-awareness of shame, honour and humiliation presupposes the transgression of moral boundaries. They relate to actions that are evaluated in light of shared, public norms. As a precursor to his discussion of humiliation, Miller laments the passing of shame proper.[4] He notes how it has contracted from the large role it played in honour societies concerned with saving face or reputation (notwithstanding huge problems in itself, e.g. gendered ideas such as protecting one's honour by having dresses down to the ankles) into a mere association with not feeling good about oneself or having low self-esteem.[5] Here, everyday locutions, 'shame on you', 'you ought to be ashamed', point to a stronger status-related concept rather than a mere subjective feeling.

Miller argues that shame and humiliation are to be distinguished along the lines of status pretension. Humiliation, he argues, is tied to a mode or quality of self-presentation. He writes:

> They seek deference from others, they mean to cut figures before others, and in doing so they presume on others; those others will get even. It is the presumption that enables the humiliation and justifies it. Vanity begs for humiliation.
>   One of the most salient distinctions between shame and humiliation is that, at root, humiliation depends on the deflation of pretension.
>
> (Miller, 1993: 139)

Before we develop the argument further, we should enquire where this distinction fits with the humiliating blowout literature. In concentrating predominantly on the score itself and quantitatively the margin between victor and vanquished, neither Dixon nor Hardman *et al.* developed their theses in relation to the modes of self-presentation of the contestants. In order to give a virtue-ethical account of these episodes it seems to me that this is critical. To be fair, Dixon makes the point that one may be humiliated where one shows character flaws but fails to expand the point. Pugilistic examples can be particularly relevant here, since the boxing world is saturated with machismo. The mode of self-presentation is critical to boxers, since part of their identity as much as their chances of winning rests in the (self-)deception they can generate both to gird themselves and psychologically to terrorise the opposition; 'respect' here is no Kantian notion, but a cultural shorthand for embodied power.

Notwithstanding this, blowout scenarios, however various they may be, are not tied to shame necessarily. For, as we have noted above, shame is linked with a failure in reaching a designated *moral* as opposed to technical standard. In addition, there is nothing in losing by a large margin that would indicate the appropriateness of such a weighty emotion. One might say that embarrassment was the proper response to a failure against inferior opposition because of poor preparation. Shame will characteristically be thought too serious an emotional response. Yet if shame occupies itself with the transgression of issues of cultural, moral or religious rules, humiliation in its attenuated form is only tied to the conventional or the decorous. Many authors have noted that it holds a perversely incongruous grip on the psyche of some. One might think of those for whom humility had descended to the pathological. Instead of weighing their talents and achievements in a proper way, their self-evaluations never reach beyond mere self-loathing. Likewise, there are others over-sensitive to 'proper' conduct who feel that any and all transgressions of etiquette are self-imposed attacks on their integrity. A form of alienation is the end point of this view. We can see its development in accounts of those who argue that they feel they do not belong within certain milieux. Their experiences are to be found in early accounts of racism encountered at golf clubs, or sexism within football cultures, where blacks and women respectively report to being acutely sensitive about observing intricate social codes or conventions. Perhaps the pathological grip is strongest though on those who act not in ignorance or gaucherie but rather in pretence. Later I will argue that those who display an arrogant form of pretension are particularly ripe for weak humiliation.

In order to develop the account of humiliation and hubris I need to appropriate some important distinctions from Miller that open the door to thinking about weak humiliation in sports. He talks of pretensions of accident where a person merely finds oneself superior in some respect to another, which is to be distinguished from an active putting on of 'airs'. It is the latter that is interesting for our purposes. It is not difficult for sports fans to remember any number of pre-fight hypes where challengers for titles describe in rich and colourful terms how bad the champion is; how he has only been matched against cherry-picked opponents; how he's past his best and should have retired before this fight to save him from the impending woe the challenger will visit on him. The litany of abuse is depressingly familiar. Why is such a person, lacking in both humility and due-respect, ripe for a humiliating defeat? Miller writes:

> Structural pretension is not merely a matter of fowl among fish. It depends on the fowl occupying, by the usual social conventions of status demarcation, the higher position. The setting must be one in which the fowl has no moral or social right to assert the higher status, but also is likely to be seen as making such a claim because the context calls for special attention to status differential.
>
> (Miller, 1993: 142)

Now one can innocently occupy the high ground, but our boxers do not fit this scenario. The boxing world has an honour code; it represents an honour community, where virtues and vices are displayed under fire and the public's gaze. So the disrespectful boxer's quest for esteem and status is cheaply sought at the price of disrespect for the champion who has earned his right to that status and can now play the role of champion (what in Ancient Greek thought would be honorifically described as *megalospuchia* – the great souled man) with the dignity appropriate to a champion. In Aristotle, we find an idea that jars on moderns: the idea that a certain level of pride is appropriate to those who are recognised for their greatness. Nevertheless, the idea that a certain status attaches to a role still remains in the strongly structured world of boxing as in other martial sports. Working out whether in particular circumstances embarrassment or humiliation attach will not be a mechanical application of criteria. Nevertheless, something general needs to be said to demarcate cases. Again, Miller writes: 'If shame is the consequence of not living up to what we ought to, then humiliation is the consequence of trying to live up to what we have no right to' (1993: 145).

As the mealy-mouthed pretender to the throne is beaten in the first few rounds, few shed tears. Where are all his hollow threats now? Where is his vaunted jab, stout defence or granite chin? He is indeed humiliated before the boxing community and perhaps the entire audience to the extent that they appreciate the standards of the practice and the significance of status ranking therein. In sports, unlike so many other practices, we are positioned publicly. He can lay no such right to that ground again without fear of ridicule.[6] So in these cases, the public deflation of a status beyond our merit occasions weak humiliation. While the negative emotion felt is a form of 'emotional punishment' for the flouting of recognised, socially conferred status it does not amount to an assault on the basic condition of the sportsperson *as* person and therefore cannot be considered a case of strong humiliation. What must be shown below is that it can amount to more than a mere loss of self-esteem.

Hubris, humility and the modes of self-presentation

What I want to do now is to show how hubris, thought of as an exaggerated pride in oneself, specifically in one's powers and status, is crucially related to the possibility of suffering weak humiliation in sports. Hubris takes its original meaning from the Greek description of those who thought themselves superior to the gods. It entails the moral failing of not knowing one's place in a hierarchical scheme and vaingloriously sticking to it. Boxing, perhaps the closest sporting cousin to war, provides the case study.

In the first title fight between (Sugar) Ray Leonard and Roberto Duran in Montreal, much bad blood was spilt in the pre-match promotion. Duran had wanted to unsettle his opponent and reduce him to an angry fighter. He did this by a number of taunts and provocations that challenged, among other things, Leonard's sexuality and heart for a battle. In the fight, Leonard eschewed his usual highly technical skills in favour of a brawl. Naturally, he lost to Duran who had seduced him into contesting the match in a manner that conduced to Duran's abrasive style. In the rematch, however, Leonard set out to prove that he had learnt his lesson. The contest was set up as a grudge match wherein two classic styles of boxing were in the starkest of contrasts. In addition to this dichotomy of 'artist' and 'slugger', much was made of personal contrasts between the two. Here there was the pitting of an articulate, college-educated, stylish, beautiful black man against a hungry and hardened opponent, notorious for never taking a backward step, who had never been knocked out, and whose overweening pride now manifested itself in an arrogance that went well beyond an all-consuming self-esteem.

In the early rounds Leonard's technical virtuosity was clearly on display. He was quicker of mind as well as fist and foot. He hit Duran so many times and with the full array of combinations. It was simply remarkable. Duran just could not get near enough to hit him with any effect. And often when he tried, and he tried often, Leonard's fluid defensive manoeuvres meant that he slipped punches by inches in with aesthetic élan, making Duran appear an amateur.

When Duran did land a punch, Leonard's elastic movements assuaged the full force, and with beautiful balance he simply countered to greater effect.

By the middle rounds, Duran was tired and frustrated at his inabilities, and this was compounded by Leonard's public demonstration of his own pugilistic excellence and Duran's limitations. Without verbal assault, Leonard's entire performances exuded élan, an aesthetic dimension of which Duran's own mien was the antithesis. In his biography of Leonard, Toperoff writes:

> In the eighth round, a round that has already become an indelible part of boxing history, one that will forever tarnish the Duran legend, Ray Leonard sensed the level of Roberto Duran's frustration at not being able to have his own way. Now it was Sugar's turn to taunt and mock the man with hands of stone. A payback for all the insults and humiliations in Montreal. Ray dropped his hands in mid-ring and exposed his chin, a look of teasing stupidity playing on his face. By merely twisting this way and that, he made Duran miss the too-tempting target. Frustration mounted. A few seconds later, again in the center of the ring, Ray wound his right arm like a pantomiming softball pitcher. The so called bolo motion is not one of boxing's classic punches, but as Duran watched the right hand warming up, Ray popped him with a quick left jab right on the schnoz [nose]. It was the sort of move my old man would have pulled on me during our first few weeks of sparring. Duran heard the crowd's derisive laughter.
>
> With only sixteen seconds left in the round, and with Ray working *him* along the ropes, Roberto Duran turned away and said to Octavio Meyeran, the referee, *"no mas no mas"* [no more, no more].
>
> Meyran said "Por que?"
>
> Duran's non-answer "No mas"
>
> Roberto Duran's quitting, unhurt in mid-fight, was so big a story that Ray Leonard's strategic and technical brilliance was overlooked. [. . .] There were strong rumors of mysterious drugs that had sapped his will. More logical was the explanation that the macho man could handle anything except being made a fool of in public – it had never happened during his life on the planet: now it was happening for the world to see. So he chose dishonor over humiliation.
>
> (Toperoff, 1989: 140–1)

Now this was no blowout victory. To be sure, Leonard was well ahead on points but, notoriously in boxing, one punch can finish the contest. As long as an opponent is standing, one had better beware. It was rather Duran's hubristic machismo, his strutting airs of masculine invincibility, which made him ripe for the humiliation. Of course, had Leonard fought him toe to toe (man to man as some may say), he would surely have lost again. For Duran was a fighter of frightening will and physical power. Leonard simply out-thought and out-boxed him and did it so publicly that he demonstrated Duran's limitations for the world to see. I think that this case is probably the limit case of weak humiliation. For the professional sportspersons, their chosen profession constitutes an identity-constituting commitment. Leonard's assault on Duran's identity as boxer was considerably harder to bear than the physical blows he received. Because of the significance of those commitments and the public deflation of his honour as boxer, the loss to Duran exceeds characterisation as a loss of self-esteem. It's not simply that he thinks a little less of himself now. Rather, in full view of the adoring public and the boxing community, his legend lost much of its lustre in the nature of his defeat. Though he may recover some of his self-esteem in the future, he can do nothing to erase the record of that humiliation.[7]

Just so it is not thought that I am putting the victor on a pedestal or engaging in some variant of ethical hegemony against a culturally specific machismo, some critical remarks are in order.[8] Having established that weak humiliation is not necessarily tied to the quantitative measure of defeat but rather its quality, and in particular the character of the humiliated, a word or two is in order of the potential viciousness of the victor. Of course, Leonard was now ripe himself for being brought down a peg or two. But not in the manner that had behoved Duran. To be sure he had mocked Duran but not in the vicious manner in which Duran had questioned his integrity. He had not 'shot his mouth off' to use the vernacular. He had not abused Duran – though this may have been as much out of prudence as virtue. To have bad-mouthed Duran may have been to motivate him further. There is an old Aesopian tale about crowing one's eminence only to be brought low by a creature greater than oneself. Even the greatest of sportsmen and women do well to mind its moral. Such is the nature of sports: they are temporal affairs; they offer time-related goods. The one sure fact a champion must come to know and to obey is that he or she will not be champion forever. Time will have its way and usually sooner rather than later.

It is worthy of note that, after Mackinnon (1999), virtue theorists have tended to focus on a range of positive dispositions and rather neglected the negative ones. So it is in the sport philosophical literature that there is little discussion of the vices that are commonplace and the qualities they take on in sporting contexts. So in our potential evaluation of humiliators we must take into account whether we will characterise their acts as vicious, and if so, enquire as to the nature of that viciousness. To what extent do they pursue the humiliation of their opponents in ignorance or full knowledge of their actions and consequences? Are their failings mere weaknesses of will or outright wickedness?

I have little doubt that the full lists of vices display themselves in and across all ranges of sports. What is less clear, but more interesting is the extent to which vicious acts are the products of 'weak' and 'strong evaluation', which was discussed in Chapter 2. Recall, that the weak evaluator is no more than a means–ends reasoner. The ends of his or her actions or desires are never problematised nor alternative visions explored. Here we have a paradigm of sports talk; winning is taken unproblematically to be the exclusive goal of professional sports. How wins are secured is only considered in terms of models of technical reason, where criteria such as efficiency and effectiveness dominate. There are exceptions of course. And the exceptions betoken a particular problem for those who wish to generalise in the ethics of sports. For the heterogeneity of sports and sports cultures makes generalisations problematic. Honda (2005) in his defence of the sportisation of the ancient art of Kendo notes how shifts from its underlying warrior ethic (*budo*) to a sporting one, have angered traditionalists. They have argued that the deployment of strategy and tactics is deceitful, ignoble and unworthy of the Kendo master. The loss of this ethic, however problematic it may be in its own right and in modern times, also represents a certain shift in ethical language from strong to weak evaluation.

Nevertheless, in the West it is clear that such technical criteria dominate and not merely at elite levels. It may well be the case that Dixon's athletes bent on achieving the widest margins fall most easily into this category of weak-evaluating sportspersons. We might think the vice of hubris and the viciousness of strong humiliation-infliction are the products of the weak evaluator, one who is simply morally negligent. Where the margin of victory and defeat are not relevant, there appears little justification for the all-out pursuit of the widest margins. Though the viciousness of such athletes or coaches cannot inflict strong humiliation, we can still ask what good it achieves for the victor, the vanquished, or even the sport itself. But that is to stray beyond my stated purpose. What is the point of the comparison of the abilities? This is the question of the strong evaluator, someone who is capable of critically reflecting the quality of the relations between means and ends and indeed of the ends themselves. How we pursue our goals necessitates discussion of virtue and vice. Here, any deontological or utilitarian vocabulary insufficiently grasps the adverbial nature of ethical discourses. Having said that an aretaic vocabulary is required to capture the phenomenology of victory and defeat, a further caveat is required. How we describe and evaluate action in sport must not be reduced to an individualistic framework. The ethos of various sports sub-cultures sometimes fosters viciousness as part of the everyday business-as-usual background of the activity. In particular, coaches who subject young athletes to regimes of physical and verbal abuse in order to improve performances are apt to be described by such a vocabulary. Humiliation may here be the product of a mere weak evaluator but we should reserve our deepest approbation for those who knowingly humiliate their athletes merely for economic gain, or sporting glory, or in the worst-case scenario, who use humiliatory strategies to bolster their domination as in the coach–coached relation.[9] To capture the wrongness in terms of respect may be apposite, but to dig beneath that disrespect requires a vocabulary more psychologically robust.

Of course, it is the case that virtues and vices display many formal similarities. As virtues are innervated through particular perceptions, so are vices. As virtues are habituated, so too are vices as patterns of feeling, judging and acting. As virtues are chosen and ramified by supporting traits, so too are vices.

And similarly, the catalogues of virtue and vice are heterogeneous. As I noted in Chapter 4, Kohlberg (1981) was not without prescience when he noted that the trouble with virtue approaches is that everyone has their own bag with its preferred contents. This is precisely why he urged developmental psychologists to move to a system of rational universal principles to evaluate moral development. Only with a consistent scale could one compare developmental stages of persons in different time and place. To the extent that this is true, it would of course follow that vices varied too in scope and significance. It would be difficult to conceive of anything we might call a society these days in which certain fundamental virtues such as justice and honesty were necessary. Yet each culture, or horizon of significance as Taylor puts it, lauds and laments particular persons and personalities. Humility played no part in Ancient Greek schemes of thought, nor later in Hume's writings when he derided it pejoratively as a 'monkish virtue'. Yet chief among the theological vices of medieval Christendom was pride. Indeed Gregory the Great labelled it the root of all evil. Similar to hubris, the proud man failed to understand his limitations in the place of the pantheon of gods and men and thereby alienated himself from both. It seems too that an understanding of status within or without a theological horizon is crucial to understanding the nature of hubris or arrogance, which is probably our closest approximation to it, as a vice.[10] I do not take the two to be synonymous. In the absence of detailed analysis, I suggest that arrogance entails hubris, though hubris does not necessitate the haughtiness or dismissiveness that arrogance demands.

In modern professional sport no less than in the great sagas, self-knowledge and self-understanding are part and parcel of the good life. Hubris, if we can situate it in modernity, is a presumption of power in excess of one's capabilities. But I want to hold to an idea that can distinguish it from mere ignorance. The arrogant know their power, but they fail to situate it properly in the contexts that give rise to their overweening pride. A crucial component then of both humiliation and hubris is the idea I set out above of thinking rather too much of oneself. It is the direct opposite of humility, which requires an understated though reasonable estimation of one's powers and status. It need not entail the failure to give others their due in an active sense. It is too self-centred, too egoistic. One may be dismissive of others without claiming greatness for oneself. So, though a dismissive attitude often accompanies hubris, it is not logically tied to it.

What fuels hubris in sports, and what makes those who display the vice so ripe for humiliation, is the bloated importance of big-time commercialised sports and sportspersons. Too many veils of economic interest cloud the athlete's own critical self-interrogation. Irresponsible agents and journalists promote players in the most outrageous of styles. Florid language conduces to the formation of would-be heroic reputations based on the shifting sands of falsely conceived superhuman abilities. Athletes too often live a cocooned world where critical coaches and commentators can either be ignored or dismissed in favour of others who will sing more sycophantic songs. To such athletes then, we may view weak humiliation as a corrective to their conceited self-conceptions. But even where we judge this to be a good, this does not license in any way a triumphalism on the part of those who render the corrective. Humility in victory and graciousness in defeat may be the stock-in-trade platitudes of the physical educator, but have a genuinely deeper import. The virtues are indeed our best travelling companions in good sporting careers no less than in good lives.

Although there is a limited place for weak humiliation, there can be no such place for its stronger counterpart. Perhaps some linguistic stipulation is necessary here. To be humbled may be no bad thing in the great scheme of things; but no one (except a masochist) is grateful for humiliation in the strong sense. So the humiliator who seeks pleasure in the degradation of another is simply wicked. The sooner a professional ethics of coaching emerges to outlaw the verbal torture that many athletes old and (especially) young endure, the better for us all.

How, as philosophers of sport or reflective coaches or physical education teachers, we are to cultivate greater powers of reflection in our sports cultures is no easy matter. One philosophical challenge is to create better taxonomies of the emotionally laden virtues and vices of our sportsmen and women. Sharper distinctions can indeed help all involved in sport to mark out the ethically acceptable from the unacceptable territories. Crucially, that will entail the analysis of concepts but in a way that is historically sensitive and socially situated. In articulating the shared roots of hubris and humiliation, we can help deliver the resources critically to initiate practitioners.

Hubris, honour, and power on loan from the gods

The honour societies of Greece and Scandinavia, where one was how one acted, and certain modern-day sports are still rich in ethical instruction – even if we must learn the modern lessons of non-discrimination to detoxify ancient honour. How one comports oneself is ethically significant. The broad-chested swagger of hubris still is as vicious now as it was in the days of Agamemnon. Yet we might also ask whether our desire for modest millionaires is merely egoistic. We want sports superstars to retain touch with the herd, with a common humanity. How then are we to think of keeping such hubris in check? Is it even possible? The worst excesses of sports talk and posturing can and must be kept in check by sports institutions that are paradoxically in the position both of exploiters and guardians of sports practices and communities. What are called the external goods of sport, such as recognition, wealth, esteem and status, are perfectly proper in sports when justly conferred. And the muscles of the institutions can indeed be flexed when badmouthing and egregious arrogance offends the best traditions of those sports. To understand the nature and sometimes positive functions of weak humiliation is in part to know the price of hubris and what makes sport the power for good it can be.

Of course, as inheritors of the Greek scheme, we are left with some of its pieces in a puzzle that just does not hang together. Phillipa Foot, long before MacIntyre and others, warned us of this. But in sports, and especially sports such as boxing, the heritage is closer to that brutal time. Even if the gods or 'fate' as sources of equilibrium between hubris and humility are no longer available, we can take a lead from Weil's recognition of the need to appropriate and rein in the power of 'force' in such warrior-sports:

> Thus it happens that those who have force on loan from fate count on it too much and are destroyed.
>
> But at the time their own destruction seems impossible to them. For they do not see that the force in their possession is only a limited quantity; nor do they see their relations with other human beings as a kind of balance between unequal amounts of force. Since other people do not impose on their movements that hold, that interval of hesitation, wherein lies all our consideration for our brothers in humanity, they conclude that destiny has given complete license to them, and none at all to their inferiors. And at this point they exceed the actual measure of force that is at their disposal. Inevitably, they exceed it, since they are not aware that it is limited. And now we see them committed irretrievably to chance; suddenly things cease to obey them. Sometimes chance is kind to them, sometimes cruel. But in any case there they are, exposed, open to misfortune, gone is the armor of power that formerly protected their naked souls; nothing; no shield, stands between them and tears.
>
> This retribution, which has a geometrical rigor, which operates automatically to penalize the abuse of power, was the mainstay of Greek thought. It is the soul of the epic. [. . .] conceptions of limit, measure, equilibrium, which ought to determine the conduct of life are, in the West, restricted to the service function in the vocabulary of technics. We are only geometricians of matter; the Greeks were, first of all geometricians in their apprenticeship to virtue.
>
> (Weil, 1983: 231)

Conclusion

I have argued that sporting contests cannot occasion 'strong humiliation', where this is taken to mean the denial of the basis of respect as a person. I have argued, however, that something more than a mere loss of self-esteem may be effected by a sporting loss and, moreover, that this is independent of the mere margin of the loss. I have argued that structural pretension is logically tied to what has been called 'weak humiliation'. In illustrating the vice of hubris, I have shown how such weak humiliation may occur and also highlighted the corrective role that humiliation may play for those who opt for hubris over humiliation. In sports, more than most cultural pursuits, greatness is indeed on loan temporarily from the gods.

8 *Schadenfreude* in sports
Envy, justice and self-esteem

Introduction

Sports administrators, media commentators and policy makers have tended to focus on the big ethical issues such as child abuse, doping and violence in their pronouncements upon the moral health and ailments of sports. Yet it is often the smaller acts of kindness and unkindness that are better indications of the moral health of sporting practices. Following directly on from the previous chapter, we are left with the worry that in celebrating (Sugar) Ray Leonard's humiliation of Roberto Duran we are endorsing the humiliation of another human who is clearly suffering. The aim of this chapter is to scrutinise that feeling crystallised in the concept of *schadenfreude* – the pleasure felt at another's misfortune – and argue that one's feeling it is both a culpable and, at the very least, undesirable aspect of the ethico-emotional ecologies of sport.

In order to attempt to show that *schadenfreude* is a morally objectionable emotion in sport as elsewhere, and one that can be curbed, I first offer some conceptual remarks about emotions generally and their differential treatment in philosophical discussions. Second, I argue that the rationality of the emotions is crucial to our self-understanding as persons in general and sportspersons in particular, attempting to live good lives and play good sport. I situate this point within an understanding drawn from both Aristotle and Kant. Third, I argue for its undesirability in the character of the one who feels the emotion (the *schadenfroh*) and their relations to those who suffer. I offer a critique of the argument for the ethical excusability of *schadenfreude* in Portmann (2000) and argue that he fails to defend his position coherently. Specifically, I show how his defence of the emotion's genesis in low self-esteem and a commitment to justice is not compelling and suggest that one's feeling *schadenfreude* is itself evidence of poor sporting character and sporting culture.

Ir/rationality and the emotions: Kant and Aristotle

When an actor at an audition says to his or her fellow actor 'break a leg', it is ordinarily understood that the saying is one of encouragement. When some sporting competitors utter the same remark, I fear, it is often tinged with a less metaphorical desire. When we see the delight on the face of a contestant whose competitor falls at the last hurdle, fails their final jump, or injures themselves in the warm-up, some of us at least are troubled by this. Ought we to be? *Schadenfreude*, the joy or pleasure felt at another's harm, is something sportspersons and coaches undeniably feel. Is it felt for reasons good or ill, one may ask? Whichever is the case, we ought first to ask, more generally, what it means to say that one feels an emotion and to consider why it is worthwhile paying philosophical attention to the emotions. I want first to observe what Bernard Williams wrote more than a quarter of a century ago, and which has applied to much recent sports ethics talk:

> Recent moral philosophy in Britain has not had much to say about the emotions. Its descriptions of the moral agent, its analyses of moral choice and moral judgement, have made free use of such notions as attitude, principle and policy, but have found no essential place for the agent's emotions, except perhaps for recognising them in one of their traditional roles as possible motives for backsliding, and thus potentially destructive of moral rationality and consistency.
>
> (Williams, 1973: 207)

The thought that emotions are themselves irrational has a long and varied history spanning folk psychology and a number of academic disciplines. Emotions appear to have a dual nature; on the one hand they refer to bodily sensations and on the other to expressions of judgement. In philosophy, no less than in certain scientific writings, a peculiarly pejorative and simplified picture of emotions emerged only to be dismissed. And this disposition is no new one. Plato talks in the *Republic* (1974: 440a) of 'reason and its civil war with desire'. He also writes in the *Phaedrus* (1962: 246a8) of the Soul being a composite power, a pair of winged horses and a charioteer. Reason, our ruling part, is the charioteer of course, and while one of the horses is of good and honourable stock, the other is not and 'makes our chariot wayward and difficult to drive' (1962: 246a8).

This picture of rationality both controlling and prosecuting the emotions remained dominant in philosophy and religion into modernity, where Kant gave it particular prominence. As I noted in Chapters 2 and 4, this picture demands correction if we are to understand engagement with sports in a manner that is more than one of mortal machines. I noted there how as part of an evaluation of the moral emotions Wollheim referred to Kant's position as being a 'singularly bleached moral psychology' (1993). Kant is traditionally attributed with denying the rationality of the emotions and therefore derogating their value, both of which are said to be conceived of as obstacles to rational moral action (Williams, 1973). More recently, however, scholars have been at pains both to look for similarities in the ethical writings of Aristotle and Kant (Engstrom and Whiting, 1998) and to give a more generous evaluation of Kant, particularly in relation to his writings in the

Metaphysical Principles of Virtue and *Anthropology from a Pragmatic Point of View* (Baron, 1995; Sherman, 1997).[1]

The widespread, though less favourable, Kantian interpretation is summarised by Montada (1993: 295) thus: (1) that emotions are transitory and capricious; (2) that conduct issuing from emotions is therefore unreliable and unprincipled, even irrational; (3) that the moral perception of right and wrong entails abstraction from our emotions; (4) that emotions are passively experienced and we are not responsible for them; and (5) being attached to particular persons and not universal principles, they are partial and therefore not belonging to the moral realm.

I will comment below partly in defence of Kant's position. I draw out some counterpoints to Montada's characterisation in respect of the relations between passivity and responsibility in our emotional experiences they often held to be part of the Kantian position. Depicting the difficulties that attend to the passivity of, and responsibility for, emotional experiences may help us to understand better the ethical import of emotions generally, but specifically here in relation to human suffering or misfortune, and the experience of *schadenfreude*.

Baldly put, Montada asserts that under a Kantian description we experience emotions passively and that, therefore, we are not responsible for them. This position, though not wholly wrong, lacks precision. Specifically, it is based on an inaccurate reading of Kant since it fails to recognise that, as a response to Hume and others, Kant distinguished between affects or emotions on the one hand, and passions, on the other in his *Metaphysical Principles of Virtue*. A point about nomenclature is necessary here. Kant refers both to '*Affekt*' and '*Leidenschaften*'. In the Mary Gregor translation '*Affekt*' is affect whereas in the Ellington translation it is referred to as 'emotion'.[2] Thus if we use the term emotion – in some recognisably modern sense – we may both (1) obscure the distinction; or worse (2) take his more negative stance to *passions* and apply it inappropriately to what we call emotions. In the Gregor translation Kant says:

> *Affects* and *passions* are essentially different from each other. Affects belong to *feeling* insofar as, preceding reflection, it makes this impossible or more difficult. Hence an affect is called *precipitate* or *rash* (*animus praeceps*), and reason says, through the concept of virtue, that one should *get hold of* oneself. [. . .] Accordingly a propensity to an affect (e.g., *anger*) does not enter into kinship with vice so readily as does a passion. A *passion* is a sensible desire that has become a lasting inclination (e.g., *hatred*, as opposed to anger). The calm with which one gives oneself up to it permits reflection and allows the mind to form principles upon it and so, if inclination lights upon something contrary to the law, to brood upon it, to get it rooted deeply, and so to take up what is evil (as something premeditated) into its maxim. And the evil is then *properly* evil, that is, a true *vice*.
> (Kant, 1991: 208)

To give a fairer reading to Kant, especially in respect of our emotional responses to human suffering or misfortune we must bear this distinction in mind. One important aspect of this distinction for Kant's understanding the emotions (in this case elicited by the suffering of others) is that in passions a 'lasting inclination' is formed and that this entails choice and judgement, which in turn carry the agent's experience into the realm of responsibility. I shall comment further on this point in the section on the culpability of *schadenfreude* below. A second point pertains to the passivity of the experience and is brought out nicely by Baron when commenting on a section from *Anthropology from a Pragmatic Point of View*:

> Kant's distinction between sensitivity and sentimentality is further evidence that in his view we play a significant role as agents in determining how we respond affectively. 'Sensitivity is a *power* and *strength* by which we grant or refuse permission for the state of pleasure or displeasure to enter our mind, so that it implies a choice.' By contrast 'sentimentality is a weakness by which we can be affected, even against our will, by sympathy for another's plight' (Kant, 1974: 236). Clearly, then, we are not always passive with respect to our emotions and feelings: sensitivity does not involve such passivity.
>
> (Baron, 1995: 196)

Sherman too offers a useful summary of Kant's point here: that his intention is to 'repudiate sentimentalism, not sentiment' (1997: 153). So, let us first allow that Montada's position is Kantian, rather than Kant's. Second, and more substantively, despite Baron's protest at the lack of agency ascribed to Kantian emotion, our passivity in the experience of sentimentality entails a lack of responsibility. But, with Kant's distinction above in mind, we should say that the point refers to emotions as affects (i.e. sentimentality) – rather than passions (i.e. sensitivity). And this is important in his consideration of the cultivation of sympathy as a moral duty. One point that Baron takes from all this, and one that I am in *sympathy* with (if you will excuse the pun) is that we should not use feelings and emotions as objects to excuse our moral responsibility. And this, I contend, is often what happens when people say that the experience of an emotion such as *schadenfreude* is felt by someone in relation to a suffering other. But the experience of emotions such as *schadenfreude* need not be considered like what might be termed 'immediate natural responses' such as a knee-jerk or anxiety at the onset of a sharp toothache.

Consider a sports physician who refuses pain relief to the athlete on the grounds that they do not believe the level of pain reported is either accurate or authentic. On reflection the physician wonders whether their mistrust and hostility to the patient is, for the purposes of example, driven by their guilt-ridden recollection of giving a questionably high dose of pain killer to an ageing athlete who played on in ignorance of the damage being done to him, and was forced subsequently to retire. In such cases colleagues might claim that the physician's judgement was 'clouded by emotion.' Thinking carefully through such scenarios requires a consideration of the relations between cognition and the relevant emotions at play.

All cognitive theorists of emotion have argued that simply characterising emotions as subjective feelings – as biological theorists do – ignores two important aspects: first, that emotions entail judgements and second that they are to a considerable degree influenced by space and time. One important part of this strategy is to argue that feelings and modes that are not in some way suffused with some cognition are not emotions proper (G. Taylor, 1985), and the very fact of our making linguistic choices signifies this. Early analyses of emotions, inspired by Wittgenstein's anti-essentialism in conceptual analysis, conceived of emotions-talk as illustrating the family resemblances idea: there is neither an essence nor unifying set of properties to them. Some are voluntary, some involuntary, some passive yet others are active. Likewise, their intensity, though typically greater than felt moods, can vary too; compare a punch in anger in the playground, to the studied resentment of a colleague's unmerited promotion where one may stew for days, weeks, even years in one's own acidic feelings, memories and thoughts. Those familiar with British soccer may recall the Manchester United player Roy Keane in his recent autobiography revealing that he harboured resentment for an opposing Norwegian player (Alfe Haaland) for a full year before exacting revenge in a violent, career-threatening tackle. Even allowing for their biological bases, we must agree with Rorty (1988: 1) that 'the emotions do not form a natural kind'. Sometimes the emotions are felt in anticipation of action; at other times they succeed it. Sometimes they are directly motivational, at other times they are not. Moreover, certain emotions such as panic are experienced as self-referring while other emotions such as humiliation or shame have a very significant interpersonal role in preserving boundaries of conduct by reinforcing norms of the acceptable and unacceptable. Emotions such as guilt, remorse, regret and shame all have a negative power that we typically seek to avoid or to work off.

The emotions can be allowed a much more positive role in our identification of what matters to us in both fleeting and more considered ways. While it is easy to recall instances when emotions have got in the way of good judgement, or indeed been obstacles to right action, we can also think of examples where our emotionally driven responses of, say, compassion or mercy are salient. To conceive of the emotions more generously opens a conceptual space in which we can consider more broadly the roles they play in our lives beyond exculpation and the denial of responsibility. To elicit the ethical import of the emotion of *schadenfreude* (or any of its close cousins in the emotional field – envy, spite, resentment, to name a few[3]) we must accept that the feeling is imbued with a judgement or an interpretation of their situation as I argued in Chapter 2.

Aristotle's writings are typically taken to afford a more generous interpretation of the emotions in the good life than Kant's, though as I hoped to illustrate above, perhaps too much has been made of the contrast. Aristotelian commentators note how the emotions record and convey our values in a manner that is constitutive of ethically defensible and desirable living (Sherman, 1989). Of course they can only perform these functions when attuned habitually to (wise) judgement. His account of emotions is not, however, encumbered, by the top-down Kantian approach where the absolute value of the moral law and the autonomous will 'shape and regulate the emotions' (Sherman, 1997: 157). Precisely what form the judgement takes is highly disputed in the literature on the philosophy of emotions. Few cognitive theorists would deny that the desires, motivations and feelings we experience involve a sense of our situation. The strongest account of the cognitive element is found in what Griffiths (1997) labels the 'propositional attitude school'.[4] Griffiths argues that in its strongest form, in Solomon's early writings, the emotion simply is a judgement about ourselves and the world. Other accounts (e.g. Roberts (1988) and Armon-Jones (1991)) have shied away from the propositional reductionism that can be attributed to Solomon and others. What is at issue among them is the extent to which language captures the construal. Charles Taylor's writings, which I employed in Chapter 2, might be criticised for having emphasised the linguistic dimension of emotional experience whereas Roberts' (1988) and Armon-Jones' (1991) accounts lean towards less propositional elements of emotion and view them under the aspect of some kind of 'construal' of events. Nevertheless, it is sufficient for my purposes here to note that in both cases language and the construal are internally related to the experienced emotion.[5]

What I shall do now is to interrogate the specific emotion of *schadenfreude* and to consider the extent to which the occurrence of the emotion in a sportsperson might make it a reason for us to think of them as lacking virtue or exhibiting vice.

Emotions, good sportspersons and good sporting lives

So, far from being blind passions, as Hume would have it, or wayward steeds as Plato preferred, I have tried to show how our emotions can shape our moral responses. We feel guilt properly at transgressions, remorse at serious violations, and shame at our inability to match well-founded social expectations. These negative emotions can act as powerful sensitisers to the worth of respective courses of action just as they can give evidence of our sensitivities, or lack of them in consequence. Whether sportspersons do experience these emotions is of course not guaranteed, however strong the social expectations for them might be. Thus, for example, many people could not understand the Argentine footballer Diego Maradona's *post facto* rationalisations of his cheating in the 1986 football World Cup quarter-final when he deceived the officials into thinking that he had headed the ball past the English goalkeeper, though in fact he had illegally punched it. His now infamous remark – that it was the 'Hand of God' – was later retracted and explained by him with reference to the more obvious motive that he was seeking a competitive advantage by a strategy that he had used successfully before. What is central to his reaction is the lack of regret (let alone remorse) expressed for his actions. (At least Ron Atkinson had publicly expressed his deep chagrin in the wake of his racist remarks.) So it is not merely, then, that we hold sportspersons responsible for their emotions and emotional outbursts, but a fortiori that we properly hold them culpable at times for their failure to experience and signal them too.

It is in this vein that Nancy Sherman writes of seeing through the emotions:

> We can think of them [emotions] as modes of attention enabling us to notice what is morally salient, important, or urgent in ourselves and our surroundings. They help us to track the morally relevant "news". . . . In addition to their role as modes of attention, emotion plays a role in communicating information to others. They are modes of responding. Putting the two together, emotions become modes both for receiving information and signalling it. Through the emotions we both track and convey what we care about.
>
> (Sherman, 1989: 40)

As I argued in Chapter 2, after Taylor, in making a strong evaluation, we are articulating the import to which the feeling aspect of emotion relates. And in doing so, we display our own moral sensitivities and insensitivities. Our emotions typically carry information to our reflections. Frequently, after a sporting encounter, and occasionally in the midst of one, we may ask ourselves, 'Why did I do and feel this and not that?', 'To what extent am I a worse or better person for feeling this and not that?' In this vein, consider the example of a recent international cricket match between Sri Lanka and England that descended into a bitter farce when members from both teams deceived and harassed each other and the umpires to such an extent that the debacle sparked a near crisis in a game renowned for its civility. After all, in how many sports does the opposing team welcome the opposing batter(s) to the crease by clapping them? In this scenario, what were thought of as hitherto unreflective professional sportsmen began asking themselves how their actions may be seen to tarnish the game irreparably. Without recourse to convenient exculpations such as the pressure of the event, the heat of the moment and so on, players came to think of themselves as having diminished a noble tradition. The players from both sides began to speak of (and therein to reconceptualise) themselves as 'custodians' of the game whose conduct and character had failed to appropriately reflect that role. The inner dialogue that prompts such questioning frequently follows our pre-reflective responses to situations that are typical of our emotional life. It was a direct consequence of the regret and even the shame many of them felt and acknowledged publicly in respect of their actions. The game emerged stronger in response to their public self-purging. Envy, like resentment and spite, can simmer. I do not want, therefore, to make too much mileage out of the episodic nature of many emotions. In a fuller discussion of the emotions in sport, and their ethical significance, there would need to be room for the full array of associated concepts such as the ranges of cognitive components and their significance. The sources of retaliatory acts of violence, for example, have a quite different aetiology than the premeditated ones that are cultivated in the locker room and practised with more or less conscientiousness on the playing field. What is important to note, however, is that our habituation into certain modes of emotionally laden attributions and responses is central to our self-development as characters of a given kind.

Thus far I have argued against the naive irrational feeling model of emotion. I have also suggested how the cognitive element of emotion renders intelligible our evaluations of good lives. It is worth developing this idea a little while connecting it more closely to the idea of virtuous and vicious character. What is required now is to interrogate the specific emotion of *schadenfreude* and to consider the extent to which the emotion is good or bad and whether the person who experiences it is necessarily to that extent a person of good or bad character.

What is *schadenfreude*?

The idea of taking pleasure in another's misfortune is one that probably translates across the world without remainder. Precisely why it is that, in modern times, only the Germans have a word for it (or as is quite often the case in German, two words joined together) is something imponderable.[6] Quite literally the word means 'harmjoy'. Before analysing the concept of *schadenfreude* and evaluating its normative status, it is worth illuminating some comical observations beyond the paradigmatic Germanic sense. Terry Lane has defined *schadenfreude* as the sensation experienced when you see two Mercedes Benz collide, but that may reflect a preference for Australian-made cars more than his misplaced egalitarianism. Philip Howard, parodying Oscar Wilde's famous remark about homosexuality, describes it as the sentiment that dares not speak its name (in English). In a similar vein, Clive James admits to feeling *schadenfreude* when he sees his rival's books in the remainders bin. Is there something distinct about the source of the feeling, which effectively designates two emotions, not one? There is something more than the comic at play in James', albeit witty, construal. One of my fellow competitors is suffering in contrast to me. What this emotion resonates with is me and my self-esteem. What seems to lie behind the first example might at least be the murky construal that the Mercedes drivers in some way deserved their comeuppance by virtue of their wealth.

Is there a morally righteous and morally repugnant conception of *schadenfreude*? Imagine a basketball player who has consistently fouled his way through a game, and done it so slyly that his actions have gone unnoticed and unpunished by the officials. In the last second of a tied match, he drives for the basket, misjudges his approach, trips over your foot, and tears his ankle liga-ments without making the shot. You smile wryly to yourself. Are you really any the worse for your reaction? Are you thereby a sportsperson of deficient character? Part of a reasoned evaluation of this type of scenario must always be particularised; it must always take account of the relations between the sufferer and the judger. Another part of our response or evaluation should concern the normative codes that structure their relations. Is the *schadenfroh* deserving of the harm? Of course, again, for these questions to make sense, we must reject the anti-cognitivist picture of the emotions. For to appreciate their sense and value is already to be committed to the cognitive dimension of emotions and thereby their rationality.

We need to be able to distinguish when what seems to be *schadenfreude* is an emotional corollary of justice – if indeed this is the case – and when it is really envy or resentment in disguise. It is clearly not born of a sense of justice when the emotion becomes active and turns into a malicious glee. In some cases of course, the experience of the emotion is not spontaneous or episodic. On the contrary, we cultivate it; sometimes cherish it; it curdles over time, and if not attended to, depletes our moral resources. This is why I have sketched the non-episodic account of *schadenfreude* in the example above. We can only attend to this task of recognition and (re)appropriation if, as Neu (2002) notes, we are able to discriminate among the sources of our emotions and thereby to understand and evaluate ourselves more judiciously. The experi-ence of *schadenfreude* is clearly not born of a sense of justice when the emo-tion becomes active and turns into a malicious glee. This is the point made specifically by Kant about the experience passion being turned into a lasting inclination. Indeed he writes specifically of *schadenfreude* (translated as 'malice' in both the Ellington and Gregor editions) in this regard:

> Malice, which is directly contrary to sympathy, is also not foreign to human nature; when it goes as far promoting evil or wickedness itself, then as a special kind of malice it reveals a hatred of mankind, and appears in all its horrors.
>
> (Kant cited in Ellington, 1994: 124–5)

This malicious glee is not, according to Portmann, *schadenfreude* proper despite the widespread understanding of it under such a description. What the matter hangs on, so to speak, is the idea of whether the harm is deserved or undeserved, and whether indeed one can take an attitude of detached impartiality towards the suffering wrongdoer.

If we wish to appraise the character of the one who feels *schadenfreude*, we need to determine the extent to which, when judging the pleasure felt at another's misfortune, they are active or passive in the generation of the emo-tion. Now, to intend that another be harmed is part of an active strategy – Portmann argues that the pleasure, which is consequent upon this, is not *schadenfreude* proper but rather a malicious glee. Portmann argues that *schadenfreude* proper requires the re-drawing of the emotion away from that particular misconception. As part of his recognition of the passivity of *schadenfreude*, he goes on to suggest an analogy between sympathy and *schadenfreude* – both come uninvited or not at all. Just as manufactured sympathy is not sympathy proper, so in experiencing *schadenfreude*, we experience a pleasure *that* they are harmed without a prior desire for them to be harmed. When set against our earlier account of emotions being necessarily partly constituted by a cognitive element (a construal), this looks odd. What sort of construal is going on then? *Schadenfreude* surely does not visit us uninvited as a guest might. Portmann (17: 27–8), in his defence, says:

> In speaking of the passivity of *Schadenfreude* I do not mean to imply that we are victims of our emotions in the sense that emotions seem to toss us about like ships in a storm. I do not claim that either malicious glee is beyond our control; indeed because we are not purely passive in the fact of feelings and emotions, our efforts to manage our emotions sometimes succeed. Alternatively, we can rationalise our enjoyment of the suffering of another; we can tell ourselves that we take pleasure in the fact that another suffers (as opposed to pleasure in the actual suffering) and that this pleasure results from the love of justice. Such mental dodges attest to the rationality of *Schadenfreude*, as well as to our responsibility for it.

The passivity of all emotions was, perhaps too swiftly, attributed to the Kantian picture of emotion and their non-existence in morally autonomous persons. And Portmann is surely right not to give in to that particular temptation in his defence of *schadenfreude*. But the key to his position is his use of the word 'rationalisation'. For that is exactly what, I will argue below, his position is. That an ethically defensible (praiseworthy?) sense of *schadenfreude* exists, where one can love a sinner while hating the sin and take pleasure in justice being served is precisely that: a rationalisation. Can we hate the foul but love the fouler? Love the cheat but hate the cheating? I will argue that this, in the context of stratified and hierarchically structured activities such as sports, is no more than a rationalisation and that its genesis is typically envy and not a love of justice or low self-esteem, as Portmann argues. But that is to move ahead of the game. Let us next consider the genesis of *schadenfreude*.

The genesis of *schadenfreude*

Articulating the genesis of *schadenfreude*, precisely why the *schadenfroh* feels pleasure at another's misfortune, should open the door to an evaluation of the ethical status of the emotion and the character of the *schadenfroh*. I take the categories from Portmann. He argues that *schadenfreude* may be born of: (1) low self-esteem; (2) loyalty and commitments to justice; (3) the comical; and (4) malice. I shall be concerned here only with the first and second categories. While Portmann maintains that the first three are still liable to be appraised in the guilt and blame we apportion to the *schadenfroh*, the latter is always to be condemned. My position, which I merely assert at this point, is that the third and fourth categories are not philosophically interesting, since the third is not a paradigmatic sense of the concept,[7] because it relates properly to instances of embarrassment rather than harm, while the fourth is obviously despicable and therefore uncontentious.

Let us consider, then, the idea that low self-esteem might give birth to feelings of *schadenfreude* that are ethically excusable. Early on in Christine Mackinnon's consideration of the cultivation of the self in virtue theory, she remarks that 'everybody is faced with the task of constructing a self, but not every-body starts with the same equipment' (1999: 37). Is it the case for those who feel *schadenfreude* that they necessarily think so little of themselves?

Francis Bacon captured something like the point nicely when he said that a recognition of others' sufferings can redeem our own.[8] This seems to be the case with our basketball player. He was on the wrong end of his opponent's cheating, made to look bad because of it, and feels relieved that the game has not been lost by virtue of his inability to master his cheating opponent. Of course, the precise identity of the other sufferer and their relation to us is a crucial variable. This is what generates remarks such as Clive James's above: it is *his* competitor's book in the remainder bin. Portmann argues that self-esteem enhances our sense that we are leading good lives. More specifically, he asserts: 'Self-esteem does not blind us to interpersonal differences; rather, it prevents us from concluding that the superiority of one person signifies the worthlessness or inherent defect in another' (2000: 33).

It seems clear to me here that he is talking about self-respect, which is not exclusive – the possession of self-respect by one does not entail its exclusion in another. Where, however, our sense of our own worth in relation to others is set in a competitive structure (going for the head coach position, achieving a promotion from one division to the next, breaking the record), it seems that self-esteem is characteristically exclusive.[9] My having won entails your loss, and vice versa. The objects of envy are typically positional goods. This is precisely the theme of a remark attributed to Gore Vidal that 'whenever a friend succeeds a little something in me dies'. Now the distinction is crucial for Portmann, since the *schadenfreude* born of low self-esteem is of a deficient sense of self; it is a weakness of character. He takes this to entail its ethical excusability. He takes his cue here from Rawls' (1972: 534–40) remarks on envy and, in quoting Rawls approvingly, conflates self-esteem with self-respect:[10] 'When envy is a reaction to the loss of self-respect in circumstances where it would be unreasonable to expect someone to feel differently, I shall say it is excusable' (Portmann, 2000: 34).

Now where resentment is felt as an affront to one's dignity – and here we can say he has shifted to self-respect again – the feeling of anger may be justi-fied. He says it reflects a healthy self-esteem, but here he is trading again on self-respect. While self-respect has a categorical status (one either has it or not), self-esteem derives and is measured from our evaluations of ourselves in social structures according to a good or range of goods or abilities.[11] He concludes: 'To the extent that a feeling of inferiority seems to invite celebration of other's woes, condemning a *Schadenfroh* person is a bit like blaming him or her for dissatisfaction with an unjust social framework' (Portmann, 2000: 35).

Now it is clear that if we feel pleasure when someone has, for example, strongly humiliated another (where the limit case is torture), then Rawls' exculpation might be reasonable. Other cases of celebration of loss by others in sport are worthy of consideration. Consider someone who is a not a regular player in the starting line-up, but is a solid and reliable substitute 'quarterback' (in American Football) or 'stand-off' (the equivalent in Rugby Union), whose fitness levels and tactical and technical abilities are not developed to the elite level of his starting team-mate. When the starting player is stretchered from the field of play, the substitute rejoices inwardly at his chance to shine and to show his talents. Where this feeling is not directly driven by the player's negative attitude towards the starting 'quarterback' or 'stand-off', I think we ought to be careful not to excuse the pleasure he experiences. On the one hand, what should rankle with us is not merely the lack of empathy and sympathy with a team-mate but the egoistic quality of his celebration, which is dependent upon a teammate's suffering. Nevertheless, the relationship between his joy and the harm of the star player is not one of cause and effect but rather mere correlation. So the concept of *schadenfreude* does not apply properly here even if we think of the substitute's inward celebration as disrespectful or callous. It is not clear to me that sports are unique in this matter. I see no reason why one would not find considerable evidence for this emotion in a whole range of competitively structured practices from work to politics. We might, however, think that paradigm cases of *schadenfreude* were those in which persons were pitted against each other in some antagonistic way. What may be slightly unusual in this example is the fact that the type of emotion can perhaps as easily be felt in relation to those with whom I share goals and aspirations. I do not want to make too much of this, however, since it is perfectly possible that competition and the exclusivity of goods on offer (especially the positional ones, such as status, ranking, hierarchy and power) might as easily obtain in other practices of an inherently competitive kind. I shall return to this issue below with a slightly more difficult example from a recent Ryder Cup contest.

Part of why I think *schadenfreude* is problematic is because of the envy that often accompanies the emotion. Both Solomon (2000) and Herzog (2000) get much closer to the relationship between envy and *schadenfreude* than Portmann. Everyone seems to agree that envy is a 'loser's emotion' resulting from a failure accurately to assess one's self-worth. We might conclude that *schadenfreude* harms no one but the *schadenfrohe* themselves. Let them stew in their bitter juices, we might think. Harm them nonetheless it does by generating false pictures of their relations with those who facilitate what it is they are committed to – sporting excellence. In developing our attitudes to these emotions dependent on self-evaluation, we might also consider the patholog-ically 'humble' who ritually deprecate themselves and seek to defer to and emulate others. Of course, we might then see envy as emulation gone bad. For emulation is, on the face of it, a good thing, and in virtue theory in particular, it is the wise person (in Aristotle, the *phronimos*) whom we seek to model our choices and character upon. In envy, however, our admiration goes awry; the negativity overtakes what benefits could be had from emulation. If we are to believe the Catholic tradition, then envy first leads to sadness, then to gossip, then to *schadenfreude*, then to hatred (Solomon, 2000). If indeed this is so, then although the lack of self-esteem that can give birth to *schadenfreude* may not be as vicious as resentment, or spite or malicious glee, it is nevertheless something we should be on our toes to avoid and/or acknowledge on our path to making ourselves better (sports) persons.

In respect of the slide between emotions of lesser and more corrosive power, Herzog picks out the comic dimension sometimes associated with *schadenfreude* that is morally unobjectionable. I have asserted above that this emotion is better conceptualised in terms of the concept of embarrassment because of the relative seriousness or significance that attaches to each. Herzog shows how our comical responses to embarrassment can slide into the deeper, nastier emotion, which can find root in envy at the same time as being productive of it:

> The heart that's heavy seeing other men more worthy in anything is the motive for a certain kind of *Schadenfreude*. Not the snicker that greets the pompous speaker who rises to the lectern with resolute gravity, obliv-ious to the lobster bisque splattered across his tie; so much doesn't require any antecedent envy. But suppose you had previously noted your dismay that he cut a more imposing figure in public than you, that the thought rankled, and that now you rejoice in seeing the fates bring him low precisely because his humiliation makes him less of a threat to your self-esteem.
>
> (Herzog, 2000: 148)

So it is often the case, and is by no means ethically excusable, that the *schadenfreude* born of low esteem masks a more or less bitter envy, not because one has been robbed of one's self-respect, but rather because one has suffered a blow to one's self-esteem that one simply cannot handle.

In this vein, Dr Johnson remarks that envy, not selfishness, is the mother of all malevolence:

> Most of the misery which the defamation of blameless actions, or the obstruction of honest endeavours brings upon the world, is inflicted by men that propose no advantage to themselves but the satisfaction of poi-soning the banquet which they cannot taste, and blasting the harvest which they have no right to reap.
>
> (Cited in Herzog, 2000: 149)

Moreover, when we think of envy, it is important to consider who is envied and what are its characteristic objects (from material goods, to appearances and talents). Like *schadenfreude*, envy is felt paradigmatically, but not exclusively, in relation to those in whom we have antagonistic relations. Consider the jealousy that drives so many of the characters of *The Iliad* against both friend and foe alike as they seek to claim that most competitive of goods, honour, from the gods. What often drives envy is not so much the desire to be the greatest; that is too limited a preserve to be psychologically credible. Rather, what motivates a sportsperson's emotional set more frequently is the desire to be seen to be (even a little bit) better than one's nearest rival. Two qualities of this desire for status strike me as important in an attempt to better understand what is going on when *schadenfreude* is felt, either in terms of opponents or indeed of team-mates occupying the starting line-up. First, it is the narcissism of minor differences, in Freud's term, that seems to drive the emotion. Second, the joy felt at our antagonist's harm is therefore driven by our familiarity with them. Or, as Hume puts it, 'tis not the great disproportion betwixt ourself and one another, which produces it, but on the contrary, our proximity' (cited in Herzog, 2000: 155).

There is a further, related point that is worthy of notice. Ought we to think of the celebration of a loss by one team, or indeed a vital mistake by our opponent, as being born necessarily of *schadenfreude*? The much discussed response of the American Ryder Cup team of 1999 who ran across the eighteenth green before the hole had been finished is paradigmatic of this category. Were they celebrating their European opponent's failed putt or their own win? It seems to me, although the matter is open to subsequent empirical refutation, that in the heat of the moment, the relief and joy expressed in their actions was symptomatic of mere catharsis and not inherently the rejoicing at their opponent's suffering. If my reading of this is correct, then it would be improper to think of their actions under the description of *schadenfreude*. It was of course still highly undesirable; the best that one can say is that it evidenced a lack of respect – and against the grain of what is undeniably among the nobler sports. This is not to say that in all such cases, the celebration of such an incident could not be classified as *schadenfreude*. If they were genuinely rejoicing the miserable failing of their opposition, and the celebration of their victory was secondary in importance, then it is clear that the description of *schadenfreude* would be properly applied – and our responses to it should alter accordingly.

I see no reason to suppose that any particular sports culture is more given to *schadenfreude* than another. What strikes me as noteworthy, if you will pardon the pun, is that in the sport where direct harm is intentionally and legally inflicted, boxing, *schadenfreude* is almost conspicuous by its absence among the boxers themselves. It might be argued more generally that spectators or followers of clubs, teams, and individual sports stars revel in opponents' harms rather more so than the players themselves. Where the clubs have intense geographical and cultural rivalries, it seems that this is perfectly plausible, though no less regrettable. For my own part, this might well be explained by a deficient sense of self, where spectators appear to believe that their self-worth is vicariously tendered by their identification with a success-ful other (be it team, club or player). Further exploration of this issue is, however, beyond the scope of the present discussion.

That we can reflect on the antecedents to our emotions is one clue as to how we may think about working upon our emotions and perceptions of others and selves, in order to go about educating ourselves in that respect.[12] They do not *all* visit us as uninvited guests might. Moreover, correct perceptions of others and selves are surely part of what we call a good life. And I want to emphasise that it is only a virtue-theoretical position that attempts to take this feature of our experience seriously. For to act well is not merely to do so for the right reasons, to the right extent, at the right time, and so on, but also to feel these reasons and responses while so construing and responding. And this, I fear, is simply ignored, not merely in much of the flourishing sports ethics literature but also in the sociology of sport.[13] Having rejected Portmann's first defence of *schadenfreude*, I will consider his second, rather stronger account for excusability: a loyalty to justice. If he is right that the feeling of *schadenfreude* may be justified as a function of justice then it might be seen as a virtuous rather than a vicious emotional response.

The sense that most of us may feel both familiar and warranted is in the *schadenfreude* felt by those who believe that another has violated an expec-tation or obligation and suffers in relation to their transgression. (How many times have you heard in post-match conferences: 'They got their just desserts!'; or 'I am glad they got their comeuppance', or, in both anticipation and desire, 'What goes around comes around'? Portmann writes:

> There is an important difference between enjoying *that* someone suffers and enjoying actual suffering. The former case must be held apart from *Schadenfreude*, for the attendant pleasure is not properly in seeing some-one suffer but in the hope that someone will learn a valuable lesson in having suffered. Thus we take pleasure not in the suffering of another, but in the hope that he or she will correct a mistake.
>
> (Portmann, 2000: 48)

The pleasure felt at seeing justice done, he argues, must not be confused with a pleasure that a given person is actually suffering themselves. But it seems to me that 'pleasure' is not the right concept here. To take pleasure in suffering is too active, too destructive of human sympathy to be evidence of a love of justice. Now lest it be suggested that I am promoting a picture of sport devoid of intense commitment, let me make it clear that I do not approve of a sport-ing ethics of indifference. To the contrary, anger is an entirely appropriate emotional response to injustice as was noted in Chapter 6.

How it is registered, how accounted for and how exacted – these are fur-ther questions. I am merely arguing that pleasure felt at another's suffering is itself not desirable, even when the suffering is experienced by a wrongdoer. I think the more appropriate model may be a legal one. What one seeks through the courts is often described as 'satisfaction'. I want my transgressor to be adjudged wrong in public and admonished. A more appropriate emotional response, then, will be a less hedonistic or egoistic one; not cold, impartial, empathy-lacking justice, and certainly not an active, hand-rubbing glee. It strikes me that the proper emotional response to justice being served, and subsequent harm befalling the wrongdoer is captured by the concept of 'satisfaction'. Such is the feeling that ought to characterise our basketball player's emotional response. This concept denotes emotional neutrality and a certain passivity that is entirely absent in the positive and corrosive *schadenfreude*.

Of course this distinction regarding our rejoicing in the seeing of justice done begs wider questions about the role of human suffering in our lives. The position here is in debt to St Augustine in *Summa Theologiae*: Love the sinner, hate the sin is the exhortation. But Portmann's gloss seems unreal. 'We take pleasure in hoping they will correct the mistake' (2000: 156), he says. Well this *may* be the emotion felt by the zealous reformer, but the attitude of the *schadenfroh* seems not of this kind. 'You're bad but look how good in contrast I am', seems closer to the mark. What is missing here is any reference to sympathy – note, *not* empathy – with the sufferer. Of course, the resenting sportsperson may well, like Keane above, have empathy with his opponent, as he writhes on the floor in agony; it is precisely that empathy that fuels his enjoyment.

Schadenfreude and sporting sympathy

I have tried to show that Portmann's defences for *schadenfreude* are unacceptable. In the first instance, his conflation of self-respect and self-esteem undercuts his defence of the emotion. Second, the idea that low self-esteem and a commitment to justice might drive an excusable pleasure at another's suffering is at odds with any basic notion of human sympathy that will be at the core of all moralities I (perhaps too boldly) assert.

In summary, it seems more felicitous to link *schadenfreude* with a lack of spirit – an othering[14] of my opponent or competitor, or a failure to connect with their humanity as opposed to a deficiency in one's self-esteem. It is clear that our attitudes towards *schadenfreude* will alter accordingly with the severity of the suffering and the greatness of their deficiencies in conduct and character. What seems clear, however, is that the 'trick' of loving the sinner but hating the sin is a perception that will not find a home in the capriciousness of human character (however much we might want to cheer with the angels). Better that we recognise the nature of the occurrence and reflect on our own motivations in relation to the sufferer before we revel too much in the baseness of others and, by contrast, our own righteousness. In sports practice communities, no less than in social science research, we do well to observe Owen Flanagan's principle of minimal psychological realism. 'Make sure when constructing a moral theory or proposing a moral ideal that the character, decision-processing, and behavior are possible, or are perceived to be possible, for creatures like us' (Flanagan, 1991: 32).

This dictum could be seen to work both for and against the position I have set out above. It is natural that our responses to competitors' sufferings will not be driven by feelings so impartial that their losses strike us as heavily as our own. To an extent this is obviously true. Of course, one cannot hope to develop in sportspersons so detached a consideration of human interests, a point made more frequently these days against modern moralities of both utilitarian and deontological persuasion. But the active pleasure at another's misfortune goes beyond the asymmetry of self and other. *Schadenfreude* passes beyond the excusable and into both the realms of culpable and responsible emotion. Worse, where it is cultivated or merely utilised to enhance and celebrate our own esteem and achievements, *pace* Gore Vidal, a little something in us dies too.

Part III

Sports ethics, medicine and technology

9   Suffering in and for sport

In the previous two chapters I have explored the emotional ecology of winning and losing and tied it closely the virtues and vices frequently found in sport. The arrogant are lowered; those who relish their suffering are to be thought of as undesirable characters. I want to extend this ethical discussion further into the limit cases of suffering, which is manifest in many ways in sports. Compare the tears of Mary Decker Slaney, the hot favourite for the women's 5,000m final of the 1984 Olympics at Los Angeles with the uncontrolled weeping of British rower Matthew Pinsent on the podium in Athens in 2004, as he won his fourth consecutive Olympic gold medal in rowing. These extreme examples of intense emotions in sport should warn us against simple classifications of the emotions. In this chapter I want to make sense of how we can better understand and appreciate the emotionally saturated concept of suffering by first distinguishing more carefully between pain and suffering than is typically done in sports medicine or sports anthropology, where they are often conflated and treated as synonymous with private or subjective feelings. I go on to present critically some philosophical accounts of the concept of suffering and in doing so begin to draw together threads of shared interest between sports ethics and medical ethics. I articulate and exemplify a range of issues that arises from thinking of suffering in sport as an extended emotional experience, which is inherently linked to the projects that we care about, are committed to, and that partly constitute our identities as sportspersons.

On suffering and pain: some conceptual geography

There is not a developed philosophical literature on pain and suffering in sport.[1] Jeff Fry (2002) recently published a very insightful overview of the theodicy of pain and suffering as it applies (and where it does not apply) to sports. In sports anthropology, David Howe (2004) has catalogued the habitus of injury-acceptance as part and parcel of the practices that are elite sport. Neither Fry nor Howe, however, directs attention significantly to the relations between the two concepts. What I shall do in this section is to set out some analytical remarks concerning the two concepts – and only hint at the theological similarities and dissimilarities in an attempt to enquire as to whether a consideration of suffering might have something interesting to say about the nature and purposes of sport, and the sportspersons' emotional components seen as part of the living of a good life.

There is often conceptual confusion in sports talk surrounding these thorny concepts. Typically suffering and pain are conflated. One is thought to be suffering when in pain, and concomitantly when pained, to be suffering. One of the ways of dealing with the complexity of the conceptual connections of pain and suffering is crudely to dualise them in the aspect of the person. Under such a dualism, pain is physical, suffering is mental. Thus Howe writes: 'Pain is a highly subjective phenomenon, and this has led to its exclusion from much discussion of injury, which may be seen as more objective' (2004: 74).

Despite disavowals to the contrary throughout the book, it is difficult to read passages in Howe's book in any way other than dualistically.[2] After Descartes, and dominating Western philosophy until Gilbert Ryle's brilliant debunking in *The Concept of Mind* (1949), people were thought to be comprised of separate substances – minds and bodies – whose natures were distinct. Howe's writing, like that of many other social scientists (especially with the rise of the sociology of the body, with authors who are not naturally inclined to a phenomenological mien) and even sports psychologists (who really should know better), has difficulty in escaping the language that separates mind and body as distinct substances. So in Howe's critical ethnographies of living with pain and injury, it is perhaps not surprising that 'mental' concepts such as 'anguish' or 'suffering' do not appear in the index. It seems clear that physical pain is the paradigmatic object of discussion. And there is of course nothing necessarily wrong with this. What is problematic, and what is found in many places elsewhere, is a particular set of relations between pain and suffering. On the one hand there is an apparently non-dualistic position where writers casually refer to 'bodily suffering' as a sensation 'usually' in the body. On the other hand there is the dualistic one: suffering is supposed to be the felt marker: pain indicates suffering.[3]

A further and less frequently observed aspect of suffering and pain is brought out by Ivan Illich[4] (1987):

> The Old Testament is very rich in words that express a deep, deep sense of suffering: anguish, fear, bitterness, the experience of being lost, forlorn, beaten up, exposed to the wrath of the Lord. It was only very much later, during the Christian epoch, that rabbis felt the need to assign a specific word for that which we moderns now call pain. When these same rabbis had to talk about physical pain they used the word that designated punishments which I inflict. The English word pain comes from the Latin poena, from being punished. The concept of a physical pain, one specifically physical, comes from the experience of being chastised by another. In our language pain does not come from the inside; it is imposed on us from outside.

In what follows I will assume that the concepts of suffering and pain are closely related and will develop some ideas more concerned with suffering that is not driven by pain. To do this I shall draw upon analyses of suffering from the medical ethics literature.

Concepts of 'suffering' in medical ethics

In a well-known medical ethics text, Cassell (1991: 33) offers the following definition of suffering:

> [S]uffering occurs when an impending destruction of the person is perceived; it continues until the threat of disintegration has occurred or until the integrity of the person can be restored in some other manner. [...] suffering extends beyond the physical.

And later says that 'suffering can be defined as the state of severe distress associated with events that threaten the intactness of person' (Cassell, 1991: 33).

The two features of this definition might be called the (1) feeling and (2) integrity criteria.[5] It is worth observing how these criteria relate to aspects of privacy and subjectivity. There can be times when there seems to be a simple causal relationship between pain and suffering – though it must be noted Cassell avoids the simple dualism of caused in the body, suffered in the mind. In such cases one suffers because one is in pain. Cassell refers (1991: 25–6) to situations 'when the pain is so severe it is virtually overwhelming', 'when the patient believes the pain cannot be controlled' and also to 'pain that is not overwhelming but continues for a very long time'. It is not difficult to find sporting examples for these instances of suffering because of pain. They represent, perhaps, a kind of paradigm for sporting suffering in that they are at least the most obvious of cases of sporting suffering.

Cassell, however, makes a couple of further conceptual remarks that are interesting for our purposes. Like Howe, he too writes dualistically in the vein of an essentially private character of suffering: 'Suffering is ultimately a personal matter – something whose presence can only be known by the sufferer' (Cassell, 1991: 35).

This privatisation of suffering runs counter to the view I shall adopt and adapt later. In that account, suffering can indeed be attributed by another. Indeed, our predication of empathy as sports spectators rests on this point. As I watch the gymnast fall on the last movement of their routine my heart goes out to them. I can appreciate at least sufficient of their misery to see how and why they suffer. In later remarks, however, Cassell captures at least some of what I take to be the inherent sociality of suffering:

> Suffering must be distinguished from its uses. In some theologies, especially the Christian, suffering has been seen as presenting the opportunity of bringing the sufferer closer to God. This 'function' of suffering is at

once its glorification and relief. If, through great pain or deprivation, someone is brought closer to a cherished goal, that person may have no sense of having suffered but, instead, may feel enormous triumph. To an observer, the only thing apparent may be the deprivation. This cautionary note is especially important because people are often said to have suffered greatly, in a religious context, when we know only that they were injured, tortured or in pain, not whether they suffered.

(Cassell, 1991: 35)

He summarises: 'Although pain and suffering are closely identified in the minds of most people and in the medical literature, they are phenomenologically distinct' (1991: 35).

Given that the concepts are so frequently run together, we should ask: precisely what does it mean to say that pain and suffering are conceptually distinct? One could think of minor ailments, when one is in pain but not suffering. One could think of fleeting twinges – for example, the type which, in my early middle age, I encounter in my knee, back and ankles when I run - where it would be a piece of gross conceptual inflation to say that I was suffering. Finally, one could imagine cases of minor injuries, knocks, bumps, soreness, that are inherent in contact sport. When we experience minor injury or dysfunction it is no more than the consequence of the graft and grind of any sporting life. These simple remarks serve to establish the point that pain and suffering are not synonymous. We may often be in pain but it does not follow that we should think of ourselves as suffering.

One further idea that might cut through the simplistic body–mind/pain–suffering complex is the idea of significance. It can be argued that what the integrity criterion attempts to secure is a quality of 'depth' in our experience. Suffering under such a description necessarily draws on both significance (extent or duration) and psychological distress. It would be odd to speak of one who suffered momentarily or in the blinking of an eye. In what follows below I consider Edwards' critique of the 'feeling' and 'integrity' criteria of Cassell's account and his own analysis of the concept.

Edwards bases his criticisms of the concepts of suffering proposed by Cassell, among others, upon a more cautious appropriation of the concept. His leading point is a rejection of the essentialism entailed in the necessary and sufficient conditions they propose; that is to say he rejects their method on Wittgensteinian grounds. Edwards says that we should attend to the uses of the concept 'suffering' in order to establish its meaning. And following our appreciation of that heterogeneity we shall find no crystallised essence but rather a family of meanings that criss-cross and overlap without containing any indisputable linguistic essence. Suffering is the kind of experience that must be felt. To suffer is to be in a state that is necessarily felt by the agent. In this respect, it is like pain. He says: 'Would it make sense to say of a person "You're in pain" if this came as a complete surprise to them?' (2003: 65). Of course, stories are legion of sportspersons who are injured without consciousness of it as they perform heroic deeds – only later to collapse in agony. One image that springs to mind is that of the bandaged American gymnast Kelly Strug as she prepared to risk even more serious injury lining up for the vault, which won the American team the gold medal at the 1996 Olympic Games. While, however, one may be injured without being in pain, one cannot be said to suffer without the cognitive aspect of the emotion registered at some conscious level. This condition seems indisputable for human suffering. Put formally we might say that it – the awareness of some seriously negative happening – is a necessary condition of suffering but not a sufficient one. Well, for the moment we may say that. I think there are some grounds for denying even that much, as we shall see.

Second, Edwards argues that suffering must be extended in time. Something as fleeting as a pinprick, or stepping on a sharp stone, cannot count. Moreover, though this seems a separate point, he argues that pain is not a necessary condition of suffering, for we may grieve deeply while experiencing no pain – where this is taken to be the unpleasant sensation produced by physical causes. Third, he argues that one cannot be happy and suffer. To suffer is to have a shadow cast – for that time – over one's enjoyment of life. He does note that in theological accounts of suffering – martyrdom is the extreme – that suffering is a central part of one's conception of the good life but he argues here one merely has a stronger preference for the suffering.[6] Edwards summarises his threefold account thus:

> The first is a 'self' component; the sufferer must realise that it is he or she that is suffering, that the experiences are his or her own. Second, the phenomenological component, the distinct way or ways it feels to suffer. And third, a temporal component; this will signal the duration of the experience of suffering. Schematically we might express such experiences thus: [S, p, t]. Where the components are the self component S, the phenomenological component p, and the temporal component t, respectively.
>
> (Edwards, 2003: 65)

We can conclude that there is at least a generic meaning here; a conceptual core but nothing as strong as an essence conceived of as a set of necessary and sufficient conditions. That general sense of 'suffering' means little more than experiencing something significantly deleterious to our well-being. In relation to human suffering we typically qualify the nature of that suffering in an adverbial way by drawing out the qualities of mind and character that attend the suffering. In addition, I want to draw attention to a specific dimension – the emotionally saturated idea of suffering. It seems to me that much suffering in sport is merely the experience of distressing pain – and this is surely worthy of explanation. But I shall not address it below, preferring instead to highlight a few remarks about the emotionality of suffering in sport. By way of summary let us agree for the moment that suffering in sport is an extended emotional response to events that are significantly deleterious to our well-being. Where will that take us?

Emotionally laden suffering

Let us say that we can articulate human suffering as a felt emotion. This point arises from Edwards' first two conditions, though he does not employ the description of suffering as an emotion as such. The idea that suffering is an emotion is denied by some. Consider Meyerfeld (1999: 50) who argues that one may suffer without cognisance. He asserts that one may be stunned, inarticulate or confused. Yet it seems that here he is presupposing that for which he must argue. For while it is true of certain moods ('distress' being one candidate) that they are to a certain extent diffused or inchoate, I cannot see what conceptual advantage there is in thinking that the epistemological condition is not necessary.

In my discussion of emotion above, I included the cognitive element of emotion, which is typically in the form of a judgement. Imagine being told by someone who looked desolate that they are suffering but they had no idea why. We might think, quite reasonably, that they had taken leave of their senses. Of course they might be experiencing a sense of foreboding, anticipating some bad event, or simply be feeling melancholic. If this were the case though, we would have moved away from emotion-talk and back into the territory of moods, which have a lower cognitive threshold and no specific intentional object where the idea of emotional construal finds more obvious application. Moreover, that someone is inarticulate or stunned or confused is a psychological condition – one that need not impinge upon our conceptualisation of suffering as an emotion. So let me assume here that to suffer is to experience an emotion with an intentional object: we suffer because of our perceptions of something significantly bad about our condition. Nevertheless, this alone is insufficient to make sense of suffering. In the light of the foregoing we should say that to suffer is to undergo some unpleasant emotion for some significant duration. Now what is to count as 'significant duration' cannot be pre-specified in some abstract way. The particularity of the phenomenology of suffering means that what counts as extended in one context may be brief in another. But that does not open the door to subjectivity of meaning. Consider the intensity of effort of the 400m runner as he or she comes down the final straight, paradoxically trying to produce and remove lactates from her or his legs. I want to maintain that to use the word 'suffering' here, as commentators do, is inappropriate. Contrast the use of the word 'suffering' to describe the efforts of marathon runners in the last mile, or Tour de France cyclists going for the last climb of a mountain stage. Here the use of the word has a more natural home. Edwards does not develop this point and so I shall say a little by way of justification for the position.

For us to speak of emotionally saturated suffering, we must at least have time to dwell (should we so desire) on our misfortune in order for us to suffer.

In this sense we could contrast suffering with more episodic emotions – such as the joy of scoring a goal – which is brief, however much we recall, re-describe and relish it on later occasions. Now if we were to evaluate the benefit or disbenefit of an emotion we might well be required to consider its duration as well as its extent. Ought we to opt for a few years of adulation, status and wealth at the expense of a lifetime's suffering, as many elite sportspersons do? Typically, the experience of the emotion in sport does not last in time in the same way as the caring love of a parent or child. Equally, though pain can range from mild to excruciating, it seems to make little sense to say that suffering could be mild. This is not to say that suffering is all or nothing. We do not need to be absolutist about this. But it makes sense to say that there is a certain threshold before we meaningfully apply the concept.

By coalescing pain and suffering, by failing to keep them analytically distinct, Meyerfeld denies this attribution. He draws on the *locus classicus* of the pain register (Melzack and Torgerson, 1971), which describes pain as ranging from mild to discomforting, and then to distressing, horrible and, finally, excruciating. Meyerfeld goes further by saying: 'These words recognisably refer to the intensity of suffering not just pain' (1999: 39).

I fail to see the coherence of this application, and Meyerfeld offers no argument for it. In order that one may be said to suffer, one must experience a certain intensity or one cannot say one suffered. To suffer mildly makes little sense, *pace* Meyerfeld, though to describe a pain as mild does. Cassell is much clearer here. He says that we suffer – in relation to pain – 'when the pain is so severe it is virtually overwhelming' (1991: 36) and later 'when the patient believes the pain cannot be controlled' or 'in relation to pain that is not overwhelming but continues for a very long time' (1991: 36). It is not an accident that in the biomedical literature, where pain and suffering co-mingle, we find that chronic pain is the paradigmatic example. Extension in time, and a certain intensity, are all present in Cassell's examples. They are part of the condition of suffering. But an articulation of that condition is not complete without the articulation of a sense of meaning that attaches inherently to it.

In addition, it seems reasonable to say that we cannot suffer in relation to things to which we are indifferent. Whereof one does not care, thereof one cannot suffer. That for which we suffer we must, in some fairly strong sense, be committed to, or care for, or identify with. There must be some sense of both attachment and value. This is the direction in which Cassell's 'intactness' condition aims, but it sets too high a threshold. Equally, Edwards holds that suffering 'must have a fairly central place in the mental life of the subject'. And while I think that this is right, it does not have normative direction; it fails to specify the inherent negativity of the concept. In contrast to this point, Cassell merely asserts that the religious martyr suffers yet experiences the suffering positively. This seems to be too open-ended. I maintain that the negative normativity is, logically speaking, internal to the concept of human suffering. Where one embraces a painful death in what sense can one be said to suffer? It strikes me that that would be contradictory. It is a mistake founded on the generalisability of experience – yes, you and I might suffer in such circumstances but our *Weltanshauungen* are radically different.

What is at stake in suffering, as I have said, is something that is not a matter of indifference to us – it is something that is part of our 'horizon of significance' to use Charles Taylor's apt phrase. As Cassell observes, we can only *see* the Christian sufferer in pain. Perhaps we can put it more strongly by saying that martyrs do not suffer the pains of fire, rather they rejoice in it. Now a chief question will be whether sportspersons find, like religious martyrs, the depths of meaning in sport that their forebears did in Christianity.

Having merely hinted at the features that I consider critical to capture our emotional sense of human suffering, I will merely point to aspects of sports suffering that would bear further analysis and note certain social and theological parameters that might serve to deepen our understanding of suffering – especially for those such as physicians or physiotherapists or sports coaches who necessarily deal with the equally necessary sense of the inevitably tragic in sport.

Suffering in and for sport: three possibilities

As I have said, the paradigmatic cases of suffering in sport relate closely to those cases wherein pain drives the suffering over time in relation to something of significance to the sufferer. It strikes me that there are three categories where this conceptualisation could usefully be explored in sports-related literatures. They help to point to what I think of as the inherently tragic in sport. I do not mean by this the myth of continual progress so dear to global capitalism and crystallised in sports marketing. The point is simply that sport careers (however humble or exalted) are not best represented in a linear fashion. Rather they are cruelly, inescapably, elliptical. They rise, they peak and then, necessarily, they fall. The simple fact can be seen in three categories of sportspersons to whom we might look naturally for suffering: (1) the elite athlete; (2) the ageing athlete; (3) the retired athlete. In each of these cases the meaning of the suffering will be coloured in distinct ways; the manner in which the sport informs the life of the elite athlete – which may be almost suffocating in its exclusivity and intensity – will be quite distinct from the more chronic experiences of the ageing athlete and the desolation of the retired athlete who may wallow in a post-sport world devoid of emotional peaks and troughs (along with other lacunae).

If we were to agree that suffering in sport (as elsewhere) is best thought of as an emotional experience, then we should be able to point to the intentional objects involved. What might 'cause' such suffering? Some potential precursors might be (1) the anticipation of loss or the infliction of a defeat; (2) the recognition of consequences of injury; (3) distress of possible termination of career, perhaps most strongly for elite athletes; and (4) sports 'death' as it were: the loss of economic and social identity. Of course the list is not exhaustive and merely attempts to suggest where one might toil for more interesting phenomenological investigations. In these cases one could ask whether sportspersons, contra Huizinga, take their sports too seriously. Here the status of the sportsperson is all important. For professional players, sports may well be 'everything' – the phrase 'it's only a game' is a banal utterance in this context. The rest of us, however, need to find a place for the sports activities we care for, love and value, in ways that are not so totalising. It also opens up at least one significant normative question: ought we really to suffer for sport?

Having merely hinted at the meaning-driven facets of sports suffering it might be worth thinking how the duration element might draw us to look for central cases in sport. Where might we find suffering in the performance of sport – as opposed to the preparation for sport? The obvious point to look is at those endurance sports where performance is not merely extended over time – a round of golf after all takes three–four hours – but also those where there is a limited array of performance factors. Typically, sports where the production of power is not dominated by technical or aesthetic concerns seem rich candidates for sites of suffering. We find not merely temporal extension in marathon or ultra-distance running, biathlon, triathlon, and in cycle races such as the Tour de France, but a quality of extension where one has time and space for a welter of factors to impinge upon one's consciousness in the experience of the activity.

A recent incident may go some way to pointing up this interesting aspect in a literal way. At the 2004 Olympics the British runner Paula Radcliffe was the favourite for the marathon. She had posted the year's fastest times for 10,000m on the track and had recently smashed the world record for the marathon. Having struggled to control the pace, in heat that made even some African athletes retire earlier in the race, Radcliffe withdrew with only three miles to go to the finish, apparently in the knowledge that she would not win a medal. Clearly she suffered over the difficult, hilly, terrain in exhausting heat. Mile after mile her face grew more contorted, more anguished. What were her thoughts over those miles, those hours and minutes as she considered personal failure, in the certain knowledge that she had 'blown' probably her best chance to gain an Olympic gold? What kind of scathing introspection went on with her every stride? And just as one can experience emotion after the fact, what emotions fuelled her anticipation of the savage British sports press in the aftermath of what would be written as a national tragedy. Or as it was later written up, even in some of the most thoughtful quarters of the British media, not so much a national disgrace as a moment of personal egoism and cowardice. Robert Philip's (2004) article, entitled 'Radcliffe was a sore loser', was as critical of the national press that supported Radcliffe as a heroine as he was of the athlete herself:

> The Tears of a Hero proclaimed one headline alongside a picture of Paula Radcliffe. Well, if it's heroes you want, then I'll give you heroes: Japan's Mizuki Noguchi, who won the Olympic marathon, was a hero. So, too,

was Briton Liz Yelling, who produced a late sprint to overtake Maria Abel, of Spain, in a photo-finish for 25th place.

Nor should we forget her team-mate Tracey Morris, who ran in the same heat and up the same hills as Radcliffe to finish 29th only to be totally ignored by Fleet Street. And was there anyone more heroic than Mongolian Lursan Ikhundeg Otgonbayar, the 66th and last competitor across the line in the Panathanaiko Stadium, a full 30 minutes behind the woman in front and almost 1½ hours adrift of Noguchi?

But no, it is poor, distraught, anguished, heroic (I could go on but you get the drift) Radcliffe sitting in a gutter by the side of the road on whom we are expected to bestow the laurel leaf for Olympic gallantry.

Call me a cynic, but the way I see it is that unless the medics in Athens can come up with a physical reason why she quit just over three miles from the finish, Radcliffe stopped running and started blubbing for the simple reason that she had just seen gold, silver and bronze medals disappear into the distance [. . .].

What most observers appear to have overlooked is that, yes, while there are only three medals on offer, every runner who completes any marathon course is a winner. Radcliffe – as brave, heroic, and dedicated as she might have proved herself to be in the past – was a loser on Sunday night and, judging by her reaction when she opted out of the race having conceded third place, a pretty sore loser at that.

What is striking in this appraisal is the adverbial quality that Philip imports to the appraisal of the athlete's character. Without knowing it, Philip has charged Radcliffe and held her to account for her suffering. He has judged her character through an emotional evaluation. Yet he has only captured a small part of the aetiology of her suffering – the anticipated failure. It might be argued that he has failed himself (on a monumental scale) to empathise with the athlete in her suffering before moving to his strong critique. The significance of the goal, the preparation of a lifetime, the realisation of a lost dream, the estimation of one's fall from esteem (and then grace) all seem to meet our criteria for suffering to the point that make her devastation comprehensible. For Philip, all that is perceived is a wallowing, egoistic, pity. Now it might be held by others, properly, that Radcliffe's response lacked courage, that it was weak in some meaningful sense – but then that is not the position before us. It is clear that she experiences herself as suffering as she ran and eventually gave up. Ought she to have experienced this emotion? Is she entitled to the empathetic responses that are proper to the perception of a suffering one? These are the questions Philip fails to ask. Instead, he arrives too quickly at his conclusion: she is a shallow loser. For my own part, and based upon the analysis of suffering above, I think it makes every sense to see Radcliffe as suffering and worthy of an aptly felt empathy. I do not say that this makes her a model of good character; one to be admired or envied, simply one for whom we may feel, with justification, some considerable sadness.

To explore such suffering further – and our ethically responsible responses to it – we would need to evaluate the adverbial character of the emotion in a more compassionate manner. Precisely how does one suffer here? Is it wallowing in the failure to achieve one's expected goal? Is it more intense as one battles to dislocate one's sensory experiences, to dull the pain of chronic injuries or heat-driven distress? Again these are only suggestions as to where we might meaningfully further explore suffering in sport.

A set of interesting questions remains that is located beyond the individualised phenomenological conception that we are naturally drawn to in the West. I take my cue here from the socio-theological writings of the Catholic intellectual and polymath Ivan Illich. Illich (1987) writes of 'communities of suffering'. It is an idea rich in possibilities for understanding the places of suffering in sport. Of course this could refer to the suffering that is closely related to intense pain: the gym, weights room, the track, the pool. Commentators frequently remark about the camaraderie wrought by the masochistic mutuality of boxing, or the tacit acknowledgement of chronic neck and back pain suffered by front row players in rugby, or American footballers on the line of scrimmage, at the tight end, protecting the quarterback at the risk of life and limb.

If we eschew a model of emotion that is pejoratively characterised as mere moods, or as uncognitive – as feelings that visit rather like a thief in the night – it makes sense to ask questions regarding the history of suffering in sport. From whom do we learn to suffer? In what ways are we initiated to it? Do we embrace it as a friend or as an enemy? What coping strategies are authentic? Are such strategies for anti-suffering (such as withdrawal) somehow inauthentic? In what sense can coaches or team-mates or indeed opponents share in the suffering of others?

Suffering, sports medicine and the ethics of sport

Finally, there is a further set of Aristotelian-inspired ethical questions that we can ask in respect to the non-theological ethical significance of suffering under the physical and emotional aspects of the concept. Might there be virtuous responses to suffering? Could we think of the boxer, humiliated by his opponent, as acting courageously while he suffers? Or ought we to think of it as courage gone awry, as rash or reckless suffering? Is the boxer's suffering (especially where self-inflicted) in some sense wrenched from virtuous ends – and means? For virtue, if Aristotle is right, is always in the service of good ends. Not any amount of courage is to be thought of as bravery – a point that Philip might have borne in mind during his verbal lasceration of Radcliffe. Should we think differently of Stoic suffering in the face of unbearable pain forced on us by another – a model of passive suffering? Lance Armstrong talks of precisely such a disposition in his account of cycling in the Tour de France, of making his competitors endure the suffering he purposefully inflicted on them. To what point do we admire their forbearance? At what point does it become pathological? Is the quality of suffering conceptually relevant when that person is ourselves, pushing through the 'pain barrier', when we are active in the construction of our own suffering?

It seems best to think of suffering in sport in a teleological way. In medicine we suffer in rehabilitation. In Christian thought we suffer for redemption. What ends are served by suffering in and for sport? There will be no global answers here, only particular ones. But we are minded as philosophers to ask of coaches, players and physicians, especially in elite sports, a question put by Plato long ago (1974: 407a): what limits should we observe in our efforts to improve our bodily performance and remove causes of suffering?

In asking such a question, though not answering it, we would begin to challenge many myths in modern sport and sports medicine. There is a pressing need to understand the moral topography of sports medicine. Key to that challenge is the need to understand sports as well as sports medicine as social practices and, in particular, to uncover that which is often latent – the idea that medicine is merely a technical, unproblematic, means to unquestioned (and unquestionably valuable) ends.[7] So when we talk of medical professionals and professionalisation of sports, we need to ask: whose ethics? Surely there is no necessarily shared ethic between the doctors' cure, the physiotherapists' care, in relation to the players' career. How this is both gendered and loaded – or not – with emotional content will be worthy of exploration and explanation.

Rather than asking whether the pain is positive or negative we might ask: 'What qualities attend the suffering?' In what ways specifically do we suffer in sports? This requires us necessarily to arrange and argue about the adverbial qualities of our selves and our sufferings. These questions force us to deny the hegemony of physicalised, biomedically explainable pain as the paradigm of negative experiences in sport. They force us to take the social and emotional aspects of the emotion of suffering more seriously than hitherto has been the case. As Illich (1987) concluded:

> I am taking the liberty of speaking of suffering as the culturally shaped way of dealing with the shadow side of life rather than with its lighted, sunny side. I shall use the term suffering to indicate a particular socially and culturally acquired art of dealing with that shadow side, of bearing burdens which come with living. I'm speaking about the art of suffering. Pain is only one narrow, but very special, kind of condition in which one would properly need the art of suffering.

I hope, in the spirit of Illich's moving testimony, that I have at least offered a framework in which to consider suffering as an emotion loaded with ethical significance, and one that should be taken more seriously by philosophers and social scientists of sports and sports medicine. I shall now turn to a topic that has had no difficulty whatever in arresting the attention of these communities of scholars, the illicit enhancement of performance otherwise known as 'doping'.

10 Doping

Slippery slopes, *pleonexia* and shame

In Book II of *The Republic* Plato reports the well-known story of Gyges' ring. Gyges, a lowly shepherd, takes his flock into a cave and there finds a corpse wearing a beautiful ring that he subsequently steals. While talking with other shepherds, he fidgets with his fingers and turning the stone of the ring became invisible. Aware of his new-found possibilities, he uses the ring's powers to seduce the king's wife and take over the kingdom. In the Platonic dialogue that follows, Socrates' interlocutor, Glaucon, argues that any sane person would do the same as Gyges. The story throws into sharp relief the value of a life lived justly where one is at peace with oneself – but with little reward – as opposed to one that is lived ignobly while accruing wealth and power and (what seems at least to be) happiness. Is there a necessary relation between the flourishing life and an ethically praiseworthy one? In a number of respects, it will be argued, the myth of Gyges' ring is directly analogous to the problem of doping in elite sports.

In this chapter I will rehearse the central arguments against doping practices and substances and their rebuttal in the literature. I will then introduce the idea of slippery slopes, which has not been deployed in the sports ethics literature, and argue that it is a powerful logical argument against doping liberalisers. Finally, returning to an aretaic vocabulary and drawing upon the moral of the story of Gyges' ring, I will articulate the viciousness of those who unjustly acquire the goods and status their own athletic abilities do not merit as an example of what the ancient Greeks called *pleonexia*. Only in apparent paradox, I argue that the cultivation of shamefulness in elite sports might well assist in the necessary task of self-regulation by athletes and coaches in their strivings for dope-free sporting excellence.

What's wrong with doping? Some standard arguments

As one might imagine the problem of doping is not a new one (Dimeo, 2007; Hoberman, 2005; Houlihan, 1999). In the literature of sports ethics a familiar range of arguments are deployed and typically defused. As it is not my purpose here to review them critically in any detail I shall merely note examples of authors who have written more or less persuasively under the following headings: (1) that doping is all about performance enhancement; (2) that doping allows more training; (3) that doping is unnatural; (4) that doping is coercive; (5) that doping is harmful; (6) that doping confers an unfair advantage.

Doping is wrong because it enhances performance

The weakest of all anti-doping arguments is oddly enough one that is commonly proposed in sports bars and cafés. It is that doping is wrong because it enhances performance. The position is straightforward enough but clearly open to two types of initial rebuttal. In the first instance one might ask whether it is indeed true that the banned substances we see on lists of prohibitions are indeed performance enhancing. Among others, Nicholson (1987) claims that the evidence is far from clear. Much of their performance enhancing effect, he suggests, is down to a placebo effect. It would be fair to say that the body of sports scientists would argue that he is wrong as a matter of fact. It may well be true, however, that we are not, or at least not always, in a position to identify clear cut explanations for enhanced performance that are caused by the doping substance or process. To the contrary, it seems to me, sporting excellence – doped or otherwise – will always be a complex product of human heart and mind, as much as extreme bodily efforts. A second, less easily dismissed, aspect of this argument refers to the very possibility of gathering such information. If one suspected x, y or z substances were performance enhancing but also likely to cause harm, how would one proceed to gain ethical approval for the research that tried to demonstrate that? So, it is said, the very idea of gaining a large and reliable inventory of doping products would be scuppered at the first stage by the inability to gain research ethics approval by the relevant regulating authority. It seemed one could not in principle claim then to *know* that the alleged substances actually enhanced performance in a reliable and valid way.

Since the time these arguments were first raised, largely in the late 1980s, empirical work on performance enhancing products and substances has indeed emerged despite the scepticism concerning research ethics approval, on the grounds of potential harm to participants (McNamee *et al.*, 2007), ever being granted to gain sufficiently large and reliable data. Recent UK studies of body-building cultures both medical (e.g. Baker *et al.*, 2006) and sociological (e.g. Monaghan, 2001) offer clear evidence of risks outside healthcare and medically related doping abuse.

Doping allows athletes to train hard, too hard

In any event, it has been said by the sceptic, elite sports is all about enhancement, why worry specifically about pharmacological modes of enhancement. All elite competitors, and a good many below their elevated status, push themselves to the very limits of their own sporting capacities, looking for that extra degree of concentration, effort, speed, strength, or whichever capacity is prized in the various sports under discussion. One response to this problem is the idea that doping is wrong because, it is said, it allows some athletes to train harder.

In many spheres we admire those who, with exceptional focus, achieve goals of almost superhuman magnitude. Ought we to find ethically problematic athletes who dope in order to work harder? I might be on a caffeine high as I write; no one worries. A great many comedians and musicians are well known to suffer from a host of psychological deficiencies and can only face the audience when bolstered by alcohol or other drugs; no public outcry. Why should chemical or pharmaceutical means in sport to enhance performance provoke our ire? Moreover, access to new facilities, higher levels of specialised coaching, increased nutritional sophistication and equipment technology (such as isokinetic resistance machines or hyperbaric chambers) all improve training effects without so much as an eyebrow being raised? We encourage other training enhancement methods, it is said, why not pharmacological enhancement?

Doping is unnatural

One direct attack on pharmacological enhancement is the claim that doping is wrong because it is unnatural. Precisely what is natural is itself problematic. Nevertheless, even on the grounds of consistency it can be asked why approved substances and procedures such as sleeping in oxygen-deprived tents or chambers is thought to be any more 'natural' (see Fricker, 2005; Loland and Murray, 2007; Spriggs, 2005; Tamburrini, 2005; Tannsjo, 2005).

Another feature of this move that is open to attack, is the idea that sport itself is not natural but an artifice: a social construction and institutionalisation of the impulse to play. So why then should we be worried about doping as unnatural? What ethical leverage is the argument supposed to apply? If it is some unstated assumption that that which is natural is good and that which is unnatural is bad then one has only to wave that logical sword, the naturalistic fallacy, at such proponents. The naturalistic fallacy, in brief, holds that one may not move directly from statements of fact (what is the case) directly to moral conclusions (what ought to be). This is the move that is illicitly made between the jump that our natural bodies are good because they are natural, but unnatural ones are bad because they are unnatural (or analogously that natural performances are good and non-natural/artificial ones bad). And of course the conclusion *might* make for some indefensible positions on those with artificial limbs or replacement joints who (apparently) fall below the limit of what is a natural body. It is reasonable to suppose that those who naively put forward the naturalistic argument have failed to consider the implications for such people who engage in sports in both able bodied and disability sports. The idea that an athlete with prostheses is somehow morally inferior to natural athletes (which is the consequence of the view) is deeply offensive to our modern egalitarian ideals.

Yet there is something in the view that our human nature deserves respect that is not fully articulated in this view of the unnaturalness of doping whether pharmacological or genetic. As Miah (2004) correctly points out, part of it is objection to an irrational fear of some kind of mythical Frankenstein. Nevertheless, his particular rejection of the natural argument is not sound. He notes that the argument that sports ought only to measure natural performances which somehow can be divorced from artificial input, raises the following issues:

> This type of argument does not constitute a reason for prohibiting the use of genetic modification in sport because its definition of the natural is contested. Indeed, I suggest that the natural is, at best, a meaningless concept though, at worst, potentially divisive, since it would seem to lead to the conclusion that some kinds of human are more valuable than others.
>
> (Miah, 2004: 151)

It must be noted, however, that a distinction need not be absolutely clear for it to be useful. We cannot tell the precise point at which night becomes day yet we are able to apply the concepts without difficulty. One cannot point to an exact point at which orange becomes red but this does not prevent the traffic cop booking the driver for failing to stop at the traffic lights. And the very idea that *because* a concept is contested it follows that it must therefore be meaningless does not hold water. Consider what are referred to as essentially contested concepts (Gallie, 1956) such as education whose nature and purposes are contested by every political ideology. The very fact of their contestedness does not render them meaningless. To be sure Miah is right to be wary of the careless or the manipulative deployment of what is a fishy concept, but there is no reason to think that the normative utilisation of naturalness in arguments against doping leads us necessarily to condemn or disvalue disabled populations who rely on artificial or technological products in their daily living. Notwithstanding all this, the idea of a non-natural body enhanced from our ideas of normal human functioning is one that troubles many philosophers and scientists alike.[1] I will return to this idea specifically in the Chapter 11 when I consider the future sports and sports ethics in the light of biomedical technologies in society more generally.

Dopers coerce non-dopers to dope

It is sometimes said by athletes themselves that doping-related bans are justified to prevent their coercion into taking drugs. Or, as Ben Johnson's coach, Charlie Francis, famously put it: 'if you don't take it you won't make it'. Allowing athletes to dope, coerces other athletes into doing the same against their will it is said. There is a close relationship between the apparent coercion argument and the train harder argument. When a colleague eschews the model of a family life and, like a hermit, works 12 hours a day, 5 days a week, and 50 weeks a year, we may just as easily admire their industry as we may mock their lack of balance. Would we have grounds for saying, at the next promotion board, that the promotion ought not go to the super-industrious on the grounds that their work habits have a coercive effect on all those who wish to achieve the said promotion in the future?[2] Not any old social pressure may count as a coercive one. But if coercion means something like the wrongful restriction of an agent's freedom then one might be hard pressed to locate our fellow, dope-driven, athletes in the ascription 'coercers'. In what sense are they coercing their opponents? Can the clean not simply choose a dope-free option to training and performance? Is it not, rather, that a free choice not to participate, or to participate in legal and legitimate ways, is still possible? We do not say to our gut-busting, Stakhanovite, colleague that they ought to be prevented from accessing their workstation, or the library, or their personal computers after so many hours. We respect their autonomy even if we deride the narrowness of their industriousness. And on a point of consistency, if our arguments were truly about the concern that others inflicted upon us, that should apply to all practices such as athletes who run for more miles or in higher climates, swimmers who do more lengths, cross-country skiers who sleep in so-called oxygen tents to boost their production of red blood cells and improve oxygen transportation around the body. What about cyclists who wear aerodynamic hats, swimmers who wear fast-skin suits, or female gymnasts who are forced to discipline their bodies by calorific control to achieve outrageous morphological norms that are inappropriate for certain ages and body types and often deeply corrosive to their psychological well-being. What about jockeys who are 'coerced' to waste (to lose weight by the excessive use of fasting, saunas and often smoking) to achieve the weight that horse trainer believes is optimum for his or her thoroughbred?

Doping is harmful

The coercion argument is itself related to a more general justification of doping bans (and *mutatis mutandis* other allegedly unethical practices that are made impermissible by the rules), that of preventing harm to athletes. Doping substances, it is claimed, are harmful to the athletes concerned. Now, as I noted above, while there is a fair degree of consensus that some doping substances and processes are harmful, not all banned substances are harmful or at least not necessarily harmful. Might blood doping under medical conditions provide such a model (though certainly a more respectful version of the East German doping scandals of the 1970s and 1980s)?[3]

Even if it were true that doping products and substances were harmful we would again have to field questions as to why we should feel bad faith and not countenance the ranges of harms associated with doping, as opposed to our benign acceptance of other sports where harm is intrinsic to the activity or where it is statistically associated with it to a significant degree? Contrast the magnitude of harm that has been caused by elite athletes who dope with the panoply of boxers who engage in their sport in legitimate ways but endure in their careers, and long afterwards, seriously debilitating injuries. What about the deaths from equestrian sports, of horse and rider alike? What about the number of paraplegics whose disability has been caused from forceful contact with the ground and with other players in rugby and American football? Less dramatically, what about the legion of football players around the world with arthritic ankles, hips and knees? How do we honestly discount the magnitude of harm here?

As with the range of other practices that might be thought impermissible in the discussion on coercion, we find ourselves confronted with the question: 'what are the limits on "paternalistic interference" in sport?' Finding a satisfactory answer to this question ought properly to precede banning doping it might reasonably be objected.

Doping confers an unfair advantage

Perhaps the most commonly discussed criterion in support of banning doping has been the argument that it represents an unfair advantage to those who undergo it. Let us assume that the bans are based on the efficacy of the substances and processes so included. In this way we can set aside the fact that advantage does accrue to the doped athlete. The standard position against the unfairness argument is the sceptical one of inconsistency: unfair advantages abound in sport, why worry about pharmacological ones. Examples spring readily to mind. What should we say of athletes born in high altitude who develop greater oxygen carrying capacities? What about those born in wealthier nations who can rely on sophisticated technological systems support? What about teams that are sponsored by multinational companies or billionaire sugar-daddies compared to relatively impoverished opponents?

Perhaps the most problematical of all of the unfairness arguments concern our ready acceptance of those whose excellence is a direct product of genetic lottery? It is through no extra merit, nor is it fair, that I or you benefit from a wonderful genetic pool. To take this to its limit consider the case of Eero Mäntyranta and Miguel Indurain[4] both of whom were born with physical abnormalities that contributed directly to their athletic excellence. Eero Mäntyranta, the Finnish Olympic skier in the 1960, 1964 and 1968 Olympic Games won three golds, two silver and two bronze medals and won a very similar tally in the World Championships during that time. He clearly was a phenomenal skier.[5] Undoubtedly, part of his quite exceptional ability is based upon a biomedical abnormality. Mäntyranta was born with unnaturally high levels of haemoglobin because of a mutation in the ethrypoetin (EPO) receptor gene which allowed for more sustained maximal performance, discovered during familial genetic screening (de la Chapelle, et al., 1993). Second, there is the case of Miguel Indurain, the five times winner of the Tour de France:

At the top of his career, Miguel Indurain had a physique that was not only abnormal when compared to statistically derived norms from the general population, but also when compared to his fellow athletes. His blood circulation had the ability to circulate 7 litres of oxygen around his body per minute, compared to the average amount of 3–4 litres of an ordinary person and the 5–6 litres of his fellow riders. Also, Indurain's lung capacity was 8 litres, compared to an average of 6 litres. In addition, Indurain's resting pulse was as low as 29 bpm, compared to a normal human's 60–80 bpm, which meant his heart would be less strained in the tough mountain stages. His VO2 max was 88 ml/kg/min; in comparison, Lance Armstrong's was 82 ml/kg/min.

(Wikipedia, 2007)

The sports world at large concerns itself with procedural fairness so that during competition athletes and teams share the same test. But unfairness prior to the contest abounds. Why worry about doping then?

I shall proceed now to one argument I think more robust in defence of the bans and two virtue-ethical considerations that support the anti-doping position.

Doping and slippery slopes

One argument, not to my knowledge explored in the copious literature on the ethics of doping, is the idea that permitting the banned substances and products that comprise doping, would be that they would lead us down a slippery slope. While one may think that this argument is straightforward enough, that we just need to go and apply it so to speak, I want to hold back. Understanding slippery slope arguments is not quite so straightforward and it is worth charting their varied conceptual geography carefully before applying them to the issue of doping.

Schauer offers the following essentialist analysis of slippery slope arguments. A 'pure' slippery slope is one where a 'particular act, seemingly innocuous when taken in isolation, may yet lead to a future host of similar but increasingly pernicious events' (1985: 361–2). Abortion and euthanasia are classic candidates for slippery slope arguments in public discussion and policy making. Against this, however, there is no reason to suppose that the future events (acts or policies) down the slope need to display similarities – indeed one might propose that they led to a whole range of different, though equally un-wished for, consequences. The vast array of proposed enhancements by those who would have no pharmacological or other technical restraints might not be captured under this conception of a slippery slope because of their heterogeneity.[6]

The excessive breadth principle can be subsumed under the latter of Bernard Williams' pair of slippery slopes distinguished thus: (1) horrible result and (2) arbitrary result slippery slope arguments. According to

Williams, the nature of the bottom of the slope enables us to determine which category a particular argument falls under. Clearly, the commonest form is the slippery slope to a horrible result argument. Walton (1992) goes further in distinguishing three types of horrible result slippery slopes: (1) thin end of the wedge or precedent arguments; (2) Sorites arguments; (3) domino effect arguments. I shall illustrate each of these arguments in relation to doping and anti-doping arguments.

In (1), the thin end of the wedge slippery slopes, allowing anabolic steroids (for example) will set a precedent that will allow further precedents (Pn) taken us to an (unspecified) problematic terminus. Is it necessary that the end point has to be bad? Of course this is its typical linguistic meaning of the phrase 'slippery slopes'. Nevertheless, one might turn the tables here and argue that the slopes might be viewed positively too (see Schubert, 2004). Perhaps a new phrase will be required to capture ineluctable slides (ascents?) to such end points. This would be somewhat analogous to the ideas of vicious/virtuous cycles. So it might be argued that the use of anabolic steroids, EPO, human growth hormone and other banned doping substances may well allow elite athletes to fulfil their Olympian dreams. *Citius, Altius, Fortius* the motto goes: faster, higher, stronger. It can present for some a legitimisation of the pursuit of limitless growth in human powers and excellences.

In (2), the Sorites idea of slippery slopes, the inability to draw clear distinctions has the effect that allowing P will not enable us to consistently deny Pn and so on. This argument has many instantiations in the literature: one allows performance enhancement by nutritional supplements, how can these rationally be distinguished? Altitude training is permitted, so hyperbaric chambers that simulate this effect cannot be banned, and if hyperbaric chambers are allowed then . . . and so on and so forth. This slope follows the form of the Sorites Paradox where taking a grain of sand from a heap does not prevent our recognising or describing the heap as such even though it is not identical with its former state.

At the heart of the problem with such arguments is the idea of conceptual vagueness. Those who wish to advocate a radically liberal stance in relation to doping might well seize upon this vagueness and apply a Sorites argument as follows: since therapeutic interventions are currently morally permissible, and there is no clear distinction between therapy and enhancement, enhancement interventions are morally permissible too. Can we really distinguish categorically between the added functionality of certain prosthetic devices and other forms of biotechnological enhancement, they might well ask? In the case of Oscar Pistorius, the champion disability athlete, the IAAF has ruled that he is precisely afforded such an advantage over an able bodied athlete. Pistorius who had both legs amputated early on in life has achieved 400m times well in excess of his competitors and sought to compete with able bodied opponents in Championship races but has been disallowed for the reason, it is alleged, that his stride length has been altered by the technology offering him an unfair advantage.[7]

In (3), the domino conception of the slippery slope, we have what others often refer to as a causal slippery slope (see, for example, Den Hartogh, 2005). Once P is allowed a causal chain will be effected allowing Pn and so on to follow, which will precipitate increasingly bad consequences.

In what ways can slippery slope arguments be used against the pro-doping lobby? Is there really an end point, a horrible result we can point to, of which we can say doping is ethically indefensible? One particular strategy adopted by proponents of doping falls clearly under the aspect of the thin end of the wedge conception of the slippery slope. While some aspects of their movement might be aimed at therapeutic effects that are undoubted goods, how would we feel if the very same lobby were to argue thereafter that there were just too many broken bones in (say) American Football (because of the new and heightened powers of their athletes) and so it was proposed that key skeletal structures such as the hip or the knee were enhanced by new construction materials such as Kevlar. And if we were to accept this would we maintain a principled position in which we could still with logical ethical authority deny the possibility of greater than 20: 20 vision for golfers or archers (despite Tiger Woods electing for such laser surgery in 2006), or artificially extended toes to lever the sprinter with reinforced feet arches to dampen the effects of the new levels of friction their legs could generate. Here pro-dopers and their typically libertarian supporters stroll half-asleep into the territory of enhancement that Kass (1997) has labelled 'repugnant'.

One strategy, therefore, to consider is the use of a therapeutically driven argument that prizes open the door with the thinnest of (morally defensible) wedges, which in principle cannot be distinguished from successive practices that we collectively feel repugnance at. While we all may recognise the repugnance, we appear to have no logical basis in denying the coherence of the first revision, and ineluctably, the later repugnant ones. I wonder how many are prepared to used therapeutic justifications to shield the more Promethean aims, less explicitly advertised. Examples of this manoeuvre can be found in medical ethics. Take for the purposes of illustration the Cognitive Enhancement Research Institute in California. Prominently on its website front page (http: //www.ceri.com/) it reads 'Do you know somebody with Alzheimer's Disease? Click to see the latest research breakthrough.' The mode is simple: therapy by front entrance, enhancement by the back door. Borgmann (1984: 36), in his discussion of the uses of technology in modern society, observed precisely this argumentative strategy more than 20 years ago:

> The main goal of these programs seems to be the domination of nature. But we must be more precise. The desire to dominate does not just spring from a lust of power, from sheer human imperialism. It is from the start connected with the aim of liberating humanity from disease, hunger, and toil and enriching life with learning, art and athletics.

Who could want to deny the powers of viral diseases that could be genetically treated? Might one want to draw the line at the transplantation of non-human capacities (sonar pathfinding)?, *in vivo* fibre optic communications backbone or anti-degeneration powers? (These would have to be non-human *ex hypothesi.*)

Nevertheless, one cannot determinately point to a precise station at which one can say 'here, this is the end we said things would naturally progress to if we allowed all and any doping'. But does this pose a problem? Well, it certainly makes it difficult to specify exactly a 'horrible result' that is supposed to be at the bottom of the slope. Equally, it makes it extremely difficult to say that if we allow precedent X it will allow practices Y or Z to follow since it is not clear how these later practices are (if at all) connected with the precedent. So it is not clear that a form of precedent setting slippery slope could be strictly used in every case against pro-dopers though it may be applicable in some.

Consider in this light, a Sorites-type slippery slope that might be used to support the lifting of doping bans. The pro-doper would have to show how the relationship between the therapeutic practices and the enhancements are indeed transitive. Or they might have to argue that the boundaries between the natural and artificial cannot be drawn sufficiently clearly since certain accepted technologies are so commonplace, such as glasses, hearing aids, prosthetic devices, vaccinations to boost the immune system and so on.

In response to this manoeuvre, which has much to recommend it, we might look first to some conceptual objections. The first was raised in relation to the natural argument. We know night from day, or orange from red, without being able to specify precisely we move from one to the other. So simply because one cannot determine a precise distinction between (say) genetic or pharmacological therapies T1, T2, T3 and enhancements E1, E2, E3 and so on, it does not follow that there are no important moral distinctions between T1 and E20. As Williams (1985) notes this kind of indeterminacy arises because of the conceptual vagueness of certain terms. Yet, the indeterminacy of so open a predicate 'heap' is not equally true of 'therapy' or 'enhancement'. The latitude they allow is not nearly as wide as this.

Instead of objecting to Pn on the grounds that Pn is morally objectionable (i.e. to depict a horrible result) one might instead, after Williams, object that the slide from P to Pn is simply morally arbitrary where it ought not to be. Here one can say, without specifying a horrible result that it would be difficult to know what, in principle, could ever be objected to. And this is, quite literally, what is troublesome. Still, the sports-libertarian might argue, 'what is wrong with arbitrariness?' Let us take one brief example. There are aspects of our lives where, as a widely shared intuition, we might think that in the absence of good reasons we ought not to discriminate among people arbitrarily. Healthcare might be considered precisely one such case. Given the ever-increasing demand for public healthcare services and products it could be argued that access to them ought typically to be governed by publicly disputable criteria such as clinical need, or potential benefit, as opposed to individual choices of an arbitrary or subjective nature.

And nothing in the pro-doping, or more broadly the pro-enhancement, position seems to allow for such objective dispute let alone prioritisation. Who does not rightly applaud advances in therapeutic medical technologies such as those from new genetically based organ regeneration to more familiar prosthetic devices? Here the ends of the interventions are clearly medically defined and the means regulated closely. This is what prevents the libertarian dopers from adopting a Sorites-type slippery slope. Where does it end though? I suggest that in the absence of a defensible *telos*, over and above the mindless mantra of more medals, more glory (the narrowly conceived *Citius, Altius, Fortius*[8]) of clearly and substantively specified ends (beyond the banner of unrestrained 'enhancement'), elite athletes, their coaches and their sports medical back-up teams alike ought to resist the potentially open-ended transformations of human nature and potentialities. For if all transformations are in principle to count as 'enhancements' then surely nothing is to count as enhancement. The very purpose of the word would fall into disuse. Thus it seems one strong argument against the pro-doping lobby generally – the arbitrary slippery slope – presents a challenge to them to show that all of what they describe as enhancements are indeed imbued with positive normative force and not merely the technological extensions of libertarianism whose conception of the good is merely an extension of individual choice and consumption.

An aretaic account of anti-doping

I have tried to show thus far that some standard arguments in favour of banning doping are either incoherent or lacking in consistency of application. I have also tried to show how we might understand slippery slopes arguments for, but in the final analysis against, doping and limitless enhancement. What might be said about a virtue-ethical account of doping and anti-doping? Well, I believe an aretaic account of what is wrong with doping and those who wish to liberalise doping products and processes will get to the heart of the matter.

The rational argument about horrible and arbitrary result slippery slopes may not convince philosophers or social scientists who think that athletes should be allowed to use any performance enhancements or indeed those athletes who wish to dope and not face sanctions or even expulsion from competition. But to limit rational argument to discussion of the rightness or wrongness of the act itself is to fail to consider the character of the doping cheat. Moreover, in aretaic ethics it is thought crucial to consider the living of good lives as an amalgam of thought, feeling and action within a relatively well-settled form of dispositions. Conceiving respect for fellow athletes is one thing, feeling it another. And virtuous action should be holistic in this regard. So we may attend not merely to what athletes think about doping, but what also they characteristically feel in relation to other athletes and their selves, which emotions are salient and why.

It is of course true that there may be many vices that attend doped athletes. Let us remind ourselves of the application of the Doctrine of the Mean, which has heuristic value even if it cannot be pressed into the service of all choices as an explanatory framework. What should we say of the praiseworthiness or culpability of the doped athlete's character? Some of these might just be a deficient – their desire to be the greatest is unhindered by reference to any rules that govern the sport. Or they may fail to feel the demands of justice; that their opponent ought to enjoy an equality of opportunity to compete and win as they do. At the other extreme, doped athletes might be thought of as vicious in their excess; the desire to emulate previous heroes may have become so strong that one becomes blinded to the demands of fair sporting competition. I want to expand, by way of example rather than by an exhaustive argument, upon two such vices that are both defects of deficiency in character; the deficiency or absence of justice that is operative (*pleonexia*) in doped athletes and the similar defect in those who have not, or not sufficient, of the quasi virtue shame (*aidos*).

The vice of *pleonexia*

In his discussion of justice as a virtue Aristotle argues that *pleonexia* is the vice that attends all acts of injustice. I shall not argue for or against that general position though I accept Williams' (1980) critique of its over-ambitious application. I am more interested in its particular application to the case of the doping cheat. First, it is typical for philosophers to distinguish two dimensions of justice: the distributional (who gets what, where, when and why) and the rectificatory (following injustice how is the matter rectified properly). Moreover, Aristotle distinguishes justice as a moral concern with 'particular justice', which is one among the virtues and related only to certain kinds of goods. In the MacIntyrean scheme we can call these external goods. Aristotle conceives of these goods as 'divisible' because as they are divided so it is the case that as one gets a portion so another cannot. MacIntyre refers to this characteristic as 'exclusivity'. They are thus typically the object of competition. With some leeway in interpretation we can think of *pleonexia* as a vice in relation to particular goods where one wants more of them, or wants more than others, or simply as greed.

As I noted in Chapter 6 on racism, it is important to follow Aristotle in distinguishing unjust acts from unjust characters. Is doping typically an act of ignorance? I shall take it that it is not. We must distinguish between an athlete who is the subject of doping in some passive sense such as the young East German athletes who were force fed illicit pharmacological enhancement under the deceit that they were nutritional supplements (Spitzer, 2006). Equally, I have considerable sympathy for the 17-year-old Romanian gymnast, Andreea Raducan, at the Sydney 2000 Olympics who took 'painkillers' on the advice of the team doctor. Subsequent tests showed that they had contained 'pseudoephedrine' a banned substance and under the strict liability ruling of doping she was expelled from the competition. Unusually, it might be thought, because the urine test showed only positive after the all-round competition Raducan was allowed to keep her medals from the floor and the vaulting competition. Perhaps this judgement displays at least some sensitivity to both distributive and rectificatory justice. Yet this irony displays the distinction: it was not suggested that Raducan's motivation was vicious merely that prior to the performance in the all-round competition an illicit substance had been found in her body and she was strictly liable for that action. It makes every sense from this perspective to say that Raducan had fallen foul of doping laws but was not herself a doping cheat.

The doping cheat is another type of character altogether. In my discussion of emotions I distinguished the episodic from those which endure over time. So too it is necessary to distinguish, as in Chapter 6, between an act that is something of a one-off, or one that has under certain conditions revealed itself, from one that is more universal and therefore thought to form part of the character of the sportsperson; that is, one which is dispositional. We can say, thus, what the doping cheat lacks and what he or she displays. He or she lacks a clear sense of justice for it is constitutive of the virtue of justice that one is habitually disposed to think, feel and judge some courses of action as just and therefore noble, while feeling revulsion at others and having the courage to resist their allures. Now the unjust person may be motivated in many ways that are not relevant to our discussion; in many different ways they may simply not care about achieving a just outcome. But the systematic nature of doping cheats – the fact that they must arrange with the help of others, the dosages of supplements, their timing, an understanding of when the active pharmaceutical agent will persist in the body and be detectable, or the duration of time they must avoid an out-of-competition test, or the other substances they must use to mask the doping substance or process – points to a systematic deception.

What is it that the doped athlete seeks to achieve? How and why should we describe him or her as pleonectic? For our purposes I want to suggest that the pleonectic doper is the one who wants not merely more, for that would simply indicate the disposition of greed. For the greedy, enough is never enough. Sparshott (1994: 188) refers to this as logically insatiable greed. It is an imperialising vice and not merely a one-off passion (Sparshott, 1994). Yet, in describing the doping cheat as pleonetic, I want to stress the connection of injustice to his or her avarice; crucially the doped athlete wants more than he or she is due. The deficit is one of not caring for justice precisely so that he or she may improperly gain the external, divisible, goods: wealth, sponsorship, fame, even honour in the form of being listed in the record books. It is to desire, avariciously, that which he or she has no right to. It is tantamount to covetousness. Williams (1980) situates one aspect of pleonexia in the heart and soul of Achilles. He wants glory and he wants it so that no one else may share it. This, it strikes me, is at least one important aspect of what the pleonectic doping cheat wants. The athlete with the vice of *pleonexia* does not simply want enough, or what is their proper reward, they want more and more than others irrespective of whether they are entitled to it by their commitment, dedication, talent, in short, not by merit.

The quasi virtue of *aidos* (or the vice of shamelessness)

In what way ought we think of shamefulness as a virtue? It is an odd idea. What has the virtuous sportsperson to feel ashamed of? On the one hand it is typical to think of modern individualistic cultures as cultures of guilt (G. Taylor, 1985). The wrongness of action is internalised to a feeling; an interiorisation of culpability and remorse for the wrong doing; for breaking a rule, or standard, or norm. Shame, it is typically said, is not so much transgression as failure and more public than private. So, as the standard account goes,[9] shame cultures are predicated on social norms such as honour. Failing to live up to the social demands that roles place upon us, we feel, when socialised into the culture, shame. We hide our face.

Why should we want to cultivate shamefulness in our athletes? Put that way, the requirement could be thought of as a perversion of an ethics of sports. Put another way, the question makes more sense: why should we wish to cultivate the capacity to feel shame? This seems much more promising. Imagine the contrary position. In contemporary elite athletics, for example, getting caught doping might be seen as little more than an occupational hazard. Charlie Francis said of Ben Johnson, that if he had simply stuck to the schedule – knowing when to come off certain drugs and doses, knowing when to apply masking agents to prevent the identification of doping substances – he would not have been caught. This manner of approaching the problem is technicist: a mere problem of timing, not one of ethics. For those who have not been taught the power of moral opprobrium, and here I am at least as much thinking of Francis as I am of Johnson, the fear of shame is not present. The fear of excommunication from the athletic community either does not register, or registers so weakly that it can be ignored. Even if felt, power diminishes in the sight of potential glory and wealth.

Shame, of course, is a powerful social regulator. When we appreciate the power of shame, of its capacity to separate us from the group, to alienate us from the communities that shape our very identities, it can indeed perform a powerful preventative function. And, we all will exhibit moral failings from time to time. Some more than others. And most, perhaps, in face of incredible rewards that are the province of some, though not all, elite sports.

Williams (1993: 87) offers a discussion of shame in Sophocles' play *Philoctetes*, which is analogous to our present concern. The cunning Odysseus is attempting to persuade Neoptolemus into a deceitful act against Philoctetes. In his sophistic strategy Odysseus appeals to Neoptolemus's virtue while at the same time attempting to assuage the power of pre-emptive shame which would prevent him from stooping low:

I know, my boy, that you are not of a nature
To say such things or use a low trick;
but it is pleasant to lay hold of victory,
so be bold

Neoptolemus's first response is what we would hope all our elite athletes would mouth:

MyLord,
I prefer to fail nobly rather than to win shabbily.

Before we cheer at his courage and the habituation of *aidos* the power of Odysseus's sophistry wins out. True to tragic Greek heroic form, he is persuaded by what he thinks is the potential glory:

All right, I'll do it, and put the shame aside.
(All cited in Williams, 1993: 87)

In this vein, but with more apparent virtue, the journalist Dag Vidar interviewed Ådne Søndrål, former Olympic skating champion and IOC member for Norway, who said that "[g]etting caught doping is the second worst crime a Norwegian can commit. In my opinion only child abuse disgusts people more. Doping is high treason against the nation." This seems to overplay the matter considerably. It should be said that the Danish scholar, Ask Vest Christiansen has said that Danish cyclists have also expressed that shame is a powerful disincentive to doping.[10] Whether this is something in a broader Scandinavian sports psyche, or the product of smaller nations with more homogeneous cultures who have always celebrated health and sports together I cannot say. On the one hand we can say that, in some cases then reports of the death of shame have been exaggerated, so to speak. Before we chide the weak-willed doper, however, there is also a word of caution about the would-be cheat. As Stewart (1892) remarks: 'If one takes credit for being ashamed, one palliates the action one is ashamed of, and is more likely to repeat it' (cited in Sparshott, 1994: 392).

It is equally true that shame has a corrosive aspect when its standards are unjustifiable. One has to only think of examples of the hegemonic force of Victorian England with its complex social codes which, among other things, prevented women even using a bicycle for fear 'it would transport them to prostitution' (Hargreaves, 1994). Equally, one thinks of honour codes in groups such as American University student fraternities or even the South African police force in the apartheid era, which, in the name of solidarity and allegiance to the group, fostered violence against women and people of colour through a large proportion of the twentieth century.

What do *pleonexia* and *aidos* point to in terms of the ethics of sport? Well, we are drawn back to the familiar pedagogical ground of Aristotle and the formation of habits: of patterns of feeling, perception, thought and action that comprise the good sportspersons and good sporting lives. Unless children are taught the import of the values of sport how will they come to feel that shame is to be avoided; how will they know what is within their reach and what beyond it; where they stand in the pantheon of mediocrity and excellence?

Here the idea of role modelling is utterly critical. One of the finest ever sports journalists, Hugh MacIlvanney, once had occasion to chastise the French footballer Thierry Henry for his tactics of "diving" (or 'simulation' in FIFA speak), a practice that has more than a family resemblance to the doping cheats. Now Henry is one of the most elegant players it has ever been my pleasure to watch on a football field. And more than that, he is regarded highly for his social responsibility outside of the game. To see him deceitfully gain a penalty kick is a sad thing indeed. Shakespeare had it just right:

> The summer's flower is to the summer sweet
> Though too itself it only live and die,
> But if that flower with base infection meet,
> The basest weed outbraves his dignity:
> For sweetest things turn sourest by their deeds:
> Lillies that fester, smell far worse than weeds.
>
> (Booth, 2000: Sonnet XCIV)

It is true, and many find unreasonable, that we hold elite sportspersons to a higher level of account than teachers or politicians. It is not only the fact of the matter that we do this but good that we do it too. Where else, in the modern age, do the masses see the morality play played out? That is the price we pay for the diminished moral resources of modernity just as it is the price the individual sportsperson pays for the grotesquely high salaries they command.

To attend to the emulative responsibilities of elite sportspersons and other virtuous considerations, is properly to be initiated into sport. This is a critical matter, as pressing as it is ancient. Often it is stories that teach us the limits. Often it is appreciation for the best standards of sporting excellence conceived of as ethically valuable practices and not mere arenas for physical excellence and the spectacles of *Citius, Altius, Fortius*; always it is about role models – exemplars of the best in us and of us. How much time is spent perfecting the forehand topspin, the head position in the sprint start, the protection of the basketball in the lay up, the perfect tuck in the somersault, the ideal timing of a hip throw? How little time perfecting ourselves; considering the appropriateness of the aims, ideals and purposes to which we strive.

Conclusion

In this chapter, I began with a consideration of the myth of Gyges' ring, I utilised some slippery slope arguments and I pointed to an illustrative example of the aretaic vocabulary that could help us understand motives for doping and anti-doping alike. At least part of what Gyges' ring teaches us, is that when people do not feel that they will be held responsible for their actions they may go to any and all lengths to achieve their (often unreflective) goals. They feel there is no power greater than their selves. They feel, perhaps, that they can bask in a glory that is not properly theirs yet feel neither ambiguity nor shame. Shame may have a chequered history, but we'd better not throw the baby out with the bath water. The shameless feel no standards beyond their own will. Character conversions are not so common outside of religion and myth, we had better attend to the cultivation of virtue and vice-aversion while these considerations have a grip on the maturing psyche of the young sportsperson.

11 Whose Prometheus?

Transhumanism, biotechnology and the moral topography of sports medicine

Introduction

The rise of sports medicine to the apex of sports science is something that I believe has not been commented upon. There are hierarchies within hierarchies. Sports medicine sits over sports science, which sits in panoramic ascendancy over what I take to be the humanities of sport: history, literature, philosophy and theology. I wish, against that hegemony, to challenge some of the more self-aggrandising possibilities of sports medicine in the final chapter of this book.

The most recent incarnation of the Promethean myth is the image of 'genetically modified athletes'.[1] Recognising limits is not, however, a prominent feature of modern medicine. Indeed it is sometimes extremely unclear where medicine begins and other social practices such as social care, welfare or education begin.[2] If, however, this conceptual inflation spreads horizontally it effects a process widely referred to as the medicalisation of everyday life. It is not the sheer spread of medicine that concerns me here, but rather its vertical ambition in transforming our very nature as humans and its impact upon our understanding of human virtue and vice.

In a recent book, the American conservative bioethicist Leon Kass has written, somewhat polemically, that

> human nature itself lies on the operating table, ready for alteration, for eugenic and neuropsychic 'enhancement', for wholesale design. In leading laboratories, academic and industrial, new creators are confidently amassing their powers, while on the street their evangelists are zealously prophesying a posthuman future.
>
> (Kass, 2002: 4)

It is against this evangelising and self-promoting backdrop that I wish to problematise the unfettered application of science and technology to the sphere of sports medicine. To do this I wish first to note elements of science derived from the English philosopher, politician and polymath, Sir Francis Bacon, from the sixteenth and seventeenth centuries, which survive and in some sense shape the hubris of modern biomedical science. Second, I wish to challenge the assumptions of transhumanism, an ideology that seeks to complete the merely 'half-baked' project of human nature (Boström, 2004). In response, I sketch out two interpretations of the myth of Promethus in Hesiod and Aeschylus that can help us see aright the moral limits of sports medicine. I conclude with a banal reminder: we are mortal beings. Our vulnerability to injury, disease and death, far from something we can overcome or eliminate, represents natural limits both for morality and medicine generally and sports medicine in particular.

Baconian science, biomedical technology and the perfection of the body

Though the Ancient Greeks and, more generally, artists throughout history have had a deep and significant aesthetic respect for the perfection of human form, the obsession with physical perfectionism arises as a moral imperative, as sociologists of the body have noted, with the increasing pervasiveness of modern technology (Shilling, 2005). In the writings of Bacon, and also Descartes, the rise of experimental philosophy (bringing together the rational and the empirical) found canonical expression in medical science. The allusion to the Baconian ideal itself belongs to Hans Jonas, whose railing against the hubris of medical technology prefigured much work in the fields of medical ethics and medical theology. Jonas wrote, as early as 1974, regarding the potential pitfalls of 'biological engineering'. Slightly less rhetorically than Kass, he argued:

> The biological control of man, especially genetic control, raises ethically questions of a wholly new kind for which neither previous praxis nor previous thought has prepared us. Since no less than the nature and image of man are at issue, prudence itself becomes our first ethical duty, and hypothetical reasoning our first responsibility.
>
> (Jonas, 1974: 141)

It will be clear that the presence of Greek myths, which raise in our imagination the proper limits of the human, cast a shadow of doubt on the uniqueness of the controlling aspects of modern biology or genetics. And despite offering two contrasting lenses with which to view biotechnology, my own posture is marked by a precautionary stance. Moreover, I will claim in the final section that there is no need for the generation of a new ethic. I claim, rather, that the moral sources for such evaluations as the proper ends of medicine and sports medicine are with us now and have been since at least the time of Plato. As Williams (1993) observed: there is no need to revive these sources since they are not dead.

It is noteworthy that the foundational drive for medical technologies in particular is one that fits with a very traditional conception of medicine as a healing art or as in the relief of suffering.

Of course the relief of suffering is a noble end associated with medicine traditionally conceived (Cassell, 1991; Edwards and McNamee, 2006; Porter, 2002). But that is neither the object of my concern nor typically those of sports medics associated with elite sports. The idea is captured brilliantly in Gerald McKenny's excellent book on bioethics, technology and the body: *To Relieve the Human Condition* (1997). It is as if the fulfilment of science's quest for domination of nature was itself to culminate in overcoming *human* nature. Now, of course, the denial or denigration of human nature is not new: early behaviouristic psychology often included a claim that human nature was no more than a myth or a hangover from a pre-scientific age, and this ideology was given further impetus in the sociobiological movements of the 1980s. Nevertheless, modern science takes the body as an object in nature, capable of precise observation and minute description. The uses of science extend not merely to intervening in, but also to re-envisioning, the body. The rise of medical technology, however, opens entire new vistas for medicine as a social practice.

Technology in medicine and sports

It is easy to think of technology as a modern social practice and to assume a particular kind of technology (such as computer technology) to represent a paradigmatic example. Nye (2006) ties technology to tool making but reminds us of the narratives in which our appreciation of those tools are rested. For example:

> In Herman Melville's *Moby Dick*, Queequeg, a South Sea harpooner visiting Nantucket, was offered a wheelbarrow to move his belongings from an inn to the dock. But he did not understand how it worked, and so, after putting all his gear into the wheel barrow he lifted it on to his shoulders. Most travellers have done something that looked equally silly to the natives, for we are all unfamiliar with some local technologies. This is another way of saying that we do not know the many routines and small narratives that underlie everyday life in other societies.
>
> (Nye, 2006: 6)

This commonplace example is a reminder of the importance of locating our views of technology historically but also brings to mind a less manipulative conception than the kind which those opposed to radical biotechnologies conjure up as counter examples. The term 'technology' has a venerable past. It derives from the conjoining of two Greek words *techne* and *logos*. *Techne* which refers to the kind of skill (practical knowledge) involved in making things. By *logos* is meant a form of reasoning aimed at understanding the nature or form of things. Although we think of the term as a modern one, it was in fact first coined by Aristotle (Mitcham, 1979) but his meaning for it was the technical skills of rhetoric; literally the *techne* of *logos* (Kass, 2002).

It is not uncommon, however, in everyday talk to slide the concept of science together with the concept of technology. Indeed, in the UK at least, sports scientists very often conflate their activities with what should properly be called sports technology.[3] Today philosophers of science clearly distinguish theory generation (science) and its application (technology), though the distinction is rather lost in the natural scientific study of sport. We could imagine then, that the domains of medical and sports technology might simply be taken to include the theoretical knowledge, practical knowledge, and the instruments and products that bring about the ends of medicine or sports respectively. If this were acceptable then their salient characteristic would be a 'means–end' structure. Technology might be thought of as the means utilised to pursue chosen ends. It would appear to follow then that technology is, in a sense, neutral. It is neither good nor bad *in itself*. Rather, its normativity is typically governed by the uses to which it is put. An example of this conceptualisation is found in the recent literature on philosophy of technology:

> Technology in its most robust sense . . . involves the *invention, development, and cognitive deployment of tools and other artifacts, brought to bear on raw materials . . . with a view to the resolution of perceived problems* . . . which, together, allow [society] to continue to function and flourish.
>
> (Hickman, 2001: 12)

An equally sympathetic account is to be found in the UN Convention on Biological Diversity (Article 2: Use of Terms) where biotechnology is defined thus:

> Biotechnology means any technological application that uses biological systems, living organisms, or derivatives thereof, to make or modify products or processes for specific use.
>
> (Wikipedia, 2006)

Less authoritatively, and even more broadly, biotechnology can also be commonsensically defined thus: 'Biotechnology is the manipulation of organisms to do practical things and to provide useful products' (Wikipedia, 2006). While such global definitions are useful as a starting point, it is important to note that they fail to distinguish ethically important characteristics of different forms of practice that fall under the headings 'technology' or 'biotechnology'.

By contrast, then, a stronger line of criticism is found especially in continental European writers who have made problematic the assumption that technology is itself a neutral means to chosen (good or bad) ends. Mitcham (1995) gives an account of this history of technological scepticism in medicine and Kapp (1877), Desauer (1927), Ortega y Gasset (1939) and Heidegger

(1977) also note more fundamental criticisms of technology as ideology where, far from being the hand-maiden of man, technology comes full circle to be his master (Foucault 1988; Habermas 1968; Marcuse 1964). Although not as radical in her writings as these latter philosophers, Lee (2003) helpfully marks the following distinction in the application of science in the form of technology whose goals are: (1) explanation; (2) prediction; and (3) control. It is the last of these aims that I want to pick up on in relation to any ethical evaluation of technologies. Nye, a historian of technology, arrives (far too swiftly for my liking) at a softer conclusion about the relations between technology and human kind. He writes: 'Stonehenge suggests the truth of Walter Benjamin's example that "technology is not the mastery of nature but of the relations between nature and man."' (2006: 7). Nevertheless, we find more classical sources that are to be interpreted less generously. Francis Bacon (1562–1626) is well known for his remarks (2000) on the development of scientific and technological methods whose aim would be 'to relieve man's estate' (i.e. of suffering/vulnerability) and likewise René Descartes (1596–1650) had wanted 'to use this knowledge [. . .] for all the purposes for which it is appropriate, and thus make ourselves, as it were, the lords and masters of nature' (2003). Of course, as C. S. Lewis pointed out in his essay, *The Abolition of Man* (1943), every time we hear the phrase 'mastery of nature' we ought to be alerted to the fact that it is some particular group that is doing the mastering for its own reasons and in light of its own version of the good, rather than the good of humanity (whatever that might look like).

Again, Lee distinguishes the types of control thus: (1) Weak: avoid the occurrence; and (2) Strong: prevent the occurrence. And the facets comprising weak or strong technological control of nature (or for my present concerns 'human nature') range from theoretical knowledge, through practical knowledge and skills, to instruments and products. Notwithstanding these cautionary considerations, I will consider biotechnology and sports technology respectively to refer to those technologies deployed to meet the ends or goals of sports medicine or sports respectively. What forms, more specifically, might this technology take? The most obvious uses by sports scientists and sports medics might be instrumentation such as hypoxic chambers (to assist the fastest recovery times for soft tissue and bone injuries[4]); gas analysers (to measure anaerobic contributions to exercise); and isokinetic strength testers or 'bod-pods' (to assess body density). Finally, the scourge of sports, many would say, fall into the category of 'technological products'. Most obvious here might be anabolic steroids, or other doping supplements such as EPO or human growth hormone. Nevertheless, it is important to note that these products are often designed, as Borgmann (1984) pointedly remarked, with medical therapies in mind. It is their use in elite sports population that is problematic, not the nature of the products themselves.

What I want to do now is to step back a little from a discussion of the enhancement mantra that governs elite sports and some sections of what is called sports medicine and consider a broader, and to my mind more problematic, application of biotechnology to enhance human nature. It is an ideology that falls under the label 'transhumanism' (TH).[5] Rather than a unified entity, TH is a broad and heterogeneous group of thinkers who give technology a grander, Promethean, aim.

What (good) is transhumanism?

A range of views fall under the label of TH.[6] The most extreme is a view according to which TH is a project to overcome the inherent limitations of human nature. Examples of these limits, which most of us take for granted as part of the human condition, are appearance, life-span, vulnerability to ageing, disease and so on. There is, however, a more extreme version of TH that sees the role of technology as one to vastly enhance both the person and his or her environment by exploiting a range of technologies including genetic engineering, cybernetics, computation and nanotechnology.

Recruitment of these various types of technology, it is hoped, will produce selves who are intelligent, immortal, etc. but who are not members of the species *Homo sapiens*. Their species type will be ambiguous, e.g. if they are cyborgs (part human, part machine). If they turn out to be wholly machines, they will lack any common genetic features with human beings. Extreme THs strongly support such developments. Less extreme THs are satisfied to augment human nature with technology where possible and where desired by the individual.

At present TH seems to command support mostly in North America, though there are some adherents from Europe (see the website of the World Transhumanism Association (WTA)). On one level it can be seen as an extension of neoliberal or libertarian thought transferred into biomedical contexts. This is because the main driver appears to be the valorisation of autonomy as expressed in economic choices of individuals. If certain technological developments enable greater defences against senescence, or if they can significantly enhance my powers of thought, speed, movement, then (as competent consumers) TH argue that anyone should be allowed to obtain them – if they can afford them of course. Sandberg attempts to give an ethical underpinning to this essentially political programme. He argues that we must consider 'morphological freedom as a right' (Sandberg, 2001).

Before TH is considered to be the product of outlandish free-thinkers who have enjoyed too much certain medico-technological products themselves, we must consider that it embodies two aims that are widely thought to be valued in the West. These are: (1) the use of technology to improve the lot of humans – work in public health, e.g. construction of sewage systems, fluoride additives to water supplies to prevent dental decay, and so on, is all work to facilitate this noble end that is shared with the entire medical enterprise; and (2) the other widely shared value is that of increased autonomy such that the individual has greater scope in governing his own life-plan.

Moreover, proponents of TH say it presents an opportunity to plan the future development of human beings, the species *Homo sapiens*. Instead of this being left to the evolutionary process and its exploitation of random mutations, TH presents a hitherto unavailable option, tailoring the development of human beings to an ideal blueprint. Typically educational, social and political reformers have been unable to carry forward their project with the kind of control and deficiency (it is said) that biologically driven technologies can.

Against transhumanism

One can ascribe to Ellul a certain prescience: without knowledge of ideologies such as TH he pointed out in 1965 that the development of technology will lead to a 'new dismembering and a complete reconstitution of the human being so that he can at least become the objective (and also the total object) of techniques' (1965: 431). One possible consequence that can be read into the grander claims of some THs is that, in effect, TH will lead to the existence of two distinct types of being, the human and the posthuman. The former are most likely to be viewed as some kind of underclass.

It is worth pursuing this argument a little. It is said that 'we' have a 'self-understanding' as human beings. This includes, for example, our essential vulnerability to disease, ageing and death. Parens (1995), in reversing the title of Nussbaum's celebrated book, captured this idea memorably when speaking of the 'goodness of fragility'. Suppose, however, that the strong TH project is realised. We are no longer so vulnerable, immortality is a real prospect. This will result in a change in our 'self-understanding'. This will have a normative element to it, most radically this may take the form of a change in what we view as a good life. Hitherto such a life would have been assumed to be finite, but now this might change.

Habermas' (2003) objection can be interpreted more or less strongly. The strongest one is that *any* change in self-understanding is a morally bad thing. But this move is not a defensible one. Consider the changes in self-understanding that have occurred over the centuries, the advent of Christianity or Islam, the intellectual revolutions that followed Copernicus and Darwin. It does not follow necessarily that any particular change in self-understanding logically entails moral decline. There are many who would advocate that this constitutes not decline but, rather, moral progress.

There are, to my mind, more telling and less abstract arguments that can be marshalled effectively against TH. These concern, in the first place, a simple argument against inequality. The second relates to the unarticulated ends of TH. What is its *telos*? What do we enhance and why? Let us consider, albeit briefly, the first consideration.

Rather than considering two species of humanities, we might (perhaps crudely) consider the two categories of economics: the rich and the poor. The former can afford to make use of TH whilst the latter will not be able to.

Given the commercialisation of elite sports one can see both the attractions (for some) and the dangers here. Mere mortals – the unenhanced poor – will get no more than a glimpse of the transhuman in competitive elite sports contexts. Note the double-binding character of this consumerism. The poor, at once removed from the possibility of choosing augmentation, end up paying for the privilege on a per-per-view basis. The weak thus pay the strong for the pleasure of their envy. By contrast, one might see less corrosive aspects of this economically driven argument. Far from being worried about it, it might be said, TH is an irrelevance, since so few will be able to make use of the technological developments even if they ever manifest themselves.

Still further, critics point out that TH rests upon some conception of the good. As seen, for one group of THs, the good is expansion of personal choice. But some critics object to what they see as consumerism of this kind. They suggest that the good cannot be equated with what people choose. With regard to the other kind of THs, those who see TH as an opportunity to enhance the general quality of life for humans, critics point out that this again presupposes some conception of the good, of what kind of traits are best to engineer into humans (disease-resistance, memory enhancement, high-speed intelligence etc.), and they disagree about precisely what 'objective goods' to try to select for installation into humans/posthumans. A further and stronger, though more abstract, objection is voiced by Habermas. It is that interfering with the process of human conception, and by implication human constitution, that deprives humans of the 'naturalness which so far has been a part of the taken-for-granted background of our self-understanding as a species' and '[g]etting used to having human life at the biotechnologically enabled disposal of our contingent preferences cannot help but change our normative self-understanding' (2003: 72). And will those TH agents (athletes and non-athletes alike), genetically and technologically modified to their autonomous heart's content, ever escape from being the objects of never ending resentment?[7]

We have seen then that there are a variety of arguments for and against TH. It will be clear that I am neither in favour of the radical nor the apparently moderate versions. It seems clear to me at least, that the project is an undesirable utopianism. We have enough problems with the human nature we struggle with let alone another nature that we neither control nor understand anywhere near as fully. It strikes me that the platitude that what is needed is nicer people not brighter ones is apposite. Perhaps that is why it is a platitude. At its heart, it seems to me, is a view of technology at the mercy of scientists generally (or in the case of athletic powers: sports '*medics*'), which is simply a case of Prometheanism. This charge is often labelled against genetic and other technologists without proper explanation. And it strikes me that the charge is not properly understood. In order that to move beyond mere slogans or name-calling, then, I shall offer two contrasting lenses through which these claims may be viewed by returning to the roots of the Promethean myth itself.

Whose Prometheus: Hesiod or Aeschylus?

In order to understand the charge of Prometheanism one might begin by asking 'What is the myth of Prometheus?' I think the better question is 'whose myth of Prometheus should we concern ourselves with?' I take my cue both from Conacher's (1980) account and also from Kerenyi's (1963) though I do not attempt fully to do justice to their theses here.[8] I merely use them for my own purpose of providing lenses to view the unrestrained enhancement ideology of TH, which it seems to me can find an easy footing in the unreflective pools of sports medicine and sports sciences more generally.

First, let us say that there is no single Greek account of Prometheus' deeds. There are at least two sources and even among these sources there are variations. The two sources, in chronology, are Hesiod and Aeschylus. In Hesiod there are two accounts: *Theogeny* and *Works and Days*. And the only full text from Aeschylus is *Prometheus Bound* though we know it to be part of a trilogy (*Prometheus Unbound, Prometheus the Firebringer*).

Theogeny is Hesiod's account of the beginning of the world. The Titans (giants) challenged Zeus and the Olympian gods for the supremacy of the world. *Works and Days* is said to be a similar account but one which celebrates the ideas that labour is the universal lot of mankind but that those willing so to do can get by. This is important to appreciate in order to evaluate the act for which Prometheus became (in)famous. Prometheus, acting against his fellow Titans, sided with Zeus and his cunning brought about the victory over the latter by the former. In consequence he was honoured by Zeus and seems to have some kind of dual nature: both God and mortal. Sometimes the two are simplistically dichotomised: Zeus as power, Prometheus as cunning reason or intellect (Conacher, 1980).

Prometheus is said to have stolen fire and to have cheated the gods out of their proper share of a sacrifice. Which came first is not always clear as there are different interpretations. But both acts, according to Kerenyi, evidence the claim that Prometheus is of deficient character. He writes:

> Prometheus, founder of the sacrifice, was a cheat and a thief: those traits are at the bottom of all the stories that deal with him. The meaning of his strange sacrifice in which the gods were cheated out of the tasty morsels is simply this: that the sacrifice offered up by men is a sacrifice of foolhardy thieves, stealers of the divinity round about them – for the world of nature that surrounds them is divine – whose temerity brings immeasurable and unforeseen misfortune upon them.
>
> (Kerenyi, 1963: xxii)

A little amplification is in order. Both Prometheus (often translated as 'foresight') and his inept brother Epimetheus (sometimes translated as 'aftersight') set out on Zeus' orders to fashion creatures to populate the Earth. Lacking wisdom (or 'foresight') Epimetheus fails to consider what qualities are necessary as he goes about making the 'animal kingdom'. Prometheus fashions mortals in the vision of the gods. Epimetheus having used all his gifts from Zeus has failed to clothe them and Prometheus watches pitifully as they shiver in the cold nights. It is here that, rebelling against Zeus' authority, Prometheus sides with mankind, and steals fire – hidden in a fennel stalk. The mortals are thus warmed.

In order to appease and honour Zeus, Prometheus reveals his disrespectful cunning. He offers him a sacrificial ox. In one half he hides the bones with a rich layering of fat which appears on the surface to be the greater and more desirable share. Under the entrails of the animal he hides in the other skin all the good meat. Zeus, apparently understanding the deception as part of the unchanging fate of mankind, accepts the lesser share.

By way of punishing Prometheus and all mortals, he withheld fire from mortals.[9] The hubris of Prometheus in particular though is captured by his punishment: he is to be chained to a tree on Mount Caucasus where an eagle will eat at his liver all day only for it to be replenished overnight for the cycle of suffering and humiliation to continue the next day and so on.

In Aeschylus we get a different interpretation of events, one that is at once more sympathetic to Prometheus. First, there is a more optimistic conception of 'human initiative' (Conacher, 1980: 13). A further aspect of this is in the fact that hope is hidden from men in Hesiod ('fortunately' it is said in Hesiod, or rather 'for their sakes') whereas in Aeschylus it is one of the gifts from Prometheus. As Conacher puts it:

> To put the point in the broadest possible terms, the Hesiodic Prometheus, by his deceptions and frustrations of Zeus in his relations with man, is presented (however 'artificially') as the indirect cause of all man's woes; the Aeschylean Prometheus, on the other hand, by his interventions on behalf of man, is presented as the saviour of mankind, without whom man would have ceased to exist and with whose help he progresses from mere subsistence to a state of civilization.
>
> (1980: 13)

Aeschylus does this by suppressing the sacrifice deception and transforms the fire-stealing act as one of daring rather than hubris. For without the deception there is no occasion for the withholding of fire, which is the consequent punishment. For fire is seen not merely as the warmth that forestalls the chill of the night but – more importantly – as the precondition of craft, trade, even civilization. But what has all this got to do with TH generally, and sports medicine more specifically?

A moral topography for sports medicine

In the rise of psychiatry, much was made of the scientism that bedevilled the then emerging profession. Disputes raged as to whether there could be such a thing as mental illness (akin to physical illness) or whether this constituted the imposition of normative patterns of thought and action by state powers. The more pharmacologically inclined argued that mental illness did indeed exist but that its basis was chemical not political. Others took it to be a case of the medicalisation of everyday life. In all of this Thomas Szasz was (and still remains) a trenchant critic. Like Kass, Szasz has been charged with providing powerful polemic more than patient argument. Notwithstanding this, he once crafted the following, memorable, remark: 'Formerly, when religion was strong and science weak, men mistook magic for medicine; now, when science is strong and religion weak, men mistake medicine for magic' (1973: 115).

This juxtaposition of religion, magic and science is a troublesome one for the public, no less than gullible and overcommitted athletes, who appear to lack any kind of moral framework within which to evaluate their Herculean efforts. Like many highly paid athletes, the models of professionalism for sports physicians are too often dominated by Koehn's (1993) models of expert or service-provider for fee. The hired hand goes out to the highest bidder. But the loss of dedication to the traditional aims of medicine, let alone the Hippocractic Oath, is palpable.

The main concern that TH raises for sports is the following, rather general, concern: 'How are we to evaluate the enhancement agenda?' It is clear that there are strong advocates such as Miah who want to extend autonomous choice by athletes in ways that may easily open the door for unprincipled biomedical and sports scientists. Equally clearly there will be traditionalists, myself included, who find the unfettered use of technology to augment human nature utterly repellent.

One way forward is to establish better spaces of dialogue between opposing camps in order to establish what Taylor (1989) calls 'moral topography'. I take this to be a loose application of what he had in mind in his articulation of the moral sources of modern identity. Moral topography in sports medicine might be about drawing out the conceptual relief, and the natural and artificial of the work of scientists therein. I use moral topography as a metaphor for teasing out what I take to be the 'traditional' work of medicine in the relief of suffering and the more recent (and artificial) goal of performance enhancement or the augmentation of natural abilities as opposed to the traditional therapeutic role of medicine. This may help develop critical but informed attitudes to, for example, the new genetic technologies that are likely to invade elite sports over the next decade and that threaten to make arcane the worries over steroids, EPO or human growth hormone.

Yet, in contrast to Miah (2004), and to Jonas (1974) and Kass (2002) before him, the new biology and biotechnology or indeed the new genetics need not require us to rethink a new ethics *ab initio*. The sources for the evaluation of medical and sports technology were revealed long ago in the Ancient Greek writings of Plato. The historian of medicine, Edelstein (1967) notes the Ancient Greek philosopher's task of undermining the glorification of the body. And building upon his insight McKenny (1997) noted Plato's observations, considering the education of the Guardians so that medicine may serve rather than hinder or dominate our moral projects. In this vein we too should ask: how much attention should we devote to our bodies in the effort to optimise our capacities?; how much control should we allow physicians to exercise over our bodies?; what ends should determine what counts as a sufficiently healthy body?; what limits should we observe in our efforts to improve our bodily performance and remove causes of suffering? In short, what kinds of life shall we lead and what kinds of persons shall we become?

Elite sportsmen and women, their coaches, sports national governing bodies and no less even than sports promoters and institutions such as the IOC, the IAAF, FIFA, all have an interest in surpassing limits. Athletes are deemed to have failed if they do not 'peak' at big events breaking their own personal best times, and heights, and distances. World records must tumble at every event it seems. At this macro-level, enhanced performances are wrapped up in celebratory spectacles primarily to sell media and marketing packages. And the circus rolls on to the next event, the next town. This denial of the necessity of limits in nature by some, the desire to remove or delay their onset in the shape of disease, or burnout-syndrome, and to control these human-limiting factors by the unfettered use of biotechnology is something that should concern us all in sports. I submit that philosophers of both sport and medicine begin to press such questions of character and conduct, of ends as well as means, in the public spaces of the media as well as the gymnasium and the university so that sports do not become the vanguard of Hesiod's Promethean character and the unmooring of ethical ends.[10]

Notes

1 What is this thing called sport?

1 Phonetically pronounced: clan-ur-tid (with apologies to my Welsh-speaking friends!).
2 The conceptual core of each of these concepts is so diffuse and contested that they have often been referred to, after Gallie, as 'essentially contested concepts'. This term of art was used to depict concepts whose core meaning was contested. It seems clear to me, and as I hope to draw out in this chapter, there are enough persisting characteristics of sport that allow us to understand the concept typically even if a certain vagueness persists at its edges. That is to say, despite the many accounts of the concept of sport that exist, I see no reason to think of the concept as an essentially contested one.
3 Suits' original essay 'What is a game?' was published in 1967 and became the cornerstone of his later (1978) book *The Grasshopper: Games, Life and Utopia*. I shall comment on his account below but do not attempt to do full justice to his rich and subtle account laid out there, nor in subsequent revisions collected as an appendix in the (2005) second edition. See instead McFee (2003b).
4 Instead see Kyle (2007: 23–53) on pre-Greek athletic cultures and art notably in Mesoptamia.
5 Though in a very limited manner: £40 ($60 US dollars), a silver trophy and a hand-held computer courtesy of the sponsors.
6 See Young (1984) for a particularly sharp destruction of the myth of amateur athletic nobility in Ancient Greece.

2 Sports, persons and sportspersonship

1 This is, of course, not to say that the possibility does not exist. In one of his thought experiments Glover writes:

> Suppose we construct a robot whose 'brain' functions just like ours, although it consists of a silicon chip, Its exterior, as in science fiction films, is metallic, But, unlike any present robots, its behaviour passes any test for consciousness that we do. It does not just play chess, but appears also to read novels, fall in love, daydream and enjoy jokes. It can take part in sophisticated conversation about whether its present feeling is shame or embarrassment.
>
> Should we say that the robot really has experiences, or just that it behaves as though it does? Its behaviour gives us more evidence in favour of its consciousness than we have in the case of cats or monkeys. Against this, there is the

argument that since it is not alive it is not conscious. But perhaps restricting consciousness to things not made of the same sort of stuff as us is just a prejudice.

(Glover, 1988: 86).

2 See instead Miah (2004).
3 The most important works, for our purposes, written by Taylor between the period 1971–84 are collected together in two volumes: C. Taylor (1985a) and (1985b). All page references are taken from the above and not the original sources.
4 See C. Taylor (1985a: 75–6).
5 One corollary of this point was highlighted by early English Utilitarian Jeremy Bentham who remarked that when deciding whether or not one might harm someone or thing the question is not so much whether they can speak but whether they can experience pain. See Midgley (1983: 203–51) *Beast and Man: The Roots of Human Nature*, Chapter 10 'Speech and other excellences'.
6 See C. Taylor (1985a: 60–75).
7 It should be noted that Taylor does account for instances where the subject may be said to be unaware of remorse without fully being able to articulate what it is that one has done wrong. In such cases, one may feel an unease about a given scenario or act and only later find oneself, perhaps through the guidance of another, to realise the proper ethical contours of the emotion.
8 Again, see Midgley (1983: 253–84), especially Chapter 11 ''On being animal as well as rational'.
9 The notion of strong evaluation is central to Taylor's thesis here and in his later explication of that theme in *Sources of the Self* (1991).
10 This idea is explored similarly in Kovesi (1972). See especially Chapter 2 on 'Following rules and giving reasons'.
11 This is not meant to imply that persons are *ipso facto* fully conscious of their motives or emotions at all times.
12 A similar point is made by Williams who reminds us that modernity is partly characterised by the unprecedented degree to which we are reflectively aware of our actions and that this self-understanding is so basic to many of the institutions of modern life such as law, medicine or business. It is also one of the reasons why past forms of life cannot be returned to. As he puts it: 'There is no route back from reflectiveness' (Williams, 1985: 163–4; see also 2–3 and 156–73). See Rorty (1976) for a discussion on the theological and legal influences of the development of the concept of personhood which requires unified location for the attribution of responsibility.
13 I discuss Radcliffe's personal tragedy in Chapter 9.
14 As it happens England lost the match to Germany (again) on penalties and so the depths of his anguish were later diffused though not extinguished.
15 For a clear discussion of the notions of, and distinction between, the constitution and institutions of games see Reddiford (1985: 41–51). However, see in contrast Mary Midgley's comment: 'Speech is not an institution [. . .] nor is games [. . .] The word "institution" would be best saved for things which were once instituted and could at a pinch be disinstituted again without taking the whole human race with them' (1974: 252). Play and games for Midgley, as for Huizinga and Berne, exist in the cultures with whom they grew up. They are not optional extras; we need them. Similarly, one might add to this point Lasch's remark, contrary to what many people intuitively assert, that '[t]he degradation of sport, then, consists not in its being taken too seriously but in its trivialization. Games derive their power from the investment of seemingly trivial activity with serious intent' (Lasch, 1979: 195). I think Midgley and Lasch raise extremely interesting points which have important implications for a philosophical discussion of the values of play, games

and sport. But I cannot address this issue here. Throughout the book, however, and especially in the next chapter, I shall reserve the term institution for the meaning of bureaucratic organisations that organise, control and often corrupt social practices such as sports.

16 Feitelson's work is cited but not referenced in Sutton-Smith (1974: 121).

17 It should go without saying that none of these remarks should rule out the possibility of disabled persons engaging in able-bodied sports whether adapted or otherwise.

18 To borrow the memorable phrase of my middle-distance Paralympic athlete friend David Howe.

19 Flanagan's article goes further to question in many respects the defensibility of the strong/weak distinction in ways that are not necessary for me to consider here. What I have written accords however with the interpretation that strong/weak evaluation can be translated without loss of meaning as ethical/non-ethical evaluation though I will not engage in any depth of meta-ethical dispute here as to the drawings of those or indeed the moral/ethical boundaries. I say slightly more about the scepticism of Taylor who, along with Alisdair MacIntyre and Bernard Williams, has expressed deep scepticism about the narrowness of modern morality. I take up this issue in relation to the subject of moral development in and through sport in Chapter 4.

20 I once had the dubious pleasure of receiving ski lessons at an Austrian resort. Moderately skilful in contexts where one runs, jumps, swings and throws, I found sliding and gliding all but impossible and immensely frustrating. The ski instructor felt the latter too. 'Stop thinking' he said, 'just do what is natural'. I remonstrated that (1) thinking was a professional hazard and (2) not having grown up on or near any wintry slopes the movement pattern was anything but natural to me despite his effortless élan. He remained unimpressed and I failed to warm to alpine skiing until on a short sabbatical with Sigmund Loland in Oslo, where I was taught with minimal instruction and elegant example, the two or three basic things to focus on. I achieved at least some measure of control over my wayward limbs on ontologically real slippery slopes and a small insight into the beauty of this sports form.

21 Indeed it was a mistake I made when presenting an earlier version of the paper back in 1991 at a Philosophic Society for the Study of Sport (now the International Association for the Philosophy of Sport) that was generously pointed out by Scott Kretchmar. His gentle provocation failed to get me to change my mind as a version of the piece was published (McNamee, 1992). But it seems clear to me now that Flanagan's critique is compelling and I regret not having been aware of it at the time as I do failing to take his advice.

22 Note, I am not saying that this cannot be done for I am persuaded by a lot of what appears in the Dreyfuss brothers account of the similarities of motoric and moral learning. It is just that is not the account Flanagan offers.

23 Or as a colleague remarked to me, tongue in cheek, 'is that *three* concepts: "sports", "person" and "ship"?!'

24 In sports psychology see Bredemeier and Shields (1995), and in philosophy see most recently, Feezel (2005, 83–96). I shall offer an extended critique of the whole program of psychological research in moral development and sports in Chapter 4.

25 For a critical review of which see Kretchmar (2007).

3   Sports as practices

1 See for example Arnold (1992, 1994), Brown (1991), Schneider and Butcher (1993, 1994), Gibson (1993) and Morgan (1994).

2 Later MacIntyre calls these internal goods, goods of excellence (1998) but without adding significantly to the clarity of the idea or ameliorating the charge of opaqueness.

3 A point that Gibson (1993) surprisingly ignores.

4 By which he means that moral attitudes, norms, rules and their like are the equivalent to emotions or feelings, themselves understood as pre- or non-cognitive. It is important for the virtue-ethical account of sport I am developing to note here that this view of emotion is itself a deeply flawed one and to be rejected *tout court*, and not simply by those wishing to develop or sustain a virtue-ethical account.

5 See MacIntyre (1985: 207–47).

6 For a critique of this and related communitarian theories of the situated self see Kymlicka (1989: 47–73).

7 This phrase was adopted in response to some research that suggested, in North America, the average viewer changed channels on his or her television every three minutes suggesting as much the failure to engage with the material as much as the banality of it.

8 Later in the 2004 Athens Olympics the British athlete Paula Radcliffe would suffer under similar heat conditions. I shall discuss her suffering during that race in Chapter 9.

9 See pp. 136–50.

10 One could cite any number of books on the history of sport and/or the Olympic Games. The socio-economic role played by the poets who celebrate heroic deeds in Ancient Greece is precisely part of the institutional logic of that epoch of heroic deeds that is often overlooked. For an extended discussion of the chains of compensation see Kurke (1991).

11 Morgan sets out in the last chapter in his 1994 book to discuss this very problem. He eschews alternative routes that offer solutions to intrapractice deliberations of ends such as are offered by Rawls (overlapping consensus) and Habermas (ideal-speech situations). His positive line draws first from MacIntyre (by using the practice-institution distinction to lever the internal logic of sports from external considerations) and then from Walzer (by implementing the 'liberal art of separation') so that the non-relevant considerations are 'bracketed from the deliberations of sporting communities'. What this amounts to is investing in the ongoing tradition the unavoidability of de facto authority. While this is an appealing move in many ways, it lends itself to a certain purist interpretation of the practice and a necessarily dim one of the institution. The efficacy of this distinction has already been questioned.

12 It is interesting that another of MacIntyre's critics, inspired by Hume, comes to a similar direction by way of distinguishing her own moral champion distinct from Aristotle. Baier writes:

> Virtues are those traits of character, involving both motivation and ability, to which we give approval when we reflect upon them from a point of view that has overcome the "continual contradictions" to which more partial points of view are prone. Hume's ultimate moral question is one about character: the good person is the one of whom the moral judge can say "his company is a satisfaction to me." The one who is "a safe companion, an easy friend, a gentle master, an agreeable husband, or an indulgent father."
>
> (1985: 257)

13 Again, I wish partly to alleviate Morgan from this charge on the basis of his comments, for example, that the leftists' critique often presupposes that the activity has itself no particular logic but is only an empty vessel awaiting institutionalisation of various forms. Morgan acknowledges this though he attributes the ability

of the practice to withstand the various institutional onslaughts to the practice's own awareness of its internal logic. On the one hand, I am not sure what it is for a practice to have such awareness other than through its participants, and, given my questioning of the sharpness of the distinction between sporting practices and institutions, I am not sure why we should not also include those members of the institution who are not entirely deaf and blind to the internal logic of sport.

14 The chess example is borrowed from Kolnai (1966).

15 See, for example, Peters (1966).

16 Following MacIntyre (1985) and Cooper (1975). It should be noted, though, that the *locus classicus* is Aristotle's *Nichomachean Ethics*, Book One (1980).

17 See more generally Taylor (1989: 115–26).

18 Such an idea has a long history of course. The idea captured in the evaluation – social before personal, cooperative before competitive – is to be found also in Green (1907) who writes that a pure notion of the good

implies interest in an object which is common to all men in the proper sense, in the sense, namely, that there can be no competition for its attainment between man and man; and the only interest that satisfies this condition is the interest, under some form or other, in the perfecting of man or the realization of the powers of the human soul.

(1907: 67)

19 More specifically he argues against the notion of equality of opportunity and its capacity to counteract systematically unjust distribution of goods (Singer, 1993).

4   Sport and ethical development

1 See Hampshire (1983).

2 In contemporary (sport) psychology, researchers refer to personality traits (which are considered quite fixed over time and context), omnibus dispositions (where proneness to act is more malleable) and situationally-specific traits or dispositions.

3 Although Kohlberg (1981) was initially adamant about the strong, if not perfect correlation, between thought and action, his confidence was not borne out by empirical evidence. Kohlberg (1984) and Power *et al.* (1989) attempted to explain the possible reasons for a less than perfect correlation. The idea of personal responsibility and the prevailing moral atmosphere came to be thought of as mediating influences in moral action.

4 Though, as Peters (1974: 303–35) famously observed, ought one not to *care* about duty? And if one agrees with the proposition, one ought immediately to be attuned both to the necessity of certain emotions in the appreciation and execution of one's moral duties (see especially Chapter 8 below).

5 It should be noted that Kohlberg's theory was not a unified matter. He made several revisions to his position but in this section we are merely sketching his theory in order to show its influence in sport psychological research. For more detailed exegesis see Jones and McNamee (2000).

6 What the term is taken to mean precisely is open to alternative accounts. Contrast, for example, D'Agostino (1981) and Loland and McNamee (2000).

7 A phrase I still shudder at.

8 It has been argued, with effect, that the kind of definition commonly used in sport psychological research is itself problematic – failing clearly and adequately to delineate assertion, aggression and violence – as it stands far apart from common linguistic usage and moral philosophical accounts. See Parry (1998).

9 It is clear that the many and various research publications constitute an extremely significant research programme in its totality. In order to find a shorthand for the critique we will simply refer to the corpus of work as Bredemeier and Shields while intending no disrespect to their colleagues. Second, it is extremely important to note that we hold this research in very high regard. This critique of it relates exclusively to philosophical considerations and the methodological implications that flow from the alternative theoretical conceptualisations of ethics, virtue and character that I set out here and elsewhere; see Jones and McNamee (2000) and McNamee and Jones (2000).

10 Within the philosophy of education Charles Bailey (1975) argued in a similar fashion that there was a logical connection between winning and the demonstration of superiority over an opponent. As such he argued that competitive games in particular were incompatible with moral education. For those interested in the psychological development of this point and the differentiation between task and ego-oriented individuals see McNamee *et al.* (2003).

11 Another issue with contemporary models like the one discussed here is that they do not account for reactive, 'in the heat of the moment' aggressive and/or immoral action. In sport contests, there is not always the time to think through the situation and then act in an intentional manner. There is an issue therefore about what is being predicted: one-off behaviours or patterns of responses, acts or agency/character?

12 Again, it is important to remind ourselves that their use of the term 'moral' here is theoretically guided (whether the researchers are aware of it or not) and can be traced specifically to its use in the cognitive development tradition, namely that morality is simply right action in accordance with moral principles. Likewise, morally mature agents are those who consistently and autonomously apply these moral principles. We have already shown that this is not a given, but rather a reflection of theoretical preference for one picture from a highly contested terrain.

13 This criticism might seem particularly harsh. It is important to note, however, that in their excellent, densely researched book *Character Development and Physical Activity*, limited space (Shields and Bredemeiers, 1995: 192–5) is given over to the elaboration of character and the four component virtues that are the object of my critique in the following paragraphs.

14 For suggestions of such positions see Hampshire (1983: 152):

> My claim is that morality has its sources in conflict, in the divided soul and between contrary claims, and that there is no rational path that leads from these conflicts to harmony and to an assured solution, and to the normal and natural conclusion.

More generally against the theoretical systematisation of ethics see Clarke and Simpson (1989).

15 I say 'most' since psychoanalytical accounts stand out in the sharpest of contrasts. See for example Wollheim (1984: 197–225) 'The growth of moral sense' and also 'The good self and the bad self' (1993: 39–63).

16 See Guivernau and Duda (2002) for a full account of the empirical support for this point.

17 For an extended discussion of which see MacKinnon (1999: 57–90).

18 Consider the remark, which I owe to Graham McFee, that scientists should on principle treat subjects *as if* they were human beings.

19 The terms of stages ('initial', 'intermediary' and 'final') and more general inspiration are taken from Tobin (1989).

20 See Nussbaum (2001: 174–236).

21 Although the quotation is Nussbaum's, she is setting out an idea from Nancy Chodorow. It is important to note, and not merely contingent, that the philosophers and social scientists most helpful in drawing our attention to the depth and salience of the emotions in ethics are women. Moreover, this maternal aspect is not tied to the female gender in a necessary way, but merely reflects the empirical dominance of women in the care-giving, care-taking, role.

22 I explore this tension in Chapter 5.

23 According to Ryle (1972) we speak better of learning than teaching here. The point is also made by Spiecker (1999) who reminds us that character traits are better thought of as complex multi-track dispositions than simple ones. Other things being equal, glass will smash when we drop it. Persons being much more complex do not simply respond with a given act in relation to any given circumstance when they are in this intermediate stage. Notoriously, with adolescents whose value-structures are in flux, their reactions are not reliable. Equally, responses from those in the final stage of moral development are not simple, triggered, responses. Often it takes a good deal of moral maturity to see the potential clash of interests that are commonly called dilemmas.

5   Codes of conduct and trustworthy coaches

1 See Morgan (1993), Butcher and Schneider (1993) and, more recently, Allison (2005).

2 Koehn (1993), cites Annette Baier's original (1986) essay 'Trust and anti-trust' that appeared in *Ethics*. All references to that essay heretoforward are from the version of it that appears in Baier (1994) *Moral Prejudices; Essays on Ethics*.

3 These points are synthesised and amended from Dawson (1994) and Brackenridge (1994). Whether or not any code can, as Dawson asserts, offer a neutral framework seems to be highly dubious. Time and space, however, does not provide further comment.

4 The *locus classicus* of this view is Kant's *Groundwork of the Metaphysic of Morals* (1953).

5 As set out by Davis (1991).

6 The elegance itself is a little deceptive as many philosophers have noted for Kant since the 'Categorical Imperative' he took to be the cornerstone of his moral system, has not one interpretation but two. In the first instance, by wedding morality and rationality, Kant sets out what is to count as a moral rule. All moral rules, he argued, must be such that we would will all persons to act in accordance with them. It is the second interpretation of the 'Categorical Imperative' I have noted above that urges us never to treat other people as means to our ends, but rather as ends in themselves, since all human agents are worthy of our unconditional respect, because they are moral agents.

7 Any utilitarian would properly object that this negative characterisation, though it fits the utilitarian rule to minimise pain, misses entirely the corresponding rule to maximise happiness or pleasure. It should be clear that the general target here is the deontological one.

8 Since the original essay was published, there have been several revisions yet I have kept the example for its clarity. I assume that it is typical of a good many such rules. Moreover, since writing the original essay the organisation changed its name to Sports Coach UK.

9 For an account of the idea of a moral principle see Schneewind (1983). He articulates three features of a classic moral principle: relative context-freedom, unexceptionability and substantiality. To these he adds a fourth, a foundational or basic feature, which, in combination with the others gives what he calls a 'classical first principal' (1983: 114).

10 An amusing anecdote illuminates the point. I hope it does not offend my feminist friends and colleagues; it ought not. In the smash hit film *Ghostbusters* the fraudulent psychology professor Venkman has gone to see would-be client who has been citing paranormal activity in her flat (the sort of activity a code of conduct might properly comment upon) whereupon he finds her body lain on the bed with another identical figure floating invitingly above her in a provocative fashion. Venkman at first rebuffs 'I make it a rule never to go to bed with more than one person at the same time' (or something very similar) but upon further exhortations gives in with a spurious self-justification 'it's more of a guideline than a rule'!
11 I am grateful to John Lyle for this observation.
12 This is not the place for Wittgensteinian exegesis. See instead Baker and Hacker (1985) and Holtzman and Leich (1981).
13 I note though that Brackenridge (2001) argues that these are not the most important variables that predispose coaches to abuse athletes.
14 See Gambetta (1988).
15 See Chapters 6 to 9 in Baier (1994).
16 As reported by Solomon (1993: 144).
17 Though, for the untrusting, I have elsewhere explored a different and greater range of principles and rules in 'Theoretical limitations in codes of ethical conduct' (1995b).
18 I am very grateful to Graham McFee, Gordon Reddiford and Tony Skillen for their helpful comments.

6 Racism, racist acts and courageous role models

1 Perhaps the best-known advocate for the former is Warren Fraleigh's (1984) *Right Action in Sport*, while the utilitarian case is less popular, Claudio Tamburrini's (2000) *The Hand of God* is the best example of a sustained defence of a utilitarian position in sports ethics.
2 Why, it might be asked, have I indicated the age of Hill? As will become clear, the reference to Hill's age is entirely relevant to the formation of racist attitudes masked as benign humour.

7 Hubris, humility and humiliation: vice and virtue in sporting communities

1 The original focus for this chapter came predominantly from Dixon (1992). Later challenges to and revisions of his thesis are relatively unimportant for my purposes as they pertain to the notion of lop-sided defeats that are not, as I argue later, necessary to understand how weak humiliation may properly be said to be felt by sportspersons. In earlier discussion of blowout victories and defeats, Dixon (1992, 1998, 2000), Feezel (1999) and Hardman *et al.* (1996) appear to favour the idea of a simple continuum between a loss of self-esteem and humiliation (weak or strong). And this fails to capture the grammar of the emotions at hand, though it should be noted that Dixon is more dismissive of the intensity of sports' emotionality than the others. Our sense of who we are and the import we attach to projects such as sports when we are deeply committed to them has an ineradicable social dimension well captured in the phrase 'practice communities'.
2 See instead Bruckhardt (1998: 135–213) and Hatab (1991: 31–42).
3 In older shame cultures the keeping of face, or of holding to the social expectations of one's roles, is central. Yet in individualistic cultures the preservation of autonomy and integrity represent a social/moral terrain that the modernist vocabulary of universal rights is designed to promote and protect. As I have said, certain martial sports are pre-modern in certain aspects of their nature and to that degree

anachronistic. This fact opens up some latitude in terms of the possibility of imposing strong humiliation on an opponent. I am reminded, however, of the case of an elite Japanese Sumo wrestler who was involved in a motorbike accident that was publicised in the national press. So strongly did he feel that he had let down the high expectations of his sport and its code of honor (*budo* is the name given to the warrior ethic) that he offered to withdraw from his club. I am clear then, that much of what I write here is cradled in the history of Western civilisation and that the anachronism may not be felt in Eastern or Latin cultures and the tradition-bound practices that constitute them. It might be argued that my later example of Roberto Duran's over-weening machismo and subsequent humiliation entails a certain Western hegemony. Though I try to make clear why I think this is not the case, I am aware that I am at the very least open to criticism here.

4   Miller is not entirely clear here. One might assume, however, that by shame proper he means something like Aristotle's account of shame as quasi-virtue: a susceptibility to recognise and publicly show one's recognition of a moral transgression. A battery of other concepts such as awkwardness, discomfort, compassion, regret and so on have refined our appreciation of responses to minor wrongdoing. Making a virtue out of a response to wrongdoing might be beyond the bounds of reasonableness for the modern mind yet I shall attempt to carve out such a response in relation to a discussion of the ethics of doping in Chapter 11.

5   I think that this is precisely the position adopted by both Dixon (1992, 1998) and Hardman *et al.* (1996).

6   I am reminded here of Mohammad Ali when he labelled Joe Frazier as an "uncle Tom" before the first of their epic fights. He was not alone in this regard; names of former world champions such as Nasseem Hamed, Chris Eubank and Gene Tunney all trip easily off the tongue in respect of those whose mouths got the better of their manners. It is only fair to note too that Frazier was no saint. In the pre-match media banter, it was Frazier who had called Ali merely a mouthpiece for Islam. He too was made to pay for his mealy-mouthed quip. Ali was scarcely able to occupy the high ground, however, as he taunted Frazier 'nigger', while hitting him in the ensuing contest. Ali's position was that he had no right to invoke such an assault on his integrity – though he would have done well to dwell on the nature of his own racial abuse of Frazier. Not surprisingly, there is still no love lost between the two, nor their daughters who recently slogged it out in a contest more to be remembered for its hype than pugilistic excellence. I have used the male gender here and throughout the essay for no better reason than the boxing world is predominantly a male world even though this is not exclusively the case.

7   I owe this point to Keith Thompson.

8   I am grateful to Cesar Torres who first raised some disquiet about locating Duran within a discourse of Latino machismo. I later benefited from a discussion with Fernando Cervantes about this and have subsequently revised the attribution. The mere historical fact of his Latino background is an accidental and particular aspect of his hubris. I am grateful to both for their advice and correction.

9   Stories are legion of the Russian gymnastics coach Bela Karoly who initiated and sustained regimes of terror in his gymnasia and for whom the strong humiliation of his charges was part of his coaching armoury. But he is only one of many targets who might be singled out. My hunch, for which there is patchy evidence, is that this pattern of domination is not uncommon in sports where children perform at an elite level. See David (2005).

10   In the final chapter, I discuss the hubris of Prometheus in the context of sports medicine and the enhancement agenda that is prevalent in its ethos.

8   *Schadenfreude* in sports: envy, justice and self-esteem

1   I shall attempt a more balanced account of Kant's stance towards the emotions in his own virtue theory here, in contrast to the more one-sided account I gave in the original publication of this essay (McNamee, 2003b) and an earlier article on the emotion of guilt as a response to injury infliction (McNamee, 2002).

2   This is the case of the 1991 translation of the *Metaphysics of Morals*. In a footnote (91n, p. 292) to this very point, however, she notes that in the earlier 1974 translation 'affect' had been preferred to the earlier translation as 'agitation' where as 'passions' were previously labelled 'obsessions'.

3   The point may be put more generally that the emotions come in clusters (Baier, 1990: 4–5). Not surprisingly, Rorty (1988) had earlier put that observation to effect in the context of virtue theory: the virtues, she says, hunt in packs. It seems only a short leap to imagine that the vices too rarely work alone. To support this point, I shall attempt to show below that it is not justice which triggers *schadenfreude*, but envy.

4   Griffiths takes Anthony Kenny's 1963 work *Act, Emotion, Will* to be seminal here. It has found its strongest expression in the work of Robert Solomon but also is a cornerstone of Charles Taylor's theory of human agency and personhood and is central to his celebrated distinction between strong and weak evaluation.

5   It might seem reasonable to suggest that the extent to which this is the case is a hostage to the heterogeneity of emotions. Typically one might think that this propositional element may be more developed according to the complexity and/or nuance of the emotion at hand. When one feels uneasy in the dark one might say one is afraid but unable to articulate the object of the fear. Or think of long-term injured athletes who go through moods of depression without some precisely focused object as their source.

6   Philip Howard identifies *schadenfreude* as one of the black holes in English. One commentator (R. C. Trench, etymologist and author of *English Past and Present* and *On the Study of Words*) celebrates this gap, saying:

> What a fearful thing it is that any language should have a word expressive of the pleasure which men feel at the calamities of others; for the existence of the word bears testimony to the existence of the thing. And yet in more than one, such a word is found: in the Greek *epikairekakia*, in the German, *Schadenfreude*.
>
>   (Retrieved at http://www.users.bigpond.com/burnside/black_holes.htm)

7   It could be argued that the comic is only a token of a wider class that might issue *Schadenfreude* vis-à-vis the trivial or insignificantly harmful.

8   As cited in Portmann (2000: 33).

9   It will probably be clear that I take my lead here from Nozick (1974: 239–46). As he puts it:

> People generally judge themselves by how they fall along the most important dimensions in which they *differ* from others. People do not gain self-esteem from their common human capacities by comparing themselves to animals who lack them. (I'm pretty good; I have an opposable thumb and can speak some language) . . . self-esteem is based on *differentiating characteristics*: that's why it's called *self* esteem.
>
>   (1974: 243, emphasis thus)

10   In the introductory section of 'Envy and equality', Rawls (1972: 604) writes:

> We are now ready to examine the likelihood of excusable general envy in a well-ordered society. [. . .] Now I assume that the main psychological root of the liability to envy is a lack of self-confidence in our own worth combined with a sense of

impotence. [. . .] This hypothesis implies that the least favoured tend to be more envious of the better situation of the more favoured the less secure their self-respect and the greater their feeling that they cannot improve their prospects.

Here, then, we see the further conflation of related concepts, since self-confidence is not a synonym either for self-respect or self-esteem. Interestingly, in the index to Rawls's magnum opus, under 'self-esteem', it actually says, 'see self-respect'.

11 I am indebted to David Sachs' (1981) paper where a more subtle version of the relations between self-respect and self-esteem can be found.

12 The phrase 'education of the emotions' sounds odd here despite its common currency. Do we not better speak of education in and through the emotions?

13 Among the sociological theories of sport, figurational explanations of sport violence centre upon the emotions, but even there surprisingly little, beyond noting the obvious emotions of anger, excitement, and frustration, is to be found. See, for example, Dunning (1999), for a collection of essays by one of the founding fathers (*sic*) of that school of thought.

14 *Othering* is a term of art invented by feminists, I believe, to capture the manner in which non-heterosexuals are pejoratively defined as non-normal as part of a subconscious psychological process of preparing them for maltreatment or at least inequitable treatment.

9 Suffering in and for sport

1 See, however, Loland *et al.* (2005).

2 Of course, the mistake was made by philosophers for centuries so this should not be thought of as a particularly damning criticism.

3 It is worth observing that so many people mistakenly believe that pain is somehow an inescapably private event that, in so far as it happens, can only be accessed and understood by the person in pain. This position was philosophically demolished in part by Ryle's famous attack on Cartesian dualism but also by Wittgenstein's private language argument about the social and learning contexts that demand a non-private reading of these types of experiences.

4 I am grateful to Martin Lipscombe for drawing my attention to this essay.

5 I am grateful to Steve Edwards for sharing with me his thoughts on suffering and also for alerting me to his critique of Cassell's account of suffering *inter alia* with which I am in general agreement. I merely revise his analysis in a minor way in what follows. I note that he refers to Cassell's criteria as the phenomenological and intactness conditions.

6 One might say here that Edwards has not embraced theodicy from the inside. But this is not the place to argue this point.

7 I am mindful that this is 'grist to the mill' of anthropologists of sports medicine such as Howe and Waddington; part of their everyday discourses. Nevertheless, the ideas are typically ignored or pejoratively dismissed by biomedical scientists in sports.

10 Doping: slippery slopes, *pleonexia* and shame

1 Though not all of course. See, for example, Miah (2004) and Savulescu and Foddy (2007).

2 See Simon (2004) for an elaboration of this argument.

3 For an insider account of the full scale of horrors of state-sponsored doping see Spitzer (2006). For an argument that doping under medical supervision would not work in practice, let alone principle, see Holm (2007).

4 I take these examples from an article on the deployment of concepts of normality and abnormality in McNamee (2008).

5 Even with his highly functional abnormality it should still be noted that his success was also partly based on hormonal supplementation before such time as it was banned.

6 Moreover, as Sternglantz (2005) notes, Schauer undermines his case when arguing that greater linguistic precision would undermine the slippery slope and that indirect consequences often bolster slippery slope arguments. It is as if the slippery slopes would cease in a world with greater linguistic precision or when applied only to direct consequences. These views do not find support in the later literature. Schauer does, however, identify three non-slippery slope arguments where the advocate's aim is to (1) show that the bottom of a proposed slope has been arrived at; (2) show that a principle is excessively broad; (3) highlight how granting authority to X will make more likely that an undesirable outcome will be achieved. It is clear that (1) could not properly be called a slippery slope argument in itself, while (2) and (3) often play some role in slippery slope arguments.

7 The ruling, however, is contestable at a number of levels. See Edwards (2008).

8 One might also observe that among the carry-overs from Ancient Greece, this particular motto is embedded in the excesses of Imperial Rome driven the arbitrary expansion of public spectacles. One might imagine Nero standing to proclaim to his fearful but worshipping plebiscite at the games: 'more Christians, more lions, more goring!' More seriously, see Allison' s critique: 'citius, altius, fortius ad absurdum' (2005).

9 Bernard Williams, however, suggests that the typical shame culture guilt culture dichotomy is too crude. See his *Shame and Necessity* (1993: 75–102).

10 The quotation from Hanstad is from personal correspondence 3.9.2007. Christiansen's remarks were made at a conference in response to a paper I gave on anti-doping where I suggested the loss of shame in elite sports was an important factor in doping.

11   Whose Prometheus?: Transhumanism, biotechnology and the moral topography of sports medicine

1 The best known advocate for which is Andy Miah (2004).

2 With respect to health see Brülde (2001).

3 The conflation of terms gets worse than this. In my view a significant portion of what is called 'sports medicine' is not medicine at all, but more commonly sports science or sports technology. See Edwards and McNamee (2006).

4 For a debate on the pros and cons of hypoxic chambers as (il)licit uses of sports medicine see Spriggs (2005) and the collected responses by Fricker (2005), Tamburrini (2005) and Tannsjo (2005).

5 For a fuller account of the nature(s) of TH see McNamee and Edwards (2006).

6 The clearest expositor is Nick Bostrom. See his 2005b 'Transhumanist values'. See also Bostrom (2005a), and contrast with the outline of one of the movement's founding fathers Max More (More, 1996, 2005). For a more detailed summary of the purported features of TH see McNamee and Edwards (2006).

7 As Rollin (2003) remarked of those who in the future might develop, and retain the secrets of, extreme longevity.

8 A short summary of the two accounts, though with no comparison or contrast can be found in Price and Kearns (2004: 453).

9 There is some ambiguity as to whether mortals had fire before. Conacher (1980: 12) is in no doubt that Prometheus stole it back for them, which entails their prior possession of it. I set to one side, here, Hesiod's misogynistic account of the first

punishment intended for Prometheus where Zeus has Hephaestus fashion women from fire (namely Pandora) whose jar (and not 'box' as is commonly thought) contains all the portents for the suffering of mankind.

10 I am grateful to Fritz-Gregor Herrman for his insight and guidance regarding the myths of Prometheus. I am especially grateful to my colleague, Steve Edwards, with whom I have collaborated closely on issues regarding both TH – especially in the light of slippery slope arguments – (McNamee and Edwards, 2006) and also regarding the conceptual relations between medicine and sports medicine (Edwards and McNamee, 2006). This chapter is an off-shoot from those discussions and conferences which was previously presented at a conference in Prague and which was published in an earlier form in Slovenian (McNamee, 2005b) and has been significantly revised.

References

Allison, L. (2005) 'Citius, altius, fortius ad absurdum', in C. Tamburrini and T. Tannsjo (eds) *Genetic Technology and Sports: Ethical Questions*, London: Routledge, pp. 149–57.

Allport, G. (1987) *The Nature of Prejudice*, Reading, MA: Addison-Wesley.

Appiah, K. A. (1996) 'Race, culture, identity', in K. A. Appiah and A. Guttman *Color Conscious*, Princeton, NJ: Princeton University Press.

Aristotle (1980) *Nichomachean Ethics*, Oxford: Oxford University Press (trans. W. D. Ross; updated J. O. Urmson and J. L. Ackrill).

Armon-Jones, C. (1991) *Varieties of Affect*, Toronto: University of Toronto Press.

Arnold, P. (1992) 'Sport as a valued human practice', *Journal of Philosophy of Education*, 26(2): 237–56.

Arnold, P. J. (1994) 'Sport and moral education', *Journal of Moral Education*, 23(1): 75–90.

Åstrand, P. O. and Rodahl, K. (1986) *A Textbook of Work Physiology*, London: McGraw Hill.

Back, L. (1996) *New Ethnicities and Urban Culture*, London: UCL Press.

Bacon, F. (2000) *Novum Organum* (ed. L. Jardine and M. Silverhorne), Cambridge: Cambridge University Press.

Baechler, J. (1992) 'Virtue: its nature, exigency and acquisition', in J. W. Chapman and W. A. Galston (eds) *Nomos*, XXXIV: 25–48 (trans. J. Chapman).

Baier, A. C. (1985) *Postures of the Mind*, London: Methuen.

Baier, A. C. (1986) 'Trust and anti-trust', Ethics, January (96): 231–60.

Baier, A. C. (1990) 'What emotions are about', *Philosophical Perspectives*, 4: 1–29.

Baier, A. C. (1994) *Moral Prejudices: Essays on Ethics*, London: Harvard University Press.

Bailey, C. (1975) 'Games, winning and education', *Cambridge Journal of Education*, 5(1): 40–50.

Baker, G. P. and Hacker, P. M. S. (1980) *Wittgenstein: Understanding and Meaning*, Oxford: Blackwell.

Baker, G. P. and Hacker, P. M. S. (1985) *Wittgenstein: Rules, Grammar and Necessity*, Oxford: Blackwell.

Baker, J. *et al.* (2006) 'Gym users and abuse of prescription drugs', *Journal of the Royal Society of Medicine*, 99: 331–2.

Balibar, E. and Wallerstein, I. (1991) *Race, Nation, Class: Ambiguous Identities*, London: Verso.

Bambrough, R. (1968) 'Universals and family resemblances', in G. Pitcher (ed.) *Wittgenstein*, London: Methuen, pp. 186–204.

Barker, M. (1981) *The New Racism*, London: Junction Books.

Baron, M. (1995) *Kantian Ethics Almost Without Apology*, London: Cornell University Press.

Best, D. (1978) *Philosophy and Human Movement*, London: George, Allen and Unwin.

Blum, L. (2002) *'I'm Not a Racist, But . . .' The Moral Quandary of Race*, Ithaca, NY: Cornell University Press.

Bok, S. (1978) *Lying*, New York: Pantheon Books.

Booth, S. (2000) *Shakespeare's Sonnets*, Yale: Yale University Press.

Borgmann, A. (1984) *Technology and the Character of Everyday Life*, Chicago: University of Chicago Press.

Boström, N. (2004) 'Human genetic enhancements: a transhumanist perspective', *Journal of Value Inquiry*, 37(4): 493–506.

Boström, N. (2005a) 'The fable of the dragon tyrant', *Journal of Medical Ethics*, 31: 231–7.

Boström, N. (2005b) 'Transhumanist values', Online. Available at: http://www. nickbostrom.com/ethics/values.html (accessed 19 May 2005).

Brackenridge, C. (1994) 'Fair play or fair game? Child sexual abuse in sport organisations', *International Review for Sociology of Sport*, 29(3): 287–9.

Brackenridge, C. (2001) *Spoilsports: Understanding and Preventing Sexual Exploitation in Sports*, London: Routledge.

Bredemeier, B. J. (1985) 'Moral reasoning and the perceived legitimacy of intentionally injurious acts', *Journal of Sport Psychology*, 7: 110–24.

Bredemeier, B. J. (1994) 'Children's moral reasoning and their assertive, aggressive and submissive tendencies in sport and daily life', *Journal of Sport and Exercise Psychology*, 16: 1–14.

Bredemeier, B. J. and Shields, D. L. (1984a) 'Divergence in moral reasoning about sports and everyday life', *Sociology of Sport Journal*, 1: 348–57.

Bredemeier, B. J. and Shields, D. L. (1984b) 'The utility of moral stage analysis in the investigation of athletic aggression', *Sociology of Sport Journal*, 1: 138–49.

Bredemeier, B. J. and Shields, D. L. (1986a) 'Athletic aggression: an issue of contextual morality', *Sociology of Sport Journal*, 3: 15–28.

Bredemeier, B. J. and Shields, D. L. (1986b) 'Moral growth among athletes and non–athletes: a comparative analysis', *Journal of Genetic Psychology*, 147: 7–18.

Bredemeier, B. J. and Shields, D. L. (1995) 'Moral assessment in sport psychology', in J. L. Duda (ed.) *Measurement in Sport and Exercise*, Morgantown, WV: FIT, pp. 257–76.

Bredemeier, B. J., Weiss, M., Shields, D. and Cooper, B. (1986) 'The relationship of sport involvement with children's moral reasoning and aggression tendencies', *Journal of Sport Psychology*, 8: 304 –18.

Bredemeier, B. J., Weiss, M., Shields, D. and Cooper, B. (1987) 'The relationship between children's legitimacy judgments and their moral reasoning, aggression tendencies and sport involvement', *Sociology of Sport Journal*, 4: 48–60

Brown, W. M. (1991) 'Practices and prudence', *Journal of the Philosophy of Sport*, 17: 71–84.

Bruckhardt, J. (1998) *The Greeks and Greek Civilization*, New York: St Martin's Press (trans S. Stern; ed. O. Murray).

Brülde, B. (2001) 'The goals of medicine: towards a unified theory', *Health Care Analysis*, 9: 1–13.

Butcher, R. and Schneider, A. (1993) 'For the love of the game', *Quest*, 45(4): 460–9.

Caillois, R. (1955) *Man, Play, and Games*, New York: The Free Press of Glencoe.

Carr, D. (1998) 'What moral educational significance has physical education? A question in need of disambiguation', in M. McNamee and S. J. Parry (eds) *Ethics and Sport*, London: Routledge, pp. 119–33.

Carrington, B. and McDonald, I. (2001) 'Whose game is it anyway? Racism in local league cricket', in B. Carrington and I. McDonald (eds) *Race, Sport and British Society*, London: Routledge, pp. 50–69.

Cassell, E. (1991) *The Nature of Suffering*, Oxford: Oxford University Press.

Clarke, S. G. and Simpson, G. (eds) (1989) *Anti-theory in Ethics and Moral Conservatism*, New York: State University of New York Press.

Coakley, J. (2001) *Sport in Society*, 7th edn, Boston: McGraw Hill.

Conacher, D. J. (1980) *Aeschylus' Prometheus Bound*, Toronto; University of Toronto Press.

Connolly, P. (2000) 'Racism and young girls' peer group relations: the experiences of South Asian girls', *Sociology*, 34: 499–519.

Connolly, W. E. (1993) *The Terms of Political Discourse*, 3rd edn, Oxford: Blackwell.

Cooper, R. (1975) *Reason and the Human Good in Aristotle*, Cambridge, MA: Harvard University Press.

D'Agostino, F. (1981) 'The ethos of games', *Journal of the Philosophy of Sport*, VIII: 7–18.

David, P. (2005) *Human Rights in Youth Sport*, London: Routledge.

Davis, N. (1991) 'Contemporary deontology', in P. Singer (ed.) *A Companion to Ethics*, Oxford: Blackwell, pp. 205–18.

Dawson, A. J. (1994) 'Professional codes of practice and ethical conduct', *Journal of Applied Philosophy*, 11(2): 145–54.

de la Chapelle A., Traskelin A. L. and Juvonen E. (1993) 'Truncated erythropoietin receptor causes dominantly inherited benign human erythrocytosis', *Proceedings of the National Academy of Sciences of the USA*, 90(10): 4495–9.

Den Hartogh, G. (2005) 'The slippery slope argument', in H. Kuhse and P. Singer (ed.) *Companion to Bioethics*, Oxford: Blackwell, pp. 280–90.

Desauer, F. (1927) *Philosofie Der Technik*, Bonn: Verlag.

Descartes, R. (2003) *Discourse on Method and Related Writings*, London: Penguin (trans. D. M. Clarke).

Dimeo, P. (2007) *A History of Drug Use in Sport: 1876–1976: Beyond Good and Evil*, London: Routledge.

Dixon, N. (1992) 'On sportsmanship and "running up the score"', *Journal of the Philosophy of Sport*, XIX: 1–13.

Dixon, N. (1998) 'Why losing by a wide margin is not in itself a disgrace: response to Hardman, Fox, McLaughlin and Zimmerman', *Journal of the Philosophy of Sport* XXV: 61–70.

Dixon, N. (2000) 'The inevitability of disappointment: a reply to Feezel', *Journal of the Philosophy of Sport*, XXVII: 93–9.

Dixon, N. (2003) 'Canadian figure skaters, French judges and realist in sports', *Journal of the Philosophy of Sport*, XXX(2): 103–16.

D'Souza, D. (1995) *The End of Racism*, New York: Free Press.

Duda, J. L. (2001) 'Achievement goal research in sport: Pushing the boundaries and clarifying some misunderstandings', in G. C. Roberts (ed.) *Advances in Motivation in Sport and Exercise*, Champaign, IL: Human Kinetics.

Duda, J. L. and Hall, H. K. (2001) 'Achievement goal theory in sport: recent extensions and future directions', in R. Singer, H. Hausenblas and C. Janelle (eds) *Handbook of Sport Psychology*, 2nd edn, New York: John Wiley and Sons, pp. 417–43.

Duda, J. L., Olson, L. K. and Templin, T. J. (1991) 'The relationship of task and ego orientation to sportsmanship attitudes and the perceived legitimacy of injurious acts', *Research Quarterly for Exercise and Sport*, 62(1): 79–87.

Dunning, E. (1999) *Sport Matters*, London: Routledge.

Edelstein, L. (1967) *Ancient Medicine*, Baltimore: John Hopkins University Press (eds O. Temkin and L. Temkin).

Edwards, S. D. (2003) 'Three concepts of suffering', *Medicine, Health Care and Philosophy*, 6: 59–66.

Edwards, S. D. (2008) 'Oscar Pistoris . . . .', *Sport, Ethics and Philosophy*, 2(2) (in press).

Edwards, S. D. and M. J. McNamee (2006) 'Why sports medicine is *not* medicine', *Health Care Analysis*, (14): 103–9.

Eichberg, H. (1990) 'Stronger, funnier, deadlier: track and field on the way to the ritual of the record's in John Marshall Carter and Arnd Krüger (eds) *Ritual and Record: Sports Records and Qualification in Pre-Modern Societies*, New York: Greenwood, pp. 123–34.

Ellington, J. W. (1994) *Immanuel Kant: Ethical Philosophy*, Cambridge: Hackett Publishing Company.

Elliott, R. K. (1974) 'Education, love of one's subject, and the love of truth', *Proceedings of the Philosophy of Education Society of Great Britain*, 8(1): 135–47.

Ellul, J. (1965) *The Technological Society*, London: Cape (trans. J. Wilkinson).

Engstrom, S. and Whiting, J. (1998) *Aristotle, Kant and the Stoics*, Cambridge: Cambridge University Press.

Erikson, E. H. (1964) *Insight and Responsibility*, New York: Norton.

Feezel, R. (1999) 'Sportsmanship and blowouts: baseball and beyond', *Journal of the Philosophy of Sport*, XXVI: 68–78.

Feezel, R. (2005) *Sport and Ethical Reflection*, Chicago: University of Illinois Press.

Flanagan, O. (1991) *Varieties of Moral Personality: Ethics and Psychological Realism*, London: Harvard University Press.

Football Against Racism in Europe (2004) 'Hill backs Big Ron', Online. Available at: http://www.farenet.org/news_article.asp?intNewsID=204 (accessed 12 September 2007).

Foucault, M. (1988) *Technologies of the Self*, London: Tavistock Publications (eds L. H. Martin, H. Gutman, and P. H. Hutton).

Fraleigh, W. P. (1984) *Right Actions in Sport*, Champaign; IL: Human Kinetics.

Frankfurt, H. (1988) *The Importance of What We Care About*, Cambridge: Cambridge University Press.

Fricker, P. (2005) 'Hypoxic air machines: commentary', *Journal of Medical Ethics*, 31: 115.

Fried, C. (1978) *Right and Wrong*, Cambridge, MA: Harvard University Press.

Fry, J. (2002) 'Coaches' accountability for pain and suffering in the athletic body', *Professional Ethics*, 9, (1–2): 5–14.

Gallie, W. B. (1956) 'Essentially contested concepts', *Proceedings of the Aristotelian Society*, LVI: 167–98.

Gambetta, D. (ed.) (1988) *Trust*, Oxford: Blackwell.

Gellner, E. (1967) 'The concept of a story', *Ratio*, 9: 49–67.

Gibson, J. H. (1993) *Performance Versus Results A Critique of Contemporary Values in Sport*, New York: State University of New York Press.

Gilligan, C. (1982) *In a Different Voice*, Cambridge, MA: Harvard University Press.

Gilroy, P. (1987) *There Ain't No Black in the Union Jack*, London: Hutchinson.

Glover, J. (1988) *I: The Philosophy and Psychology of Personal Identity*, London: Penguin.

Gough, R. W. (1998) 'Moral development research in sport and its quest for objectivity', in M. McNamee and S. J. Parry (eds) *Ethics and Sport*, London: Routledge, pp. 135–47.

Green, T. H. (1907) *Prolegomena to Ethics*, 5th edn, Oxford: Clarendon.

Griffiths, P. (1997) *What Emotions Really Are: The Problem of Psychological Categories*, Chicago: University of Chicago Press.

Guillaumin, C. (1972) *L'Ideologie raciste: Genèse et langage actuel*, The Hague: Mouton.

Guivernau, M. and Duda, J. L. (2002) 'Moral atmosphere and athletic aggressive tendencies in young soccer players', *Journal of Moral Education*, 13(1): 67–85.

Guttman, A. (1978) *From Ritual to Record*, New York: Columbia University Press.

Haan, N. (1975) 'Moral reasoning in hypothetical and actual situation of civil disobedience', *Journal of Personality and Social Psychology*, 32: 255–70.

Haan, N. (1978) 'Two moralities in action contexts: relationship to thought, ego regulation, and development', *Journal of Personality and Social Psychology*, 36: 286–305.

Haan, N. (1983) 'An interactional morality of everyday life', in N. Haan *et al.* (eds) *Social Science as Moral Inquiry*, New York: Columbia University Press, pp. 218–50.

Habermas, J. (1968) *Knowledge and Human Interests* (reprinted 1986), Cambridge: Polity.

Habermas, J. (2003) *The Future of Human Nature*, Cambridge: Polity.

Hall, S. (1992) 'New ethnicities', in J. Donald and A. Rattansi (eds) *'Race', Culture and Difference*, London: Sage, pp. 252–9.

Hampshire, S. (1983) *Morality and Conflict*, Oxford: Blackwell.

Hardman, A. *et al.* (1996) 'On sportsmanship and "running up the score": Issues of incompetence and humiliation', *Journal of the Philosophy of Sport*, XXIII: 58–69.

Hargreaves, J. (1994) *Sporting Females: Critical Issues in the History and Sociology of Women's Sports*, London: Routledge.

Harris, E. M. (2007) 'The rule of law in Athenian democracy, reflections on the judicial oath', *Ethics and Politics*, 9(1): 55–74.

Hart, H. L. A. (1955) 'Are there any natural rights', *The Philosophical Review*, 64(2): 175–91.

Hart, H. L. A. (1961) *The Concept of Law*, Oxford: Clarendon.

Hartshorne, H. and May, M. A. (1928) *Studies in the Nature of Character*, New York: Macmillan.

Hatab, L. J. (1991) 'The Greeks and the meaning of athletics', in J. Andre and R. Double (eds) *Rethinking College Athletics*, Philadelphia: Temple University Press, pp. 31–42.

Heidegger, M. (1977) *The Question Concerning Technology and Other Essays*, San Francisco: Harper Row (trans. W. Lovitt).

Herzog, D. (2000) 'Envy', in R. C. Solomon (ed.) *Wicked Pleasures*, Oxford: Rowman and Littlefield, pp. 141–60.

Hickman, L. A. (2001) *Philosophical Tools for Technological Culture: Putting Pragmatism to Work*, Bloomington: Indiana University Press.

Hoberman, J. M. (1988) 'Sport and the technological image of man', in W. J. Morgan and K. V. Meier (eds) *Philosophic Inquiry in Sport*, Champaign: IL: Human Kinetics.

Hoberman, J. M. (2005) *Testosterone Dreams: Rejuvenation, Aphrodisia, Doping*, Berkeley: University of California Press.

Holm, S. (2007) 'Doping under medical control – conceptually possible but impossible in the world of professional sports?', *Sport, Ethics and Philosophy*, 1(2): 135–45.

Holt, R. (1989) *Sport and the British*, Oxford: Clarendon Press.

Holtzman, S. and Leich, C. (eds) (1981) *Wittgenstein: to Follow a Rule*, London: Routledge and Kegan Paul.

Honda, S. (2005) 'Kendo as sport', unpublished PhD dissertation, University of Gloucestershire.

Houlihan, B. (1999) *Dying to Win*, Brussels: Council of Europe Press.

Howe, D. (2004) 'It was not a lapse: Atkinson was up to his neck in football's endemic racism', *New Statesman*, 3 May, Online. Available at: http://www.newstatesman.com/200405030005 (accessed 12 September 2007).

Howe, P. D. (2004) *Sport, Professionalism and Pain*, London: Routledge.

Huizinga, J. (1970) *Homo Ludens: a Study of the Play Element in Culture*, London: Paladin.

Illich, I. (1987) 'Some theological perspectives on pain and suffering: the meaning and management of pain', Institute for Theological Encounter with Science and Technology, Online. Available at: http://itest.slu.edu/dloads/80s/suffer.txt (accessed 13 November 2003).

Inglis, F. (1977) *The Name of the Game*, London: Heinemann.

Jacobs, J. (2001) *Choosing Character: Responsibility for Virtue and Vice*, New York: Cornell University Press.

Jonas, H. (1974) *Philosophical Essays: from Ancient Creed to Technological Man*, Chicago: University of Chicago Press.

Jones, C. and McNamee, M. J. (2000) 'Moral reasoning, moral action and the moral atmosphere of sport: some critical remarks on the limitations of the prevailing paradigm', *Sport, Education and Society*, 5(3): 131–48.

Kant, I. (1953) *Groundwork of the Metaphysic of Morals*, London: Hutchison (trans. H. J. Paton as *The Moral Law*).

Kant, I. (1974) *Anthropology from a Pragmatic Point of View*, The Hague: Nijhoff (trans. M. Gregor).

Kant, I. (1991) *The Metaphysics of Morals*, Cambridge: Cambridge University Press (trans. M. Gregor).

Kapp, F. (1877) *Grundlinien einer Philosophie der Technik*, Braunshcweig: Westermann.

Kass, L. (1997) 'The wisdom of repugnance', *New Republic*, 216: 17–26.

Kass, L. (2002) *Life, Liberty and the Defense of Dignity*, San Francisco: Encounter Books.

Kekes, J. (1989) *Moral Tradition and Individuality*, Princeton, NJ: Princeton University Press.

Kenny, A. J. (1963) *Act, Emotion, Will*, London: Routledge.

Kerenyi, C. (1963) *Prometheus*, Princeton, NJ: Princeton University Press.

Koehn, D. (1993) *The Ground of Professional Ethics*, London: Routledge.

Kohlberg, L. (1981) *Essays on Moral Development. Vol 1. The Philosophy of Moral Development*, San Francisco: Harper and Row.

Kohlberg, L. (1984) *Essays on Moral Development. Vol 2. The Psychology of Moral Development*, San Francisco: Harper and Row.

Kolnai, A. (1966) 'Games and aims', *Proceedings of the Aristotelian Society*, 66: 103–27.

Koukouris, K. (2000) 'An examination of coaches' responsibilities for premature athletic disengagement of elite Greek gymnasts', in M. J. McNamee, C. Jennings and M. Reeves (eds) *Just Leisure: Policy Ethics and Professionalism*, Brighton: LSA Publications No. 71, pp. 211–26.

Kovesi, J. (1972) *Moral Notions*, London: Routledge.

Kretchmar, R. S. (2007) 'Dualisms, dichotomies, and dead ends: limitations of analytic thinking about sport', *Sport, Ethics and Philosophy*, 1(3): 266–80.

Kurke, L. (1991) *The Traffic in Praise: Pindar and the Poetics of Social Economy*, New York: Cornell University Press.

Kyle, D. G. (2007) *Sport and Spectacle in the Ancient World*, Oxford: Blackwell.

Kymlicka, W. (1989) *Liberalism, Community and Culture*, Oxford: Clarendon.

Lasch, C. (1979) *The Culture of Nacissism*, New York: Warner Bros.

Leamon, O. (1988) 'Cheating and fair play in sport', in W. Morgan and K. V. Meier *Philosophic Inquiry in Sport*, Champaign, IL: Human Kinetics, pp. 277–82.

Lee, K. (2003) *Philosophy and Revolutions in Genetics*, London: Palgrave.

Lehman, C. (1981) 'Can cheaters play the game?', *Journal of the Philosophy of Sport*, VIII: 41–6.

Lewis, C. S. (1943) *The Abolition of Man*, Oxford: Oxford University Press.

Llanwrtyd Wells Coming Events (2007) 'Bog snorkelling', Online. Available at: http://llanwrtyd-wells.powys.org.uk/bog.html (accessed 7 June 2007).

Loland, S. (2002) *Fair play: A Moral Norm System*, London: Routledge.

Loland, S. and McNamee, M. J. (2000) 'Fair play and the ethos of sports: an eclectic philosophical framework', *Journal of the Philosophy of Sport*, XXVII: 63–80.

Loland, S. and Murray, T. H. (2007) 'Editorial: the ethics of the use of technologically constructed high-altitude environments to enhance performance in sport', *Scandinavian Journal of Medicine and Science in Sports*, 17: 193–5.

Loland, S., Skirstad, B. and Waddington, I. (eds) (2005) *Sport, Pain and Injury*, London: Routledge.

Long, J. and McNamee, M. J. (2004) 'The moral economy of racism and racist rationalisations in sport', *International Review for the Sociology of Sport*, 39(40): 405–20.

Long, J., Hylton, K., Dart, J. and Welch, M. (2000) *Part of the Game? An Examination of Racism in Grass Roots Football*, London: Kick It Out.

Long, J., Nesti, M., Carrington, B. and Gilson, N. (1997) *Crossing the Boundary: A Study of the Nature and Extent of Racism in Local League Cricket*, Leeds: Leeds Metropolitan University.

McDowell, J. (1981) 'Virtue and reason', in S. H. Holtzman and C. M. Leich (eds) *Wittgenstein: to Follow a Rule*, London: Routledge and Kegan Paul, pp. 332–3.

McFee, G. (2003a) 'Art, essence and Wittgenstein', in S. Davies and A. Sukla (eds) *Art and Essence*, Westport, CT: Praeger, pp. 17–38.

McFee, G. (2003b) *Sports, Rules and Values*, London: Routledge.

MacIntyre, A. C. (1985) *After Virtue*, London: Duckworth.

MacIntyre, A. C. (1998) *Whose Justice, Which Rationality?*, London: Duckworth.

MacIntyre, A. C. (2001) *Dependent Rational Animals*, London: Duckworth.

McKenny, G. P. (1997) *To Relieve the Human Condition*, Albany, NY: State University of New York Press.

Mackinnon, C. (1999) *Character, Virtue Theories and the Vices*, Toronto: Broadview.

McNamee, M. J. (1992) 'Physical education and the development of personhood', *Physical Education Review*, 15(1): 13–28.

McNamee, M. J. (1995a) 'Sporting practices, institutions and virtues: a critique and a restatement', *Journal of Philosophy of Sport*, XXII–XXIII: 61–82.

McNamee, M. J. (1995b) 'Sport, relativism, communality, and essential contestability, in S. Eassom (ed.) *Sport and Value* Bedford: Casper, pp. 86–119.

McNamee, M. J. (1995b) 'Theoretical limitations in codes of ethical conduct', in G. McFee *et al.* (eds) *Leisure Values, Genders, Lifestyles*, Brighton: LSA Publications, pp. 145–55.

McNamee, M. J. (1998) 'Celebrating trust: virtues and rules in the ethical conduct of sports coaches', in M. J. McNamee and S. J. Parry (eds) *Ethics and Sport*, London: Routledge, pp. 148–68.

McNamee, M. J. (2002) 'Hubris, humility and humiliation: vice and virtue in sporting communities', *Journal of the Philosophy of Sport*, 29(1): 38–53.

McNamee, M. J. (2003a) '*Schadenfreude* in sport: envy, justice and self-esteem', *Journal of the Philosophy of Sport*, 30(1): 1–16.

McNamee, M. J. (2003b) 'Is guilt a proper emotional response to the causing of an unintentional injury?', *European Journal of Sport Science*, 2(1): 1–10.

McNamee, M. J. (2005a) 'Suffering in and for sport: some philosophical remarks on a painful emotion', in S. Loland, B. Skirstad and I. Waddington (eds) *Pain and Injury in Sport*, London: Routledge, pp. 229–45.

McNamee, M. J. (2005b) 'Transhumanizem in moralna topografija sportne medicine', *Borec*, 57: 626–9 (translated in Slovenian) .

McNamee, M. J. (2007a) 'Whose Prometheus? Transhumanism, biotechnology and the moral topography of sports medicine', *Sport, Ethics and Philosophy*, 1(2): 181–94.

McNamee, M. J. (2007b) 'Nursing schadenfreude', *Medicine, Health Care and Philosophy*, 10(2): 289–99.

McNamee, M. J. (2008) 'Normality, abnormality and disability sport', *Sport, Ethics and Philosophy*, 2(2) (in press).

McNamee, M. J. and Edwards, S. D. (2006) 'Transhumanism, medical technology, and slippery slopes', *Journal of Medical Ethics*, 32: 513–18.

McNamee, M. J. and Jones, C. (2000) 'Value conflict, fair play, and a sports education worthy of the name', in M. Leicester, *et al.* (eds) *Education, Culture and Values (Vol. 4)*, London: Cassell, pp. 103–11.

McNamee, M. J., Jones, C. R. and Duda, J. L. (2003) 'Ethics, psychology and sports: back to an Aristotelian "Museum of Normalcy"', *International Journal of Sport and Health Science*, 1: 15–29.

McNamee, M. J., Oliver, S. and Wainright, P. (2007) *Research Ethics in Exercise, Health and Sport Sciences*, London: Routledge.

Macpherson, Sir William, of Cluny (1999) 'Report of the Stephen Lawrence Inquiry' (Cm 4262–I, 1999), London: Stationery Office, Online. Available at: http://www.archive.official-documents.co.uk/document/ cm42/4262/4262.htm (accessed 1 April 2004).

Mangan, J. A. (1986) *The Games Ethic and Imperialism*, Harmondsworth: Viking.

Marcuse, H. (1964) *One Dimensional Man*, Boston: Beacon Press.

Margalit, A. (1996) *The Decent Society*, London: Harvard University Press (trans. N. Goldblum).

Massara, A. (2007) 'Stain removal: on race and ethics', *Philosophy and Social Criticism*, 33: 429–528.

Melzack, R. and Torgerson, W. S. (1971) 'On the language of pain', *Anaesthesiology*, 34: 50–9.

Meyerfeld, J. (1999) *Suffering and Moral Responsibility*, Oxford: Oxford University Press.

Miah, A. (2004) *Genetically Modified Athletes*, London: Routledge.

Midgley, M. (1974) 'The game game', *Philosophy*, 49: 231–53.

Midgely, M. (1983) *Beast and Man*, Hassocks: Harvester Press.

Miles, R. (1989) *Racism*, London: Routledge.

Milgram, S. (1964) 'Group pressure and action against a person', *Journal of Abnormal and Social Psychology*, 69: 137–43.

Mill, J. S. (1859) 'On liberty', in M. Warnock (ed.) (1962) *Utilitarianism*, Glasgow: Fontana.

Mill, J. S. (1972) *Utilitarianism* (ed. M. Warnock), London: Fontana.

Miller, S. (1991) *Arete*, Berkeley: University of California Press.

Miller, W. I. (1993) *Humiliation: And Other Essays on Honor, Social Discomfort and Violence*, London: Cornell University Press.

Mitcham, C. (1979) 'Philosophy and the history of technology', in G. Bugliarello and D. B. Doner (eds) *The History and Philosophy of Technology*, London: University of Illinois Press, pp. 2477–84.

Mitcham, C. (1995) 'Philosophy and technology', in W. T Reich (ed.) *Encyclopedia of Bioethics*, London: Simon and Shuster, pp. 2477–84.

Modood, T. (1997) '"Difference", cultural racism and anti-racism', in P. Werbner and T. Modood (eds) *Debating Cultural Hybridity*, London: Zed Books, pp. 154–72.

Monaghan, L. (2001) *Bodybuilding, Drugs and Risk,* London: Routledge.

Montada, L. (1993) 'Understanding oughts by assessing moral reasoning or moral emotions', in G. G. Noam and T. Wren (eds) *The Moral Self*, London: MIT Press, pp. 292–309.

More, M. (1996) 'Transhumanism: towards a futurist philosophy', Online. Available at: http://www.maxmore.com/transhum.htm (accessed 25 September 2007).

More, M. (2005) 'Transhumanism', Online. Available at: http://www.mactonnies.com/trans.html (accessed 13 July 2005).

Morgan, W. J. (1993) 'Amateurism and professionalism as moral languages: in search of a moral image of sport', *Quest*, 45: 470–93.

Morgan, W. J. (1994) *Leftist Theories of Sport*, Chicago: University of Illinois Press.

Morgan, W. J. (1998) 'Multinational sport and literary practices and their communities: the moral salience of cultural narratives', in M. McNamee and J. Parry (eds) *Ethics and Sport*, London: Routledge, pp. 184–204.

Morgan, W. J. (2004) 'Moral antirealism, internalism, and sport', *Journal of the Philosophy of Sport*, XXXI: 61–83.

Nicholson, R. (1987) 'Drugs in sport: a reappraisal', *Institute of Medical Ethics Bulletin*, 7: 1–25.

Nilsson, P. (1993) *Fotbollen och moralen*, Stockholm: HLS Forlage.

Nozick, R. (1974) *Anarchy, State, Utopia*, Oxford: Blackwell.

Nue, J. (2002) *A Tear Is an Intellectual Thing: The Meaning of Emotion*, Oxford: Oxford University Press.

Nussbaum, M. (2001) *Upheavals of Thought: the Intelligence of the Emotions*, Cambridge: Cambridge University Press.

Nye, D. E. (2006) *Technology Matters*, Cambridge, MA: MIT Press.

Ortega y Gasset, J. (1939) 'Man the technician', in *Towards a Philosophy of History*, New York: Norton.

Parekh, B. (1995) 'The concept of national identity', *New Community*, 21: 255–68.

Parens, E. (1995) 'The goodness of fragility: on the prospects of genetic technologies aimed at the enhancement of human capacities', *Kennedy Institute of Ethics Journal*, 5(2): 131–43.

Parry, J. (1998) 'Violence and aggression in contemporary sport', in M. J. McNamee and S. J. Parry (eds) *Ethics and Sport*, London: Routledge.

Peters, R. S. (1966) *Ethics and Education*, London: Routledge and Keegan Paul.

Peters, R. S. (1974) *Psychology and Ethical Development*, London: Allen and Unwin.

Phillip, R. (2004) 'Radcliffe was a sore loser', Online. Available at: http://www.telegraph.co.uk/sport/main.jhtml?xml=/sport/2004/08/25/sorp25.xml (accessed 25 August 2004).

Piaget, J. (1932) *The Moral Judgment of the Child*, London: Routledge and Keegan Paul.

Pincoffs, E. L. (1986) *Quandaries and Virtues: Against Reductivism in Ethics*. Lawrence, KS: Kansas University Press.

Plato (1962) *Phaedrus*, London: Penguin.

Plato (1974) *Republic*, 2nd edn, London: Penguin (trans. D. Lee).

Porter, R. (2002) *Blood and Guts: a Short History of Medicine*, London: Penguin.

Portmann, J. (2000) *When Bad Things Happen to Other People*, London: Routledge.

Power, C., Higgins, A. and Kohlberg, L. (1989) *Lawrence Kohlberg's Approach to Moral Education*, New York: Columbia University Press.

Price, S. and Kearns, E. (2004) *Oxford Dictionary of Classical Myth and Religion*, Oxford: Oxford University Press.

Rawls, J. (1972) *A Theory of Justice*, Oxford: Clarendon Press.

Reddiford, G. (1985) 'Constitutions, institutions and games', *Journal of the Philosophy of Sport*, XII: 41–51.

Reid, H. (2002) *The Philosophical Athlete*, Durham, NC: Carolina Academic Press.

Rest, J. R. (1984) 'The major components of morality', in W. Kurtines and J. Gewirtz (eds) *Morality, Moral Behaviour and Moral Development*, New York: Wiley, pp. 24–40.

Roberts, G. C. (2001) 'Understanding the dynamics of motivation in physical activity: the influence of achievement goals on motivational processes', in G. C. Roberts (ed.) *Advances in Motivation in Sport and Exercise*, Champaign, IL: Human Kinetics, pp. 1–50.

Roberts, R. C. (1988) 'What an emotion is: a sketch', *The Philosophical Review*, XCVII: 183–209.

Roberts, T. (1998) 'Sporting practice protection and vulgar ethnocentricity: why won't Morgan go all the way?', *Journal of the Philosophy of Sport*, XXV: 82–102.

Rollin, B. (2003) 'Telos, value and genetic engineering', in H. W. Baillie and T. K. Casey (eds) *Is Human Nature Obsolete?*, Cambridge, MA: MIT Press, pp. 317–26.

Rorty, A. O. (1976) 'A literary postscript: characters, persons, selves, individuals', in A. O. Rorty (ed.) *The Identities of Persons*, Berkeley: University of California Press.

Rorty, A. O. (1980) *Explaining Emotion*, Berkeley: University of California Press.

Rorty, A. O. (1988) *Mind in Action: Essays in the Philosophy of Mind*, Boston: Beacon Press.

Rorty, A. O. and Wong, D. (1997) 'Aspects of identity and agency', in A. O. Rorty and D. Wong (eds) *Identity, Character and Morality*, Cambridge; MA: MIT Press, pp. 19–36.

Roth, S. and Cohen, L. J. (1986) 'Approach, avoidance, and coping with stress', *American Psychologist*, 41: 813–19.

Russell, J. S. (1999) 'Are rules all an umpire has to work with?', *Journal of the Philosophy of Sport*, XXVI: 27–49.

Russell, J. S. (2004) 'Moral realism in sport', *Journal of the Philosophy of Sport*, XXXI: 142–60.

Ryle, G. (1949) *The Concept of Mind*, London: Hutchinson.

Ryle, G. (1972) 'Can virtue be taught?' in R. F. Dearden, P. H. Hirst and R. S. Peters (eds) *Education and Reason: Part 3 of Education and the Development of Reason*, London: Routldege, pp. 44–57.

Sachs, D. (1981) 'How to distinguish self-respect from self-esteem', *Philosophy and Public Affairs*, 10: 346–60.

Sandberg, A. (2001) 'Morphological Freedom – why we not just want it but need it', paper presented to TransVision 2001 conference, Berlin, Online. Available at: http://www.nada.kth.se/~asa/Texts/MorphologicalFreedom.htm (accessed 5 October 2005).

Sandel, M. (1982) *Liberalism and the Limits of Justice*, Cambridge: Cambridge University Press.

Sansone, D. (1988) *Greek Athletics and the Genesis of Sports*, Berkeley: University of California Press.

Santayana, G. (1894) 'Philosophy on the bleachers', *Harvard Monthly*, XVIII: 181–90.

Savulescu, J. and Foddy, B. (2007) 'Performance enhancement and the spirit of sport: is there good reason to allow doping?' in R. Ashcroft *et al.* (eds) *Principles of Healthcare Ethics*, Chichester: Wiley, pp. 666–70.

Schauer, F. (1985) 'Slippery slopes', *Harvard Law Review*, 1988(99): 361–83.

Schneewind, J. B. (1983) 'Moral principles and moral knowledge', in S. Hauerwas and A. C. MacIntyre (eds) *Revisions: Changing Perspectives in Moral Philosophy*, London: University of Notre Dame Press, pp. 113–26.

Schneider, A. J. and Butcher, R. B. (1993) 'For the love of the game: A philosophical defense of amateurism', *Quest*, 45: 460–9.

Schneider, A. J. and Butcher, R. B. (1994) 'Why Olympic athletes should avoid the use and seek the elimination of performance-enhancing substances and practices from the Olympic Games', *Journal of the Philosophy of Sport*, XX–XXI: 64–81.

Schubert, L. (2004) 'Ethical implications of pharmacogenetics: do slippery slopes matter?', *Bioethics*, 18: 361–78.

Seung, T. K. (1991) 'Virtues and values: a platonic account', *Social Theory and Practice*, 17(2): 207–47.

Sherman, N. (1989) *The Fabric of Character*, Oxford: Clarendon Press.

Sherman, N. (1997) *Making a Necessity of Virtue*, Oxford: Clarendon Press.

Shields, D. L. L. and Bredemeier, B. J. L. (1995) *Character Development and Physical Activity*, Champaign, IL: Human Kinetics.

Shields, D., Gardner, D., Bredemeier, B. and Boström, A. (1995) 'Leadership, Cohesion and team norms regarding cheating and aggression', *Sociology of Sport Journal*, 12: 324–39.

Shilling, C. (2005) *The Body in Culture, Technology and Society*, London: Sage.

Simon, R. (2000) 'Internalism and internal values in sport', *Journal of the Philosophy of Sport*, XXVII: 1–16.

Simon, R. (2004a) *Fair Play*, 2nd edn, Boulder, CO: Westview Press.

Simon, R. (2004b) 'From ethnocentrism to realism: can discourse ethics bridge the gap?', *Journal of the Philosophy of Sport*, XXXI: 122–41.

Singer, P. (1993) *Practical Ethics*, Cambridge: Cambridge University Press.

Skillen, A. (1985) 'Rousseau and the fall of social man', *Philosophy*, 60: 105–22.

Solomon, R. (1976) *The Passions*, New York: Doubleday.

Solomon, R. C. (1993) *Ethics and Excellence: Co-operation and Integrity in Business*, Oxford: Oxford University Press.

Solomon, R. C. (2000) 'Introduction', in R. C. Solomon (ed.) *Wicked Pleasures*, Oxford: Rowman and Littlefield, pp. 1–17.

Solomos, J. and Back, L. (1996) *Racism and Society*, Basingstoke: Macmillan.

Sparshott, F. (1994) *Taking Life Seriously: A Study of the Argument of the Nichomachean Ethics*, Toronto: University of Toronto Press.

Spiecker, B. (1999) 'Habituation and training in early childhood', in D. Carr and J. Stuetel (eds) *Virtue Ethics and Moral Education*, London: Routledge, pp. 217–30.

Spitzer, G. (2006) 'Sport and the systematic infliction of pain: a case study of mandatory state sponsored doping in Germany', in S. Loland, B. Skirstad and I. Waddington (eds) *Sport, Pain and Injury*, London: Routledge, pp. 109–26.

Spriggs, M. (2005) 'Hypoxic air machines: performance enhancement through effective training – or cheating?', *Journal of Medical Ethics*, 31: 112–13.

Stephens, D. E., Bredemeier, B. J. and Shields, D. L. (1997) 'Construction of a measure designed to assess players' descriptions and prescriptions for moral behaviour in youth sport soccer', *International Journal of Sport Psychology*, 28: 370–90.

Sternglantz, R. (2005) 'Raining on the parade of horrible slippery slopes, faux slopes and justices: Scalia's dissent in Lawrence v Texas', *University of Pennsylvania Law Review*, 153: 1097–120.

Stornes, T. (2001) 'Sportspersonship in elite sports: on the effects of personal and environmental factors on the display of sportspersonship among elite male handball players', *European Physical Education Review*, 7(3): 283–304.

Stout, J. (1988) *Ethics After Babel*, Boston: Beacon.

Strawson, P. (1967) 'Persons', in D.F. Gustaffson, *Essays in Philosophical Psychology*, London: Macmillan, pp. 306–403.

Strawson, P. F. (1968) 'Freedom and resentment', in *Studies in the Philosophy of Thought and Action*, Oxford: Oxford University Press.

Suits, B. (1967) 'What is a game?', *Philosophy of Science*, 34(2): 148–.

Suits, B. (1978) *The Grasshopper: Games, Life and Utopia*, Toronto: University of Toronto Press.

Sutton-Smith, B. (1974) 'Towards an anthropology of play', *The Association for the Anthropological Study of Play Newsletter*, 1(2): 8–15. Reprinted in M. Hart and S. Birrell (1981) *Sport and the Socio-cultural Process*, Dubuque, IA: Brown, pp. 114–22.

Szasz, T. (1973) *The Second Sin*, London: Routledge.

Tamburrini, C. (2000) *The Hand of God*, Gothenburg: University of Gothenburg Press.

Tamburrini, C. (2005) 'Hypoxic air machines: commentary', *Journal of Medical Ethics*, 31: 114.

Tamburrini, C. (2006) 'Educational or genetic blue prints. What's the difference?', in C. Tamburrini and T. Tannsjo (eds) *Genetic Technology and Sport: Ethical Questions*, London: Routledge, pp. 82–90.

Tannsjo, T. (2005) 'Hypoxic air machines: commentary'. *Journal of Medical Ethics*, 31: 112–13.

Taylor, C. (1985a) *Human Agency and Language: Philosophical Papers 1*, Cambridge: Cambridge University Press.

Taylor, C. (1985b) *Philosophy and the Human Sciences, Volume 2*, Cambridge: Cambridge University Press.

Taylor, C. (1989) *Sources of the Self*, Cambridge: Cambridge University Press.

Taylor, G. (1985) *Pride, Shame, Guilt*, Oxford: Clarendon Press.

Tobin, B. (1989) 'An Aristotelian theory of moral development', *Journal of Philosophy of Education*, 23(1): 195–211.

Toperoff, S. (1989) *Sugar Ray Leonard*, New York: Simon Schuster.

Ture, K. and Hamilton, C. (1992) *Black Power: The Politics of Liberation*, New York: Vintage Books.

Walsh, A. and Giulianotti, R. (2007) *Ethics, Money and Sport*, London: Routledge.

Walton, D. N. (1992) *Slippery Slope Arguments*, Oxford: Clarendon.

Weil, S. (1983) 'The *Iliad* or poem or force', in A. C. MacIntyre and S. Hauerwas (eds) *Revisions*, London: University of Notre Dame Press, pp. 224–49.

Weinberger, D. A., Schwartz, G. E. and Davidson, R. J. (1979) 'Low anxious, high anxious, and repressive coping styles: psychometric patterns and behavioural and physiological responses to stress', *Journal of Abnormal Psychology*, 88: 369–80.

Wellman, D. T. (1993) *Portraits of White Racism*, 2nd edn, Cambridge: Cambridge University Press.

Whiting, B. B. (ed.) (1963) *Six Cultures: Studies of Child Rearing*, New York: Wiley and Sons.

Wieviorka, M. (1995) *The Arena of Racism*, London: Sage.

Wikipedia (2006) 'United Nations Convention on Biological Diversity', Online. Available at: http://en.wikipedia.org/wiki/Convention_on_Biological_Diversity (accessed 10 June 2006).

Wikipedia (2007) 'Miguel Indurain', Online. Available at: http://en.wikipedia.org/wiki/Indurain (accessed 21 August 2007).

Williams, B. A. O. (1973) *Problems of the Self*, Cambridge: Cambridge University Press.

Williams, B. A. O. (1980) 'Justice as a virtue', in A. O. Rorty (ed.) *Essays on Aristotle's Ethics*, Berkeley: University of California, pp. 189–99.

Williams, B. A. O. (1985) *Ethics and the Limits of Philosophy*, London: Fontana.

Williams, B. A. O. (1993) *Shame and Necessity*, Berkeley: University of California Press.

Wittgenstein, L. (1953) *Philosophical Investigations*, Oxford: Blackwell.

Wittgenstein, L. (1967) *Philosophical Investigations*, 3rd edn, Oxford: Blackwell, (trans. G. E. M. Anscombe).

Wollheim, R. (1984) *The Thread of Life*, Cambridge: Cambridge University Press.

Wollheim, R. (1993) *The Mind and its Depths*, Boston: Harvard University Press.

Young, D. C. (1984) *The Olympic Myth of Greek Amateur Athletics*, Chicago: Ares.

Index